PRACTICAL
BLACKSMITHING.

PRACTICAL
BLACKSMITHING.

A COLLECTION OF ARTICLES CONTRIBUTED AT DIFFERENT TIMES BY
SKILLED WORKMEN TO THE COLUMNS OF "THE BLACKSMITH
AND WHEELWRIGHT" AND COVERING NEARLY THE
WHOLE RANGE OF BLACKSMITHING FROM
THE SIMPLEST JOB OF WORK TO
SOME OF THE MOST COM-
PLEX FORGINGS.

Compiled and Edited by

M. T. RICHARDSON,

Editor of "THE BLACKSMITH AND WHEELWRIGHT."

ILLUSTRATED.

FOUR VOLUMES IN ONE,
ORIGINALLY PUBLISHED IN
SEPARATE VOLUMES IN 1889, 1890, AND 1891.

WITH A FOREWORD BY
DONA Z. MEILACH.

WEATHERVANE BOOKS, NEW YORK

FOREWORD.

"Old" is not necessarily outdated. "New" is not necessarily better. These statements underscore the reasons for reprinting *Practical Blacksmithing*. The techniques and tools illustrated and their application to the handmade object are as valuable to the modern blacksmith as they were to his forefathers of the late 1800s. Blacksmithing, as a craft, had a rapid demise when industrialization, mass production, and modern technology set in, but it didn't die. Rather, it smoldered, as did the coals of the forge. Today those coals are once again being fanned into brightly lit flames as craftsmen take up blacksmithing as a hobby, as an art form, and as a creative endeavor for any variety of reasons and satisfactions.

In the 1970s, the heated and hammered metal began to assume an entire range of forms that differed greatly from those made in Richardson's day. The horseshoe, the nail, the plowshare tine do not stimulate the imagination of the modern smith. He is more apt to be interested in creating some object that is not made by industry, one that may be decorative and practical such as an unusual hinge or a door knocker. He may forge the iron into an expressive and unique form such as a sculpture, a carved head at the end of a banister, the base for an avant-garde table, or a personalized weather vane.

No matter what the form, the approach and the techniques have not changed appreciably from those of Richardson's era; perhaps the bellows is now activated by electricity rather than a foot pump or hand crank, and the composition of available metals differ—Richardson and his peers were able to secure wrought iron while today the blacksmith has a variety of different steels to use.

The four original volumes that have been combined unabridged into this single new volume are offered as a basic resource for the modern blacksmith. It will lead him to a discovery of old tools that may no longer be in existence, to learn how they were shaped and why. It will help him recreate such tools, especially tongs, hammers and chisels, for his own further forays into smithing.

The collector of old tools will welcome the information and find it an invaluable aid for identifying items found at flea markets, farm sales, and in antique shops.

Practical Blacksmithing—with its emphasis on technique and craftsmanship, its homey style, its glimpses into the distant and recent past of this ancient craft—will excite the historian and nostalgia enthusiast. It will help bring the new blacksmithing activity into a sharper focus and a brighter future.

DONA Z. MEILACH
1978

VOLUME I.

CONTENTS

PREFACE.

Although there are numerous legendary accounts of the important position occupied by the blacksmith, and the honors accorded him even at a period as remote in the world's history as the time of King Solomon, strange to relate there is no single work in the language devoted solely to the practice of the blacksmith's art. Occasional chapters on the subject may be found, however, in mechanical books, as well as brief essays in encyclopedias. While fragmentary allusions to this important trade have from time to time appeared in newspapers and magazines, no one has ever attempted anything like an exhaustive work on the subject; perhaps none is possible. This paucity of literature concerning a branch of the mechanic arts, without which other trades would cease to exist from lack of proper tools, cannot be attributed to a want of intelligence on the part of the disciples of Vulcan. It is perfectly safe to assert, that in this respect blacksmiths can hold their own with mechanics in any other branch of industry. From their ranks have sprung many distinguished men. Among the number may be mentioned Elihu

Burritt, known far and wide as the "learned black-smith." The Rev. Robt. Colyer, pastor of the leading Unitarian Church in New York City, started in life as a blacksmith, and while laboring at the forge, began the studies which have since made him famous.

Exactly why no attempt has ever been made to write a book on blacksmithing, it would be difficult to explain. It is not contended that in the follow-ing pages anything like a complete consideration of the subject will be undertaken. For the most part the matter has been taken from the columns of *The Blacksmith and Wheelwright*, to which it was con-tributed by practical men from all parts of the American continent. *The Blacksmith and Wheel-wright*, it may be observed, is at present the only journal in the world which makes the art of black-smithing an essential feature.

In the nature of things, the most that can be done by the editor and compiler of these fragmentary articles, is to group the different subjects together and present them with as much system as possible. The editor does not hold himself responsible for the subject matter, or the treatment which each topic receives at the hands of its author. There may be, sometimes, a better way of doing a job of work than the one described herein, but it is believed that the average blacksmith may obtain much information from these pages, even if oc-

casionally some of the methods given are inferior
to those with which he is familiar. The editor has
endeavored, so far as possible, to preserve the exact
language of each contributor.

While a skillful blacksmith of extended experience,
with a turn for literature, might be able to write a
book arranged more systematically, and possibly
treating of more subjects, certain it is that no one up
to the present time has ever made the attempt, and
it is doubtful if such a work would contain the
same variety of practical information that will be
found in these pages, formed of contributions from
hundreds of able workmen scattered over a wide
area.

THE EDITOR.

INTRODUCTION.

Some time since, Mr. G. H. Birch read a paper before the British Architectural Association entitled: "The Art of the Blacksmith." The essential portions of this admirable essay are reproduced here as a fitting introduction to this volume:

"It is not the intention of the present paper to endeavor to trace the actual working of iron from primeval times, from those remote ages when the ever-busy and inventive mind of man first conceived the idea of separating the metal from the ore, and impressing upon the shapeless mass those forms of offense or defense, or of domestic use, which occasion required or fancy dictated.

"Legends, both sacred and profane, point retrospectively, the former to a Tubal Cain, and the latter to four successive ages of gold and silver, brass and iron. Inquiry stops on the very edge of that vague and dim horizon of countless ages, nor would it be profitable to unravel myths or legends, or to indulge in speculation upon a subject so unfathomable. Abundant evidence is forthcoming not only of its use in the weapons, utensils and tools of

remote times, but also of its use in decorative art ;
unfortunately, unlike bronze, which can resist the
destructive influence of climate and moisture, iron—
whether in the more tempered form of steel or in
its own original state—readily oxidizes, and leaves
little trace of its actual substance behind, so that
relics of very great antiquity are but few and far
between.   It remains for our age to call in science,
and protect by a lately discovered process the works
of art in this metal, and to transmit them uninjured
to future ages.   In the

RETROSPECTIVE HISTORY OF THE BLACKSMITH'S ART

no period was richer in inventive fancy than that
period of the so-called Middle Ages.   England,
France, Italy, and more especially Germany, vied
with each other in producing wonders of art.   The
anvil and the hammer were ever at work, and the glow
of the forge with its stream of upward sparks seemed
to impart, Prometheus-like, life and energy to the
inert mass of metal submitted to its fierce heat.
Nowhere at any period were the technicalities of iron
so thoroughly understood, and under the stalwart
arm of the smith brought to such perfection, both of
form and workmanship, as in Europe during this
period of the Middle Ages.

   The common articles of domestic use shared the
influence of art alike with the more costly work
destined for the service of religion ; the homely

gridiron and pot-hook could compare with the elaborate hinge of the church door or the grille which screened the tomb or chapel. The very nail head was a thing of beauty.

Of articles for domestic use of a very early period handed down to our times we have but few specimens, and this can easily be accounted for. The ordinary wear and tear and frequent change of proprietorship and fashion, in addition to the intrinsic value of the metal, contributed to their disappearance. "New lamps for old ones," is a ceaseless, unchanging cry from age to age. In ecclesiastical metal-work, of course, the specimens are more numerous and more perfectly preserved; their connection with the sacred edifices which they adorned and strengthened proved their salvation.

IRON TO PROTECT THE HUMAN FORM.

Without going very minutely into the subject of arms and armor, it is absolutely necessary to refer briefly to the use of iron in that most important element, in the protection of the human form, before the introduction of more deadly weapons in the art of slaying rendered such protection useless. In the Homeric age such coverings seem to have been of the most elaborate and highly wrought character, for, although Achilles may be purely a hypothetical personage, Homer, in describing his armor, probably only described such as was actually in use

in his own day, and may have slightly enriched it
with his own poetic fancy. From the paintings on
vases we know that sometimes rings of metal were
used, sewn on to a tunic of leather. They may have
been bronze, but there is also every reason to
believe that they were sometimes made of iron.
Polybius asserts that the Roman soldiers wore chain-
mail, which is sometimes described as "*molli lorica
catena,*" and we find innumerable instances on
sculptured slabs of this use, and in London, among
some Roman remains discovered in Eastcheap and
Moor Lane, actual specimens of this ringed armor
occurred, in which the rings did not interlace as in
later specimens, but were welded together at the
edge. From this time there is authentic evidence of
its constant use. The Anglo-Saxons wore it, as it is
frequently described in manuscripts of this period.
Later on, the Bayeux tapestry represents it beyond
the shadow of a doubt, both in the manner as before
described and also in scales overlapping one another;
while the helmet of a conical shape, with a straight
bar in front to protect the nose, is also very accurately figured. What we call

CHAIN-MAIL

proper did not appear before Stephen's reign, and
its introduction followed closely after the first
Crusade, and was doubtless derived from the East,
where the art of working in metals had long been

known and practised. The very term "mail" means hammered, and from Stephen's time until that of Edward III. it was universally used; but long before the last mentioned period many improvements, suggested by a practical experience, had modified the complete coat of chain-mail. Little by little small plates of iron fastened by straps and buckles to the chain-mail, to give additional safety to exposed portions of the person, gradually changed the appearance, and developed at last into complete plate armor, such as is familiar to us by the many monumental brasses and effigies still extant; the chain-mail being only used as a sort of fringe to the helmet, covering the neck, and as an apron, until even this disappeared, although it was near the end of the sixteenth century—so far as Europe is concerned—before the chain-mail finally vanished. After this date armor became more elaborately decorated by other processes besides those of the armorer's or smith's inventive genius. Damascening, gilding and painting were extensively employed, and more especially engraving or chasing; and the collections at the Tower—and more particularly the rich collection formed by her Imperial Majesty, the ex-Empress of the French, at Pierrefonds, now at the Hotel des Invalides—show us to what a wonderful extent this ornamentation of armor could be carried.

The seventeenth and eighteenth centuries still gave employment to the smith, until the utter in-

ability of such a protection against the deadly
bullet, rendered its further use ridiculous, and in
these days it only appears in England in the modified form of a cuirass in the showy but splendid
uniform of the Horse and Life Guards or occasionally in the Lord Mayor's show, when the knights
of old are represented by circus supernumeraries, as
unlike these ancient prototypes as the tin armor in
which they are uncomfortably encased resembles the
ancient.

With the armor the weapons used by its wearers
have been handed down to our time, and magnificent
specimens they are of an art which, although it may
not be entirely dead among us in these days, is certainly dormant so far as this branch of it is concerned. The massive sword of the early mediæval
period, which depended on its own intrinsic weight
and admirably tempered edge rather than on its ornamentation ; the maces, battle-axes, halberds and
partisans, show a gradual increase of beauty and
finish in their workmanship. The sword and dagger
hilts became more and more elaborate, especially in
Germany, where the blade of the sword is often of
most eccentric form and pattern, as if it was intended more to strike terror by its appearance than
by its actual application.

Many of the ancient sword-hilts preserved in
England, at the Musée d'Artillerie in Paris, and at
Madrid, Vienna, Dresden and Turin, are of the

most marvelous beauty and workmanship that it is possible to conceive, more particularly those of the sixteenth century.   Italy and France vied with each other in producing these art treasures of the craft of the smith ; Milan, Turin and Toledo were the principal seats of industry, and in Augsburg, in Germany, there lived and died generations of men who were perfect masters in this art of the smith.

The decadence with regard to the weapon was as marked as that of the armor ; the handle of the sword became more and more enriched with the productions of the goldsmith's and lapidary's art until the swords became rather fitted to dangle as gilded appendages against the embroidered cloaks or the silken stockings of the courtier, than to clang with martial sound against the steel-encased limbs of the warrior.

It would be beyond the limits of the present paper to enumerate the many examples of ancient work in

WEAPONS AND ARMOR

contained in the public museums of Europe, and also in private collections.   Armor is only mentioned here to give an idea of the extent to which the art of working in iron was carried, of the perfection it attained, and how thoroughly the capabilities of metal were understood, noting well that the casting of the metal into molds was scarcely ever practised, that it was entirely the work of the hammer and the anvil, that the different pieces were welded and riveted by manual labor of the smith, and then subsequently finished in the same manner by the various processes of engraving, chasing and punching.

The next division of the subject is the use of

IRON IN ECCLESIASTICAL ART,

and this comprises hinges of doors, locks and fastenings, screens, railings and vases. We have already seen to what perfection it could be brought in defending man against his fellow man ; its nobler employment in the service of his Maker remains to be considered. The church door first engages our attention, the framing of the door requiring additional strength beyond the ordinary mortising, dovetailing and tenoning of the wood, and this additional strength was imparted by the use of iron, and so completely was this attained that we have only to turn to numerous examples, still existing, to prove the manner in which it was done and the form it took. The hinge was usually constructed in the following manner : a strong hook was built into the wall with forked ends well built into the masonry ; on this hook was hung the hinge, which, for the convenience of the illustration, we will consider as simply a plain strap or flat bar of wrought-iron, its ornamentation being a matter of after consideration ; this strap had at one end a hollow tube or ring of metal which fitted on to the hook, allowing the

hinge to turn ; the strap on the outside of the door
was longer than the one on the inside, with sufficient
space between the two to allow for the framing of
the door and its outside planking, and the back and
front straps were united by bolts, nails or rivets,
which passed through the thickness of the wood,
and firmly secured all, the form of the opening in
the masonry preventing, when once the door was
firmly fastened by a lock or bolt, its being forced up
from the hooks on which it hung. Allusion has been
made to the planking, which invariably covered the
framing ; beside the security of the strap this planking was also fastened to the frame by nail heads and
scrolls of metal, sometimes covering the whole of
the outside of the door with very beautiful designs ; in
most cases the scrolls started from the plain strap,
but sometimes they were separate. This was the
usual construction, irrespective of century, which
prevailed in England. On the Continent, especially
in Italy, at Verona and Rome, and at other places,
the exteriors of doors were entirely covered with
plaques of bronze. A survival of the ancient classic
times, that of Saint Zeno, Verona, is one of the most
remarkable, and is probably of Eastern work.
Although of bronze, and beyond the limits of the
present paper, allusion is made to it in consequence
of the ornamentation and nail heads, reminding one
of some of the earliest specimens of Norman or
twelfth-century metal in England and France.

It would be difficult to decide which is really the earliest

SPECIMEN OF AN IRON HINGE

in this country. Barfreston Church, in Kent, has some early iron work on the doors, and the Cathedrals of Durham and Ripon and St. Albans. It would be hazardous to say that this last-mentioned specimen is absolutely Norman ; although generally accounted such, it is more probably twelfth-century. It occurs on the door leading from the south transept into the "Slype," the said door having two elaborate scroll hinges, more quaint than beautiful, the scrolls being closely set, and the foliage very stiff, the edge of the leaves being cut into a continuous chevron with a stiff curl at the termination ; the main part of the band or strap, before it branches out into the scrolls and foliage, being indented with a deep line in the center. From this the section slopes on each side, on which are engraved deeply a zigzag pattern whose pointmeet forms a sort of lozenge, the sections of the scrolls and foliage being flat and engraved with a single chevron. The whole of the hinge is studded with small quartrefoil-headed nails at regular distances. On the band from which the foliage springs there is a peculiarly-formed raised projection like an animal's head, slightly resembling a grille at Westminster Abbey, to which reference will be made : the hinge is either a rude copy of a thirteenth-century one, or it may be a prototype of the later and richer work of the next era. On the door of Durham Cathedral nave there is a very fine specimen of a

KNOCKER,

called the "sanctuary" knocker, of a lion or cat looking with erect ears, and surrounded by a stiff conventional mane, from which the head projects considerably ; and from the mouth, which is well garnished with sharp teeth, depends a ring, the upper part of which is flattened, and at the junction of the circular and flat part on each side is the head of an animal, from whose open mouth the flat part proceeds. It is a wonderfully spirited composition with an immense deal of character about it, the deep lines proceeding from the nose to the two corners of the mouth reminding one of some of the Assyrian work. The eyes project and are pierced ; it is supposed that they were filled at the back with some vitreous paste, but of this there is no proof. This grim knocker played a very important part in early times, for Durham Cathedral possessed the privilege of " sanctuary" and many a poor hunted fugitive must have frantically seized the knocker and woke the echoes of Durham's holy shade, and brought by its startling summons the two Benedictine monks who kept watch and ward by day and night in the chambers above the porch, and at once admitted him

into the sacred precinct, and, taking down the hur-
ried tale in the presence of witnesses, passed him to
the chambers kept ready prepared in the western
towers, where for the space of thirty-nine days he was
safe from pursuit, and was bound to be helped beyond
seas, out of the reach of danger. The peculiarity
attached to this Durham knocker must be the
excuse for this digression.

Examples of this sort of knockers, although not
necessarily "sanctuary" ones, are by no means uncommon. Beautiful examples exist at the collegiate
church of St. Elizabeth, Marburg, at the cathedral
of Erfurt, in Germany, and at the church of St.
Julian, Brionde, in Auvergne, France. The Erfurt
example is just as grim a monster as the Durham
one; the mane in each case is very similar, but it
has the additional attraction of the figure of a man
between its formidable teeth, the head and fore part
of the body, with uplifted arms, projecting from the
mouth; but the ring is plain, and it has an additional
twisted cable rim encircling the mane.

Farringdon Church, Berks, possesses a very beautiful specimen of early metal-work in the hinges on
one of its doors, very much richer in detail than the
St. Albans example, a photograph of which is shown.
Roughly speaking, there are two hinges of not quite
similar design, with floriated scrolls and a very rich
band or strap between them, floriated at each end,
and at the apex a curious perpendicular bar terminat-

ing at the lower end in the head of an animal, and at the upper with scrolls fitting to the shape of the arch; the whole of the hinges, bands and scrolls are thickly studded with nails and grotesque heads and beaten ornaments. The church has been restored; the stone carving, which is of thirteenth-century character, is entirely modern, and therefore misleading, and must not be taken as the date of the door with its metal work.

At Staplehurst Church, Kent, there was formerly on one of the doors a very characteristic Norman hinge, of a very early type; but this church has also undergone restoration, and a friend, to whom we are indebted for the photograph of the Farringdon example, states that this hinge was not there at his last visit; but in general form it resembles one at Edstaston Church, Shropshire, which retains its original hinges on the north and south doors of the nave. There are many other examples scattered about England, but all these Norman or twelfth-century hinges follow more or less the same idea—a broad strap terminating in scrolls, and whose end next the stonework is intersected by another broad strap forming nearly two-thirds of a circle, with scrolls at the ends; and between the two hinges by which the door is actually hung, there is one or more flat bands, also floriated, the iron-work protecting the whole surface of the woodwork, but not so completely as in the next era.

In France the work was, like the architecture, a little more advanced. Foliage was more extensively used, the scrolls generally finished with a well-molded leaf or rosette ; but the form of the scrolls is still stiff and lacks the graceful flow of the thirteenth century. Some of the best specimens are preserved at the cathedrals of Angers, Le Puy, Noyeau, Paris, and many others, especially at the Abbey of St. Denis.

DOOR WORK.

In addition to the metal-work on the doors, in many of the large churches in France of the twelfth century, the large wheel windows are filled with ornamental iron grilles. Noyeau has a noted example. These grilles were more particularly used when there was no tracery, the ramifications of the iron-work almost supplying the want of it. Viollet le Duc in his *Dictionnaire Raissonne* gives a very beautiful example of this. The grilles referred to are not the iron frames in which the twelfth and thirteenth century stained glass is contained, as at Canterbury, Bourges and Chartres, and in innumerable other instances, but were designed especially to fill these large circular openings, and the effect is very beautiful.

The next era during which the smith's art seems to have arrived at a culminating point is the thirteenth century. We have an immense number of examples, nor have we to go far to find them ; they are as well represented in England as on the Continent. The idea is much the same as in the preceding century, only the scrolls are easier in their curves, the foliations more general, and the wood-work almost entirely covered. In the cloisters of St. George's Chapel, Windsor, is a nearly perfect example; the door occurs in Henry III.'s work, some very beautiful wall arcading still remaining in juxtaposition. The door itself is of more recent date, probably Edward IV.'s time, but the iron-work has belonged to an earlier door. It can scarcely be called a hinge; it is more correctly a covering of metal-work, and although mutilated in parts, the design is exceedingly beautiful. Each leaf of the door has three pointed ovals, known technically as the "vesica" shape; these are intersected in the center perpendicularly by a bar of iron, and from this and the vesicæ spring very beautiful curves, filling up the whole interstices. The sides and arched top have an outer continuing line of iron, from which spring little buds of foliage at intervals; the lower vesicæ are now imperfect, having one-third cut off, and the top continuing line on the left is wanting. Between the first and second panels are two circular discs with rings for handles, seemingly of later date; the intersecting bar is not continuous, but terminates close to the point of each oval, with an embossed rosette, thickly studded with small nails to attach it to the wood-work, and with heads, bosses and leaves at intervals.

At York Minster there are splendid specimens of metal work on two cope chests ; these chests are of the shape of a quadrant of a circle, so as to obviate folding the cope, often stiff with gold embroidery. The lids open in the center more than once, and the hinges with their scrolls cover the whole surface ; the design and execution of the work being similar to the previous example.

At Chester Cathedral there is an upright vestment press in the sacristy, opening in three divisions of one subdivision ; but in this case, as at Windsor, the iron-work is more as a protection than as a hinge, for the hinges are separate, being only small straps of metal and not connected with the scrolls. The design is irregular, the center division having a perpendicular line from which spring five scrolls on each side, with floriated ends ; the left-hand division has one bold scroll in three curves, and the right-hand division opens in two subdivisions, each having a horizontal bar in the center, with scrolls springing from each side, but reversed, the lower being the boldest ; the center and right have continuing lines on each side, but none at the top or bottom. This example at Chester Cathedral is a very beautiful one, and not so much known as it should be, or deserves.

At Ripon Cathedral there is also another vestment press, but the hinges are plain strap hinges with a stiff conventional series of curves on each side, more curious, perhaps, than beautiful. The handle is a simple circular disc, with punched holes round the outer circumference, and a drop ring handle. Ripon Cathedral possesses also some very good hinges on the south door of the choir, which may be twelfth century, but if not, are certainly thirteenth century, and they have no back straps.

Eaton Bray Church presents, on the south door, a very fine specimen of early metal-work. Here the door is again covered with the scrolls diverging from three strap hinges reaching quite across the door, the apex of the arched head being also filled with scroll work; portions of the bands are also ornamented with engraved work; the leaves and rosettes are punched. The ring and plate are perfect. This specimen is in a very good state of preservation, only some of the scrolls at the bottom being imperfect. In the same church is another hinge of more simple character, but of a very quaint design, and possessing the peculiarity of being alike on both the inner and outer sides of the door. In the Cathedral Close at Norwich there are the remains of a beautiful specimen of iron work covering one of the doors, but it is in a sadly mutilated condition, the upper hinge being the only one perfect; this has an outer iron band following the outline of the door, though only one portion remains, and between the two hinges is a horizontal bar starting from a central raised boss from which hangs the handle, the ends of the bar being floriated.

The examples enumerated here are only a few

among many, a detailed description becoming monotonous, for they all more or less follow one general arrangement.   The French examples differ slightly in treatment, but there the strap is rather broader and does not branch out into scrolls until it reaches more than half across the door; the scrolls are shorter and the foliage richer than in the English examples, and the scrolls do not bear the same proportion to the strap.   A very good hinge is still to be seen on the north door of Rouen Cathedral, Portes de Calendriers, and at Noyon Cathedral, on the door of the staircase leading to the treasury.   But hinges were not the only things upon which the smith of the Middle Ages exerted his skill and ingenuity.   The grilles which protected the tombs in the interior of churches and the opening in screens demanded alike the exercise of both, and at Westminster Abbey there is still preserved and replaced *in situ*, after having been for many years thrown by on one side among useless lumber, a specimen which any age or any clime might justly be proud of.   Around the shrine of Edward the Confessor repose many of his successors, and this chapel and shrine was exceedingly rich in costly gifts, silver, gold and jewels being there in great abundance.   Originally the only entrance to the chapel was through the doors in the screen forming the reredos of the high altar, and though considerably elevated above the level of the pavement of the surrounding aisle, it was not sufficiently secure to protect its precious contents, and there must have been some screen or railing. At the close of the thirteenth century the only royal tomb besides that of the royal founder, Henry III., was that of his daughter-in-law, Eleanor of Castile. Henry's tomb was of a good height, but Eleanor's was not so lofty, and there was the dread of the robbers making free with the offerings to the shrine, as they had done only a short time previously with the treasure which the king had amassed for his Scotch wars, and which was stolen from the treasury in the cloisters hard by.

A grille of beautiful workmanship was accordingly placed on the north side of the tomb toward the aisle, the top of the grille being finished with a formidable row of spikes, or "chevaux de frise," as we now term them, completely guarding the chapel on that side. The framework of forged bars projects from the tomb in a curve, and on the front of these bars is riveted some exquisite scrollwork. It is difficult to describe in detail this art treasure—a photograph only could do it justice; the wonderful energy and beauty and minute variety thrown into the little heads of animals, which hold the transverse bars in their mouths, and the beauty of the leaves and rosettes, scarcely two of which are alike, are things which must be seen to be appreciated. On the score of anything very beautiful attributed to foreigners, this iron work, like the beautiful effigy of the queen whose tomb it guards, has been attributed to French or Italian influence ; and the English Torell, who molded and cast the bronze effigy, has been Italianized into Torelli, a name which he never bore in his lifetime. With regard to its being French, France has now nothing existing resembling it in the slightest degree ; while the work in the cloister at St. George's Chapel, Windsor, before referred to, does resemble it slightly in some points. A very beautiful grille exists at Canterbury Cathedral, screening St. Anselm's Chapel from the south aisle and the tomb of Archbishop Meopham. This grille does remind one of Italian or foreign work, but there is every reason to believe it to be English ; its great characteristic is its extreme lightness, for it is formed of a series of double scrolls, only ½ inch wide by ⅛ inch in thickness, 7½ in. high and 3⅛ in. broad, placed back to back and fastened together and to the continuous scrolls by small fillets or ribands of iron wound round ; these being fixed into iron frames, 6 ft. 6 in. high by about 2 ft. 10 in. broad. This extreme lightness makes it resemble the foreign examples.

THE EFFECT OF THE GREAT LONDON FIRE ON THE ART.

There is one particular phase of the smith's art in England which deserves more than a passing notice. The great impetus given to the industrial arts by the universal re-building after the great fire of London exercised a considerable influence on the art of the

smith, and there is the peculiarity attaching to the
revival that the productions are essentially English
and are unlike the contemporary work on the Continent, preserving an individuality perfectly marked
and distinct. One might almost call it a "school"
and it lasted for nearly a hundred years.

St. Paul's Cathedral, which was commenced in
1675 and the choir so far completed that it was
opened for service in 1697, possesses some of the
finest specimens of this date in the grilles and gates
inclosing the choir, and although one is bound to
confess that it was to a foreign and not to a native
artist that these are due, yet in many particulars they
resemble genuine English work. One has but to
compare these gates with others of the same date in
France to directly see the immense difference between them, as in the inclosures of the choir of the
Abbey church of St. Ouen, at Rouen, and at the
cathedral at Amiens The artist's name was Tijau
or Tijou, for the orthography is doubtful. In addition to these large gates, the original positions of
which have been altered since the rearrangement of
the cathedral, there are several smaller grilles in
some of the openings and escutcheons to some of
the internal gates with the arms of the Dean and
Chapter very beautifully worked into the design.
The whole of the ironwork at St. Paul's deserves a
close inspection. The outer railings, which are part-

ly cast, are of Sussex iron and were made at Lamberhurst.

Most of the city churches have very good iron-work, especially in the sword rests and communion rails, some of the finest of the former being at All-hallows Barking, St. Andrew Undershaft, and St. Mary at Hill, and the latter at St. Mary, Woolmoth. The altars of some of these city churches are marble slabs supported on a frame of wrought iron-work. In the church of St. Michael, Queenhythe, now destroyed, there was a very curious iron bracket, with pulley and chain for the font cover, and some wrought-iron hat rails. Though the hinges and locks of these churches are not remarkable, many of the vanes are curious. St. Lawrence Jewry has a grid-iron in allusion to the martyrdom of the saint. St. Mildred, Poultry, and St. Michael, Queenhythe, both destroyed, bore ships in full sail; St. Peter's, Corn-hill, the cross keys; St. Mary-le-Bone has a flying dragon; and St. Antholin, Budge Row, had a very fine vane surmounted by a crown. The destruction of this church and spire, one of the most beautiful in the city, will ever be a lasting disgrace to those who brought it about. In the church of St. Dionis Back-church, at the west end, supporting the organ gallery, stood square columns of open work of wrought iron, and with very nicely wrought caps, but the church has also been destroyed, and the pillars probably sold for old iron. Some of the brass chandeliers, where they had not been made away with, to be replaced by gas standards or brackets, are suspended by iron-work more or less ornamented and gilded, a good specimen having existed at the church of St. Cathe-rine Cree, and there is still one remaining at St. Sa-viour's, Southwark. At St. Alban's, Wood street, a curious hour-glass is preserved in a wrought-iron frame, a relic of Puritan times ; and though hour-glasses and their stands are not uncommon, it is a comparative rarity when found in a church of the date of St. Alban's, Wood street.

The smith also found plenty of occupation in mak-ing railings and gates for public bodies and for pri-vate houses, and wrought-iron handrails to staircases. One of the most beautiful specimens of the art of the seventeenth century is to be seen in a pair of gates at the end of a passage or hall in the building occu-pied by the managers and trustees of the Bridewell Hospital, Bridge street, Blackfriars ; the wrought leaves and scrolls are very rich, being designed for internal work, and date from very soon after the fire of London.

The honorable and learned societies of Gray's Inn, and the Inner Temple have fine scroll entrance-gates to their respective gardens, and scattered about in the suburbs at Clapham, Chelsea, Fulham, Stoke Newington, Stratford-by-Bow and Hampstead are fine entrance gates, whose designs are doubtless very familiar, since there is scarcely an old brick mansion

with red-tiled roof and dormer windows and walled
garden that does not possess them. There is considerable beauty about these gates; notably in the
way in which the upright standards are a¹ternated
with panels of scroll-work, and the upper part enriched with scrolls and leaves and the initials of the
owner or his arms worked in, some of this work indeed being very delicate and refined, especially with
regard to the foliage. But the chief glory of the
English school of this date is the wonderful work upon
the gates, now preserved at Kensington Museum,
formerly adorning the gardens at Hampton Court
Palace, and the work of Huntingdon Shaw. These
are far superior to the gates in St. Paul's Cathedral,
for the latter are a little too architectural in their
treatment, Corinthian pilasters being freely introduced, while these Hampton Court ones are free
from any approach to architectural forms in iron and
rely for effect solely upon the bold curves and sweeps
of the scrolls, the richness of the acanthus-like foliage and the delicacy of the center medallions. The
wreaths, which are suspended from the top, are wonderfully modeled, some of the flowers introduced
being almost as delicate as the natural ones they
represent, or rather reproduce in iron; one
medallion in particular, being truly exquisite. At
the top of each of the gates are some fine masks, in
some cases surrounded by foliage, and each gate
is different in design, although they resemble one

another in general form. South Kensington Museum possesses six of these gates—one with a rose, another with the rose of England surrounded by small buds and leaves, a thistle; this last one is superbly modeled, the peculiarity and bend of the leaf being accurately rendered. Another has the harp of Ireland, but with strings rent and broken, emblematic of the present state of that unhappy country; and three have the initials of William of Orange and Mary Stuart. If William's name in these days may not be quite so popular as it once was, and if he did but little for the country over which he was called to govern by a dominant party, at least he was the means of calling into existence these exquisite works of art, which hold their own against any foreign production, and place the smith, Huntingdon Shaw, foremost among those who, working with stalwart arm, with anvil and hammer, were able to throw life and energy into the dull mass of metal before them.

In the staircase of a house in Lincoln's Inn Fields, at No. 35, there is a wonderful specimen of a wrought-iron staircase. At present this wrought work terminates at the first floor, but there is evidence of it having been continued to the second floor, a panel having been once sold at Christy's for £40 which purported to have come from No. 35 Lincoln's Inn Fields, and had been removed in consequence of extensive alterations in the interior. The rail is composed of separate standards, with scrolls and leaves, until it reaches the landing, which sweeps round a circular well-hole ; round this the standards cease, and are replaced by an extraordinarily fine panel, in which one can recognize the same hand as in Hampton Court gates.   There is the same wonderfully modeled mask with foliage proceeding from it, the same sort of wreath depending in advance of the other work, the rich acanthus foliage partly masking the boldly designed scrolls beneath, betraying the hand of Huntingdon Shaw or his school.   The date would also fit, for this house and the next are traditionally supposed to have been designed by Christopher Wren for the Solicitor and Attorney-Generals about 1695–96, the date of the Hampton Court work. The center oval medallion of this panel has unfortunately gone, and is replaced by some initials in cast iron ; but it probably contained some of those beautifully modeled bunches of flowers which appear on the Hampton Court gates.

CHAPTER I.

ANCIENT AND MODERN HAMMERS.

A trite proverb and one quite frequently quoted in modern mechanical literature is, "By the hammer and hand all the arts do stand." These few words sum up a great deal of informa-

ELEVATION.   SECTION.

FIG. 1—A TAPPING HAMMER OF STONE.

tion concerning elementary mechanics. If we examine some of the more elaborate arts of modern times, or give attention to pursuits in which complicated mechanism is employed, we may at first be impressed that however correct this expression may

have been in the past, it is not applicable to the
present day. But if we pursue our investigations
far enough, and trace the progress of the industry
under consideration, whatever may be its nature

END ELEVATION.

SIDE ELEVATION.

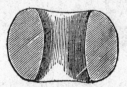

SECTION.

FIG. 2—PERFORATED HAMMER HEAD OF STONE.

back to its origin, we find sooner or later that both
hammer and hand have had everything to do with
establishing and maintaining it. If we investigate
textile fabrics, for instance, we find they are the

products of looms. In the construction of the looms the hammer was used to a certain extent, but back of them there were other machines of varying degrees of excellence, in which the hammer played a still more important part, until finally we reach a point where the hammer and hand laid the very foundation of the industry. It would be necessary to go back to this point in order to start anew in case by some unaccountable means our present equipment of machinery should be blotted out of existence. The wonderful mechanism of modern shoe factories, for another example, has superseded the cobbler's hammer, but on the other hand the hammer and hand by slow degrees through various stages produced the machinery upon which we at present depend for our footwear. And so it is in whatever direction we turn. The hammer in the hands of man is discovered to be at the bottom of all the arts and trades, if we but go back far enough in our investigation. From an inquiry of this kind the dignity and importance of the smith's art is at once apparent. While others besides him use hammers, it is to the smith that they all must go for their hammers. The smith, among all mechanics, enjoys the distinction of producing his own tools. A consideration of hammers, therefore, both ancient and modern, becomes a matter of special interest to blacksmiths of the present day as well as to artisans generally.

The prototype of the hammer is found in the clinched fist, a tool or weapon, as determined by circumstances and conditions, that man early learned to use, and which through all the generations he has found extremely useful. The fist, considered as a hammer, is one of the three tools for external use with which man is provided by nature, the other two being a compound vise, and a scratching or scraping tool, both of which are also in the hand. From using the hand as a hammer our early inventors must have derived the idea of artificial hammers, tools which should be serviceable where the fist was insufficient. From noting the action of the muscles of the hand the first idea of a vise must have been obtained, while by similar reasoning all our scraping and scratching tools, our planes and files, our rasps, and, perhaps, also some of our edged tools, were first suggested by the finger nails. Upon a substance softer than itself the fist can deal an appreciable blow, but upon a substance harder than itself the reaction transfers the blow to the flesh and the blood of nature's hammer, much to the discomfort of the one using it. After a few experiments of this kind, it is reasonable to suppose that the primitive man conceived the idea of reinforcing the hand by some hard substance. At the outset he probably grasped a rounded stone, and this made quite a serviceable tool for the limited purposes of the time. His arm became the handle,

while his fingers were the means of attaching the
hammer to the handle. Among the relics of the
past, coming from ages of which there is no written
history, and in time long preceding the known use
of metals, are certain rounded stones, shaped, it is
supposed, by the action of the water, and of such a
form as to fit the hand. These stones are known
to antiquarians by the name of " mauls," and were,
undoubtedly, the hammers of our prehistoric ancestors. Certain variations in this form of hammer
are also found. For that tapping action which in
our minor wants is often more requisite than blows,
a stone specially prepared for this somewhat delicate operation was employed, an illustration of
which is shown in Fig. 1. A stone of this kind
would, of course, be much lighter than the " maul "
already described. The tapping hammer, a name
appropriate to the device, was held between the
finger and the thumb, the cavities at the sides being
for the convenience of holding it. The original
from which the engraving was made bears evidence
of use, and shows traces of having been employed
against a sharp surface.

The " maul " could not have been a very satisfactory tool even for the work it was specially calculated to perform, and the desire for something
better must have been early felt. To hold a stone
in the hollow of the hand and to strike an object
with it so that the reaction of the blow should be

mainly met by the muscular reaction of the back of the hand and the thinnest section of the wrist is not only fatiguing, but is liable to injure the delicate network of muscles found in these parts. It may have been from considerations of this sort that the double-ended mauls also found in the stone age were devised. These were held by the hand grasping the middle of the tool, and were undoubtedly a great improvement over the round mauls. Experience, however, soon suggested that in even this form there was much wanting. It still lacked energy to overcome reactions, the office which the wooden handle so successfully performs. Experiments were, therefore, early made in the direction of a more suitable handle than the unassisted arm and of a proper connection between the hammer and the handle. The first attempts were doubtless in the use of withes, by which handles were attached to such of the double-ended mauls as may have seemed suitable for the purpose. This means of fastening the handle is seen to the present day among half-civilized nations, and in some cases is even practised by blacksmiths to whom are available other and more modern means. Evidences of a still further advance are, however, found at almost the same period, for in the geological records of the stone age are met double mauls with holes through their centers for the insertion of a handle In some instances these holes are found coned, and

are almost as well adapted for the reception of
hammer handles as the best tools of modern times.
An illustration of one of these primitive tools is
presented in Fig. 2.

From this it will be seen that the advance toward
a perfect hammer in the earliest periods was important as well as rapid. All the preliminary experimenting to the development of a perfect tool was
done by men who lived and worked before history
commenced to be written. What remained to be
done by the fraternity was entirely in the direction
of more suitable material, and in the adaptation of
form to meet special requirements. While principles were thus clearly established at an early day,
very slow progress seems to have been made in
applying them and in perfecting the hammer of the
modern artisan. Between the " maul " of the sav-
age of the stone age and a " Maydole " hammer,
what a gulf! From the " tapping hammer " of
stone, illustrated in Fig. 1, to a jeweler's hammer of
the present day, what a change! Between the
double-faced perforated stone hammer, shown in
Fig. 2, and the power forging hammers of modern
practice, what a series of experiments, what a record
of progress, what a host of inventors! In whatever
direction we turn and from whatever standpoint we
view the hammer there are clustered around it facts
and legends, historical notes and mechanical principles, to the consideration of some of which a portion
of our space may be well devoted.

To trace the origin of the hammer, commencing
with its prototype, the human fist, and advancing
step by step through the stone age, where fragments
of rocks were made to do roughly the work that better
tools afterwards performed, and so down the ages until
the finished hammer of the present day is reached,
would read like a romance. Like a pleasing story
it would, perhaps, be of very little practical value,
however entertaining the narrative might be, and,
therefore, we shall not follow the development of
the hammer too minutely. We desire to interest
our readers, but we also hope to do more than
simply amuse them.

The hammer has been justly called the king
of tools. It has been sung by poets, and made
the central figure of graphic scenes by some
of the world's most noted writers. Sir Walter Scott
has turned it to good account in some of his stories.
The poet of modern history, however, is yet to
come ; but when his day appears there will be much
of suggestive incident from which he can fashion his
song. Some of the most beautiful and delicate
works that has ever been produced by the hand of man
has been wrought by the hammer, and the skillful
hammerman is well worthy of admiration. The
fabled hammer of Thor is scarcely an exaggeration of
the giant tools in actual use to-day in scores of iron
works, and it would appear that the mythology makers
of ancient times really saw visions of the coming ages,

when they wove the wonderful stories that were a part of the religion of our ancestors.

We are very apt to look upon the hammer as a rude instrument. We overlook the scientific principles involved in its construction and use, and pay too little attention to the materials of which it is fashioned and the forms in which it is made. We frequently look upon it merely as an adjunct to other tools, and forget that it is entitled to consideration as a sole independent and final tool. In some handicrafts, and these, too, involving a high class of finished work—the hammer is the only tool employed. That great artistic skill in the use of the hammer as a finishing tool can be acquired is manifest from the many beautiful specimens of *répoussé* work to be seen in silversmiths' shops. The details of the ornamentation are not only minute, but they so harmonize as to give elegance and expression to the whole, exclusive of the form of the articles themselves. A glance into the art stores in any of the cities will reveal specimens of hammered work of this sort, or of duplications of them, made by electroplating or by stamping with dies. The excellence, and, consequently, the value of these copies depends upon the closeness of imitation to the original ; and as they are for the most part very clever specimens in this particular, they serve as illustrations in point almost as well as the originals. Those of our readers who are interested in the capabilities and possibili-

ties of the hammer will be interested in an examina-
nation of some of these pieces of work. They are
mostly of brass and copper, and in both originals
and copies the tool marks are faithfully preserved.
The esteem in which they are held may be judged
from the statement that a piece of work of this kind
about half the size of one of these pages sometimes
fetches as much as $25, while shields of a larger
size frequently sell for three and four times this
sum. Choice originals are cherished in museums
and are beyond the reach of money to buy. Other
examples of hammer work might be mentioned, for
example, the ancient wrought-iron gates, hinges and
panels, representations of which are frequently met
in art books. The suits of mail, and choice armor,
most of which the ancient warriors were wont to
clothe themselves in, are also examples in point.
As marvelous as these examples of ancient work
may seem, we think there are modern applications
of the hammer that are quite as wonderful.

THE HAMMER.*

* * * The hammer is generally known as a
rude instrument, but as a matter of fact it is in some
of its uses a very refined one, requiring great care
and skill in its use. * * *

Time forbids that I should refer to more than a
few prominent forms of hammers. The carpenter's

* [From a lecture delivered before the Franklin Institute, by Joshua Rose, M. E., Philadelphia.]

mallet has a large rectangular head, because, as his tools are held in wooden handles, he must not use a hard substance to drive them with, or he will split the handles. Wood being light, he must have a large head to the mallet in order to give it weight enough.

THE STONE-MASON'S MALLET.

The stone-mason uses a wooden mallet, because

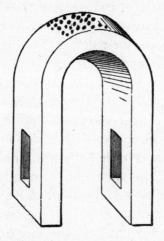

FIG. 3—AN ILLUSTRATION OF THE PROCESS OF STRETCHING WITH THE HAMMER.

it delivers just the kind of dull blow that is required. His mallet head is made circular, because his tools are steel, and have no wooden handles, and he is able to use the whole circumference, and thus prevent the tools from wearing holes in the wooden mallet face. The handles of both these mallets are short, because they will strike a sufficiently powerful blow without being used at a great leverage. On the other hand, the stone-breaker's hammers have long handles, to avoid the necessity of stooping. The pattern-maker's hammer is long and slender; long, that it may reach down into recesses and cavities in the work, and slender, because, being long, it has weight enough without being stout. Now, take the blacksmith's sledge, and we find the handle nearer to the pene, or narrow end, than it is to the broad-faced end, while the pavior's sledge has the handle in the middle of its length. If we seek the reason for these differences, it will readily occur to us that the blacksmith's helper or striker delivers most of his blows in a vertical direction, and uses mainly the face and not the pene of the hammer, and by having the eye, and therefore the handle, nearest to the pene end, the face end naturally hangs downward, because, as held by the handle, the face end is the heaviest, and, as a result, he needs to make but little, if any effort, to keep the face downward. The pavior's work, however, lies near the ground, and he uses both faces, his hammer not requiring a pene. Hence the handle is placed central, balancing both faces equally.

THE MACHINIST'S HAMMER.

The machinist's hammer is also made heavier on the face than on the pene end, so that the face which he uses the most will hang downward without any special effort to keep it so. His chipping hammer, which he also uses for general purposes, weighs in the heaviest kinds 1¾ pounds, and the handle should be 15 inches long. He wields it for heavy chipping, with all the force he can command, obeying the law that it is velocity rather than weight that gives penetration. Thus, supposing a hammer weighing 100 pounds is traveling at a velocity of ten feet per second, and the power stored up in it is 1,000 foot-pounds. Another hammer, weighing one pound and traveling 1,000 feet per second, would also have stored up in it 1,000 foot-pounds. Hence the power is equal in the two, but the effects of their blows would be quite different. If they both struck a block of iron we should find that the effects of the quick moving hammer would sink deeper, but would spread out less sidewise, giving it a penetrating quality; while the slow-moving one would affect the iron over a wider area and sink less deeply. To cite an important operation in which this principle must be recognized : Suppose we have a wheel upon a shaft, and that the key is firmly locked between the two. In driving it out we know that, if we take a heavy hammer and strike slow, moving blows we shall spread the end of the key riveting it up and making it more difficult to drive out ; so we take a hammer having less weight and move it quicker.

USES OF THE HAMMER.

In whatever form we find the hammer, it is used for three purposes only, namely, to crush, to drive and to stretch. And the most interesting of these operations are stretching and driving. The gold-beater, the blacksmith, the sawmaker, the plate straightener and the machinist, as well as many others, employ the hammer to stretch; while the carpenter, the machinist, and others too numerous to mention, use the hammer to drive. Among the stretching operations there are many quite interesting ones. Here in Fig. 3, for example, is a piece of iron, two inches wide, and an inch thick, bent to the shape of the letter *u*. This piece of wire is, you observe, too short to fit between the jaws, and I will now bend the piece and close the jaws by simply hammering the outside of the curved end with a tack hammer. The proof that the blows have bent the piece is evident, because the piece of wire now fits tightly instead of being loose, as before the hammering. The principle involved in this operation is that the blows have stretched the outer surface, or outside curve, making it longer and forcing the jaws together. If we perform a similar operation upon a straight piece of metal, the side receiving the blows will actually rise up, becoming convex and making the other side concave, giving us the seeming anomaly of the metal moving in the opposite direction to that in which the blows tend to force it. This process is termed pening, because, usually, the pene of the hammer is used to perform it. It is sometimes resorted to in order to straighten the frame-work of machines, and even to refit work that has worn loose.

STRAIGHTENING PLATES AND SAWS.

Straightening thin metal plates and saws form very interesting examples of the stretching process, and are considered very skillful operations. Some few years ago I was called upon to explain the principles involved in this kind of straightening, and having no knowledge of the subject, I visited a large saw factory to inquire about it. I was introduced to one of the most skillful workmen, and the object of my visit was made known to him. He informed me that it was purely a matter of skill, and that it was impossible to explain it.

" I will show you how it is done," said he, and taking up a hand-saw blade, he began bending it back and forth with his hands, placing them about eight inches apart upon the blade.

" What do you do that for ?" I asked.

" To find out where it is bent," he replied.

      *   *   *   *   *

I spent two hours watching this man and questioning him, but I left him about as much in the dark as ever.

Then I visited a large safe-making factory, knowing that the plates for safes required to be very nicely straightened. The foreman seemed very willing to help me, and took me to the best straightener in the shop, who duly brought a plate for a safe door and straightened it for me. Then he brought another, and as soon as he stood it on edge and began to sight it with his eye, I asked him why he did that.

"Because the shadows on the plate disclose the high and the low patches."

"In what way?" I asked.

"Well, the low patches throw shadows," he replied, and the conversation continued about as follows:

"When you have thus found a low place, what do you do?"

"I hammer it out."

I sighted the plate and made a chalk mark inclosing the low spot, and he laid the plate upon the anvil and struck it several blows.

"Why did you strike the plate in that particular spot?" I asked.

"Because that is where I must hit it to straighten it."

"Who told you that this particular spot was the one to be hammered?"

"Oh! I learned some years ago."

"But there must be some reason in selecting that spot, and that is what I wanted to find out."

"Yes, I suppose there is a reason for it, but if it

had been a different kind of hollow place I wouldn't have hit it there at all."

" Why not ? "

" Because I should have had to hit it somewhere else."

And so it went on, until finally I got some pieces of twisted plate, one with a bulge on one edge, another with a bulge in the middle, and he straightened them while I kept up my questions. But still the mystery remained, nor did I seem any nearer to a solution ; so I abandoned the attempt.

About six months after this I met by chance, an Eastern plate straightener, and on relating this experience to him he offered to go into the shop and explain the matter.

We went, and taking up a plate one-eighth inch thick, two feet wide and four long, he laid one end on an anvil and held up the other with his left hand, while with his right hand he bent or rather sprung the plate up and down, remarking as he did so :

" Now you just watch the middle of this plate, and you will see as I swing it the middle moves most, and the part that moves most is a *loose place*. The metal round about it is too short and is under too much tension. Now, if I hammer this loose place, I shall stretch it and make it wide, so I hammer the places round about it that move the least, stretching them so that they will pull the loose place out. Now, with a very little practice you could take out a loose place as well as I can, but when it comes to a thick plate the case is more difficult, because you cannot bend the plate to find the tight and loose places, so you stand it on edge, and between you and the window, the light and shades show the high and low patches just as a landscape shows hills and valleys."

I selected several examples of twisted and crooked

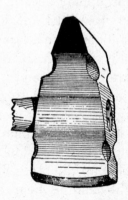

FIG. 4—THE LONG CROSS-FACE HAMMER.

plates and he straightened them for me, explaining the reasons for each step in the process, and as this forms one of the most interesting operations performed by the hammer, I may as well speak somewhat in detail of hammers, the way they are used, and the considerations governing their application to the work.

Fig. 4 represents what is called the long cross-face hammer, used for the first part of the process, which is called the smithing. The face that is parallel to the handle is the long one, and the other is the cross-face. These faces are at a right angle one to the other, so that without changing his position the operator may strike blows that will be lengthways in one direction, as at *A*, in Fig. 5, and by turning the other face toward the work he may strike a second series standing as at *B*. Now, suppose we had a straight plate and delivered these two series of blows upon it, and it is bent to the

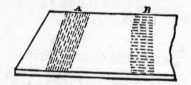

FIG. 5—SHOWING HOW THE CROSS-FACE HAMMER OPERATES IN TWO DIRECTIONS.

shape shown in Fig. 6, there being a straight wave at *A*, and a seam all across the plate at *B*, but rounded in its length, so that the plate will be highest in the middle, or at *C*. If we turn the plate over and repeat the blows against the same places, it will become flat again.

FORM OF HAMMER FOR STRAIGHTENING SAWS.

To go a little deeper into the requirements of the shape of this hammer, for straightening saws, I may

say that both faces are made alike, being rounded
across the width and slightly rounded in the length,
the amount of this rounding in either direction being
important, because if the hammer leaves indentations, or what are technically called "chops," they will
appear after the saw has been ground up, even
though the marks themselves are ground out, because in the grinding the hard skin of the plate is
removed, and it goes back to a certain and minute
extent toward its original shape. This it will do
more in the spaces between the hammer blows than
it will where the blows actually fell, giving the surface a slightly waved appearance.

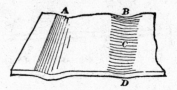

FIG. 6—ANOTHER ILLUSTRATION OF THE STRAIGHTENING
PROCESS.

The amount of roundness across the face regulates the widths, and the amount of roundness in
the face length regulates the length of the hammer
marks under any given force of blow. As the
thicker the plate the more forcible the blow, therefore the larger dimensions of the hammer mark.   *
    *   *   This long cross-face is used again after the
saws have been ground up, but the faces are made

more nearly flat, so that the marks will not sink
so deeply, it being borne in mind, however, that
in no case must they form distinct indentations or
"chops."

In Fig. 7 we have the twist hammer, used for precisely the same straightening purposes as the cross-
face, but on long and heavy plates and for the following reasons :

When the operator is straightening a short saw

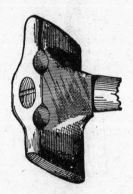

FIG. 7— THE TWIST HAMMER.

he can stand close to the spot he is hammering, and
the arm using the hammer may be well bent at the
elbow, which enables him to see the work plainly,
and does not interfere with the use of the hammer,
while the shape of the smithing hammer enables
him to bend his elbow and still deliver the blows
lengthways, in the required direction. But when a
long and heavy plate is to be straightened, the

end not on the anvil must be supported with the
left hand, and it stands so far away from the anvil
that he could not bend his elbow and still reach the
anvil. With the twist hammer, however, he can
reach his arm out straight forward to the anvil,
to reach the work there, while still holding up the
other end, which he could not do if his elbow was
bent. By turning the twist hammer over he can

FIG. 8—THE DOG-HEAD HAMMER.

vary the direction of the blow, the same as with the
long cross-face. * * *

Both of these hammers are used only to straighten
the plates, and not to regulate their tension, for you
must understand that a plate may be flat and still
have in it unequal strains ; that is to say, there may
exist in different locations internal strains that are not
strong enough to bend the plate out of truth, as it is,

but which will tend to do so if the slightest influence is exerted in their favor, as will be the case when the saw is put to work. When a plate is in this condition it is said to have unequal tension, and it is essential to its proper use that this be remedied.

The existence of unequal tension is discovered by bending the plate with the hands, as has been already mentioned, and it is remedied by the use of the dog-head hammer, shown in Fig. 8, whose face

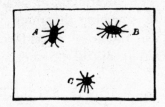

FIG. 9—SHOWING THE DIFFERENCE IN THE EFFECTS OF TWIST AND DOG-HEAD HAMMER BLOWS.

is rounded so that the effects of its blow will extend equally all around the spot struck. It will readily be understood that the effects of the blow delivered by the smithing, or by the twist hammer, will be distributed as in Fig. 7, at *A B*, while those of the dog-head will be distributed as in Fig. 9, at *C*, gradually diminishing as they pass outward from the spot struck; hence the dog-head exerts the more equalizing effect.

USE OF THE DOG-HEAD HAMMER.

Now, while the dog-head is used entirely for

regulating the tension, it may also be used for the
same purposes as either the long cross-face, or the
twist hammer, because the smith operates to equalize
the tension at the same time that he is taking down
the lumps ; hence he changes from one hammer to
the other in an instant, and if after regulating the
tension with the dog-head he should happen to require to do some smithing, before regulating the tension in another, he would go right on with the dog-
head and do the intermediate smithing without
changing to the smithing hammer. Or, in some
cases, he may use the long cross-face to produce a
similar effect to that of the dog-head, by letting the
blows cross each other, thus distributing the hammer's effects more equally than if the blows all lay in
one direction.

CHAPTER II.

ANCIENT TOOLS.

A paper that was recently read before a scientific association in England, gives interesting particulars about tools used by the artisans who worked on the ancient buildings of Egypt, and other moribund civilizations. The subject proved specially valuable in showing how skilled artisans performed their work 4,000 years ago. The great structures whose ruins are scattered all over North Africa and Asia Minor, demonstrate that great artisan and engineering skill must have been exercised in their construction, but when parties interested in mechanical manipulations tried to find out something about the ancient methods of doing work, they were always answered by vague platitudes about lost arts and stupendous mechanical powers which had passed into oblivion. A veil of mystery has always been found a convenient covering for a subject that was not understood. The average literary traveler who helped to make us the tons of books that have been written about Oriental ruins, had not the penetration or the trained skill to reason from the character and marks on work what kind of a tool was employed in fashioning it.

A trained mechanic, Flanders Petrie, happened round Egypt lately, and his common-sense observations and deductions have elucidated many of the mysteries that hung round the tools and methods of ancient workmen. From a careful collection of half finished articles with the tool marks fresh upon them —and in that dry climate there seems to be no decay in a period of four thousand years—he proves very conclusively that the hard diorite, basalt and granite, were cut with jewel-pointed tools used in the form of straight and circular saws, solid and tubular drills and graving tools, while the softer stones were picked and brought to true planes by face-plates.

That circular saws were used the proof is quite conclusive, for the recurring cut circular marks are as distinctly seen on these imperishable stones as are the saw marks from a newly cut pine plank. This proof of the existence of ancient circular saws is curious, for that form of saw is popularly believed to be of quite modern invention. That another device, supposed to be of recent origin, was in common use among Pharaoh's workmen is proved by the same authority. We have met several mechanics who asserted that they made the first face-plate that was ever used in a machine shop, and we have read of several other persons who made the same claims, all within this century. Now this practical antiquary has gone to Egypt and reported that he found the ochre marks on stones made by face-plates that were used by these old-time workmen to bring the surfaces true.

As steel was not in use in those days the cutting points for tools must have been made of diamond or other hard amorphous stone set in a metallic base. The varied forms of specimens of work done, show that the principal cutting tools used were long straight saws, circular disc saws, solid drills, tubular drills, hand grainers and lathe cutters, all of these being made on the principle of jewel points, while metallic picks, hammers and chisels were applied where suitable. Many of the tools must have possessed intense rigidity and durability, for fragments of work were shown where the cutting was done very rapidly, one tool sinking into hard granite one-tenth inch at each revolution. A curiosity in the manner of constructing tubular drills might be worthy of the attention of modern makers of mining machinery.

The Egyptians not only set cutting jewels round the edge of the drill tube, as in modern crown drills, but they set them in the sides of the tube, both inside and outside. By this means the hole was continually reamed larger by the tool, and the cone turned down smaller as the cutting proceeded, giving the means of withdrawing the tool more readily.

As indications on the work prove that great pres-

sure must have been required to keep the tools cutting the deep grooves they made at every sweep, the
inference is that tools which could stand the hard
service they were subjected to, must have been mar-
velously well made.

AN AFRICAN FORGE.

In describing his African journey up the Cam-

FIG. 10—AN AFRICAN FORGE.

eroons River from Bell Town to Budiman, Mr. H.
H. Johnston refers to a small smithy, visited at the
latter town, in which he came across a curious-look-
ing forge. Many varieties of African forges had

been noted by him, but this differed markedly from any he had seen. Ordinarily, he says, the bellows are made of leather—usually a goat's skin, but in this case they are ingeniously manufactured from the broad, pliable leaves of the banana. A man sits astride on the sloping, wooden block behind the bellows, and works up and down their upright handles,

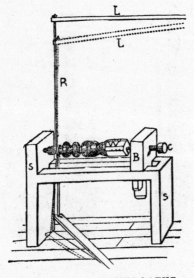

FIG. 11—A PRIMITIVE LATHE.

thus driving a current of air through the hollow cone of wood and the double barreled iron pipes (fitted with a stone muzzle) into the furnace, which is a glowing mass of charcoal, between two huge slabs of stone. Fig. 10 is an illustration of this remarkable specimen of the African smith's ingenuity.

ANCIENT AND MODERN WORK AND WORK-MEN.

Forging is a subject of interest to all smiths. Excellent work was made in the olden days, when stamps, dies and trip hammers were unknown.

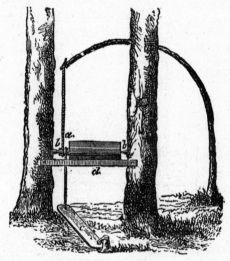

FIG. 12—A LATHE NOW IN ACTUAL USE IN ASIA.

I saw some examples of ancient forging in the exhibition of 1851, made in 1700, that were simply beautiful, both in design and execution. They were a pair of gates in the scroll and running vein class of design. The leaves were beautifully marked and not a weld was to be seen. Now I am not one of

those who think we cannot produce such work now-
adays, for I feel sure we can if we could spare the
time and stand the cost, but undoubtedly blacksmithing as an art has not advanced in modern
times, and in this respect the blacksmiths are in
good company, as was shown in the ancient Japanese
bronze vases (in the Centennial Exhibition at Philadelphia), which brought such marvelous prices.
Some of the turned works of the last century were
simply elegant, and in this connection I send you
two sketches of ancient lathes. Figure 11 is that
from which the lathe took its name. A simple wood
frame, *S* and *S*, carried a tail stock, *B*, and center
screw, *C*, carrying the work, *W*. The motion was
obtained from a lathe *L* (from which the word
lathe comes), *R* is a cord attached to *L*, wound once
around the work and attached to the treadle, *T*.
Depressing *T* caused the lathe *L* to descend to *L*
while the work rotated forward. On releasing the
pressure on *T* the lathe rotates the work backward
so that cutting occurs on the downward motion of
T only.

A very ancient device you may think. But what
do you think of Fig. 12, a lathe actually in use to-day
in Asia, and work from which was exhibited at the
Vienna exhibition. Of this lathe, London *Engineering* said :

"Among the exhibits were wood glasses, bottles,
vases, etc., made by the Hercules, the remnants of

an old Asiatic nation which had settled at the time of the general migration of nations in the remotest parts of Galicia, in the dense forests of the Carpathian Mountains. Their lathe (Fig. 12) has been employed by them from time immemorial."

We must certainly give them credit for producing any work at all on such a lathe ; but are they not a little thick-headed to use such a lathe when they can get, down East, lathes for almost nothing ; and if they know enough of the outside barbarian world to exhibit at an exhibition, they surely must have heard of the Yankee lathe.—*By* **F. F.**

CHAPTER III.

CHIMNEYS, FORGES, FIRES, SHOP PLANS, WORK BENCHES, ETC.

A PLAN OF A BLACKSMITH SHOP.

The plan on page 34 shows the arrangement of my shop. I keep all my tools and stock around the sides of the shop so as to have more room in the center. I do all my work, repairing, iron or wood work on the one floor, shown in Fig. 13. My forge is two feet four inches high, and four feet square ; it is made of brick and stone. My chimney has a 12-inch flue, which gives me plenty of draught. My tuyere-iron is set four inches below the surface of the forge ; this arrangement gives me a good bed o coal to work on. My vise bench is two feet wide and seven feet long ; it has a drawer in it for taps and eyes. My wood-work bench is two and a half feet wide and eight feet long. The blower takes up a space of four feet ten inches ; I can work it with a lever or crank. The drill occupies two by two feet. The tool-rack is built around the forge, so that it does not occupy much room and is handy to get at. The forge is hollow underneath, which allows me to dump the fire and get the ashes out of a hole left for the purpose. I use a blower in preference to the

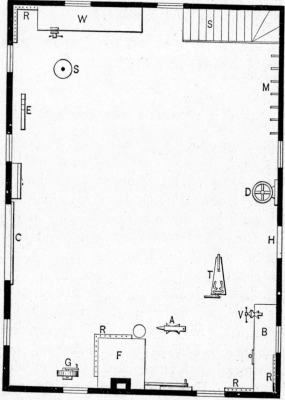

FIG. 13--PLAN OF A BLACKSMITH SHOP.

old-fashioned bellows, and consider it far superior in every way.

In the illustration, *A* denotes the anvil; *B*, is a

vise bench for iron work ; *RR*, are tool racks for
taps, dies and other small tools ; *C*, is a large front
door ; *D*, is an upright drill ; *E*, is a tire bender ; *G*,
is a grindstone ; *H*, is a back door, and my tire stone
is directly opposite, so I can step to it easily with a
light tire from the forge ; *I*, is my blower ; *V*, is a
vise for iron work ; *T*, is a tire upsetter ; *M*, is an iron
rack ; *S*, a pair of stairs ; *W*, is my wood-working
bench ; *R*, is a rack for bits and chisels ; *S*, is a wheel
horse for repairing wheels ; *F*, is the forge ; and near it
is a rack for tongues and swedges. The round spot
at the corner of the forge is a tub. I have a small
back attached to my anvil block for holding the tools
I use while at work on any particular job.—*By* J. J. B.

AN IMPROVED FORGE.

My hood for smoky chimneys, shown in a previous
communication, is a good one, generally speaking,
but there are some kinds of work that will not go
between this hood and the bottom of the hearth, and
to get over this difficulty I have devised the arrangement shown in the accompanying illustration, Fig. 14.

I derived the leading idea from a forge in Dundee,
but in making mine I deviated from this pattern to
suit myself. The great secret in having a good fire
is to have a good draft, and to have a good draft it
must be built after scientific principles. First, a
vacuum must be made so large that when your fire is

built, the blaze immediately burns the air, thereby
forming a draft which acts after the balloon principle,
having an upward tendency. The chimney should be
at least sixteen feet in height. Now, for the forge:

FIG. 14—AN IMPROVED FORGE.

I tore the old one away clear down to the floor, and
built a new one with brick, making it on the side four
feet and two inches (that is, from the back part of the
chimney), three feet and six inches in width and two

feet and eight inches in height. I placed my tuyere four inches lower than the surface of the hearth, leaving a fire-box nearly semi-circular in shape, about fourteen inches across the longest way and ten inches the other way. I then finished the hearth, making it as level as I could conveniently. I then put a straight-edge on the face of the chimney four inches from each corner, marked it, and cut all of the front away for the distance of four feet and six inches, leaving the heavy sides undisturbed. I then commenced laying brick on the surface. beginning at the edge of the chimney; the front part of the extension chimney was allowed to come within three inches of the hole in the tuyere. I laid three courses of brick and left directly over the tuyere an opening four inches by eight inches—this is large enough for a draft opening. I then completed the chimney up as high as I had the old chimney, drawing in at the top, and the job was complete, and a better drawing forge cannot be found. The noise it makes in drawing, reminds one of the distant rumbling of a cyclone.

Now I would like to say just a little in reference to the tuyere I am using. It is manufactured by J. W. Cogswell, and I think it is the finest working tuyere I ever had the pleasure of using. It is made on the rotary principle, the top turning one quarter around. It suits almost any kind of work. By opening the draft a large fire can be obtained and by closing it you have a light one.

You can have a long blast lengthwise, crosswise, or at any angle, and for welding light or heavy work, I can say the Cogswell tuyere is hard to beat.

In the illustration (Fig. 14), *A*, shows the position of the tuyere three inches from the face of the chimney. *F*, is the face of the chimney. *G*, is the upper section of the hearth. *B*, is the draft rod. *C*, is the rod that lengthens or shortens the blast. *E*, *F*, *D*, constitute the new part of the chimney. *I*, is the old chimney. *H*, is the draft, which is four inches

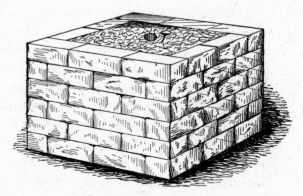

FIG. 15—THE FORGE-STAND.

by eight inches in the clear, and is six inches above the hearth. *J*, is the cinder box.—*By* L. S. R.

A SIMPLE FORGE.

The illustration herewith shows a simple forge at which may be performed some of the most difficult forgings.

The forge-stand, as shown in the illustration, is square in shape, but may be made round or any other shape to suit. *A*, Fig. 15, is the tuyere. The size of the forge must be made to suit the work. One that would answer for average purposes should be about twenty-four inches square, and about twenty or twenty-two inches high, and detached

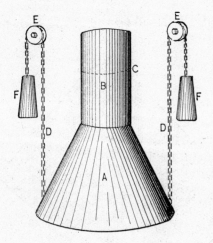

FIG. 16—THE SMOKE-STACK AND BONNET.

from the walls so as to allow of getting all around it. Fig. 16 shows the smoke-stack and bonnet. *A*, is the bonnet; *B*, the smoke-stack; *C*, is a dotted line showing the next joint of pipe as telescoped. *D D*, are chains running over the pulleys, *E E*, which are secured to the wall or ceiling. *F F*, are counterweights, which balance the bonnet when raised or lowered to accommodate the work in hand.—*By* I. D.

CURING A SMOKY CHIMNEY.

I had a chimney in which the draught was bad, and it may be of interest to many to learn how I remedied the trouble. I did so by making a hood of boiler iron.

I first cut the hood to the shape shown in Fig. 17

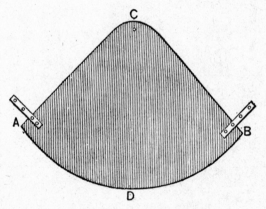

FIG. 17—THE HOOD.

of the accompanying engraving. The distance from *A* to *C* is two feet, and from *A* to *B* the distance is four feet, eight inches. From *C* to *D* it is two feet, five inches. I then cut away all projecting parts of the chimney, and next bent the hood to fit the chimney as closely as possible. I then put the hood up where I wanted it to be, that was about fifteen inches above the tuyere iron, and marked out the outline of the chimney, I then removed all the bricks inside the mark and riveted two straps, each eight inches long, on the hood at the points *A* and *B*. I also punched a hole at the top at *C*. I next drove a twenty-penny spike through the hole *C* to the middle of the chimney, being careful to set the nail in the mortar between the bricks. I then nailed the straps to the chimney and taking a strong wire drew

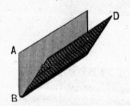

FIG. 18—THE CINDER CATCH.

the slack at *A* and *B* so that it fitted snugly. I next plastered it around the edge and gave it two coats of whitewash. The job was then finished and it is the best arrangement for a smoky chimney I have ever seen.

I have a very good cinder catch, also made of boiler iron, in the form shown in Fig. 18 of the illustrations. It was made by taking a piece eight inches wide and long enough to reach across on the inside of the chimney, and bending the piece as shown in the sketch. The catch should fit in tightly.

Fig. 19 represents the chimney with the hood attached.—*By* L. S. R.

A BLACKSMITH'S CHIMNEY.

The illustration, Fig. 20, shows my method of making a blacksmith's chimney so that it will draw

FIG. 19—SHOWING THE HOOD ATTACHED TO THE CHIMNEY.

well. I know what it is to have a smoky chimney. I had my chimney torn down and built up again four times in two years. The last time it was built I think

I struck on the right plan. The forge is built of
stone. I use a bottom blast tuyere. The space *B*,
in the illustration, is left open to receive the handle
of the valve, and to allow the escape of the ashes.
The front of the chimney, *F*, is built straight or perpendicular from the hearth, *H*. *C* denotes the open-

FIG. 20—A BLACKSMITH'S CHIMNEY THAT WILL NOT SMOKE.

ing for the smoke. The distance from *H* to *C* is
about four inches, or the thickness of two bricks.
Let me say here that the mouths of most all flues are
too high up from the fire, and this allows the smoke
to spread before it reaches the draught. The fire
should be built as close to the flue as possible, and

the top of the chimney should be a little larger than
the throat.

I think this is the handiest flue that can be built
for general blacksmithing.—*By* J. M. B.

ANOTHER CHIMNEY.

As there are a great many who do not know how

FIG. 21—A BLACKSMITH'S CHIMNEY THAT WILL DRAW.

to build a chimney that will draw well, I send you a
sketch, Fig. 21, of a chimney that I have been

using for fifteen years and that has given me perfect satisfaction.

It is made of brick or stone and is joined to the

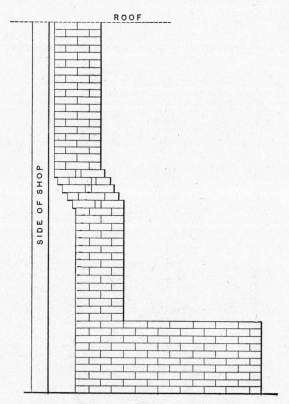

FIG. 22—ANOTHER BLACKSMITH'S CHIMNEY THAT WILL DRAW.

hearth, the latter being six bricks below the jamb. The round hole in the bottom side is the bellows hole, and the square hole in the end of the jamb is very convenient for small tools, etc. The hearth and jamb can be built in size and height to suit the builder.—*By* J. K.

STILL ANOTHER CHIMNEY.

The illustration on page 45, Fig. 22, represents

FIG. 23—STILL ANOTHER CHIMNEY THAT WILL NOT SMOKE.

my method of building a blacksmith's chimney so that it will draw well and will not smoke. The original chimney from which this sketch is taken has been in use in my shop for four years, and is as free from soot and cinders as it was the first day it was used. Its peculiar construction is due to the fact that the mason who built it made a mistake of eight inches in locating the forge, and, therefore, he had to give the chimney a jog of eight inches to get it out at the place intended for it. In making one it is best to run it out three feet, and if on the side run two feet above the comb.—*By* J. S. H.

ANOTHER FORM OF CHIMNEY.

My way of building a blacksmith's chimney, and one that will take up the smoke and soot, is shown in the accompanying engraving, Fig. 23.

It will be seen that there are five bricks across the base up to a height of five bricks, then a gradual taper to four bricks, and then two bricks and a half by one and a half. The flue or smoke hole is ten inches in diameter. This chimney will draw.—*By* G. C. C.

AN ARKANSAS FORGE.

The accompanying sketch, Fig. 24, with brief description, will give a good idea of the forge I use.

The shell of the forge is a section of iron smoke-stack, four feet in diameter, filled in with sand and brick. I use a water tuyere, and find it the best I ever tried. I use a blower in place of a bellows, and could not be hired to return to the bellows. My forge is at least six feet from any wall. The water keg rests on a bracket fastened to the wall, and, as shown in the illustration, the pipes extend downward and along the ground to the forge, and then beyond it. The pipes have caps on the ends. I use an angle valve, as shown,

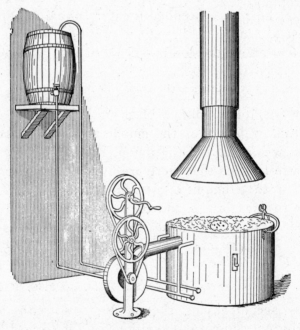

FIG. 24—AN ARKANSAS FORGE.

for shutting off water from the pipes. A rack for tongs is fastened to the back of the forge. A stationary pipe extends from a few feet above the forge through the roof. A smaller pipe with a hood on the lower end extends up into the large pipe, and this is suspended by weights so as to be raised or lowered at will.—*By* E. C.

SETTING A TUYERE.

Dropping into a small smithy on the west side of New York City, a short time ago, I found the

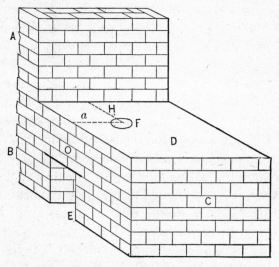

FIG. 25—SHOWING THE FORGE AND BACK WALL.

proprietor much perplexed. He was trying to raise a welding heat on the center bar of a phaeton dash which had dog-ears or projections on each side. A dozen attempts were made while I looked on, and all

were failures. " I'll have to send this job out to my
neighbor," said the smith. Then I suggested that
there was no necessity of doing so. The trouble was
owing to the fact that the tuyere was about eight
inches out from the back wall of the forge and the
dog-ears on the dash projected about fourteen inches.
With the old-fashioned back blast, the smith could
have banked out a blow-hole with wet coal the whole
length of his forge, and thus have accomplished his
weld in short order, but there would have been more
or less waste of coal. His tuyere was a bottom-blast
one, and to him there was apparently no way out of
the difficulty.

I asked the privilege of trying my hand at the job
and was given permission. My first trick was to
locate the objectionable brick and remove it. Then
one of the dog-ears of the dash could enter. I raised
the heat, made the weld, and suggested to my friend
that a handful of cement would repair the breach.
Since then it has occurred to me that a short chapter
on setting tuyeres would not be amiss, and I now
present my ideas in type and illustrated.

In Fig. 25, *A* represents a section of the back
wall of a brick forge; *B* is the working side; *C*,
the face; *D*, the top; *F*, the center of the
tuyere; *O*, the rod hole of the tuyere; and *E*,
the ash pit. Measuring from *A* and *B*, the center
of the tuyere is as shown by the line drawn, *a*
and *H ;* the distance should not be less than eighteen

inches or more. The distance will be sufficient for most of the work that is done by the average wagon or carriage smith. Set the tuyere top from four inches to six inches below the level of the forge. The heavier the irons to be manipulated the deeper must the top of the tuyere be set.

In building a new forge it is a wise precaution to build a recess in the back of the forge or forge wall as deep as the construction of the chimney will allow. If the wall be sixteen inches thick let the recess be

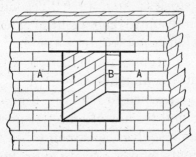

FIG. 26.—SHOWING HOW THE RECESS IS MADE.

not less than eight inches deep and twenty-four inches high and at least twenty-four inches or more wide; then, with the tuyeres set eighteen or more inches out, the most intricate forging can be handled with care. The sparks and ashes which ascend part of the way and then return, settle in the recess and thus keep the fire clean and clear. Fig. 26 shows the manner of constructing the recess, *A A* being the back wall, and *B* the recess.—*By* I. D,

A MODERN VILLAGE CARRIAGE-SHOP.

Prize Essay written for The Carriage-Builders' National Association by WM. W.
WETHERHOLD, of Reading, Pa.

In building a carriage shop, room, light and ventilation are the three great points to attain, and the builder who does attain these points and at the same time has everything convenient will have a perfect shop. In selecting a site I have taken a corner lot and have arranged my plans to run back to the ten-foot alley, using my full length of plot and getting light from three sides. Size of lot, 110x65 ft. (Height of stories: first, 12 ft.; second and third, 10 ft. For size and arrangement of room, see floor plan.) The office is fronting the main street, adjoining the wareroom, and is fitted with desks for clerks and a fire and burglar-proof safe, a table at side window at which to take the time of the hands in going to and from work, a letter-press, a stationary wash stand, shelves, speaking tubes to the different departments, and a private desk for the use of the proprietor. There is a door leading to the wareroom, one to the stock room, and is convenient to the elevator and stairway leading upstairs. The walls are plastered and kalsomined. The wareroom adjoins the office, facing the main street. The elevator opens into it, and there are sliding doors connecting it with the wood shop. The walls and ceilings are covered with cypress wainscoting, two inches wide, plowed and grooved, and finished in oil, and the windows have inside shutters.

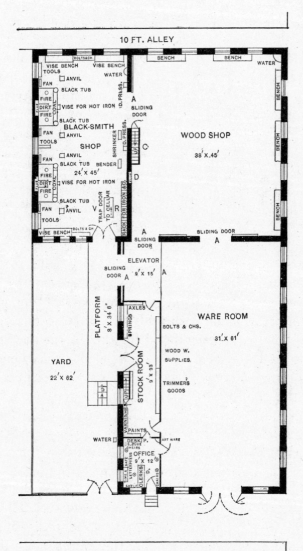

FIG. 27.—PLAN OF THE FIRST FLOOR.

The stock room is next to the office, and is fitted with shelves and racks for proper storing and accounting of stock. There is a door to the elevator and a stairway leading upstairs ; also a door to the yard for the unloading of goods without interfering with the workmen. The upper half of the partitions are ash with glass to admit light. The elevator is next to the stock room and is so arranged that the work of the smith shop can be put on and hoisted without going outside in unpleasant weather.

The wood shop is at the rear of the main building, adjoining the smith shop, and is fitted with five benches. It is next to the elevator and has a stairway leading to the second floor. The second floor is used entirely for the paint department. Going from the wood shop we get into the paint room, which has a paint bench with mill and stone to mix colors, etc. Shelves are arranged for the proper keeping of cups and brushes. There is also a vise bench in this room, with tools, bolts, screws, oil, washers, etc., for the taking apart and putting together of work. There are two spaces with cement floor, one for gears and the other for bodies. The elevator and stairway are in this room. The front of the second floor is partitioned off for varnish rooms. I have used the front so as to be removed from the smith and wood departments as far as possible. The windows are double and the ceilings and walls finished with cypress the same as the wareroom. These rooms have inside shutters also.

The trimmer room is on the third floor back, and is fitted with benches for three men. The floor plans will show position of shelves, closets and sewing machine. I have a small room connected with the trimming room to be used entirely for the stuffing of cushions, etc. It is of great help in keeping the trimming room and all the work clean. The third floor, front, is intended for the storage of bodies in stock, ironed and in the rough, and for a wareroom for second-hand work after it is rebuilt. Here, also, I have shelves for all cushions, carpets, curtains, etc., belonging to any job which is being rebuilt and repainted.

In case of my painters being crowded with work, I can have all new bodies brought upstairs and taken ahead in paint, thus giving them more room on the second floor. The smith shop I have placed in an annex, so as to remove all dirt and dust as much as possible from the main building. It is made to run four fires. The windows on the side are placed high to prevent looking into the next yard, but the large front and back windows allow plenty of light. The second floor of this annex will be used for storage of lumber, wheels, wheel stock, shafts, etc., for the wood-workers ; the door in the yard can be used to unload lumber, and I have also one of the rear windows arranged with a roller by which to take in lumber. The trap door in the floor can be used to slide lumber down into the wood shop, as it is on a line with the sliding doors connecting the wood and smith departments.

I have arranged a heater in the cellar of the smith shop, and will heat the whole shop with steam generated by it.

It will work automatically, and will require attention only twice daily except in extremely cold weather, when more attention will be needed.

To stock a shop of this kind completely at once would be a very difficult matter. I should proceed as follows : I would order 5,000 feet of lumber, assorted into 500 feet $\frac{5}{16}$ and $\frac{3}{8}$-inch poplar surfaced on both sides ; 2,000 feet $\frac{1}{2}$-inch poplar, surfaced on both sides ; 500 feet ash, $\frac{3}{4}$-inch ; 1,000 feet ash, $1\frac{1}{4}$ to 2 inch ; 1,000 feet hickory, $1\frac{1}{4}$ to 2 inch. I would order wheel stock for 25 sets of wheels, as follows : 5 sets for $\frac{3}{4}$-inch tire, 10 sets for $1\frac{1}{8}$-inch tire, 5 sets for $\frac{7}{8}$-inch tire, and 5 sets for $1\frac{5}{16}$-inch tire ; 2 dozen pair shafts, 2 dozen pair drop perches, wood screws, nails, glue, etc.; 25 sets of axles to suit wheel stock ; 25 sets of springs, bolts and clips in assorted sizes, and paints and varnishes. Bows and trimming goods I would not order at once, as I would now open up shop, and try to book a few orders, and see what quality of work was wanted to suit my new customers.

I believe that in ordering a little sparingly at first I could do better in the end by watching the run of my trade, as I could then change my stock, if necessary, without any loss.

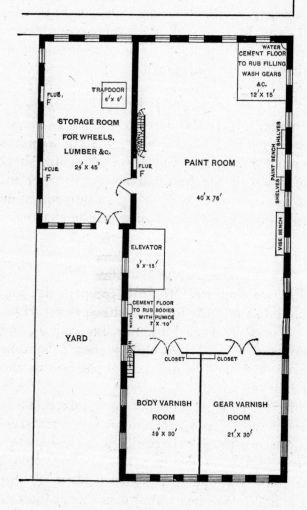

FIG. 28.—PLAN OF THE SECOND FLOOR.

The floor plans of the shops are shown in the accompanying illustrations, in which Fig. 27 represents the first floor, Fig. 28 the second floor, and Fig. 29 the third floor. The drawings are on the scale of 24 feet to the inch.

BEST ROOF FOR A BLACKSMITH SHOP.

In answer to your correspondents, G. H. & Son, who inquire about the best roof for a blacksmith shop, let me say that I prefer a corrugated sheet-iron roof, made of the best galvanized Number 20 iron, fastened down with copper wires wrapped around the rafters. Nails will work out with the changes in the weather.—*By* J. B. H..

HOLLOW FIRE VS. OPEN FIRE.

For welding steel to iron I always use an open fire, or I should say for the last ten years have done so. Formerly I used a hollow fire, but as I became more experienced in welding dies I became convinced that a hollow fire was not the best or cheapest for that purpose.

I have seen a great deal of work welded in a hollow fire, and have seen much of it burnt and rendered entirely worthless. In welding a steel plate to an iron one, I want my iron much hotter than I can get it in a hollow fire without burning the steel. As a hollow fire heats almost as fast at the top as it does at the bottom, it will be seen that in order to

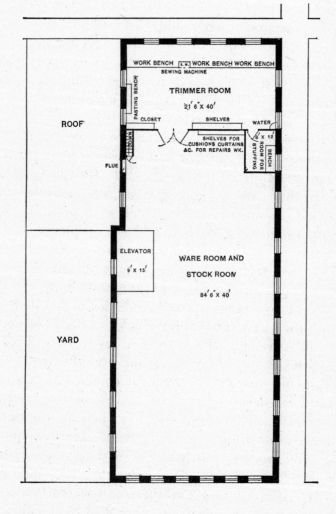

FIG. 29.—PLAN OF THE THIRD FLOOR.

get a welding heat on the iron you are pretty sure to get the steel too hot, and if you do not get a welding heat on the iron of course the steel will not weld. It may seem to be welded a great many times when it is only stuck in one or two places, and if it is not thoroughly welded it is sure to start off when it is being hardened or used.

I have not used a hollow fire for several years for welding steel to iron, for many reasons, among which I may mention the following : First, because it takes more time, and, of course, is more expensive ; and second, because I cannot do the work as well. My way of building a fire is this : I put on plenty of coal to make a fire of sufficient size for the work I have to do, and with respect to this part of the operation each man must be his own judge. I build up the sides of my fire pretty well, and let the middle burn out ; then I fill the middle with good hard coke, and my fire is ready. Then I put in my work and cover it with small pieces of coke, and give the fire a slow blast, increasing it as the heat comes up. In this way I can bring my heat up from the bottom, getting a good welding heat on my iron when the top of the steel is at an ordinary working heat. In this kind of a fire you can see your heat better than you can in a hollow fire and tell when your steel is at the right heat. It is claimed that there are several ways to tell when the heat is right other than by looking at your iron, but I am satisfied to trust to my eyes to

inform me when the proper result has been reached.
—*By* G. B. J.

A POINT ABOUT BLACKSMITHS' FIRES.

A common trouble in country blacksmith shops
is the going-out of the fire while the smith is doing
work away from it. This annoyance can be prevented by keeping at hand a box containing sawdust. When the fire seems to be out, throw a handful of sawdust on the coals and a good blaze will
quickly follow. This may seem a small matter, but
there are many who will find my suggestion a useful one.—*By* D. P.

TO KEEP A BLACKSMITH'S FIRE IN A SMALL COMPASS.

If clay or mortar soon burn out, mix them with
strong salt brine and the trouble will be avoided—
when an intense heat is required use fine coal wet
with brine. Use a thin coating on top and around
the fire. Salt and sand mixed and thrown on top of
the fire also serves a good purpose.

BLACKSMITH'S FIRE FORGE.

With reference to the manner of managing a
blacksmith's fire so as to accomplish the best results,
I will describe the forge I am using. It is 2 feet 6
inches high ; the bed is 3 feet 10 inches long and 3
feet wide, and in construction is a box. The legs
are made of 4x4 stuff. The tuyere is placed 5 inches
below the surface. I use a common bellows, size 32

inches. With this forge I have no difficulty in welding a 2¼-inch axle or facing a 10-pound sledge-hammer. The chimney is an inverted funnel, and is made of sheet-iron. At the bottom it is 2 feet 5 inches in diameter. It joins a 7-inch pipe at the top.—*By* H. B.

CEMENTING A FIRE-PLACE.

To cement a fire-place so that the cinders will not stick, I use old axes instead of bricks. I put the polls of the axes out at the front of the breast of the forge. I use from 12 to 15 axes in one forge, putting two axes below the pipe and two on each side, and as many above as are needed. I use what is called yellow clay for mortar, putting a handful of salt in the clay, and then beating it thoroughly so that there will be no lumps in the mortar. I put the axes and mortar in as I would bricks and mortar. The fire-place is left deep enough to have a bed of dust in the bottom. A fire-place fixed in this way will last for twelve months. The cinders are lifted while hot. —*By* F. M. G.

CEMENTING A SMITH'S FIRE.

My way of cementing a blacksmith's fire so that the cinders will not stick is as follows: I use Power's patent fire-pot. I have used this fire-pot nine years, and it is as good now as it was the day I put it in my shop. There is no sticking of cinders, and no cementing or fitting up of the fire is necessary, and the saving in my coal-bill for one month amounts to more than the cost of the fire-pot.—*By* J. McL.

BLACKSMITH COAL.

Though little is said regarding the coal used in a blacksmith shop the subject is one well worthy the attention of all interested in the working of iron. The three coals in use are charcoal, anthracite and bituminous. For all purposes charcoal is the best, but its drawbacks are such as to curtail its use. These are the cost and the time needed to secure the proper combustion. Except in extreme cases, it is not likely to come in use again, and the blacksmith must therefore depend upon the mineral coals.

Bituminous coal possesses more of the essentials requisite than the anthracite, but the quality is an important matter. Some is more gaseous than others; then, too, there is the oily coal, and that charged with an excess of sulphur; in others there is a great deal of earthy matter. All these faults exist, and they do much toward retarding the work of the blacksmith if they are not guarded against. It is not many years ago when all blacksmith coal was imported, but the Cumberland coal of this country is without doubt the best that can be procured. It is remarkably free from earthy matter, ignites quickly and gives a powerful heat. Anthracite "dust," as the fine siftings are designated, works well if the blast is all right, but, no matter how fine it is, it does not run together and make the close fire of the Cumberland. It also contains greater quantities of sulphur, which operates to the injury of the iron. Coke has

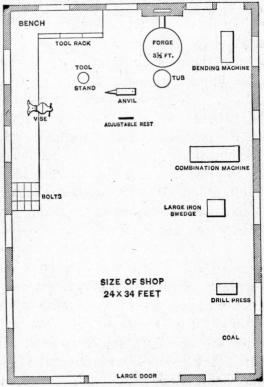

FIG. 30.—PLAN OF SHOP CONTRIBUTED BY "D. F. H."

been used to a good advantage where the fire-bed is large and the blast strong, but it does not lie close, and unless the blast is kept up it smoulders and fouls.

PLAN OF A SHOP.

I inclose you a sketch, Fig. 30, of my shop, which I think a very good one for a country place. The forge is a home-made article of tank iron, 3½ feet in diameter, the bed being filled with brick and sand. The bellows are hung overhead, and are connected with the forge by a tin tube. A place is made in front for coal. I have a fire alarm that I am intending to connect with the house, about 30 feet away. —*By* D. F. H.

PLAN OF SMITH SHOP IN A NEW YORK CITY CARRIAGE FACTORY.

Fig. 31 makes the arrangement of forges, anvils, benches, etc., quite plain.

The style of forge used in this shop is shown in Fig. 32. It consists essentially of an oblong iron pan, a hole in the bottom of which communicates with the tuyere, contained in the box-like appendage clearly shown in the engraving. The entire structure is supported on four legs made in the shape of angle iron. A long, narrow compartment at the end of the forge contains fuel, while a second compartment of about the same shape and size contains water, thus putting it in a much more desirable position and in more convenient shape for use than the old tub so common in country shops. Attached to the outside of the water-trough is a small, square bench, to

BLACKSMITHING.

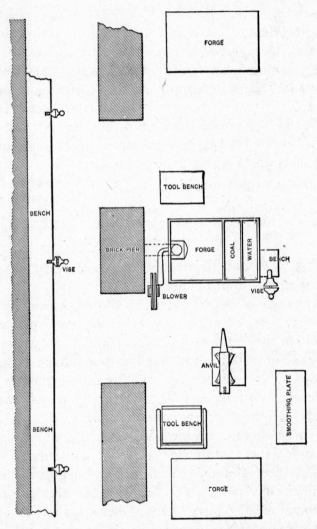

FIG. 31.—SMITH SHOP IN A NEW YORK CARRIAGE FACTORY.

which is fastened an ordinary machinist's vise, as may be seen by the engraving.

This forge possesses important advantages over the common brick forge. It occupies considerably less space, without lessening the capacity for work.

FIG. 32.—IMPROVED STYLE OF FORGE.

Its construction admits of the shop being kept clean around it, which alone is a feature of sufficient importance to warrant its introduction. Its probable cost is about the same as that of a brick forge. The fact that it is portable, however, gives it a claim for preference in this particular. It is asserted by those who have used this forge, and who have also worked at the common brick forge, that it will save its own cost in a single year, in convenience over the latter. The position of the water-trough is an important feature. It is true that a water-trough of similar construction and arrangement might be attached to a brick forge, but not with the same facility. The character of the material, brick, would necessitate a thick surrounding wall, which would render the arrangement at once somewhat awkward in appearance, and in comparison with the iron forge quite inconvenient.

A rack for supporting the ends of bars of iron in the process of heating is so arranged as to swing clear, under the forge, and yet to be ready whenever required. The brace or leg shown in the engraving is long enough to support this rack in any position that may be required.

The tool bench employed in this shop consists of a heavy wooden frame, proportioned somewhat to the load it is to carry and the use that is to be made of it. See Fig. 33. A shelf in the lower part, located but a few inches above the floor, is used as a receptacle for odd tools, bits of iron, and the general accumulation to be met with around any blacksmith's fire. The sides on the upper part are carried several inches above the top and are surmounted by an iron guard, which extends outward and is continued three-quarters of the way around the bench, thus forming an opening through which the handles of the various tools may be dropped. By referring to Fig. 32 all these particulars will be made clear.

The top of the bench is also perforated by two slots and by sundry odd holes, into which tools are

FIG. 33.—IMPROVED TOOL BENCH.

dropped. A small guard extends across the front of the bench, on a level with the top, answering a similar purpose.

To aid those who may wish to construct a similar bench a top view is shown in Fig. 34, and another one of the side or end as shown in Fig. 35, upon each of which dimensions are given in such a way as to enable any one to work from them if desired.

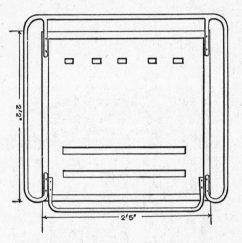

FIG. 34.—TOP VIEW OF WORK BENCH.

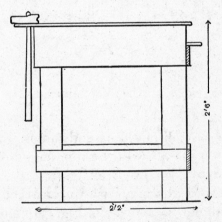

FIG. 35.—END VIEW OF WORK BENCH.

Fig. 36 shows a style of smoothing-plate or smooth-ing bench in use in this shop, which, it is claimed, answers a very satisfactory purpose, and would con-stitute a most useful adjunct for any blacksmith's shop. A heavy wooden frame supports a cast-iron plate, a

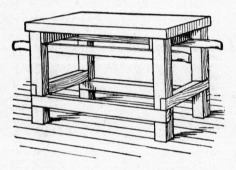

FIG. 36.—SMOOTHING BENCH.

section of which is shown in Fig. 37, and which is something like an inch and a half or two inches thick. This plate is made quite smooth on its upper surface. For straightening up various light irons used in

FIG. 37.—SECTIONAL VIEW OF SMOOTHING PLATE.

wagon and carriage work, it serves a useful pur-pose.

Fig. 38 shows an adjustable trestle used for sup-porting the ends of vehicles. A screw in the center raises the upper bar to any desired height, while the guides at the side, by means of holes in them, and pins to fit, give it stability at whatever height it is placed.   The upper bar is padded to prevent scratching.   The entire construction is light yet strong.

A PLAN OF A BLACKSMITH SHOP.

I find the arrangements of the shop I am about to

FIG. 38.—ADJUSTABLE TRESTLE.

describe very convenient, and, with the aid of the illustration, Fig. 39, they can be very easily understood. *A* denotes the shoeing floor.   *B* is the floor for plow work.   *C* is the machine and wagon floor.   *D* is the front door, which opens outwardly.   *E* is a side

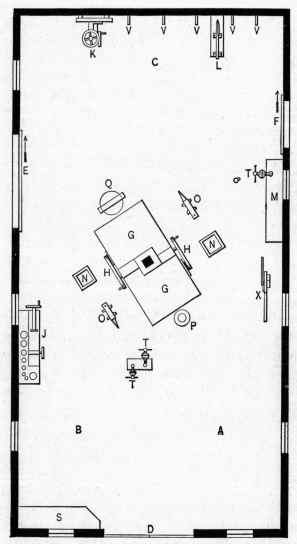

FIG. 39.—PLAN OF "J. E. M.'S" BLACKSMITH SHOP.

door that slides. *F* is another sliding door. *G* is a double forge. *HH* are No. 1 Root blowers. *I* is a vise post. *J* is a bolt cutter. *K* is a drill. *L* are iron shears that will cut 1-inch square iron. *M* is the vise bevel. *NN* are tool benches. *OO* are anvils. *P* is a mandrel. *Q* is the swedge block. *RR* are windows. *S* is an erecting bench. *TT* are vises. *U* is the chimney. *VVVVV* are pins for iron. *X* is the tire sprinkler.

In the west gable there are two windows, and in the east gable one. The platform in front of the shop is 12 x 24 feet. That on the south side is 12 x 12 feet. Both are of 2 inch plank. The sides of the shop are 9 feet high. The roof is one-third pitch. The shop is 24 feet wide and 44 feet long.

The forges are open underneath, and the blowers that set under them are connected with the tuyere by gas-pipe passing through the base of the chimney. A good hand will earn for me a dollar a day more with these blowers than with the best 36-inch bellows I ever owned.—*By* J. E. M.

CARE OF THE SHOP.

To do good work one must have good tools, as it is impossible for a smith to forge his work smooth unless his tools are in good order. It is likewise necessary for him to have good coal; but with a shop conveniently arranged, and with perfect tools and the best of coal, there is much which depends upon the way in which they are used that determines the character of work and the relative economy with which work is performed. There is no other branch of carriage making that requires so much skill as that of the smith. This is because he has no patterns, like the wood-workman, and is under the necessity of shaping all irons by his eye. A smith has more to endure than any other mechanic, for if there is anything wrong about a job the smith is sure to get the blame, whether it be his fault or not. The strength and durability of a buggy, for example, depends principally upon the blacksmith. If smiths would go to work and wash their windows, clean out behind their bellows, pick up their scrap that lies promiscuously about the shop, gather up the bolts, etc., they would be surprised at the change that it would make, not only in the general appearance of their shop, but also in the ease and convenience of doing work. One great disadvantage under which most smiths labor is the lack of light. Frequently blacksmith shops are stuck down in a basement or in some remote corner of a building. It is a fact, whether it be disregarded or not, that it is easier to do good work in a clean, well-lighted shop than in one which is dirty and dark.

A word about economy in work, for the benefit of the younger men in the trade especially. Don't throw away a bolt or clip because a nut strips, but go to

work and tap out a new one and fit a new nut. Old
bolts that are sound and that are often thrown in the
scrap are just as good for repairs as new. Careful
attention to these points will make a material differ-

FIG. 40.—A HANDY WORK BENCH.

ence in the expenses of the shop in the course of
time.—*By* B. P.

A HANDY WORK BENCH.

The plan of a work bench shown in Fig. 40 shows
a very handy arrangement for tools.

The legs and top are of hard-wood. Birch is very
good. The ends, back and open space in the bottom
are boarded up on the inside. The height of the legs
is 2 feet 10 inches, length of body 4 feet 4 inches,

width of end 1 foot 7 inches. The tops can project at the ends to suit your taste. Three drawers, 5 3-4 x 11 inches, are on the left side. On the right there are three 5 3-4 x 11 inches and two 2 1-4 x 11 inches. The middle drawer is 2 1-4 x 7 1-2 inches. I hinged a strip up and down the ends, so two padlocks would lock all the drawers except the middle one. Bolt the vise in the center of the bench, and it will be found

FIG. 41.—PERSPECTIVE VIEW OF TOOL BENCH.

very convenient. Such a bench ought not to cost over ten dollars.—*By* H. A. S.

BLACKSMITH'S TOOL BENCH.

Inclosed I send drawings of a tool bench, such as is used by me, which I think handy in all respects.

The bench was made originally from an old box that had been lying around our shop for some time. Fig. 42 shows how the box has been adapted to the purpose. The size of the box was 2 feet 8 inches square, and

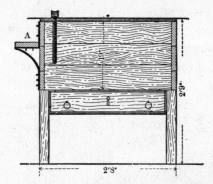

FIG. 42.—SIDE VIEW OF BENCH, SHOWING DIMENSIONS.

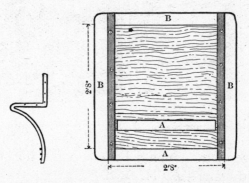

FIG. 43.—PROFILE VIEW OF BRACKET.   FIG. 44.—TOP VIEW OF BENCH.

19 inches high. Four posts or legs were attached, as indicated in Fig. 41. One board was taken off from the end of the box, and out of it was made the shelf

shown in perspective, in Fig. 41. This left the opening
into the box below the shelf. In the box I keep
my punches, heading tools, etc.; on the shelf I keep
cold chisels, gouges, punches and pins. Below the
box on the right-hand side I have placed a drawer in
which I keep papers, slate pencils, chalk and new
files. This is provided with a lock not shown in the
sketch. Fig. 42 of the accompanying sketches represents a side view of the bench, and also shows the

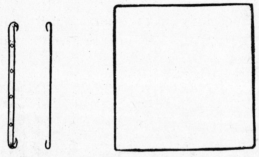

FIG. 45.—IRONS BY WHICH THE
FRAME IS FASTENED TO
THE BENCH.

FIG. 46.—THE IRON FRAME
EXTENDING AROUND
TOP OF BENCH.

shelf *A* in profile. The different dimensions are indicated in figures upon this sketch. Fig. 43 shows
a profile of the iron which forms the brackets that
support the shelf. Fig. 44 is a top view of the bench.
A A represent the front where the bottom swedges
are placed. *BBB* shows the position of the handle
swedges. Fig. 45 presents the shape of the two irons
which hold the frame shown in Fig. 46 to the bench,

a general view of which is also afforded by Fig. 41.
Fig. 46 represents an iron frame which goes entirely
around the bench, and serves as a rack for tools. It
is made of 5-8 inch oval iron. The two irons shown
in Fig. 45 are made of 7-16 x 3-16 steel tire. In fastening these two irons to the frame, the hooks come
on the underside, so as to bring the frame level with
the bench.—*By* Now and Then.

A CONVENIENT WORK-BENCH.

The dimensions of the work bench shown in
sketch, Fig. 47, are, length 16 feet, width 32 inches,

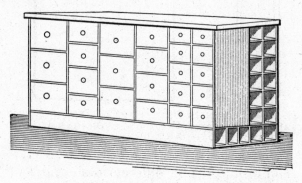

FIG. 47.—A WORK-BENCH DESIGNED BY " L. S. T."

height about the usual. It contains sixteen to
twenty drawers and twelve to sixteen boxes that
extend through its length and are six inches
square or larger. These boxes are for iron bars
such as 1-4, 5-16, 3-8, 7-16, 1-2, 9-16, 5-8, 7-8, round,

and other light irons. The drawers may be used for horseshoes, nuts, washers, etc., etc.—*By* L. S. T.

HOME-MADE PORTABLE FORGE.

I made a small portable forge a short time since, as

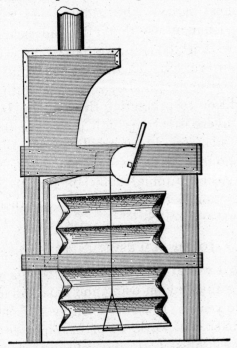

FIG. 48.—HOME-MADE PORTABLE FORGE.

shown in sketch, Fig. 48. In size it is two feet square and three feet high; it is made entirely of wood; the bellows are round and are sixteen and a half inches in size. I covered them with the best sheepskin I could get.   The bed of the forge consists of a box six inches deep.   It is supported by corner posts, all as shown in the sketch.   Through the center of the bottom is a hole six inches in diameter for the tuyere ; this is three inches in outside diameter and is six inches high.   The bed is lined with brick and clay.   I find by use that it does not heat through. The bellows are blown up two half circles with straps from a board running across the bottom, all of which will be better understood by reference to the sketch.

In addition to protecting the bed by brick and clay, the tuyere is set through a piece of sheet iron doubled and properly secured in place.   The hood which surmounts the forge was made out of old sheet iron, and has been found sufficient for the purpose. The connection between the tuyere and the bellows is a tin pipe.—*By* S. S.

IMPROVED BLACKSMITH'S TUYERE.

Perhaps it would not come amiss if I gave you a sketch of a tuyere I am using and have had in use for twenty-five years.   It works entirely satisfactory up to a certain size of work.   For example, it will answer for the lightest work, and weld up to about a four-inch bar, and is made complete, or the castings only are furnished by the Pratt & Whitney Company, of Hartford, Conn., who are using it in their own shops. It consists, as will be seen from the accompanying sketch, Fig. 49, of a wind-box *A*, supported on brick-

work which forms an ash-pit *G* beneath it. To this
box is bolted the wind-pipe *B*, and at its bottom is
the slide *E*. In an orifice at the top of *A* is a triangular and oval breaker *D*, connected to a rod operated by the handle *C*. This rod is protected from the
filling, which is placed between the brick-work and
the shell *F* of the forge, by being encased in an iron

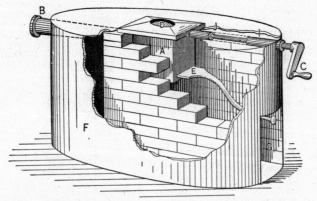

FIG. 49.—SHOWS POSITION "J. T. B.'S" TUYERE ON THE FORGE.

pipe *I*. The blast passes up around the triangular
oval piece *D*. The operation is as follows: When
D is rotated, it breaks up the slag gathered about
the wind passage or ball in taking a heat, and it falls
into the box below. At any time after a heat the
slide *E* may be pulled out, letting the slag and dirt
fall into the ash-pit beneath. A sectional view is
seen in Fig. 50. It is a great advantage to be able to
clear the fire while a heat is on without disturbing

the heat. You will see that there is nothing to get out of order, and as a matter of fact the tuyere will last fifteen years or more. The top of the wind-box is two inches thick and the sides ½ inch thick; it weighs altogether about sixty pounds.—*By* J. T. B.

THE SHOP OF HILL & DILL.

Prize Essay written for the Carriage Builder's National Association.

The carriage shop that produces one hundred new vehicles annually, without steam or power machin-

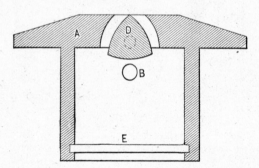

FIG. 50 IS A SECTIONAL VIEW THROUGH SLAG BREAKER D.

ery, has joined the "Society of the Obsolete," but the shop of about that capacity without power, which makes repairing its chief dependence, and builds enough new vehicles to keep the shop open and the help at work through seasons when repairing is dull seems to have or ought to have a place in the industrial economy of mankind. To such an establishment Messrs. Hill & Dill have pinned their industrial faith and their sign-board. They cater to the wants of those who desire special vehicles out of the usual line of sale work. They build extra wide carriages for fat people, give extra head and leg-room to tall people, and welcome the butcher, the baker, and the coal money-maker, when they come to order business vehicles with special features. Even the cranky doctor, minister or school superintendent, who thinks he has *invented* a vehicle which will revolutionize the business, is not frowned upon. He will probably want a good sensible Goddard to ride in after he gets through fooling with inventions.

To thoroughly know the establishment, we must know the firm. Mr. Hill, the capitalist of the firm, was formerly in the livery-stable business. He is a solid-built, shrewd, tidy-looking, affable business man. He has a large knowledge of carriages as a buyer and user, and paid repair bills for many years. He knows a good horse, a good carriage and a good customer at sight, and knows how to use them so as to get the most out of them.

Mr. Dill is some ten years younger than his partner, tall and bony, hair rather long and trousers rather short. The corners of his mouth point upward, and he looks as though he was on the point of laughing out loud, but no one ever caught him in the act. He talks but little, and is endowed with excellent judgment and numerous offspring. He

was formerly a body-maker, but degenerated or developed into a foreman of a repair shop.   He takes

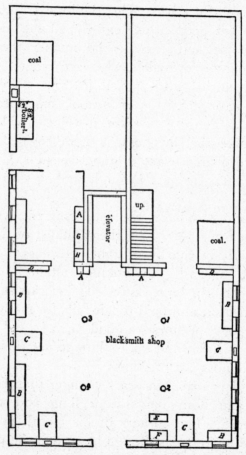

FIG. 51.—PLAN OF THE BASEMENT OF HILL & DILL'S SHOP.
AAA, Closets.   BBB, Benches.   CCC, Forges.   DD, Bolts.   E, Bender.
F, Bolt-cutter.   G, Sink.   H, Water-closet.

the world at its best and makes the best of his mishaps; if he falls down he manages to fall forward, and rise just a little ahead of where he fell. Both he and his partner are liberally endowed with the instinct that leads to accumulation, as evidenced by Mr. Hill's snug bank account and numerous blocks of real estate which he owns; and a visit to Mr. Dill's attic and cellar would convince the most sceptical that he also "lays up" everything for which he has no present use.

The first floor of the shop is level with the sidewalk and the grade is such that at 60 feet from the corner there is a full-size window (24 lights, 8 x 10 in.,) the bottom of which is 3 ft. above the basement floor, which is 11 ft. 8 in. below the first floor. The lot is 64 ft. on Main st. and 130 ft. on Glen st.

The shop is 54 x 100 ft. It is built of brick, three stories high above the basement, and has a flat graveled roof. The upper story is 10 ft. high between the joists, the other stories and basement are 10 ft. 6 in. between joists. The floor joists are all 12 in. apart to centers, 2 x 12 in. timber for the upper floor and 2 x 14 in. for the other floors except the basement, which will be explained further on. The outer walls are 16 in. thick up to the upper floor and 12 in. above that. There are two brick partitions, as shown in the plans, 12 in. thick, one running across the shop, the other from the front to the cross partition. These run to the upper floor but not above it.

The top story is all one room, except the elevator. It is unfinished and has the necessary posts to sup-

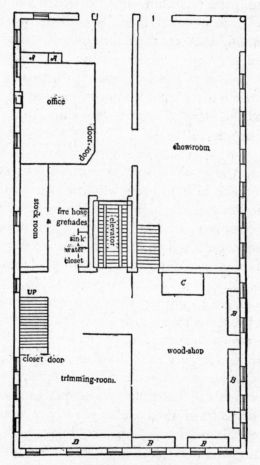

FIG. 52.---PLAN OF THE FIRST FLOOR.
AA, Closets. BBB, Benches. C, Rack.

port the roof. It is used entirely for storage. The three lower floors have gas fixtures in such positions as convenience has indicated. Having described the building in a general way, we will now consider the different departments, beginning with the basement.

The blacksmith shop in the east end of the basement is 40 x 41 ft., entirely above ground, and lighted on three sides by thirteen full-size windows and glass in the upper panels of the outside door. Four forges are located as shown in Fig. 51 of the accompanying cuts. The bellows are hung overhead, and the chimneys are set out from the wall enough to admit of the wind pipe going through the back of the chimney. This brings the front of the forges 6 ft. from the wall. The flues are 8 x 20 in., and the chimneys are curved back and into the wall near the top of the room. The tool benches are of the usual sort, except that at the side farthest from the anvil there is a double slot for swages, so that the top and bottom tools can be kept in pairs together. The anvils are wrought-iron.

There is a smith's and a finisher's vise for each fire, attached to the benches in convenient places. The tire-upsetter is bolted to the southeast post. A horizontal drilling machine for tires, and an upright one for other purposes, bolt cutter, tire bender, two bolt clippers, two axle seats, and numerous wrenches are among the tools of the smith shop. There is a good-sized drawer under each bench for taps and dies and other small tools, two cases of drawers for bolts and clips (located as shown on plan) and also part of the "furniture." Another convenience, and one not usually found in a smith shop, is a set of differential pulley-blocks. They are very handy on repair work. If a heavy vehicle comes in with a spring or axle broken it can be run under one of the several rings overhead and easily raised and the broken part removed. With them one man can raise 1,000 lbs., and they cost $13.00. Coat closets are provided here, as in all the other workrooms except the varnish rooms. A clock, broom and grindstone are also found here. The floor is 2-inch chestnut plank laid on joists bedded in concrete. (It is the same in the wheel jobber's room.) The remainder of the basement has a concrete floor. The northwest part of the basement is used as a blacksmith store-room, and occasionally an old wagon finds its way in there. The coal-bin, rack for bar iron and tire steel, box for old scraps, place for old tire, etc., all find accommodations here.

The wheel-jobber's room on this floor is fitted up with special reference to his work. He is required to do all the wheel work, examine and draft all wheels, old and new, before they are ironed, set the boxes, fix spring bars and axle heads, etc. He is provided with wheel horses, hub boring machines, a press for setting boxes, two adjustable spoke augers, cutting from $\frac{3}{8}$ to $1\frac{1}{4}$ inches. One of these he is ex-

pected to use exclusively on new spokes, the other
for old work. He is supplied with bits of all sizes
from ⅜ to 1¼ inch to be kept and used exclusively
for boring rims. He has also a dozen wood hand-
screws and a dozen iron screw clamps. By having
a jobber near the smith shop it saves a good deal of
travel to the wood shop and back. The shop is
heated by steam, and as no steam is used for power
a low-pressure 18-horse power heating boiler does
the business. It is located in the basement, as
shown on the plan. It is 6 ft. 2 in. high, 3 ft. 9 in.
wide and 8 ft. 4 in. long outside of bricks, and cost
about $500 ready for piping. It is supplied with
water from the elevator tank on the upper floor, and,
as the steam returns to the boiler after passing
through the building, but little water is used. The
radiating surface consists simply of coils of pipe
placed against the walls in convenient places in the
rooms it is desired to heat. On the north side of
the boiler, 4 in. from the floor, is our steam box for
use in bending. It is a galvanized sheet-iron cylindrical affair, 8 ft. long x 1 ft. diameter, with the open
end toward the wheel jobber. The other end is 4
inches lower and has a drip outlet. It is supplied
with steam from the boiler. It is a simple, inexpensive contrivance, but as most of the bent stock is
bought ready for use, it answers the purpose very
well. Besides the boiler and coal bin, this part of
the basement has a bin for shavings and waste wood,

and the remainder is used for general storage purposes.

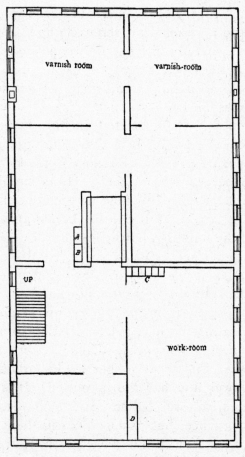

FIG. 53.—PLAN OF THE SECOND FLOOR.
A, Sink.   B, Water-closet.   C, Wardrobe.   D, Paint-bench.

The elevator occupies the position (as shown on plan) near the center of the building at the intersection of the two brick partition walls, which make two sides of the elevator shaft strong and fire-proof. The other two sides are brick, 12 in. thick from the foundation in the basement to the upper floor, and 8 in. thick above that. The elevator walls are continued 2 ft. 6 in. above the roof, and provided with openings on all four sides for ventilation. The shaft is covered with a metal frame skylight. The elevator and shaft (or, rather room), serve several purposes : First, in its legitimate and more important work of raising and lowering carriages and stock from floor to floor ; second, as a ventilating shaft ; and, third, as a wash room. It is a hydraulic telescope elevator, run by water from the street main which passes the premises to supply the neighboring city with water. We are fortunate in being located on a street which has what is known as the high service main, with a pressure of 125 lbs. to the inch. 75 lbs. will run it satisfactorily with 2,000 lbs. load, but not so fast. There is a tank on the upper floor to hold the exhaust water, which is forced up by the descent of the elevator. It is then carried in pipes for use in different parts of the building. By using the exhaust water for other purposes, the cost of running the elevator is quite small. The doorways are arched ; the doors are made of light lumber tinned on the inside, hung on hinges (opening out-

ward, of course). They close by a spring and fasten
by a catch which cannot be released from the outside except by pressing a short lever, which, for purposes of safety, is placed in an unusual place near
the floor. At each floor above the basement, there
is a light hatch covered with tin sanding on its edge,
so hung with hinges that by releasing it (which can
be done from the outside) it will fall and cover the
hatchway, thus cutting off draft in case of fire. The
car or platform of the elevator is made of spruce
lumber, and the floor is 2-inch plank, laid crosswise
with 1-inch spaces between the planks. The floor of
the shaft in the basement is concrete, concave, with
an outlet near the center (the plunger is in the center) connected with the sewer and provided with a
stench trap. With the elevator thus arranged, we
have a wash room on every floor, and, on the first
and second floors, doors opening on opposite sides
give plenty of light. The elevator shaft also serves
a good purpose as a ventilator, ventilation being as-
sisted by the elevator passing up and down. The
shaft is 15 x 9 ft.

The show-room is in the north front corner (see
Fig. 52). It is 56 x 24 ft., and has two plate-glass
windows at the northwest corner. It is sheathed
with good pine sheathing and painted like the varnish rooms, a very light drab. This room, like the
office and varnish rooms, has drab window curtains of
the same shade as the paint. The furniture of this

department consists chiefly of a display horse. A few harnesses are kept for sale, and a team is kept hitched up continually.

The office is in the south front corner; it is 8 x 17 ft., has two windows, and lights in the door. It is finished the same as the show room, but is varnished instead of painted. It is warmed by steam from the boiler and has an ornamental radiator. It has a wash bowl connected with the water pipes and the sewer. It is finished with a desk, safe, four chairs (no lounge—none of that business done in this shop), an umbrella stand and a couple of spittoons. There are two closets in this room, one (the smaller) for coats, etc. The other has three drawers, and the remainder in shelves. This closet is for back numbers of the trade journals, drawings of vehicles it is desired to preserve, etc.

The wood shop is in the northeast corner of the first floor. It is 40 x 25 ft., and has four benches, as shown on the plan. There is also a smaller bench at the northeast corner of the room on which there is a saw-filing clamp and saw set. The only stove on the premises is in this room. It is a sheet-iron drum stove with a lid on top, but no door except the ash door at the bottom. Its principal business is warping panels. It has a strong, smooth piece of horizontal pipe with a parallel rod, $\frac{3}{4}$ in. iron, under which one edge of the panel may be placed while passing it around the pipe. The other furniture of this room consists in part of a clock and a broom, grindstone, two body-makers' trestles, four horses, four dozen wood hand-screws, one dozen each 4, 5 and 6 in. iron screw clamps, and four long clamps to reach from side to side of bodies.

The trimming room occupies the southeast corner of the first floor. It is 23 x 25 ft., and has a bench running the whole length of the east side. It is large enough to accommodate three trimmers and a man to do general work, such as oiling straps, polishing plated work, helping hang up work, fitting axle washers, shaft rubbers, etc. His bench is on the north side and has a vise on it. The sewing machine is on the opposite side. There is a closet for cloth and other stock under the stairs leading to the second floor. The small room (stock room on plan) is fitted up with shelving, and part is used for trimming stock, the rest for other materials, such as varnish and color cans, sandpaper, files, etc.

The paint shop occupies the entire second floor (see Fig. 53), and in case of necessity the room back of the office on the first floor can be used for such heavy jobs as are to be done without unhanging. The room at the northeast corner is the general work-room, and contains paint bench, where paints are mixed, paint mill, press for squeezing colors out of the cans, water boxes for paint brushes, coat closets, etc., but there is no corner or place in this room nor on the floor suitable for a collection of paint rags, worn sandpaper and discarded tins. A sheet-metal can holding about a bushel is provided for this debris, and it is expected that it will be emptied each day. The room is sheathed overhead with $\frac{3}{4}$-in. matched sheathing, as are also the partition walls.

The outer brick walls are bare. The two rooms at the west end (front) are varnish rooms. Both are finished alike, sheathed with $\frac{3}{4}$-in. matched pine on all sides and overhead, and painted two coats very light drab with enough varnish in the second coat to give it an egg-shell gloss. Each room has a ventilating flue in the wall. The furniture of these rooms consists simply of the necessary trestle, etc., on which to place the work while varnishing, cup stands and brush keepers. There is also a thermometer in each of these rooms. On the north side between the varnish room and the work room is a room into which work can be put when it is necessary to empty the varnish rooms before the work is dry enough to hang up. When not needed for this purpose it can be used for varnishing running parts or for storage; this room is also sheathed and painted. The small room at the east end is for sandpapering and all very dirty work. The workroom is 40 x 23 ft., the varnish rooms 25 x 24 ft. and 25 x 26 ft. respectively.

The lumber shed is 20 x 40 ft. It stands at the northeast corner of the lot. The posts are 18 ft. high. The roof is graveled and has just slope enough to carry the water off. It has four compart-

ments on the ground, 9 ft. high, for heavy plank, and
has lofts above for lighter lumber. It is boarded
with matched boards, and has ample openings for air
at the top and bottom of each story. The west side
of the lower portion is entirely open, and the doors
to the loft above may be left open when desirable.
South of this shed is a place for a fire and a stone
on which to set heavy tires. The water for cooling
this is brought from the smith shop by means of a
rubber hose.—*By* WARREN HOWARD.

CHAPTER IV.

ANVILS AND ANVIL TOOLS.

HOW ANVILS ARE MADE.[*]

"So the carpenter encouraged the goldsmith, and he that smootheth
with the hammer him that smote the anvil."

This is the first and only mention of the anvil
found in the Bible. But it is of more remote origin
even than the prophet Isaiah, as we read of Vulcan forging the thunderbolts of Jupiter, and he must,
of course, have had an anvil of some sort for that
style of blacksmithing; probably, however, nothing
better than a convenient boulder.

The anvil and the anchor are two of the oldest
implements known, and for thousands of years about
the only ones that have not changed in general form.

The modern "vulcan" now has a hardened steel
face provided with the necessary holes for his
swedges, which with the round projection at the
other end terminating in a point, called the "horn,"
is sufficient for every kind of work.

---

[*] This article on the history, description, and manufacture of anvils
will undoubtedly be found of interest to our readers. We have taken
some pains to inform ourselves on this subject in consequence of some
unfavorable comments which were made on an article on the same topic
which appeared in the columns of *The Blacksmith and Wheelwright*
a few years ago.—EDITOR.

Except those made in the United States, every manufacturer of anvils has a body of wrought iron under the steel face. The horn also is simply of wrought iron. With slight modification, the method of making these has not changed for hundreds of years.

The body is roughly shaped out under tilt hammers. In the better grades this is in one piece, and called "patent," while in the German and most English works the four corners and the horn are "jumped" on in separate pieces. Though called "wrought" this is of the lowest grade of iron, adopted both on account of cheapness, and because the subsequent process of welding the steel face to it is easier than with the more refined of these materials.

For the same reason only the lower grades of steel —viz., "shear" steel, or even "blister" steel, are used for the face, cast steel never being used on account of the greater uncertainty of a perfect weld under the hammer to a large mass of wrought iron.

The common grade of English anvils and all those of German make weld the steel on in two or three pieces according to the size of the anvil ; the best English brand, however, of late years, has the face in a single piece of shear steel.

For this the wrought iron mass is brought to a welding heat, as also the steel plate, the welding of which begins at one end.

Four strikers swinging heavy sledge hammers together, do this welding in portions of about five inches of its length at a time, and this process is continued by successive heatings until the whole length of the face is finished.

The cutter hole and the small round hole in the tail are then punched out, the iron horn rounded off, and the whole dressed up into its finished shape at a subsequent heating. By long years of experience at this work a symmetrical, good-looking job is made.

Any inequalities or imperfections in the face are taken out by grinding crosswise on a large stone, and the anvil is then ready for the final process of hardening.

This is done by reheating the upper portion to a red heat, and a stream of water is let down upon it under a ten-foot head. The temper will be more or less uniform according to the quality of the steel which has been used, and the greater or less care in the heating at the previous stages. The soft spots so much complained of by blacksmiths are due to these inequalities of the material and workmanship. The thickness of the steel used varies from three-eighths to three-quarters of an inch, according to the size of the anvil.

The whole process is almost entirely one of manual labor and judgment. Extreme care must be used not to burn some portions of the steel during the welding operation, resulting in cracked faces and crumbling edges, which the blacksmith frequently finds to his sorrow developed in his anvil, apparently of the best when new.

A perfectly welded, wrought iron anvil has a clear "ring" when struck; otherwise it is a pretty good sign that there is somewhere an imperfection.

From the nature of the operation as above described, it is evident that the size of such an anvil must be limited. They vary in weight from one hundred to five hundred pounds; the largest ever made being one exhibited at the Philadelphia Centennial, which weighed 960 pounds.

There are no wrought iron anvils made in the United States. As it is almost entirely a question of skilled manual labor, and as there has never been any but a nominal duty imposed (it is the same as on spikes, nuts, and washers), all the wrought anvils used in this country are imported from Europe.

In 1847, the late Mr. Mark Fisher, believing in the possibility of welding cast steel to a high grade of cast iron, which had up to that time been unknown, discovered a perfect and successful process by which the two metals could be welded together in any desired dimensions. [The largest anvil in the world was made by the Fisher Eagle Anvil Works for the Centennial Exposition in 1876. Its weight was 1,600 lbs.] The value of this process for anvils was apparent, as there could thus be obtained a perfect working surface of the best quality of cast steel, capable of hard and uniform temper on a body which from its crystalline and inflexible structure would never settle or get out of shape in use — one of the defects liable to occur by continued hammering in anvils with a fibrous wrought iron body under the steel.

It also enabled a steel working surface to be applied to the horn, which previously had been only of plain iron.

The first manufacture of these anvils in this country began under his patent in 1847, and though requiring many years to perfect and establish this new and essentially American anvil, it is now recognized as a better article than the old-fashioned imported kind, over one-half of the anvils used in this country, it is said, being made by this process, and so certain and successful is it that they are the only ones in the market fully warranted against breakage, settling of the face, or failure in any respect.

It is needless to say that ordinary cast iron would not answer for a tool subject to such severe usage as an anvil.

The metal employed must have a strength equal to that in gun castings, a certain elasticity to stand the strain of high heating and sudden cooling of the tempering process, and perfectly sound in all parts. Though many so-called "cast" anvils have from time to time come upon the market, only one concern in the country, and that the original one operating under the Fisher patents, has continued to produce anvils with all the qualities described as necessary in these tools. The mode of manufacture is naturally quite different from that of wrought iron anvils.

The steel used is one piece for the face, of best tool cast steel.

The anvil is cast bottom side up, having this steel, as also the steel horn, placed in the "drag" or lower part of the mold.

Before filling it with the metal, which is not only to form the body of the anvil, but also to effect in its passage the perfect welding required, the steel face and horn are heated to a bright color, and every part of their exposed surface is covered by the molten metal. After the necessary annealing this rough anvil is removed, trimmed, planed true, and put into its finished shape, the cutter-holes made exact, and it is then ready for the hardening and tempering process. This last is the crucial test, for both iron and steel must be heated to a high point and then suddenly plunged into the cold hardening liquid. Should there be any spot between the two metals not perfectly welded, the steel will separate, or the whole anvil will crack and fly into pieces; so that if it passes this stage successfully it is reasonably sure to be perfect, and therefore the makers can safely give a full warranty to the purchaser.

Recent improvements have added much to the value of this make of anvil. By extending the steel part of the horn down into the body, all danger of breakage of the horn where it joins the main part is prevented. Also both edges of the steel face are made of double thickness, which prevents crumbling or splitting off of those places most exposed to severe usage, so common with the old-fashioned anvils.

Two peculiarities distinguish the American from the foreign anvil. They are more *solid* from the crystalline structure of the body, and therefore do not bounce back the hammer or sledge, thus retaining all the effect of the blows in the piece worked on, and the steel face always retains its original true surface for the same reason. Also there is very little " ring " in them, and this peculiarity is sometimes urged as an objection by those accustomed to the wrought iron anvils.

Nearly every metal trade has its special form of anvil, and differing from that of the blacksmith—such as saw, axe, razor, silversmith, coppersmith, shovel, hoe, plough, and many others, which are simple blocks of iron with steel faces, made by one or the other of the two above-described distinct and opposite methods and materials.

The annual importations of anvils from England and Germany into the United States exceeds one and a half million pounds.

The price of all anvils is now less than *one-half* that of former times, when we were compelled to obtain our entire supply from foreign manufacturers and importers, and before the discovery of the process above referred to made American competition possible.—*By* "EXPERT."

DRESSING ANVILS.

The expression, "I wish my anvil was dressed," can be heard every few weeks in very many blacksmith shops. The work which the smith has to do oftentimes requires some little thought in the make-up of the anvil in which it is deficient, hence a considerable hammering of the iron is required to obtain the shape wanted. I have noticed that nearly all the new anvils I have seen are wrong in the design of the face. The corners of both sides toward the horn, half way the length of the face, should be rounded to the radius of about one-quarter of an inch. This prevents the cutting of small fillets which are often required in iron work for strength, and enables the smith to get his work near the anvil without danger of cutting the fillet. This is a source of comfort in many cases. It is also more agreeable to scarf iron on a round corner, because it does not cut the scarf and cause it to break it, as a sharp corner does.

To dress an old anvil requires some knowledge. It is necessary to know how to go about it. In the first place, if the shop is provided with a crane it will be found useful in the work to be done. The tools required to handle an anvil are two bars of 1¼ inch iron, one of them six or eight feet long and the other five feet long, according to the size and weight. The length of the bars can be chosen for the work according to the smith's judgment. The carrying bars are pointed to fit the holes in the anvil under the heel and horn and also the bottom. These holes afford the most convenient way of holding an anvil either in forging it or dressing it. The construction of the fire is a most important feature of the work in hand. Throw away the fine burnt coal that is around the fire, and build the fire large enough with good, fine soft coal. Do not be afraid of using too much coal, because in rebuilding the fire there will be plenty of coke, which will be found useful. When the fire has obtained a good bottom, place the anvil face nearest the horn on the fire, thus heating parts of the face at a time. Next put some fine cut pine wood alongside the anvil, about 3 inches high and 8 or 10 inches long, and cover it all over with soft coal. When the wood burns out there will be a hollow space around the part that is being heated, which will allow free circulation of heat and flame. By this plan it will also be possible to see into the work through the openings made in front through the crust of the coke or fire cover. Through these openings on either side the operator can feed the fire with broken coke as it burns away. If the top burns through, recover the burnt parts with fine soft coal in time so that it will not fall. Do not let the coke touch the face underneath, because it hinders the proper heating.

When the anvil is hot enough, place it on the floor or block, as may be deemed best, and then let two men work up the sides together at the part heated with their hammers. This brings up the metal to build out the corners with, and also to level the roundness of the face. Smooth every part heated with the flatter or hammers as much as possible, because this lessens the work of grinding the face. Use a square in order to see that the work is level. Heat again along the face and finish. When it comes to the heel, have a square pin to drift the hole out, so that it will not be necessary to alter the tongs of the bottom tools employed in it. Round off the corners for about eight inches on each side of the horn. Further out let the corners be sharp. If a piece is broken off the corners, make a wedge of tough toe-calk steel, amply large enough to fill the space. Have a clean fire and plenty of coke to bank up with. Heat the broken part and raise up the edges with a fuller, rounded to about the size of a silver dollar, ⅜ of an inch thick; then, when hot enough to work, sink the chisel in far enough for the purpose and drive the steel wedge in the opening thus formed. Then heat until soft enough to work and fill up the space. Sprinkle the iron with cherry heat welding compound in such a manner that it will get between the iron and steel. Heat slowly with plenty of clean coke and flux with compound. If the heat is good there will be no difficulty in working with hand hammers. Cut off the waste on the side with a sharp chisel. If the horn wants setting up a little, it may be next taken in hand, as there will be sufficient coke to cover it. Do not let the point of the horn set above the level of the face, because it interferes with straightening along the iron.

To heat the anvil for hardening, place supports under the carrying bars when they are in the anvil. This prevents the anvil settling in the fire. Keep the coal from the face. Build with fine kindling wood all along the sides and heel. Cover with soft coal, not too wet, then blow up. When the wood is burned up, open a hole through the back and front of the fire for circulation. When the anvil is red hot on the face it is ready to harden. Lower it in a box of water until there is about three inches over the face. A piece of chain with hooks to it, passing around the horn and underneath the heel, the point dropped through the hole to prevent the chain slipping, a long bar passed through the chain loop, will be sufficient to keep the operators far enough from the steam to prevent danger from scalding. A stream of water from hose on the upturned face of the anvil will quickly cool it, or pails of water speedily used from an extra supply barrel will answer. Anvils are usually hardened, not tempered. The grinding can be done with a travel emery wheel, or the anvil may be

hung with a rope or chain in front of the breast of a
stone driven by machinery. Taken thus, it may be
passed to and fro across the stone, and twisted and
turned without the least inconvenience from its
weight.—*By* C. S.

SHARP OR ROUND EDGES FOR ANVILS.

" Would an anvil of any make be more convenient
if both edges of its face were to be rounded for one-
third or one-half its length ?"

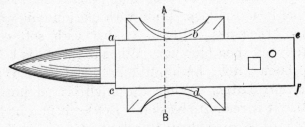

FIG. 54.—SHOWING THE EDGES.

It is not my desire at this time to discuss the relative merits of different makes of anvils. What I
would like to know is whether, in any anvil, there
is any reason for having the edges that are represented by the lines *a b* and *c d*, in Fig. 54 of the
accompanying illustration, sharp instead of rounded
to a curve of a quarter of an inch or more radius ?

I believe that it is impossible to forge an interior
angle sharp and have the forging round. It does
not matter how small the work, nor how insignificant

the shoulder that is formed by the re-entering angle, if sharp in the corner, the structure of the iron at that point is destroyed and the forging weakened. The weakness may not at first be apparent, the forging may look well enough, for it is only in exaggerated cases that the crack or "cut" is actually found. Now, if it be a fact that sharp inside corners in the work cannot be made safely, what possible use can there be for sharp outside edges on the anvil? True, I have seen blacksmiths cut off excess of stock

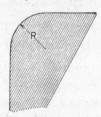

FIG. 55.—PARTIAL SECTIONAL VIEW OF ANVIL SHOWING ROUNDED EDGES.

over the edge of the anvil when their hardy was duller than the anvil; but who will defend them in such an operation?

For my own part, I am satisfied not only that the sharp edges are useless, but that they are also destructive of good work. I cannot account for their existence except as a relic of a time when the principles of forging were but little understood. I want both edges of my anvil rounded, not simply for a part of their length, but for their whole length. To my mind the ideal anvil of 130 pounds is one having its edges from *a* to *b* and from *c* to *d*, Fig. 54, rounded to a curve of three-eighths of an inch radius (as at *R*, Fig. 55, which is a partial section enlarged on the line *a*, *b*, Fig. 54), and its edges from *b* to *c* and from *d* to *f* rounded to a curve of three-sixteenths or one-quarter of an inch radius. The edge from *e* to *f* can be sharp to satisfy the unconverted.—*By* X.

DEVICE FOR FACILITATING THE FORGING OF CLIPS FOR FIFTH WHEELS.

About fourteen years ago I was engaged in the manufacture of fifth wheels on a small scale, and having to devise appliances and often to extemporize means to more effectually facilitate matters, among other "kinks" I introduced the following, which has given me a good return for the trifling change it makes in the usual method of using the "ass" of the anvil. It is well known that in the ordinary style of working this part of the anvil soon becomes imperfect or depressed, as shown at *D* in the accompanying illustration, Fig. 56. My plan is to drill immediately below the steel face, and about two inches from the front end of the anvil face, three ¾-inch holes, thus forming a round angled triangular hole, *C*, through the anvil. On removing the core left, I have a conveniently shaped hole that will accommodate almost any size clip, and enable me to swage it very true, quick and perfect, with less effort

to retain it square, than is required by the old plan.
I have not seen this idea put into practice anywhere
else, although, having been otherwise engaged for
the last twelve years, it may have been used by others
without my knowledge. The hole does not weaken
the anvil enough to injure it, and I was surprised at

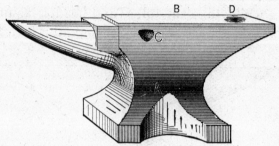

FIG. 56.—DEVICE FOR FACILITATING THE FORGING OF CLIPS FOR
FIFTH WHEELS.

the durability of this portion of the face after two
years' constant use on four or five anvils. They were
as good anvils as we could get.—*By* W. D.

PUTTING A HORN ON AN ANVIL.

I have put three horns on broken anvils, and I
have worked on one of these anvils for fourteen
years. My method of doing the job is as follows :
I first cut the mortise, cutting in straight about
three-quarters of an inch, then cut out the corners ; of
course it has to be done cold. Commence well down

below the steel, then lay out the tenon on the horn, heat it and cut with a thin chisel, fit tight, and drive together with a sledge. If there are any open places between the anvil and horn, drive in thin wedges as hard as possible. Cut off very close, and take the fuller and head the iron over them, and then put in the die and head that in. If it gets a little loose after a while, take the fuller and head it again. It has always taken me about a day to do this job. In the

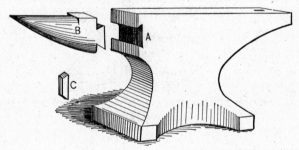

FIG. 54.—PUTTING A HORN ON AN ANVIL BY THE METHOD OF "C. H."

accompanying illustration, Fig. 57, is shown my way of doing it. *A* represents the dove-tail mortise, *B* is the horn, and *C* is the die used to fill up the mortise after the horn is driven to its place.—*By* C. H.

FASTENING AN ANVIL TO THE BLOCK.

A simple and effective way to fasten an anvil to a block is to make a square iron plug to fit tightly the hole in the bottom of anvil, and a similar hole in center of block. Then you can have the block just the size of the anvil and no fixings in the way, or even in sight.—*By* WILL TOD.

FASTENING ANVILS.

Concerning the proper method of fastening anvils in position, I would say that it only requires to flatten each corner of the anvil. Drill a half-inch hole and pass a half-inch square-headed bolt, ten inches long, down through the hole into the block, with the nut so arranged as to receive the end of the bolt. By fastening the anvil in this way there will be no obstructions whatever. I am not able to send a drawing of this means of fastening an anvil, but think every practical smith will readily understand it from the description.—*By* J. W. F.

HOLDING AN ANVIL TO THE BLOCK.

To fasten an anvil to the block, I use a chain of the proper length with an eye bolt. It is passed over the anvil, and the eye is then screwed into the block on the front and back.

The eye bolt is then passed through the eye in the block and screwed down until it is tight. When fixed in this manner an anvil cannot move. The device is so simple that it is not much work to make it. —*By* H. N. P.

SHARPENING CALKS—A DEVICE FOR HOLDING SHOE AND OTHER WORK ON THE ANVIL.

In all places where the roads are icy, it pays those who use horses to have steel calks in the heels as

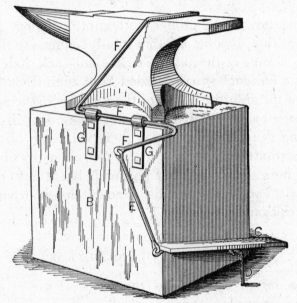

FIG. 58.—DEVICE FOR HOLDING WORK ON THE ANVIL.

well as in the toes of their shoes. In different places where I have worked various methods have been employed to obtain a self-sharpening and durable calk. The best plan I have ever tried is to split the heel-calks with a thin chisel, and insert a piece of steel (old sickle sections are good) previously cut to the proper size ; then weld solid, draw sharp, and temper hard. It used to require a helper to hold the shoe with tongs on the anvil, or it would jump off in split-ting the heels ; but I have studied out a contrivance that I think may be of use to all brother smiths who think my way worth adopting. I will try to explain it, with the aid of the accompanying illustration, Fig. 58, in which *C* is a foot lever hung in the center by two staples on a right-angle iron, *D*, which is sharpened at each end, one end being driven into the anvil-block, *B*, and the other into the floor. To this foot-treadle is bolted or riveted a strap with an eye connected to the rod *E*, which latter has eyes on both ends, and is connected with *FF*, which is in one piece of 5-8 round iron, flattened where it comes on the anvil face. Before being bent, *F* is passed through two eyes which are fastened to the front of the anvil-block with screw-bolts. When a man has no helper, this device is often useful in holding other kinds of work on the anvil for punching, etc., and saves one man's time. When there is no such work to be done, it can be taken off and laid aside.—*By* C. H. W.

MENDING AN ANVIL.

I will try to describe a job that was done lately in the shop I am working in.

The base of a wrought-iron anvil had been broken off as shown in Fig. 59. Not wishing to throw the anvil away, the boss told us to try to repair it, and we did it in the following manner :

We first looped a piece of 1⅛-inch iron around the end of the anvil, with a flat spot just above the loop on which to catch a hook so as to enable us to handle it better.   We next put what I call a binder of 5-8

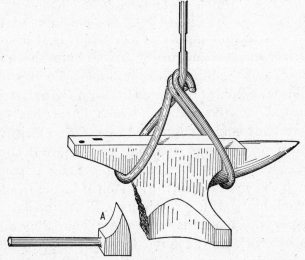

FIG. 59.—THE ANVIL AND THE PIECE USED IN MENDING IT.

round iron around the beak iron to prevent the por-ter bar from slipping off.   Next we got out a piece of iron something the shape of the piece *A*, in Fig. 59, with a bar welded on the side for handling.   This piece was about as wide as the body of the anvil. We then put the anvil in the fire to prepare it for welding, which was done by cutting away the uneven

places and scoring it with a chisel. We then put
the anvil in the fire for a weld, building the fire up
especially for it. The piece to be welded on was

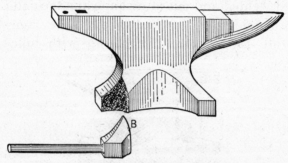

FIG. 60.—SHOWING HOW THE PIECE WAS WELDED ON AND SHAPED.

brought to a heat in a separate fire. When all was
ready the anvil was carried out of the fire by the aid
of a bar of iron run through the loop, and turned

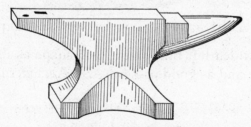

FIG. 61.—THE ANVIL AS MENDED.

into position by the use of the hook and the flat spot
on the bar. The piece was then welded on and put
into shape with a big fuller, which left the job as
seen in Fig. 60. The side was then scored and the

anvil put back into the fire for a side heat while the piece *B* was made. It was brought to a heat by the time the anvil was hot, and then they were brought out and welded and put into shape like the end piece. The other side was then put through the same process, and the whole touched up with fuller and

FIG. 62.—METHOD OF HOLDING AN ANVIL IN POSITION.

flatter, which left the job in good shape as shown in Fig. 61, and as good as new.—*By* APPRENTICE.

FASTENING AN ANVIL IN POSITION.

I enclose you a drawing which shows a method for fastening an anvil down to the block that may be of interest to some of your readers. The fastening irons consist of two 3-8-inch round rods or clips that are bent around the anvil and block, as shown by *A A* in Fig. 62. At *X* there is a piece of 7-8-inch square iron run through the block. Four holes are drilled in this piece, the square iron through which the clips *A A* pass and into which they are fastened with nuts. The threads on the rods should be one inch longer on each end than they are needed, so that in case the anvil ever becomes loose it will be possible to draw it down by means of the nuts. Fig. 63 of the sketches shows the details of the parts. I think this fastening is one of the best that I have ever seen, and it is easy to make. It keeps

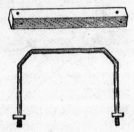

FIG. 63.—DETAILS OF DEVICE SHOWN IN FIG. 62.

the block from being split and driven full of spikes. I have never seen a better plan for holding an anvil than this.—*By* H. R. H.

FASTENING AN ANVIL IN POSITION.

I enclose some rough sketches setting forth my ideas of the fastenings for an anvil. In the first place I do not have my anvil block any larger than the anvil base. I use braces as shown in the engraving, Fig. 64. The strap is made of 1¼ by ½-inch iron bent and flatways. Each end has a piece of ¾-inch round iron welded on to it. Referring to the letters in the engraving, *A* represents the strap going around the foot of the anvil to receive *B*. On each

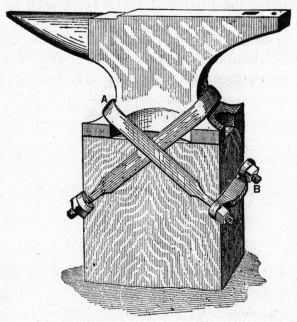

FIG. 64.—"J. T. B.'S" METHOD OF FASTENING AN ANVIL.

side of the block on which the anvil rests a notch is cut to receive *B*. Referring to "H. R. H.'s" plan (see page 120), I would say that to me it appears that his fastenings would not amount to much unless their size was greatly increased. With this I think

there is at least four times as much work to cut a
square hole quite through the block as there is to
have notches cut one on each side as indicated in my
sketch.—*By* J. T. B.

I enclose a sketch, Fig. 65, representing my own plan
for holding an anvil in position.   It serves the pur-

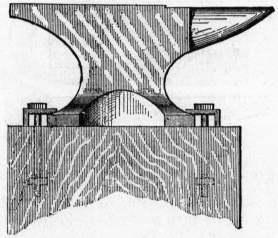

FIG 65.—"M. R. R.'S" METHOD OF FASTENING AN ANVIL.

pose well and is easily applied. The drawing so
clearly shows the idea that very little explanation is
necessary. By means of mortises in the sides of the
block, nuts are inserted, into which bolts are screwed,
as shown in the sketch. The short pieces, against
which the heads of the bolts rest, are shaped in such

a manner as to be driven by their outer ends into the
block, thus holding them securely in place, and acting as a leverage in connection with the bolt for
holding the anvil more securely. The depth at
which the mortises in the sides of the blocks is made
should be far enough from the top to give sufficient
strength for clamping the anvil solidly in position.
The braces at the side of the foot of the anvil need

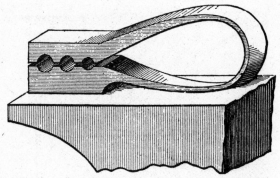

FIG. 66.—SELF-ACTING SWEDGE DESIGNED BY "E. M. B."

not project more than 1-2 or 3-4 of an inch from the
anvil. Bolts 1-2 inch in diameter, or larger, should
be used, according to the weight of the anvil to be
held.

A SELF-ACTING SWEDGE.

I send herewith a representation, Fig. 66, of a self-
acting swedge for rounding up small work on the anvil without a striker or help. It sets into the anvil
like an ordinary swedge, and the blacksmith strikes

with his hand-hammer on top. It is made of iron, with a steel spring, which should be 1 to 1 1-2 inches wide by 1-4 inch thick.—*By* E. M. B.

MAKING A PUNCH.

I send a sketch, Fig. 67, of a punch which I made for my own use and find a very convenient tool. It can be constructed so as to punch to the center of any sheet. The part *D*, shown in the illustration, is dove-

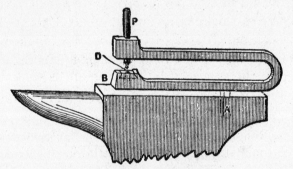

FIG. 67.—PUNCH MADE BY "H. S."

tailed, so that any size of die can be used. The punch is made of 3-4 or 7-8 inch square steel, with the point forged to the required size and with a small center to catch the center mark of the work. The machine is made to lie on the anvil, and part *A* is welded on to fit the square hole in the anvil. In using it, the punch is placed in the center mark of the work by hand, and the work is held firmly while the helper gives a good solid blow with the sledge. I have used one for four years. It will punch 7-16-inch round and square holes through 1-4 and 5-16-inch plow steel.—*By* H. S.

MAKING AN ANVIL PUNCH.

I will try to describe an anvil punch that I made in my shop at an expense of two dollars only. I have a set of six, the sizes being 1-4, 3-8, 1-2, 5-8, 3-4 and 1 in., and I think every blacksmith should have a set of them. With the 1-4 in. and 3-8 in. size I can punch cold iron up to 5-16 in. thickness. With the 1-2, 5-8, 3-4, and 1 in. sizes I can punch 3-8 in. iron cold. I can punch steel saw blades as easily as band irons, and as the punch is used in the square hole in the anvil like any other anvil tool it does not take long to c hange from one size of punch to another. The tool is made as follows : I take a piece of Swedish iron 1½ in. x ¾ in. and 10 inches long, upset it a little on one end, then take a piece of good steel and cut off a square piece 1½ in. x 1½ in. and weld it firmly on the large end of the iron. Then I take a hand punch and punch a hole in the center of the steel, making the hole a little larger than that which the punch is to cut when finished. The punch should be driven from the iron side to make the hole largest on the bottom, so that the punchings will drop out. I then heat the other end, cut it half off 1½ in. from the end, bend it over and weld it well, then take a square punch and punch and work out a 3-4 in. hole which must be perfectly

true. The punch will then look as in Fig. 68. Then I
take an iron the same size as the square hole in my

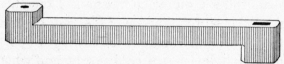

FIG. 68.—SHOWING THE PIECE AFTER WELDING, SHAPING AND
PUNCHING.

anvil, and weld it on the bottom side of the punch
2½ in. from the round hole in the punch, which is now

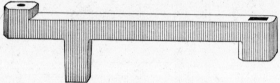

FIG. 69.—SHOWING THE PIECE READY FOR FILING, DRESSING AND
BENDING.

like Fig. 69, and is ready to be filed off and dressed.
Then I take a piece of 3-4 in. square cast steel, cut off

FIG. 70.—THE TOP DIE OF THE PUNCH.

6 inches, draw it down and file one end so as to fit the
round hole in the die of the punch. I make the top

die of the 1-4 in. punch 5-16 in. long on the round part. For larger punches the dies should be larger. Fig. 70 represents the top die when finished. I then heat the punch, bend it so that the two holes will be in a line, fit in the top die and make sure that it goes perfectly true into the hole. Let it cool slowly, and when it is

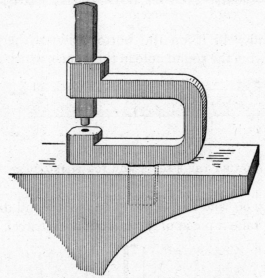

FIG. 71.—THE ANVIL PUNCH COMPLETED.

cool see that the face of the bottom die is all right, and that the die works straight and easily. Temper as you would for any tool intended to cut iron. Fig. 71 represents the punch when finished.—*By* N. C. M.

FORGING A STEEL ANVIL.

I would like to say a few words about forging cast steel anvils. Fig. 72 of the engraving annexed shows

the steel split and ready for the fullering. In Fig. 73
it is seen fullered and forming the outline of an an-

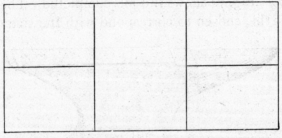

FIG. 72.—SHOWING THE PIECE SPLIT AND READY FOR FULLERING.

vil. The ends, when fullered to the proper shape,
will form the face and bottom. In doing this it must

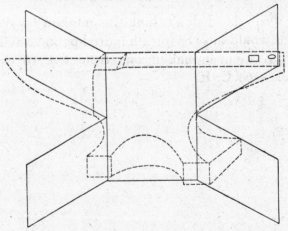

FIG. 73.—SHOWING THE STEEL FULLERED AND FORMED INTO THE
OUTLINE OF AN ANVIL.

be fullered on four sides and at the bottom, and
drawn to the thickness proper for a face. After it is

fullered it is brought back into place and trimmed to the right length, as indicated in the dotted lines of Fig. 73. Fig. 74 shows the job completed. The steel should be chosen to correspond with the size of the

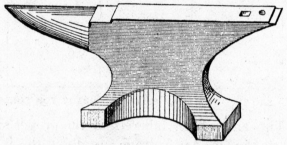

FIG. 74.—SHOWING THE FINISHED ANVIL.

anvil desired. I don't think this method I have described would answer for a hundred-pound anvil, but it is convenient in making one from five to twenty pounds.—*By* C. E.

CHAPTER V.

BLACKSMITHS' TOOLS.

In this connection, tongs, hammers (not mentioned elsewhere) and various other tools commonly used by blacksmiths, will be illustrated and described.

THE PROPER SHAPE OF EYES FOR TOOL-HANDLES.

To properly fasten a handle in a tool is not so

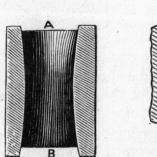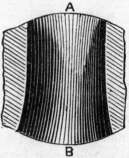

FIGS. 75 AND 76.—CORRECT SHAPE OF EYE FOR TOOL-HANDLE.

simple as it appears, and that is the reason that we so often see them improperly handled, as is evidenced by their so easily coming loose. I have a chipping-hammer that I once used for two consecutive years when working at the vise. It has been in intermit-

tent use for some ten years since, and its handle
shows no signs of coming loose, for the simple reason that it was properly put in in the first place.

The correct shape for an eye to receive a tool-
handle is shown in Figs. 75 and 76, which are sectional views. *A* is the top and *B* the bottom of the
tool. Two sides of the hole, it will be observed in
Fig. 75, are rounded out from the center towards
each end. The other two sides are parallel from the
top to the center, as shown in Fig. 76, while the bottom half of the hole is rounded out as before. The

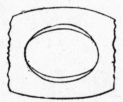
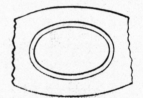

FIG. 77.—TOP VIEW.   FIG. 78.—BOTTOM VIEW.

shape thus obtained may be clearly understood from
Fig. 77, which is a view of the top, or face *A*, and
Fig. 78, which is a view of the bottom, or face *B*.
The handle is fitted a driving fit to the eye, and is
shaped as shown in Figs. 79 and 80, which are side
and edge views. From *C* to *D*, the handle fills the
eye, but from *D* to *E* it fills the eye lengthways only
of the oval. A saw-slot, to receive a wedge, is cut in
the handle, as shown in Fig. 80. The wedge is best
made of soft wood, which will compress and conform
itself to the shape of the slot. To drive the handle

into the eye, preparatory to wedging it permanently, it should be placed in the eye, held vertically, with the tool head hanging downward, and the upper end struck with a mallet or hammer, which is better than resting the tool-head on a block.   The wedge should be made longer than will fill the slot, so that its upper end may project well, and the protruding part, which

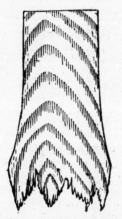 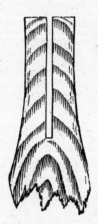

FIG. 79.—SHAPE OF HANDLE.   FIG. 80.—SHAPE OF HANDLE.
ANOTHER VIEW.

may split or bulge in the driving, may be cut off after the wedge is driven home.

The wedge should be driven first with a mallet and finally with a hammer.   After a very few blows on the wedge, the tool should be suspended by the handle and the end of the latter struck to keep the handle firmly home in the eye.   This is necessary, because driving the wedge in is apt to drive the handle partly out of the eye.

The width of the wedge should equal the full length of the oval at the top of the eye, so that one wedge will spread the handle out to completely fill the eye, as shown in Fig. 81. Metal wedges are not so good as wooden ones, because they have less elasticity and do not so readily conform to the shape of the saw-slot, for which reason they are more apt to come loose. The taper on the wedge should be regulated

FIG. 81.—SHAPE OF WEDGE.

to suit the amount of taper in the eye, while the thickness of the wedge should be sufficiently in excess of the width of the saw-cut, added to the taper in the eye, to avoid all danger of the end of the wedge meeting the bottom of the saw-slot.

By this method the tool handle is locked to the tool eye by being spread at each end of the same. If the top end of the tool eye were rounded out both ways of the oval, two wedges would be required to spread the handle end to fit the eye, one wedge standing at a right angle to the other. In this case one wedge must be of wood and one of metal, the one standing across the width of the oval usually being the metal one. The thin edge of the metal wedge is by some twisted, as shown by Fig. 82, which causes

FIG. 82.—SHAPE OF METAL WEDGE.

the wedge to become somewhat locked when driven in.

In fitting the handle, care must be taken that its oval is made to stand true with the oval on the tool eye. Especially is this necessary in the case of a hammer. Suppose, for example, that in Fig.

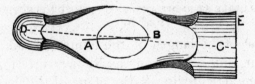

FIG. 83.—FITTING THE HANDLE.

83 the length of the oval of the handle lies in the plane *A B*, while that of the eye lies in the plane *C D;* then the face of the hammer will meet the work on one side, and the hammer will wear on one side, as shown in the figure at *E*. If, however, the eye is

not true in the hammer, the handle must be fitted
true to the body of the hammer; that is to say, to
the line *C D*. The reason for this is that the hand
naturally grasps the handle in such a manner that
the length of the oval of the handle lies in the plane
of the line of motion when striking a blow, and it is
obvious that to strike a fair blow the length of the
hammer should also stand in the plane of motion.

The handle should also stand at a right angle to

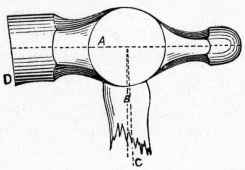

FIG. 84.—HANDLE AT RIGHT ANGLE TO PLANE OF LENGTH OF HAM-
MER HEAD.

the plane of the length of the hammer head, viewed
from the side elevation, as shown in Fig. 84, in
which the dotted line is the plane of the hammer's
length, while *B* represents a line at a right angle to
A, and should, therefore, represent the axial line of
the hammer handle. But suppose the handle stood
as denoted by the dotted line *C*, then the face of the
hammer would wear to one side, as shown in the figure at *D*.—*By* JOSHUA ROSE, M.E.

BLACKSMITHS' TONGS AND TOOLS.

[Prize Competition Essay.]

My knowledge of tools is confined to the class known as the machine blacksmith's tools. But these may be of interest to the horseshoer and carriage ironer, and their tools may interest the machine blacksmith.

The list of tools would not be complete unless the smith's hand hammer was mentioned, and as a rule the smith takes great pride in it. These ham-

FIG. 85.--THE BALL PANE HAMMER.

mers are of the class known as the ball pane, as shown in Fig. 85 of the accompanying illustrations. The weight of the hammer is according to the taste of the man who uses it, but the average weight is about 2 lbs. 4 ozs. Fig. 86 represents a pair of double calipers, one side of which is used for taking the width and the other side for the thickness when working a piece of iron. Fig. 87 is a pair of single calipers for general use and needs no explanation. Fig. 88 is a pair of common dividers which are used for describing the circles on pieces that need to be cut round, and they can be used as a gauge in welding up pieces to a given length. Fig. 89 is a T-square, which is as useful a tool as ever got into a shop for squaring up work with. The short leg can be dropped into a hole while squaring the face with the T, or it can be used for a handle while using the

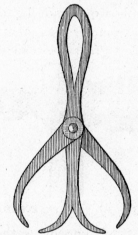

FIG. 86.—THE DOUBLE CALIPERS.

back to square up flat pieces. These tools should belong to every smith and be his private property. The ordinary 2-ft. square which every smith ought to be provided with is usually supplied by the owner of the shop. A good 2-ft. brass rule is something that every smith ought to have.

Opinions differ as regards the fire and anvil of the machine smith. But a neat outfit is a portable forge

made for general work, and a 300-lb. Eagle anvil
with all the sharp corners ground off, and made a
little more rounding next to the beak iron than on
the other end. The sledges usually found to be most
convenient are the straight pane pattern, Fig. 90,
of 8 lbs., 12 lbs., and 16 lbs. weight, the 12-lb. sledge
being for general use, and the others for light or
heavy work as occasion demands.

In addition to these, each fire usually has what is

FIG. 87.—THE SINGLE CALIPERS.

called a backing hammer, which is of the same style
as the smith's hammer, but weighing only 3½ lbs.
This is used to assist the smith in backing up a
piece of iron when scarfing for welding, and for finishing up work where the sledges are too heavy.

Tongs rank among one of the most important
things in a blacksmith's outfit. Fig. 91 represents
the pick-up tongs, which are especially the helper's

tongs and are used to pick up tools and small pieces generally.

Fig. 92 represents a pair of ordinary flat tongs for holding flat iron, and they need little explanation. Fig. 93 represents a pair of box tongs for holding square or flat iron, the lip on each side preventing the iron from slipping around. Figs. 94 and 95

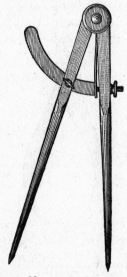

FIG. 88.—THE DIVIDERS.

show a pair of tongs, one pair of which can be made to fit several sizes by making the box piece to fit the size of iron to be used. Fig. 94 shows the pieces apart, and Fig. 95 shows how they are used. Fig. 96 represents a pair of round bit tongs for holding round iron. Fig. 97 shows a pair of hollow bits for holding round iron, and for pieces having a larger end than the body, such as bolts, etc. Fig. 98 represents a pair of square, hollow bits that answer the same purpose as the bits shown in Fig. 97, except that the square bits will hold square or round iron.

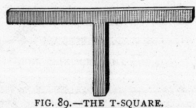

FIG. 89.—THE T-SQUARE.

Fig. 99 represents a pair of flat tongs for holding large pieces, the diamond-shaped crease in the bits making them handy for holding large pieces of square or round iron. Fig. 100 shows a pair of pin-

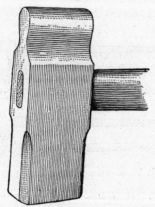

FIG. 90.—THE STRAIGHT PANE SLEDGE.

cer tongs, useful for many purposes. Holding work that has a round piece raised off the main body, they can be made still more useful by cutting out the tops of the bits, as shown in the figure. Fig. 101 shows tongs for holding work where the iron is bent flatwise. The tongs shown in Fig. 102 are useful, for they can be made to suit any size. Those shown

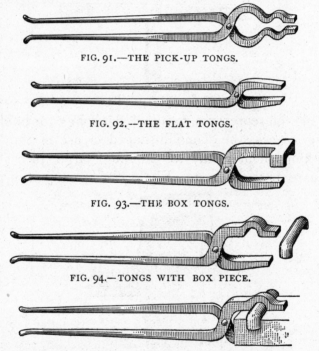

FIG. 91.—THE PICK-UP TONGS.

FIG. 92.--THE FLAT TONGS.

FIG. 93.—THE BOX TONGS.

FIG. 94.—TONGS WITH BOX PIECE.

FIG. 95.—SHOWING HOW THE TONGS AND BOX PIECES ARE USED.

in Fig. 103 are for work that cannot be held in an ordinary pair of flat tongs on account of the bits not being long enough. The bits are bent at right angles, so that the work will pass by the joints. Fig.

104 shows a pair of the same style of tongs with the bits bent to hold round iron.

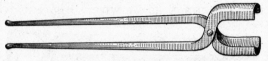

FIG. 96.—ROUND-BIT TONGS.

Another style of crooked-bit tongs is shown in Fig. 105, in which the bits are bent down instead of

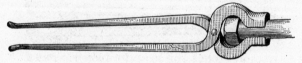

FIG. 97.—HOLLOW-BIT TONGS.

sidewise as in Fig. 103. They are useful for handling rings of flat iron and for holding flat iron while

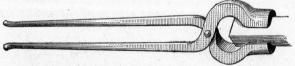

FIG. 98.—TONGS WITH SQUARE, HOLLOW BITS.

bending flatways. For holding work while the iron is being bent on edge, the tongs shown in Fig. 106

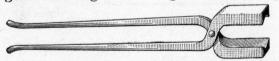

FIG. 99 —FLAT TONGS FOR HOLDING LARGE PIECES.

are good, the lip bent on one of the bits preventing the iron from pulling out of the tongs. Fig. 107 represents a pair of tongs for holding chisels while sharpening them, or for holding any such tools while they are being repaired. For making bolts out of round iron the tongs as shown in Fig. 108 will beat

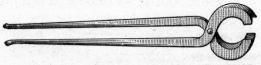

FIG. 100. PINCER TONGS.

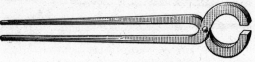

FIG. 101.—TONGS FOR BENDING IRON FLATWISE.

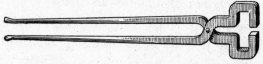

FIG. 102.—TONGS FOR HOLDING PIECES OF DIFFERENT SIZES.

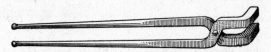

FIG. 103.—TONGS WITH BENT BITS.

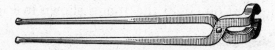

FIG. 104.—TONGS WITH BENT BITS FOR HOLDING ROUND IRON.

any I ever saw. They have the ordinary hollow bit, with a piece cut out of each bit crosswise to hold the round iron in upsetting. The swell in the bits allows the head to be taken in while straightening the other end. All of the foregoing named tongs can be made of·any size, large or small; and the smith shop that has all of these different shapes is pretty well equipped.

Next in importance are the chisels, punches and tools for the anvil. Fig. 109 represents the ordinary hot chisel, or hot-set, as it is known in some localities. The ordinary cold chisel is shown in Fig. 110. The

FIG. 105.—CROOKED-BIT TONGS.

hardy for the anvil is so well known as to need no illustration. The gouge chisel, as shown in Fig. 111, is for cutting off round corners at one operation. It can be ground inside or out, thus making an inside or outside tool. The round punch shown in Fig. 112

FIG. 106.—TONGS USED IN BENDING IRON ON THE EDGE.

needs no explanation of its uses, but it can be used for a gouge, where a good stiff one is required, by grinding it off bevel. In some work a square chisel comes very handy; one made as shown in Fig. 113 is very good. The square punch shown in Fig. 114 can also be ground bevel and used for a square or corner chisel. The long or eye punch is shown in Fig. 115. For countersinking holes and such work the bob punch or countersink, as shown in Fig. 116, is about what is needed, while for cupping or round-

FIG. 107.—TONGS USED IN SHARPENING CHISELS.

ing off the heads of bolts and nuts, and for similar work, the cupping tool as shown in Fig. 117 is used.

FIG. 108.—TONGS USED IN MAKING BOLTS OF ROUND IRON.

A tool of this kind comes handy many a time if made to fit the hardy hole.

For setting down work and getting into small

FIG. 109.—THE HOT CHISEL.

places in which the latter cannot be used we have the set hammer shown in Fig. 118. It is made with square edges, and when made with the edges

rounded off it is called a round-edge set hammer.
These hammers are also made with the face cut off
at an angle, in order to get down into corners and

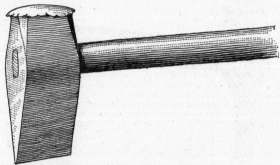

FIG. 110.—THE COLD CHISEL.

to settle work down very square. Fig. 119 represents the ordinary top swage for rounding up work,
and Fig. 120 shows the bottom swage. Every

FIG. 111.—THE GOUGE CHISEL.

smith knows the value of a good set of swages.
They can be made long, that is, the full width of the
anvil, or they can be made very short: the short ones

take the name of necking swages. Fig. 121 represents a side swage, the eye being punched in opposite from the ordinary swage. These are used for

FIG. 112.--THE ROUND PUNCH.

rounding off the ends of flat pieces, being handier
than the ordinary swage. Fig. 122 shows an anvil

FIG. 113.--THE SQUARE CHISEL.

side swage or bottom swage, a swage being made on
the end to overhang the edge of the anvil, so that
bent pieces that need to be swaged can be dropped
over the edge of the anvil and swaged up without
much trouble.

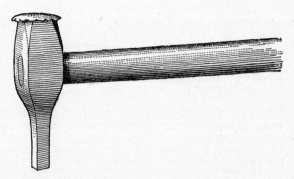

FIG. 114.--THE SQUARE PUNCH.

FIG. 115.--THE LONG OR EYE PUNCH.

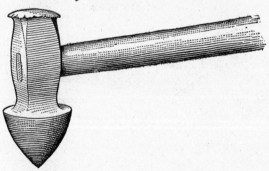

FIG. 116.—THE BOB PUNCH OR COUNTERSINK.

FIG. 117.—THE CUPPING TOOL.

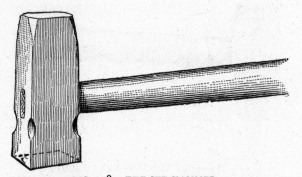

FIG. 118.—THE SET HAMMER.

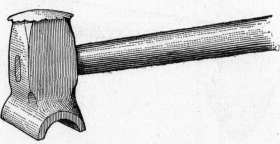

FIG. 119.—THE TOP SWAGE.

The top and bottom fullers shown in Figs. 123 and 124 are familiar to every smith. The horn on the bottom fuller is to prevent the piece to be fullered

FIG. 120.—THE BOTTOM SWAGE.

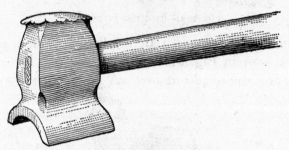

FIG. 121.—THE SIDE SWAGE.

FIG. 122.—THE ANVIL SIDE OR BOTTOM SWAGE.

from being knocked off the tool at every blow of the striker's sledge. For smoothing up work the smith has the flatter, Fig. 125, which takes out the lumps and uneven places and gives the work a finished appearance.

Sometimes a piece is so bent that a flatter cannot

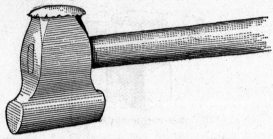

FIG. 123.—THE TOP FULLER.

be used, and the smith then falls back on his foot tool, shown in Fig. 126. The foot goes in on the work, and the head outside. A glance at the sketch

FIG. 124.—THE BOTTOM FULLER.

will show how useful it can be in almost any smith's shop.

It sometimes happens that it is necessary to leave round corners on a piece of work, and in finishing it up the ordinary flatter would mark it and spoil its appearance. The smith then makes use of the round-edge flatter shown in Fig. 127. This tool is also useful in bending flat iron, the round edge preventing galling.

FIG. 125.—THE FLATTER.

The smith sometimes has a lot of small rings to make, or to work out holes which are too small for the beak iron. For such work a small cone to fit the

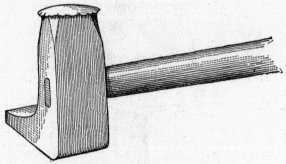

FIG. 126.—THE FOOT TOOL.

anvil, as shown in Fig. 128, is very useful. Or he may have some collars to weld on round iron, and after making one or two he wishes he had a quicker way and one that would make them all look alike. He bethinks himself of the collar swages he heard that " Tramp Blacksmith " talk about, so he makes

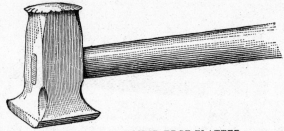

FIG. 127.—THE ROUND-EDGE FLATTER.

a pair of collar swages as shown in Fig. 129. Only the bottom swage is shown, as the impression in the top is like the bottom. After making three or four pieces he "gets the hang " of the tools, and the work goes merrily on, each piece looking like the other.

FIG. 128.—THE ANVIL CONE.

He sometimes has to make bends in his work, and then the fork shown in Fig. 130 comes in very handy. I have seen this tool used for making hooks on the end of long rods, one fork being used to press against and the other to bend the hook around. Fig. 131 represents a tool for bending flat pieces at right angles and making T-pieces.

FIG. 129.—THE COLLAR SWAGE.

The smith drops the iron in the slot, and he can bend or twist it any way he likes.

Sometimes work needs fullering, but is so offset

FIG. 130.—A FORK USED IN BENDING.

that one end rests on the anvil and the other towers away above the fuller. The smith then uses the fuller shown in Fig. 132, the outside edge of the fuller being brought flush with the side of the anvil, thus enabling the smith to drop his work down the side of the anvil and proceed as with an ordinary fuller.

In most machine blacksmith shops they have more or less bolts and nuts to make. Fig. 133 represents

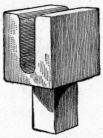

FIG. 131.—A TOOL FOR BENDING FLAT PIECES AND MAKING **T** PIECES.

the ordinary nut swage used for swaging nuts or finishing up the heads of hexagon bolts. Fig. 134 shows a better tool for making bolts. Only one-half

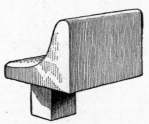

FIG. 132.—A FULLER FOR OFFSET WORK.

is sunk hexagon, the other half being the ordinary bottom round swage, so, that in making a bolt as it is turned around in the swage the shank of the bolt is brought central with the head. Smiths who

have trouble in getting the head of the bolt central
with the shank, will, by using this tool, be able to
make a good bolt.   The tool shown in Fig. 135 has
grooves cut in until they meet at the bottom, so
that many different-sized heads or nuts can be made

FIG. 133.—A NUT SWAGE.

in it, the small ones going far down and the larger
ones filling it up.   In Fig. 136 is shown the ordinary
heading tool.   Fig. 137 represents a nut mandrel in

FIG. 134.—A TOOL FOR MAKING BOLTS.

which the shank is made smaller than the body part,
in order to drive it through the nut.

Fig. 138 shows a bridge or saddle used for drawing
out forked pieces, making open-end wrenches and
similar work.

I have not attempted to describe the hand punches,

but, as is known, hand punches, round, flat and hexagonal, are very useful in the smith's shop.   Pins for

FIG. 135.—A TOOL FOR MAKING HEADS OR NUTS OF VARIOUS SIZES

driving through holes to expand them are so well
known to all smiths that I do not deem it necessary to

FIG. 136.—THE HEADING TOOL.

take up space in describing them.   The tools that I
have attempted to describe are in every-day use, and

FIG. 137.—A NUT MANDREL.

I think they form altogether a good outfit for a
machine blacksmith shop.—*By* WARDLEY LANE.

PROPER SHAPE FOR BLACKSMITHS' TONGS.

The proper shape for blacksmiths' tongs depends
upon whether they are to be used upon work of a

uniform size and shape or upon general work. In the first case the tongs may be formed to exactly

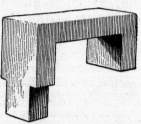

FIG. 138.—SADDLE USED FOR DRAWING OUT FORKED PIECES.

suit the special work. In the second case they must be formed to suit as wide a range of work as convenient.

Suppose, for example, the tongs are for use on a

FIG. 139.—PROPER SHAPE OF TONGS FOR SPECIAL WORK.

special size and shape of metal only. Then they should be formed as in Fig. 139, the jaws gripping the work evenly all along, and being straight along

FIG. 140.—IMPROPER SHAPE.

the gripping surface. The ends *A B* are curved so that the ring *C* shall not slide back and come off. It will readily be perceived, however, that if these tongs were put upon a piece of work of greater thickness, they would grip it at the inner end only, as in Fig. 140, and it would be impossible to hold the work steady. The end of the work, *W*, would act as a pivot, and the part on the anvil would move about.　It is better,

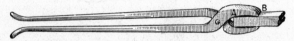

FIG. 141.—PROPER SHAPE OF JAWS FOR GENERAL USE.

therefore, for general work, to form the jaws as shown in Fig. 141, putting the work sufficiently within the jaws to meet them at the curve in the jaw, when the end *B* also grips the work.　By putting the work more or less within the tongs, according to its thickness, contact at the end of the work as at *A*, and at

FIG. 142.—SHAPE OF TONG JAWS　FIG. 143.—SHAPE OF SQUARE
FOR ROUND WORK.　　　TONG JAWS FOR ROUND WORK.

the point of the tongs as at *B*, may be secured in one pair of tongs over a wider range of thickness of work than would otherwise be the case.　This applies to tongs for round or other work equally as well as to flat or square work.

For round work, the curve in the tong jaws should always be less than that of the work, as shown in the end view, Fig. 142, in which *W* represents the work or if round work be held in *square* tongs, it should

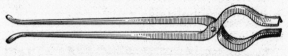

FIG. 144.—PROPER BOW OF JAWS.

touch the sides of the square as shown in Fig. 143, and in all cases there should be a little spring to the jaws of the tongs, to cause them to conform some-

FIG. 145.—PROPER SHAPE FOR BOLTS.

what to the shape of the iron. This not only causes the tongs to hold the work firmer, but it also increases the range of the capacity of the tongs. Thus

FIG. 146.—SHAPE FOR IRREGULAR SHAPED WORK.

in the shape of tongs shown in Fig. 144, the bow of the jaws would give them a certain amount of spring, that would enable them to conform to the shape of the work more readily than those shown in Fig. 139,

while at the same time it affords room for a protection head or lug.   For short and headed work, such
as bolts, the form shown in Fig. 145 is the best, the
thickness at the points always being reduced to give
some elasticity, and in this case to envelope less of
the length of the bolt also.

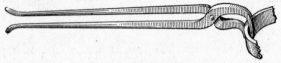

FIG. 147.—HOOP TONGS.

For holding awkward shaped work containing an
eye, the form shown in Fig. 146 is best, the taper in
this case running both ways, as shown, to give increased elasticity.   The same rule also applies to the
hoop tongs shown in Fig. 147.

Perhaps the best example of the advantage of hav-

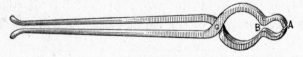

FIG. 148. —PICK-UP TONGS.

ing a certain amount of spring, or *give*, in the jaws of
tongs is shown in the *pick up* tongs in Fig. 148,
the curves giving the jaws so much elasticity that the
points at *A* will first grip the work, and as the tongs
are tightened the curves at *B* will, from the spring of
the jaws, also come in contact, thus gripping the work

in two places, and prevent it from moving on a single point of contact on each jaw as a pivot.

It follows from this that all tongs should first meet the work at the point as in Fig. 149, and spring down

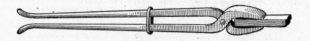

FIG. 149.—PROPER SHAPE.

to meet it at the back end as the tongs tighten upon the work, and it follows also that the thickness of the jaws should always be well tapered, and not parallel, as many unthinking men are apt to make them. —*By* J. R.

BLACKSMITHS' TOOLS.

[Prize Essay.]

In the accompanying illustrations of blacksmiths' tools, No. 1, in Fig. 150, represents a stay that goes from the axle to the perch in buggy gear. The pieces *A* and *B* are made from 7-16-inch round iron and *C* is 1-2 inch. No. 2, in Fig. 150, is the bottom tool used in forming the offset, and No. 3, Fig. 150, is the top tool.

To make the stay, cut off two pieces of 7-16-inch round Lowmoor iron of the length required for *A* and *B*, No. 1, Fig. 150, cutting *B* about 3 inches

longer than it is to be when finished. Then cut a
piece of 1-2-inch iron for *C*, Fig. 150. Next heat the
ends of *A* and *C*, upset and weld, leaving it a little
larger than 1-2 inch at the weld. Next heat *B* at the
end and double it back about 2 1-2 inches, weld and
upset a little to make up for loss in welding. Now

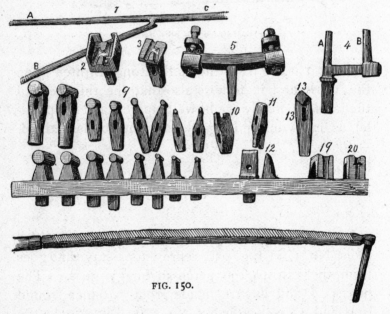

FIG. 150.

draw out as shown in *A*, Fig. 151, bend as in Fig. 152,
and insert the fuller at *A*. Then heat the end *A*,
Fig. 152, and with a thin splitting chisel split and
scarf. Then place it on the bar marked *A* and *C*,
Fig. 153, put it in the fire, take a nice welding heat,

and with a light hammer weld it lightly working in
the corners of the scarf. Then return it immediately
to the fire, get a good soft heat, and place it in the
tool No. 2, Fig. 150, with the tool No. 3, Fig. 150, on

FIG. 151.—SHOWING HOW THE PIECE IS DRAWN OUT.

top. Let the helper give it three or four sharp blows
and the job is finished. If there should be any surplus stock it will be squeezed out between the tools

FIG. 152.—SHOWING HOW THE PIECE IS BENT.

and can be easily removed with a sharp chisel.

The reader will notice that there is a box in the
tool No. 2, Fig. 150, which serves to bring No. 3 in

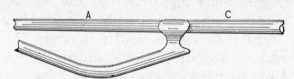

FIG. 153.—SHOWING HOW THE PIECES ARE JOINED AND WELDED IN
MAKING AN OFFSET.

the right place every time. If the tools are made
properly the job will look like a drop-forging without
any sign of a weld. Two offsets for gears can be

made in this way in fifteen minutes by any good mechanic.

No. 4, Fig. 150, is a bending crotch. The prongs *A* and *B* are made oval, and *B* is adjustable to any size needed. This tool is made of cast steel throughout. To make it take a piece of cast steel 1 1-2 inches square, fuller and draw down the end to fit the square hole of the anvil, then flatten the top and split; next bend *C* at right angle to *A*, and finish to 7-8 inch square. Then draw out *A* to about an inch oval

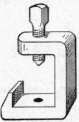

FIG. 154.—THE CLIP USED ON THE TIRE-SETTER MARKED NO. 5, IN FIG. 150.

on the angle, fuller and draw out the end *B*, cut off and punch the square hole, and work up the socket to 7-8 inch square, and it is ready for use. Then make a top wrench as shown at No. 57, Fig. 182. I like to have two top wrenches, one for light and one for heavy work.

No. 5, Fig. 150, is a home-made tire upsetter, but I do not claim that it is equal to some others now on the market. Still it will be found convenient in many shops where they do not have any.

To make it, take a piece of iron 1 x 2 inches and 11 inches long, take a heat in the center, weld on a square piece to fit the square hole in the anvil, and bend to suit large sized tire. Next make two clips, one for each end, and shape it as in Fig. 154. These clips are made from 1 3-4 x 3-4 inches iron. Drill two holes in each, one below to fasten the clip to the main plate, and one on the top end for the pinching or set screw, making the top holes 9-16 inch, and the bottom one, 5-8 inch, as a screw thread must be cut in the top for a 5-8-inch set screw. Now make four set

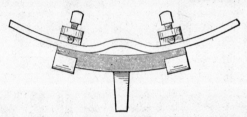

FIG. 155.—SHOWING THE METHOD OF USING THE TIRE-SETTER, NO. 5, FIG. 150.

screws, 5-8 inch full. The upper two should be made of steel or have steel points and be sharpened like a center punch. Now place the two clips on the ends of the main piece marked for holes. Drill two 9-16 inch holes and make a screw thread for 5-8 inch screws, put the screws in and cut the ends off the bottom screws level with the main plate and it is ready for use.

To use it, set the screws to fit the tire, heat to a soft heat and bend as shown in Fig. 155. Then

place it in the upset, and let your helper tighten one
of the set screws while you tighten the other, and
then hammer down with two hammers. In this way
a tire can be easily upset 3-8 inch at a heat.

No. 6, Fig. 150, is a very useful implement for
cleaning off plow shares or for reducing surplus
stock which cannot be removed conveniently otherwise. The cutting face is made of blister steel and

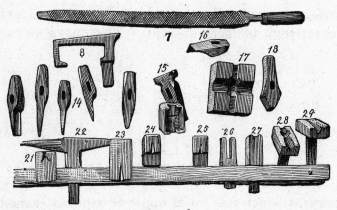

FIG. 156.

the back is of iron welded together. The length is
three feet, exclusive of the handle, and the width is
1 1-2 x 3-4 inches. The teeth are cut hot and like a
mill saw's teeth. To cut them take a sharp wide
chisel, commence at the front, cut one tooth, then
place your chisel back of the tooth and slide it forward until it comes against the first tooth. This
will make your gauge for the second tooth, and you

go on in this way until the teeth are all cut. To temper the tool, heat it for its full length to a blood heat, cool, then cover with oil and pass it backward and forward through the fire until the oil burns off. It can then be straightened if it has sprung. The front handle that stands up at right angles to the other part of the tool is screwed in. When the tool becomes dull, it can be softened and sharpened by a half-round file.

No. 7, Fig. 156, is a home-made rasp, made of solid cast steel 1 1-2 x 3-4 inches and 2 feet long (without tang). It has three cutting faces, two sides, and

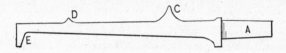

FIG. 157.—SHOWING HOW THE TOOL MARKED NO. 8, IN FIG. 156, IS DRAWN AND FULLERED.

one edge; the cutting edge is swaged round, which makes it very convenient for rasping around collars or similar places; the square edge is left smooth, which makes a good safety edge. It is double cut, similar to the ordinary blacksmith file. It has to be cut hot, and in cutting the second side it will be necessary to place it on the end of a wooden block. It will be found very useful for hot rasping large step-pads, or reducing stock on difficult work.

No. 8, Fig. 156, is made of 1 3-8 inches square machinery steel. To make it, draw it down as at *A*,

Fig. 157, to fit the square hole in the anvil, then
fuller in, work out the corner at *C*, draw out and
leave the corner at *D*, and form the foot as at *E*.
Then bend at *C* and fuller out the corner
as at *A*, Fig. 157, bend *D*, Fig. 157, as shown
at *B*, Fig. 158, and it will be ready for use. It
will be found very handy in making wrenches and
different kind of clips, scaffing, dash irons, etc. In
many cases it will be preferred to the little anvil at
No. 22, Fig. 156, being much firmer on account of

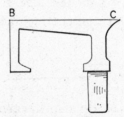

FIG. 158.—SHOWING HOW THE PIECE SHOWN IN FIG. 157 IS BENT
AND FULLERED.

the extra leg. At *C*, Fig. 158, it is 1 3-8 inches wide,
and 7-8 inch deep, and at *B*, 1 1-4 x 3-8 inch.
The length of the face is 7 inches.

No. 9, Fig. 150, is a collection of fullers ranging
from 1 1-2 inches to 3-16 inch. The top ones are
made of cast steel. Some of the bottom ones are
made of iron, and faced with steel, but lately I have
made them altogether of machinery steel, which is
less trouble to make and answers the purpose very
well. I do not think any further description of them

is necessary, as any blacksmith can see how they are made by a glance at the illustrations.

No. 10, Fig. 150, is a tool for cutting off round iron. In using it place the bottom swage in the anvil with the long end of the face toward the helper so as to be flush with the front of the anvil.   Then place the iron that is to be cut off in the bottom swage, and

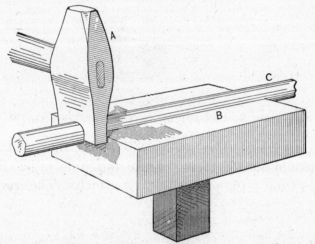

FIG. 159.—SHOWING THE METHOD OF USING THE TOOL MARKED AT NO. 10, IN FIG. 150.

put the top tool on; let the helper give it a sharp blow and off it goes.   Iron from 5-16 inch to 5-8 inch can be cut off thus with one blow.   This tool should be made of cast steel.   The recess should be made to fit 3-4-inch iron and so deep that the points will rest against the front of the swage and to prevent the tool and the swage from cutting each other.

In Fig. 159 a tool of this kind is shown with the iron in position ready to cut. *A* is the top tool, *B* is the bottom swage, and *C* is the round iron to be cut off.

In No. 12, Fig. 150, are shown two hardies for

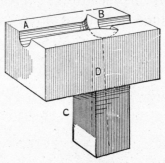

FIG. 160.—SHOWING THE BOTTOM OF THE SWAGE NO. 15, FIG. 156.

cutting iron. The reader will notice that there is a hole in one of them. I use this hole in bending rings from 7-16 inch round to 1-4 inch. The iron is

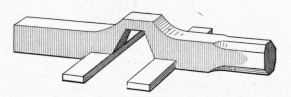

FIG. 161.—A FRENCH CLIP.

cut off to the desired length, one end is placed in the hole of the hardy, and on the other end I put a suitable heading tool. I then describe a circle around the hardy and the ring is made without heating it.

No. 13, Fig. 150, is a diamond-shaped fuller. It is made the same as those shown at No. 9, with the exception that the face is diamond shape. It is very useful in heavy work in working out corners and will often save considerable filing. Its shape tends to raise the corners, or make it full.

No. 14, Fig. 156, is a number of fine chisels. The first is a hollow or gouge chisel and is very convenient where you want to cut anything circular or hollow. The second is the ordinary hot chisel for cut-

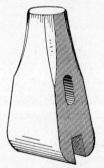

FIG. 162.—SHOWING A TOOL USED IN MAKING A FRENCH CLIP.

ting off hot iron. The third is a thin splitting chisel and should be rounded on the side toward you, which gives a rounding finish to the cut which is a great deal better where you wish to bend the branches. The fourth is a paring chisel, and is very useful often in trimming where the swell on both sides would be inconvenient. The fifth is an ordinary chisel for cutting cold iron, and should have a stronger edge than any of the others.

No. 15, Fig. 156, is a top and bottom collar swage. The top tool is about the same as any ordinary collar swage, but the bottom tool differs from any other I have ever seen. In the first place it will be noticed that there is a band around it, projecting above it fully one inch and cut out at each end. This band insures that the top tool will come in the right place every time. In the ordinary collar swage, I have always found more or less trouble in keeping the bottom tool perfectly clean from scales so as to

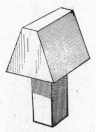

FIG. 163.—A TOOL USED IN MAKING FRENCH CLIPS.

make a sharp collar. To avoid this difficulty I have a hole from the bottom of the collar down through the shank so that the scales work out as fast as made, and now I find the collar comes out clean and sharp every time. To make this tool, forge the swage as usual, with a steel face, then commence at the bottom of the shank and drill a 3-8 inch hole to within 1-2 inch of the face. Drill the rest of the way with a drill about 1-8 inch. The place where the drill comes through is just where the large part of the collar should be. Then prepare it for the collar, then place the top tool exactly over it, mark around and cut so as to have both alike; then put on your band and finish up, and you will have a tool that will give satisfaction.

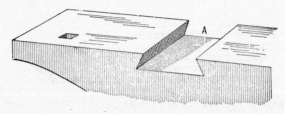

FIG. 164.—SHOWING A METHOD OF USING AN OLD ANVIL IN MAKING FRENCH CLIPS.

In Fig. 160, the bottom block is shown before the band is put on. *A* is the face of the tool, *B*, the part used to form the collar, *C* is the shank, and the dots, *D D*, indicate the hole for the escape of the dirt or scales.

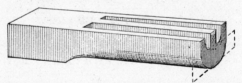

FIG. 165.—SHOWING HOW THE IRON IS FULLERED IN MAKING A FRENCH CLIP.

No. 16, Fig. 156, represents a V-chisel which is convenient for trimming out corners, and is especially useful in making French clips; it saves filing and time as well.

Fig. 161 represents a French clip, and Figs. 162, 163, and 164, and Nos. 17 and 18 in Fig. 156, are tools for making such a clip. No. 17 has no shank, but is intended to be used in a cast iron block being held in position by a key so as to be perfectly solid. An

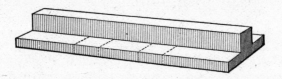

FIG. 166.—SHOWING FRENCH CLIP READY TO FULLER DOWN WITH TOOL 28, FIG. 156.

old anvil can be made to answer the same purpose by cutting out a recess as shown in *A*, Fig. 164. To make the clip shown in Fig. 161 proceed as follows:

Take iron of the proper size and extra quality, place it in the large oval bottom tool and with the

FIG. 167.—SHOWING EYE MADE WITH TOOL NO. 26, FIG. 160.

recess fuller shown in Fig. 162. Then place the iron in the bottom tool, as shown at No. 36, Fig. 175, and flatten out as shown by the dotted lines Fig. 165. The iron will then look as in Fig. 166. Then place it in the tool, No 17, Fig. 156, fuller down and trim up, finally using the tool No. 18, Fig. 156, and the tool shown in Fig. 163, to finish on, and the clip will then be in the shape shown in Fig. 161.

No. 19, Fig. 150, represents one-half of a tool used.

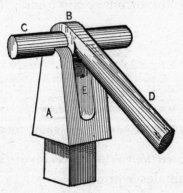

FIG. 168.—SHOWING METHOD OF USING TOOL NO. 26, FIG. 156.

in welding drop steps on body loops. It is used in the vise. It is recessed out to fit shank of step, and

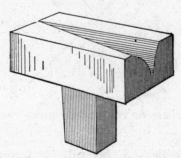

FIG. 169.—SHOWING A TOOL FOR MAKING HARROW TEETH.

the top is rounded so as to leave it strong where it is welded to the loop.

No. 20, Fig. 150, is one-half of a vise tool intended to be used in forming collars for seat wings, etc.

No. 21, Fig. 156, is a tool for making clips, Nos. 23, 24 and 25 are the ordinary clip tools. Nos. 24 and 25

FIG. 170.—SHOWING HOW THE HARROW TOOTH IS BENT.

are set back so as to be convenient for draw-jacks or work of that description.

No. 22, Fig. 156, is a small anvil intended to be

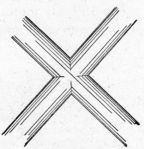

FIG. 171.—SPECIMEN OF THE WORK DONE BY THE TOOL NO. 32, FIG. 175.

used on a larger one. It will be found very useful in light work, such as welding small bends or socket and working up small eyes.

Nos. 26 and 27, Fig. 156, are used in making eyes

like those in the ends of top joints, as shown in Fig.
167, and for working up clevis ends. It is very convenient for the latter purpose, because it enables the
smith to make a good square corner without straining
the iron, and so prevents splitting. Fig. 168 shows

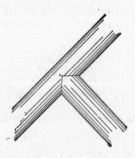

FIG. 172.—SPECIMEN OF THE WORK DONE WITH THE TOOL NO. 33,
FIG. 175.

method of using tools No. 26 and 27. *A* is the
bridge of the tool, *B* the eye and *C* the pin, while
D is the part which is held in the hand. The
slot *E* allows the part *D* to be raised or lowered

FIG. 173.—SPECIMEN OF THE WORK DONE WITH THE TOOL NO. 34,
FIG. 175.

while hammering on *B*. In making this tool I use
machinery steel. I draw down for the shank, split,
fuller out and then dress up.

No. 28, Fig. 156, is a tool for forming heads for body

loops. It is recessed to the shape of the top of the body loop. It will be found very convenient, and insures getting all the heads of the same shape. I place the head in the tool in punching, which forces the tool full in every part. To provide for the shank the front of the tool is a little higher around the head than at the oval part.

FIG. 174.—SECTIONAL VIEW OF THE TOOL NO. 35, FIG. 175.

No. 29, Fig. 156, represents a tool for making harrow teeth similar to the duck's foot that is thought a good deal of in some parts of the country. Fig. 169 will perhaps give a better idea of the tool, and Fig. 170 will show how the tooth is bent.

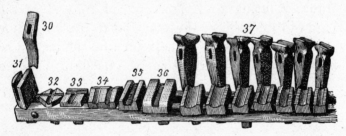

FIG. 175.

No. 30, Fig. 175, represents a crooked fuller for use in difficult places, such as gridiron steps, for which it is almost indispensable.

No. 31, Fig. 175, shows an anvil tool used in welding up oval gridiron steps.

No. 32, Fig. 175, is the bottom tool of a cross swage. The same tool is also shown in No. 27, Fig. 156. Fig. 171 represents some of the work done with this tool.

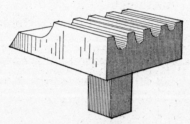

FIG. 176.—THE BOTTOM TOOL SHOWN IN NO. 38, FIG. 178.

No. 33, Fig. 175, is the bottom tool of a T-swage. The same tool is shown in No. 28, Fig. 156. It is used a good deal for ironing iron dickey seats, as is

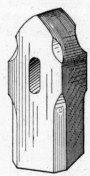

FIG. 177.—SHOWING A SLEDGE FOR HEAVY WORK.

also No. 32, Fig. 175, when a double rail is used. Fig. 172 is a specimen of the work done by this tool. No. 34, Fig. 175, is a tool for making corner irons for seats which have rounded surfaces on the inside and flat on the outside. One of the grooves is swedged on both sides of the point or apex of the tool. The other groove is flat on the other side from the one shown in the cut. I use this groove when I wish to make an iron with a foot for only one screw.

No. 35, Fig. 175, is a tool for making horseshoes similar to the Juniata pattern, excepting that the crease is set back so that the center of the shoe projects above the nail heads, thus insuring a good grip

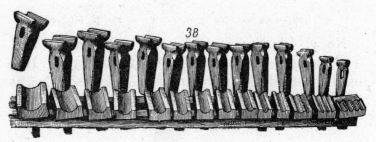

FIG. 178.

of the ground. Fig. 174 is a sectional view of the tool. It is made deeper at one end than at the other so that different weights of shoes can be made with it.

No. 36 is another punch clip tool.

No. 37 is a group of top and bottom oval swages. They range from 1-2 inch to 1 1-4 inches, there being 1-8 inch difference between each tool. I think they should range up to 2 inches, but at present I am out of top tools. The latter are of cast steel which I find to give the best satisfaction. For the bottom tools I

use iron faced with steel. To make them, I take a
piece of square Lowmoor iron, a trifle larger than the
square hole in the anvil, reduce it to proper size, cut
off about three-fourths of an inch above the part reduced and form it to a head with thin edges. I then

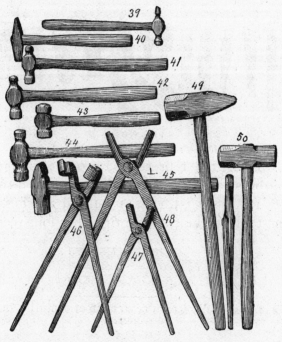

FIG. 179.

take a piece of common iron of suitable size for the top
and jump-weld a shank on it, then take a piece of blister steel of suitable size, take separate heats and weld
on, then cut off level with the back of the anvil, fuller

in the recess and finish up. In finishing up I am
careful to have the center a little fuller than the ends,
as if it is left perfectly straight it will cut the iron at
the ends and in working there is always a tendency
for the center to lower.

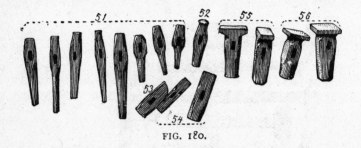

FIG. 180.

No. 38, Fig. 178, represents a group of swages for
round iron sizes, being 5-16, 3-8, 7-16, 1-2, 9-16, 5-8,
3-4, 7-8, 1, 1 1-8, 1 1-4, 1 1-2, 1 3-4, and 2 inches. The
bottom tool at the extreme right has four recesses,

FIG. 181.—SHOWING A FAULTY METHOD OF SPLITTING OUT
CROTCHES.

5-16, 3-8, 7-16, and 1-2 inch, and is made as shown in
Fig. 176. The reader will notice that the back edge projects over the anvil and slants, which makes it very
convenient for swaging different kinds of clips and by
having the swage short it is rendered very conveni-

ent also for cutting off surplus ends as shown at No. 10, Fig. 150, but for doing this work the top swage only is used. The swage next to the one on the extreme right at No. 38, Fig. 178. has three recesses, 3-16, 1-4, 5-16-inch. I do not have top tools for the 3-16 or 1-4-inch size but I find them useful in mak-

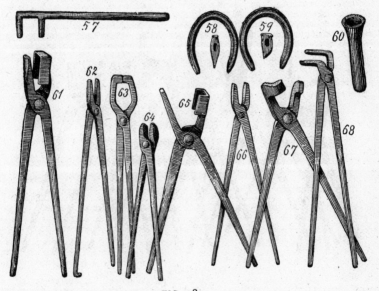

FIG. 182.

ing small half round iron. They are made in the same way as the oval tools. I mark the sizes of the top and the bottom tools.

No. 39, Fig. 179, is a small riveting hammer with a round pein or pane of about 3-8-inch diameter. I think this kind of hammer is best for riveting purposes, as it spreads the rivet every way alike.

No. 40, Fig. 179, is another riveting hammer. It is a cross pane which for some purposes is better than the round pane.

No. 41, Fig. 179, is a light hand hammer, commonly called a bench-hammer, with a globular pane.

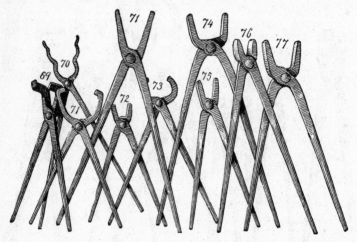

FIG. 183.

It is very useful for chipping with a cold chisel, and for light work at the anvil, such as welding dashes, etc. It weighs one pound.

No. 42, Fig. 179, is the ordinary hand hammer. It weighs 1 3-4 pounds.

No. 43, Fig. 179, is a horseshoe hammer, very

short and compact, being two-faced, one end being
slightly globular to answer for concaving.   Its weight
is 1 3-4 pounds.

No. 44, Fig. 179, is a heavy hand hammer similar
to Nos. 41 and 42.   It weighs about 2 1-2 pounds.

No. 45, Fig. 179, is a large cross pane hammer
made very plainly.   It is useful in straightening heavy,
irons, and also for the helper as a backing hammer
on light fullers.

No. 49, Fig. 179, is an ordinary sledge hammer in
which the eye is near the center.

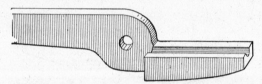

FIG. 184.—SHOWING A RIGHT HAND JAW FOR TONGS.

No. 50, Fig. 179, is a horseshoe sledge, but it should
be rather shorter and more compact than it appears
in the illustration.

Fig. 177 represents another sledge.   It will be
noticed that the eye is nearer the top of the sledge,
and I think this is an improvement for heavy work
where the smith wants to swing overhead.

No 51, Fig. 180, is a group of punches.   The first
two on the left hand side are oval or eye punches.
The oval stand on the corner of the square so as to
have the handle in the most convenient position, and

are used for punching eyes, or where the smith wishes
to swell out in order to strengthen by punching an
oval hole first and then driving a round pin in afterwards. They can be used to good advantage in
splitting out crotches, as there is less danger of cold
sheets than when the smith cuts right up with the
chisel as shown in Fig. 181.

The next two in the illustration are square punches,
and the next four are round punches of different sizes.

No. 52, Fig. 180, is a bob punch. It has a face
similar to a countersink only more rounding. It is

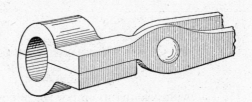

FIG. 185.—SHOWING HOW THE JAWS OF THE TONGS NO. 46, FIG. 179,
ARE MADE TO FIT ROUND IRON.

useful to press a cavity in a flat piece of iron where
a jump-weld is to be made, as in welding shanks to
bottom swages, also for T welds.

No. 53, Fig. 180, is a side-set hammer which is
very handy for working up an inside corner or any
place where you have to weld two irons in the shape
of angle iron, or on the landside of a plowshare.

No. 54, Fig. 180, represents two set hammers, one
being 1 inch and the other 1 1-2 inches square. They

are very useful in making many kinds of clips, and numerous other jobs.

No. 55, Fig. 180, also represents two set hammers similar in make but with the eyes punched from different sides. They are useful in plow work and are often used as flat hammer, where there is not room enough for the ordinary flat hammer.

No. 56, Fig. 180, represents two flat hammers, the smaller having a face 2 1-4 inches square, while the larger is 2 1-2 inches. This tool is to the blacksmith what the plane is to the woodworker. It is what we generally calculate to finish all flat surfaces with.

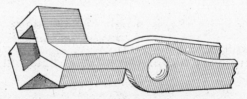

FIG. 186.—SHOWING TONG JAWS MADE FOR HOLDING LONG SQUARE IRON.

We now come to the tongs, and just the same as with everything else, there is a right and a wrong way to make them as tongs are right and left-handed. The accompanying illustration, Fig. 184, represents a right hand jaw. It is not often that a pair of left hand tongs are made, and, as a rule, if a smith does such a thing by mistake in a shop where there are many working, it produces so much merriment that

he scarcely ever forgets it, yet I have seen a man of
several years' experience do such a thing.

No. 70, Fig. 183, is a pair of pick ups. They
should be kept in a staple in front of anvil block, or
else hung convenient on the side of tool bench.
They are used by the helper to pick up pins or any-

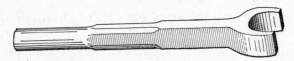

FIG. 187.—TOOL USED IN MAKING KEEPERS FOR DEMAREST WAGON
SEATS.

thing else. They will easily catch anything from 2
inches downward.

No. 69, Fig. 183, is a pair of side tongs. No. 67,
Fig. 182, is another pair of the same kind, but larger,
which are very useful for holding flat iron. There

FIG. 188.—KEEPER MADE WITH THE TOOL SHOWN IN FIG. 187.

is a sort of calk turned on one jaw to prevent the
iron slipping sideways.

No. 62, Fig. 182, is a pair of snipe bills, which are
very handy for small bands, sockets or eyes. One
of the jaws is round and the other is square, and a
fuller mark is made up the center, which I think is

better than making both round, as it fits both the outside and inside of band. They are drawn quite
small at the point. The back ends answer for a pair
of clip tongs to draw on clip bars with.

No. 48, Fig. 179, is a pair of hollow jaw tongs which
are very useful for holding round iron. Every blacksmith should be provided with three or four pair
ranging from 3-4 inch upward. I always fuller up
the center of my ordinary tongs so that they will

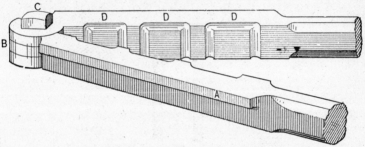

FIG. 189.--TOOL USED IN MAKING CLIPS.

hold small round iron well. They will hold flat iron
all the better for it.

No. 60, Fig. 182, is a cupping tool. It is hollowed
out with a countersunk drill and is very useful for
finishing off nuts or the top of square-headed bolts.
Four sizes of these make a very good set, but the
largest one should have a handle.

No. 58, Fig. 182, is a horseshoe stamp which is to
common to require any description.

No. 59, Fig. 182, is a creaser. I like it to be hollowed slightly on the inside face, as I think it follows the round of the shoe better.

No. 64, Fig. 182, represents a pair of horseshoe tongs.   The jaws are short and round so as not to project far inside of the shoe and be in the way of the horn of anvil, and at the same time to allow the smith to shift the position of the tongs without losing their grip.

No. 68, Fig. 182, is a pair of clip tongs which are indispensable in welding up whiffletree clips.   The

FIG. 190.—CLIP MADE BY THE TOOL SHOWN IN FIG. 189.

outside jaw is rounding, while the inside or short jaw is concaved to fit outside of the clip.

No. 71, Fig. 183, is a pair of coulter tongs.   One of the jaws turns down on each side of the coulter shank which makes the tool very convenient for holding.   No. 65, Fig. 182, are similar tongs which are very useful for holding square iron.

No. 46, Fig. 179, is a pair of tongs for holding large round iron.   They are very convenient for holding large bolts as the smith can let the

head project back of the jaws.   They are similar to
to the tongs shown in No. 69, Fig. 183, excepting that
both jaws are hollowed to fit the round iron as shown
in Fig. 185.   Fig. 186 represents a pair of tongs for
holding long square iron.

Fig. 187 represents a very simple and handy tool
for making keepers for Demarest wagon seats.   I
usually make them of 7-8-inch band iron.   To make
them I place a piece of 1-2-inch round iron on the
anvil, lay the band iron across it, then place the top

FIG. 191.—SHOWING HOW THE CLIP IS BENT BY THE MANDRIL.

tool, Fig. 187, strike two or three blows, and the job
is done as shown in Fig. 188.

Fig. 189 shows a tool for making clips of round iron
as illustrated in Fig. 190.   This tool will save a great
deal of time and do good work.   The clips are used
largely in some shops for clipping on springs, etc.
The tool is intended to be used in the vise and has
a projecting part, as shown at *A*, to rest on the vise.
It is intended for three different sizes of clips, 1 1-4,

1 1-2 and 1 3-4 inches. To make it take a piece of
1-inch square iron, fuller along the center with a
3-8 inch fuller the length of jaw. Then use the set
hammer on the lower side and reduce to 3-4 inch
thick; then use the side set hammer to true up;
plunge and form the joint as at *B*, taper down for
handles and weld on a piece of 5-8 inch round iron
so as to make a handle one foot long. The jaw is 9
inches long, measuring from the bolt hole. After
both jaws are made put in the bolt *C*, clamp firmly
together and drill six holes the size and width of
your clips. Be careful not to drill any larger as the
clips require to be held firmly. If a little small they

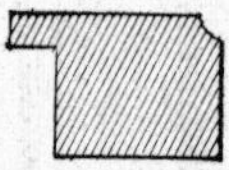

FIG. 192.—SECTIONAL VIEW OF A SIDE OF THE TOOL SHOWN IN
FIG. 189.

can easily be opened a little on the sides with a round
file. Then with a rounding chisel cut the corners as
shown at *D, D, D*, and smooth out with the end of the
file and it is ready for use. To make the clip, cut off
the desired length of iron and screw ends, bend on a
clip mandril as shown at Fig. 191, then place in the
tool, grip firmly in the hand, give a few sharp blows
on the top with a suitable swage and you have a clip
similar to that shown in Fig. 190. Fig. 192 is a sectional view of the tool.—*By* AMATEUR,

ABOUT HAMMERS.

Nearly every one has noticed the name of David Maydole stamped upon hammers. David Maydole made hammers the study of his lifetime, and after many years of thoughtful and laborious experiment he had actually produced an article to which, with all his knowledge and experience, he could suggest no improvements.

Let me tell you how he came to think of making hammers. Forty years ago he lived in a small village of the State of New York; no railroad yet, and even the Erie Canal many miles distant. He was the village blacksmith, his establishment consisting of himself and a boy to blow the bellows. He was a good deal troubled with his hammers. Sometimes the heads would fly off. If the metal was too soft the hammer would spread out and wear away; if it was too hard it would split. At that time blacksmiths made their own hammers, and he knew very little about mixing ores so as to produce the toughest iron. But he was particularly troubled with the hammer getting off the handle—a mishap which could be dangerous as well as inconvenient. One hammer had an iron rod running down through the handle with a nut screwed on at the end. Another was wholly composed of iron, the head and handle being all one piece. There were various other devices, some of which were exceedingly clumsy and awkward. At last he hit upon an improvement

which led to his being able to put a hammer upon a
handle in such a way that it would stay there.   He
made what is called an adze-handled hammer, the
head being attached to the handle after the manner
of an adze.

The improvement consists in merely making a
larger hole for the handle to go into, by which device
it has a much firmer hold of the head, and can easily
be made extremely tight. Each hammer is hammered out of a piece of iron, and is tempered over a
slow charcoal fire, under the inspection of an experienced man. He looks as though he were cooking
his hammers on a charcoal furnace, and he watches
them, until the process is complete, as a cook
watches mutton chops.

The neighborhood in which David Maydole lived
would scarcely have required a half-dozen new hammers in a year, but one day six carpenters came to
work on a new church, and one of these men left his
hammer at home and came to David Maydole's
blacksmith shop to get one made. The carpenter
was delighted with it, and when the other five carpenters saw it, they came to the shop the next day
and ordered five more hammers made. They did
not understand all the blacksmith's notions about
tempering and mixing the metals, but they saw at a
glance that the head and handle were so united that
there never was likely to be any divorce between
them. To a carpenter building a wooden house, the

removal of that one defect was a great boon. A
dealer in tools in New York City saw one of these
hammers, and then David Maydole's fortune was
made, for he immediately ordered all the hammers
the blacksmith could make. In a few years he made
so many hammers that he employed a hundred and
fifty men.—*From " Captains of Industry," by* JAMES
PARTON.

DRESSING UP OR FACING HAMMERS, REPAIRING BITS OR DRILLS.

Good tools are among the most essential things
about a blacksmith shop. You need a good fire, a
good anvil, and also a good hammer. You may
have fire, anvil, and all your other tools in good
shape, but if your hammer is rough and broken you
cannot do good work, nor do so much in a day. I
think that every man who calls himself a good blacksmith should be capable of dressing his hammer.
But for the benefit of those who are just beginning
the trade I will give my way of doing this job.

In the first place I open the middle of my fire and
fill it up with charcoal, using the mineral coal only
as a backer. Heat only the face you wish to dress
as by so doing you will not change the shape or disturb the eye. Upset on the face and draw down
on the sides. If the face is broken very badly it
may be necessary to trim off a little, but by upsetting
and drawing down several times you can get quite a

large break out without much trimming. After you
have completed the forging it is a good plan to put
the hammer in the dust of the forge and let it anneal;
and then it can be leveled with a file and ground off
smooth.

To temper it, heat only the part you wish to hard-
en, to a good red, dip and hold under water until
cold. Then have a thick ring (an old ax collar will
do) that the face of the hammer will go through
while the sides will come in contact with the ring,
heat the ring hot and place it over the hammer, turn
the ring slowly so as to keep the heat even on all sides
at once, draw until it shows a little color, then try with
a fine sharp file, and when you can make the file take
hold it has drawn enough. There are so many grades
of steel and different temperatues of heat and water
that you cannot always rely on the colors. The
middle of the face should be left as hard as you can
keep it, for if you let the heat from the eye part run
down and draw the face, it will be too soft and settle, leaving the outside circle the highest. If the
tool is double-faced do all your forging and finishing
before you temper. Then after you have tempered
the largest face, wind a wet cloth around it and keep
it cold while you are heating the other face.

I think that round sides with the outside edge
rounded in a little, stand better than the square or
octagon. Get a good handle and put it in so that it
will stay.

Every one who does repairing breaks a good many bits, especially small ones. They usually break at the end of the twist, leaving the shank long enough to make another bit by flattening about an inch of the end and twist once around. Then hammer down the edge, file a diamond point leaving the cutting part a little larger than the seat of the bit, temper and you have a drill as good as new. Drills can be made in the same way.—*By* F. P. HARRIMAN.

HAMMERS AND HANDLES.

Almost every blacksmith has a different style of hammer or handle, and every one thinks that his way of making them is right. One wants a heavy hammer and another a light hammer, for the same kind of work.

One wants a long hammer and another wants a short one. One wants his hammer to stand out and another likes his to stand in. One wants a long handle and another prefers a short handle. One wants his handle to spring and another does not. And so it goes on in that way all through the country.

Everyone will tell you that his way is the best, and will explain why it is the best. Now, my opinion in regard to the above is that they are all in almost every case right. I make all my hammers and handles, and think they are the right kind, simply because they suit me and I can do the work required with them satisfactorily.

I do not claim that there is any *right* way to make a blacksmith's hammer, But, of course, there is a certain line that you cannot pass without going to extremes.

For instance, if you should make a hammer a foot long, with a handle ten inches long, that would be out of all proportion, and would not be convenient to work with, and it could not be said by anyone that it was right. But supposing one man makes an ordinary hammer with a long pane, another makes one with a short pane; each one will claim that his hammer is right and that he could not do his work as well with another.

Now, how shall we determine which hammer is the nearest right? I should say both are right, for as long as they can do the work required, and they are satisfied with their hammers, that is all that is necessary.—*By* G. B. J.

A HAMMER THAT DOES NOT MARK IRON.

I was in a country blacksmith's shop the other day, and while talking with the boss I noticed a workman who was trying to get the kink out of an axle spindle with a hammer and swage. Every "lick" made it worse and filled it with hammer marks. I offered to show him how to make a hammer that would do the job properly. The offer was accepted, and this is the way the hammer was made. I first called for about four or five pounds of old

lead. This was furnished, and I then took a piece of
three-quarter-inch round iron about fifteen inches
long and upset the end, as shown in *A,* Fig. 194 of
the accompanying illustrations, to about 1 1-8-inch
and tapered it to *B,* a length of 2 inches. This left
the handle portion *C* about 12 inches long. I next

FIG. 193.—SHOWING THE HAMMER-HEAD.

got a box full of yellow mould, formed a circle in it
of about two inches in diameter and placed the
handle at the center. With a piece of sheet-iron
I made a ladle, melted the lead and poured it into
the impromptu mould. After a wait of twenty
minutes I lifted my hammer out of the sand,

FIG. 194.—SHOWING THE HANDLE.

dressed it up with a hand-hammer and then the
job was finished.

In Fig. 193 *D* is the hammer, and *E* is the place
occupied by the handle. Fig. 195 illustrates a simpler method of making the tool. A hole is made in
the sand as at *D,* and the handle is stuck in at *E,*

then the lead is heated and poured in. These hammers will not mark the iron.—*By* IRON DOCTOR.

AN IMPROVED TUYERE.

When I first began to work at the forge, nearly
fifty years ago, the old bull's-eye tuyere was the
best in use, but soft coke (or "breese" as it was
called, being the refuse of the rolling mill furnaces),
coming into use disposed of the bull's-eye, so the
water tuyere was invented as a necessity. For more
than thirty years I heard its gurgling waters, always
looking upon it as an evil to be tolerated because it
could not be avoided. Fancy all your fires started
on Monday morning in the winter, temperature
below zero, water just getting warm and then find-

FIG. 195.—SHOWING A SIMPLER METHOD OF MAKING THE TOOL.

ing pipes all bursted, new ones to be fitted, corners
to be bent in one of the forges at the risk of spoil-
ing a tuyere for want of water in it, customers waiting, foreman swearing, men freezing and shop liter-
ally upside down.

Next came the tank and tuyere in one, a good
improvement; also the coal back made of wet
"slack," but owing to its extravagant use of fuel not
to be tolerated. Then came the bottom blast. I

do not know when or where its first originated (invent or a "crank," no doubt).

As I was determined to do without a water tuyere, if possible, I tried most of the fancy "turn 'ems and twist 'ems" in the market, patented and otherwise, and all of them spread the fire too much for economy, in fact, some of them made a series of fires all over the hearth—the tuyere getting hot and clinging to the "clinker" with a matrimonial tie

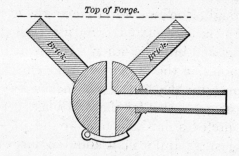

FIG. 196.—IMPROVED TUYERE, AS MADE BY "IRON JACK."

never to be divorced until one or both of them was deadly cold—making me hot, too, both in body and temper. I then got the tuyere craze and schemed all sorts of "jimcracks," if possible, worse than the others, until at last I concluded that moving blast orifices in tuyeres at the bottom of a forge fire were out of place, worse than useless, the poker being all sufficient; and to keep the tuyere sufficiently cool to prevent the clinker from clinging, it only wanted a lump of iron big enough where the fire could not touch it to keep the part cool where it did touch. Coming across an old cannon-ball, which, I suppose, had been used to knock down the walls of Petersburg during the war, and big enough it was, for the matter of that, to knock down the walls of—well, I won't say where—it being about nine inches in diameter and weighing upward of one hundred pounds, I said to myself, " Here is my tuyere." So I bored a hole in one side and screwed a piece of 3-inch wrought iron pipe into it, then giving it a quarter turn on the face plate I bored a 2 1-2 inch hole at right angles and into the other. I then drilled three 3-4 inch holes in the other side and chiseled them into a mouth for the blast 2 1-2 inches by 3-4 inch, which is a good size for the fan blast for regular work. I prefer a flat hole to a round one for the bottom blast, as it does not allow so large a cinder to fall through when the blast is off. After putting a trap door at the bottom to empty the tuyere I fixed it on the hearth 6 inches below the level of the top of the hearth, making a fine brick basin, as shown in section in the accompanying engraving. The success of this tuyere is complete, the blast coming straight out of the mouth like shot from a gun, making the fire very intense at the proper place (not spreading all over the hearth), which economizes the fuel as far as possible consistent with the work to be done, and the mass of metal always keeps the tuyere cool and cakes the clinker so as to make it easy to lift out of the fire with the poker, no matter how long or how heavily it is worked. Should anyone feel disposed to try it he will be more than pleased. The forge and anvil should be both on a level to permit the crane to operate easily without trouble.—*By* IRON JACK.

HOME-MADE BLOWER.

I commenced business without tools and without any other resources than my own strong right arm. After getting an anvil I experienced the need of a blower. Those which were for sale were high priced, and nothing but the cash in hand would buy one. In order to do the best possible under the circumstances, I took a good look at one in a store, by which I obtained the principle on which it was operated, and then went home and commenced work upon one upon my own account. I made it of wood, and succeeded so well as to make something by which a sort of a fire could be started. When it was in motion, however, my neighbors thought I was running a threshing machine. It could be heard of a still morning nearly a mile away. After using this for a short time, I concluded I would try to make a better one, and now I will tell you how I set about it.

I took three pieces of white pine plank, 12 by 14 inches and 1 1-2 inches thick. I dressed and glued them together crosswise, in order to obtain the greatest

possible strength. I took the piece to a jig-saw,
and had a circle, perfectly true, taken out of the
center, 8 inches in diameter. I then closed this hole
by placing a half-inch poplar board on each side, the
same size as the large block. These thin pieces I
screwed down tight with eight screws on each board.
Removing one of them I got the center of the edge
of the hole on the inside of the one that remained,
and by reversing the operation, got the center upon
the opposite one. From this measurement I cut a
hole 4 inches in diameter through each of these thin
pieces, which was to serve to let the air into the

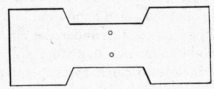

FIG. 197.—GENERAL SHAPE OF THE PADDLES OR FANS IN "NO
NAME'S" BLOWER.

blower. By placing the boards back in their original
position the holes would be in the center of the hole
cut in the large block.

I next took two pieces of iron 1-2 by 1 1-4 inches
and drilled a 5-16-inch hole through them in the
middle. I took a piece of 3-8-inch steelrod and
made two thumbscrews of it; cut threads upon
them to work tightly in the holes in the irons. I
made them very pointed and chilled them very
hard. Next I took a piece of 3-8-inch steel rod and

cut it the right length to fit between the points of
the two thumb-screws, and with the center punch I
made a small puncture in the center of the ends of
this rod to receive the pointed ends of the thumb-
screws, above described. Next I drilled two holes

FIG. 198.—SHAPE OF SIDE IRONS HOLDING THE AXLE OF FAN
IN "NO NAME'S" BLOWER.

in this shaft, one about 1 1-2 inches from one end,
and the other about 2 inches from the pulley
end. On the long end I placed a small cotton
spindle pulley, and 1 1-4 inches in diameter and

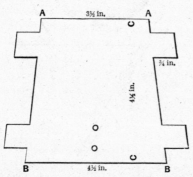

FIG. 199.—PATTERN OF FANS, TO BE MADE OF GALVANIZED IRON.

1-4 of an inch thick, having a groove in its surface for
a small round bolt, such as is frequently used on
sewing machines. I next took a piece of sheet iron,
heavy gauge, and cut some paddles or fans 4 by 8

inches, in shape as indicated by Fig. 197, accompany·
ing sketch.   I riveted these fans to shaft and bent
them up, thus forming four paddles, located at
equal distances apart.   The   fan was now done, except putting together.   I screwed fast the straight

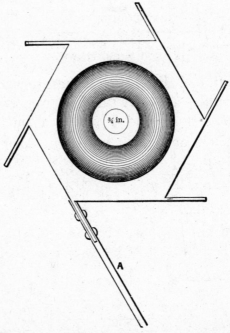

FIG. 200.—CENTER-PIECE TO WHICH FANS ARE ATTACHED.

pieces of iron that held the thumb-screws and took
care that the screw came exactly in the center of the
hole, in order that the fan should turn freely.   I
turned the box over and placed the fan in the hole,

with two pivots together, and then fastened in position the other piece of iron, which was made in the shape shown in Fig. 198 of the sketches. I exercised great care that it also should come exactly in the center and at the same time be in such a position as not to come in contact with the bolt. I took care also that the face hung perfectly true in the center and then screwed down the second board. I

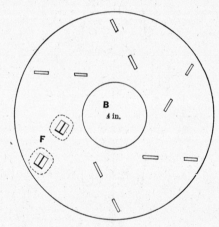

FIG. 201.—SIDE PLATES, BETWEEN WHICH FANS ARE FASTENED.

next made a hole in the end of the box 3 inches in diameter, making it to intersect with the hole in the box at the upper part. I took care that it should be smooth and clean. I made a frame of 2 by 3 hard wood in such a way as to mount the blower in a convenient position near my forge. A driving-wheel grooved on the fan to accommodate a bolt of the

kind above described, and operated with a crank, is
fastened to two standards at the front of the frame,
thus affording motive power.   My fan, constructed
in this manner, has now been in use over two years,
and is in perfect condition at the present time.   It
gives all the blast that I require, and runs noiselessly.
—*By* No Name.

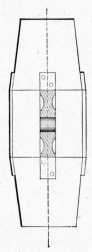

FIG. 202.—CROSS SECTION THROUGH COMPLETED FAN.

HOME-MADE FAN FOR A BLACKSMITH'S FORGE.

I think anyone with ordinary mechanical skill, by
following the directions which I shall attempt to present, will have no difficulty in building a fan which
will perform satisfactorily.

First cut twelve piece of galvanized iron to the
shape and dimensions shown in Fig. 199.   These

should be about 1-16 of an inch thick. Four square
studs about three-quarters of an inch long, are left
on the edges of each plate. The distance from *A*
to *A* is 3 1-2 inches, from *B* to *B*, 4 1-2 inches, and
from *C* to *C*, 4 1-2 inches. Punch two full quarter-
inch holes in each piece. Make a middle piece of

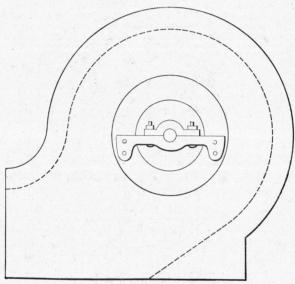

FIG. 203.—SIDE ELEVATION OF COMPLETED FAN.

metal like Fig. 200, which should be about five
inches in diameter, and seven-eighths or an inch
thick. This can be made of brass, zinc, or iron.
Drill two holes in each arm to match the holes in
plates shown in Fig. 199. Then put two of these
plates on each arm, with quarter-inch bolts as is

shown at *A* in Fig. 200. Then cut two circular
plates after the pattern shown in Fig. 201. These
are to be dished as shown in Fig. 202, in order to
fit the middle of the fan nicely. Have them quite as
large as the middle of the fan. In the center of
these plates are draught holes, *B*, through which the

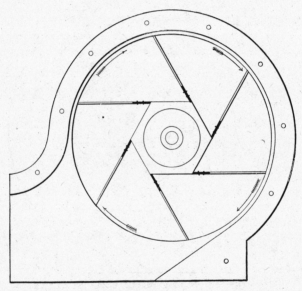

FIG. 204.—LONGITUDINAL SECTION THROUGH COMPLETED FAN.

air will enter the fan. These are to be four inches
in diameter. Each plate has twelve long narrow
holes punched in it as shown in Fig. 201, and a
strong zinc washer is soldered upon it. This plate is
now forced on to the side of the fan. The studs will

of course project through this plate rather more than half an inch. By taking a chisel or screw driver, and putting it between the studs or lugs, one part can be turned one way and the other the other, as in Fig. 201, and the plates will be fast. A good bit of solder should then be run over the whole, as shown by the dotted lines at *F* in Fig. 201. The next thing is to take two of pieces 1 1-4 inch plank, and cut them to the shape shown in Fig. 203. They should be grooved as shown by the dotted line about one and one fourth inches from the edge. This portion is to form the box for the fan. Fig.

18 in.

FIG. 205.—SPINDLE AND PULLEY FOR DRIVING THE FAN.

204 shows the fan put together, but with one side and one plate removed. Now a sheet of iron 3-32 of an inch thick, and say five inches wide, must be bent to the shape of the groove shown by the dotted line in Fig. 203. Put this into the grooves between the two wooden sides, and bolt all together with quarter-inch bolts and nuts. The bolts should be put in four inches apart all around. Zinc bearings four inches wide should be used, and the whole made to fit firmly to a one-inch board about twelve inches wide. Turn a wooden pulley, about three

inches in diameter, with a convex face, something like that shown in Fig. 205. The spindle of this pulley should be three-fourths of an inch in diameter, and eighteen inches long. The outlet at the mouth of the fan is four inches square. The nozzle in the fire can be made two inches, or any desired size.—*By* **K.**

MINERS' TOOLS AND SMITH WORK.

When I was on Ballarat Diggings from 1852 to '59 there were sledge hammers in use for various purposes; thus in my shop I had sledge hammers for the ordinary strikers, which weighed say, 14 lbs. each, and as a sort of corps de reserve, one of 28 lbs.; and as a good striker was not always to the fore, I usually wielded a hand hammer myself of 4 lbs. for sharpening the miners' picks, for which I received when a "rush" was on, 2s. per point, never less than 1s. 6d. per point, 2s. 6d. for steeling, and 5s. for laying and steeling; also I got 10s. for making an ordinary Cornish hammer-headed driving pick. I think that the weight I stated would be about the average for striking the heads of jumpers for quartz reef, and what we termed cement, which might be likened to masses of stone, imbedded in a slaggy sort of glass; but as those engaged in the search for the precious metal were representatives of, say, every country, calling and want of calling upon this sublunary sphere, so were the tools and the "shooting irons" which came to me for repair.

I was renowned for tempering the miners' gear. I think that about 1 in 500 smiths is fit to be trusted to manfacture any tool from cast steel without over-heating same. I have not been brought up a black-smith, being more in the line of a fitter of the knotstick species, and I have not yet met with a blacksmith that I would trust to forge me any kind of tools for lathe, etc. Now, please to bear in mind that this does not apply to men who make a specialty of tool-making but only to the ordinary general men of the shops. A dull red in a dusty place is not enough for the welfare of cast steel, but this entails a lot of additional hammering, which tells upon a man's wrist in an unpleasant manner. At same heat I dip drills or jumpers steadily into ordinary water not containing any sort of quack medicines therein.

A proper smith's hand hammer always has a com-paratively small rounded pane, the pane for drawing-out purposes being upon the sledge hammer, but I employed out on the Diggings for all-round jobs a German, who probably could make anything com-plete with hammers alone, from an elbow for stove-pipes to figures and foliage, and he spoke of having alongside the anvil in Germany, say some fifty dif-ferent sorts and weights of hammers.

To stop the ring of an anvil. Let the spike, which ought to be in the block to keep the anvil *in situ*, fit the hole in it tight, and let the adjacent iron of the anvil's bottom bed upon said block, and its vibration will be stopped once for all. The reason why we don't have more articles upon smithwork is undoubtedly because, in the bulk, English smiths are uneducated, and like all such, grudge to afford any information upon that or any other subject, and they abound in quasi nostrums for accomplishing many things.

With regard to making a weld, one of your correspondents says : " Dip each piece in sand," etc. Now, there are many varieties of sand, such as that about here, which is deficient in the matter of silica, which I opine is the material which, by melting at the necessary heat just previous to the melting of the iron, forms a coating of glass over the iron, and so prevents its oxidation during its heating and transit to the anvil; therefore, I find it better to collect the bottoms out of a grindstone trough, taking care that no debris of zinc, copper, lead, tin or anything abounding in sulphur, be used upon said stone; and he has omitted to mention that an important factor in a sound weld is that, at the instant of taking the two pieces to the anvil, the operator, or operators, should strike each piece gently, behind the heated part, upon the anvil, in order to knock off all impedimenta; with lightning rapidity, place one upon the other, tap gently upon the " center " of the weld, and quickly close up the two thin ends, but bearing in mind to work from the center to the outside

An amateur will find that a serious difficulty will

be encountered when he tries to hold anything, more
especially cast steel, in a tongs.   When learning how
to turn the work upon its side, be sure to turn so
that the "back" of the hand is uppermost, or a bad
striker will be likely by lowering his back hand to
plant a lot of the hot slag into the palm of your hand,
or you may accomplish this by bad striking upon
your own account.   When hitting a job upon the
anvil, do not strike in various places, as a rule, unless when necessary to place the work over a particular part, as the edge or on the beak.   Keep your
hammer going up and down, as if it were in guides,
drawing the work back or forward as required.

There is an art in making and keeping up the
fire.   It depends very much upon the fuel used.   If
a heavy welding heat be required, we must take two
or more shovels of wet slack (after, of course, light-
ing up) and tamp this down gently with the shovel,
so that it forms an arched oven, as if were, and poke
a hole or holes to run in the bar or plural.   If we
observe a blue or greenish tinge in the flames, we
will probably consider as to the advisability of
shoveling off "all" the fire and beginning again, as
sulphur is in the ascendant.

Sulphur would cause the white-hot iron to run
away in drops.   Mine is a portable forge, and by
drawing out the plug at the back in the air-pipe when
knocking off for a spell, this not only allows the entrance of air to keep fire alight, but prevents the lia-

bility there is to blowing up a bellows, if fresh coal is put on, and immediately after, more especially if it be wet slack, the blowing be stopped, as in this event the large quantity of gas generated finds its way into the said elbows, and when the culprit next draws down the handle, he mixes it with the air, and a violent explosion is the result, as well as probably the splitting of the inside middle board. This is the reason why the nozzle of an ordinary bellows ought not to be jammed into the tuyere; but there should be, say, 1 4 inch clear space around its end. A steady continuous blast is far more efficacious than short jerky forcing.

The putting of salt or anything else in the water for tempering is bosh.

When a smith applies to me for a job, I always set him—if in want of one—to make his hammer and a pair of tongs. When an amateur can make a tongs that does not open when it ought to shut he will know a thing or two anent forging, and when a smith can make a good cast-steel hammer, it is tolerably certain that he is up to the hammer, and if he doesn't want to wet it too often, deserves taking on.

As to the silent language, it would never do if one had to say to a striker, "Will you be kind enough to hit so and so?" therefore if we want the striker, we ring on the hand hammer; he is all attention. We whip out the bar and gently tickle it together whilst in a melting mood; next, we tap it in an inviting

manner upon the spot where he ought to strike it,
which, as before stated, should, as a rule, be in the center of the anvil. At first both strike alternately,
but as the reducing effect of the sledge becomes evident, we, the smith, judiciously intersperse our blows
upon the jobs by taps upon the anvil, always shifting
our irons; but unless we touch a certain spot with
our hammer he is to keep on striking in the middle,
and when we require him to knock off we bring down
our hammer in such a way that it in a sense rings
upon the anvil.—*English Mechanic and World of
Science.*

THE HACK SAW.

Probably no tool devised for the use of iron workers in recent years can be employed to greater

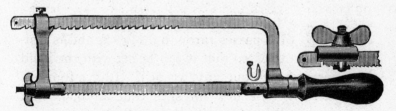

FIG. 206.—-SHOWING THE HACK SAW.

advantage by a blacksmith than a hack saw. In
many shops it has almost supplanted the cold chisel,
as it can be used in nearly all cases where the latter
tool comes in play, and does its work more ex-

peditiously.   It will cut iron almost as rapidly as an
ordinary saw cuts wood.   Its cheapness brings it
within the range of every mechanic having iron to
cut.   The engraving, Fig. 206, gives a correct idea
of its appearance.

ADJUSTABLE TONGS.

I lately came across about as handy a blacksmith's
tool as one could wish to find.   It was an adjustable pair of tongs that will hold tight enough for any
light work.   The jaw, *J*, Fig. 207, is provided with
a slot, *S*, and the rivet is carried at that end in a

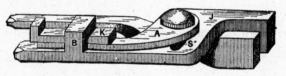

FIG. 207.—ADJUSTABLE TONGS, AS DESCRIBED BY "NEW YORKER."

tongue, *A*, that passes through a lug, *B*, and is fastened by a key, *K*, so that it can be set with the hand
hammer and without any wrench.   I have found it
an excellent tool, and am sure that anybody that
makes one will be pleased with it.—*By* NEW YORKER.

TONGS FOR MAKING SPRING CLIPS, SLEIGH JACKS, ETC.

I send you a sketch, Fig. 208, of a pair of tongs for
making sleigh jacks, spring clips, staples, etc.   *A* is
a clip to be bent as at *B*, Fig. 209.   The pair of

tongs has in jaw, *C*, Fig. 210, a hole for the stem, the width of the jaw, *D*, being that required between the jaws of the clip.   If both jaws have holes through

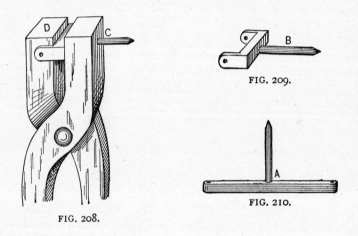

FIG. 209.

FIG. 208.

FIG. 210.

them and are of different widths two sizes of clips can be bent on one pair of tongs.—*By* R. R. M.

END OF VOLUME I.

INDEX.

VOLUME II.

CONTENTS.

PREFACE.

In Vol. I. the editor of this work gave a brief account of the early history of blacksmithing, so far as known, and described a few ancient and many modern tools.

Numerous plans of shops were given with best methods of building chimneys and constructing forges.

This volume opens with a brief treatise on the early history of iron and steel. Artistic iron work is then considered, and the tests employed to show the strength of iron are given.

It was the original intention to compress all the material relating to tools in Vol. I., but this was found to be impracticable without largely increasing the size of the volume, and possibly the price as well. It was deemed best therefore to devote so much of Vol. II., as might be necessary, to the fur ther consideration of tools, and the reader will doubtless agree with us that the space has not been wasted.

Vol. III. will be devoted mainly to the consideration of jobs of work.

THE EDITOR.

CHAPTER I.

IRON AND STEEL.

THEIR ANTIQUITY AND GREAT USEFULNESS.

All mechanics, irrespective of the trades which they follow, have so much to do with iron in its various forms, either by working it or by using tools and instruments in the construction of which it forms an important part, that a brief consideration of the material, both retrospective and present, cannot fail to be of interest. To trace the development of iron from its earliest known existence to the present, and to glance at its use as a material of construction, that, unlike all others can rarely be dispensed with in favor of a substitute equally desirable, cannot fail to be of the greatest interest.

In the description of the building of Solomon's Temple there is no specific statement that iron was employed, although by inference it is understood that this material must have been used in the tools of the workmen, if for no other purpose. It is not to be forgotten that the record says there was neither hammer nor axe, nor tool of iron heard in the house while it was being built. A plausible construction to place upon this assertion is that the parts were fashioned and fitted together at distant places, and were joined noiselessly in completing the structure. This view of the case serves to point out the excellence of the skill of that day, for, however great the care that is exercised at the present time by mechanics, few buildings are put up in which the sound of tools in the shaping of the various parts, after they have been sent to the building for putting up, might be dispensed with.

King David, it is said, had in his collection of materials "iron in abundance for the doors of the gates and for the joinings." Other allusions to iron are to be found in the Old Testament Scriptures. Some passages are of figurative character, where iron is the emblem of hardness, strength and power. Others are descriptive, and indicate its uses in those early times.

The manufacture of iron existed in India from very remote antiquity, though carried on in a very primitive manner. Vast accumulations of slag and cinder are found spread over large areas in various districts, and the manufacture of iron is still carried on with little change from the ancient process. In one of the temples near Delhi there is a wrought-iron pillar sixty feet in length, which dates as far back as the fourth century of the present era. It is only of late years that the production of a shaft of these dimensions has been possible to the present race of iron-workers.

The extent to which iron was employed by the ancient Egyptians is a problem difficult of solution. When the enormous labor expended upon the masonry and sculpture in the hardest granite, and the beautiful surface and high finish generally displayed in the architectural works of that country are considered, it seems difficult to imagine that tools inferior to the hardest steel could have produced the result, yet the evidence is exceedingly slight that anything of the kind was employed. Bronze is some times found in ancient tombs in that country in a variety of forms, but iron is almost entirely wanting. Iron mines have been discovered in Upper Egypt, and the remains of iron-works have been found recently near Mount Sinai. An iron plate was found in one of the pyramids, and a sickle in one of the tombs at Thebes.

The use of iron by the Romans was of comparatively late introduction. The fine specular iron of the Isle of Elba had been smelted by the Etruscans from an early date, but it does not seem to have been extensively used in Italy. It was not until the time of the second Punic War that the Romans, extending their conquests beyond their narrow original seat, obtained supplies of iron and steel from Spain, and discarded their bronze weapons for the harder and keener metal. Iron was little used by any of the ancient nations in building construction. When Virgil describes the splendors of Dido's rising city, no mention is made of iron in any form. Stone, with the addition of bronze for plating, are the materials especially alluded to.

In the New Testament mention is made of an iron gate which would seem to indicate that at that period iron had been brought into use in many forms, more, however, in the way of machinery, armor and weapons, than in building construction. For all constructive purposes bronze was gradually superseded by iron, and during the middle ages was worked with great skill and success. Iron employed at this period was not made by the process of fusion and puddling, but was obtained direct from the ore by roasting with charcoal and working it under the hammer. The metal thus obtained was of excellent quality, and such examples as have come down to us indicate that it was very skilfully manipulated. Armor and weapons attained a high degree of efficiency, and were finished with great taste.

There are very few specimens remaining in anything like perfection of the mediæval smith's work. Enough fragments, however, are in existence to indicate the extreme beauty of the workmanship of this age. The rich and graceful curves of the work done at this time, together with their lightness and strength, show what capabilities exist in iron when freely treated in accordance with its nature. Probably the grills or screens and the gates of the middle ages exhibited the art of the smith in its greatest perfection. Nothing that has been made in modern times is equal to the specimens which remain of that period. The wonder arises that, with such simple means as were at the command of the mechanics and artists of that day, such wonderful effects could be produced.

During the Romanesque period iron does not seem to have been employed, even in carpentry or masonry. At the end of the twelfth century iron cramps were employed at the Cathedral of Notre Dame, Paris, to connect the stones of the cobbled corners. The oxidation of these cramps in the course of time had the effect of fracturing the stones. Experience in this practice does not seem to have taught wisdom, for, even at the present day, the mistake of using iron in similar positions has frequently led to like results.

We owe to Germany the discovery of the process by which fusible iron could be smelted from the ore. It probably arose from the gradual improvement of the blowing apparatus, by which the old blast bloomeries were transformed into blast furnaces. Cast iron was unknown prior to the middle of the sixteenth century. About 1550 the German system, above alluded to, was introduced into England, where there already existed great facilities in the enormous quantity of scoriæ accumulated about the ancient bloomeries and in the abundance of timber for fuel. Progress in the art was so rapid that cast-iron ordnance was an article of export from England early in the seventeenth century. As the art of casting made progress, the art of the smith declined. The cheapness of cast iron and the facility with which it could be manipulated, led to its extensive use in every department of life.

In 1735, the problem of smelting iron with pit coal was successfully solved, but it was not until within a very recent period that the advantages of iron on any great scale developed themselves. Down to the commencement of the present century the casting of iron pipe was so difficult and costly an operation, that in schemes for the supply of water to towns, wooden pipes were adopted for the mains. In 1777 the first experiment was made with iron as a material in bridge building. At present scarcely a bridge of any importance is constructed of other material.

Having thus glanced hastily at the progress of manufacture and the use of iron from the earliest historical periods to the present time, the inquiry comes up, what is to be its influence in the future? That it will contribute materially to aid man's power over the elements of nature is certain, but the moral results which are likely to follow lie beyond our province. All true designs arise out of construction. Every style which has attained any eminence owes its effect to the adoption of its essential parts as sources of beauty rather than an attempt to conceal them. The use of iron in any construction or design is a source of power and effect, put into the hands of the architect for good or for evil.

The Strength of Wrought Iron and Steel.

There is something very interesting, but not altogether as yet understood, in the behavior and strength of iron and steel when loaded.

It is all very well to institute certain tests to find the number of pounds it requires to break a piece having a sectional area of one square inch, and from this pronounce what is the strength of the iron ; because, with our present knowledge and appliances, it is all we can do, and a test of some kind is of course imperative. It is a curious fact, however, that the strength of a piece of iron or steel varies according to the manner in which the load is applied, If the metal receives its load suddenly, it will break under a less weight than if the load comes on slowly and gradually increases ; and the difference is not a minute one either, for it is as great as 20 per cent under the two extremes of conditions. One of the most eminent constructing engineers in this country stated not long since, in reply to a question, that he would make as much as 20 per cent difference in the strength of two beams to receive the same load, one to have the load suddenly, and the other to have it gradually applied. From this it is a fair and reasonable deduction that if the load, when applied, caused vibration, the beam would require still greater dimensions to be of equal strength, because vibrations are simply minute movements, and, in the case of horizontal beams, on moving downward increase the pressure of the load.

A short time since some experiments were made to ascertain the strength of iron and steel wire, two specimens of each size of wire being used, one just as the iron came from the mill and the other an annealed specimen.

The wires were suspended vertically, and a certain weight, as say 10 lbs., was hung on them. Then in some cases a ½ lb. weight per day was added, in others 1 lb. per day, in yet others the weights were increased as fast as they could be put on, and in every instance it was found that the breaking strains increased according as the time between the increases of weight was made longer, the amount varying from 10 to 20 per cent. The failure of the boiler plates of the English steamship *Livadia* elicited some interesting facts and strange opinions upon the behavior of low-grade steel. The facts concerning these plates are given below. The boiler was 14 feet 3 inches diameter by 16 feet long. The plates were ¾-inch thick, lap-jointed and treble riveted. The plates were all punched, then slightly heated and bent to shape, afterwards put together, and the rivet holes reamed out to size. While under this treatment one of the plates fell out of the slings on to an iron plate and was cracked right across the rivet holes. Naturally this gave some anxiety, but after the plates were all in the boiler itself, they cracked across the rivet holes in nearly all directions; that is, many of them did.

Investigation was immediately set up, chemically and mechanically, when it appeared, as nearly as could be ascertained, that although the stock was good of which the plates were made, it had not been thoroughly worked under the hammer before rolling.

Dr. Siemens, the inventor of the process which bears his name, asserts that annealing plates, either before or after working (punching), is of no advantage; tending, if anything, to injure rather than benefit the materials. Many practical men, however, hold views in opposition to Dr. Siemens on this question.—*By* JOSHUA ROSE.

The Rotting and Crystallization of Iron.

I noticed an article lately, in which an iron worker, who claims an experience of fifty years in his trade, says that iron rots as well as crystallizes under strain and jar. The latter part of this statement is correct in degree only. The springs of vehicles

deteriorate by use and excessive strain, but not to
the extent which the writer of the article I refer to
represents, as the springs of thousands of old vehicles will attest, in which not a leaf is broken, although the remainder of the gear is worn out.

And although iron may be crystalline in the fracture it does not lose its tensile strength to any great
extent, unless under a very great strain or jar, as in
the case of quartz-mill stamp stems, which are lifted
and dropped about once a second, are run night and
day, including Sundays, and even then will stand
several years of this hard usage before breaking.
The danger of iron losing its tensile strength is
greatly exaggerated in the article in question. If it
were not so people would be afraid to go over and
under the Brooklyn bridge.

The statement that iron rots is absolutely untrue,
and if the crowbars referred to in the article mentioned would not weld readily, and had a bad smell
when heated, the odor was from the sulphur and
phosphorus which the iron contained, and which was
present in the iron when it was made, like much of
the first iron in early attempts at iron making by
using stone coal. The iron did not absorb, it could
not have absorbed sulphur and phosphorus from
age or exposure to the atmosphere.

The art of iron making has progressed in spite of
all statements to the contrary, and iron is made
smelted with stone coal, which is as good as the best

Swedish charcoal iron, and even better for some purposes, and the iron makers manufacture any grade of iron to suit price or purpose.

When iron, by reason of long-continued strain or jar, breaks, showing a crystalline fracture, its chemical constituents are still the same as when it was made, and when heated and welded it will resume its fibrous appearance and its original toughness, as I know from much practical experience in welding broken stamp stems and heavy iron axles.

Rolling mills were invented about a hundred years ago, but if the practical wiseacre is in favor of the old system of laboriously pounding out a bar of iron filled with hammer marks by the trip hammer, why that settles the rolling mills of course.—*By* R. R.

Steel and Iron.

I have been turning in my mind some of the generally accepted theories about iron and steel, and wondering when the general public will drop the notion that the main distinguishing feature between the two is that one will harden and the other will not.

Does a piece harden ?   It is steel.

Is it found impossible to harden another piece? It is iron.

Many people go no further than this in deciding the character of pieces under examination, and still there is steel that will not harden which is almost equal to tool steel. Growing out of these wide differences between different steels and irons there is a continuous discussion and much misconception as to real facts. That a piece of Swedes iron of irregular structure, with minute seams, sand streaks and impurities, should contain sufficient carbon to harden would hardly make it valuable for edge tools. Nor would a piece of cast-steel of the most unexceptionable structure be of any great value for the same use, in a commercial sense, if the necessary carbon were lacking. How often is heard the very positive assertion in regard to certain articles which should be made of steel and hardened, "They are nothing but iron," and quite recently there has appeared in trade journals an article on cutlery, in which it is charged that "table knives are made of iron, on account of the greater facility with which iron can be worked."

That cast-iron shears and scissors with chilled edges, and cast-iron hammers and hatchets sandwiched in with malleable iron and steel castings, to take the place of instruments which are generally supposed to be forged from steel and hardened and tempered in the regular way, are to be found on the market is true, but when it comes to goods which are made in the regular way, we need not believe that wrought iron is used to any great extent where steel should be. That a tool is soft does not prove that it might not have been hardened to be one of the best of its kind. That a tool proves to be as brittle as glass, breaking at the very beginning of service, does not prove that the steel of which it was made was of poor quality, for, properly treated, it might have been hardened to be of the very best.

In this matter of deciding as to the merits of steel there is too much of jumping at conclusions, and so the self-constituted judges are continually called upon to reverse their decisions. No decision would be considered to be in order on a matter of law until the evidence was all in, and not till the evidence was laid before a judge and jury would they be asked to render a decision. No more can a man expect to decide off-hand the character of steel, for what may be attributed to poor quality may be due to bad condition caused by unfair treatment, while to know what would have been fair treatment one must know the quality of steel. Much stress is put upon the fact that only certain brands of imported steel are used by some American manufacturers, who tell us that "they can depend upon it every time—well, nearly every time," and that "they don't have to be so particular about heating it. If it is heated a little too hot it won't crack, but will stand to do something. They like a little leeway." These men seem to think that it is just that particular brand of steel which possesses the qualities of safety of which they think so much, and we hear them say, ——'s steel does this and that, but you cannot do it with ——'s steel, it would fly all in pieces treated the same way."

How is it? Does anybody who has studied upon the subject a little, suppose that when a particular grade of steel of any brand has been found to be right for a certain use, while the first bar used of some other brand without reference to the grade has proved to be apparently of no value, that that settles it, or that ground is furnished for saying that the steel from one manufacturer shows certain characteristics which the other does not?

Then, after a certain grade of any brand of steel has been settled upon as right, it will not do to condemn too broadly steel of another brand, which with the same treatment accorded to the favorite steel fails, for it is quite likely that, with the different treatment which this grade of the new brand requires, it might prove equally as good as the "long-tried and only trusted steel," or, if not of the right grade, a grade could be furnished of the new brand fully as good as the best of the old brand, while it is reasonably certain that had a change of grade without change of brand been made the result would have been much the same. Too much weight is put upon a name; and we hear steel-workers lauding the especially good qualities of this or that steel and condemning the bad qualities of others, when the fact is that both the words of praise and blame apply to the grades of steel and their treatment and condition, not to the fact that this or that was made in Pittsburg or Sheffield. The steel maker, whether he will or not, must, and does, make a variety of grades—tempers—of steel; and upon a judicious and honest selection of the right temper for any particular use, and upon just the treatment required—especially in hardening—hang the desired results.

" Jessup steel doesn't do this,", says one of its admirers, but a grade of Jessup's can be had which will, without doubt.

Said an enthusiastic admirer of a "special" brand of imported steel to the writer:

" That steel stands to do what no American steel will do at all; on this work-tools from it have stood to work five and even six hours without grinding."

A few months later this same man said, in speaking of the same work:

" The result in using tools made from the pieces of American steel which you sent by mail were simply wonderful; some of them stood to work without grinding two entire days of ten hours !"

With steel of proper temper from reliable makers, there are possibilities of which many men who look upon steel as steel simply, and who judge its quality in advance by the brand it bears, have never dreamed ; and of those who pride themselves on being thoroughly American, and still persist in using English steel, what can be thought, except that they have not carefully investigated to learn the merits

of American steel? For it is well known that for
every difficult job done with English steel there is

Fig. 1—Wrought Iron Balustrade by M. Baudrit, of Paris.

the equal done daily with American steel.—S. W.
GOODYEAR, *in the Age of Steel.*

Modern French and English Wrought Ironwork.

Attention has been called at different times to the possibilities in wrought iron work in the art line,

Fig. 2—Wrought Iron Railing by Ratcliff & Tyler, of Birmingham.

and examples of work have occasionally been presented showing what has been done and may be

done in this direction.   Figs. 1 and 2 show two very
handsome designs, Fig. 1 being a specimen of
wrought ironwork from the establishment of M.
Baudrit, of Paris.   It is original in design and admirable in execution. There is a charming variety in
the work, characteristic of the high productions of
French artists.   The lower portion is solid, as the
foundation of the terminal post of a balustrade
should be, but it lies on the stairs naturally and
elegantly.   The upright pillar and hand-rail are
sufficiently massive, while the decorative portion has
all the light elegance of a flower.

In this country our designers are wont to draw
work of this kind for execution in cast iron, and so
accustomed have we become to casting all ornamental work of a similar character that our blacksmiths scarcely know what it is possible to accomplish with the hammer and anvil.   Fig. 2 is not less
striking, and is an example of work in good taste for
a similar purpose to that shown in the first instance.
It is as unlike it, however, in character and execution
as the two nations from which these two pieces of
work come. Fig. 2 represents a continuous balustrade
executed by Messrs. Ratcliff & Tyler, of Birmingham. An oval in the center is very happily arranged
panel fashion between the scroll work which serves
the purpose of pilasters.   The design is neither too
ornamental nor is it poor.   The connecting links of
the work, including the attachments to the stairs, are

graceful and effective. This pattern also, if made in this country, would very likely be executed in cast metal, and would lose all those peculiar character-istics that render it attractive, and, as at present, considered an example of true art workmanship. The mechanical ingenuity of our smiths is univer-sally acknowledged, but in artistic taste and in the ability to execute ornamental work they are very much behind those of other nations.

Upsetting Steel and Iron.

I have recently read some things in relation to the upsetting of iron and steel, which are so much at vari-ance with the generally accepted ideas on the subject, and at the same time so flatly contradict what the every-day experiences of many mechanics show to be facts, as to prompt me to offer some testimony.

First, as to the "Upsetting of Iron," for under this heading may be found in a trade journal of recent date a very interesting reference to the "quality of movements of the particles of iron under pressure or percussion." . . . "Red-hot iron can be pressed to fill a mold as clearly and exactly as so much wax could be." . . . "Cold iron can also be molded into form by pressure." . . . "The heading of rivets, bolts and wood-screw blanks shows some surprising results in the compression of iron ; a No. 6 1-inch screw requires a piece of wire slightly

more than 1 1-2 inches long to form it. Yet the
total length of the screw blank headed is just one
inch. . . . Now, it has been proved by experiments with shorter bits of wire that less than five-
sixteenths of an inch of the extra eight-sixteenths is
required to form the screw head. What becomes of
the remaining more than three-sixteenths of an inch
in length of an original 1 1-2 inches that make the
1-inch screw blank? There can be but one answer
—the iron is driven upon itself, . . . so that
1 1-16 inches of wire are compressed into seven-
eighths of an inch in length without increasing the
diameter of the wire."

This flatly contradicts the assertions of scientific
investigators, who have, after making many exhaustive experiments, concluded that cold working of iron
and steel, such as hammering, rolling, drawing, pressing, upsetting. etc., do not increase the specific
gravity. Is it likely that in the many careful experiments made by the most painstaking of men, the
experiments involving the most accurate measurements possible, added to the unquestionable tests of
specific gravity, there has been uniformly a misconception of the real facts, and that experiments made
by measuring a blank piece of wire—possibly with a
boxwood rule—before heading, and again measuring
the length of blank produced by heading the same
wire, are to upset this proven fact, that ordinary cold
working does not make iron and steel more dense?

Where does the iron go, then? It goes to round up the contour of the die in which the blank is headed, that entire part of the block constituting the body, and to fill the die for the entire length of the body of the blank, through the upsetting process, to a fullness which in solid dies defies the efforts of any but the best of carefully hardened and tempered steel punches, from best of steel, to push out of the dies after heading rivets and screw blanks, making the question of what steel to use for "punching out in solid die heading," one of the most important connected with the business.

In heading a screw-blank or rivet, the first effect produced by the longitudinal pressure applied is to upset the piece of wire for its entire length. The diminution in length will produce an exactly proportionate increase in diameter up to the point when the wire fills the die so tightly as to transfer the most of the upsetting effect of the continued pressure to that part of the wire not encircled by the die, and then comes the heading, which begins by increasing diameter and proportionately decreasing length, the metal being in a measure held by contact with the die and heading punch from lateral expansion. As the pressure continues, it assumes first a pear shape, simply following the not necessarily written law under which all metals under pressure yield in the direction of the least resistance, and soon a shoulder is formed, which, coming in contact with the face of the die, or bottom of countersink, depending upon the shape of die, the direct or entire resistance to the pressure applied has no longer to be supplied by the body of the wire as at first. But still, as the pear-shaped bulb is gradually pressed out of that shape into the shape required in the completed blank or rivet, a time will come when a portion of the superfluous metal back of the body of the blank, or representing the center of the head, can escape more easily in the direction of the pressure, thereby still further increasing the diameter of the body of the blank, than to escape altogether in a lateral direction under the immense pressure required toward the completion of the heading process.

"Without increasing the diameter of the wire," we quoted, it would not be possible, in any commercial sense, to do anything of the kind. Did the writer who stated as a fact that this was the rule realize the improbability of the statement which he virtually makes, i. e., that over 17½ per cent of the wire entering into the body of the blank described by him has been lost, if, as he says, the diameter remains unchanged?

I once made some carefully conducted experiments to prove or disprove the truth of the assertion, which I had often made, that cold swaging did increase the specific gravity of steel, but which was denied by those who, having learned by actual experiment that other cold working did not, felt sure that the effect of cold swaging would be the same as that of other methods. My experiments were made with pieces of steel rod, each two feet in length, by reducing them by cold swaging until they were nearly eight feet long, and, having first carefully measured the original length and diameter, the increased length and decreased diameter was to show by measurement whether the specific gravity had been increased by swaging. I have not the figures at hand, but they showed on my side; still, when I presented them to my opponents, they met me with the statement that "there was too little difference to talk about, and, if my measurement had been absolutely correct, I had established nothing further than to appear to show the exception, which proved the rule. Cold working did not increase density; this was a well-known principle." Well, it was not much. The fraction of an inch which showed the difference in length of pieces from what they should have been, had the specific gravity remained unchanged, was represented by a figure in the third or fourth place in decimals, not much like the 0.1875= 3-16 of an inch, which the writer from whom we have quoted would have us believe was lost from 1½ inches in length, when it is considered that in my experiments there were pieces sixty-four times as long in which lost metal might hide, and still not more than the one-hundredth part as much had hidden in the eight feet as is claimed for 1½ inches.

Some facts are hard to swallow unless dressed up

to appear reasonable. " Upsetting iron," as applied
to heading, cannot be easily upset by anybody who will
take the time to compare diameters and specific gravity of wire before heading with those of headed
blanks.

" Upsetting steel " is spoken of by some persons,
whose information on the subject of steel working is
very extensive, as one of the most pernicious of
practices, and, by the way the subject is treated, one
might suppose that they fully believed that steel was
made up of fibres, which must be always worked in
one direction. Steel is of a crystalline nature—not
fibrous—and such of it as will be ruined by upsetting
within reasonable limits, the operation being performed intelligently, is not good, sound steel.

Pursuing the subject of heading, I can testify that
in the days when our grandfathers worked steel I
made heading dies of two inches diameter by upsetting 1¼-inch octagon steel, which stood to do as
much work as any that I could make from steel of
other shape and size Of hundreds which were made
in this way, I do not remember that seams or cracks
resulted from upsetting in a single instance. If the
steel was sound, and the work in upsetting was so
distributed as to affect all parts of the mass alike,
why should they ?

As to upsetting cold chisels, strips of sheet-steel,
iron, or pieces of steel of any shape which are so
slender as to double up like straws from the power

of the blow, there are not enough blacksmiths wasting time and injuring steel in that way to call for any protest. Steel is hammered with a view to improve it many times, in these latter days, in a manner so much like that in vogue with the "old chaps" that it is a wonder that so many of them have ceased from labor without ever having been told that they had "monkeyed" steel. Well, if the devil has only got those smiths who hammered cold steel, there are not many smiths in his ranks yet. Heating steel as hot as it will bear and working it while hot, with injunctions not to try to draw cold steel, never to upset, may be construed to mean: hot as is best for steel, no hotter; not cold, but continue hammering till the grain of the steel is well closed up and finer for hammering at a low heat than it could possibly be made if the hammering was all done while the steel was hotter. It don't seem that everybody does write in the papers against heating steel too hot, and nobody can come to the conclusion that half the trouble is caused by too little heat, if his experience and opportunities for observation have been the same as mine.

What a difference it makes where a chap, old or young, stands to look at a thing. But I am off the track. Upsetting steel is the question. The screw blanks which were headed in the upset dies were threaded with rotary cutters. These cutters may be described as a section of a worm gear, the shape of tooth being that of the space between threads on a

wood screw, and the cutter having a rotary motion
in keeping with the rotary motion of the screw and
with its own longitudinal motion as it traversed the
length of the screw which it cut.   The b st of steel,
according to our best judgment, was used for these
cutters, but running through many of the best
brands, from "Jessup's" to "Hobson's Choice Extra
Best," these cutters did not stand as it seemed they
ought to do.   I was anxious to try a high grade of
a certain brand, of which I could get none of the
right size till it could be imported (this was in the
days of the old chaps—grandfathers).   I had some
one-half of an inch or five-eighths of an inch round;
the cutters were to finish round, over three-fourths
of an inch diameter.   I could not wait, so I made
some cutters by upsetting the steel which I had.
These cutters stood to do five times the work of the
cutters I had been using; and, willing to "let well
enough alone," I continued using the same size of
steel and upsetting.

I once had for my job the lathe work on the hook
for the Wheeler & Wilson sewing machine.   As it
came to me it was nothing more nor less than a
round-headed steel bolt, made in just the same way
that a blacksmith would make any solid headbolt, by
drawing a body to pass through the heading tool
and upsetting the head.   After this lapse of time—
thirty years—I can hardly be expected to remember
the character of each particular hook, but I do not

remember that one of them was unsound as a result of upsetting. If steel gets too much work in one part and not enough in another, in any direction, hot or cold, it is likely to get broken up. Upsetting need not take all the blame.

How much difference in fracture does anyone suppose will be found between breaking a bar of steel crosswise and breaking a piece of the same length of the width of the bar the other way of the grain? Cut two pieces of steel, each two inches long, from a two-inch square bar and draw one of them down to one inch square, or eight inches long in the direction of the length; draw the other piece to the same size and length by upsetting at every other blow, or drawing crosswise. Who believes that the tool made from this last piece will be inferior to the one made the right way of the grain? Some bars of steel, and steel for some uses, can be improved by the work which they can get on a smith's anvil. Some bars of steel, and steel for some uses, will be injured by the same treatment. When it is necessary or desirable to use the center of a bar of steel, and it is found to be in a coarse condition by reason of having been brought to shape and size by blows disproportioned to its cross-section, there is, perhaps, no better way of improving the grain at and near the center of the bar than to upset, and alternate the upsetting with work from the outside of the bar.

Upsetting is not a cheap, easy or desirable thing to

do, and is not likely to be resorted to often except
when necessity compels ; but I see no use in making
a bugbear out of it, when, if properly done, there is
no harm in it, and in some cases actual good is done
by it. It does not at least break up the center of the
bar, as blows at right angles with its axis often do ;
and, after seeing, as I have, thousands of good cutters made by upsetting, for uses requiring the utmost
soundness and best condition of steel, I do not like
to see the process tabooed without saying a word in
its favor.—S. W. GOODYEAR, in *The American Machinist*.

Heating Steel in the Blacksmith's Fire.

In heating steel, two faults are especially to be
guarded against. First, over-heating ; secondly, unequal heating of the parts to be operated on
(whether by forging or tempering). Referring to
the first, many blacksmiths do not recognize that
steel is burned unless it falls to pieces under the
hammer blows, whereas that condition is only an advanced stage of the condition designated as *burnt*.
This is the secret of their partial failure, or, that is
to say, of the inferiority of their work. Others recognize that from the time a piece of steel is *overheated*,
to its arrival at the stage commonly recognized as
burnt, a constant deterioration is taking place.

In the practice of some, this excessive heating
may be carried to so small a degree as not to be dis-

cernible, except the tool be placed in the hands of an operator whose superior knowledge or skill enables him to put it to a maximum of duty, less skillful manipulators being satisfied with a less amount of duty.

But in the case of stone-cutting tools especially, and of iron cutting tools when placed in the hands of very rapid and expert workmen, the least overheating of the tool will diminish its cutting value as well as its endurance. A piece of steel that is burnt sufficiently to break under the forging hammer, or to be as weak as cast iron, will show, on fracture, a coarse, sparkling, granulated structure, and this is the test by which working mechanics, generally, judge whether steel is burned or not. But it is totally inadequate as a test to determine whether the steel has not suffered to some extent from overheating. Indeed, although the grain becomes granulated and coarse in proportion as it is overheated, yet it may be so little overheated as to make no *visible difference in the grain of the fracture, although very plainly perceptible in the working of the tool, if placed in the hands of a thoroughly good workman.*

When the results obtained are inferior, it is usual to place the blame on the steel, but in the case of well-known brands of steel, the fault lies, in ninety-nine cases in a hundred, in over-heating, either for the forging or for the tempering.

In determining from the duty required of it,

whether a tool comes up to the highest standard of
excellence, the best practice must be taken as that
standard.   Thus, if it is a metal cutting tool, as, say,
a lathe tool, let the depth of cut be that which will
reduce, at one cut, say, a four-inch wrought-iron
shaft down to 3¼ inch diameter, the lathe making,
say, 16 revolutions, while the tool travels an inch,
and making from 25 to 30 revolutions per minute.
Under these conditions, which are vastly in excess of
the duty usually assigned in books to lathe tools, the
tool should carry the cut at least four feet along the
shaft without requiring grinding.

If the tool is for stone work, let it be tested by
the most expert and expeditious workman.   These
instructions are necessary because of the great difference in the quantity of the work turned out in the
usual way and that turned out by very expert workmen.

At what particular degree of temperature steel
begins to suffer from overheating cannot be defined,
because it varies with the quality of the steel.   The
proper degree of heat sufficient to render the steel
soft enough to forge properly and not deteriorate in
the fire is usually given as a *cherry red*, but this is
entirely too vague for entirely successful manipula-
tion, and, in practice, covers a wide range of temperature.   The formation of scale is a much better
test, for when the scales form and fall off of themselves, the steel, in fine grades of cast steel, is over-

heated, and has suffered to some extent, though the common grades of spring or machine steel may permit sufficient heat to have the scale fall off without the steel being worked. As a rule, the heat for tempering should be less than that for forging, and should not exceed a blood red. There are special kinds of steel, however, as, for example, chrome steel, which require peculiar heating, and in using them strict attention should be paid to all instructions given by the manufacturers.

Steel should be heated for forging as quickly as compatible with securing an even degree of heat all through the part to be forged, and heated as little as possible elsewhere. If this is not done the edges or thin parts become heated first, and the forging blows unduly stretch the hottest parts, while the cooler parts refuse to compress ; hence a sort of tearing action takes place, instead of the metal moving or stretching uniformly.

The steel should be turned over and over in the fire, and taken frequently from the fire, not only to guard against overheating, but because it will cool the edges and tend to keep the heat uniform.

The fire may be given a full blast until the steel begins to assume redness at the edges or in the thin parts, when the blast must be reduced. If the thin part is heating too rapidly it may be pushed through the fire into the cooler coals or taken out and cooled in the air or in water, but this latter should be avoided as much as possible.

When the steel is properly heated, it should be forged as quickly as possible. Every second of time is of the utmost importance.

There must be no hesitation or examining while the steel is red-hot, nor should it be hammered after it has lost its redness. There is, it is true, a common impression that by lightly hammering steel while black-hot it becomes impacted, but this only serves to make the steel more brittle, without increasing its hardness when hardened.

If the tool has a narrow edge, as in the case of a mill pick or a chisel, the first hammer blows should be given on those edges, forging them down at first narrower than required, because forging the flat sides will spread the edges out again. These edges should never be forged at a low heat ; indeed, not at the lowest degree of red heat, or the steel at the outer edge is liable to become partly crushed.

What is known as jumping or upsetting—that is, forging the steel endways of the grain should be avoided, because it damages the steel.

As the steel loses its temperature, the blows should be delivered lighter, especially upon the edges of the steel.

The hammer blows for drawing out should have a slight lateral motion in the direction in which the steel is to be drawn, so that the hammer face, while meeting the work surface, fair and level, shall also draw the metal in the lateral direction in which the face of the hammer is moving at the moment of impact.—*By* JOSHUA ROSE, M.E.

Testing Iron and Steel.

The English admiralty and " Lloyds'" surveyor's tests for iron and steel are as follows :

Two strips are to be taken from each thickness of plate used for the internal parts of a boiler. One-half cf these strips are to be bent cold over a bar,

Fig. 3—Clamping in a Steam Hammer for the Purpose of Bending.

the diameter of which is equal to twice the thickness of the plate. The other half of the strips are to be heated to a cherry red and cooled in water, and, when cold, bent over a bar with a diameter equal to three times the thickness of the plate—the angle to which they bend without fracture to be noted by the surveyor. Lloyds' circular on steel tests states that strips cut from the plate or beam are to be heated to a low cherry red, and cooled in water at 82° Fah. The pieces thus treated must stand bending double to a curve equal to not more than three times the thickness of the plate tested. This is pretty se-

Fig. 4.—Bending under a Steam Hammer over a Hollow Anvil and by means of a Round Bar.

vere treatment, and a plate containing a high enough percentage of carbon to cause any tempering is very unlikely to successfully stand the ordeal. Lloyds' test is a copy of the Admiralty test, and in the Admiralty circular it is stated that the strips are to be one and a half inches wide, cut in a planing machine with the sharp edges taken off. One and a half inches will generally be found a convenient width for the samples, and the length may be from six to ten inches, according to the thickness of the plate. If possible, the strips, and indeed all specimens for any kind of experimenting, should be planed from the plates, instead of being sheared or punched off. When, however, it is necessary to shear or punch, the pieces should be cut large and

Fig. 5—Bending Still Further by means of a Steam Hammer.

dressed down to the desired size, so as to remove the injured edges. Strips with rounded edges will bend further without breaking than similar strips with sharp edges, the round edges preventing the appearance of the small initial cracks which generally exhibit themselves when bars with sharp edges are bent cold through any considerable angle. In a homogeneous material like steel these initial cracks are very apt to extend and cause sudden fracture, hence the advantage of slightly rounding the corners of bending specimens.

In heating the sample for tempering it is better to use a plate or bar furnace than a smith's fire, and care should be taken to prevent unequal heating or burning. Any number of pieces may be placed together in a suitable furnace, and when at a proper

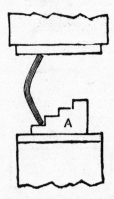

Fig. 6—A Simple Contrivance by which a Common Punching Machine may be converted into a Testing Apparatus.

heat plunged into a vessel containing water at the required temperature. When quite cold the specimens may be bent at the steam-hammer, or otherwise, and the results noted. The operation of bending may be performed in many different ways; perhaps the best plan, in the absence of any special apparatus for the purpose, is to employ the ordinary smithy steam-hammer. About half the length of the specimen is placed upon the anvil, and the hammer-head pressed firmly down upon it, as in Fig. 3. The exposed half may then be bent down by repeated blows from a fore-hammer, and if this is done with an ordinary amount of care it is quite possible to avoid producing a sharp corner. An improvement upon this is to place a cress on the anvil, as shown at Fig. 4. The sample is laid upon the cress, and a round bar, of a diameter to produce the required curve, is pressed down upon it by the hammer-head. The further bending of the pieces thus treated is accomplished by placing them endwise upon the anvil-block, as shown in Fig. 5. If the hammer is heavy enough to do it, the samples should be closed down by simple pressure, without any striking. Fig. 6 is a sketch of a simple contrivance, by means of which a common punching machine may be converted temporarily into an efficient test-bending apparatus. The punch and bolster are removed, and the stepped cast-iron block, *A*, fixed in place of the bolster. When a sample is placed endwise upon one of the lower steps of the block *A*, the descending stroke of the machine will bend the specimen sufficiently to allow of its being advanced to the next higher step, while the machine is at the top of its stroke. The next descent will effect still further bending, and so on till the desired curvature is attained. It would seem an easy matter, and well worth attention, to design some form of

machine specially for making bending experiments;
but with the exception of a small hydraulic machine,
the use of which has, I believe, been abandoned on
account of its slowness, nothing of the kind has
come under the writer's notice.

The shape of a sample after it has been bent to
pass Lloyds' or the Admiralty test is shown at Fig.
7. While being bent the external surface becomes
greatly elongated, especially at and about the point
A, where the extension is as much even as fifty per

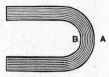

Fig. 7—Shape of a Sample after being Bent to pass the Admiralty Test.

cent. This extreme elongation corresponds to the
breaking elongation of tensile sample, and can only
take place with a very ductile material. While the
stretching is going on at the external surface, the
interior surface at B is being compressed, and the
two strains extend into pieces till they meet in a
neutral line, which will be nearer B than A with a
soft specimen. When a sample breaks the difference between the portions of the fracture which
have been subject to tensile and compressive strains
can easily be seen. Fig. 8 shows a piece of plate

olded close together ; and this can generally be done with mild steel plates, when the thickness does not exceed half an inch.

Common iron plate will not, of course, stand anything like the foregoing treatment. Lloyds' test

Fig. 8—A Piece of Plate Folded Close Together.

for iron mast-slates ½ inch thick, requires the plates to bend cold through an angle of 30° with the grain, and 8° across the grain ; the plates to be bent over a slab, the corner of which should be rounded with radius of ½ inch.

The Treatment of Steels.

I think it possible that some ideas of mine on the subject of the treatment of steel may be of interest, but I do not make these remarks for the purpose of attacking any opinions that have been advanced on this matter by others.

My purpose is simply to call attention to some important facts which appear to have been unknown or overlooked by the advocates of certain methods of treating steel.

First, let me say that I have no faith in the idea

that the operator can be guided correctly by color in the tempering or hardening of steel. If the word steels is used instead of steel, and if the teacher in the mysteries of hardening and tempering is thoroughly familiar with the character of each particular steel—and their name is legion, with the exact heat at which each would harden to the best advantage, and the precise color at which the temper should be drawn—this would not be enough to justify him in laying down the color or any other specific rule. He should also be able to make millions of pupils see a color exactly alike, use the same kind of fuel, work in the same light and remember the precise heat and color necessary for each particular steel. Then, and not till then, he may speak of specific rules.

Is it asked what can be done if no specific method will apply? The reply is, that with so great a variety of steels and such a variety of grades of the same steels, with such a variety of treatments required for pieces of different sizes of precisely the same steel, we must look for successful hardening and tempering to the intelligence and powers of observation and comparison to be found among those who do this most important part of tool-making.

These rules will, however, apply in every case. Try to learn the lowest heat at which each particular steel will harden sufficiently to do the work for which it is intended, and never exceed that heat. Harden at a heat which calls for no drawing down to a blue to remove brittleness. Hardened at the proper heat, steel is stronger without drawing the temper than it is before hardening. Whenever hardened steel snaps off like glass at a little tap, and shows a grain as coarse, or coarser than it showed before hardening, don't say " It is too hard," but say "It was too hot." Steel is hardened by heating to the proper heat and cooling suddenly. Good results can never be obtained by heating steel too hot for sudden cooling, and then cooling in some mixture or compound which will cool the overheated steel more gradually. Overheating steel does mischief which cooling gradually only partially removes. Many a man who hardens in some mixture or compound to prevent cracks or distortion, may learn that at a lower heat he may use a bath of cold water with equal safety and better results.—*By* S. W. G.

Hints About the Treatment of Steel.

A practical worker in steel gives the following hints in reference to the treatment of tool steel.

He says: " Bosses of machine and other shops where considerable steel is used would be astonished could they see the amount of loss to them in broken taps, dies, reamers, drills and other tools accumulated in one year. I do not mean to say that tools can be made and hardened that will not break, but I do say fully one-third, especially taps, are broken by being improperly tempered. * * * Thousands of dollars are lost in waste of steel and loss of time by men who try to do what they have never learned.

"First of all, never heat steel in any fire, except a charcoal fire, or a lead bath, which gives it a uniform heat (I mean steel tools of any kind). Rainwater is the best water for hardening, as it contains less lime than either well or river water. Water should never be very cold for hardening tools, as the sudden contraction of the steel will cause it to crack, more especially in cutting dies, where there are sharp corners.

"To insure thorough hardness, salt should be added to the water until the same becomes quite brackish. The salt will cause the water to take hold of the steel and cool it off gradually. I find rock or fish salt to be the best, though table salt will answer. The salt is also beneficial to the carbon in steel.

"For removing scale from steel when put into water, ivory black should be used, putting it on the steel while it is heating, and letting it remain till the steel goes into the water.

"In tempering taps, reamers, twist drills and other like tools, great care should be taken to put them in the water in a perpendicular line, and slowly, not allowing them to remain stationary in the water, as there is danger of there being a water crack at the water line.

"A good way to draw the temper is to heat a collar, or any suitable iron with a hole in the center, and draw the tool backward and forward through it until the right temper is obtained, which will be uniform."

On the Working of Steel.

Allow me to express a few thoughts in regard to the degree of heat steel can be worked for edge tools. And in doing so I shall no doubt differ with many; but what of that? If we all had one way of doing work what would be the use of giving "*our method*" for doing anything? Some tell us that steel should never be heated above a cherry-red, others say it should not be hot enough to scale, and many suppose if heated to a white heat the steel is burnt and utterly worthless. Now if all this be true, how in the world could an edge tool ever be made, and of what practical use would they be when they *were* made?

Can steel be put into an axe or any other tool without heating the steel above a cherry-red heat? If so, I would like to have some one tell me how, as I have never learned that part of the trade. I do not believe that iron or steel can be welded at a cherry heat.

My experience in the working of steel during the past fifteen years has been mostly confined to the axe business. I have made and repaired during this time, several hundreds of axes, and the work has given unparalleled satisfaction. My experience in the mat-

ter has convinced me that the degree of heat steel
should be worked depends very much upon circumstances. For instance, if I am going to fix over an
axe, and wish to reduce the steel to one-half or three-
fourths of its present thickness, I have no fears of
any bad results if the steel is brought to a white
heat to commence with. But when nearly to the
required thickness, I am careful not to heat above
a cherry-red. And when the last or finishing touch
is given by the hammer it is at a low heat, when but
a faint red is discernible. I never finish forging an
edge tool of any kind at a cherry-red heat. The finishing should be done at as low a heat as to refine
the steel, and leave it bright and glossy.

In heating to temper, the greatest care should be
observed that an even cherry wood heat is obtained.
I do not deny that injury may occur by overheating.
This every smith knows to be true; but I *do* claim
that it can be remedied, and the fine grain of the
steel restored when the nature of the work will
admit of a suitable amount of forging. When it
will not, I never heat above a cherry-red.—*By* W.
H. B.

Hardening Steel.

On the subject of the hardening of steel I will say
that salt water is not more liable to crack steel in the
hardening process than is fresh water. In fact, clear

and pure water is the best thing that can be used in making steel hard.

The best mode of annealing heavy blocks of crucible cast-steel is to heat the block to a uniform red heat, and as soon as you have obtained this heat place the steel in a cast-iron or sheet-iron box, made as shown in Fig. 9, of the accompanying illustrations. This box is filled with common lime and wood ashes, equal parts of each. In placing the steel in the box

Fig. 9—Showing the Box used in Hardening Steel by the Method of "H. R. H."

try to keep about 4 or 5 inches of lime below the steel, then put 4 or 5 inches on top of the steel, close up the box and let it remain there to cool off slowly, which will require from 24 to 48 hours. Generally crucible cast-steel will anneal best at a low red heat, if treated as described.

The only secrets in annealing steel, that I know of, are to exclude air from the steel as much as possible, while it is annealing, and to avoid overheating.

For hardening drop hammer dies, I would suggest the use of the water tub, shown in Fig. 10. In the illustration, *A* is the water supply pipe, which, as shown by the dotted lines, runs down to the bottom of the tub and over to its center, where the pipe is bent up, as shown at *D*. At *x*, *x*, *x*, *x* there are four holes, which represent waste pipes that carry off all the water that comes above their level. This water passes on down through to the main waste pipe *O* at

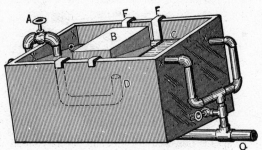

Fig. 10—Showing the Water Tub.

E. The cut-off shown is used when cleaning the tub or box.

To harden a heavy die proceed as follows: Get a uniform bright red heat on the steel, then place it in the water tub with the face of the die in the water, the steel being supported in the tub by the two hangers, *F F*, as shown in Fig. 10. *C* indicates the water's edge and depth, and shows the position of the die in the water. Before placing the die on

the hangers be sure to have the two hangers in
their proper places, have the water in the supply
pipe, A, turned on with full force, and be sure that the
die is placed directly over the middle of the supply
pipe at D. We will say the die B, in Fig. 10, is
10 x 5 x 6 inches; a bulk of steel like this will heat
much water, and therefore while the supply pipe
furnishes cold water, the waste pipes, x, x, x, x,
carry off all the hot or warm water as fast as the steel
heats it. In Fig. 11 I give a side view of the die on the
hanger, F, F, showing the ends that hook over the

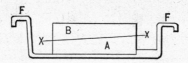

Fig. 11—Side View of the Die.

sides of the tub. The cut also shows how the die
is placed at an angle in the water. B indicates
the portion of the die out of the water line, and
A represents the part in the water. It is not
necessary to keep the dies moving during the hardening process, but keep the water moving, and there
will be no trouble.

The best way to harden trimming dies is to always
examine thoroughly the die before you dip it, and
turn it while dipping so that all the thick or heavy
parts enter the water first.

The best mode of hardening punches is to harden them first in cold water, and then draw the temper

Fig. 12—The Furnace for Heating and Drawing Temper.

to suit the work they are intended for. While the die is hanging in the tub, as in Fig. 10, it would do no harm to utilize a tin cup in pouring water on the bottom of the die, which is out of the water. I have seen hundreds of blocks of steel hardened this way with the best of success. I never have the temper drawn for drop hammer dies. The harder you can get them the better.

In Fig. 12 I show a furnace for heating and drawing temper. This furnace is 3 feet 6 inches wide and 4 feet 4 inches long. At *E* it is 2 feet 6 inches from the ground to the top of the cast-iron plate *B*. From plate *B* to the under side

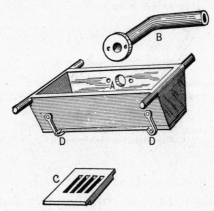

Fig. 13—Showing the Grate-Box, Blast-Pipe and Grate.

of the top, *F*, it is 16 inches in height. *A* is the grate, *D* is the ash-pan, *C* is the door, and *X* is the damper. Hard coke is the best fuel I know of for this furnace except charcoal. In using the coke start the fire, close the door and get the coke red,

then put in the steel that is to be annealed or
hardened. In heating you can gain much by regulating the damper X. Fig. 13 shows the grate
box used in the furnace. At D, D, the box has
two hooks, which hold up the box door. This door
is fastened to the other side of the box with two
hinges. At A is a blast pipe hole to which the
point of pipe B is bolted. C is part of the grate
used. Three pieces of this kind are used to make
the full grate. This is done to allow the use of

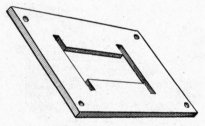

Fig. 14—The Plate for Holding the Grate-Box.

two blank grates and one open grate when a small
fire is desired, or you can use two open grates
and one blank, or all three may be open grates,
just as your work requires. Fig. 14 shows the plate
in which the grate box is hung when in use. This
plate is bolted to two iron bars in the furnace, and
on this place the brick work is laid. The chimney
can be used on the side, end or middle. I prefer
it in the center, as shown in the illustration. The

plate, *B*, of the furnace is cast-iron 1 1-4 inches thick, 10 inches wide, and the length is the same as the width of the furnace. The best steel I can get for drop and trimming dies is made at the Crescent Steel Works, Pittsburgh, Pa. I think the illustrations fully explain themselves without any further description—*By* H. R. H.

To Select Good Tool Steel.

One way is to break a bar of steel and observe the grain, which should be fine and present a silvery look, with sometimes an exfoliated appearance. The best test of steel is to make a cold chisel from the bar to be tested, and, when carefully tempered, try it upon wrought iron, a piece of old wagon-tire, for instance. The blows given will pretty correctly tell its tenacity and capability of holding temper. If it proves tough and serviceable take this temper as a guide, and temper your steel in like manner. Inferior steel is easily broken, and the fracture presents a dull, even appearance, which might be appropriately termed a lifeless look.—*By* W. B. H.

Different Kinds of Steel.

Blister steel is made by causing the carbon of charcoal to penetrate iron in a heated state. German steel is blister steel rolled down into bars. Sheet steel is made by hammering blister steel. Double shear steel is made by cutting up blister steel and putting it together and hammering again. Crucible steel is made by melting in a pot blister steel and wrought iron or unwrought iron and charcoal and scrap. Bessemer steel is made by blowing air through cast-iron, burning out the silicon and carbon. Open hearth steel is made by melting pig-iron and mixing wrought iron or scrap steel, or iron ore to reduce the silicon and carbon.

Restoring Burnt Steel.

To restore the original qualities to steel which has been burnt in the forge, plunge the metal at red heat into a mixture of two parts of pitch, two parts of train oil, one part of tallow, and a small quantity of common salt. Repeat the operation two or three times. Excellent results have frequently been so obtained.

Cold Hammering Iron.

To the statement by a writer on this subject that "it either is, or ought to be known to all practical men that hammering a piece of the best and toughest iron in the process of forging until it ceases to be red hot, will remove and destroy its tenacity so as to render it capable of being broken with the slightest blow," practical men must say, "depends."

It depends upon the character of the iron, and upon how the hammering is done. As between hot work-ing, and the finishing blows " of cold hammering," *i. e.*, hammering at black heat—not cold—there are two reasons why the effect so strongly deprecated is produced.

First, the iron is less yielding in this semi-cold state and so would not be affected clear through, or as nearly through, by the same blows it received when hot.

Second, the blows during the cold hammering are light compared with what were used when the heat was greater. Thus, if the best condition of the mass is considered, we have the heaviest blows when least force is needed and the lightest blows when to move the mass the heaviest are needed, and so, while the "requisite finish and fine surface" result from the cold hammering there is an evil effect produced, not from the hammering *per se*, but, from the fact that only the surface being affected to any considerable extent, the desirable homogeniety of condition is de-stroyed and unequal strains are set up which can only be relieved by annealing.

Quoting again, " By subjecting wrought-iron to the most violent hammering or compression at a low temperature, and then submitting the iron work so treated to the simple process of heating red hot and slow cooling, we enhance its tenacity, or shock sus-taining qualities at least twenty times."

Now, without questioning the accuracy of this statement, is it not fair to ask if cold working is done in a way to affect the entire mass acted upon clear through, putting all parts as nearly as possible in the same condition would there not be *greater* " tenacity or shock-sustaining qualities" *without* subsequent annealing ?

In cold working of both wrought iron and steel, the writer has had to do with, and opportunity for observing the effect of reduction as great as from 25 per cent. to 75 per cent. often from drawn wire, not annealed after drawing, and without heating or annealing after such cold working, millions of these pieces have been bent, flattened, riveted and otherwise treated in a way to test their tenacity, without showing any sign of having had the " tenacity removed or destroyed," but on the contrary greatly increased, while actual tests for tensile, torsional, or transverse strength showed great increase in these directions, but which increase would, in a great measure, be lost by " heating red hot and slow cooling." If, in the article under consideration, the term cold-hammering had been used only, this would not have been written, but, as the terms " swaging" and " compression" were used, the door was opened. What is the difference ? It is immense in its effect, as between simple hammering and swaging, between compression—squeezing—blows and hammering.

Hammering implies working between two plain faces which allows some parts of the metal acted upon to escape from the compressive effect of the blows more easily than other parts, hence unequal conditions result. Swaging implies the use of dies, which hold all parts of the metal acted upon up to the work they are to receive, and so produce an equable condition all through the mass. Again, compression, as against blows, produces effects peculiar to itself in that the work takes place in a gradual, gentle manner, rather than through shock and violence. Just why there is so marked a difference, whether it is because the parts composing the mass having more time are able to arrange themselves differently from what they do under the sudden effect of blows, whether the less friction of changing parts and less consequent heat, or any other of many guessed at causes lie back of what strikes the average mechanic as a phenomena, a paradox, will probably remain an open question for some time to come. That compressive swaging, properly done, however, will increase tenacity and strength tested in any way we choose, by bending, twisting, pulling, etc., is an unquestionable fact.

Pieces of cast-steel wire of high carbon percentage, suitable for drills, have been reduced by cold swaging sufficiently to become elongated more than 700 per cent, and then tied in knots and drawn up almost as tightly as would be possible in the case of a string.   That this could be done when the fact is taken into consideration that the wire had been cold-worked—drawn since annealing—and was consequently in that condition so deprecated in the article under notice, the subsequent cold-working—swaging —taking place without annealing or heating after the drawing, and the knots being tied after the swaging with no heating or annealing, should settle the question, to some extent at least, whether cold-working *per se*, is the destructive agent which some believe it to be.—*By* S. W. GOODYEAR.

CHAPTER II.

BOLT AND RIVET CLIPPERS.

A Bolt and Rivet Clipper.

Cutting off bolts and rivets with a cold chisel is not very convenient in a shop where only one man is working : for instance, a blacksmith shop in a small town. Very good bolt and rivet clippers are now manufactured, but many blacksmiths cannot afford to pay eight or ten dollars for a bolt clipper, and so they have some one to hold a hammer or bar on one side of the bolt while the smith cuts from the other

Fig. 14—Showing how the Knife is made for Bolt and Rivet Clipper.

side with a dull chisel, and now and then hits his hand, or the end of the bolt flies in his eye or in the eye of the man that holds the bar. Then very often the end of the bolt goes through a window, and before they get through with their job the smith is very mad.

About three years ago I made a good and cheap bolt clipper, which is shown in the accompanying il-

lustrations, Figs. 14 to 17. It is made as follows:
A piece of steel ½ x 1 inch and 6 inches long is
welded to a ¾-inch round rod 12 inches long, and

Fig. 15 – Showing the two Jaws together.

the end of the steel is turned up half an inch for a
nipper or knife, as at *A* in Fig. 14. In Fig. 15 the

Fig. 16—The Purchase Lever.

two jaws or nippers are together. *B*, in Fig. 15, is a
spring used to raise one jaw when the tool is applied

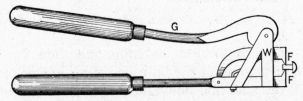

Fig. 17 —Showing the Clipper completed.

to a rivet. The upper jaw works loosely in a slot
hole at *C*. A small hole is punched six inches from
the end for the spring. A nut is used to fasten the

spring. In Fig. 16 the purchase lever is shown.
This is made of inch-square iron and 12 inches of
¾-round iron, or just as the lower handle is made.

A ½-inch round hole is punched in one side at *D*,

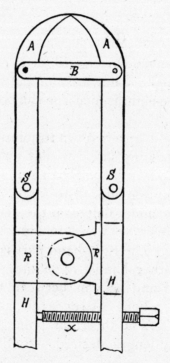

Fig. 18—Cut Nippers as made by "Steel Square.

as in Fig. 16. In Fig. 17 the clipper is shown as it
appears when put together and ready to be applied
to a bolt.

Fig. 17 is a side view of the clipper. The jaws, *F*, *F*, must be close to the piece *W*. When you press down the lever the lower side of the head commences to press down. This clipper can be made in half a day and will answer for most jobs.—*By* E. H. WEHRY.

Cut Nippers.

I send you a sketch, Fig. 18, of a pair of cut nippers I invented. They are not patented, nor will they be. Three-eighths-inch iron can be cut with them with ease.

A A are steel cutters down to joints *S S*, and they may be made of any shape to suit. At *B* there are two links bolted to the cutter, one on each side. The joint *R R* would be difficult to forge, so it is made of malleable iron, and is bolted on the side of the handle *H*. There are two of these made with a shoulder on the inside. The right-hand part is bolted on the edge of the other handle *H*, is the same thickness as the handle and sets in between the other two, being held by a bolt. A set screw, as shown, stops the handles *H H* at the right point. The handles may be of any length desired.—*By* STEEL SQUARE.

Bolt Clipper.

I inclose sketches illustrating a bolt clipper which may be made by any good blacksmith in four hours' time. Fig. 19 represents the tool complete, while the other sketches represent details of construction. For the parts shown in Fig. 21 take a piece of spring steel 2¼ inches wide by ¼ inch thick and flatten out

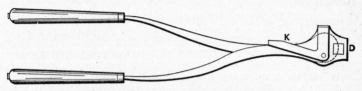

Fig. 19—The Bolt Clipper complete.

about 2½ inches wide at *B*. That will leave the part 3-16 of an inch thick. Punch holes as shown at

Fig. 20—Portion of Bolt Clipper. Elevation, Sectional View and Details of " D. H. E.'s " Bolt Clipper.

A and *B*. Shape a small piece of steel as indicated by *C* in the same cut and place it on the end. Take

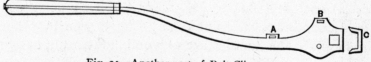

Fig. 21—Another part of Bolt Clipper.

a light heat and weld it fast in that position. That will keep the end from pushing out. The square hole marked *O* in Fig. 21 is made large enough to

pass it over the nuts. The part shown in Fig. 20 is
made of cast-steel and sharpened in the parts shaded
as shown at *H*. The construction of the guard is
shown in Fig. 22. It is to be bent at the dotted
lines, giving it the shape indicated by Fig. 23. It is
then ready to clinch into the holes provided for it as
shown in *A* and *B* of Fig. 21. The bolt uniting the
two parts should be made of cast-steel 5-16 inch in
diameter. The entire length of the tool should be
15 inches. Made of these dimensions leverage

Fig. 22—Shows how the Guard   Fig. 23—Shows Shape of
is Constructed.   Guard.

enough will be afforded to clip bolts 3-16 to 5-16
inches in diameter.—*By* D. H. E.

A New Bolt Clipper.

I enclose a sketch, Fig. 24, of a bolt clipper which
is a handy tool and unlike any I have seen in other
shops. The handles are of wood, and are about two
feet long. The band or clamp prevents the twisting
of the knives to one side when they close on the bolt.
The plate shown in the sketch is duplicated on the
other side. This arrangement enables me to get a
leverage near the hinge or heel.

This tool can be used for bolts ranging in size from the smallest up to half inch.—*By* R. D. C.

A Handy Bolt Cutter.

I enclose sketches of a bolt cutter of my own make, which I will describe as well as I can. I think the tool may be of some benefit to some of my brother

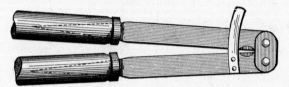

Fig. 24—A New Bolt Clipper as made by " R. D. C."

smiths. It saves labor and is easily made. To make it I first take a bar of iron 7-8-inch square and cut off two pieces, each two feet long, for the levers *A*

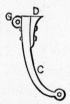

Fig. 25—A Handy Bolt Cutter. The Bow.

and *B* shown in the engravings, Figs. 25 and 26. In making the lever *A*, I first square up the end where the hole, *G*, is made. I then punch, six inches below

the hole G, another hole, I, to receive the bow C.
The lever B is of the same length as A and has on
the upper end at G a coupling made the same as a
joint on a buggy top brace. This coupling connects
the lever B and bow C. The hole in the coupling

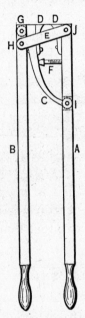

Fig. 26—The Bolt Cutter as completed.

and the hole shown at H, Fig. 27, are one inch apart
from center to center. I next take a piece of steel
¾-inch square to make the bow. I first stave it up
on one end to put the ear on it for the coupling G,
then I put an eye in it to fit in the long holes shown

at *I*, and bend it so that the knife *D* will fit closely against it when the two are put together. To forge the knife I take a piece of ¾-inch good cast-steel. I dress up the knives, harden them and then rivet one

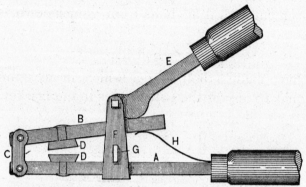

Fig. 27—Side View of Bolt Clipper made by "C. N. S."

on the lever *A* and the other on the bow *C*, using two rivets in each one. The plates *E*, are made of 1 7-8-inch by 3-8-inch iron, the holes in them being

Fig. 28—Showing the Piece F, used in the Bolt Clipper.

four inches apart from center to center. The holes are 3-8 inch. The plates are placed as indicated by the lines in Fig. 26, and are held in position by steel rivets inserted in the holes *H* and *I*. The set screw

F is used to prevent the edges of the knives from striking together. The jaws must be open about three-quarters of an inch when the levers are straight. In this tool the cutting is done, not by pressing the levers together but by pulling them apart.

I can cut with it all bolts from ½-inch down.—*By* L. G.

Making a Bolt Clipper.

I have made a bolt clipper which, in my opinion, is equal to any of the patent ones in the market. In

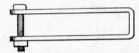

Fig. 29—Showing the Piece F Bent.

Fig. 27 of the illustration, *A* denotes the long handle made of ¾-square iron; *B* is the other piece, *C* is the

Fig. 30—Showing one of the Pieces used for the Hinge.

double hinge, *D D* are the knives, *E* the purchase lever, *F* the piece that holds the purchase lever in

Fig. 31—Showing how the Knives are Fastened to the Handle.

place. In Fig. 28 the piece *F* is shown ready to bend, and in Fig. 29 it is shown bent, *G* is a key for fastening the piece *F* on the piece *E* or the main lever. It is also used to keep the knives apart. *H*, in Fig. 27, is the spring used to open the jaws. The piece shown in Fig. 30 is one of those that form the hinge, one goes on one side and one on the other, being fastened together with two rivets. Fig. 31 shows how the knives are put on the handle.—*By* C. N. S.

Tool for Cutting Rivets.

I send you sketches of a pair of cut-nippers, Figs. 32 and 33. They are adapted to cutting bolts and rivets up to ¼-inch in diameter. The jaws do not

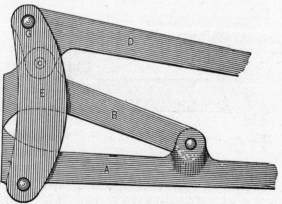

Fig. 32—" O. F. F.'s " Rivet Cutter.

project, so as to cut long wire, and whatever is cut must be inserted end-ways. When finished the tool is 10 inches long, and weighs 14 ounces. [The portions represented in the engravings are full size, the handles being broken at the points indicated, to save space. The plate *E* is represented partially broken away in Fig. 33, so as to show clearly the method of construction.—ED.] *A* is the fixed jaw or leg, having a pivoted jaw, *B*. A lever, *D*, is pivoted to *B*, at *C*. Two plates, *E*, on each side of the

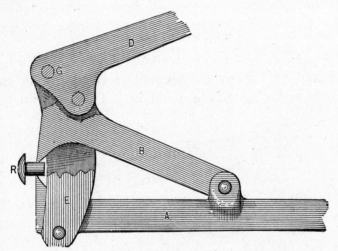

Fig. 33—Another View of " O. F. F.'s " Rivet Cutter.

jaws, are pivoted to *A*, at *F*, and to *D*, at *G;* *D* is moved outwards, a rivet, at *R*, put in, and *D* is closed, cutting off the rivet, the operation being obvious. The plate, *E*, must be 1-3 of an inch thick, and riveted to *A* and *D*, on both sides, with at least 3-16 rivets, as the strain is very great. If well made and carefully used, one of these cut-nippers will last a long time. I have used one seven years, and it is in good condition yet, though I have averaged to iron fifty sleighs a year, and they have done all the cutting, besides all my other work, where they could be used.—*By* O. F. F.

Rivet Cutter.

I have a tool which will cut a rivet or bolt one-half inch in diameter very easily. It is very handy and useful in cutting points of bolts, in ironing wagons,

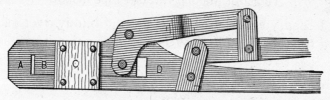

Fig. 34—Showing Rivet Cutter Closed.

buggies, etc. In my sketch, Fig. 34 represents the tool nearly closed. The part marked *A* is one shear or knife, which is a piece of steel (best) welded on

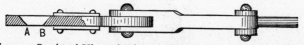

Fig. 35—Sectional View of Rivet Cutter showing Edges of Shears.

the iron frame or body, and beveled from the opposite side so as to make an edge. The part marked *B*, is the main or sliding shear, made of the best steel. It also has a beveled edge the same as *A*.

C is a plate, and there is one on each side so as to hold the shear or knife, *B*, to its place. These plates can be fastened on either with rivets or small bolts· as desired. *D* is the main frame or body of the tool, which is iron. Fig. 35 is a top view with a portion of the outer jaw removed, showing the points or edges of shears or knives, *A* and *B*, and the method of securing the plates referred to.- -*By* CYRUS G. LITTLE.

Tools for Making Rivets—Pipe Tongs.

I send you a sketch, Fig. 36, of a handy rivet-making tool. The hole at *A* is just deep enough to make

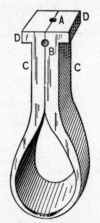

Fig. 36—Rivet-making Tool.

the required length of rivet; the wire is cut off long enough to make the body and head, and is riveted with a button rivet set; the lower part of the tool is bowed as you see and naturally holds the two jaws a little open. The vise jaws grip at *C C*, the two flanges, *D*, resting on top of the vise jaws: as the vise is

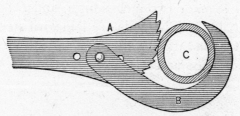

Fig. 37   Best form of Pipe Tongs.

opened or shut the jaws of the tool open and release or close and grip the rivet.

I also send you a sketch, Fig. 37, of, I think, the best form of pipe tongs. The jaw *B* points to jaw *A*. Moving *A* in the direction of arm causes pipe *C* to be very firmly gripped.—*By* "SOUTHERN BLACKSMITH."

A Tool for Making Rivets.

The accompanying illustration, Fig. 38, represents a tool which is very convenient for making the rivets that are used to fasten the brass on the plow share and the bar, and also the frog when wooden stock plows are made. The tool will make rivets of two lengths, namely, 1½-inch and 1-inch. I used 3-8-inch round Norway iron for rivets because it is the only kind fit for that purpose. Rivets made of common iron will always break if they are put in hot.

I make the tool as I would an ordinary heading tool, but am careful to get the ends *A B*, high enough where the holes are. The end *A* is for the 1½-inch rivets and the other end is for the 1-inch rivets; *A* is made two inches high, and *B* is an inch and a half high. The ends are laid with steel on the tops, and I then take a 3-8-inch bit the size of the round iron used and bore holes at *C* and *D*, so that

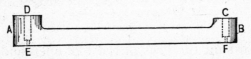

Fig. 38—A Tool designed by "L. G." for making Rivets.

they lack but half an inch more to come through the piece, and then bore through the rest of the way with a 3-16-inch bit at *E* and *F*. This is to facilitate the driving out of the rivets after they are made. The iron should be cut long enough to allow for a head. After making the rivets I drive them out with a small punch. If a little oil is used in the tool they will come out easier.—*By* L. G.

Making a Bolt Clipper.

I have a bolt clipper that will cut easily bolts of half an inch or smaller ones. It is made as follows :

I first make a pattern of tin. For the jaws, which are marked *A A* in the accompanying illustration,

Fig. 39, I used a piece of bar iron, 3-8 x 3 inches, cutting off two pieces about 10 inches long, then forming them according to the pattern and welding on a piece of steel for the cutting edge. The hole *B* is made 5-8-inch in diameter. The holes *C C* and *D* are ½-inch in diameter. The distance from the hole *B* to *C C* is 6 inches, from *C C* to *D* it is 1¼ inches, and from *C* to *C* is 1½ inches. The handles *G G* are made of iron 5-8 x 1½ inches and are joined at *D*.

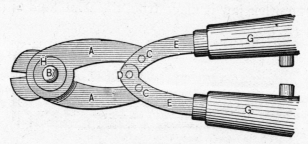

Fig. 39—Bolt Clipper made by " W. R."

The jaws, *A A*, are joined to the handles at *C C.* The other parts of the handles, *G G*, are of wood, about three feet long, with ferrules on the ends. The total length of the handles, measuring from *D,* is 3½ feet. The washer, *H,* is 2 inches in diameter, and is forged to a thin edge around the outside. I put one on each side. The rivets should be of steel.—*By* W. R.

How to Make a Bolt and Rivet Cutter.

I have made a bolt and rivet cutter that works spendidly, and will tell how it is made.

Take a piece of square iron, twenty-four inches long, for the bottom piece. In the end weld a piece of tool steel for a cutter   This should be 3-4 inch so as to have solid steel cutters.   In the bottom piece, seven inches from the end, punch a hole with a flat punch and round down from above the hole.

The other jaw is made from the same kind of iron

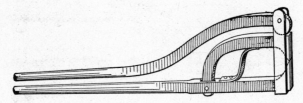

Fig. 41—Showing C. V. Marsh's Bolt and Rivet Cutter complete.

with steel welded on the end for cutter.   The upper handle can be made from round or square iron whichever is handiest.   The spring can be made from any piece of old spring, and is put on with two small rivets.   The end piece can be made from 3-4-inch stake iron.   It is in one piece and bent so as to fit around the lower jaw. Fig. 41 shows the cutter complete and will give a good idea as to how it is made. I think that some of the boys will find this cutter very useful. It is powerful and will cut easily small bolts and pieces of iron. It is also, as will be seen by the engraving, simple in construction and not difficult for any smith to make.—*By* C. V. MARSH.

CHAPTER III.

CHISELS.

The Chisel and Chisel-Shaped Tools.

The subject upon which I have been invited by the Franklin Institute to speak this evening is that of the chisel and chisel-shaped tools, and the object of my remarks will be similar to that I had in view in a former lecture, namely, to demonstrate, as far as it is possible in a talk of this kind, that in skillful handicraft the very foundation lies in a knowledge that may be obtained altogether independent of any actual use of the tool.

The first day I entered the machine-shop I was given a hammer and a cold chisel wherewith to chip the ends of some bolts level. I had looked forward to my entry into the shop with a great deal of pleasure, for my heart and mind were set upon becoming a skillful workman. The idea of being able to cut and shape metal to my will, and form it into the machines that were to save mankind the exercise of mere brute force, had such a charm for me that it was the height of my ambition. An apprentice of some two years' standing was to show me how to use the chisel, which he did as follows: "You hold the chisel so, and the hammer so, and then you chip this way," and he cut off the end of the first bolt very nicely and quickly. I tried to follow him, but after the first blow, which by chance struck the chisel-head sideways, I became aware that my hand was

Fig. 42—Showing a Flat Chisel.

dangerously near to the chisel-head. I realized this more thoroughly at the second blow, for the hammer fell upon my thumb, to the great amusement of my neighbors. After that I could not be persuaded to hold the chisel near the head unless I held the

hammer pretty close to its head, so that I could take
better aim.   For two days I struggled on, left to
myself to find out by bungling along how to grind
the chisel, and all the other points that could have
been taught me in an hour.   What was worse, I

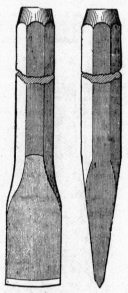

Fig. 43—Showing Another Shape of Flat Chisel.   Side and End Views.

became disheartened, for instead of finding all plain
sailing with nothing to do but to master the principles of tool using, feeling every day that I had made
some progress, I found myself floundering in the
dark, not understanding anything of what I was
doing, asking others to grind the chisels because I

had no idea how to do it properly myself, and at the
end of the first month I should, but for the authority of my parents, have tried some other business.
The machinist's trade seemed to be nothing but one-
half main strength, one-quarter stupidity, and the

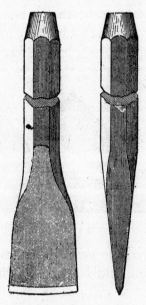

Fig. 44—Broad Chisels.

other quarter hand skill that every man had to work
out for himself, for nobody seemed able to help me.
Many a boy meets just this same experience, and
getting discouraged drifts about a month at this
trade, two months at that, until he finds himself at

last without any trade at all, and very often in his old age without the means of earning an honest livelihood. Examples of this kind are, I believe, within the personal knowledge of most of us, and the fault is often attributed to the absence of an apprenticeship system, but if we go deeper I am persuaded that it will appear that it is more in the want of intelligent preparation for the workshop.

Parental authority, as I have said, saved me from this misfortune, but since then I have, in the course

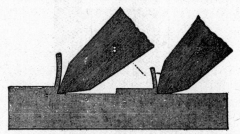

Fig. 45—Correctly and Incorrectly Ground Chisels.

of years, mastered the principle involved in the use of this cold chisel, and I can now draw you two pictures, which I hope will not be uninteresting. Suppose when I went to the shop doors to ask for employment the superintendent had said to me:

"Want to be a machinist, do you? Well, why do you think you are fitted for it; do you know anything about it, or about tools? On what foundation have you built the opinion that you will ever make a good machinist?"

What could I then have answered except that I
thought so, hoped so, and meant to try my best. But
suppose I was again a boy, and again found myself
at the shop door, having previously taken enough
interest in mechanics to have remembered the principles I had already been taught, I could take a
pencil and a piece of paper and answer him thus :

" I can only say, sir, that I have prepared myself
somewhat for a trade ;" here, for example, in Figs. 42

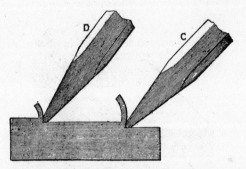

Fig. 46—Chisels for Brass and Steel.

and 43, are shown the shapes in which flat chisels are
made.   The difference between the two is, that the
cutting edge should be parallel with the flats on the
chisel, and as Fig. 42 has the widest flat, it is easier
to tell with it when the cutting edge and the flat are
parallel, therefore the broad flat is the best guide in
holding the chisel level with the surface to be
chipped.   Either of these chisels is of a proper width
for wrought iron or steel because chisels used on

these metals take all the power to drive that can be given with a hammer of the usual proportions for heavy chipping, which is, weight of hammer, 1 3-4 lbs.; length of hammer handle, 13 inches; the handle to be held at its end and swinging back about vertically over the shoulder.

If I use so narrow a chisel on cast iron or brass, and give full force hammer blows, it will break out the metal instead of cutting it, and the break may

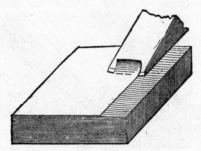

Fig. 47—Chisel for Fine Cuts.

come below the depth I want to chip and leave ugly cavities. So for these metals the chisel must be made broader, as in Fig. 44, so that the force of the blow will be spread over a greater length of chisel edge, and the edge will not move forward so much at each blow, therefore it will not break the metal out.

Another advantage is that the broader the chisel the easier it is to hold its edge fair with the work surface and make smooth chipping. The chisel-point I must make as thin as possible, the thickness shown in my sketches being suitable for new chisels,

Fig. 48—Improperly Ground Chisel.

In grinding the two facets to form the chisel, I must be careful to avoid grinding them rounded as shown at *A* in the magnified chisel ends in Fig. 45, the

Fig. 49 – Magnified View of the Chisel Shown in Fig. 48.

proper way being to grind them flat as at *B*. I must make the angle of these two facets as acute as I can, because the chisel will then cut easier.

The angle at *C*, in Fig. 45, is about right for brass, and that at *D* is about right for steel. The difference is that with hard metal the more acute angle dulls too quickly.

Considering the length of the cutting it may for heavy chipping be made straight as in Fig. 42, or curved as in Fig. 44, which is the best, because the corners are relieved of duty and are therefore

Fig. 50—Showing a Common Error in Grinding.

less liable to break. The advantage of the curve is greatest in fine chipping because, as you see in Fig. 47, a thin chip can be taken without cutting with the corners, and these corners are exposed to the eye in keeping the chisel-edge level with the work surface.

In any case I must not grind it hollow in its length, as in Fig. 48, or as shown exaggerated in Fig. 49,

because in that case the corners will dig in and cause
the chisel to be beyond my control, and besides that,
there will be a force that, acting on the wedge principle and in the direction of the arrows, will opera'e
to spread the corners and break them off.

I must not grind the facets wider on one side than
on the other of the chisel, as in Fig. 50, because in

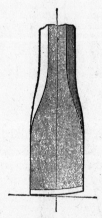

Fig. 51—Showing Another Error in Grinding.

that case the flat of the chisel will form no guide to
let me know when the cutting edge is level with the
work surface.

Nor must I grind it out of square with the chisel
body, as in Fig. 51, because in that case the chisel
will be apt to jump sideways at each hammer blow.

I can remove a quantity of metal quicker if I use
the cape chisel in Fig. 52 to first cut out grooves, as

at *A*, *B* and *C*, in Fig. 53, spacing these grooves a little narrower apart than the width of the flat chissel, and thus relieving its corners. I must shape the end of this cape chisel as at *A* and *B*, and not as at *C*, as in Fig. 53, because I want to be able to move it sideways to guide it in a straight line, and the

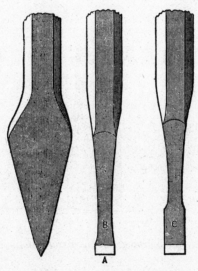

Fig. 52—Proper and Improper Shapes for Cape Chisels.

parallel part at *C* will interfere with this, so that if I start the chisel a very little out of line it will go still farther out of line, and I cannot move it sideways to correct this.

The round-nosed chisel, Fig. 53, I must not make straight on its convex edge; it may be straight from

H to G, but from G to the point it must be beveled so that by altering the height of the chisel head I can alter the depth of the cut.

The cow-mouthed chisel, Fig. 55, must be beveled in the same way, so that when I use it to cut out a round corner, as at L in Fig. 53, I can move the

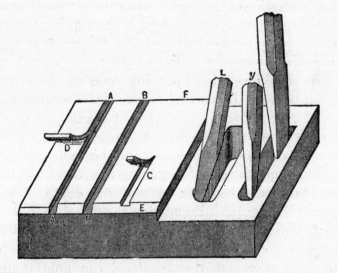

Fig. 53—Showing the Application of the Cape Chisel to Facilitate the Work of the Flat Chisel.

head to the right or to the left, and thus govern the depth of its cut.

The oil groove chisel in Fig. 56, I must make narrower at A than it is across the curve, as it will wedge in the groove it cuts.

The diamond-point chisel in Figs. 57 and 58 I

must shape to suit the work, because if it is not to be used to cut out the corners of very deep holes, I can bevel it at M, and thus bring its point X central to the body of the steel as shown by the dotted line Q, rendering the corner X less liable to break, which is the great trouble with this chisel. But as the bevel at M necessitates the chisel being leaned over as at Y, in Fig. 53, it could, in deep holes, not be kept to its cut; so I must omit the bevel at M, and make that edge straight as at R R in Fig. 58.

The side chisel obeys just the same rule, so I may give it bevel at W, in Fig. 59, for shallow holes and lean it over as at Z in Fig. 53 or make the side V W straight along its whole length, for deep ones; but in all chisels for slots or mortises it is desirable to have, if the circumstances will permit, some bevel on the side that meets the work, so that the depth of the cut can be regulated by moving the chisel head.

In all these chisels, the chip on the work steadies the cutting end, and it is clear that the nearer I hold the chisel at its head the steadier I can hold it and the less the liability to hit my fingers, while the chipped surface will be smoother.

Now, what I have said here is what I might have learned before I applied at the shop, and is it not almost a certainty that if there was a vacancy I should have obtained the position? Nay, more, I venture to say that I should have received the appointment before I had made half my explanation, unless, indeed, the superintendent heard me through out of mere curiosity, for it certainly would, as things now are, be a curiosity for a boy to have any idea of the principle involved in using tools before he had them actually placed in his hands—unless, indeed, it be the surgeon's tools.

There is an old saying that an ounce of practice is worth a pound of theory, but this sounds to me very much like saying that we should do a thing first and find out how it ought to be done afterwards. Yet I should not care to patronize a young dentist or a young surgeon who was pursuing his profession in this way.

I may, however, illustrate to you some of the points I have explained by adding to the pound of theory I have advanced an ounce of practice. Here, for example, I have to take a chip off a piece of wrought-iron, and, as it is a heavy chip, I stand well away from the vise, as an old hand would do, instead of close to it, as would be natural in an uninstructed beginner. In the one case you will observe that the body is lithe and supple, having a slight motion in unison with the hammer, while in the other it is constrained, and not only feels but looks awkward. If, now, I wish to take a light chip, I must stand nearer to the work, so that I can watch the chisel's action and keep its depth of cut level. In both cases I push the chisel forward to its cut and hold it as steadily as I can.

It is a mistake to move it at each blow in this way, as many do, because it cannot be so accurately maintained at the proper weight.

Here I take a deep cut on a piece of brass, and the full force blows have broken it out, for the reasons I explained just now. Next we will take a

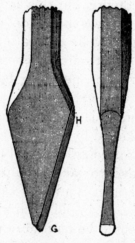

Fig. 54—The Round Nose Chisel.

finishing cut across, leaving the surface smooth and more level for the filing that is to follow. Light and quick blows are always necessary for the finishing cuts, whatever the kind of metal may be.

Here are two cape chisels, one formed as at *B* and the other as at *C*, in Fig. 52, and a cut being taken with each, you will see that I have been able to direct the path sideways of *B*, but that I could not do so with *C*.

With the side chisel alone I can illustrate the points made with reference to the chisel shown in Figs. 54, 55, 57, 58 and 59, namely, that there must be a bevel made at the end in order to enable the depth of cut to be adjusted and governed, for if I happened to get the straight chisel too deeply into its cut I cannot alter it, and unless I begin a new cut it will get imbedded deeper and will finally break. But with this side chisel, Fig. 59, that is slightly beveled, I can regulate the depth of cut, making it less if it gets too deep, or deeper if it gets too shallow.

The chisel that is driven by hammer blows may be said to be to some extent a connecting link between the hammer and the cutting tool, the main difference being that the chisel moves to the work while the work generally moves to the cutting tool. In many stone-dressing tools the chisel and hammer are combined, inasmuch as that the end of the hammer is chisel-shaped, an example of this kind of tool being given in the pick that flour millers use to dress their grinding stones. On the other hand we may show the connection between the chisel and the cutting tool by the fact that the wood-worker uses the chisel by driving it with a mallet, and also by using it for a cutting tool for work driven in the lathe. Indeed, we may take one of these carpenter's chisels and fasten it to the revolving shaft of a wood-planing machine, and it becomes a planing knife ; or we may put it into a carpenter's hand plane, and by pushing it to the work it becomes a plane blade. In each case it is simply a wedge whose end is made more or less acute so as to make it as sharp as possible, while still retaining strength enough to sever the material it is to operate upon.

In whatever form we may apply this wedge, there

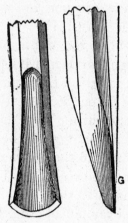

Fig. 55—Showing how the Cow Mouth Chisel is Beveled.

are certain well-defined mechanical principles that govern its use. Thus when we employ it as a hand tool its direction of motion under hammer blows is governed by the inclination of that of its faces which meets the strongest side of the work, while it is the weakest side of the material that moves the most to admit the wedge and therefore becomes the chip, cutting, or shaving. In Fig. 60, for example, we have the carpenter's chisel operating at *A* and *B* to cut out a recess or mortise, and it is seen that so long as the face of the chisel that is next to the work

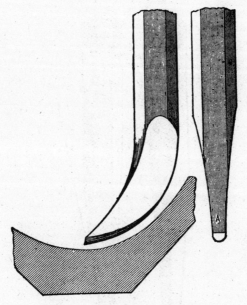

Fig. 56—The Oil Groove Chisel.

is placed level with the straight surface of the work the depth of cut will be equal, or, in other words, the line of motion of the chisel is that of the chisel face that lies against the work. At *C* and *D* is a chisel with, in the one instance, the straight, and in the other, the beveled face toward the work surface. In both cases the cut would gradually deepen because the lower surface of the chisel is not parallel to the face of the work.

If now we consider the extreme cutting edge of

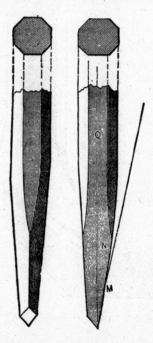

Fig. 57—The Diamond Point Chisel for Shallow Work.

chisel or wedge-shaped tools it will readily occur that but for the metal behind this fine edge the shaving or cutting would come off in a straight ribbon and

that the bend or curl that the cutting assumes increases with the angle of the face of the wedge that
meets the cutting, shaving or chip.

I may, for example, take a piece of lead and with
a pen-knife held as at *A*, Fig. 61, cut off a curl bent

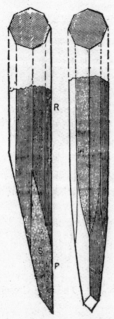

Fig. 58—The Diamond Point Chisel for Deep Work.

to a large curve, but if I hold the same knife as at *B*
it will cause the shaving to curl up more. Now it
has taken some power to effect this extra bending or
curling, and it is therefore desirable to avoid it as

far as possible. For the purpose of distinction we may call that face of the chisel which meets the shaving the top face, and that which lies next to the main body of the work the bottom face. Now at whatever angle these two faces of the chisel may be to the other and in whatever way we present the

Fig. 59—The Side Chisel.

chisel to the work, the strength of the cutting edge depends upon the angle of the bottom face to the line of motion of the chisel, and this is a principle that applies to all tools embodying the wedge principle, whether they are moved by a machine or by hand.

Thus, in Fig. 62, we have placed the bottom face
at an angle of 80 degrees to the line of tool motion,
which is denoted by the arrow, and we at once perceive its weakness. If the angle of the top face to

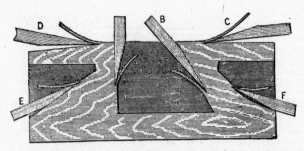

Fig. 60—Showing that the depth of the Cut depends upon the position
and direction of the lower surface of the Chisel.

the line of tool motion is determined upon, we may
therefore obtain the strongest cutting edge in a

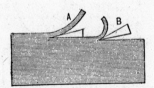

Fig. 61—Showing that the Effect of the Cutting Edge depends upon
the Angle of the Bottom Face to the Chisel's line of motion.

hand-moved tool by causing the bottom angle to lie
flat upon the work surface.

But in tools driven by power, and therefore accurately guided in their line of motion, it is preferable

to let the bottom face clear the work surface, save at the extreme cutting edge. The front face of the wedge or tool is that which mainly determines its keenness, as may be seen from Fig. 63, in which we

Fig. 62—Showing the Bottom Face at an Angle of 80 degrees to the Line of Motion.

have the wedge or tool differently placed with relation to the work, that in position *A* obviously being the keenest and least liable to break from the strain

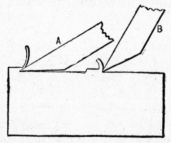

Fig. 63—Showing two Positions of the Wedge.

of the cutting process.—*From a lecture delivered by* Joshua Rose *before the Franklin Institute, Philadelphia.*

Chipping and Cold Chisels.

Permit me to make some remarks on my experience with chipping chisels.

"There's not much of interest in the subject," you may say, "for everybody knows all about cold chisels."

Not exactly, for there are a good many chisels that are not properly shaped. Figs. 64 and 65 represent common shapes of cape chisels. That in Fig. 64 is faulty because it is a parallel or nearly so from

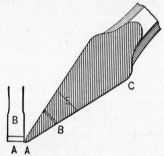

Fig. 64 – Chipping and Cold Chisels. A Chisel Faulty at the Point.

A to *B* and a straight taper from *B* to *C*; its being parallel from *A* to *B* causes it to stick and jam in the groove it cuts, or even to wedge when the corners of the cutting edge get a little dulled; while if they should break (and these corners sometimes do break) there is the whole of the flat place to grind, if the side is ground at all, as it is desirable when the break extends up the chisel and not across its cutting edge.

" The sticking don't amount to much nor does the grinding," is the answer.

It amounts to some unnecessary sticking that makes it very difficult to alter the angle of the chisel if it is going too deep or not deep enough, and so it is an impediment to smooth, even chipping. The grinding amounts to *some* unnecessary grinding, and furthermore, the chisel thus shaped is more difficult to forge, very little more difficult I grant, but more difficult all the same.

Haven't you seen men tug at a chisel to get it out

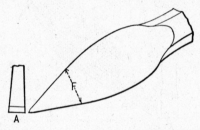

Fig. 65—A Better Shape for Cold Chisels.

of a keyway? Haven't you seen them hit it sideways with a hammer to loosen it in the sides of the cut? I have.

Fig. 64 would do very well for a keyway in a bore, but for outside work it is also faulty because it is too weak across *E;* hence Fig. 65 is, for outside work, the best shape, being stiffer and therefore less springy.

All these I think are plain and well grounded points, and so to settle a discussion on them I was blindfolded and given three cape chisels, two like Fig. 65, and one like Fig. 64, and in a dozen trials at chipping told each time I was given the one like Fig. 64. I claim that the shape makes a tangible difference. I could tell by the chipping, for it was a piece of machine steel I was chipping, and the corners of Fig. 64 soon began to round and the chisel to wedge.

As to the flat chisel, haven't you often seen it hollow along the cutting edge, and isn't that more likely to break and more liable to stick than one a little rounding ?

There is one more point that I will mention, and that is a habit many have of pulling the flat chisel back from the cut after every blow. I have seen some good workmen do it, and I am not disposed to find particular fault with it, but I think it is unnecessary, at least I see no end that it accomplishes. I like the chisel to lie steadily under a little hand pressure against the cut so that I can feel that the lower face of the chisel rests fairly and evenly upon the bottom face (as it must do to chip straight), and having got it at the proper angle to the work, I like to carry the cut clear across without moving it once. It is a kind of machine chipping that reminds one of Rowell's running, on, on, on; it goes without a falter. Now a word about using the hammer, not that there is much to discuss about it, but simply to round off the subject. The old style was a 1 3-4 lb. hammer with handle 15 inches long, and this is all right for the man who does chipping enough to keep his muscles well hardened and can swing his hammer ten hours a day without feeling it next day, but it is better to get broke in with a 1 1-4 lb. hammer.

I had at one time a 1 3-4 lb. hammer and a 1 1-4 (or a little heavier than that) hammer, and was well broke in at chipping, having had about a year at getting out work with hammer, chisel and file; the 1 3-4 hammer broke and I took to the smaller one; I found that I could not do as much work with it and it began to tell on my hands, because I could use the lighter hammer quicker, and in doing this I naturally gripped it tighter and it told on me, indeed it would sometimes be a minute before I could straighten my fingers out after releasing the hammer; of course the handle was a little less in diameter, and that had something to do with it, but not all, because my left hand, gripping the chisel, which I always did firmly, never tired, nor did the fingers stiffen, though the diameter of the chisel was smaller than the small hammer handle.

The palm of my hand would, with the small hammer, get red and feel nervous and twitchy, while it would not do so with the heavy one.

Did you ever notice what different styles there are in using a chipping hammer, how much more the wrist and elbow are used by some than by others? Yes, and there are graceful and ungraceful chippers. I like to see (I am talking of heavy hand chipping of course) the chipper stand, for the heavy cuts, not too close to the vise, use the wrist very little, the elbow not much, the shoulder a good deal, and to let the body swing a little with the hammer, the hammer head going as far back as about vertically over the shoulder, and that is the time when every blow tells.

For the last or smoothing cut I like to see the hammer handle held a quarter way up from the end, the chipper to stand pretty close to his work, using the wrist a little and the elbow, but not the shoulder joint; and just in proportion as the chisels are smaller, the wrist used more and the elbow less.

"What is a good day's chipping for a man thoroughly broken in?"

Well, I should say on a chipping strip of cast iron 3-4 inch wide, taking a cut, say, a full 1-16 inch deep, 600 running inches is a good day's work, to keep it up day after day.—*By* HAMMER AND TONGS.

How to Make Cold Chisels.

What I have to say about cold chisels is from purely practical experience. In the first place we do not get the best quality of cast steel, and the kind we do get is very inferior to what we used to have in

years gone by (say "befo' de wa'"). We now use
what is called the Black Diamond, and this is not

Fig 66—Showing a Faulty Method of Making a Chisel.

often very suitable for heavy cutting such as steel
rails. When a chisel comes from the hammer of the

Fig. 67—Showing how the Hammer Marks are Ground out.

smith, as a general rule, it is taken to the grindstone
and given a bevel and then it is called ready for use.

But it is not. If a chisel is made, tempered and ground properly it will stand until the head wears down to the eyes. In Fig. 66 of the accompanying illustrations, the reader can readily see that the chisel is not true with the hammer marks on each side, and that it also has hammer marks on the edges when it is made and tempered. It may seem as if this would not make a great difference, but never-

Fig. 68—Showing how the Chisel is Beveled.

theless it does. When I make a chisel and temper it (I have to find the proper temper to put in the steel I am working, as steel differs in grade), I take it to the grinding stone and grind out the hammer marks on each side half way up to the eye, and on edges as seen in Fig. 67, so that it will be in the center of the chisel represented by dotted line in Fig. 67. By grinding all the hammer marks out on each side the tool becomes less liable to jar or chatter, and it is jarring or chattering which generally causes

the chisel to break.   I grind it rounding from the
eye or half way from the eye to the point on both
sides, after which I give it the bevel as in Fig. 68.
I round it on the sides as an axe is rounded and
also on the edge.

Cast steel should be worked with charcoal, which
adds to instead of diminishing the most important
element in steel, which is carbon, while stone coal,
through its sulphur, takes away the carbon.   The
continual use of stone for smith coal reduces the
steel and makes it almost worthless for tools.—*By* W.

Forging Cold Chisels.

Many blacksmiths find a difficulty in drawing out
a cold chisel so that it will cut steel, but if they forge
their chisels as I do, the trouble will disappear.
Thus, let Fig. 69 represent the chisel to be drawn

Fig. 69 — Chisel to be   Fig. 70—Shows Shape After Forging.
Drawn out.

out to the dotted lines.   Heat the chisel about as far
up as shown in the cut to a blood red, and first forge
it down to the dotted lines in Fig. 70 ; then flatten
out the sides, but do not hammer the steel after it is
cooled below a red heat.   Strike quick and not too
heavy blows, especially on the edge.—*By* O. P.

CHAPTER IV.

DRILLS AND DRILLING.

Making a Drill Press.

The drill press shown in the accompanying engraving, if properly made, will drill a perfectly

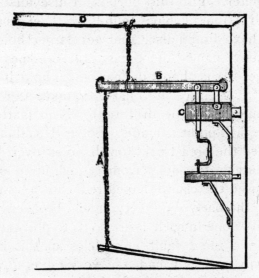

Fig. 71—A Drill Press as Designed by "R. E."

straight hole. It will drill from the smallest to the largest hole without any danger of breaking the bit.

The lever B, in Fig. 71, is 1¼ x ½ inch and five feet long. The part C is 3 x 6 inches. The chain A can be of the length most convenient for the operator.—*By* R. E.

Drilling in the Blacksmith Shop.

In my shop there is not much drilling done, and what there is done is composed principally of small holes and countersinking for holes ¼ inch and less in diameter. For this purpose I use an ordinary hand drill, but I have found, as I expect other people have found also, that for larger holes than those above named the breast drill becomes quite a nuisance. It is almost impossible to hold it steady, and it drives entirely too hard. It takes a great deal of pushing to get the drill to feed, no matter how thin the drill point is made. So, as I said above, I discarded the breast drill for all holes over ¼ inch in diameter. For holes from ¼ inch up to about ½ inch I used the clamp-shaped rest shown in Fig. 72. I made the back of A very much broader than is generally done in such cases, so as to prevent it from bending, a great fault in articles of this kind, as commonly made. I made the work table, T, about 6 inches square and gave the feed screw, S, a much finer pitch than is usual. I employ 12 threads per inch, by means of which I can feed as lightly as I like. I use all square shank drills, and let the end of the shank pass through the socket so that I can knock the drill out easily. This answers very well for holes that are not too deep. A man can stand the work in such cases, For deep holes and those from ½ inch in diameter upwards I have a small machine, shown in Fig. 73, which I had made to order. The reader will see that it has no self-feed

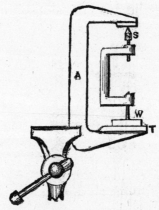

Fig. 72—An Ordinary Hand Drill Improved.

on it. Inasmuch as the operator has got to stand by the machine and mind the wheel it is just as easy, it seems to me, to put on the feed, and in doing so he can increase or diminish it according to the feel of the drill. In this case, as in the other already mentioned, I made the feed screw, S, with a pitch of 12 threads to the inch, and bushed the feed wheel, F, so that I could put in a new nut whenever the

threads wore.   I made the cap, *C*, screw on so that I
could easily take it off and put in a washer for taking up any lost motion in the feed screw collar.   I
bought cut gear, *G*, for I think every drill should
have such gear, because they run so much easier.
The drilling takes enough hard work to drive without losing any power through cast gear wheels.   I
made the driving wheel, *W*, larger than usual, and
fastened the handle, *H*, in the slot so that I could move

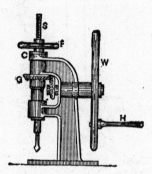

Fig. 73—A Bench Drill.

it further away or closer to the hub, according to circumstances.   Every one of the alterations from the
ordinary form here described, I am convinced, are
substantial improvements.

In the course of time work came along that I
could not get under the machine last mentioned, and
other work came in that required holes too big to be
bored in a hand machine at all.   For them I had to

resort to the ratchet brace. The rig for the ratchet brace I found, as I presume every other one has found who does an odd job, to be a complete nuisance; still, I had no choice. One day, I put a new hand, a repairer I had hired, on a ratchet-brace job, and left him at it, going away from my business for two days' time to see about some other work. When I got back I found he had rigged up what he called the blacksmith's drill-frame, and which he said was common enough in Scotland, but of which I only knew of one other in this country. I did not like the look of the thing. It appeared like a cross between a gallows frame and some sort of a weighing machine. However, I did not say a word to my man, because I felt a degree of uncertainty about the matter. It might be all right, and so I waited developments. I asked him :

" What, will it drill any better than can be drilled by the method we have formerly used?" He made reply :

" It will drill anything you can get between the posts, and from ¼-inch hole up to a 2-inch hole or more.

He proved this assertion by drilling first a ¼-inch hole, and then a 1½-inch hole, that being the largest drill at hand. For the large hole he used the ratchet brace, using the frame as a feeding fulcrum. Fig. 74, of my sketches, represents the device in question. It has two posts, *A*, and two posts, *B*, fast to the

floor and ceiling.   The fulcrum lever is pivoted at
C, and has a feeding weight at the opposite end.
The lifting lever is pivoted at D, and has, at F, a
link connected to the end of the fulcrum lever.   At
E is an iron plate for the drill brace to rest against,
and G is a handle to operate the lifting lever.   The
work is rested in a movable, or it may be a fixed

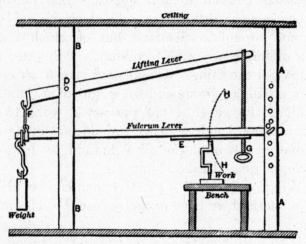

Fig. 74—The Device Invented by " Blacksmith's " Man.

bench.   The one in question, however, is made movable.   By pulling the handle, G, the fulcrum lever
is raised, and the drill brace or ratchet brace may be
put in position on the work.   When G is released
the weight pulls down the fulcrum lever to feed the
drill brace to its cut.   If the weight is too heavy the
pressure may be relieved by pulling upon G, or by

moving the work further from the posts A, the pressure becomes less, because the leverage of the weight is less. This device has one fault, which is that as the fulcrum lever descends in the arc of a circle, as indicated by H, it may, in deep holes, become necessary to move the upper end of the brace to drill the hole straight in the work. The fulcrum lever may

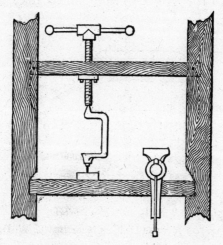

Fig. 75—Simple Drill Press, as Made by Will Tod.

be raised or lowered for different heights of work by shifting the pin C higher, there being holes at A, at intervals, for that purpose. This device may be a very old one. It is certainly good for the purpose, however, and very desirable for use where there is no power drill-machine. I would not be without it for many times its cost.—*By* BLACKSMITH.

A Simple Drill Press.

I send, as shown in the accompanying engraving,
Fig. 75, a rig which is simple and also avoids the
"arc" direction which has been complained of. A
common iron bench screw is inserted in a 4 x 4 scantling, mortised, over the bench, into upright posts.
The cut explains itself. The screw (two feet long)
may be had for $1.00, or the smith may make one

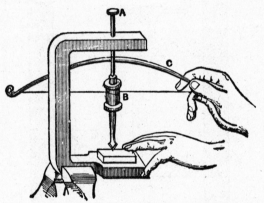

Fig. 76—A Small Drill, as Made by "C. W. D."

himself, having a hand wheel. This arrangement
takes no room.—*By* Will Tod.

Making a Small Drill.

A very serviceable drill may be made by welding
the socket of a shoemaker's awl into a 3-8-inch rod,
5 inches long, with a countersink at the upper end
forming a cup to hold lubricating oil and in which

the conical center of the feed screw can work. In the engraving, Fig. 76, *A* represents the screw and *B* the spindle. Bore a hole through a block of wood to receive the center of the spindle and put the spindle in a two-centered lathe. Move it with a "dog" and a turn pulley like a common thread spool. The drill is run with a bow *C*, holding all in a vise. Tempered awl blades make good drill bits.—*By* C. W. D.

To Drill a Chilled Mold-Board.

If you want to drill a hole or file a notch in a stove plate or ploughshare, or other piece of cast-iron, lay it on the fire level until it is cherry red, and then with tongs lay a bit of brimstone on the spot you wish to soften, the piece of brimstone being a trifle less in diameter than the hole you need. Leave the iron on the fire until cold enough to handle and it will yield to your tools.—*By* D. T.

Holding Long Bars in Drilling.

A good method of holding long bars of iron, such as sled shoes, so that the holes can be drilled in them easily by one person, is as follows: Take a strong ¼-inch cord or rope and fasten it to the ceiling about five, six or seven feet from the drilling machine, then fasten a pound nut on the end of the rope and let it reach nearly to the floor. When you wish to drill iron, wrap the rope around the iron once at

the height you want and you will find that you will
have a very handy tool.   You can drive a nail so as
to hang it up out of the way when not in use.—*By*
A. W. B.

Drilling Glass.

Stick a piece of stiff clay or putty on the part
where you wish to make the hole.   Make a hole in
the putty the size you want the hole, reaching to
the glass, of course.   Into this hole pour a little
molten lead, when, unless it is very thick glass, the
piece will immediately drop out.

Straightening Shafts or Screws—A Remedy for Dull and Squeaking Drills.

Every machinist who has ever attempted to
straighten a polished shaft or screw knows the difficulty of marking the point of untruth when the work
is revolved on the centers of a lathe.   By procuring
a piece of copper pointed on one end and of a shape
suitable to fill the tool post, and allowing it to touch
the work as it turns, a red mark will be left, even on
a brightly polished surface, and this will furnish the
desired guide for correction, and at the same time if
a short piece of octagon steel about 1¾ inches
diameter is allowed to partly lie beside the tool post
in its T slot, the straightening bar used may be ful-
crumed on this with the copper tool still remaining

in the tool post, thus expediting the work. If a piece of sheet copper is screwed or riveted to the end of the bar used for straightening, no injury will result to the work from its contact therewith.

Blacksmiths and machinists who use twist drills, have probably been bothered when drilling moderately hard steel by the squeaking and slow cutting of the drill caused by the rapid dulling of its edges. To remedy this, first sharpen the drill, then procure a small piece of tool steel, say 4 inches long, half an inch wide, and 3-16 to ¼ of an inch thick, and, after rounding and tempering one end, place the offending drill in a vise, between a pair of copper clamps, gripping it so that the cutting points will be well supported. Then by holding the tempered point of the tool I have described, against the lips of the drill and striking lightly with a hammer on the opposite end, the lips will be upset so that a good clearance will be secured, and the results will be satisfactory if the operation has been carefully done.

This upsetting will, of course, slightly enlarge the diameter of the drill, but in most cases this will do no harm.—*By* J. F. Ross.

A Chinese Drill.

Some time ago I read an account of the high quality of Chinese steel. I think there must be some mistake about it. During five years' residence in China, I often examined and remarked the inferior

quality of their drills, gravers, etc., and I think their
best steel is all imported from England, as I know their
finer iron is. They have an ingenious arrangement
for drilling, which is remarkably rapid. As shown

Fig. 77—A Chinese Drill as Described by Will Tod.

in the accompanying engraving, Fig. 77, the drill is
fixed in an upright bamboo, which is weighted by a
stone (not unlike an old grindstone), at top. It is
attached by strings from the top to a handpiece
which slides up and down the lower end of the rod.

When the rod is revolved and the hand piece held still, the strings wind on the rod and raise the hand piece, and the machine is "wound up." To start drilling, press the hand piece down the rod till the

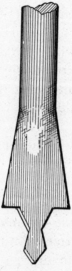

Fig. 78—A Drill and Countersink, as Made by C. H. Preble.

strings become unwound by the rod revolving; lighten the pressure and the momentum will wind the machine up the reverse way, when pressure is again resumed.—*By* WILL TOD.

A Drill and Countersink Combined.

I enclose sketch, Fig. 78, of a tool made by myself last Summer, and which may be of some in-

terest to carriage-smiths and blacksmiths who do
tiring.

It is a drill and countersink combined, for use on
buggy tires. It can also be applied to drilling and
countersinking sleigh and sled shoes. It makes quite
a saving in time by removing the necessity for using
a drill and a countersink separately.

It is made so that when the drill part begins to go
through the tire, the countersink begins to cut, and
when the work is countersunk to the proper depth it
is stopped by a shoulder on the tool. Any blacksmith can make this tool in a very short time, and
after using one he will never go back to the old
method.—*By* C. H. Preble.

A Handy Drill.

I have a drill made by myself that is simple,
strong, and very effective. Any blacksmith can make
it in the following manner:

Take a two-inch rod of iron long enough to reach
from the bench to the shop loft, then take two bars
of iron, 1½ by 5-8 inches, and turn good solid eyes

Fig. 79—Showing the Bars with Eyes Turned in them.

on them, as shown in Fig. 79 of the illustration. The
pieces should be about three feet long. Then shape
them as shown in Fig. 80, the top and bottom pieces

being twisted to fit the shaft. Then take a drill brace made as shown in Fig. 81. The top part of brace

Fig. 80—The Bars Bent.

works as a ratchet. The four eyes on the shaft have set screws to hold them in position. The pieces

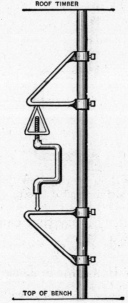

Fig. 81—The Drill Completed.

shown in Figs. 80 and 81 can, by means of the set screws, be easily adjusted to the work to be drilled, and will take in larger work than most drills. The drill stock works the same as a ratchet drill. The bottom side of the top cap should be slotted so as to hold the drill stock in place. The thread on the drill can be made four inches long or longer as desired. The threads should be cut very coarse so that they will not wear out too soon. Fig. 81 shows the drill completed.

This drill can be used to good advantage on steam

Fig. 82—A Home-Made Drill, showing How the Shank *H* is Formed and the End *A* Upset.

boilers and other machinery that cannot be brought into the shop.—*By* J. W. J.

A Home-Made Drill.

I make a drill brace as follows:

I take a round rod of iron, size 1¼ inches, shape it as shown in Fig. 82 of the accompanying illustration, upset it at *A*, and make it about 1½ inches square there. I then punch a hole in this end about the same as if for an old-fashioned bit brace, to receive the drill shank. I then take a flat piece of iron about a foot long, and draw the ends shown in Fig. 83 at *B, B*. I next take a large nut or a plug of

Fig. 83—Showing the Flat Piece Ready for Welding.

iron 1½ inch square, and weld it on the flat piece at *C*, making it 2 inches thick. I then punch or drill a hole large enough to take in the shank *H*, shown in Fig. 82, and cut a very coarse thread to prevent it from wearing loose. I next weld the ends

Fig. 84—Showing the Piece of Scantling Used.

B, B, together, and the brace is then ready to be put together as shown in Fig. 85. I next take a piece of scantling 4x4, cut a mortise in one end as shown in Fig. 84, and bore a half-inch hole at *R*, and fasten this scantling over a joist directly over the back of

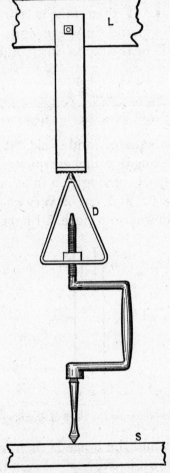

Fig. 85—Showing the Joist, Vise Bench, and Drill.

the vise bench. I put a steel plate on the lower

end of the piece shown in Fig. 84, and "dot" it well
to keep the drill from slipping off. In Fig. 85 the
brace is shown completed, *L* being the joist and *S*
the vise bench. This is a handy and cheap way to
make a drill, and answers well in a small shop where
room is scarce. This make of drill works on the
same principle as the ratchet drill, and can be adapted

Fig. 86—A Stone Drill as Made by W. O. West.

to heavy or light drilling. As the drill cuts itself
loose it can be tightened by turning the ratchet *D*.
It is the best home-made drill I know of.—*By* J. W. J.

Making and Tempering Stone Drills.

My method of sharpening and tempering stone
drills may be of interest to some fellow craftsmen.

First, in making a drill do not draw down the steel,
but cut off each side and then upset back to widen

the bit, making strong or light to suit the hardness or softness of the stone to be drilled. Next place the drill in the vise and trim off as shown in the accompanying cut, Fig. 86, then lay it down until cool, and then file and temper. Draw the temper twice to a deep blue and you will then have a tool that will drill without cornering a hole, and one

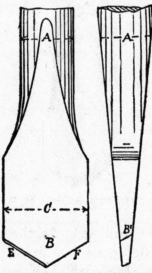

Fig. 87—Form of Drill for Smooth, Straight, or Round Hole.

that will also stand much better than an ordinary drill.—*By* W. O. WEST.

Some Hints About Drills.

To drill a smooth, straight and round hole with a flat drill let the diameter, as at *C*, in Fig. 87, be enough larger than the shank A to allow the cuttings to pass freely and parallel, to steady the drill in the hole. Let the bevel at E and F be, for iron and

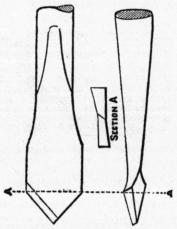

Fig. 88—Form of Drill to Cut Freely in Wrought Iron or Steel.

steel, just enough to clear well, and for crass, give more bevel, as at $B\mathbf{1}$. To make a drill cut freely on

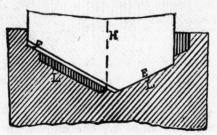

Fig. 89—Showing center of rotation at H.

wrought iron or steel, give it a lip by setting the cutting-edges forward as in Fig. 88.

To make a drill drive easily, first be sure that it runs true and that it is ground true. Suppose, for example that the center of rotation of the drill shown in Fig. 89 is at H, and the cutting edges be ground

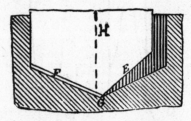

Fig. 90—Shows Drill Ground too Much on One Side.

as shown. Then E will cut a certain-sized hole, and F will simply act to enlarge it, so that the rate of feed can only be sufficient for one cutting-edge instead of for two. If the drill be ground to one side,

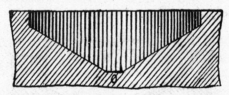

Fig. 91—Showing another Improper Way of Grinding.

as in Fig. 90—H being the center of rotation—all the cutting will be done by the edge F, and the rate of feed must again be only one-half what it could be if both edges acted as cutting-edges.

Another secret in making a drill cut easily is to

keep the point thin, so that it shall not cut a flat place at the bottom of the cone, as shown in Fig. 91 at *O*, which increases the force necessary to feed the drill.

Drills for brass work should have the cutting edges form a more acute angle one to the other than drills for the fibrous metals, such as steel or iron.

Oil should be supplied to a drill when used on wrought iron, steel, or copper, but the drill should run dry on cast iron, brass and the soft metals, such

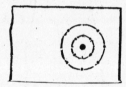

Fig. 92—Showing how to Mark a Piece of Work to be Drilled.

as babbitt metal, tin, lead, etc.; but very hard steel is easier cut dry than with oil.

For all ordinary work, a drill should be tempered to a bright purple, but for extra hard metal a brown temper may be used.

To drill a hole very true to location, mark it as in Fig. 92, the outer circle being of the diameter of the hole to be drilled, and the smaller one simply serving as a guide to show if the drill is started true. Both circles should be defined by small center-punch marks, as shown, as the oil and cuttings would obscure a simple line.

Drifts and Driftings.

The drift is a useful tool, once extensively employed, which has been pushed aside by improved
machinery.   Still, as many a country shop is unsup-
plied with a slotting machine, the drift may often be
used with advantage yet. Indeed no other hand tool
will cut with precision a small angular hole where
there is no thoroughfare; and even where the tools

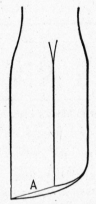

Fig. 93—Showing the Simplest Form of Drift.

can pass through, if the metal be thick or there be a
number of holes to cut, the drift will be more
economical than the file.

The simplest form of a drift is a steel plug, as
shown in Fig. 93 of the accompanying illustrations.
This is used to dress out a square hole, especially
one with no thoroughfare. It is driven into the hole,

the edge *A* cutting a chip as it descends. The underside slopes back slightly from the cutting face to allow room for chips when the hole does not go
through the metal.

To take a second cut, a thin strip of brass or steel,
such as shown in Fig, 94, is inserted behind the drift
before driving it again, and further cuts are taken by

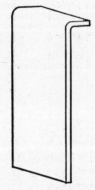

Fig. 94—Showing the Strip used in making a Second Cut.

backing up the drift with similar strips until the hole
is cut to gauge.

The commonest form of drift is made of a tapered
bar of steel, around which teeth—about eight to the
inch—are cut with a file, as in Fig. 95. It will readily
be seen how a round hole is squared, or a square
hole enlarged by driving such a drift through it.
The teeth will cut better if filed somewhat diagonally. The tool being very hard, must be fairly struck

or it will be liable to break at one of the notches. A round hole can be converted into a hexagonal one in a similar way by means of a six-sided drift, more quickly and much more exactly than by filing.

To square a round hole with no thoroughfare, in a

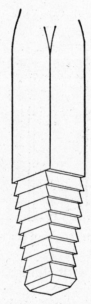

Fig. 95—Showing the Commonest Form of Drift.

box wrench for instance, it is first made flat on the bottom, say with a D bit. Then a half round plug is inserted as backing. and a flat drift driven in and gradually fed to the work by strips of brass till half of the hole is cut square. The half round plug is then withdrawn, the drift faced the other way, and the other half of the hole cut, suitable backing being inserted. A half round drift, cutting on its flat face,

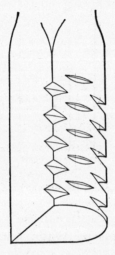

Fig. 96—Showing a Drift used for making Round Holes Oval.

could be used for this job, instead of the flat one but would not be so easily backed up and directed.

Half round drifts, cutting on the round face as shown in Fig. 96, are used to make round holes oval, in hammer eyes for instance. They are backed up first by a half round plug and then fed to the work by slips of brass or steel. In this instance, however, the half round plug must have a shoulder, as shown in Fig. 97, to keep it from slipping through the hole.

These are but the simplest styles of drifting, but

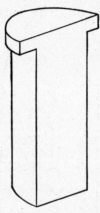

Fig. 97—Showing how the Shoulder is made on the Plug.

they show that the drift can be used to cut almost any shape of hole.—*By* WILL TOD.

CHAPTER V·

FULLERING AND SWAGING.

The Principles of Fullering.

I should like to say a few words about swaging, which will, I think, be of interest to the younger members of our trade if not to the older ones. Suppose, then, that we take a bar of iron, such as *B*,

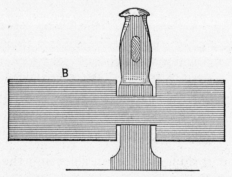

Fig. 98—A Bar in which a Square Recess is being Forged.

in Fig. 98, and forge on it a square recess. The bar will get a certain amount longer, and, in the neighborhood of the recess, a certain amount wider also. Just what the amount would be under any given condition is a matter concerning which I am not aware, but it would, doubtless, vary with the shape and size of the bar, and perhaps also with its degree of temperature I should suppose that the greater the heat the more the metal would spread sideways and the less the bar would elongate, but I may be wrong in this view.

This is a matter of more importance to blacksmiths than at first sight appears. Suppose, for example, a blacksmith is given a pair of dies to make

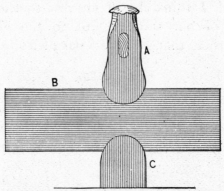

Fig. 99—A Round Fuller Substitute.

some drop forgings with; in selecting the best size and shape of bar, the question at once arises as to how much the bar will spread in each direction under the action of the blows.

To take a specific case, suppose we require to forge in a die some blocks of iron that must measure $\frac{15}{16}$ inch by $1\frac{1}{16}$ inch, and be, say, four inches long, there being enough taper on them to permit their easy extraction from the die; now, what would be the best size of iron to use, and how far should it be placed in the die? Would it be better to cut off the pieces, lay them in the die, and let the blows spread them out, or to take a bar, place it a certain distance over the die and depend upon the elonga-tion of the bar to fill the die?

One could, of course, make an experiment for any

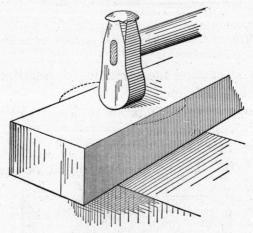

Fig. 100—Spreading a Bar.

given job, but it seems to me there could be got from experiments a rule upon the spreading of iron under compressive blows that would be of great use-fulness.

If, instead of a square fuller, we take a round one, as in Fig 99, *A* and *C* representing top and bottom fullers, and *B* the bar, the effect is to increase the elongation of the bar and diminish its spread across the width.

If we require to spread the bar as much as possible and increase its width, we turn the fuller around, as

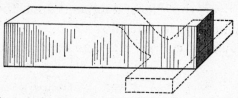

Fig. 101 — The end of a Bar to be Forged as shown by the Dotted Lines.

in Fig. 100, causing the spreading to occur, as denoted by the dotted lines.

Suppose it were required to forge the end of the bar in Fig. 101 to the shape denoted by the dotted lines, the first operation would be to fuller, as at *A*, Fig. 102. Then the fuller would be applied as

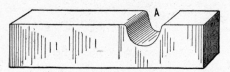

Fig. 102—The First Operation.

in Fig. 103, being slanted, as shown, to drive the metal outwards, as denoted by the arrows.

Thus the fuller is shown to require considerable judgment in its use, and to be one of the most useful blacksmith tools.

If we were to follow the plan of the scientific men, we could very easily claim that a flatter is simply a fuller, on the ground (as the scientists state with reference to gear wheels and racks) that if we suppose

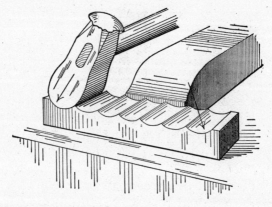

Fig. 103—The Fuller Applied to drive the Metal Outward.

the radius of a fuller curve to be infinite in length, then a portion of its circumference may be represented by a straight line; hence, a flatter becomes a fuller whose radius is of infinite length.—*By* R. J.

About Swages.

The old method of forging a swage was to take a piece of the best quality band iron and roll it up to make the body of the swage, and then weld a face of shear or double shear steel on it, the finished tool appearing as in Fig. 103½. This forms a good and durable tool, possessing two advantages : First, that a chisel-rod can be used as a handle, instead of requiring to have an eye punched and a trimmed or turned handle ; and secondly, that when the head is

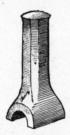

Fig. 103½—Old Method of Forging a Swage.

worn down a new one can readily be welded on, and the tool need not be thrown away.

In modern practice, however, solid steel swages are employed which, on account of the cheapness of

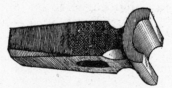

Fig. 104—Semi-circular Top Swage for Round Work.

steel and the cheapness of production when made as at present in quantities, obviates to a great extent the necessity for a blacksmith to forge his own tools. A swage for round work may be semicircular, as in Fig. 104, which represents a top swage only, or V-shaped, as in Fig. 105, which shows a top and bottom swage. There is, however, this difference between the two. That shown in Fig. 104 makes a neater and more truly circular job, but is more apt to draw the work hollow than that shown in Fig. 105. The reason of this is that the impact of Fig. 104 is on two sides only, tending to crush the work to an oval instead of clo-ing it to the center, while that shown in Fig. 105 compresses the work on four

Fig. 105—V-shaped Top and Bottom Swage.

sides, and prevents its bulging sideways. When iron is compressed on both sides, and liberty is given it to move sideways, the fibers are apt to work one past the other, and a sort of disintegrating process sets in, so that, if the forging be carried to excess on these two sides, without being carried on on the two sides at right angles, the iron will finally split. But if the compression is carried on on four equidistant sides, the forging may be carried to an indefinite extent without separating the fibers, or "hammering hollow," as it is termed.   For these reasons, the form shown in Fig. 104 is used to finish work, and, indeed, is used exclusively on small work; while on large work, under steam-hammers, the form shown in Fig. 105 is used to rough out the work, and that in Fig. 104 to finish with.   It is obvious that heavier blows may be used without injury to the iron, while

Fig. 106—Shows a Spring Swage for Light Work.

the form shown in Fig. 105 is used, the shape of the working face only being, of course, referred to.

On very light work, when the hand-hammer only is used, a spring swage, such as shown in Fig. 106, is often used because the top swage guides itself, and the operator, holding the work in one hand and the hand-hammer in the other, is enabled to use the swage without the aid of a helper.

Another method of guiding a small swage is shown in Fig. 107, in which the bottom swage is shown to contain a recess to guide the top one by inclosing its outside surfaces.

The holes of circular or round swages are always made of larger circle than the diameter of the work, so that the hole between the two swages, when placed together, will be an oval.   This is necessary to

Fig. 107—Recessed Swage.

prevent the swage hollow from wedging upon the work, and it becomes obvious that in consequence of this form the hollow of the swage must not envelop half the diameter.   In practice it usually envelops one-third, or, in large work, still less.

In collar-swages, such as shown in Figs. 106 and 107, the recess for the collar is (to prevent the work from wedging in the recess) made narrower at the bottom than at the top, so that the work may easily be revolved by hand and easily removed from the swage.

Swage-blocks, such as shown in Fig. 108, should have the holes passing through them, as at *A*, a true circle or square, as the case may be, and parallel for the full length of the hole. But the recesses, *B*, should be oval, as in the case of hand-swages. Swage-

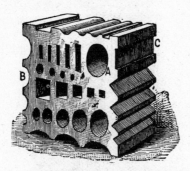

Fig. 108—Swage Block for General Work.

slots, such as shown at *C*, should, for parallel work, be parallel in their lengths, but taper in their depths, being narrowest at the bottoms of the recesses or slots.

Swages for steam-hammers should have flanges on two opposite sides, as shown in Fig. 109, in which *B* is an anvil block, *S* a block swage, and *S* a hand-swage, and this flange should pass below and envelop the angle block so as to prevent the swage from

moving the anvil-block when the work is pushed
through the swage ; and it follows that the flanges
should be on the sides of the swage where the swage-
hole emerges, or in other words, the length of the
flanges should be at a right angle to the working
curved face of the swage.   The handle, *H*, of the
hand-swage should be below the level of the striking
face, *S,* so that the hammer-face shall, in no case

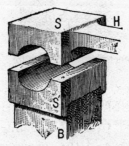

Fig. 109—Form of Swage for Steam Hammers.

strike it, which would cause it to vibrate and sting,
or perhaps injure the operator's hands.

If the position of the steam hammer or other
causes renders it necessary, on account of the length
of the work, to have the length of the swage-block
run at a right angle to the hammer (as in the case of
long work done under a trip-hammer, where the
parts of the machine under the helm would be in the
way of the work), then the flange must fit the sides
instead of the front of the anvil-block, as shown in
Fig. 110.   For small work intended to be neatly fin-

ished under a trip-hammer, hinged stamps, finishing
tools or dies are often used.   Suppose, for example,
it be required to forge pieces such as shown in Fig.
111 ; then, after being roughed out, they may be
neatly and cleanly finished to size and shape in a pair
of hinged dies, such as shown in Fig. 112.   The

Fig. 110—Another Form of Swage for Steam Hammers.

curves in the dies, however, require to be of larger
radius than those of the work, so that they may not
jam the work and prevent it being revolved in the
dies.   But the depth of the recess in the dies is made
correct for the diameter of the dies, so that when the
faces of the two halves of the die meet the work will

Fig. 111—Specimen of Forging.

be of correct diameter.   To free the dies of the oxidized scale falling from the forging, a supply of
water is necessary, otherwise the scale would drive
into the work-surface, making it both rough and hard
to cut.   Sometimes, instead of the pivoted joint, *P*,

Fig. 112, the ends are composed of a spring similar to that shown in Fig. 106, which enables the flat

Fig. 112—Hinged Dies for Forging Fig. 111.

faces of the dies to approach each other more nearly parallel one to the other.

Rules for Swaging.

To make a good jump weld it requires good judgment on the part of the smith in getting the two pieces fullered properly before welding. Many smiths

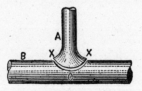

Fig. 113—Correct method of Fullering or Swaging.

do not think or use good judgment when making a weld of this kind. To make a jump weld for a

shank, carriage-step, or for any other purpose, proceed as in Fig. 113.   Fuller at *C*, upset the shank

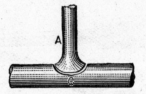

Fig. 114—Incorrect Method.

A, as at the projecting parts, *X, X*.   The shank, *A*,
at *X, X*, is the important point to take notice of when

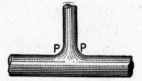

Fig. 115—Correct Way of Finishing.

making the weld.   Always let the shank, *A*, extend
over the fullered part, *C*, as at *X, X*.   This will give

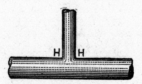

Fig. 116—Incorrect Way of Finishing.

you a good chance in using the fuller when welding
so as to get the scarfs, *X, X*, solid to the part *B*.

Never fuller the part *C*, or forge the part *A*, as is shown in Fig. 114. If you do, you will not get a solid weld. To make a neat as well as a strong job, finish as is shown at *P, P*, in Fig. 115. Never finish as is shown at *H, H*, in Fig. 116. A weld made as at *H, H*, in Fig. 116, is not as strong as if made as shown in Fig. 115.—*By* NOW AND THEN.

A Stand for a Swage-Block.

A blacksmith of my acquaintance once abused the swage-block because he stubbed his toes against it.

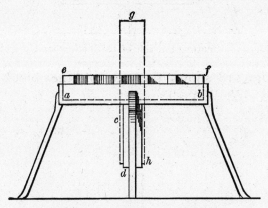

Fig. 117—Stand for a Swage-Block.

I want to tell him and others how to save their toes and the swage-block, too.

Let him make a stand for it with four legs, like Figs. 117 and 118, shown herewith. Fig. 117 shows the

block, *e, f*, lying flat, resting on the ledge shown by
the dotted line, *a, b*. The dotted lines, *g, h*, show how
the block would stand when upright in the stirrup,

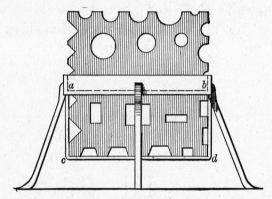

Fig. 118—Showing the Side of the Block when Upright.

c, d. Fig. 118 shows the side of the block when
upright.—*By* WILL TOD.

CHAPTER VI.

MISCELLANEOUS TOOLS.

The Principles on which Edge Tools Operate.

All cutting and piercing edge-tools operate on the principle of the wedge. A brad-awl furnishes an example which all can readily understand. The cutting edge of the awl severs the fibres of wood as the instrument enters, and the particles are compressed into a smaller compass, in the same manner as when a piece of wood is separated by a wedge. A chisel is a wedge in one sense ; and an ax, drawing knife, or jack-knife is also a wedge. When a keen-edged razor is made to clip a hair or to remove a man's beard, it operates on the principle of the wedge.

Every intelligent mechanic understands that when a wedge is dressed out smoothly, it may be driven in with much less force than if its surface were left jagged and rough. The same idea holds good with respect to edge-tools. If the cutting edge be ground and whet to as fine an edge as may be practicable with a fine-gritted whet-stone, and if the surface

back of the cutting edge be ground smooth and true,
and polished neatly, so that one can discern the
color of his eyes by means of the polished surface,
the tool will enter whatever is to be cut by the application of much less force than if the surfaces were
left as rough as they usually are when the tool leaves
the grindstone. All edge-tools, such as axes, chisels
and planes, that are operated with a *crushing* instead
of a *drawing* stroke, should be polished neatly clear
to the cutting edge, to facilitate their entrance into
the substance to be cut.

Hints on the Care of Tools.

The following hints on the best means of keeping
tools in good condition cannot fail to be useful :

WOODEN PARTS.—The wooden parts of tools, such
as the stocks of planes and handles of chisels, are
often made to have a nice appearance by French
polishing; but this adds nothing to their durability.
A much better plan is to let them soak in linseed oil
for a week, and rub them with a cloth for a few minutes every day for a week or two. This produces a
beautiful surface, and at the same time exerts a solidifying and preservative action on the wood.

IRON PARTS.—*Rust preventives.*—The following
receipts are recommended for preventing rust on
iron and steel surfaces :

1. Caoutchouc oil is said to have proved efficient

in preventing rust, and to have been adopted by the German army. It only requires to be spread with a piece of flannel in a very thin layer over the metallic surface, and allowed to dry up. Such a coating will afford security against all atmospheric influences, and will not show any cracks under the microscope after a year's standing. To remove it, the article has simply to be treated with caoutchouc oil again, and washed after 12 to 24 hours.

2. A solution of india rubber in benzine has been used for years as a coating for steel, iron, and lead, and has been found a simple means of keeping them from oxidizing. It can be easily applied with a brush, and is as easily rubbed off. It should be made about the consistency of cream.

3. All steel articles can be perfectly preserved from rust by putting a lump of freshly-burnt lime in the drawer or case in which they are kept. If the things are to be moved (as a gun in its case, for instance), put the lime in a muslin bag. This is especially valuable for specimens of iron when fractured, for in a moderately dry place the lime will not want any renewing for many years, as it is capable of absorbing a large quantity of moisture. Articles in use should be placed in a box nearly filled with thoroughly pulverized slaked lime. Before using them, rub well with a woolen cloth.

4. The following mixture forms an excellent brown coating for protecting iron and steel from

rust : Dissolve 2 parts crystallized iron chloride, 2 antimony chloride, and 1 tannin, in water, and apply with sponge or rag, and let dry. Then another coat of the paint is applied, and again another, if necessary, until the color becomes as dark as desired. When dry it is washed with water, allowed to dry again, and the surface polished with boiled linseed oil. The antimony chloride must be as nearly neutral as possible.

5. To keep tools from rusting, take ½ oz. camphor, dissolve in 1 lb. melted lard ; take off the scum and mix in as much fine black lead (graphite) as will give it an iron color. Clean the tools, and smear with the mixture. After 24 hours, rub clean with a soft linen cloth. The tools will keep clean for months under ordinary circumstances.

6. Put 1 quart fresh slaked lime, ½ lb. washing soda, ½ lb. soft soap in a bucket; add sufficient water to cover the articles ; put in the tools as soon as possible after use, and wipe them up next morning, or let them remain until wanted.

7. Soft soap, with half its weight of pearlash ; one ounce of mixture in about 1 gallon boiling water. This is in every-day use in most engineers' shops in the drip-cans used for turning long articles bright in wrought iron and steel. The work, though constantly moist, does not rust, and bright nuts are immersed in it for days till wanted, and retain their polish.

Names of Tools and their Pronunciation.

Pane, Pene, Peen, which is correct? Pane is the correct word for the small end of a hammer head, Pene or Peen being corruptions. As soon as you leave without any necessity or reason the correct word Pane, you enter a discussion as to whether Pene

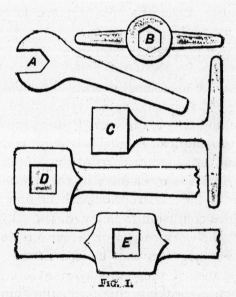

Fig. I.

Fig. 119—Shows various Styles of Wrenches.

or Peen shall be substituted, with some advocates and custom in favor of both. If custom is to decide the matter, Pane will have it all its own way, because, of the English speaking people of the earth, there are, say, thirty-six millions in England, four millions

in the West Indies, six or seven millions in Austra-
lia with the Cape of Good Hope and other English
colonies to count in, who all use the original and
correct word Pane, besides Canada and the United
States ; the former having a majority in favor of
Pane from their population being largely English,
Scotch, etc., and the latter having some of its greatest authorities, Pane-ites and therefore uncorrupted.
Don't let us, as Tennyson says,

> " Think the rustic cackle of your burg,
> The murmur of the world."

Peen may be used in all parts of the country where
" Old Fogy" has been, but it is not used where I
have been and that is in Great Britain, the West Indies, South American English-speaking countries, as
Guiana, and not in some parts of the United States ;
or rather by some mechanics in the United States.

The fact is these corruptions are creeping in and
creating dire confusion in many cases. For example :   A lathe-work carrier or driver has now got to
be called a " dog" in the United States. This is
wrong, because if the word *carrier* is used as in
other English-speaking countries, the thing is distinct, there being no other tool or appliance to a
lathe that is called a carrier. But if the word used
is " dog" we do not know whether it means a dog to
drive work between the centers of the lathe, or a
dog to hold the work to a face-plate, the latter being the original and proper " dog."

Again, in all other English-speaking countries, a key that fits on the top and bottom is a "key," while one that fits on the sides is a "feather." Now a good many in the United States are calling the latter a "key," hence, with the abandonment of the word "feather," a man finding in a contract that a piece of work is to be held by a key, don't know whether to let it fit on the top or bottom or on the sides, and it happens that some mechanics won't have a feather when a key can be used, while others won't have a key at any price.

Let us see what has come of adopting other corruptions in the United States, and I ask the reader the following questions : If I ask a boy to fetch me a three-quarter wrench, is he not as much justified in bringing me one to fit a three-quarter inch tap as a three-quarter inch nut wrench ? How is he to know whether a solid wrench, hexagon wrench or a square wrench is meant ? In other English-speaking countries, an instrument for rotating the heads of tools, and having a square hole to receive such heads, is a wrench. Thus a three-quarter wrench is a wrench that will fit a three-quarter tap. A "wrench" that *spans* the side of a nut, and is open at the end, is termed a "spanner." There can be no mistake about it, it is a *spanner* or a thing that spans.

Now, suppose the "wrench" goes on the end of the nut head, you call it a box wrench, because its hole is enclosed on all sides but one, and it boxes in the bolt head.   Thus the term wrench is properly applied to those tools in which the head of the work is enveloped on all sides by the tool (but not of course, at the end or ends).

For example, in Fig. 119, *A* is a spanner, *B* a box wrench, *E* a double (handled) and *D* a single wrench, and from these simple elements a name can be given to any form of wrench that will indicate its form and use.   Thus, Fig. 120 will be a pin spanner, so that if a boy who did not know the tools was sent to pick out any required tool from its name he

Fig. 120—A Pin Spanner.

would be able to do so if given the simple definitions I have named.   These definitions are the old ones more used among the English-speaking people than "monkey wrench," which indicates a cross between a monkey and a wrench.

No, no, don't let the errors of a minority influence us simply because we happen to be in a place or town where that minority is prominent, and if we are to make an American language let it be an American improvement, having system and reason in its composition. A man need not say p-e-n-e, *pane*, because the majority of those around his locality were Irishmen and would pronounce it that way whether you spell it pane, pene, or peen. A man need not spell h-a-m-m-e-r and pronounce it *hommer* because the majority of those in the place he is in are Scotchmen. And we need not alter pane to pene or peen promiscuously because a majority of those around us do so, they being in a minority of those speaking our language, especially since pene or peen does not signify the thing named any plainer than pane, which *can* be found in the dictionary, while the former *can't* be found there.

We have got now to some Americanisms in pronunciation that are all wrong, and that some of our school-teachers will insist on, thus : d-a u-n-t-e-d is pronounced by a majority of Americans somewhat as darnted, instead of more like dawnted : now, if daun, in daunted, is pronounced darn, please pronounce d, a, u in daughter and it becomes "darter." I shrink from making other comparisons as, for example, if au spells ah or ar, pronounce c-a-u-g-h-t.

We are the most correct English-speaking nation in the world, and let us remain so, making our alterations and additions improvements, and not merely meaningless idioms.— *By* HAMMER AND TONGS.

NOTE.—This writer talks learnedly, but nevertheless he is condemned by the very authority which he cites (and correctly too) in support of his pronun-

ciation of the word *Pane*. Webster's Unabridged
gives the *au* in *daunted* the sound of *a* in *farther* so
that the word (our contributor to the contrary notwithstanding), should be pronounced as though
spelled *Darnted.*—ED.

Tongs for Bolt-Making.

I send a sketch of a pair of tongs suitable for making bolts. The jaws are eight inches and the reins
ten inches long. A glance at the engraving, Fig.

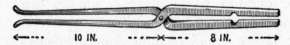

Fig. 121—Tongs Designed by "Southern Blacksmith."

121, will show that it is not necessary to open the
hands to catch the head on any size of bolt. These
tongs should be made very light. The trouble with
all nail grabs is that the rivet is put too near the
prongs, and when you try to get nails out of the bottom of a keg the reins catch in the top and the tongs
can't open far enough.—*By* SOUTHERN BLACKSMITH.

Home-Made Fan for Blacksmith's Use.

To construct a home-made hand blower proceed as
follows : Make two side pieces of suitable boards of
the shape shown in Fig 122 of the accompanying
sketches. Make a narrow groove in the line marked

A. Procure a strip of sheet-iron of the width the blower is desired to be, and bend it to correspond

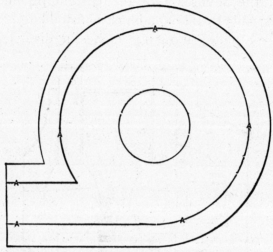

Fig. 122—Side Elevation of " E. H. W.'s " Blower.

with the groove. Then the two sides are to be clasped upon the sheet-iron, with small bolts. This

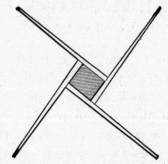

Fig. 123—Manner of Attaching the Fans to the Shaft of Blower.

will form the blower case.　The small circle shown
in the center of Fig. 122, incloses a portion to be cut
out for the admission of the current of air.　The
shaft is made by taking a block of wood large enough
to make a pulley about 1¾ inches in diameter, the

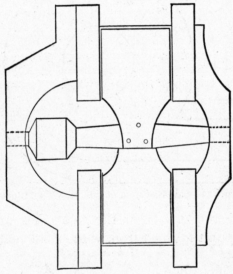

Fig. 124—Cross-section Through Blower, showing Bearings for Shaft.

length of the block being from bearing to bearing of
shaft.　Bore a central longitudinal hole ½-inch in
diameter in the block, turn a plug to fit the hole.
Put the plug in place and place all on the lathe and
turn, leaving the part where fans are to be attached
about 1 2-5 inches in diameter.　Square this part
and fasten the fans thereto, as shown in Fig. 123.

Constructed as there shown they are intended to re-
volve from left to right.   On removing the block
from the lathe the wooden plug is withdrawn and
a rod of half-inch iron is put in, projecting at
each end an inch and a quarter for journals.   The
bearings for the shaft are simply blocks of wood
screwed to the sides of the case, with holes bored to

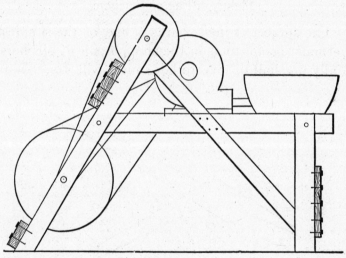

Fig. 125—General View of Blower, in connection with Forge.

fit the shaft as shown in Fig. 124.   The dimensions
of my blower are as follows : Case, 9 inches in diameter inside of sheet-iron; width of case, 3 inches; central opening, to admit air, 3 inches in diameter ; pulley, 1¾ inches in diameter.   The fans are of pine,
one-quarter inch thick at the base, diminishing in

thickness to one-eighth inch at the point.   Fig. 125
shows my portable forge, upon which the above described fan is employed.   The frame is made of four-
foot pine fence pickets.   The fire-pot is an old soap
kettle partly filled with ashes to prevent the bottom
from getting too hot.—*By* E. H. W.

Making a Pair of Pinchers.

The subject of my remarks is one of the simplest
yet most useful tools in the shop, a pair of pinchers.
Fully one-half of my brother smiths will say, " Who

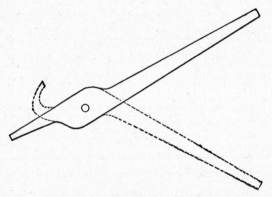

Fig. 126—Shows Method of Forging.

doesn't know all about pinchers?" From the appearance of two-thirds of those I see in use, I am convinced that if the makers knew all about them, then
they slighted their work when they made them.   To

make a neat and strong pair of pinchers, forge out of
good cast steel such a shape as is shown in Fig. 126,
and then bend to shape, as in the dotted lines. When
one-half of the forging is done, forge the other jaw

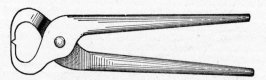

Fig. 127—Showing the Pinchers Finished.

in same way, and make sure that they have plenty of
play before riveting them together. Then fit and
temper, and you will have a strong neat tool, as
shown in Fig. 127. Fig. 128 represents the style of

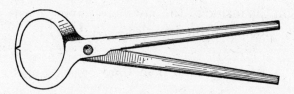

Fig. 128—Showing a Faulty Method of Making Pinchers.

pinchers generally made. They are awkward and
weak looking, and work about as they look. The
cutting edge is entirely too far from the rivet.—*By*
J. O. H.

A Handy Tool for Holding Iron and Turning Nuts.

Fig. 129 represents a small tool I use in my shop and find very handy to hold round iron and turn nuts, etc., in hard places. Wheelwrights and carriage painters, as well as blacksmiths, will find it a very

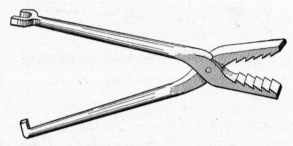

Fig. 129—Tool for Holding Iron and Turning Nuts.

convenient tool. It is of steel and is quite light. It is made the same as a pair of tongs, having teeth filed on the inside of the jaws and having clasp pullers on the end of the handles.—*By* L. F. F.

A Handy Tool to Hold Countersunk Bolts.

A handy tool to hold countersunk bolts in plows, etc., is made as follows: I take a piece of iron, say ¾-inch square and ten inches long, as shown in Fig. 130, and punch a slotted hole four inches from the pointed end. The hole should be ¾ x ¼ inch. I then take a piece of iron ¾-inch square and make a slotted hole in this at one end and a tenon in the

other, as shown at A in Fig. 131. I next punch a
¼-inch hole in the slotted end, and then take a piece
of iron ¾ inch x ½ inch and 6 inches long, and draw
one end out to ½ inch and turn a hook on it, as
shown in Fig. 132. I then punch two or three holes
in the other end, take a piece of steel ¾ inch x ¼

Fig. 130—The First Stage in the Job.

inch, draw it to a point like a cold chisel; then take
the piece shown in Fig. 13, split the end, and put
in the small pointed piece I have just mentioned, and
weld and temper. I then put all my pieces together
in the following manner: After heating the tenon
end of the piece A in Fig. 131 to a good heat, I place

Fig. 131—Two additional parts of the Tool.

it in my vise and place on the piece shown in Fig.
130, letting the tenon of the piece A go through the
piece shown in Fig. 130, and while it is hot rivet or
head it over snugly and tightly. If this is done right,
the tenon and slotted hole in A will point the same way.
I then take the piece B shown in Fig. 131, and place

it in the slot of *A* and join the two pieces with a loose
rivet, as shown in Fig. 132, so that the piece can be
moved about to suit different kinds of work.   I next
place the pointed end of the bolt holder against the
bolt head and give the other end a tap with the ham-

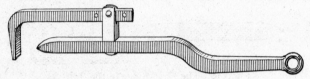

Fig. 132—The Parts united and Tool complete.

mer; then hook the piece shown in Fig. 131 over the
plow bar and bear down on the cutter end with my
knee, while with my wrench I take off the top.   A
ring may be welded in the end to use in hanging the
tool up.—*By* C. W. C.

Making a Pair of Clinching Tongs.

The following is my way of making clinching
tongs :   I take a piece of 5-8 square steel and forge
it out the same as I would for common tongs, making the jaws ½ inch wide by 3-8 inch thick, one jaw
1½ inches long and the other 2½ inches in length.   I
then draw out the short jaw to 10 inches and draw
the long one to 12 inches.   I then turn the long jaw
back as shown at *A* in Fig. 133 of the accompanying
engravings, and shape the short jaw as in Fig. 134.   I
next take the ¼-inch fuller and notch the inside of

the short jaw as shown at *B* in Fig. 134. I then put
notches in the long jaw at *A*, and next drill a 5-16-

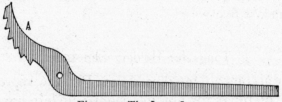

Fig. 133—The Long Jaw.

inch rivet hole as in other tongs and take a 5 16-inch
bolt with a long thread and screw one nut on the

Fig. 134—The Short Jaw.

bolt down far enough to receive both jaws and
another nut. I then temper the curved jaw at *A*

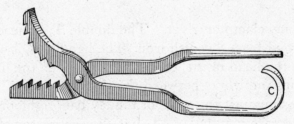

Fig. 135—The Tongs Complete.

until a good file can just cut it. I next put in the
bolt and bend the reins as shown in Fig. 135. The

object of bending at *C* is to prevent the jaws from
pinching your fingers if they slip off a clinch.   I have
a pair of tongs made in this way that I have used
for the last five years.—*By* J. N. B.

Tongs for Holding Slip Lays.

The accompanying illustration, Fig. 136, represents
a pair of tongs for holding right and left hand slip
lays while sharpening and pointing, and making new
lays. This tool does away with the clamping or
riveting of the steel and bar before taking a welding
heat, because it holds the two parts together better

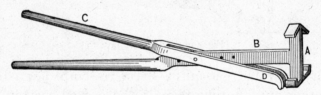

Fig. 136—Tongs for Holding Slip Lays.

than any clamp or rivet.   The double T, or head *A*,
is forged from Swedish iron. The handle, *B*, is welded to the head in the center, as shown in the illustration, and works between the forked handle *C*.   *D*
pushes against the end of the lay bar (right or left
as the case may be), and that draws the top T up
tight, and as it is bent in the same angle as a plow
lay, but little power of grip is needed to hold the
tongs to their place while sharpening or pointing.

They clamp up so tight that often you have to tap them on the end of the handles to release the lay. Both handles have ¼-inch holes through them and I use ¼-inch bolts or pins in them to hold them together after they have been adjusted to fit the lay. Any good blacksmith can make these tongs and will certainly find them very useful.—*By* A. O. K.

CHAPTER VII.

MISCELLANEOUS TOOLS.

Mending a Vise.

I will make a few remarks about the vise, a tool which blacksmiths use every day. Some smiths believe that when the threads or screws are worn out, it is necessary to buy a new vise. But this is an error; for the old vise can be mended so as to be as good as a new one. The job is done as follows:

First cut the old vise screw off where the screw stops, or about two inches from the collar of the large end, then weld on a new piece of round iron and turn threads on it the same as if for a new vise screw. To get them in line these threads should be done with a lathe. It is better to have the screws taper slightly. The next thing in order will be to get the screw threads in the box. First, take a drill and turn the old threads out, smoothly and true. Care must be taken to have a space of at least 3-16 of an inch all round the screw when it is placed in the threadless box. Then take a long piece of Swedish iron just thick enough to be bent in the screw, and about 3.16, or a fraction under, than the depth of the threads on the screws. Bend this flat iron from one end of the screw to the other, then make another piece of iron that will fit in the screws that the first piece of iron left after it was bent. This second piece we find will be as thick as the screws on the vise screw, and as wide as the first piece extends above the screws. This being done, all is closed up smooth, the second piece holding the main threads firm after the screw is turned out. Now the threads are on the vise screw, and it is nearly ready to be put in the box. First dress the outside of the threads off, so the screw can be driven in the box when it is a little warm, then drive screw threads all into the box at about the place where they belong, then let the box cool, and turn the screw out of the threads and braze the screws; put the brass on end side. When you are melting it, keep turning the box so it will be brazed all over. When cool, grease the screw and threads well and slowly turn it in. The main thread must not fit too tightly in the screws. This makes the best vise screw. By measuring the depth of the hole in the box you can tell how long to make the threads on the screw—*By* J. W.

A Cheap Reamer.

The following may be an old idea, though I have discovered it for myself: Heat an old three-cornered file; hammer one corner down, then grind the same round and the other corner sharp, temper, and you have a cheap taper reamer, cutting both ways.—*By* WILL TODD.

Shapes of Lathe Tools.

Every toolsmith knows the trouble he has to contend with in tool dressing. One man wants a tool this shape, another a different shape. One wants his tools fully hardened, while another prefers a straw temper. Of course, in a shop large enough to keep a toolsmith for this special work, the smith makes the tools to the shape he has found by experi-

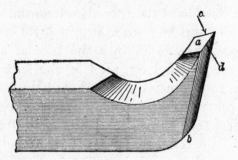

The Shape and Use of Cutting Tools for Lathes. Fig. 137—The Diamond Point Tool.

ence to be the most suitable for general work, only varying it to suit some special occasion.

But in a small shop tool forging becomes a part of the duty of the ordinary blacksmith, and in order that he may know what shapes tools should be given he must understand the principles governing their action. These principles I will now explain so plainly and carefully that no one can fail to comprehend them.

Fig. 137 of the accompanying illustrations represents what is commonly called the diamond-point
tool, *a* being its top face, *b* its bottom one, and *c* and
d the cutting edges. This is a very common form of

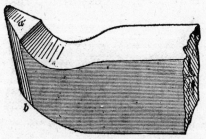

Fig. 138—Showing a Tool Easy to Forge and Grind.

tool, but I do not believe it is the best one even for
the purpose of plain outside turning, a much easier
tool to forge and to grind being the one shown in

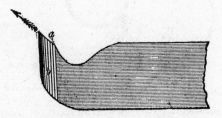

Fig. 139—Showing the Rake of the Top Face.

Fig. 138. The rake of the top face is its angle in
the direction of the arrow in Fig. 139, and the rake
of the bottom face *b* is its angle in the direction of
the arrow in Fig. 140.

The efficiency and the durability of the cutting edge depends upon the degrees of rake given to these two faces.   Obviously the less rake the stronger the cutting edge, but the less keen the tool.

If we give a tool an excess of top rake, as in Fig.

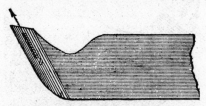

Fig. 140—Showing the Rake of the Bottom Face.

141, the cutting edge will soon dull, but the cutting C will come off clean cut and in a large coil, if the

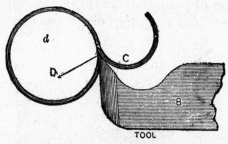

Fig. 141—Showing a Tool with an Excess of Top Rake.

tool is fed into the work.   The strain on the top face, however, will be in the direction of *D*, and the tool will be liable to dip into the cut when the cut deepens, as it will in some places on account of a want of roundness in the iron.

If, on the other hand, we give too much bottom rake, as in Fig. 142, the cutting edge will be weak, and there being but little top rake, the pressure will be in the direction of *D*.   Furthermore, the cutting will come off in almost straight pieces and all broken up.

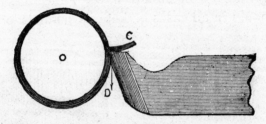

Fig. 142—Showing a Tool with too much Bottom Rake.

A fair amount of top and bottom rake for wrought iron is shown in Fig. 143, the top rake being diminished for cast iron and for steel.

The best guide as to the efficiency of a tool is its

Fig. 143—Showing a well proportioned Tool for Wrought Iron.

cuttings or chips, as they are commonly called. When the tool is fed upward only, the cutting should come off in a large circle as in Fig. 141, and if the coil is small there is insufficient top rake.   But when

fed level along the work the cutting comes off in a
spiral, such as in Fig. 144. The more top rake the
tool has the more open the coils will be, the cutting
shown being as open as it should be even for the
softest of wrought iron. The harder the metal the
less top rake a tool should have, while the bottom
rake should in all cases be kept as small as possible,

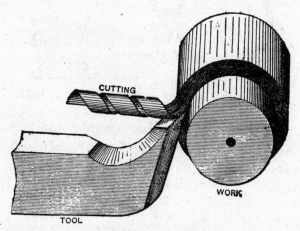

Fig. 144—Showing how the Cutting comes off when the Tool
is fed Level.

say 10 degrees for the rate of feed of an average 16-
inch lathe. The tool point should never stand far
above the top of the tool steel, the position shown in
Fig. 138 being for a newly-forged tool.

The practiced hand may have these tools fully
hardened, but the beginner should temper them to
a light straw color.

The top of anvil should be perfectly level and smooth, and the center of the same should be harder than the edges, because it receives the brunt of the blows. When used on the upper floors of a building, when a solid foundation can not be had, resort is had to a device by means of which the jar of the blows is obviated. This consists in mounting the anvil upon a stout spring whose upward rebound is counteracted by smaller springs placed above.—*By* JOSHUA ROSE.

Useful Attachment to Screw Stock Dies.

Having an order to fill for a small quantity of iron pins 2½ by 1-8 inch in diameter, to be threaded at each end with a wood screw thread, and having no tools to cut the threads with, I devised and used the following plan, which answered so satisfactorily that I think the idea may be of service to others, and hence send you sketches of it.

C, in Fig. 145, is the die stock having in it the dies *B B*, with the requisite pitch of thread. On the die stock is fastened a tool post and tool at *F* and a copper steadying piece at *A*. The tool may be made from ¼-inch square Stubbs or Crescent steel carefully filed to the shape of the thread to be cut and carefully tempered. *E* is a steel sleeve screwed with a thread of the same pitch and sawn through its axis one way to point *D*, and the spring tempered in oil.

The pin to be threaded is inserted through the sleeve *E*, which on being gripped in the vise secure-

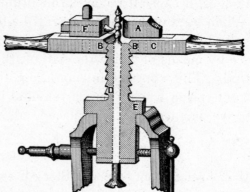

Fig. 145—Attachment to Screw Stock Dies as designed by "W. D."
Side View.

ly holds the pin. When the stock is revolved *E* regulates the pitch of the thread that the tool will

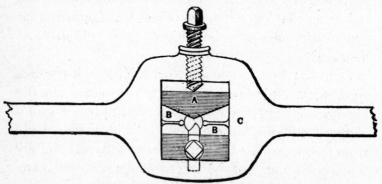

Fig. 146—Plan View of "W. D.'s" stock.

cut on the pin. Hence the stock may be used in the ordinary manner. A plan view is shown in Fig. 146.

If many bolts are wanted it would be well to make a pair of blank or soft dies or otherwise a piece of thin sheet-brass between the dies, and the sleeve will be of service. I may state that the thread cut by this tool when well made, is equal to any wood screw, whether made of iron, steel, or manufactured brass. —*By* W. D.

Wear of Screw-Threading Tools.

It is well-known that a tap can be sharpened by grinding the tops of the teeth only, and since the reason of this explains why the work goes together tighter as the tools wear, permit me to explain it. In

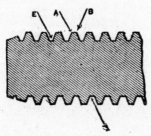

Fig. 147—Section of Tap showing Wear of Screw-Threading Tools.

Fig. 147, which presents a section of the tap, *A B* are the top corners and *E F* the bottom corners of the thread. Now, as the thread is formed by cutting a groove, and the teeth cut the groove, it is evident that *A B* cut continuously, but as *E F* do not meet the work until the thread is cut to its full depth, they do no cutting, providing the tapping hole is the right size, as it should be. It follows then that the corners *A B* wear the most, and like all sharp corners they wear rounding.

Now take the case of the die in Fig. 148, and it is evident that the corners *C D* do the cutting, and, therefore, wear rounding more than the corners *G H*, which only meet the work when it has a full

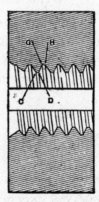

Fig. 148—Section Through a Die.

thread cut on it. Now take a bolt and nut with a thread cut on it by worn dies, and we shall have the c ndition of things shown in Fig. 149 ; rounded corners at *A B* on the nut and at *C D* on the bolt, and sharp corners at *E F* on the nut and at *G H* on the bolt. Hence corners *G H* jam against corners *A B*, and corners *E F* jam against corners *C D*. So much for the wear, and now for the sharpening of

the tap. It is evident that as the tops of the teeth
do the main part of the cutting, they get dull quickest,

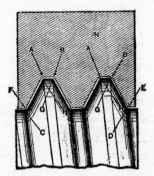

Fig. 149—Enlarged Section Through a Bolt and Nut cut by Worn Dies.

and therefore by grinding them the teeth are greatly
sharpened.—*By* J. R.

Tool for Wagon Clips.

The following tool for use in bending buggy,
saddle and wagon clips, is easily made and will save
much time where a number of clips are used. Figs.
151 and 152 show the tool taken apart. In making
it have the width from axle to axle the required
width of the clip, and have the part *A* so that it will
fit up tight in the slot *H*. The part *B*, shown in Fig.
151, is of the same width as *A*. Fig. 150 shows the
tool put together with the clip fastened in it ready
for bending. In bending clips in a tool of this kind,
they can be formed half round, if desired. Round

and square iron may be used as required. In using
the tool proceed as follows : Place *A*, of Fig. 151, in
the slot *H*, then place the clip in the slot at *O*. Next

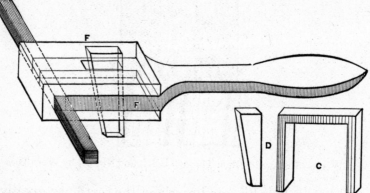

Fig. 150—Device for Bending Clips, with Detail of Wedge and a View
of a Finished Clip.

drive the wedge-shaped key *D* in the slots of *C* and
B. When the clip is fastened in the tool, as shown

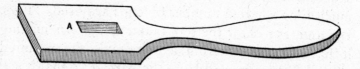

Fig. 151—The Principal Part of the Tool.

in Fig. 150, with a hand hammer bend the ends
against the parts *F F* of the tool. In taking the clip
out of the tool drive the pin out of the slots and drive

the clevis from the mandrils.   At this stage the clip
will be finished, or in other words it will be shown in
the shape as shown at *C* and ready for swedging the

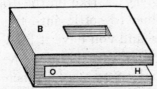

Fig. 152—Detail of the Clamping Device.

parts for the nuts.   By a little practice any smith
will be able to bend nearly a square corner on the
outside of the clip.—*By* H. R. H.

A Handy Tool.

Many times, iu taking old carriages apart, considerable trouble arises from the turning of bolts, as

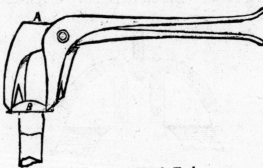

Fig. 153—A Handy Tool.

the small square under the head will not hold the
bolt if the nut turns hard.   In such cases it is usually

necessary to split the nut, to get the bolt out.   The
tool in question will save many bolts and much
vexation of spirit.   Set the jaws down over the head
B of the bolt, Fig. 153, strike on the top of the jaw
at *A* with a hammer to settle into the wood; then
pinch the handles and you have it held fast, and the
nut can then be readily turned off.   The tool is about
10 inches long, and 5-8 to ¾ of an inch in thickness,
measuring through the points joined by the rivet.   It
will work on bolts from 3-16 to 3-8, and even larger.
A blacksmith can make a pair in one hour, and save
many hours of valuable time.   For the want of a
better name we call it a " Polly."—*By* O. F. F.

False Vise-Jaws for Holding Rods, etc.

Here is a simple device for holding bolts in a vise.
Though an old invention it is not as well-known as

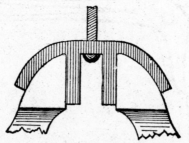

Fig. 154 — False Vise-Jaws.   End View.

it ought to be.   Fig. 154 of the illustration shows the
end of a pair of cast-brass jaws fitting on the vise.

Fig. 155 shows one jaw. The same pattern will do for both. Clamp the jaws and drill the holes, filing them afterward to the shape desired. Square

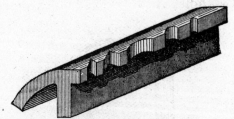

Fig. 155—Showing one of the Jaws.

holes are most useful, as they hold both round and square rods. Do not make the holes larger than need

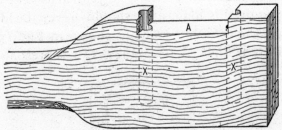

Fig. 156—The Bottom Tool for Making Spring Clips.

be, and then they may be redressed when worn, or altered to suit new work.—*By* WILL TOD.

Making Spring Clips with Round Shanks and Half-Round Top.

The accompanying illustrations represent my method of making short spring clips. The bottom tool shown in Fig. 156, should have a handle about 12 inches long. To make this tool take cast steel, say 3 x 1 inches, and first forge out the handle, then drill the two holes $X X$. These holes should be for

Fig. 157—Showing how the Clip is Bent.

5-16 iron, and drilled with a 11-32 drill as deep as the shaft required is long, and should never be drilled through the tool, but made as shown in Fig. 157 by the dotted lines $X X$. Fig. 159 represents the

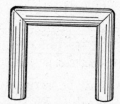

Fig. 158—The Finished Clip.

top swage. This is made of cast steel, the same as any common top swage. First cut out the impression C the full length of the tool, then cut down the recess $B B$, then punch out the eye D for the handle.

This top swage is made to fit the bottom swage or handle tool, Fig. 156. To make the clips proceed as follows : Cut 5-16 inch round iron the proper length, bend it as shown in Fig. 157, place it in the tool, Fig. 156, set the swage, Fig. 159, on top of the

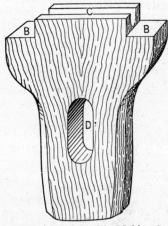

Fig. 159—The Top Tool used in Making Spring Clips.

iron, and with five or six blows from the sledge you get the clip with both corners bent, as shown in Fig. 158. Any smith after two or three trials will know just how long to cut the iron to get the best results. The tool must be kept cool, for when it gets hot it will stick the clip.- -*By* H. R. H.

Handy Tool for Marking Joints.

Not wishing to secure everything and give nothing in return, I send you a sketch, Fig. 160, of a

handy tool to mark off joints where one cylindrical
body joins another. *A* is a stem on a stand *E*. A
loose sleeve, *B*, slides on *A* carrying an arm *C*, hold-
a pencil at *D*. A piece of truly surfaced wood or
iron, *W*, has marked on it the line *J*. Two Vs, *G
G*, receive the work *P*. Now, if the centers of *G G*

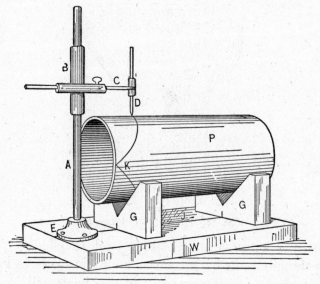

Fig. 160—Handy Tool for Marking Joints.

and of the stand *E* all coincide with the line *J*, then
E will stand central to *P*, and *D* may be moved by
the hand around, *P* being allowed to lift and fall on
A so as to conform to the cylindrical surface of *P*,
and a line will be marked showing where to cut away
the wood on that side, and all you have to do is to

turn the work over and mark a similar line diametrically opposite, the second line being shown at K. —*By* S. M.

Tools for Holding Bolts in a Vise.

I send sketches of what I find a very handy tool for holding bolts or pins. It consists of a spring

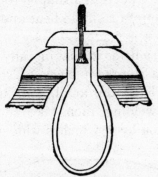

Fig. 161—Showing how the Bolt is held by device of " M. S. H."

clamp that goes between the vise jaws, as in Fig. 161

Fig. 162—Showing the Device adapted for Holding Round Pins.

of the accompany engravings, and has a groove in its jaws to hold the round stems of bolts to the vise

jaws, without damaging the heads.   It may be made
also, as in Fig. 162, with a hole on its end as well to
hold round pins.   It doesn't fall off the vise as other
clamps do.—*By* W. S. H.

A Tool for Making Singletree Clips.

I have recently devised a simple tool for making
singletree clips from a single heat and will endeavor
to explain how it is made.

Proceed the same as in making any kind of a bottom swage, that is, take a piece of square iron the
size of the hole in the anvil, and upset one end
sufficiently for welding, then take another piece of
iron ⅛-inch thick by 2½ inches wide and 8½ inches

Fig. 163—Showing How the Ends are Shaped.

long and draw the ends down to the shape shown in
Fig. 163 of the accompanying illustrations.   Upset
in the center, or, if your anvil is small, a little to one
side of the center, or enough so that when your
swage is in place, the end will not project over the
end of the anvil.   Weld on the stem and fit to the
anvil.   Next, make two ½-inch grooves in each end
of the swage commencing near the end and pointing
to the center, as shown in Fig. 164.   Have the

measurements as near as possible to the following: From *A* to *B*, 8 inches; from *C* to *D*, 1½ inches. Next, take a piece of iron 1 x 1¼ inches and weld on the ends of the swage, extending over the swage about

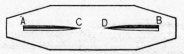

Fig. 164—Showing How the Grooves are Made.

¼ of an inch. Open up the ends of the grooves and the tool is ready for use, as in Fig. 165.

To make the clips take ½-inch round iron, cut off 8½ inches long, heat in the center and bend sufficiently to allow it to go in the tool, then flatten the

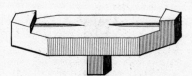

Fig. 165—The Finished Tool.

center, take the clip out and bend it over the horn into shape. A smith can easily make a clip at each heat. Of course, for making clips of different sizes the tool must be made accordingly.—*By* J. W. C.

Tool for Making Dash Heels.

I send sketches of a tool for making dash-heels for buggies or phaetons, and will attempt to describe the manner of making and using the tool. Fig. 166 represents the article. It is made of cast steel as far as the dotted line shown to the right. At this point is welded on a piece of 7-8-inch round iron for the handle. The tool proper is four inches long, and

Fig. 166—Tool for Making Dash Heels. General Appearance of the Tool.

the handle twelve inches long. The thickness or depth of the tool is two and one-half inches. It is made wider at the bottom than at the top. Through the center of the tool, as shown in Fig. 166, a hole is

Fig. 167—Tapering and Splitting the Piece of Iron to form the Article.

made, passing from face to face. This hole is 7-8 by 5-8 inch, which adapts the tool to making a heel of these dimensions. This weight is ample for a piano box, or phaeton body. The oval cavity in the upper face of the tool is five-eighths of an inch deep.

The manner of using the tool is as follows : Use Norway iron, 7-8 x ½ inch in size, and draw it out wedge shape, as indicated in Fig. 167, heat the end marked *A A*, and place the iron in the tool ; let the

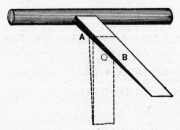

Fig. 168—Appearance of the Article upon Removing from the Tool.

helper strike it four or five blows with the sledge ; next take a splitting chisel and while the iron is in the tool, split it, as shown in Fig. 167 at *O* ; replace the iron in the fire, and obtaining a good welding

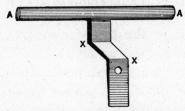

Fig. 169—Form of the Article Made in the Old Way.

heat, put it in the tool again and hammer down the split ends in the oval part of the tool. With the same heat edge up the iron ; this is done by letting the piece come up two or four inches in the tool and

holding it with the tool while edging it up. With
the same heat also knock the iron down into the tool
and swage with a top oval swage to match the oval
of the tool. Take the iron out. It will be found
that a heel has been formed as shown in Fig. 168.
If the heel is required for a phaeton body, all that
remains to be done is to punch the holes ; if, on the
other hand, however, the heel is wanted for a piano-
box or any other body with a panel in the front, it
is necessary to bind the corner *A*, Fig. 168, as shown
by the dotted lines.

The old way of forging a dash heel was to split it,

Fig. 170—Tongs for Making the Bend shown at *A* in Fig. 168.

forge and swage the oval ends *A A*, Fig. 169, and
then bend the corners as shown by *X X* in the same
figure. By forging a dash heel with the tool above
described, bending one corner is saved, and the
piece, when finished, does not set up like a stilt.
The oval iron comes down on to the body. In fastening the dash to the body always let the oval iron project one-eighth of an inch beyond the edge, so as to
have the leather of the dash lie straight against the
edge of the body. For making the bend *A* in Fig.

168, I use a pair of tongs shown in Fig. 170. The lower jaw is one inch in depth and the upper jaw 1⅛ inches. The length of the jaws is four inches, and their width 1⅛ inches. The manner of using these tongs is so evident upon inspection of the sketch that further explanation is unnecessary.—*By* H. R. H.

Mending Augers and other Tools.

It often happens that a good auger with the screw broken off is thrown away as useless. Now I will try to tell how I have often made a quarter repairing such augers.

Take a file of suitable size and cut a groove the width of the old screw about 3-16 inch deep, a little wider at the bottom than the top (dovetail form). Then form a piece of steel the shape of the screw with a base to it neatly and tightly in the groove. Then coat the edges with a mixture as follows :

Equal parts of sulphur and any white lead with about a sixth of borax. Mix the three thoroughly, and when about to apply the preparation wet it with strong sulphuric acid, press the blank screw tightly in the groove, lay it away five days, and then you will find it as solid as if welded ; then smooth up and file the threads on the screw. The job will not take a half hour's work, or cost three cents for material, and the same process may be used for mending almost any broken tool, without drawing the temper. —*By* D. F. KIRK.

An Attachment to a Monkey Wrench.

I enclose sketches of a tool that I have found very useful in my shop. It is an attachment for a monkey wrench. It is made of steel and of the same size as

Fig. 171—Showing how the Teeth are made.

the head of the wrench. The teeth are filed in so that they slant downward toward the wrench, as shown in Fig. 171. A small tire-bolt holds the attachment in place. Fig. 172, represents the attach-

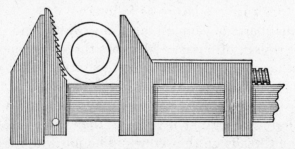

Fig. 172—Showing the Attachment in operation on the Wrench.

ment in position on a wrench and gripping piece of pipe. This device will hold round rods or pipe as well as a pair of gas-pipe tongs would.—*By* G. W. P.

A Handy Tool for Finishing Seat Rails, etc.

Fig. 173 represents a tool that I have found very handy in finishing eyes in seat rails, braces and other work that requires to be fitted exactly. I made this tool like a number of others that I use, for a particular job. It answered the purpose so well that I made others, of different sizes. It can be made by any

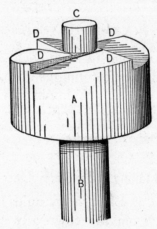

Fig. 173—A Tool for Finishing Eyes in Seat Rails, etc.

machinist.   The shank, B, is 2-1-2 inches long and 1-2 inch in diameter to fit the drilling machine. The head, A, and the follower, C, can be made to agree with the work they are to be used on. The cutting lips, D, are filed to shape, and tempered to straw color. With this tool you can smooth up.—*By* " BLACKSMITH."

A Tool for Pulling Yokes on Clips.

The illustration, Fig. 174, represents a very handy and useful tool of my own invention, which I use for putting yokes on clips or as a clip puller. *A* and *H*, as shown in the illustration, are of 3-8 inch square steel,

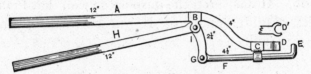

Fig. 174—A Tool to Pull Yokes on Clips.

A has two ears welded to it on each side at *B*, and a loop is welded on at *C*; *F* hinges on to *H* at *G*, and *H* hinges on to *A* at *I*; *E* hooks into the yoke; *D* hooks on the end of the clip. By closing the handles, the yoke is pulled to the clip or vise.—*By* A. D. S.

Making a Candle Holder.

I was driving, and full thirty miles from a railroad and three miles from the town I wished to reach, when I lost a jack bolt. Fortunately a little smithy was near, but it was late in the day, and before the son of Vulcan had finished his evening meal and was ready to attend to my wants it was dark. With tallow candle in hand, the smith, with his man and I, went to his shop and the job was done; the smith doing the work, the helper holding the candle. I asked the smith if he found it profitable to pay a helper to hold the candle, and he answered that he knew no better way. I told him that I would pass by his shop again the next day and would show him then how to make a cheap and handy candle-holder. I kept my word and did the job before his eyes, as follows:

I took a piece of band iron, 1¼ inches wide and 10 inches long, bent it as shown in the accompanying illustration, so as to join the two angles, each 3 inches long, leaving the back, *A*, 4 inches. I then

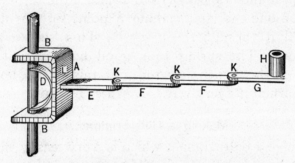

Fig. 175—Showing Candle Holder Complete.

bored the holes *B B*, 1-2 inch, and at *L* (on *A*) made a 3-8-inch hole. I next took iron ¾ x 3-16-inch and 6 inches long, turned a shoulder on it after upsetting, squared the hole at *L* and fitted into it the end on *E*. I next took a piece of 1 x 12 inch hoop iron and made the spring *D*, concaving the ends, which I riveted on the inner side of *A* by means of the shoulder on *E*. I next made the pieces *F F* and *G*, and drilled and riveted them as at *K K K*. I next took a block of wood, *H*, 1 1-2 inches diameter, 3 inches long, in which I bored a hole to suit the candle, which I secured with a screw on the under side, and my candlestick was complete, as seen in accompanying illustration, Fig. 175.

My friend watched me patiently all the way through, and was inclined to believe that he had me at my wits' end and suggested that he was no better off than before. I asked him to have a little patience. I soon found a piece of 7-16 round iron, turned an eye on one end, and, making a point on the other, passed it through the bracket. This served as a support. The spring took good hold. I put the stake in the bench, lowered and raised the holder and turned it every way.—*By* Iron Doctor.

Making a Bolt Trimmer.

I have a bolt trimmer which is very easily made, and cannot help giving satisfaction.

It is shown complete below. The cutting jaws

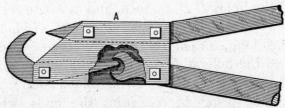

Fig. 176—Showing "C. C. O.'s" Bolt Trimmer Complete.

are of good tool steel. The stationary jaw is welded to the iron handle at *A,* making the handle and cutter one piece. The movable cutter works in a fork, as seen in Fig. 176.

I have my cutter made with side plates, 3 x 7 inches, and handles two feet long.

For convenience in sharpening I have put it together with bolts.—*By* C. C. O.

A Labor-Saving Tool.

I send drawing of a tool that I have found to be very handy. It is my own idea and a handy tool, especially in plow or buggy work. For plow work it cannot be beaten. The holder is of cast steel and

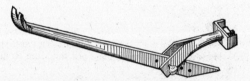

Fig. 177—Showing " B. F. C.'s " Labor-Saving Tool.

made with two spurs to fit against bolt heads. The steel is welded into a ¾-round iron, 18 inches long. Drill four or five holes for the pin that runs through the holder.

To make the holder take two pieces of 1¼ by 5-16 flat iron, weld to make as shown in Fig. 177. Round the end and cut threads for burr brake or pin to hold. When in use the other end is made to pull the bolts to the jaw.

It will be seen from Fig. 177 that this holder is made to turn in any direction and will hold on any shear.—*By* B. F. C.

Making a Spike-Bar.

I will try to describe a handy spike-bar and tie-fork for mine road men. This tool enables them to do a third more work than they could do with the spike-bar generally used in coal mines. In making the bar I weld 1-inch square steel to 1-inch round

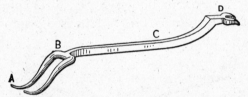

Fig. 178—Handy Spike-bar and Tie-Fork for Mine Road Men.

iron and use 7-8-round for the fork-prongs. *A*, in the accompanying illustration, Fig. 178, represents the part that goes under the tie, and *B* is where the tool rests on the rail. The man, while driving, sits at *C*. *D* should be made ½ inch longer on the under side than the spike is.—*By* R. DELBRIDGE.

How to Make a Tony Square.

This is a very simple thing to make, and very useful for trying six or eight-square timber or iron. It

is very handy in making wheelbarrow hubs or anything of that sort.

Take an ordinary try square and saw a slit in it
opposite the blade ; next take a piece of steel plate of

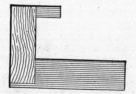

Fig. 179—Showing " Village Smith's " Tony Square.

the same thickness of the blade and cut it to about
one-third of the length of blade in the try square.
Insert the short blade in the slit as shown in Fig.
179 and you have a "tony" square that will do its
work as nice as you please.—*By* VILLAGE SMITH.

An Easy Bolt Clipper.

I have a bolt clipper of my own invention and
which I think is a very good one. It is simple and
easily made The lever *E*, in Fig. 180, and the jaw
I are of one piece of solid steel. The lever *L* and
jaw *M* are also of steel, but in two pieces, as shown
by the dotted line at *H*, which is a joint that works
by the opening and closing of the handle or lever *L*.
F is a steel plate, there being another on the opposite

side. The plates are three-sixteenths of an inch thick. The distance from *A* to *B* is five inches from center to center of bolt holes. From *B* to *C* is two inches from center to center, and from center of bolt hole *C* to joint *H* is three and one-half inches.

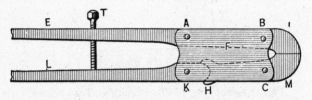

Fig. 180—An Easy Bolt Clipper, as made by Chris. Vogel.

From joint *H* to center of bolt hole *K* is one and one-half inches. The handles or levers are two feet six inches in length. The set-screw *T* is used to prevent the jaws *I* and *M* from coming together. With this clipper I can cut anything up to a one-half inch bolt.—*By* CHRIS. VOGEL.

A Tool for Pulling on Felloes.

The illustration, Fig. 181, shows a tool I have for drawing on felloes when making or repairing wheels. The ring, *A*, which goes over the nut is about 10 inches in diameter ; the rod, *B*, is 2 feet long and made from 5-8 iron. It has a thread cut one-half the length. *C* is a comet nut about one foot long before being bent. *D* is a piece of 1½ x 3-8 inch flat iron and bent as shown. It is drilled 11-16 so that it will easily slip over the rod; the end is widened and

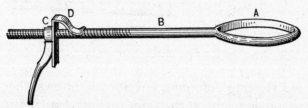

Fig. 181—Tool for Pulling on Felloes, made by Louis Tuthill.

slightly turned up. There is power enough in this to draw a small wheel all out of shape.—*By* LOUIS TUTHILL.

How to Make a Handy Hardy.

I have a very handy hardy which can be made with little expense. Take an old saw file and break off a short piece from each end. Draw the temper and it is ready for use. If it should stick to the iron when cutting, grind the sides a little. If you are careful to lay it level on the anvil you will have no difficulty in cutting heavy tires—by turning the iron. I have used one of these hardies for a year without breaking it.—*By* R. C.

A Handy Clincher.

The accompanying illustration, Fig. 182, represents a clincher which I believe to be a little better than any I have ever seen. It can be made from

Fig. 182—The Handy Clincher, as made by A. F. Reinbeck.

an old shoeing hammer. The cut shows the construction so clearly that no further explanation is necessary.—*By* A. F. REINBECK.

A Bolt Holder.

I have a bolt-holder that gives good satisfaction, see Fig. 183: it is very useful in preventing bolts from turning. The eye is forged from 7-8 square iron, the eye 5-16 x 1½ inches; the part that presses against the bolt-head is steel, the iron being split

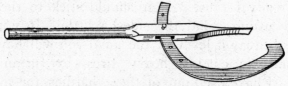

Fig. 183—Bolt Holder.

and spiral inserted; the square part being 5 inches long; from the square to the point, about 4¼ inches; the handle welded out of ¾-inch round iron. The curved piece passing through eye is made from 1 x ¼-inch stake iron—*By* J. F. SMALL.

Making a Cant-Hook.

Some smiths may think that the making of a cant-hook is a job too simple to write about, but to make a hook that will catch hold every time is not so easy after all. My way of making such a hook is as follows:

First, make an eye to go around the handle, then make the hook almost any shape, or bend it so that

Fig. 184—Cant-Hook.

you can then rivet it to the eye and put on the handle. Bend the point so that it will lie flat on the handle when closed, as shown in the accompanying illustration, Fig. 184. Then it will always catch and hold.—*By* E. P. A.

Making a Cant-Hook.

The accompanying illustrations represent my way of making a cant-hook.

The clasp is made of 1¾ inch by ½-inch Norway iron. I get the exact measure around the handle, and if it be 9 inches around, I measure 4½ inches on the Norway bar (which is of the right length to handle conveniently), then I take a heat, and with a fuller let in about 7-8 inch to 1 inch from each end. I next draw down the center to nearly the right thick-

ness, bend the ends nearly to a square angle, and set
down with the hammer, and make the ends or corners square.   I then take a chisel and cut in about
1⅛ inch or 1 inch from one edge, for the jaw, leaving this for the thickest part of the clasp.   I then set

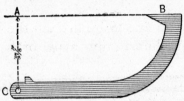

Fig. 185—Making a Cant-Hook.   Showing Method of making Shoulder.

the remainder down with the set-hammer.   When
both ends are down, I draw to the right length, turn
and bend to fit the handle.

For the hook, I use 7-8-inch by ½-inch steel, 14
inches long.   At the end where the hole is, I upset

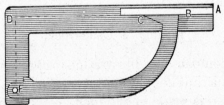

Fig. 186—Showing Method of Setting the Draw.

to make a shoulder, as shown in Fig. 185 of the illustrations, which prevents the hook from cutting away
the soft iron of the clasp, and prevents the point of
the hook from striking the pick.

I give 4 7-8 inches draw as shown by the dotted

lines *A C*, Fig. 185, and to get this exactly every time, I make the tool shown in Fig. 186. In making it I take a bar, 1 foot 6 inches long, 1¾ inches by ½-inch, and bend it 13 inches from *A* to *D*. At

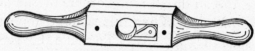

Fig. 187—Screw Box.

B, Fig. 186, I weld on a piece of iron. 6 inches long by ½-inch, with the edge to the *D* bar, and previously bent to the right shape. I then make the piece *B*, Fig. 186, true on the face (along *C*) with the square *D*. I next measure off from *D* 4 7-8 inches to *F*, and here set a 7-16-inch pin. I make the hook bend and lay as shown in the illustration, Fig. 186, being careful to have the hook true at *B D*. I file to a point from the inside of the point. For the bands, the

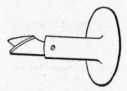

Fig. 188—The Knife.

first is of 1-inch band iron, the two next are of 1½ inch, and the toe bands are of 2-inch band iron. This pick is of 7-8-inch square steel, 10 inches long. —*By* W. W. S.

Making Screw Boxes for Cutting Out Wooden Screws.

To make wooden screws by my plan, first take a square piece of steel and with a three-cornered file make the thread on all four corners of the steel for about two inches. When this is done you will have a tap as seen in Fig. 187. To make the screw box

Fig. 189—The Tap.

as shown in Fig. 188, turn a piece of word (apple wood is the best), with two handles, and bore a hole in the center to the size of the tap with the thread off. Then cut a thread in it with the tap and cut away the wood at one side to admit the knife. This is made as in Fig. 189 with two screws in it, one in the center and the other set. Put the knife in the

Fig. 190—Piece of Wood used to Secure the Knife in its Place and Admit the Tap.

box so it will match the thread, and screw in over it a piece of wood one-quarter of an inch thick with a hole in it the size of the tap with the thread on, as represented in Fig. 190. The box is then complete—*By* H. A. S.

Mending a Square.

In this communication I will tell your readers how to mend a square. Very often a good steel square is rendered useless by having the foot or short end broken off, as in Fig. 191 of the accompanying illustrations. I then work a piece of good iron into the

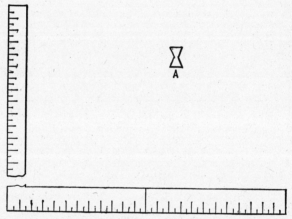

Fig. 191—Showing the Square and the Piece used in Mending.

shape shown at *A*, in Fig. 191, and taking a hack saw, I cut a notch in each piece in which the piece *A* will fit tightly. I have a square at hand to ensure accuracy, and then having my coal well charred, I take good clean brass and lay it on. When it begins to get hot I put on borax powdered fine—I can't braze much without borax. When the brass is all melted it is removed from the fire, allowed to cool, and when it is cool the surplus brass and iron are ground off, and the square will then be as good as ever.

Copper is about as good as brass to braze with.

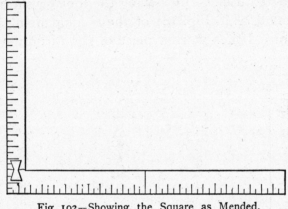

Fig. 192--Showing the Square as Mended.

Fig. 192 shows the square when finished.—*By* J. W. J.

Stand for Carriage Bolts.

From an old buggy shaft, three cheese boxes and four strips of wood I made a very handy stand for carriage and tire bolts, the general appearance of which is afforded by the inclosed sketch, Fig. 193. In the center of each box I nailed a square block. I put partitions on two sides, and also two partitions crossways, in order to make six different sized boxes for different sized bolts. I bored a hole through the center and slipped the box down over the shaft.

I fastened it both above and below by nails through the shaft. On the outside surface of the boxes I fastened four strips, using ordinary felloe strips for the purpose, placing them equidistant. Their pur-

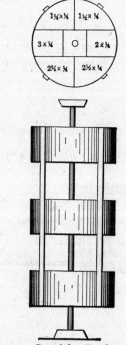

Fig. 193 —Stand for Carriage Bolts.

pose was to keep the boxes steady. Below and on top I fastened two blocks with holes (bushed) in which the pointed ends of the shaft turn. The device stands in the corner of the shop and is very handy, inasmuch as it easily turns round. Each compartment in the box is marked on the outside in plain figures, thus indicating the size of bolt that it contains.—*By* F. D. F.

An Improved Crane and Swage Block.

In the line of cranes I have something differing from the usual style. It is new, I think, and certainly very good. The engraving, Fig. 194, will ex-

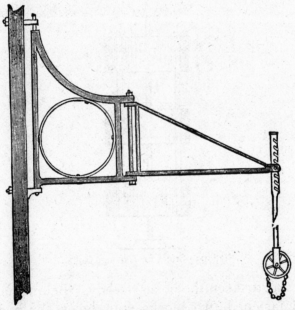

Fig. 194—Improved Crane.

plain it. It can be attached to a post in the most convenient position. Mine is hung in thimbles built in the front of the forge chimney. Next in order shall be the swage block. Of all the much abused tools in a smith's shop, I think the greatest quantity of curses have been bestowed on that patient and unoffending tool. I have known the English language riddled, picked and culled for epithets with the strongest adjectives to hurl at this useful tool. You can hear some of them any time by walking across the shop and stubbing your toe against it as it lays on the floor, and you need not be afraid of hurting it (the swage block I mean). Now, as I consigned mine to the scrap heap many years ago, I will describe a substitute. Get a cast-iron cone mandril, 7 inch diameter at the top and 10 inch at the bottom, with an outside flange at the bottom to form a base, and a strong inside one at the top, having a 4-inch hole in the top, into which cast or wrought-iron collets and swages can be fitted for every kind of work, including farmers' and other tools. The cone can be made the height of the anvil and forge, so as to be right for the crane to swing to as easy as the anvil.—*By* IRON JACK.

A Cheap Crane for Blacksmiths.

The accompanying sketch, Fig. 195, of a cheap crane for blacksmiths needs but little explanation, for any practical man will understand it at a glance. *E* is a round pole with a band on each end and a gudgeon and mortise to receive the bar *C,* which is 30

inches x ¾ inch.   At *A A* make holes and put in
rough pins.   Then a part, *B*, is ¾-round iron, with

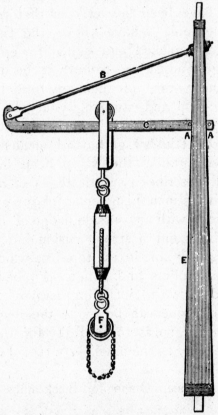

Fig. 195—Cheap Crane.

nuts at the top and joint at the bottom. *F* is a small
sheave, with chain to hold your work, and as you
turn your work in the fire or on the anvil it revolves.

I am using one of these cranes, and have had eight hundred pounds on it. In every case it answers well. —*By* SOUTHERN BLACKSMITH.

Repairing an Auger.

I will tell your readers my way of putting a screw in an auger. I take the old auger and file a notch in it where the old screw was broken off. I do this work with the edge of the file, making the notch no wider than the old screw was. I then take a 3-square

Fig. 196—Repairing an Auger. Showing Notch and Piece to be Fitted into it.

taper file and file the notch wider until it appears as at *A* in the accompanying illustration, Fig. 196. I next take a small piece of steel, forge out the size desired for the screw, file the piece "dovetailing," as shown at *B*, and then slip it sidewise into the auger. It is put in so it can be driven rather snug. When it is fitted it must be brazed.

Then, commencing inside next to the lip, I file with a 3-square file, and boring the thread half way around, I then commence at the other lip and file a double thread, keeping the two threads side by side and even with each other, by fitting first one a little and then the other about as much, and so on. By

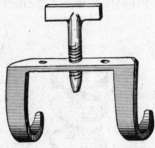

Fig. 197—A Clamp for Holding Countersunk Bolts.

this means they can be kept true. An auger repaired in this way is just as good as new. It does not pay to mend small ones in this way, but it is a good plan for large augers, for the operation is simple and requires but a short time.—*By* ERNEST.

A Clamp for Holding Countersunk Boltheads.

I enclose an illustration, Fig. 197, of a clamp that I use in holding countersunk boltheads, while removing the taps from the bolts on spring wagon and buggy felloes. There. is no patent on it and it is quickly put on and taken off. It is made of 7-16 inch horseshoe bar with three holes, and has a T headed bolt with threads to tighten. The points hook over the felloe and the point of the bolt, which should be tapering at the point, so it will tighten against the bolt without coming in contact with the tire. I have seen different devices for the purpose but like this the best. It should be made from four to five inches long. It will answer the same purpose for a large wheel by making it larger and stronger. —*By* W. E. S.

A Handy Machine for a Blacksmith.

A useful machine for any blacksmith is made as follows : Take a piece of lumber 1½ x 8 and 6 feet long, cut a hole in the middle 2 feet from the end, the dimensions of the hole being 2 x 14, take two cog wheels from some old fan mill, bolt journal box-es for the crank wheel down to the bench on each side of the slot and make an emery wheel mandrel for the small wheel to work on. The mandrel should be of ¾-inch iron 12 inches long. Plug up the hole in the small wheel and bore a hole for the mandrel, having the mandrel square to avoid turning in the wheel, then weld on a collar. If you have no lathe you can true it up with the hammer and file. Next cut a good screw on the end and put your collar on the end, which should be about 2 inches, and put on a small emery wheel ¾ inch thick and 8 or 10 inches in diameter. But first put on a washer of thick leather, also another one against the wheel, screw the tap up tight and if it does not turn true you can trim your leather washer down on one edge and by this means get it perfectly true. On the other end of the bench you can attach a good pair of hand shears. For sharpening drills, cold chisels, and a variety of other work, this machine has no equal.—*By* J. M. WRIGHT.

A Clamp for Framework.

The accompanying illustration, Fig. 198, represents a hand clamp for drawing together framework, such as wagon beds, wheelbarrows, etc.

It is made as follows:

The bar *A* is of narrow tooth steel which will not bend so easily as iron. It should be five feet long by 1 x ½ inch. *B* is a piece of iron which should

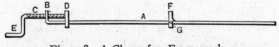

Fig. 198—A Clamp for Framework.

be 3 inches high by 1½ wide, welded to the end and with a ¾-inch hole having good threads in it. *C* is a screw to fit the same. It is made one foot long with a crank *E* which is attached to the end. *D* is a slide to fit over *A*, and it should have 3 inches above it a hole ¼ inch deep to allow the screw *C* to get a good bearing. *F* is made the same as *D*, except that it has a shoulder back of it to keep it from leaning too far back, and a set screw *G*, at the side, to hold it stationary. I use this clamp almost every day, and I never saw or heard of one just like it.—*By* V. D. B.

A Tool for Holding Bolts.

I send a sketch, Fig. 199, of a tool for holding loose bolts while screwing nuts off. To make it, take a piece of ⅝-inch round iron of suitable length, draw down oval and tapering about 5 inches, and about 7 inches from the pointed end drive in a piece of steel,

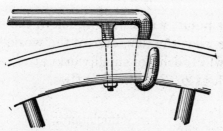

Fig. 199—A Tool for Holding Loose Bolts.

wedge-shaped, weld securely and sharpen like a chisel; one inch is long enough for this. Then five inches from the end turn it down at right angles, edgewise, and then curl to the left as shown in the illustration. This is better than all the patented tools for this purpose.—*By* EDWIN CLIFTON.

A Hint About Callipers.

Let me give some of your young readers a hint how to chamfer off the ends of their callipers from the outside and slightly round them across as in Fig. 200, and not make them rounding as in Fig. 201,

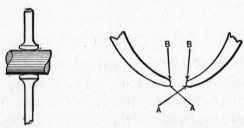

Fig. 200—Right way to Shape   Fig. 201—Wrong way to Shape
    Calliper Ends.   Calliper Ends.

The outer points will always touch at the same point no matter what the diameter of the work. If rounding they will touch, for small work, at *A, A*, and for large work at *B, B.—By* SHAFTING.

Vise Attachment.

I inclose a paper model of a device that I am using for holding beveled edge iron for filing. It is also useful for chamfering flat iron. In use it is to be screwed in a large vise. The spring shown in the cut, Fig. 202, throws the jaws apart when the vise is released. I think many of your readers will find this idea useful, and as it is one that every blacksmith can

put into practical operation, I commend it to the at-
ention of my fellow craftsmen.—*By* E. M. B.

Note.—The accompanying engraving has been
made from the paper model inclosed in our corres-

Fig. 202—Vise Attachment.

pondent's letter, and, we believe, correctly represents
his idea. As he did not show how the spring was
attached, or in what form it was to be made, we have
nothing to govern us in this particular.—Ed.

Bolt Set

We have been using a tool in this community for
a long time, which can be applied to wheels very

Fig. 203—Bolt Set.

quickly. Any blacksmith who can make a pair of
tongs can produce it. It is made of good steel, *A* in

the engraving being chisel-pointed and hardened, so that it can be set into the head of bolt, when it is necessary, by a slight rap with the hammer.—*By* W. H. S.

A Home-Made Lathe.

The accompanying drawings represent a turning lathe that I have been using for some time and find very convenient, not only in turning, but also in drilling small holes. Fig. 204 is a side view of the head stock, and Figs. 205 and 206 show the front and back ends of Fig. 204. In beginning to make

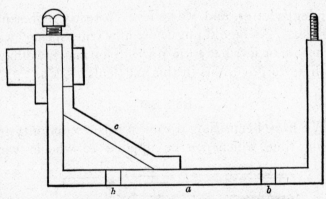

Fig. 204—Side View of the Head Stock.

the lathe, I take a piece of flat iron 12 inches long, 3 inches wide and ¼ inch thick, and cut 3 inches at each end, tapering down to 1¾ inches, as shown at *a*, Fig. 206. I then turn 3 inches of the same ends up at right angles, as at *a*, Fig. 204, and drill two 3/8-inch holes at *b* to bolt the head stock. The head stock is braced at *c* to prevent the springing of

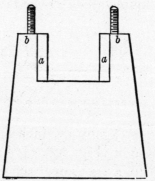

Fig. 205—Front End of the Head Stock.

the back end of the frame, as all the end pressure comes on that end. I next drill a 3/4-inch hole through the back end and 2½ inches from the bot-

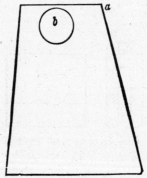

Fig. 206—Back End of the Headstock.

tom, *a*, as shown in Fig. 206 at *b*, and fit to *b* a piece of round iron 1½ inches long, with one end coun-

tersunk as in Fig. 207 at *a*. This is to fit the spindle
and take up the wear. To prevent this piece from
coming out, I double a piece over the end at *a*, Fig.

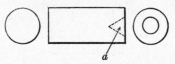

Fig. 207—Showing the Piece to be Attached to the Spindle.

205. This piece is 1¾ by 1¼ inches, with a ¾-inch
hole, as shown at *a*, Fig. 208. It has a ¼-inch set
screw at *b*. This piece goes over the end *a*, Fig. 206,
and the piece shown in Fig. 207 goes through the
¾-inch hole, and the set screw bears on the head
stock. By turning up the set screw the piece, Fig.
207, can be clamped at any place desired, thus forming the bearing for that end. The front end has

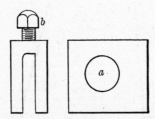

Fig. 208—Showing the Piece used to Secure in Position the Part Shown
in Fig. 207.

a place cut out at the center, 1½ by 1 inch, to receive the boxes. The edges at *a*, Fig. 205, are
beveled to a V, so the two boxes will slide down and

fit tightly. The boxes are 1½ x 1¾ x ¾ inch. With the ends cut out to fit the V shown in Fig. 205

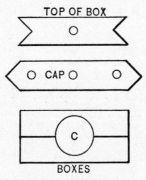

Fig. 209—Showing the Boxes and Plate.

at *a*, I next drill in each prong at *b*, cut a thread and fit a bolt to clamp the boxes. *C*, in Fig. 209, is the

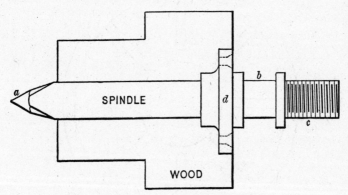

Fig. 210—The Spindle.

plate that goes over the boxes. The bolts go through the plate into *b*, Fig. 205. I put the boxes in, placing a

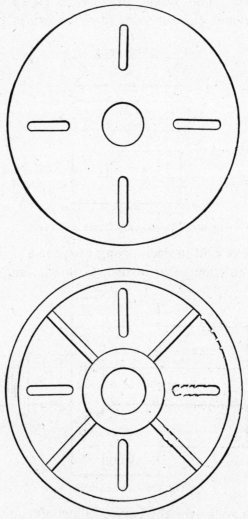

Fig. 211—The Face Plate.

thin piece of pasteboard between them, and then
clamp them tightly and drill a ¾-inch hole through

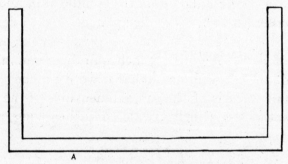

Fig. 212—Side View of the Tail Stock.

them at *C*. Composition is the best material for the
boxes.

The spindle must be turned, for it could not be
filed true enough to run well. Fig. 210 represents the shape. The end *a* should fit into Fig. 207

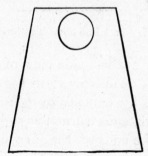

Fig. 213—End View of the Tail Stock.

at *a*. The bearing at the other end is at *b*, ¾ inch
in diameter. *c* is turned down a little smaller, and a

thread cut on it so as to screw on the face plate.
The spur center goes into the spindle with a taper.
You can shrink a flange on the spindle at *d*, and bolt
the pulley to that. The face plate needs no description. A glance at Fig. 211 will give anyone a clear
idea of it. It might be 5 inches in diameter, and it
would answer well enough if it were 3 inches only.
The tail stock is of the same dimensions of the head
stock, that is, 3 inches wide, 6 inches long, and 3

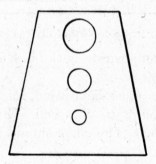

Fig. 214—Back End of the Tail Stock.

inches high. Fig. 212 is a side view of the tail stock;
Figs. 213 and 214, end views; in Fig. 215 is shown
a piece 1½ inches by 9 inches by ¼ inch thick, with
1½ inches of both ends turned at right angles to *a*.
This goes over the ends of Fig. 212 at *A*.

To clamp the arbor, drill a ¾-inch hole in both
ends of Figs. 213 and 214, 3½ inches in front of *a*,
and going also through the ends of the piece shown
in Fig. 216 at *b*. This hole must match the holes in

s. 213 and 114. The purpose of the arrangement

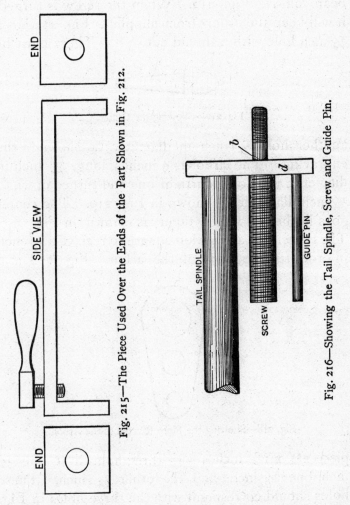

Fig. 215—The Piece Used Over the Ends of the Part Shown in Fig. 212.

END

SIDE VIEW

END

Fig. 216—Showing the Tail Spindle, Screw and Guide Pin.

TAIL SPINDLE

SCREW

GUIDE PIN

is to hold the arbor and keep the work from coming

out of the lathe. The set-screw shown in Fig. 215
bears on *A*, Fig. 212. When the screw is turned,
it will keep the arbor from slipping. Fig. 214 has a
½-inch hole with a thread cut in it. There must be

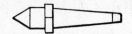

Fig. 217—Showing the Center.

another hole ¼ inch in diameter, as shown in the
engraving. The arbor is 9 inches long, ¾ inch in
diameter, with one-fourth of one end turned down to
½ inch diameter, as shown in Fig. 219. The center
goes in the end with a taper as shown in Fig. 217.
The center has a place left square to receive a wrench
in order to take it out of the arbor. Fig. 218 is a

Fig. 218—Showing the Piece Riveted to the Arbor.

piece 2¾ x 1¼ inches with three holes in it, one ½
inch, one ⅜ inch, and the other ¼ inch. These
holes should correspond with the three holes in Fig.
214. Fig. 218 is riveted to the arbor, which is

worked with a screw.   The guide-pin is fastened to

TAIL SPINDLE

Fig. 219—The Tail Spindle.

the plate and goes through the smallest hole in the

piece Fig. 214.   Fig. 220 is a hand wheel which fits on to a very tight nut.   To fasten it, there must be work in the plate, so that the screw can be turned in and out.   In turning the screw so, you carry the arbor with it.   The rest is a flat piece of iron ¼ inch thick, 8 inches long and 3 inches wide, with 2

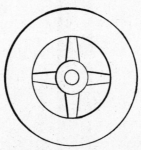

Fig. 220—The Hand Wheel,

inches of one end bent at right angles.   There must be two holes near the end, so a piece of wood can be bolted on for turning different lengths.   To fasten the rest to the bed cut a hole the size of the bolt, 4 inches long, in the bottom of the rest to let it slide to and from the work.—*By* H. A. SEAVEY.

CHAPTER VIII.

Blacksmiths' Shears.

I enclose a sketch, Fig. 221, of a pair of shears to be used in the square hole of the anvil. They are very useful and cheap. Any blacksmith can make them. Use good steel and make the blades eight inches long, measuring from the rivet. Make the

Fig. 221—Blacksmiths' Shears.

short blade with a crook, as shown in the illustration, to go in the anvil, and have the long blade extend back about two and a half feet to serve as a handle. With these shears I can cut quarter-inch iron with ease and cut steel when it is hot.—*By* A. J. T.

Shear for Cutting Round and Square Rods.

I would like to give a description of a shear for cutting round and square iron constructed by me. The inclosed sketch, Fig. 222, is an attempt to represent it. The lower member of the shear is a bar

an inch thick, three inches wide and fourteen inches
long, and is furnished with a steel face at that part
where the cutting is done.   The upper member is of
the same general description, except that it is seven-
teen inches long.   The lower blade is fastened to the
bench at the back part by cleats, as shown in the
drawing.   A guide for the upper blade, just wide

Fig. 222—Shear for Cutting Round and Square Rods.

enough in the opening to allow of easy play, is made
to serve a like purpose for the front part. The handle of the shear is hinged to the lower blade, and is
connected also with the upper one by the link shown
in the sketch. The handle is five feet long and is
one by three inches in size down to a taper.   Three
holes are provided in it for connecting the link

attached to the upper blade, thus opening the shear more or less as may be required. With this shear I can cut round or square iron up to seven-eighths in size.—*By* SOUTHERN BLACKSMITH.

Cheap Shears for Blacksmiths' Use.

I inclose a sketch, Fig. 223, of a cheap shears for smiths' use, and submit the following directions for

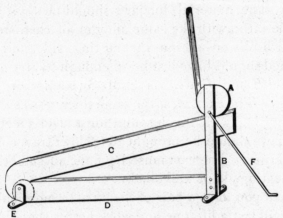

Fig. 223—Cheap Shears for Blacksmiths.

making : The under jaw, *D*, should be 10 inches long, 3 inches wide and 1 inch thick. The upper jaw must be 13 inches long, but otherwise the same as the lower jaw, except where it couples with the latter. Then it must be forged by the dotted lines. The coupling at *E* is made with a ⅞-inch cast-steel bolt, which takes a brace on each side of the shears,

this brace taking one half-inch bolt at the foot
through the bench.   The braces at the other end
take two bolts through the bench.   That next to the
lower jaw takes two half-inch rivets through the same
and a ¾-inch cast-steel bolt at the top through the
the cam.   The upper jaw is brought up by two strips
of sole leather connected to the cam A by two bolts.
The two braces, F (only one of which is shown in
the cut), are ½-inch round and take a ⅜ bolt at the
foot.   The material for jaws should be ⅝ x 3 inch
Swede's iron with the same amount of cast steel or
English blister laid on the cutting side, and when
finished should have just bevel enough to give a good
edge. E and B are made of Swede's iron ½ x 3
inches.   The cam, A, is the same thickness as the jaw
and finished with 1 inch round for a lever 3 feet long.
The jaws should be brought to a low straw color in
tempering.   The cam must be finished smooth and
the bearings kept well oiled.

Then you have a pair of shears at a nominal cost
that will last a lifetime and work better than most of
the shears in the market.   It is a good plan to use a
guard with the shears ; let it bolt on to the bench,
rising ⅜ of an inch above the edge of the lower pair,
and then run parallel with the jaw to the other end,
where it is secured by another bolt.   The brace, B,
which rivets to lower jaw, must have an offset of one
inch to come flush with the inside of the jaw.—*By*
J. M. W.

Blacksmiths' Shears.

I send a sketch, Fig. 224, of shears made by myself. They are cheap and I have found them very convenient. The engraving from my design requires no explanation. A glance at it will be sufficient for any smith who understands his trade. I

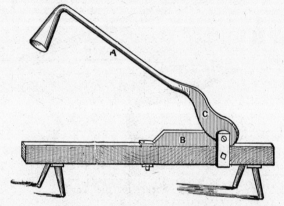

Fig. 224—Blacksmith's Shears.

will, however, give some of the dimensions. *A* is 1¾ round, *B* 9 x ¾ and *C* 6½ x ¾ inch. The main point in making is to get the edges to come together as in the common shears.—*By* J. J.

Shears for the Anvil.

I send you a sketch, Fig. 225, of a very handy tool, a pair of shears for the anvil. Any blacksmith that understands his trade can make them. They are

good for trimming cultivator shovels when they
have just been painted and they will take the place
of a helper on many jobs where striking is needed.
The cutting jaws are 4 inches long, 3 inches wide

Fig. 225—Shears for the Anvil.

and ¾ inch thick, and bevel to the edge and to the
back.   One jaw has a square hole for a square
shoulder bolt.   The handles are two feet long.   I
use them on hot iron or steel and they cut sheet iron
cold.—*By* G. W. P.

CHAPTER IX.

EMERY WHEELS AND GRINDSTONES.

Emery Wheels.

I have polishing wheels in daily use, and put the emery on them with good glue. The way I employ the glue is as follows: I heat it to the proper degree, and then with a brush I cover from six to eight inches of the wheel with it. Then I put the emery on the covered part, and with a roller run over it so as to pass the emery down into the glue. I then apply the glue for another six or eight inches and repeat the same operation. I keep on in this manner until I get around the wheel. I then lay it away for twenty-four hours to dry, after which time it is ready for use.

In making emery wheels, nothing but the best glue is satisfactory for use. Poor glue is worse than nothing. Care must always be taken to keep oil and grease of all kinds from getting on the wheel. I have had some trouble with wheels of this general character, but I have always found the fault to be poor glue or oil that squirted from the shafting on the wheel. I make it a rule always to wash and clean the wheels in warm water when I find them greasy, and then let them dry, and put the emery on anew as above described. By following this plan I have always met with good results. No glue, however good, will hold emery or other parts together when the surfaces to which it is applied are oily or greasy.—*By* H. R. H.

Making an Emery Wheel.

It will not pay to put emery on wooden wheels because it flies off in pieces. I know this from experience. It is better to use felt that is made for the purpose. I use felt about 4 inches wide and 1 inch thick. I make a wooden wheel of about 12 inches diameter and 4 inches face and nail the felt on it with shingle nails at intervals of 1½ inches. I then drive the nails half way through the felt by means of a punch, spread glue over the felt and roll the wheel in emery. This makes a good wheel for finishing off.—*By* "SHOVELS."

How to Make Small Polishing or Grinding Wheels.

The general method of making small polishing or grinding wheels is to glue together pieces of wood, making a rough wheel, which, when dry, is put upon a spindle or mandrel and turned to the required shape. The periphery is covered with leather, coated with glue and rolled in emery until a considerable portion adheres to the glue-covered surface.

Wheels of this character will wear but a short

time before the coating process must be repeated to form a new abrasive surface. They can scarcely be called grinding-wheels, and are more properly termed polishing wheels, and are used but very little except to produce a polished or finished surface. What are termed grinding-wheels, or " hard-wheels," are formed of emery in combination with some plastic mass that is preserved in moulds, in course of time becoming very hard like a grindstone.

If the mechanic desires a small grinding-wheel of this character, and cannot readily obtain one, he can make a very good substitute himself. To do this, procure a block of brass or cast iron, in which make a recess of the same diameter, but a little deeper than the desired thickness of the wheel. Make a hole centrally to the diameter of the recess and extending through the block, corresponding in size to the spindle on which the wheel is to be used. In this hole fit a strong bolt with one end threaded and a stout head on the other end. On the threaded end fit a nut. Make a thick washer that will fit pretty tight on the bolt, and at the same time fill the recess in the block. Make a follower of the same size that will fit in the same manner.

The materials for the wheels are glue and good emery. Make the glue thin, as for use on wood, and thicken with emery, and keep hot to be worked. When ready to make the wheels, oil the recess or mould as well as the washer and follower. This will prevent the hot mass from adhering to these parts. Put the washer at the bottom of the mould. Insert the bolt in the hole with the head at the bottom side of the block. Put in the hot glue and emery, well mixed together, spread it evenly in the mould, almost filling it. Put the follower on the bolt, letting it enter the mould and rest upon the glue and emery ; then put on the nut and screw it down tight with a wrench. The mass is compressed according to the force employed.

If the wheel be small and thin it will cool and harden in a few minutes so that it can be removed. Take off the nut and follower and drive out the bolt, and if the recess be properly made a blow with a hammer on the bottom of the block will expel the wheel and washer.

In place of a recess cut in a block of metal, a ring may be used, care being taken to place it so that the bolt will be central, to insure equal radius on all sides.

Oiling the parts prevents the glue and emery from sticking. The washer put in the bottom of the mould facilitates the removal of the soft wheel, and also tends to prevent it from injury while being removed. The wheels must be dried in a warm place before being used, and must be kept away from moisture.

Above the size of two or three inches it would be hardly advisable to attempt making this kind of wheel.

Common shellac may be used in place of glue, but the objections to its employment are the greater cost, difficulty to mix with emery, and it is also more difficult to put in the mould. It has the advantage over the glue and emery wheel, inasmuch as it is proof against moisture or water. For a small, cheap wheel, and one that can be readily made, the one made of glue and emery is preferable.—*By* W. B.

Making an Emery Wheel.

Having a few articles to polish I thought I would make an emery wheel. After turning my truck and fastening it to the arbor I tried several times to glue the leather to the truck or wheel and failed. The splice was what bothered me most. Looking

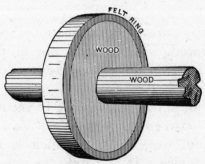

Fig. 226—Making an Emery Wheel.

around for a way out of this difficulty, I came across an old pair of woolen or felt boots such as are worn by loggers. I took the leg of one of these boots, cut off a ring the width of my truck, glued it on the truck and turned it off as well as I could. I held a hot iron over it until it was very smooth, and then covered it with glue. I next heated emery as hot as I thought necessary, spread it on a board and rolled the truck in it and pounded it in. When it was dry I gave it another coat and then another. Three coats are enough, at least they were sufficient for the wheel I am using. A glance at the accompanying engraving, Fig. 226, will give anyone a fair idea of how the job should be done.—*By* H. A. SEAVEY.

Something About Grindstones and Grinding Tools.

In the matter of the average grindstone, its use and misuse, I would state that the result of my observation and experience is :

First—It is too small in diameter. Second—It is too broad-faced. Third—It is not properly speeded. Fourth—It is not properly cared for. Fifth—It is not properly used.

Stones should be narrow-faced to secure a greater proportion between that which is worn from its surface by useful work and that which is removed by the truing device. It is patent to every practical mechanic that the portion of a stone most in use is a very narrow line at each corner, and the reason for this is plain when we consider that after a tool is once properly shaped the workman will endeavor to

confine his grinding to the top or cutting-face of the
tool, leaving the sides and clearance angles intact, if
possible, and to do this, keeping in mind the desired
cutting-lip, he must have recourse to the corners to
secure the proper inclination of the tool for that result. So it comes about that the corners are rapidly
worn rounding.

It is a matter of experience that the faster a stone
runs the faster it does its work and the longer it remains in working shape. But they are weak, and if
run too rapidly, have an uncomfortable habit of disintegrating themselves. Water has to be used for
the two-fold purpose of keeping the tools cool, and
the stone clean and free from glaze, but water has a
decided tendency to disassociate itself from a stone
that capers around too lively. So we are compelled
to reduce the speed to the fastest possible, compatible with safety and freedom from a shower bath.
Now, of all the inconsistencies that exist in modern
machine-shop practice, I think that the running of
the average grindstone is the most pronounced, because it has not the adjunct of a variable speed due
to the losses of diameter.

In regard to the choice, care and use of a stone, I
would discourse as follows : The desiderata in the
selection of a stone are, that it should cut fast,
should not glaze, and should remain true. To secure the cutting and anti-glazing qualities—for they
are associated—a stone should be close and sharp-

grained, and not too firmly cemented or hard. It must be just soft enough to slowly abrade under the mark ; such abrasion constantly brings new cutting points into prominence, and prevents the lodgment of the abraded particles of steel upon the stone, which would finally result in glazing. For the proper maintenance of its truth, it is essential that the stone be homogeneous, as uneven hardness *must* result in uneven wear. The condition of homogeneity is one that cannot exist in a natural stone, but ought reasonably to be expected in an artificial one, and I believe that the grindstone of the future will be manufactured—not quarried.

To get the best results from a stone filling the above requirements, it should be hung in a substantial frame, properly balanced, supplied with *clean* water, never allowed to stand immersed, because that softens locally and thus throws it out of balance. Therefore, I say that the average stone is not properly cared for and used, because these conditions for well-being are rarely met.

For ordinary tool-grinding, I would recommend that the "front" side of the stone be used, not because better work can be done there ; but because it can usually be done there faster ; and that it be fitted with an adjustable narrow-edged rest, used close to the stone, and extending around the sides toward the center about two inches. Such a rest enables one to incline his tool in any possible direction, and hold it firmly with adequate pressure, while running small risk of the dreaded " dig."

In all sorts of tool-grinding, my experience tells me that the cutting edge of a tool should *always* be toward the approaching side of the stone or wheel. —BEN ADRIANCE, *in American Machinist.*

Hanging a Grindstone.

To hang a grindstone on its axle so as to keep it from wabbling from side to side requires great skill. The hole should be at least three-eighths or one-half inch larger than the axle and both axle and hole square. Then make double wedges for each of the four sides of the square, all alike and thin enough so that one wedge from each side will reach clear through the hole. Drive the wedges from each side. If the hole through the stone is true the wedges will tighten the stone true. If the hole is not at right angles to the plane of the stone it must be made so or the wedge must be altered in the taper to meet the irregularity of the hole.

Device for Fastening a Grindstone.

The device, a sketch of which I send you herewith, is very simple and effective for fastening a grindstone. The illustration, Fig. 227, shows the method so well that only a brief description appears to be necessary. Almost any mechanic will see at a glance that the tightening of the screws or bolts (either can be used, according to the size of the

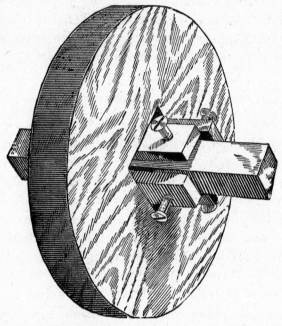

Fig. 227—Device for Fastening a Grindstone, as described by " H. G. S."

grindstone), as shown in the engraving, cannot fail to hold the stone securely upon the shaft.—*By* H. G. S.

Note.—It was not thought necessary to show the device of our correspondent attached to the grindstone frame, because that is a simple matter which probably every blacksmith or wheelwright understands thoroughly. The stone can be set true by

loosening or tightening the opposite screws or bolts.
—Ed.

Mounting a Grindstone.

I send you some illustrations representing a convenient method of mounting a grindstone. The

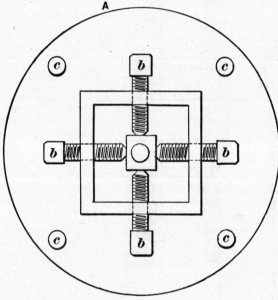

Fig. 228—Mounting a Grindstone. End View of the Mounting Flange.

casting will cost about 50 cents for a 30-inch stone. Anyone can make the pattern and core box. *A* in Fig. 228 of the engraving annexed, is a cast-iron flange, *b b b b* are set-screws tapped into the flange and impinging on the square bar, which is turned up

with gudgeons, and will constitute the axis of the
grindstone.   Top holes corresponding to those

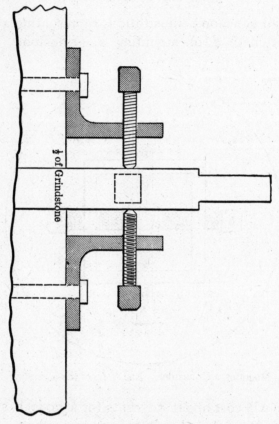

Fig. 229—Sectional View of the Flange.

marked *C* in the flange are drilled through the stone
and a flange like *A* is bolted to each side of the

stone.   Fig. 229 is a sectional view of the flange.
By slacking and setting the screws *b* the stone can
be made true to a hair.—*By* J. H. S.

How to Make a Polishing Machine.

An emery wheel is a good thing for every smith
to have about his shop, for burnishing axles, chisels,
knives, and a thousand things that should be kept
bright.   But owing to the high price of wheels,
together with the fact that few shops have any steam
or water power to run them, but very few are used.

Now any smith can get up a rig for polishing that
will answer every purpose and cost very little.   First
make a driving wheel, as shown in the accompanying
illustration, Fig. 230, 2½ feet in diameter by 4 to 6
inches in thickness.   It can be made with arms, or
solid, by nailing together several thicknesses of
boards.   Hang it in a frame as you would a grindstone.   Put upon one end of the crank a balance
wheel of not less than 50 lbs. weight and attach the
other end to the foot piece by a rod ; or, what is
better, a piece of hard wood, which will not wear on
the crank.   Bolt two pieces of hardwood board, 4 x
8 and 1 inch in thickness, upon the inside of the
frame.   Cut a slot at the wide end to go astride of
the crank ; also, one at the narrow end to receive the
spindle of the emery wheel.   The emery wheel
should be some 10 or 12 inches in diameter, by 3
inches in thickness, with a small pulley bolted upon

one side for the belt. Now, put on the belt, apply the foot power, and turn the emery wheel as true as possible with a sharp tool. Then cover it with sole leather. The leather should be well soaked in hot

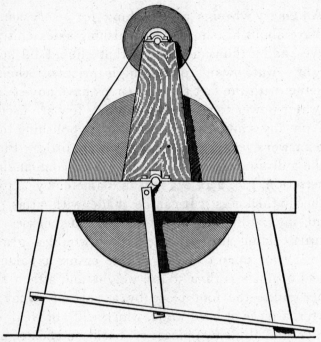

Fig. 230—A Polishing Machine.

water and pegged on wet; one row of pegs at the edges, one inch apart, will be sufficient. After the leather is put on, fix a rest and true it again as before.

To emery the wheel, make a box 2½ feet long

and a little wider than the wheel, in which to put the emery. After putting on a coat of thin glue with a brush, roll the wheel in the box and the coating is done at once. It should stand a few hours before using. Whenever the wheel gets smooth and doesn't cut, apply another coating as before. After several coatings have been put on the old emery should be removed, which can be done by soaking in hot water and scraping with a knife or piece of glass. It is a good thing to have two wheels, one for coarse and the other for fine emery. I have a rig which I made in this way ten years ago and it works like a charm. The expense of running it is next to nothing : try it and you will not be without one.—*By* W. H. BALL.

END OF VOL. II.

INDEX.

VOLUME III.

CONTENTS.

PREFACE.

In Vol. III. the subject of tools is continued in the first and second chapters, after which the volume is devoted chiefly to a description of a great variety of jobs of work. This volume is, therefore, in many respects, the most valuable thus far of the series, as it shows how the improved tools described in Vols. I. and II. can be used practically.

Vol. IV. will continue the topic of jobs of work and complete the series.

CHAPTER I.

BLACKSMITH TOOLS.

THEIR PRESERVATION.

In continuing the construction of blacksmith's tools from Vol. II. some general directions for their care and preservation will not be out of order, as even the best tools soon become useless if they are not well cared for. The following valuable hints on their preservation will be appreciated by every mechanic who has a desire to make his tools last as long as possible, and who wishes to have them always in good condition :

WOODEN PARTS.—The wooden parts of tools, such as stocks of planes and the handles of chisels, are often made to have a nice appearance by French polishing, but this adds nothing to their durability. A much better plan is to let them soak in linseed oil for a week and rub them with a cloth for a few minutes every day for a week or two. This produces a beautiful surface and exerts a solidifying and preservative action on the wood.

IRON PARTS.—*Rust Preventatives*—1. Caoutchouc oil is said to have proved efficient in preventing rust, and it has been used by the German army. It only requires to be spread with a piece of flannel in a very thin layer over the metallic surface and allowed to dry up. Such a coating will afford security against all atmospheric influences and will not show any cracks under the microscope after a year's standing. To remove it, the article has simply to be treated with caoutchouc oil again and washed after twelve to twenty-four hours.

2. A solution of India rubber in benzine has been used for years as a coating for steel, iron and lead, and has been found a simple means of keeping them from oxidizing. It can be easily applied with a brush and as easily rubbed off. It should be made about the consistency of cream.

3. All steel articles can be perfectly preserved from rust by putting a lump of freshly-burnt lime in the drawer or case in which they are kept. If the things are to be moved, as a gun in its case, for instance, put the lime in a muslin bag. This is especially valuable for specimens of iron when fractured, for in a moderately dry place the lime will not need renewing for many years, as it is capable of absorbing a large amount of moisture. Articles in use should be placed in a box

nearly filled with thoroughly slaked lime. Before using them rub well with a woolen rag.

4. The following mixture forms an excellent brown coating for preserving iron and steel from rust: Dissolve two parts crystallized iron of chloride, two of antimony of chloride and one of tannin in four of water, and apply with sponge or rag and let dry. Then another coat of paint is applied, and again another, if necessary, until the color becomes as dark as desired. When dry it is washed with water, allowed to dry again and the surface polished with boiled linseed oil. The antimony chloride must be as nearly neutral as possible.

5. To keep tools from rusting, take one-half ounce camphor, dissolve in one pound melted lard; take off the scum and mix in as much fine black lead (graphite) as will give it an iron color. Clean the tools and smear with this mixture. After twenty-four hours rub clean with a soft linen cloth. The tools will keep clean for months under ordinary circumstances.

6. Put one quart freshly slaked lime, one-half pound washing soda and one-half pound soft soap in a bucket, and sufficient water to cover the articles; put in the tools as soon as possible after use, and wipe them next morning, or let them remain until wanted.

7. Soft soap, with half its weight in pearlash, one ounce of mixture in one gallon of boiling water, is in everyday use in most engineers' shops in the drip-cans used for turning long articles bright in wrought-iron and steel. The work, though constantly moist, does

not rust, and bright nuts are immersed in it for days, till wanted, and retain their polish.

8. Melt slowly together six or eight ounces of lard to one ounce of resin, stirring until cool; when it is semi-fluid it is ready for use. If too thick it may be further let down by coal oil or benzine. Rubbed on bright surfaces ever so thinly, it preserves the polish effectually and may readily be rubbed off.

9. To protect metal from oxidation, polished iron or steel, for instance, it is requisite to exclude air and moisture from the actual metallic surface; therefore, polished tools are usually kept in wrappings of oil-cloth and brown paper, and thus protected they will preserve a spotless face for an unlimited time. When these metals come to be of necessity exposed, in being converted to use, it is necessary to protect them by means of some permanent dressing, and boiled linseed oil, which forms a lasting covering as it dries on, is one of the best preservatives, if not the best. But in order to give it body, it should be thickened by the addition of some pigment, and the very best, because the most congenial of pigments, is the ground oxide of the same metal, or, in plain words, rusted iron reduced to an impalpable powder, for the dressing of iron and steel, which thus forms the pigment of oxide paint.

10. Slake a piece of quicklime with just enough water to crumble in a covered pot, and while hot add tallow to it, and work into a paste, and use this to cover over bright work; it can be easily wiped off.

11. Olmstead's varnish is made by melting two ounces of resin in one pound of fresh, sweet lard, melting the resin first and then adding the lard and mixing thoroughly. This is applied to the metal, which should be warm, if possible, and perfectly clean; it is afterward rubbed off. This has been well proved and tested for many years and is particularly well suited for Danish and Russian oil surfaces, which a slight rust is apt to injure very seriously.

Rust Removers.—1. Cover the metal with sweet oil, well rubbed in, and allow to stand for forty-eight hours; smear with oil applied freely with a feather or with a piece of cotton wool after rubbing the steel. Then rub with unslaked lime reduced to as fine a powder as possible.

2. Immerse the article to be cleaned for a few minutes, until all the dirt and rust are taken off, in a strong solution of potassium cyanide, say about one-half ounce in a wineglass of water; take it out and clean it with a toothbrush with a paste composed of potassium cyanide, castile soap, whiting and water mixed into a paste of about the consistency of thick cream.

Bench Tools.

The tool shown in Fig. 1 is very convenient where there is much bundle iron to open, as it is made heavy enough so that any ordinary band can be easily cut with it at one blow. It has an eye large enough to admit a small sledge handle, and the handle should be made of good hickory with some surplus stock near the eye, as it is liable to get many bruises from careless handling

Fig. 1—Hatchet for Opening Bundle Iron.   Made of 1⅝ square Steel.

and mis-blows.   It should have a little less blunt edge than a cold chisel and be tempered a "pigeon-blue," if it is made of good steel; but if it is made of the fancy brands the temper must be a matter of experiment.

Fig. 2—Collaring Tool for Shouldering Down Round Iron.   Made of 1¼ square Steel.

For shouldering down round iron or steel to form a collar or neck, there is no tool that is any better than that shown in Fig. 2.   The concave should be of a size to fit the circumference of the bar to be worked or larger. The cut does not show the cutting part quite plainly; the edge all the way around the hollow should

Fig. 3—Light Flatter for Finishing Flat Iron. Made of 1¾ square Steel. Face 2½ inches square.

be flat on the inside and rounded out on the other side the same in section as Fig. 8.

Fig. 3 is simply a good handy size for a light flatter. It is about 5½ inches high. There is a great advantage in having a flatter light, not only because it is easier handled, but because it is more efficient. When a flatter is too heavy in proportion to the weight of the

Fig. 4—Round-cornered Set Hammer. Made of 1¾ square Steel.

sledge it absorbs more force than it gives down. It kicks. It spends its elasticity in reacting against the sledge, instead of letting the blow through it and de-

livering it to the work on the other side.   It is all nonsense to suppose that big flatters are best on big work.
It is not the work that governs the size of hand tools,
it is the power of the men who are to deliver the blows.

Fig. 5—Heavy Flatter for Straightening Cold Iron. Made of 2-inch
square Steel.

Fig. 4 is a tool that does not feel as good in the hand,
and is not quite as nice to handle.   It some way does
not hang as well as a flatter, but it is a tool that should

Fig. 6—Large Siding-Down Tool.   Made of 1½ square Steel.

be used in the formation of all inside corners, for it is a
deadly enemy to cold shuts and broken fibers, which
are the vital seeds of death in any work of iron in which
they find lodgment.

The heavy flatter, Fig. 5, for straightening cold iron, is made very strong, and a sledge must be used with it proportionate to its weight. There is not such partic-

Fig. 7—Small Siding-Down Fuller. Made of 1¼ square Steel.

ular need of activity, spring, and haste in getting a blow on cold iron as there is on hot, and blows that count in bending or straightening, are slow and solid. Steel rails are straightened under a press. If this flatter is

Fig. 8—Small Siding-Down Chisel. Made of 1¼ square Steel.

not made very strong it will soon crystallize and break in the weakest place across the eye.

The tools, Figs. 6, 7, 8, are for the purpose of siding-down work or making offsets, leaving good shoulders standing up, without having to use the backing ham-

mer. There is a tendency to make tools heavier than
is necessary simply to perform the office in blacksmithing that the jointer plane does in carpentering. The
carpenter jacks off the rough stock and then smooths
up with his " jointer." In dressing tools a heavy large-
faced hammer is used by some first-class tool dressers.
I have known them to call it the " jineter." The siding-down tool, Fig. 8, need not be wider than a man
can sink an eighth of an inch into hot iron or steel at a
blow. When the impression is deep enough, or if, in
crossing wide iron, it gets crooked sidewise, the wider
bitted one shown in Fig. 6 can be used to make the
impression straight and uniform, and afterwards the
siding-down fuller, Fig. 7, may be used. On a large
amount of work these tools suffice; but where there is
much wide iron to work it will pay to have a wide
fuller, the width, say two and one-half inches, of Fig. 6.

Blacksmith Tongs.

The blacksmith who will do his work well and
quickly, whether on carriage work or the ordinary
work of the country shop, must be well supplied with
tongs, and they well made. It is no uncommon
thing to see a man working at the forge depending
upon two or three tongs for holding all kinds of work.
If the jaw opens too wide it is heated and a blow from
the hammer closes it; if too narrow the same operation is gone through to open it; this makeshift business costs dear, and brands the workman as a botch.

A complete list of tongs for one man might not be a complete list for another, as some workmen are particular as regards specialties, but an assortment that comprises those that should be on every bench consists of two pairs of tongs for ⅛-inch iron, two pairs for ¼-inch iron, two pairs for ⅜-inch iron, two pairs for ½-inch iron, and one pair for each succeeding one-eighth of an inch up to 1¼ inches and above that a pair for each succeeding quarter inch up to the limit of size.

Blacksmiths, as a rule, prefer to make their own tongs. For these they should use Lowmoor or Burden's "best." Drill all holes, instead of punching, and be careful to see that the face of the jaws are parallel when closed to the required size ; jagging or otherwise roughing the face of the jaw is an unnecessary operation, for if the tongs work easily and true, as they should, they will hold the iron without extra pressure. If the jaws wobble or twist the fault is at the joint and should be corrected. The blacksmith who stands all day at the forge working with poor tongs will find, when night comes, the hand that held the tongs is much more wearied than the one that held the hammer.

How to Make a Pair of Common Tongs.

I will describe my method of making a pair of common tongs, which is so simple that any blacksmith can follow it. I take a piece of ½ x 1¼ inch iron, 14 inches long, and draw down the ends as shown in Fig. 9.

Fig. 10 shows a side view. Then split as shown in Fig. 11 and draw the handles to the proper shape. Punch the holes, rivet, and the tongs are completed

How to Make a Pair of Common Tongs. Fig. 9—Shape to which " J. M. W." would Draw the Iron.

and can be shaped to suit your own notion.—*By* J. M. W.

Tools for Farrier Work.

Fig. 12 shows a shoe-spreader. To make it take ¾ or ⅞-inch square Norway iron, shoulder and turn down as shown at *A* and *B*. Fig. 13 shows a side

Fig. 10—Side View of Fig. 9.

view of *B* of Fig. 12. For *C* use three-fourths rod with thread up to the jaw *A* and riveted through it. File notches in points so that they will not slip.

Fig. 11—How the Iron is Split.

This tool is very useful and can be used to spread a shoe that has been on two or three weeks, or when only one side is nailed. *D*, of Fig. 12, is marked in inches, so that one can tell the exact distance the shoe has been spread.

Fig. 14 shows a farrier's pick for removing dirt and

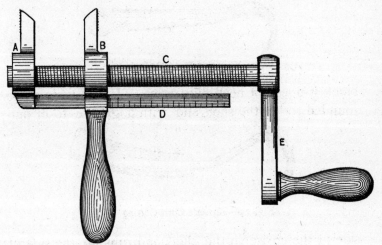

Fig. 12—Shoe Spreader Complete.

gravel. It is made of ½-inch steel and has a hole in the end that it may be hung on box.

Fig. 15 is a farrier's corn-cutting tool. It is made of

Fig. 13—Side View of *B*, Fig. 12.

¼-inch round steel and has the point ground to a sharp diamond tip. It is worth its weight in gold to any horseshoer. The handle is that of a farrier's broken knife.

As every blacksmith is acquainted with the clinch

Fig. 14—Farrier's Pick.

block it does not need illustrating. I have mine made rounded to fit the shoe and with a groove to fit out-

Fig. 15—Farrier's Corn-Cutting Tool.

side of the crease in the shoe, and runs up the side of the shoe, the idea being to hold nails that are sunk too deep for corn block.

Fig. 16—Handy Tongs for Handling Wagon Tires.

Fig. 16 shows a pair of fire-tongs made like the ordinary fire-tongs but having the handles bent four or five inches above the jaws. These tongs are to be used in cases where it is desirable to keep the hands away from the fire. Especially are they handy to use in handling wagon tires.

Fig. 17 shows tool used in sharpening toe calks.

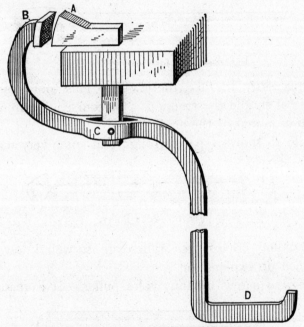

Fig. 17—Tool used in Sharpening Toe Calks.

The part *A* is made of tool steel, and is swaged same as an ordinary bottom swage, raised at *A*, and slightly rounded, so that the toe of the shoe will stand out. The part *B, C, D* is made of one by one-fourth inch iron, and to the shape shown in Fig. 17. It should be long enough so that the smith can keep his heel on the floor and place his toe on D.   No weights

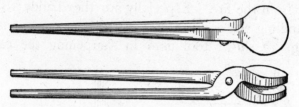

Fig. 18—Tongs for Holding Horseshoes.

are necessary to raise the jaw B.   This tool has the merit of simple construction.   Of course it is intended for use on end of the anvil.

Fig. 18 shows a pair of tongs that come very handy

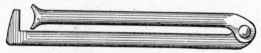

Fig. 19—Yoke Puller.

for holding horseshoes.   These are so well known as to need no explanation.

Fig. 19 shows a handy yoke puller.   It is made of

Fig. 20—Plow Clamp.

⅜-inch round iron and hinged and riveted.   One point is turned up to fit in hole of yoke, the other is rounded to fit clip, as seen in cut.

The plow clamp shown in Fig. 20 is made of 3-4 x

7-16 horseshoe bar, turned and welded. It fits the
share edgewise. The space is for 5-16 bolt, and bolts

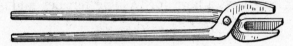

Fig. 21 —Tongs for Holding Cultivator Shovels.

to share with cam. The bolts keep the share from
springing when being sharpened.

Fig. 21 shows the tongs I use for holding cultivator

Fig. 22—Horn for Welding Ferrules.

shovels. The under piece has forks that pass on either
side of the casting on the shovel or ball tongue. The

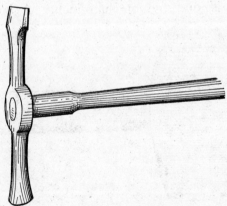

Fig. 23—Light Riveting Hammer.

upper jaw is similar to that of ordinary tongs, except
that it is a little shorter than the forks. The

handles are bent a little so that the ball tong point stands nearly straight.

Fig. 22 shows a horn for welding ferrules and small

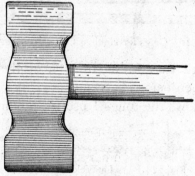

Fig. 24—Light Plow Hammer.

bands, also for rounding the same. It is made to fit anvil and is one and one-half inches at bottom and

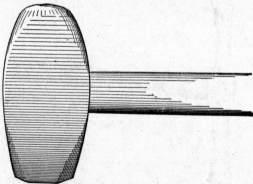

Fig. 25—Turning Hammer.

tapers to a point. The length of horn is eight inches.

Fig. 23 shows a light riveting hammer. It is made

of five-eighths steel. Draw and make like ordinary hammer, except that the handle should be very light

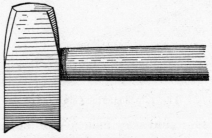

Fig. 26—Round Chisel.

and elastic. This hammer is very handy in riveting light castings, light welds, etc.

A plow hammer is seen in Fig. 24. It weighs two pounds, and has the pene set lengthwise with the handle and enables the smith to weld in throat of plow.

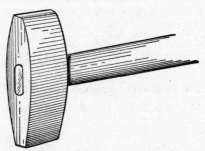

Fig. 27—Hoop Set-Hammer.

Fig. 25 shows a turning hammer with two faces; one is made rounding for concaving shoes, it is also handy for drawing any kind of iron. It weighs from two and one-half to three pounds.

Fig. 26 shows a round chisel. It is made similar to the ordinary handle chisel, except that it is made round

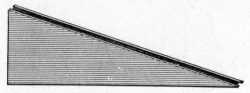

Fig. 28--Singletree Clip Wedge.

in two sizes—1 and 1¾ inches—for cutting holes in wagon plates, roller plates, etc.

A hoop set-hammer is seen in Fig. 27. It is made

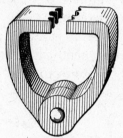

Fig. 29—Vise Tool for Holding Short Bolts.

lighter than the ordinary set-hammer and tapering on sides only. It is used for band hoops or any kind of band drawing.

Fig. 30—Heavy Wrench or Bending Tool.

Fig. 28 shows a singletree clip wedge. It is made of ½ x 2-inch iron with a groove on bevel side, and is used to draw tight single and doubletree clips. In putting them on, slip on clip, drive in wedge tight

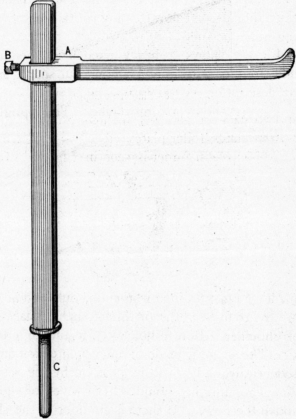

Fig. 31—Forge Crane.

down, and cool, drive out the wedge and the job is done.

Fig. 29 shows a vise tool for holding short bolts.

It is made of 2 x 2½-inch iron bent square, and has three grooves cut for three sizes of bolts, shouldered off, and riveted at bottom. This tool is handy in cutting threads on plow, or any short bolts, or in working nuts on same.

Fig. 30 shows a heavy wrench or bending tool. This tool is so common among our smiths as to need no description.

Fig. 31 shows a forge crane. The upright post is

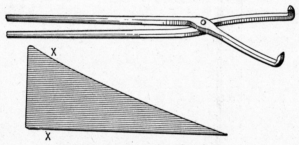

Fig. 32—Tongs for Plowshare.

made of 1½ x ½-inch iron and shouldered at *C*; draw around to five-eighths or three-fourths; place collar on at shoulder. Bore a hole close to the forge to receive *C*. The crane is made of inch square iron and should slide easily, and is held in position by the set-screw at *B*. The upright should extend seven or eight inches above the forge. If there is no floor in the shop then drive or set a post level with the dirt. Blacksmiths will find this to be a great labor-saving tool.

Fig. 32 shows a pair of handy tongs for plowshares. The jaws are made to fit top and bottom of share, being turned to fit the bevel as shown at $x\ x$ of share. These tongs are used in either welding or sharpening.

Fig. 33 shows a clip for making round clips. It is made to fit the anvil and can be made in any size. C

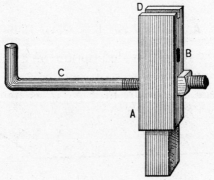

Fig. 33—Tool for Making Round Clips.

is the gauge, B the hole, and D the groove in top. Cut the iron to the right length for clip wanted, cut threads on both ends, heat and run through the hole B,

Fig. 34—Tool for Rounding Rivet Heads.

gauge by C, and bring the end over to D, tap down gently until true.

Fig. 34 shows a tool for rounding rivet heads. It is made of one-half inch steel shaped like a punch. Make a tool to the shape that you want the head of the rivet

to be when finished.   Heat the steel and place it in the
vise, then drive the special tool, or rivet head, into the
steel until it is sunk enough.   Then dress up and temper to a light blue.—*By* REX.

A Tool for Holding Plow Bolts.

I will try to give a description of a handy tool for
holding plow bolts.

The piece *A* shown in Fig. 35 is made of ⅜ or

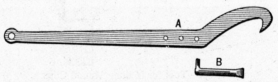

A Tool for Holding Plow Bolts.   Fig. 35 – Showing how the two Pieces
are made.

½-inch iron, and is about 20 inches long.   It has holes in
it into which the piece *B* can be inserted and moved
forward or backward so as to catch any bolt.   The

Fig. 36—Showing the Tool completed.

piece *B* is made of steel with a rounded end to fit in
the hole in *A*.   The other end is made like a cold
chisel in order to catch the bolt.   Fig. 36 represents
the tool ready for use.—*By* A. G. BUNSON.

Tongs for Holding Plow Points.

I have a pair of tongs for holding plow points while sharpening or laying, that are simple, easily made, and I like them far better than any other tongs for the purpose that I ever saw. I forged them from a one and a quarter inch square bar just like ordinary straight jawed tongs. The edges are about two inches long (not longer), quite heavy, with one-half inch handles. After they were finished I heated them and then caught them edgewise in the vise and bent them, just

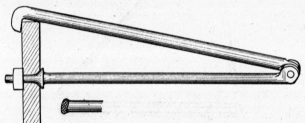

Fig. 37—Tool made by " H. H. K." for holding Plow Bolts.

at the rivet, to an angle of nearly forty-five degrees, and I find they never slip or work off, but answer every purpose.—*By* Earles J. Turner.

A Tool for Holding Plow Bolts.

A handy little tool which I use to prevent plow bolts from turning when the wrench is on the nut is shown in Fig. 37. The tool is one that will be appreciated by every smith who does plow work. It is made of ⅝-inch round iron, but having steel at one end which is cross-cut as shown in the illustration.—*By* H. H. K.

A Tool for Holding Slip-Shear Plows in Sharpening.

To make a tool for holding slip-shear plows in sharpening them, take ⅝-inch round iron, cut off two

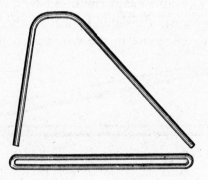

A Tool for holding Slip-Shear Plows in sharpening.   Fig. 38—Showing how the two Pieces are shaped,

pieces, making each 2½ feet long, and bend one in the middle and weld the ends as shown in Fig. 39, so that a plow bolt will fit in and slip along.   I then bend the other piece as shown in the cut, then weld the ends of this piece to those of the other, and the tool is finished as shown in Fig. 40.   In Fig. 41 the tool is shown fastened to a plowshare with plow bolts.   This tool will hold either right or left-hand plows.—*By* A. G. B.

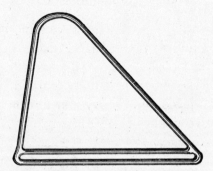

Fig. 39—Showing the Tool as finished.

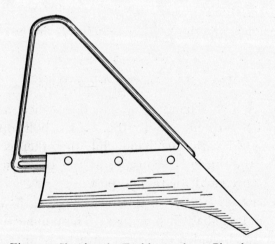

Fig. 40 —Showing the Tool fastened to a Plowshare.

Making a Plow Bolt Clamp.

To make a plow bolt clamp take a piece of steel 14 inches long, and 5⁄8-inch square ; make a two-pronged claw to fit the bolt-head on one end and draw the other to go into the wooden handle marked *A*, Fig. 41. Then draw a piece of 1¾ x ½ inch iron to an edge and bend two inches to a right angle at *B*. Punch a

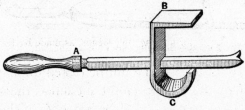

Fig. 41—A Plow-Bolt Clamp as made by G. " W. P ".

square hole to fit the steel, two inches from the bend.— *By* G. W. P.

Tongs for Holding Plow Bolts.

This is a very handy tool and one which no shop should be without. With this tool a bolt in the lay can be held with one hand while the other is free to remove the burr. I consider it the only successful tool ever invented for this purpose.

The jaw *A*, Fig. 42, is five inches in length, while *B* is four and one-half inches long. The point *C* is made of steel and welded to *B*, and must be tempered hard. It is made with a sharp point like a chisel or screw point. The handles are two feet long and of five-eighths inch iron. The jaws are of three-fourths inch square iron.

To remove a bolt from a plow-lay with this tool place the point *C* on the bolt head, and let the jaw *A* come in any convenient place on the other side of the lay, grip tightly and the bolt will be held tight while the nut

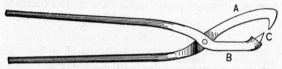

Fig. 42—Iron Tongs for holding Bolt Heads, as made by E. K. Wehry.

is being removed. If the nut be rusted on and hard to turn, then with a sharp chisel cut across the bolt head same as a screw head. Then place *C* in the cut and the bolt cannot turn. You will seldom have to do this.—*By* E. K. WEHRY.

How to Point a Plow.

My plan for pointing a plow is as follows : Make a pair of blacksmith's tongs, somewhat heavier than or-

Fig. 43—Pointing a Plow, as Done by "H. L. C." The Tongs.

dinary tongs, let one jaw be two inches and the other one five inches long. Make the long jaw very heavy and shaped as shown in Fig. 43 ; then take a piece of suitable steel and cut out a point the desired shape,

and, after shaping and filing the edges, place it on the
plow lay and clamp it with the tongs, as shown in Fig.
44; then take a light heat on the point and bend it
under, as shown by the dotted lines.   Make the point
of such a length that when bent under it will lap on
the original point from one to two inches.   Then take
a thin piece of soft iron and place it between the lap

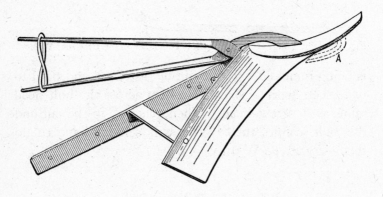

Fig. 44—Showing the Clamping and Bending Processes.

at *A* in Fig. 44—this is to make the point heavier and
to cause it to weld better—then take a welding heat
on the point, after which the tongs may be taken off
and the job finished up.   This plan is a great advantage over the old way of drilling the point and share,
and riveting the point to hold it in place while taking
the first heat.   It not only saves time and labor, but
it makes a stronger and neater job.—*By* H. L. C.

Hints for Plow Work.

Some of the plow manufacturers send out lays that are so badly welded that after being sharpened once or

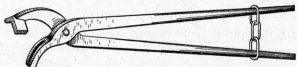

Hints for Plow Work. Fig. 45—Showing Tool used in sharpening Lays.

twice they fall away from the landside, and then the

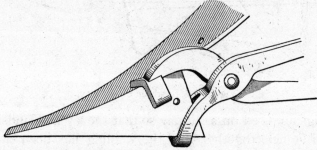

Fig. 46—Showing how the Tongs are used.

farmer blames the blacksmith. For the benefit of

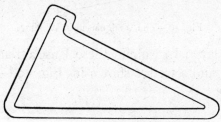

Fig. 47—The Triangle used in Welding.

smiths who have to handle such plows I give a few hints which may prove valuable. Fig. 45 represents

the tongs I use in sharpening lays when there is danger
that they will be loosened.   Fig. 46 shows how the

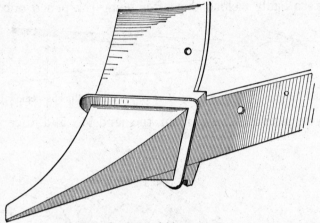

Fig. 48—A Landside or Bar Lay.

tongs are used on a slip lay so that the lay and landside
will be held together until the welding has been done
up to the tongs.   Fig. 48 represents a whole landside

Fig. 49—The Wedge used in Welding.

lay or bar lay.   In welding these I use a triangle shown
in Fig. 47 and a wedge shown in Fig. 49.—*By* G. W.
PREDMORE.

A Tool for Holding Plowshares.

A device invented by me for holding plowshares,
which I think is one of the best tools in use for

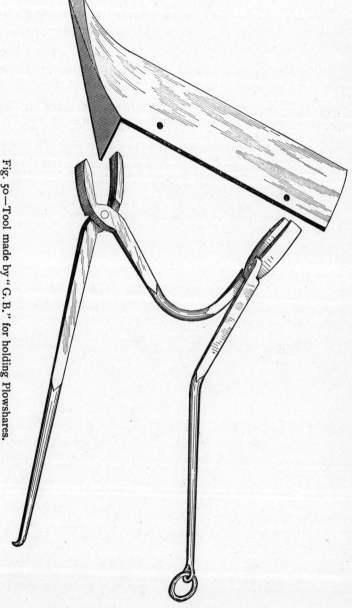

Fig. 50—Tool made by "G. B." for holding Plowshares.

holding plowshares when sharpening or pointing them, is shown by Fig. 50.   It consists of two pairs of tongs welded together, one holding the bar and the other holding the wing.   The tongs holding the wing should have round jaws.   When taking hold of the share the handles come together within three inches or so, and the ring on one of the handles is then slipped over the other.—*By* G. B.

CHAPTER II.

WRENCHES.

Forging Wrenches.

My way of making a wrench is as follows: For a 3-inch wrench take iron 1 x 2 for piece *A*, in Fig. 51

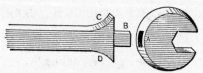

Fig. 51—Forging a Wrench.

(Fig. 52 shows it more plainly), and punch a hole at *A*

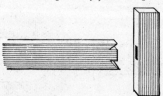

Fig. 52—How to Form the Ends as seen in Fig. 51.

to receive *B*, and take a weld, using the fuller at *C D*.

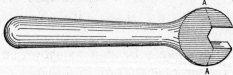

Fig. 53—Finished Wrench.

Fig. 53 shows the wrench complete. It should be very

strong at dotted lines *A A*, where the greatest strain comes.   Fig. 52 shows how to cut the end to form *C D*, in Fig. 51.   Fig. 54 shows how to make small wrenches.

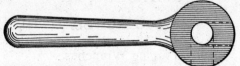

Fig. 54—Method of Making Small Wrenches.

Punch hole in the center and cut to any desired angle ; see dotted lines.—*By* SOUTHERN BLACKSMITH.

Making Wrenches.

My plan of forging a wrench is as follows : Take any piece of iron corresponding in size to the wrench

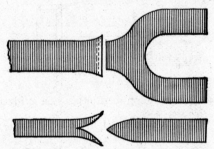

Fig. 55—"J. T. B.'s" Method of Making Wrenches.

it is desired to make.   Bend it as shown in Fig. 55. After welding, proceed to form into shape.   Any practical man, it seems to me, will admit the advantages of the plan shown in the sketch.—*By* J. T. B.

Curve for an S Wrench.

I inclose sketches of my way of curving an S wrench. I always make the curve so that the jaws run parallel

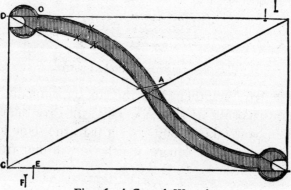

Fig. 56—A Curved Wrench.

with each other, as is shown in Figs. 56 and 57. Fig. 56 is a curved wrench, while Fig. 57 is a straight

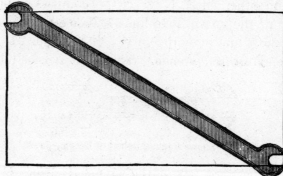

Fig. 57—A Straight Wrench.

wrench. Both of these wrenches will answer for the

same purpose. The only difference I can see is that Fig. 56 may suit one brother smith and Fig. 57 another. To make the bend in Fig. 56 proceed as follows: First mark the square space on a board to

Fig. 58—Shows Points to be Fullered.

the size required, then draw the lines diagonally from corner to corner as shown. This will give the center at *A*. Now take a compass, set it to the same length as the sides of the square, which we will find from *C*

Fig. 59—Shaping the Jaw.

to *D* on either side. Now set the compass point at *E* and draw the curve *X* to line *A*, then set the compass point on *F* and draw the curve *X X* to line *A*, which is one-half of the wrench. The point *E* is as far from

Fig. 60—Shows Faulty Method of Forging Jaws.

C as the head or jaw of the wrench is from *D* to *O*. The space between *E* and *F* is the same as the width of the wrench. With the other end of the wrench proceed the same as with the first end. By bending a wrench this way over the draft a true curve will be obtained from the center of the wrench.

Fig. 57, I think, explains itself. To make a wrench of this kind I proceed as follows : Fuller Fig. 58 at *A A*, forge and round *D* as *C* in Fig. 59 ; now get the center of *C* and punch the hole, letting the outside of the hole strike the center of *C*, as shown in cut. This gives us a strong corner at *X X*. Then split out as per dotted lines and finish. Never make a corner in a wrench as is the case at *X O* in Fig. 60, as it is more apt to break than when made rounding as shown in both Figs. 43 and 44. I always make these wrenches of spring or cast steel.—*By* Now & THEN.

Another Method of Making Wrenches.

My idea of the right way to make a wrench is to get at it in the way that takes the least labor, provided equally good results are obtained. I have two steel S

Fig. 61—First Step in Making Wrench.

wrenches in use. One is a 5-16 and ¼-inch, made from spring steel. This I have had in constant use for the last eight years. The other is a 5-16 and ⅜-inch, made from blistered steel, which I have used for the last seven years. Both are in good order still. I will try to describe my way of making a wrench of this description.

I take a piece of steel of the required dimensions

Fig. 62—Handle of Wrench Drawn Out.

and fuller it, as shown in Fig. 61. I then punch a hole, as is also shown in the same figure. I next draw out the handle, cut out from the hole, as in Fig. 62,

Fig. 63—The Finished Wrench.

then work up to shape and fuller. A wrench can be made very quickly in this manner and as strong as you please. It is shown finished by Fig. 63.—*By* W. I. G

An Adjustable Wrench.

My method of making an adjustable wrench is as follows :

I take a piece of soft steel and forge out the jaw as shown in Fig. 64. I next take a piece of ¾-inch gas pipe, cut a thread on one end, then cut a thread in the jaw, and screw the jaw and pipe together tightly. I

then heat gently, and when hot flatten down the jaw
and about two-thirds of the pipe. I then heat again,
having a drift key ready to fit the hole tightly. I drive

Fig. 64—Showing how the Jaw of an Adjustable Wrench is forged.

the key in, taking care not to split the pipe by making
the corners round, and then heat the other end and
finish the handles to shape. I next make a ring of

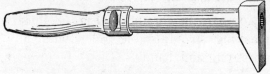

Fig. 65—Showing how the Handle and Nut are made.

1½ inches by 3-16-inch iron to go on the handle
where the hole for the nut is to be made. The ring is
heated and pressed on red hot. When it is in place

Fig. 66—Showing how the other Piece is forged.

and fitted down closely it will never become loose.
The hole in which the nut works is made by drilling
two holes close together and filing them out. The
tool then looks as shown in Fig. 65. I next forge out

the other part, as shown in Fig. 66, of one solid piece.
I cut a thread in the end, make a round nut, finish off,

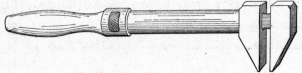

Fig. 67—The Wrench completed.

put together, and have the strong, neat-looking wrench
shown completed in Fig. 67.

Making an Adjustable Wrench.

The accompanying engraving, Fig. 68, illustrates my
way of making an adjustable 2-inch wrench, which I
find very strong and handy. First, I forge one jaw

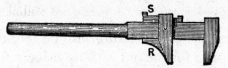

Fig. 68—Making an Adjustable Wrench

and the handle solid in the usual way; then I forge the
the sliding jaw *J* with a web at *R*, and slip behind it a
gib-wedge *S*, which will tighten or loosen the jaw
quickly and effectively.—*By* A. M. B.

Forging a Bolt, a Nut and a Wrench.

I would like to give my way of forging a bolt, a nut
and a wrench.

A great many blacksmiths take exception to making a bolt by welding the head on. I claim that if the bolt is upset as it should be, and the head properly

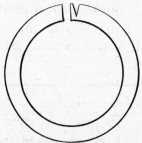

Fig. 69—Preparing to Weld a Bolt Head.

welded on, it is as good, if not better, than a solid head.

The way I do such a piece of work is this: Before welding the collar on to form the head, I upset my

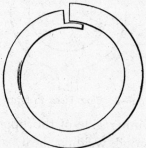

Fig. 70—Formation of Lip.

iron to the extent that the diameter of the bolt under the head will be the same or a little larger than the original diameter of the bolt. If this is done properly the bolt will not be weakened at all. Should you fail to upset the iron sufficiently, however, and let the collar cut into the bolt, then, of course, you will have a weak spot at the inner end of the head.

If I have a large nut to forge I do it in this way : I take iron of the required size and bend it around a mandrel, leaving the ends about an inch apart. Then,

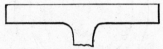

Fig. 71—Forging a Wrench.

with my chisel, I cut one end down about one-half the thickness of the iron, as shown in Fig. 69.

With a small fuller I draw out the part cut down, on the horn of the anvil, so as to form a lip, as shown in Fig. 70.

Drive the ends together so that the lip described will

Fig. 72—Bending Piece to form Jaw.

be close to the inner side of the opposite end of the ring. Take a good welding heat, and weld on the mandrel, and you will have a good, sound nut, with a smooth inner surface. If you undertake to forge a nut by jumping the ends together you will not make a good job of it; at least, that is my experience in such cases.

Now, in regard to a wrench. If I have a large wrench to forge, I pursue the following plan : Take a piece of iron the required width and thickness to draw out to the shape shown in Fig. 71.

Bend it as represented by Fig. 72 and scarf the part

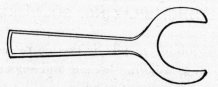

Fig. 73—The Wrench Complete.

A as for an ordinary weld. Then forge the handle and weld on and complete the wrench, as shown in Fig. 73. —*By* G. B. J.

CHAPTER III.

WELDING, BRAZING, SOLDERING.

The act of joining metals by the aid of heat is technically known as welding, brazing and soldering. The first is applied to iron and steel by heating the surfaces to be joined to a fusible state, then, by repeated blows, or by pressure, unite the particles and restore the whole to a condition similar to that existing before the metal was severed.

Brazing is the act of joining iron or composition metals by the use of brass heated to a fluid state in conjunction with the edges to be joined, and then allowed to cool slowly.

Soldering is the joining of metals of like or different kinds by another metal that fuses at a lower degree of heat than those which are joined, in which case the solder, only, is reduced to a fluid state. The degrees of heat, the condition of the surfaces, and the skill of the workmen, are all important factors.

The following tables will be found useful for reference :

Degrees Fah.

The greatest heat of a smith's forge (common) is.........2346
Welding heat of iron...................................1892

MELTING POINT OF METALS.

	Degrees Fah.
Brass.... 1900	
Copper..1996	
Lead.. ... 612	
Solder (common).................................. 4¯5	
" (plumber)................................. 360	
Tin................................. 442	
Zinc.. ... 680	
Lead 1, tin 1, bismuth 4....................... .. 201	
Lead 2, tin 3, bismuth 5........................... 212	

Solders.

Under this head is grouped compositions used for uniting metals, the proportions being by weight.

	Copper.	Lead.	Tin.	Bismuth.	Zinc.	Silver.	Gold.	Antimony.	Calcium.
Tin	..	75	25						
"	..	16	58	16	..	..	..	10	
" (melts at 360°)............	..	33	67						
Spelter (soft).................	50	..	..	..	50				
" (hard).................	67	..	..	..	33				
Lead........................	..	67	33						
Steel......................	13	..	..	..	5	82			
Brass or copper..............	50	..	..	..	50				
Fine brass...................	47	..	..	..	47	6			
Pewter (soft).................	..	45	33	22					
" "	..	25	50	25					
Gold.......................	4	..	..	..	..	7	89		
" (hard)	66	..	..	..	34				
" (soft)..................	..	34	66	..	..	80			
Silver (hard).................	20	..	..	..	..	67	..	..	21
Pewter......................	..	20	40	40					
Iron	66	..	..	33	..	..	..	1	
Copper......................	53	..	47						

FUSIBLE COMPOUNDS.

	Copper.	Lead.	Tin.	Bismuth.	Zinc.	Silver.	Gold.	Antimony.	Cadmum.
Rose's (fusing at 200°)	..	25	25	50					
" (fusing at less than 200°)	..	33.3	..	33.4	33.3				
Fusing at 150° to 160°	..	25	12	50	..	..	..	..	20

FLUXES FOR SOLDERING OR WELDING.

Metal.	Flux.
Iron	Borax.
Tinned iron	Resin.
Copper or brass	Sal-ammoniac.
Zinc	Chloride of zinc.
Lead	Tallow or resin.
Lead and tin pipes	Resin and sweet oil.

Theory of Welding.

The generally received theory of welding is that it is merely pressing the molecules of metal into contact, or, rather, into such proximity as they have in the other parts of the bar. Up to this point there can hardly be any difference of opinion, but here uncertainty begins.

What impairs or prevents welding? Is it merely the interposition of foreign substances between the molecules of iron and any other substance which will enter into molecular relations or vibrations with iron? Is it merely the mechanical preventing of contact between molecules by the interposition of such substances? This theory is based on such facts as the following: 1. Not only iron, but steel, has been so perfectly united that the seam could not be discovered, and that the strength was as great as it was at any point, by accurately planing and thoroughly smoothing and cleaning the surfaces, binding the two pieces together, subjecting them to a welding heat and pressing them together by a very few hammer blows. But when a thin film of oxide of iron was placed between similar smooth surfaces, a weld could not be effected.

2. Heterogeneous steel scrap, having a much larger variation in composition than these irons have, when placed in a box composed of wrought-iron side and end pieces laid together, is (on a commercial scale) heated to the high temperature which the wrought iron will stand, and then rolled into bars which are more homogeneous than ordinary wrought iron. The wrought iron box so settles together, as the heat increases, that it nearly excludes the oxidizing atmosphere of the furnace, and no film of oxide of iron is interposed between the surfaces. At the same time, the inclosed and more fusible steel is partially melted, so that the impurities are partly forced out and partly diffused throughout the mass by the rolling.

The other theory is that the molecular motions of the iron are changed by the presence of certain impurities, such as copper and carbon, in such a manner that welding cannot occur or is greatly impaired. In favor of this theory it may be claimed that, say, two per cent of copper will almost prevent a weld, while, if the interposition theory were true, this copper could only weaken the weld two per cent, as it could only cover two per cent of the surfaces of the molecules to be united. It is also stated that one per cent of carbon greatly impairs welding power, while the mere interposition of carbon should only reduce it one per cent.

On the other hand, it may be claimed that in the perfect welding due to the fusion of cast iron, the interposition of ten or even twenty per cent of impurities, such as carbon, silicon and copper, does not affect the strength of the mass as much as one or two per cent of carbon or copper affects the strength of a weld made at a plastic instead of a fluid heat. It is also true that high tool-steel, containing one and one-half per cent of carbon, is much stronger throughout its mass, all of which has been welded by fusion, than it would be if it had less carbon. Hence copper and carbon cannot impair the welding power of iron in any greater degree than by their interposition, provided the welding has the benefit of that *perfect mobility* which is due to fusion. The similar effect of partial fusion of steel in a wrought-iron box has already been mentioned. The inference is that imperfect welding is not the result of a change in molecular motions, due to impurities, but of imperfect mobility of the mass—of not giving the molecules a chance to get together.

Should it be suggested that the temperature of fusion, as compared with that of plasticity, may so change chemical affinities as to account for the different degrees of welding power, it may be answered that the temperature of fusion in one kind of iron is lower than that of plasticity in another, and that as the welding and melting points of iron are largely due to the carbon they contain, such an impurity as copper, for instance, ought, on this theory, to impair welding in some cases and not to affect it in others. This will be further referred to.

The next inference would be that by increasing temperature we chiefly improve the quality of welding. If temperature is increased to fusion, welding is practically perfect; if to plasticity and mobility of surfaces, welding should be nearly perfect.

Then how does it sometimes occur that the more irons are heated the worse they weld?

1. Not by reason of mere temperature; for a heat almost to dissociation will fuse wrought iron into a homogeneous mass.

2. Probably by reason of oxidation, which, in a smith's fire especially, necessarily increases as the temperature increases. Even in a gas furnace, a very hot flame is usually an oxidizing flame. The oxide of iron forms a dividing film between the surfaces to be joined, while the slight interposition of the same oxide, when diffused throughout the mass by fusion or partial fusion, hardly affects welding. It is true that the contained slag, or the artificial flux, becomes more fluid as the temperature rises, and thus tends to wash away the

oxide from the surfaces; but inasmuch as any iron, with any welding flux, can be oxidized till it scintillates, the value of a high heat in liquefying the slag is more than balanced by its damage in burning the iron.

3. But it still remains to be explained why some irons weld at a higher temperature than others; notably, why irons high in carbon or in some other impurities can only be welded soundly by ordinary processes at low heats. It can only be said that these impurities, as far as we are aware, increase the fusibility of iron, and that in an oxidizing flame oxidation becomes more excessive as the point of fusion approaches. Welding demands a certain condition of plasticity of surface; if this condition is not reached, welding fails for want of contact due to excessive oxidation. The temperature of this certain condition of plasticity varies with all the different compositions of irons. Hence, while it may be true that heterogeneous irons, which have different welding points, cannot be soundly welded to one another in an oxidizing flame, it is not yet proved, nor is it probable, that homogeneous irons cannot be welded together, whatever their composition, even in an oxidizing flame. A collateral proof of this is that one smith can weld irons and steels which another smith cannot weld at all, by means of a skillful selection of fluxes and a nice variation of temperature.

To recapitulate : It is certain that perfect welds are made by means of perfect contact, due to fusion, and that nearly perfect welds are made by means of such contact as may be got by partial fusion in a non-oxidizing atmosphere, or by the mechanical fitting of surfaces, whatever the composition of the iron may be, within all known limits. While high temperature is thus the first cause of that mobility which promotes welding, it is also the cause, in an oxidizing atmosphere, of that "burning" which injures both the weld and the iron. Hence, welding in an oxidizing atmosphere must be done at a heat which gives a compromise between imperfect contact, due to want of mobility on the one hand, and imperfect contact, due to oxidation on the other hand. This heat varies with each different composition of irons. It varies because these compositions change the fusing points of irons, and hence their points of excessive oxidation. Hence, while ingredients, such as carbon, phosphorus, copper, etc., positively do not prevent welding under fusion, or in a non-oxidizing atmosphere, it is probable that they impair it in an oxidizing atmosphere, not directly, but only by changing the susceptibility of the iron to oxidation.

The obvious conclusions are : First, That any wrought iron, of whatever ordinary composition, may be welded to itself in an oxidizing atmosphere at a certain temperature, which may differ very largely from that one which is vaguely known as a "welding heat;" second, That in a non-oxidizing atmosphere, heterogeneous irons, however impure, may be soundly welded at indefinitely high temperature.—*From the report of the United States Board appointed to test iron and steel.*

Welds and Welding.

A weld to be sound, must, like everything else, be made according to sound common sense.

The theory of welding is simple enough, and only requires a little thought to make it easy to put into practice.

If the iron is got to a proper welding heat all through its mass, there are just three things to guard against in order to get a sound job. (1) the air ; (2) scale ; and (3) dirt. Referring to the first, suppose the pieces are scarfed as in Fig. 74 (which is a form that beginners are very likely to make), and when the two pieces are put together, they will meet all around the edges. This simply forms a hollow pocket enclosing a certain amount of air, and also whatever amount of dirt or scale there may be upon the surfaces, and a sound weld becomes impossible. Another fault that a beginner is apt to fall into, is to make the scarf too short, as in Fig. 75, where it is seen that blows upon the top piece, *A*, will act to force it down, sliding it off the lower pieces.

We might simply lap the pieces as in Fig. 76, but the result will be an indentation in the corners *C* and *D*, and we may forge the lap down to the thickness of the base without getting this indentation out.

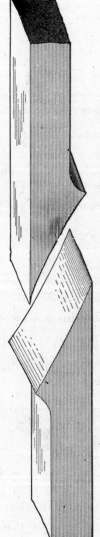

Welds and Welding.　Fig. 74—Showing a Faulty Method of Welding.

Fig. 75—Showing an Instance in which the Scarf is too Short.

A similar indentation would be formed at *C* if lapping the end of a bar, as in Fig. 77. Furthermore,

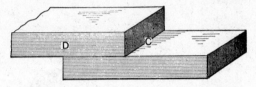

Fig. 76—Showing how the Pieces might be Lapped.

the surfaces coming together flat are apt to enclose scale, hence such a weld can only be made either in small pieces, when the dirt has not to travel far to be

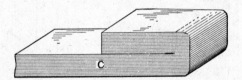

Fig. 77—Showing another Case in which an Indentation would be Formed.

worked out, or else in pieces that are heavily forged at a high heat so as to drive out the impurities.

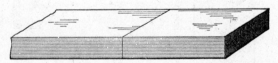

Fig. 78—Show'ng how the Weld may be effected by butting the Ends.

The ends of two pieces, if short, may be butted as in Fig. 78, the bar being struck endwise, but this is a poor weld. In the first place only a short piece can be welded soundly in this way, because the force of the

Fig. 79—Showing a good Method of Shaping the Surfaces.

blow is lost in traveling through the weak and springy bar.

The secret of a sound weld (assuming of course that

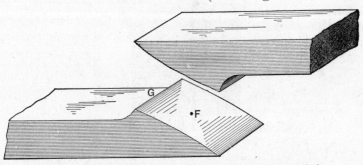

Fig. 80—Showing how the Scarf may be rounded endwise.

the iron is properly heated) lies in letting the surfaces meet at first in the middle of the weld, so that as they come together they will squeeze out the cinder, etc., and in hammering quickly.

But there are several ways of shaping the surfaces so that they will squeeze out the foreign matter : thus we may round the surfaces crosswise, as in Fig. 79, in which case a piece of scale, say at *E*, would be squeezed out, moving across the scarf as the surfaces were hammered together.   Or we may round the scarf endwise,

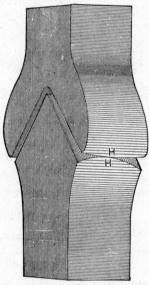

Fig. 81—Showing a Weld in which both Surfaces are rounded.

as in Fig. 80, but in this case the piece of foreign matter shown at *F*, would have to move up to *G* before it would be repelled.

A compromise between these two plans is to round the surfaces slightly both ways, and this is the best plan all things considered.

As soon as the heat is taken from the fire, it should be quickly cleaned with a brush the instant before putting the weld together. The first hammer blows

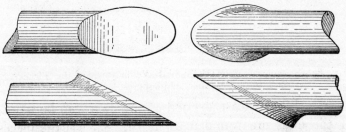

Fig. 82—Showing how round Bars are scarfed before being Welded.

should be comparatively light and follow in quick succession.

To weld up the outer edges of the scarf and make a sightly job, a second heat should be taken if the job is large enough to require it.

An excellent example of a weld is shown in Fig. 81 where both surfaces are rounded so as to meet at *H*. In this case dirt, etc., will squeeze out sidewise as the

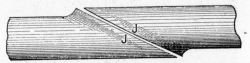

Fig. 83—Showing how the Bars come together.

welds come together. In all these examples the air, as well as foreign matters, is effectually excluded.

We now come to the welding of round bars, which are scarfed as shown in Fig. 82, so that when the two pieces are put together, as in Fig. 83, the surfaces bunch at *J* in the middle of the weld, and foreign matter is squeezed out all around the edges.

If the pieces to be welded are short and light, the

Fig. 84—Showing a good Method of Welding when the Pieces are short and light.

butt weld is at least as good as any that can be made, if the ends are rounded as in Fig. 84. If the pieces

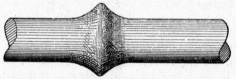

Fig. 85—Showing the Appearance of the Weld before the Swaging.

are heavy and can be stood up endwise under a steam-hammer, it is still the best weld, but if the pieces are

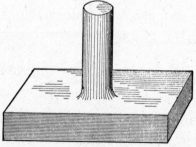

Fig. 86 – Showing a Weld in which a Stem is welded to a Block.

long, too much of the force of the hammer blow is lost in traveling from the end of the bar to the weld.

The appearance of the weld when made and before swaging down, is shown in Fig. 85, and it is seen that

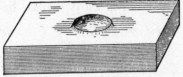

Fig. 87—Showing how the Block is cupped.

the air and any dirt that may be present, is always excluded as the pieces come together.

Fig. 88—Showing how the Stem is shaped.

We now come to another class of weld where a stem is to be welded to a block, as in Fig. 86. The block

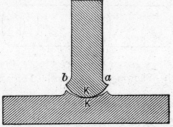

Fig. 89—Showing how the Stem and Block are put together.

is cupped as in Fig. 87, and the stem rounded and cut back as in Fig. 88, so that when the two are put together, they will meet at the point *K*, Fig. 89. The dirt and air will be forced upwards and outwards in this case. If the stem is short it may be driven home

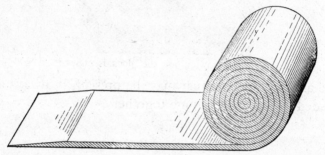

Fig. 90—Showing how the Heads of Swages and Fullers are made.

on the end, and fullered afterwards at the shoulders *a* and *b*, but if long the fullering only can be used to make the weld, and a good shoulder at *a*, *b*, is necessary.

In the days when blacksmiths made their own swages and fullers (and this is done in most first-class

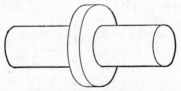

Fig. 91—Showing a Collar welded on a Stem.

blacksmith shops at the present day in England), the heads of swages and fullers were made by rolling up a band of iron, as in Fig. 90. In this case the first hammering must be given to the outside and not to the ends of the roll, the end of the band being turned down so that it will roll down in the center. With good iron and first-class workmanship, this makes a good tool.

An example of welding a collar on a stem is shown in

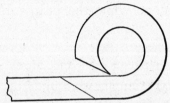

Fig. 92—The Collar ready to be cut.

Figs. 91, 92, 93 and 94. Fig. 91 is the finished iron ; Fig. 93 the stem jumped up in the middle to receive the collar ; Fig. 92 the collar ready to be cut off the

Fig. 93—The Stem prepared to receive the Collar.

bar ; and Fig. 94 the collar placed on the stem, ready for the welding heat.

Unless the stem is jumped up as shown, and the

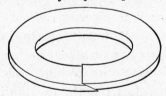

Fig. 94—The Collar ready for the Welding Heat.

collar well beaded on it, there will be a depression or crack at the corners. Very thin washers are welded with the scarf made, as in Fig. 94, and made to over-lap well.

In any weld, dispatch and decision are necessary elements as soon as the heat has left the fire, the thinking being mainly done while the heat is in the fire.—*By* JOSHUA ROSE.

Welding Iron and Steel.

A series of experiments were undertaken by Prof. J. Bauschinger at the instance of an engineering firm. Similar experiments had been previously made at the Royal Technical Experimental Institute, at Berlin, and by Mr. W. Hupfield, at Prevali, which gave very different results, those at Berlin being very unfavorable, those at Prevali very favorable, as regarded the welding capacity of steel. Prof. Bauschinger recapitulates the main results of these tests before describing those made by himself. The test pieces were flat, round and square in sections, the largest being 3.149 by 1.181 inches. Each piece was swelled up on the anvil, when hot, 0.196 to 0.392 inch, and after heating to the proper degree, the two pieces were laid on each other and welded together by hand or steam hammer.

In the chief experiment the steam hammer was employed. Every piece after welding was tested in the usual way for tensile strength, the limit of elasticity, contraction, extension and ultimate strength being determined, the same quantities having been measured for pieces of exactly similar quality, section and length, but without a weld. The limit of elasticity in both steel and iron is nearly always reduced by welding, and this is, without exception, the case as regards the extension ; the contraction of welded is less than that of unwelded pieces when the fracture takes place in the welded portion. The general conclusions arrived at are that for steel the best welding temperature is just at the transition from a red to a white heat ; a quick fire and smart handling are necessary, as the pieces should not be long in the fire.—*Midland Industrial Gazette.*

Points About Welding.

To obtain a good sound weld, the following points should be observed :

The scarf should be sufficiently larger than the finished size to permit the weld to be full size after welding. The joint surface of the scarf should be slightly rounding, so that, when the two pieces are placed together to weld, there will be no air inclosed between them.

They should be heated in a clear fire of bright and not gaseous coal. Thick pieces should not be heated too quickly, or the interior metal will not be brought up to the required heat. They should be frequently turned in the fire, to insure uniformity of temperature, and be made as hot as possible without burning them.

They should be withdrawn from the fire occasionally and sprinkled with sand, which serves to exclude the air from the surface and prevent oxidation, and at the same time cools the outer surface and thin edges, giving the interior metal and thicker parts time to become heated all through.

When the pieces are placed upon the anvil to weld them, they should be quickly cleaned with either a wire brush or a piece of wood made ragged by having been hammered. The scarfs should be placed to well overlap each other, and should receive light and quickly succeeding blows at first, and heavier ones afterward.

As soon as the pieces are firmly joined, the hammer blows should be delivered with a view to close the edges of the scarf, so that the joint of the weld shall not show when the job is finished.

Welding Cast Steel Forks.

I desire to say with regard to springs, cast steel forks and other similar articles of this general kind, also with regard to spring-tempering in a country job shop, that I have been troubled in the same manner as other smiths. I have tried the same remedies that they have tried.

When I learned my trade I had occasion to mend forks, and had experience on other difficult jobs of the same kind. Not knowing how to hold the parts until I could weld them, I commenced by scarfing and punching, and then welding, also by riveting the parts together. This was not satisfactory, as they frequent ly broke at the riveting holes. I tried every device that I could think of, splitting and locking them together, sometimes putting in a good piece of iron or steel as the occasion required. At last I tried scarfing and lapping the ends together, and holding them together with forge tongs at one end of the lap until I could get a light borax heat to fasten the other end of the lap together. Then, by taking another good heat and welding the whole together, and drawing to their proper size and shape, I obtained a satisfactory job. Of late years I have found it a very great help in welding to keep some clean filings, and to use them between the laps. The filings cause the parts to unite very much more readily.—*By* A. H.

Welding Steel.

I have seen men try to weld steel in a fire where it would be impossible to weld iron; they prepared the pieces for welding skillfully, but they did not use borax in the best manner. They used it at times too freely, at other times not enough, using at the wrong time and not applying it on the right place. I will give my way of welding steel:

See that your fire is clean from all cinders and ashes, then take selected coal and build a fire so large that you will not have to add any unburnt coal while welding. Then prepare the steel which you wish to weld by upsetting both pieces near the ends, scarfing carefully, and when you can do it, punch a hole and rivet them to-gether.   Let the lap be from half an inch to an inch, ac-cording to the size of steel you wish to weld, and have the lap fit as snug as possible all around.   Place the steel in the fire and heat to a low cherry, then apply borax to the part which is to be heated.   Apply the borax not only on the lap but also next to the lap, but do not use too much.   Then bring to a welding heat and strike quickly with light blows.—*By* G. K.

Welding Steel Tires.

Bessemer steel tires may be welded almost as readily as iron with the ordinary borax flux.   Crucible steel tires require a little more coal and a lower heat.—*By* OLD TIRE.

Welding Tires.

No. 1. My plan in welding small tires, which works well, is to put good iron filings between the scarfs and avoid heating hot enough to burn.   This plan will work fully as well on old tires as on new, and especially when you do not happen to get a weld the first heat.—*By* H. A. S.

No. 2. Open the unwelded lap of your tire and insert (if your tire is steel) steel filings (if iron, iron filings); close the lap, add your flux and weld at a fluxing heat. —*By* TIRE SETTER.

No. 3. Our way of welding tires is to cut the bar three times and three-fourths the thickness of the iron longer than the wheel measures. We then upset it thoroughly enough to get a good heavy scarf. In welding, instead of laying one end on top of the other, we put the ends of the scarf band together, place them in the fire, and bring them to a nearly white heat, then put them on the anvil and lap the welds, then sand and put in the fire. By so doing we have the top lap hot and get a weld thoroughly, without burning off any at the bottom in so doing. We get a nice, smooth weld, and the outside corners are flush and full, and show no canker spots on the tire. This method is specially for heavy tires, but it is a good plan for all sizes of tire.—*By* B. & S.

Do Not Burn Your Tires in Welding.

I would like to call the attention of carriage smiths to a great evil that many fall into when welding tires, viz.: of allowing the tire to burn on each side of the lap while taking a heat.

Many smiths fail to take into consideration the fact that it is impossible to heat a piece of iron two inches thick, especially when it is formed of two pieces of equal thickness, one placed upon the other, as quickly as one of half the thickness could be heated, and hence, having lapped their tire, the full force of the blast is thrown upon it.

As a result, the tire is put into service with a weakness at each side of the weld, caused by being burnt while the weld was being brought to the required heat. That there is not a particle of need for such carelessness every smith knows, no matter how poor a workman he may be.

Give your weld a gradual heat; attend to it yourself and not throw the responsibility upon your helper. Have a clean lot of coal and under all a clean fire, and you will never lose a good customer by having him discover a rotten place in his tire, causing it to break when far from a forge.—*By* J. P. B.

Welding Axles.

I will try to describe the way we weld axles in our shop. We first get the length between the collars and then cut them off, allowing on each piece three-fourths of an inch on each back axle for waste in welding. If we wish to make a hole in the front axle, the piece is made one and one-half inches longer. The piece is then heated to near a white heat and the end is pounded down on the anvil, until an end is made which is of good size, and also as flat as possible. Notches about half an inch apart, and a quarter of an inch deep are then made in the end with a chisel. The two pieces are then put in the fire with the ends together, and when they get to a welding heat, one man takes one piece, a second man takes the other, and the ends are put together true, and one of the men strikes a few blows on them with a wooden maul. Then the joint is hammered with the pene of a small hammer, set in a long handle. The piece is kept in the fire, with the bellows blowing all the time, so as to get a good welding heat. Finally five or six heavy blows are given with the maul, and the piece is then taken out and hammered on the anvil to the size desired. If it is a nut axle, the nuts should be put on to avoid battering the threads.—*By* J. K.

Welding Cast Iron.

The question is often asked, Can cast iron be welded to wrought iron? I will give you what I call a practical job: To weld cast iron sleigh shoes that have been broken when not worn out, I take the ends that I wish to weld together, cover them with borax, heat them to a nice mellow heat, lay them on a plain table of iron, so that when put together they will be straight on the runner. One of the pieces is held by a pin at the end; then I press the other end against it sufficiently to upset it a little, rubbing it with the face of my hammer until it is smooth. Allow it to cool and the job is done. I broke one in pieces and put it together, marking the welds with a prick punch, so as to know where it broke. It has been on a sled carrying heavy logs two and a half months, and has stood well on bare ground.—*By* FRANK E. NILES.

Cast iron can be welded by heating it nearly to a melting point in a clear fire, free from dirt, and hammering very lightly. But this job requires practice and great care. A plow point can be made as hard as glass by heating nearly to a welding degree, then having a piece of cast iron hot enough to run over the joint and finally putting it in the slack tub.—*By* M. T.

Welding Malleable Iron.

Malleable cast iron may be welded together, or welded to steel or iron by the same process as you would weld two pieces of steel. Experiment first with two useless pieces. A few attempts will enable you to become an expert at the business.—*By* H. S.

Welding Malleable Cast Iron Plates.

You can weld malleable cast iron plates by riveting them together and using a flux of powdered borax and Norwegian or crucible steel filings, equal parts. Let the first blows with your hammer be tender ones.—*By* DANDY.

Welding Cast and Wrought Iron.

It is no trick, but is easily done, if you know how. When a cast iron point is worn out, I break it off square and weld on another from one-quarter to one-half pound weight, making the point as good, and many say better than it was when new, from the fact that it sticks to the ground better.—*By* A. D.

Welding Steel to a Cast Iron Plow Point.

My experience in welding cast steel to a cast iron plowshare has not been very much, although I succeeded in welding the first one I tried. My plan is first to heat the metal hot enough so that you can spall it off (on the end you wish to weld to) as square as possible. Then make the steel point square also, to fit the metal as neatly as possible. Take heats on both with borax, heating the steel as high as possible without burning it, and the metal also as hot as can be heated without crumbling. Then jump them together, applying the hammer smartly, but not too hard, on the steel end for several seconds. When you see the heat getting off, stop hammering, and lay the job away where it will not be disturbed until perfectly cool. You may then heat the point and sharpen or dress it to suit yourself. Do not strike on the weld, as you will knock it loose. Let it wear smooth. I do not exactly call this welding, but rather cementing the parts together, which I think is the only way that it can be done.

Welding Plow Lays to Landsides.

I have found a good method for welding steel plow lays to landsides. It is as follows: After heating to a good bright red, put on plenty of wax, and when the wax is melted, put on dust from the anvil block, then take a good mellow heat and keep the top part of the lay from burning by throwing on sand. Use a light hammer and a stiff pair of tongs large enough to squeeze the lay and landside together and hold them solid while using the hammer. My object in using a light hammer, is to enable me to strike quicker and light blows, such blows being less likely to make the steel fly to pieces.—*By* C. N. LION.

To Weld Cast Steel.

Take rock saltpetre, one-quarter pound, dissolve in one-quarter pound oil of vitriol, and add it to one gallon of water. After scraping the steel, get it hot and quench in the liquid, and then heat, and it will weld like iron. Better than borax.—*By* A. D. S.

To Weld Steel Plate to Iron Plate.

To weld a steel plate to an iron plate, I would say, for a common fire you want a stout porter bar on your iron plate first—something to hold on to. If you have much of that work to do, you want a grate-fire and to use anthracite coal on the grate, with soft coal on top. A grate gives more heating area and uniformity of heat in the fire surrounding the work. The opening to the fire can be made with a piece of iron about fourteen inches long, bent at each end about three inches, and arched in the center. Place this in front and fill the center with cut wood, and cover all with soft coal ; let the wood burn out, and you have a good fire with a clear entrance, like a furnace. Feed the fire till mellow, and insert the iron and steel together till red-hot, Have fluxing matter in a pepper-pot, and dust over the surface to be welded. Let it vitrify. Now place the steel and iron together, draw heat, flux at pleasure with a spoon five feet long. When the spoon sticks, the heat is nearly up. Draw, when ready. A single "drop" blow will weld, or ten blows with a heavy sledge. Cut off and finish. A charcoal, coke, or anthracite muffle-furnace is a fine thing for this work. If you are a good mechanic this will help you out. If inexperienced, you will be apt to get the fidgets, and had better let the job out.—*By* S. C.

A Practical Method of Welding Broken Spring Plates.

First heat, upset and scarf the broken ends of the "plate" (leaf we generally call it), just the same as if it were iron, and to be welded by separate sand heats; then place them in a clean fire and take separate borax heats ; heat as high as the safety of the steel will permit. I then let my helper take out one end while I take the other, and when "stuck" come on to it lively with the sledge, and nine times out of ten I get a good sound weld at the first heat. Care must be taken to leave it as "heavy" at the weld as the original size of the steel.

The loss of length can generally be made good—if a "bed leaf"—by letting out, or taking up (as the case requires) the scroll at the end of the bottom "bed leaf," or, if it is an outside or intermediate leaf, the little loss in length is of no importance.

Now the welded end of the "leaf" must be tempered —a spring temper—or, no matter how perfect the weld, it will not prove a good job. Tempering properly is the most important feature of the job, and a majority of smiths overlook it altogether.

My plan is (and it is the most satisfactory and practical that I have heard of), after hardening, draw to temper by passing forth and back over a clear fire until it will ignite a pine stick when rubbed over the surface. If it is high steel, heat until the pine will blaze when rubbed hard. If it is low steel, let it sparkle only ; lay down to cool.

Since I have learned through my own observation the importance of tempering, I seldom weld a spring which fails to stand as well as its fellows.—*By* HAND HAMMER.

Welding Buggy Springs.

A good way of welding buggy springs is to first scarf the broken ends down to a sharp edge, and then split them back three-quarters of an inch. Then turn one point up, the other down, as shown by Fig.

95, having ready two thin strips of iron made pretty wide in the middle, and nearly to a point at the ends. Drive the ends together, and then drive the

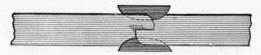

Fig. 95—Welding a Buggy Spring, as done by John Zeck.

strips of iron in between the laps from each edge, as shown in the accompanying illustration. The inside edges of the strips of iron should be made thin and sharp.

I have welded springs in this way for many years, and it has never failed. The iron insures a perfect weld, and also makes up for the waste in working.— *By* JOHN ZECK.

Welding Springs.

NO. 1. It is a fact that steel will waste away some by heating at a welding heat, and if it wastes away it will be thinner at each side of the weld than elsewhere, and more liable to break at the weak point, and more especially after taking two welding heats to one weld, and if not upset it must necessarily leave an imperfect job.

I hardly see the necessity of taking more than one heat on a weld, provided it is well executed. I will give you my method. I first upset each piece of steel, weld and chamfer nicely; then punch a small hole in each piece for a rivet. I then, at the lap, slip between the two pieces a thin piece of steel with a rivet hole in it, and rivet the three together. Each end of the middle piece is hammered sharp, and the amount must be about what will waste away in welding. Put each end of the weld alternately in the vise and hammer down the opposite end so that it lies close to the bar, then borax and weld down with one heat. Let the helper come down lively. It is not necessary to let the under point of lap come in contact with the anvil while welding, but it may extend beyond till a few blows are struck on the opposite end, and the reason is that the anvil would, perhaps, cool the thin part below the welding point.

The main object is to get a good weld, and one heat is far better than more for this purpose. Perhaps I had better add, make as short a lap as possible.—*By* FRANK.

No. 2. I don't believe that a substantial weld can be made by the use of rivets.

I upset each piece of steel one inch back from the end, leaving the end its natural size. I then split the end twice and chamfer nicely; turn the center point of the split end down and the two outside points up. After preparing both pieces in this way, I slip them together and fit them both edgewise and flatwise, forming a lock and making the lap as short as possible. I try to make my weld at one heat.—*By* A. F.

No. 3. I will state how I have had the best results. Heat to a cherry red, chamfer the ends short, split into three equal parts about five-eighths up. Bend the two outsides one way and the center the other way of both pieces to be welded. Then put together and close the laps down, making them so they will stick together; then take a light borax heat and work quick. Do not hammer too much on one side, but turn in quick succession to prevent from chilling the scarf. This way of lapping springs requires no upsetting of the ends, and is the best way I ever saw to put springs together to get a heat. Hammer all the temper in that you give them.—*By* G. W. W.

No. 4. My way of welding springs is as follows:

I first upset the ends, then draw them down to a point, as shown by Fig. 96, then punch, rivet, and weld in a fire, taking care to first burn all gas out of the coal. I apply borax freely, heat slowly and make the ham-

Fig. 96—Welding Springs as done by "C. D."

mer blows quick and hard. To ensure success I usually take two welding heats. There will be no thin edges in the laps, and if care is taken to avoid burning the steel, the job will be one that can be warranted every time.—*By* C. D.

No. 5. My plan for welding springs is to upset to

about the original thickness. Make a neat short scarf and weld the same as two pieces of common iron. I never split or punch holes. I find I can get a far better job otherwise. If, by accident, I should not get a good job, and some part is inclined to scale up and not weld thoroughly, I take a small piece of rusty hoop-iron and insert under the scale and take a second heat. There is a good deal in having a good, clean, well-charred fire in work of this kind.—*By* A. M. B.

No. 6. Will you permit me to say a few words about welding springs? Some years ago I was told by Mr. Frank Wright, of Waltham, Mass., to try one and pin or rivet it. I did so, and have employed that method ever since. If the end is split twice and the pieces locked together it is impossible to get a good solid weld, as it is necessary to weld the ends down, three on each side, and to weld the split lengthwise. Several years since I welded the main and second leaf of a 1¾-inch 5-leaf spring for the hind end of a wagon that was calculated to carry from 1,200 to 1,700 pounds, three trips per week. I know that it was used for three years after the time I repaired it, and it never broke or settled. By riveting the pieces together I find I can weld seven out of every ten and do the work so perfect that the line of weld cannot be discovered.— *By* L.

No. 7. My plan is to scarf each end and to punch a hole in about a half inch from the end, as at *A*, Fig. 97, then get a thin piece of iron and punch a hole in it, and lay it between the laps and put a rivet through it and the laps as at *C*, and then weld with borax. By welding in this way I never met with a failure, and I consider it better than splitting the ends.—*By* W. B.

No. 8. I will tell you my way of welding springs. I do not upset the pieces, but chamfer them off fine, and punch two holes in each end, giving them about one and a half or two inches lap ; rivet them firmly together, to prevent any possible displacement. Then I give them as low a borax heat as practicable to make a weld on one side near the chamfer of one end, and fol-

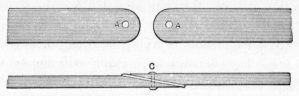

Fig. 97—Welding Springs by the Method of " W. B."

low by a like operation on the other side ; the drawing of the weld to the natural thickness and breadth of the leaf will fetch it also to its proper length. The loss of the metal in such a weld is not noticeable. I seldom ever have any springs come back after such treatment. My objection to heating the pieces separately is that it requires too strong heat to make them stick. Though the steel may not be actually burnt, it will lose much of its strength by overheating, and will be very liable to break at the same place again, though the weld may be perfect. Besides, it requires more quick and accurate movements to bring the pieces to-gether on the anvil. I give no other temper than a gentle hammering, which I keep up a little while after the leaf is black.—*By* O. D.

Welding and Tempering Springs—Mending a Spring with a Broken Ear.

My way of welding springs may be of some interest. I first upset, then scarf a little, next split, care being taken not to split too deep, or you are liable to get too long a lap. Next turn the ends each way and scarf with the ball of the hammer, letting them flatten towards the center of the spring. Next warm them up, let the helper take one end and then press together. Beat down the laps and the welding will be almost as strong as if rivets had been used, without the disadvantage of rivets. In heating to weld, most of us make the mistake of heating too fast. The best results are got by heating as slowly as possible. I want the helper in welding to strike quickly and not too hard, as heavy blows are apt to drive the laps over to one side.

In tempering I take a light hammer, and hammer the spring until it is nearly cold. A spring treated in this manner will stand as much as any weld.

To repair a spring with the ears broken off, close up. I upset it, then take a piece of good iron, scarf the edges, cut half way through it, lap the ends over the end of the spring, weld it up in good shape, turn the ears on a bottom fuller; finish the end; and after filing it up, it cannot be distinguished from the other without close inspection.—*By* OBSERVER.

How to Mend Wagon Springs.

To mend a wagon spring so that it will be as strong and durable as before it was broken is no easy job, and nine-tenths of the smiths will tell you it cannot be done. I am of the opinion that if the work is carefully and properly done, nineteen-twentieths of the springs mended will do good service. There are various ways of mending a spring, and every smith has a way of doing the work peculiar to himself, and, of course, thinks his method is the best.

I first upset the pieces to be mended to such a thickness that when the work is done, there shall be no waste near the weld, the place where mended springs usually break. I next carry the pieces about one inch back, punch and put in a small rivet to keep them in place while taking a welding heat. After obtaining a good borax heat I make the weld. If it is not perfect I take a second or a third borax heat until a solid and uniform weld is obtained. Much depends upon uniformity of the weld. If the spring is left thickest at the weld a break near it is liable to occur, especially in the case of an inside leaf. The weld should be so perfect and uniform that it cannot be easily seen where the spring was welded. I never attempt to put any temper into a spring, any more than what can be done by hammering.—*By* W. H. B.

Welding Springs.

My way of welding a spring is as follows: I chamfer the ends and split them, as shown by Fig. 98, then place them together as closely and as firmly as possible. I then give the spring a bright red heat, next roll it in calcined borax, then place it in a clean fire of coal well coked, and blow very lightly, frequently baring the splice to see that the heat is strictly in the right place and to also make sure that it does not burn. The blower can hardly be worked too slowly, for the steel must have time to heat all through alike. It will take

Fig. 98—Welding Springs as Done by a "Jersey Blacksmith."

longer when the blower crank is moved so slowly, but the time is not wasted. Near the end of the heat I keep the steel bared nearly all the time, watching it closely and just before it comes to a sparkle I cover it and give it three or four good heavy blasts, then take it out and strike as rapidly as possible upon the several lips or splices. Before drawing it down to its usual size I see that all the welds are perfect, and if they are not I go over the work again paying particular attention to the unwelded parts. I hammer until it is black for the temper. No spring I ever welded in this way has been broken, and I warrant everyone if the steel is good.—*By* JERSEY BLACKSMITH.

How to Weld a Buggy Spring.

I will give my way of welding a spring which I learned from a tramp six years ago, have used ever since, and have never had a spring break at the weld. I first lay the broken ends of the springs together to get the length, which I take with the dividers set to small center punch marks in each piece. I then place

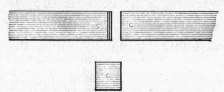

Fig. 99- Shows how "D. F. K." Welds a Buggy Spring.

the two ends in a clean fire and hammer back a short scarf, thus giving the necessary upset.

I next punch a small hole close to the ends of each piece to receive the rivet that holds them together while welding.

I next take a piece of good Norway iron, flatten to one-sixteenth of an inch in thickness, the width of the spring, and just long enough to pass the laps when placed between them, punch a hole in this for the rivet, place this piece between the laps and rivet them together; heat enough to melt borax. Lift out of the fire and soak well with borax (for you can't use too much on this kind of weld), replace in fire and heat carefully. Weld with rapid light blows, sticking both sides safely before striking on the edge; finish with as few heats as possible to make a solid job. Allow it to cool slowly, as it will require no other tempering. Fig. 99 shows how the spring and piece of Norway iron are prepared for welding. By following these directions you can weld a spring that you can safely warrant.—*By* D. F. K.

Welding Shaft Irons for Buggies.

My method of welding such work as shaft irons for buggies is as follows: Fig. 100 shows the two pieces

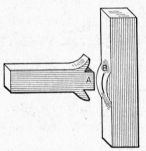

Welding Shaft Irons for Buggies. Fig. 100--Showing the Two Pieces Prepared for Welding.

prepared for the welding process, and Fig. 101 shows the finished iron. The projection on Fig. 101 is split to receive the tongue *A* on Fig. 100. I get the rounded corners at *C* (where the strain comes) by widening at *A*, and by the projection at *B*. Fig. 102 shows the old way of forming the weld, the fault in this being that there are no rounded corners as at *C* in Fig. 101,

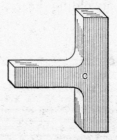

Fig. 101—The Finished Iron.

and therefore the iron is apt to break in the neck.—*By* SOUTHERN BLACKSMITH.

Welding a Collar on Round Iron.

My method of welding a collar on round iron is as follows: Suppose the bar to be one inch in diameter.

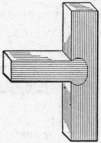

Fig. 102—Showing the Old Way of Forming the Weld.

The seat of the collar must be jumped one-eighth of an inch larger, as at *A* in Fig. 103. Leave the collar

C open one-quarter inch, and while the washer is cold and the bar red-hot, swage the collar on so that it will hold. Then take a welding heat. If the bar is not

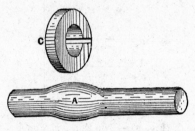

Welding a Collar on Round Iron, as Done by " J. R." Fig. 103—Showing the Bar Jumped at *A*, and the Collar *C*.

jumped the neck will shrink in as at *B* in Fig. 104, and will probably show a crack there.—*By* J. R.

Welding a Round Shaft.

I will describe my method of welding a round shaft. *A* and *B*, Fig. 105, represent the two pieces to be welded. I make one end of one piece the shape of a

Fig. 104—Showing the Point *B*, where the Neck will Shrink if the Bar
is not Jumped.

dot punch and one end of the other piece is counter-sunk to fit the punch shaped piece. I then place them in the fire together, as shown in the illustration, and weld them in the fire. After they are welded I take a good welding heat, lay the piece on the anvil and work the part smooth. This plan insures a good weld

Fig. 105—Welding a Round Shaft, by the Method of " H. H. L."

every time, no matter what may be the size or length of the rod. In welding it be sure to place it in the position shown in the illustration, and strike at both ends while heating.—*By* H. H. L.

Welding.

Here are some examples of heavy welding, such as jump welding long shafts, and scarf and swallow fork

Fig. 106.

welds for the same. In my opinion the jump weld is decidedly the best, if properly done, as it can be bent

Fig. 107.

after welding to a right angle without showing any sign of the weld,

To make a jump weld properly the ends should be rounded, as shown in Fig. 106, and, after being

Fig. 108.

brought to a welding heat with a good blast, drive them together with very light hammer blows, as a

Fig. 109.

heavy blow would cause them to bounce. As the welding proceeds employ heavier blows and the weld

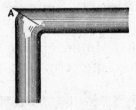

Fig. 110.

will drive up as in Fig. 107, after which the weld may be forged and swaged down. This weld will bend to a right angle, as shown in Fig. 108, without showing the scarf, whereas a scarf weld, such as shown in Fig. 109, would show, when bent, its scarf, as at *A*, in

Fig. 111.

Fig. 110, while a swallow fork weld, such as is shown in Fig. 111, when bent will show its scarf, as in Fig. 112. Only the jump weld, you will see, will stand

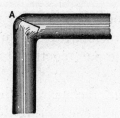

Fig. 112.

such bending and show a sound and complete weld.— *By* SOUTHERN BLACKSMITH.

Welding Shafts to an Exact Length.

An old blacksmith gives the following method of welding a shaft to an exact length, which he says he has used with unfailing success for many years.

Cut the ends of the two pieces to the exact length the shaft is to be when finished, leaving the ends quite square. Each end is then cut out as in Fig. 113, the length and depth of the piece cut out being equal in all cases to one-half the diameter of the shaft. The shoulder *A*, Fig. 113, is then thrown back with the

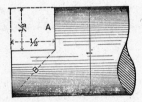

Fig. 113.

hammer, and the piece denoted by the dotted line *B* is cut off, leaving the scarf as shown in Fig. 114.

The two ends are put together to weld as shown in Fig. 115.

The advantage of this plan is that the quantity of metal allowed for wastage during the weld is a known quantity, bearing the necessary proportion to the diam-

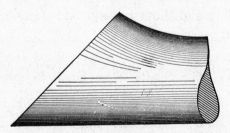

Fig. 114.

eter of the shaft, so that when the weld is swaged down to the proper diameter the length of the shaft will be correct.

Welding a Heavy Shaft.

My plan is, dress the two ends you are going to weld, level, or somewhat rounding, for a four-inch shaft. Then punch a five-eighths-inch hole two inches down each end; then take a piece of five-eighths-inch round iron four inches long and dowel the two together with the same. Next, place the shaft in the fire and revolve it slowly until the welding heat is ob-

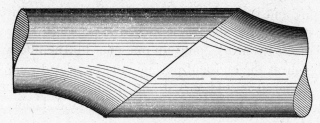

Fig. 115.

tained, and then by means of sledges or a ram, butt it together while it is in the fire. The other end must be held firm if the shaft is very long. In doing this job I would prefer to use a ram made by taking a piece of shafting and swinging it in a chair. When the butting together has been accomplished, take the shaft out and swage it. The swage should be in front of the forge so that the shaft will lay in it while heating, and then it can be easily moved for swaging.—
By L. B. H.

Welding Boiler Flues.

In welding boiler flues in a shop where you have only such tools as you make yourself, let the flue be held in a vise, then take a diamond point and cut off square, then cut off a piece of the length desired, scarf both the pieces, one inside and the other outside, drive them together and take a borax heat all around, being careful not to burn a hole through. Open the fire a little on top, keep turning the flue, weld the end of the lap down in the fire lightly, then take the flue out of the fire and round it on an old shaft or any round iron, but don't let the shaft or iron be too large.

To test the work, plug up one end, fill the flue with water, heat the end and put in lime or ashes to anneal it. When it is cold anneal the other end. To put it in the boiler you need an expander and beader.— *By* H. R.

Making a Weld on a Heavy Shaft.

There is only one kind of a weld that will stand for a stem for oil tools, and that is a forked or "bootjack" weld. The accompanying cut, Fig. 116, shows the mode of handling the shaft. It has to be done with the beam *A*, pulley *P*, and chains *C*, revolving around the lower pulley, and the iron shaft or auger stem as seen in or running through the forge or fire. The crotch should be placed so that the blast shall drive the current of heat sidewise on the crotch. Catching any

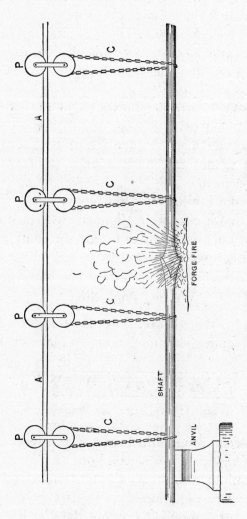

Fig. 116—Making a Weld on a heavy Shaft, as done by " A. D. G."

one of the four chains and drawing it down will revolve the shaft without misplacing the crotch in the fire until you have a welding heat. Then by drawing the shaft lengthwise, moving the upper pulleys, you can bring the weld to the anvil and with sledge or hammer make your weld.

It has been clearly demonstrated in the oil regions that a weld made with a sledge stands better on heavy stems than one made with a steam hammer. Why this is so I cannot say, but it appears to be a fact that cannot be denied.

I will make a weld after the above plan, and will guarantee that it cannot be jumped, whereas the ordinary lap or buck weld will not stand the continued jars that oil tools have to contend with.—*By* A. D. G.

Welding Angle Iron.

To be a good angle-iron smith is a thing to be proud of, for it requires skillful forging to make good, true,

Fig. 117—Angle Iron for Bending.

clean work of proper thickness at the weld. Some simple examples are given as follows :

It is required to bend the piece of angle iron shown in Fig. 117 to a right angle.

The first operation is to cut out the frog, leaving the

piece as shown in Fig. 118, the width at the mouth A of the frog being three-quarter inch to every inch of breadth measured inside the flange as at B.

The edges of the frog are then scarfed and the piece bent to an acute angle; but in this operation it is ne-

Fig. 118—First Operation.

cessary to keep the scarfs quite clean and not to bend them into position to weld until they are ready for the welding heat; otherwise scale will form where the scarfs overlap and the weld will not be sound.

The heat should be confined as closely as possible to the parts to be welded; otherwise the iron will scale and become reduced below its proper thickness.

The iron is then bent to the shape shown in Fig. 119, and the angle to which it is bent is an important con-

Fig. 119—Bending to Shape.

sideration. The object is to leave the overlapping scarf thicker than the rest of the metal, and then the

stretching which accompanies the welding will bring
the two arms or wings to a right angle.

It is obvious, then, that the thickness of the metal at

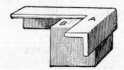

Fig. 120—How the Welding is Done.

the weld determines the angle to which the arms must
be bent before welding.   The thicker the iron the more
acute the angle.   If the angle be made too acute for the
thickness of the iron at the weld there is no alternative
but to swage the flange down and thin it enough to

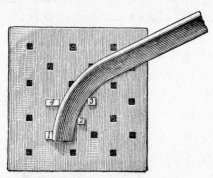

Fig. 121 –Bending Angle Iron into a Circle.

bring the arms to a right angle.   Hence it is advisable
to leave the scarf too thick rather than too thin, because
while it is easy to cut away the extra metal, if necessary,

it is not so easy to weld a piece in to give more metal.
In very thin angle irons, in which the wastage in the
heating is greater in proportion to the whole body
of metal, the width of the frog at *A* in
Fig. 118 may be less, as say nine-sixteenths inch for every inch of angle iron
width measured, as at *B* in Fig. 118.

Fig. 122—Shape
of Pins.

For angles other than a right angle the
process is the same, allowance being
made in the scarf-joint and bend before
welding for the stretching that will accompany the
welding operation.

The welding blows should be light and quick, while
during the scarfing the scale should be cleaned off as
soon as the heat leaves the fire, so that it will not drive

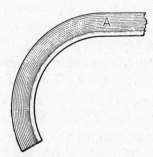

Fig. 123—Showing Flange Inside of Circle.

into the metal and prevent proper welding. The outside corner should not receive any blows at its apex ;
and as it will stretch on the outside and compress on

the inside, the forging to bring the corner up square should be done after the welding.

The welding is done on the corner of an angle block, as in Fig. 120, in which A is the angle iron and B the angle block.

To bend an angle iron into a circle, with the flange at the extreme diameter, the block and pins shown in Fig. 121 are employed. The block is provided with the numerous holes shown for the reception of the pins. The pins marked 1 and 2 are first inserted and the iron bent by placing it between them and placed under strain in the necessary direction. Pins 3 and 4 are then added and the iron again bent, and so on; but when the holes do not fall in the right position, the pins are made as in Fig. 122, the length of the heads A varying in length to suit various curves.

To straighten the iron it is flattened on the surface A and swaged on the edge of the flange B, the bending and straightening being performed alternately.

When the flange of the angle iron is to be inside the circle, as in Fig. 123, a special iron made thicker on the flange A is employed. The bending is accomplished, partly by the pins as before, and partly by forging thinner, and thus stretching the flange A while reducing it to its proper thickness.—*By* Joshua Rose.

Welding Collars on Round Rods.

I bend the rod for the collar as shown by Fig. 124, and cut off at A. In welding I hit first at B, and go on around to *A*. I weld either at the anvil or on a swage—it doesn't matter which. For large collars I cut off a piece to make the collar, and leave it straight,

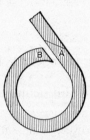

Fig. 124—Welding Collars on Round Rods by " Southern Blacksmith's " Method. Showing how the Rod is Bent and Cut off.

then I heat the bar and collar separately, and weld one end of the collar first, and bend and weld as I go around, taking separate welding heats after the bending.—*By* SOUTHERN BLACKSMITH.

Shall Sand be Used in Welding?

The rule among smiths generally seems to be that the more sand they can get on in welding the better, the idea being that the iron will be heated more evenly by this process. Some time ago I got out of sand and could get no more for a time. After I had worked awhile without it I did not want any more, and have not used it since.

Some of the reasons for not using it I will name. The forging is cleaner, and it takes less time to do work without than with sand. I have done just as good work since I stopped using it as before, and have done it in less time.

The sand used by me is from molders' castings.— *By* W. B. G.

Fluxes or Welding Compounds for Iron or Steel.

No. 1. Here is a welding compound equal to *cherry heat* :

Take ten ounces borax, one ounce muriate of ammonia, pound them roughly together, put them in an iron vessel, and roast them over the fire till all spume has disappeared, then turn it out to cool, afterwards pulverize and keep in a close tin box. Use about like borax, only not so much. I use this all the time and consider it equal to any compound in the market.

I can weld any kind of steel I ever tried with it —springs, fork tines, etc.—*By* J. C. McM.

No. 2. I will give a recipe for welding steel that I have used twenty years successfully : one ounce of copperas, half an ounce of saltpetre, quarter of an ounce of sal ammoniac, three ounces of salt, one and a half pounds of sand. Pulverize and mix together and keep in a dry place.—*By* R. S.

No. 3. An excellent welding compound for steel is composed as follows : two ounces of copperas ; four ounces of salt ; four pounds of white sand.

Mix the whole and throw it on the heat as is done with sand only.

No. 4. Equal quantities of borax and pulverized glass, well wetted with alcohol and heated to a red heat in a crucible. Pulverize when cool, and sprinkle the compound on the heat.

No. 5. Take copperas, two ounces; saltpetre, one ounce; common salt, six ounces; black oxide of manganese, one ounce; prussiate of potash, one ounce. Pulverize these ingredients and mix with them three pounds of nice welding sand. Use this compound as you would sand. The quantity I have named will cost twenty cents and last a year.—*By* T.

No. 6. Take one part of lime to two or three parts of river sand, such as a plasterer would use for a finishing coat.—*By* R.

No. 7. One part copperas, two parts salt, four parts sand. Thoroughly mix. This makes a splendid welding compound.—*By* A. G. C.

No. 8. Take one ounce of carbonate of iron and mix it with one pound of borax. In using it on plows, always fit the lay very close to the land side and rivet it to get a good weld.—*By* G. W. P.

No. 9. I offer below a recipe for welding steel without borax:

Copperas, two ounces; saltpetre, one ounce; common salt, six ounces; black oxide of manganese, one ounce; prussiate of potash, one ounce. All should be pulverized and mixed with three pounds of nice welding sand. With this preparation welding can be done at a cherry heat.—*By* ANXIOUS.

No. 10. I like this better than borax, but it takes a little more time when it is used. It is cheaper than borax. Those who want to try it can make it by taking a quarter of a pound of rock saltpetre, and dissolving it in a quarter of a pound of oil of vitrol and adding to one gallon of rain water.

After scarfing the steel get it red hot and quench it in this preparation, then heat and weld the same as iron, hammering very quickly with light blows. Keep the compound in stone jars with a tight, fitting lid, and it will be good for years.

Sand in Welding—Facing Old Hammers.

No. 11. I wish to say a few words with respect to the use of sand in welding. The question seems to be shall we or shall we not use sand in making welds. I consider it a very essential point in working steel, and use a composition, which I prepare as follows: Take a quart of quartz sand, one pint of common salt, one pint of pulverized charcoal, half a pound of borax well burnt. These I mix well together in a sand box, and consider the preparation much better than raw borax for working steel. In working iron I omit the borax from the compound.—*By* E. T. BULLARD.

Composition for Welding Cast-Steel.

Borax, ten parts ; sal ammoniac, one part ; grind or pound them roughly together ; fuse them in a metal pot over a clear fire, continuing the heat until the spume has disappeared from the surface. When the liquid is clear, pour the composition out to cool and concrete, and grind to a fine powder, and it is ready for use.

To use this composition, the steel to be welded should be raised to a bright yellow heat ; then dip it in the welding powder and again raise it to a like heat as before ; it is then ready to be submitted to the hammer.

Brazing Cast-Iron.

"What is the reason that I cannot braze cast-iron?" asked a machinist the other day. "Every time I try, I fail. Sometimes the cast-iron burns away, and sometimes the brass will not stick. What is the reason ?"

Cast-iron may be easily brazed, if, like doing other peculiar jobs, "you know how to do it." Have the iron clean ; make it free from grease and acids, which may be injurious ; choose any soft brass, or make some for this purpose. The yellow brass used in brazing copper will do ; it must contain a large percentage of zinc, or its melting point will be not much lower than that of the cast-iron itself.

Put on the borax before heating the iron. Dissolve the borax, and apply the solution freely to the parts to be brazed. By doing this before heating, a film of oxide is prevented from forming upon the iron. Fasten the parts together, and heat in a clear charcoal fire. Soft coal is not suitable ; there is too much sulphur in it.

Heat the work gradually. Apply heat to the largest piece, and keep that piece the hottest. Sprinkle on powdered borax and brass filings, and use plenty of borax. Watch carefully, and get the iron up to a red heat before any of the brass melts. The brass will not adhere unless the iron is hot enough to melt the brass.

Be very careful not to get the iron too hot, or away it melts and the job is lost. When the brass "runs," remove from the fire immediately, and wipe off the superfluous brass, cool off slowly, and finish up the joint.—*American Machinist.*

Brazing Ferrules.

Chamfer the ends of the piece to be brazed on opposite sides, and file them so that the iron will be bright and clean, bend and let the ends lap about one-eighth of an inch ; then lay on a piece of brass. (I use old lamp tops or burners.) Put on a little pulverized borax with a stick or finger, throw on a few drops of water, and it is ready for the fire. Of course all that remains to be done is to melt the brass, and the ferrule is finished. You may or may not, as you like, dip it in water and cool immediately, as it only makes the brass the softer. Hammer on it or drive it, and it will not break in the brazed part. I have made this summer at least two hundred, and have yet to break the first one. They will stand more hammering than will the solid iron.—*By* A. L. D.

Brazing a Ferrule.

I will describe my way of brazing ferrules. If a lap is wanted I file both edges sharp, as in Fig.

Fig. 125—Brazing Ferrules by the Method of Chas. W. Kohler.
Showing how the Edges are filed.

125 of the accompanying illustrations, and then make the bend as shown in Fig. 126, put a strip of copper or brass inside, apply burnt borax pulverized, place the

Fig. 126—Showing how the Ferrule is bent.

ferrule in a clear fire and keep it there until I see a clear flame and then take it out to cool.

If I wish to make the ferrule without a lap, I file

the ends square, bend around to the proper shape,. bind it with iron wire so it won't open when it gets warm in the fire, and then proceed as in making one with a lap.—*By* C. W. KOHLER.

Brazing.

You cannot braze with cast brass filings. Use granulated " brazier spelter," or sheet brass clippings ; white sheet metal for bright work. Wet with water the part to be brazed, then apply powdered borax. The water holds the borax until it calcines or slakes. Then lay on your brazing material. Use a clean coke fire, and as the metal melts poke it with a *wet*, pointed iron where you want it, and remove from the fire at once. Before the flux gets cold, scrape it off with a file or sharp cold-chisel and trim it off. Continue this process until all the flux is removed, heating slightly occasionally if necessary.—*By* COLORED BLACKSMITH.

Brazing an Iron Tube.

If it is anything very particular, I should make two small holes in the tube and two small holes in the piece of iron, and pin them together and wrap binding wire around them. Then take a piece of iron, say one and one-quarter inches thick by two inches wide, and make in it a slot longer than the piece of iron to be brazed. Lay your tube on the iron sideways, and you will see what packing you want under the iron that you are going to braze on to the tube. The larger the tube, the thicker the packing it will require if you want to get it on straight. I think if you follow the directions given you will come out all right. There may be a better way of doing it, but I know of none. —*By* G. P.

Brazing a Broken Crank.

It may be worth while for me to describe my way of brazing. It is as follows: I fasten the broken parts together just as they were before being broken. For example: The accompanying illustration, Fig. 127,

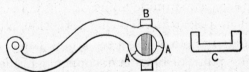

Fig. 127—Brazing. Showing a Method of Mending a Broken Crank.

represents a corn sheller crank broken at two places in the eye. *A A* indicate the places where the breaks exist. I dampen the broken ends, dip in very fine borax and then put on clamp *C*, which is made of iron as thick as the eye of the crank, and is put on the crank hot, the latter being cold. The hot clamp will make the crank swell and this will prevent the clamp from dropping off. I use plenty of brass or brazing solder, or pieces of an old clock frame, but never use cast brass, for it is useless for brazing. I use plenty of borax with the brass, but apply the brass first because if borax is put on first it will swell. When the brass is dropped in the fire and melts, the heat will look like a steel weld. After taking it out of the fire I dip it carefully in the water.—*By* I. N. Bailey.

Brazing with Brass or Copper.

To braze brass or copper, I file the parts to be joined clean, wire them in place or rivet them ; then take a few lumps of borax and burn them on a piece of sheet iron, then pulverize them, dissolve some, dip the article to be brazed in it, then lay on the piece of brass or copper, tie it fast, sprinkle some of the borax over it, and put it in a clear fire, blowing very slow at first till the iron gets red ; then I will see a blue flame, which is the melting point of brass and copper. I allow it to lie in the fire a minute with blowing, then take it out, and lay it down gently on the hearth to cool.

Very delicate articles should be dipped in a batter of clay to keep them from burning. When the clay begins to glaze it is time to take them out of the fire.

Brass or copper should be brazed with silver. Copper can be brazed with brass, but the melting points of copper and brass are only a few hundred degrees apart, and so such work is not safe unless you have to deal with a large piece of copper. Brass and copper for brazing should be milled. When silver is used it should be old coin or Mexican coin, the silver being purer. The blowpipe is the best to braze with, but it requires some practice to use it successfully.—*By* CHAS. W. KOHLER.

Soldering Fluids.

Some of the soldering fluids used are injurious to tools, and also to parts that have been laid on the bench where such fluids have been used. The following recipe will do the work well, and will not rust or tarnish any more than water would : Take two ounces of alcohol and put it into a bottle, and add about a teaspoonful of chloride of zinc and shake until dissolved. Use it in the same manner as the muriate of zinc, or muriatic acid and zinc. It has no bad smell.

A good flux for soldering iron, brass, etc., is made by dissolving chloride of zinc in alcohol.

CHAPTER IV.

STEEL AND ITS USES.

Tempering, Hardening, Testing.

Extracts from a lecture by Henry Seebohm, of Sheffield, Eng.

I fear that the advantages supposed to be derived from the use of manganese in the manufacture of cast-steel are to a large extent illusory. I have frequently conversed with consumers of steel who knew the trade before the introduction of spiegel iron into Sheffield, and it is remarkable how many of them expressed the opinion that the crucible cast-steel now in use is not so good as it was when they were young. Something may, perhaps, be allowed to the illusions of youth. But, nevertheless, I am convinced there is truth in the opinion that the quality of cast-steel has degenerated. In the present day we sacrifice much to appearances. For my part, I always distrust a bar of steel that has not a " seam " or a " roak " in it. The introduction of manganese into cast-steel is a rough-and-ready way of obtaining soundness at the expense of quality, instead of obtaining it by the tedious care and attention which the steel melter who knows his business gives to each individual crucible.

The question that should come before the consumer of cast-steel is the percentage of carbon which he wishes it to contain. When I first began business the "temper" of steel, or the percentage of carbon which it contained, was concealed from the consumer. The despotic sway of the rule of thumb was absolute. If the consumer discovered that chisel steel contained less carbon than tool steel he owed his discovery entirely to his own wit. My firm was the first to take the consumer into our confidence, and the success which has attended our efforts, and the extent to which our labels have been imitated, have completely justified our act. We have always labeled the steel we supplied to consumers with the percentage of carbon it contained, and the purposes to which, in our opinion, steel containing such percentage of carbon was applicable. The following is a list of the most useful "tempers" of cast-steel :

Razor Temper (one and a half per cent carbon).— This steel is so easily burnt by being overheated that it can only be placed in the hands of a very skillful workman. When properly treated it will do twice the work of ordinary tool steel for turning chilled rolls, etc.

Saw-file Temper (one and three-eighths per cent carbon).—This steel requires careful treatment, and although it will stand more fire than the preceding temper should not be heated above a cherry red.

Tool Temper (one and one-fourth per cent carbon).—The most useful temper for turning tools, drills and planing-machine tools in the hands of ordinary workmen. It is possible to weld cast-steel of this temper, but not without care and skill.

Spindle Temper (one and one-eighth per cent carbon).—A very useful temper for mill-picks, circular cutters, very large turning tools, taps, screwing dies, etc. This temper requires considerable care in welding

Chisel Temper (one per cent carbon).—An extremely useful temper, combining, as it does, great toughness in the unhardened state, with the capacity of hardening at a low heat. It may also be welded without much difficulty. It is, consequently, well adapted for tools, where the unhardened part is required to stand the blow of a hammer without snipping, but where a hard cutting edge is required, such as cold chisels, hot salts, etc.

Set Temper (seven-eighths per cent carbon).—This temper is adapted for tools where the chief punishment is on the unhardened part, such as cold sets, which have to stand the blows of a very heavy hammer.

Die Temper (three-fourths per cent carbon).—The most suitable temper for tools where the surface only is required to be hard, and where the capacity to withstand great pressure is of importance, such as stamping or pressing dies, boiler cups, etc. Both the last two tempers may be easily welded by a mechanic accustomed to weld cast-steel.

We may divide consumers of steel into three classes. First, those who use their own judgment of what percentage of carbon they require, and instruct the manufacturer to send them steel of a specified temper; second, those who leave the selection of the temper to the judgment of the manufacturer, and instruct him to send them steel for a specified purpose; and third, those who simply order steel of a specified size, leaving the manufacturer to guess for what purpose it is required. Fortunately, the size and shape generally furnish some clue to the purpose for which it is likely to be used. For example, oval steel is almost sure to be used for chisels, and small squares for turning tools. One and one-fourth square may be used for a turning tool or a cold set, one and one-fourth round for a drill or a boiler-cup, and the manufacturer has to puzzle his brains to discover whether the chances are in favor of its going into the lathe-room or the blacksmith's shop. It cannot too often be reiterated of how much importance it is, when ordering steel, to state the purpose for which it is going to be used.

When the steel has arrived in the user's hands, the first process which it undergoes is the forging it into the shape required. This process is really two processes. First, that of heating it to make it malleable, and second, that of hammering it, while it is hot, into the required shape. The golden rule in forging is to heat the steel as little as possible before it is forged, and to hammer it as much as possible in the process of forging.

The worst fault that can be committed is to over-heat the steel. When steel is heated it becomes coarse grained ; its silky texture is lost, and it can only be restored by hammering or sudden cooling. If the temperature be raised above a certain point, the steel becomes what is technically called "burnt," and the amount of hammering which it would require to restore its fine grain would reduce it to a size too small for the required tool, and the steel must be condemned as spoiled. Overheating in the fire is the primary cause of cracking in the water.

The process of hammering or forging the steel into the shape required has hardened the steel to such an extent as to make the cutting impossible or difficult; it must consequently be annealed. This process, like the preceding one, is a double process. The steel must be reheated as carefully as before, and afterward cooled as slowly as possible.

We now come to the culminating point in our manufacture, where the invaluable property which distinguishes steel from wrought iron or cast metal is revealed.

The part of the tool required to be hardened must be heated through, and heated evenly, but must on no account be overheated. Our tool must be finished at one blow—the blow caused by the sudden contraction of the steel produced by its sudden cooling in the water—and if this blow is not sufficient to give to the steel a fine grain and silky texture—if, after the blow is given, the fracture, were it broken in the hardened part, should show a coarse grain and dull color, instead of a fine grain and glossy luster, our tool is spoiled, and must be consigned to the limbo of "wasters." The special dangers to be avoided in hardening each kind of tool must be learned by experience. Some tools will warp or "skeller," as we say in Yorkshire, if they are not plunged into the water in a certain way. Tools of one shape must cut the water like a knife; those of another shape must stab it like a dagger. Some tools must be hardened in a saturated solution of salt, the older the better, while others are best hardened under a stream of running water.

In some tools, where the shape necessitates a great difference in the rapidity of cooling, it is wise to drill holes in the thicker parts where they will not interfere with the use of the tool—holes which are made neither for use nor ornament, but solely with a view of equalizing the rapidity of the various parts, so as to distribute the area of tension and thus lessen the risk of cracking in hardening. So many causes may produce water-cracks that it is often difficult to point out the precise cause in any given case. Perhaps the most common cause is overheating the steel in one or more of the processes which it passes through in the consumers' hands, or it may have been overheated in the process of forging, or rolling it into the dimensions required while in the hands of the manufacturer. A second cause may be found in the over-melting, or too long boiling of the steel, causing it to part with too much of its confined carbonic acid, a fault which may be attributed to the anxiety of the manufacturer to escape honeycomb in the ingot. A third cause may be sometimes discovered in the addition of too much manganese, added with the same motive. A fourth cause may, curiously enough, prove to be a deficiency of carbon, while, in some cases, too much will produce the same effect. A fifth cause may be one which, as a steel manufacturer, I ought to mention in a whisper— the presence of too much phosphorus in the steel; but, after all, this may not be the fault of a greedy manufacturer, who wants to make too great a percentage of profit. It might be the fault of a stingy consumer, who begrudges him the little profit he makes. You may depend upon it there is nothing so dear as cheap steel. It must be more economical to put five shillings' worth of labor upon steel that costs a shilling, to produce a tool that lasts a day, than to put the same value of labor upon a steel that costs only ninepence, to produce a tool that only lasts half a day.

Our difficulties are not quite over when the process of hardening has been successfully accomplished. Our steel was originally lead; it has now become glass. To attain its proper condition our tool must pass through the final process—that of tempering.

If you heat a piece of hardened steel slightly, and allow it to cool again, it becomes tempered. It suddenly changes from glass to whalebone ; and in the process of changing its nature, it fortunately changes its color, so that the workman can judge by the hue of the color the extent of the elasticity which it has acquired, and can give to each tool the particular degree of temper which is most adapted to its special purpose. The various colors through which tempered steel successfully passes are as follows : Straw, gold, chocolate, purple, violet and blue. Of course, in passing from one color to another, the steel passes through the intermediate colors. It really passes through an infinite series of colors, of which the six above mentioned are arbitrarily selected as convenient stages.

It is supposed that the maximum of hardness and elasticity combined is obtained by tempering down to a straw color. In tempering steel regard must be had to the quality most essential in the special tool to be tempered ; for example, a turning tool is required to be very hard, and is generally taken hot enough out of the water to temper itself down to a degree so slight that no perceptible color is apparent, while a spring is required to be very elastic, and may be tempered down to a blue. If you ask me to give you a scientific explanation of the process of tempering steel, I must confess my absolute ignorance.

Hardening in oil is another mode of treating steel, which appears to a certain extent to attain by one process the change from lead into whalebone without passing through the intermediate glass stage, and is of great value for certain tools.

There are many kinds of steel to which your attention should be called, but which can only obtain from me the briefest mention. A special steel for taps, called mild-centered cast-steel, is made by converting a cogged ingot of very mild cast-steel, so that the additional carbon only penetrates a short distance. These bars are afterward hammered or rolled down to the size required, and have the advantage of possessing a hard surface without losing the toughness of the mild center.

Another special steel, somewhat analogous to mild-centered cast-steel, is produced by melting a hard steel on to a slab of iron, or very mild steel heated hot enough to weld with the molten steel, so that a bar may be produced, one-half of which is iron and the other half steel, or three-fourths iron and one-fourth steel, as may be required.

A third kind of special steel, which is used for turning tools for chilled rolls, magnets and some other purposes, is made by adding a certain percentage of wolfram, or, as the metal is more generally called, tungsten, sometimes with and sometimes without carbon, sometimes to such an extent that it can be used without hardening in water. Special steel of this kind is the finest-grained that can be produced, but it is so brittle that in the hands of any but exceptionally skilled workmen it is useless.   The addition of chromium, instead of wolfram, has somewhat the same effect.

TESTING.

It is much to be regretted that no easy method of testing cast-steel has been invented. The amount of breaking strain and the extent of contraction of the area of the fracture are all very well for steel which is not hardened, and not required to be used in a hardened state, but for hardened and tempered steel it is practically useless. It is very difficult to harden and temper two pieces of steel to exactly the same degree. A single test is of comparatively small value, as a second-rate quality of steel may stand very well the first time of hardening, but deteriorates much more rapidly every time it is rehardened than is the case with high quality steel. Nor am I at all sure that the breaking strain is a fair test of the quality of steel. For many tools the capacity to withstand a high amount of breaking strain slowly applied is not so much required as its capacity to withstand a sudden shock. The appearance of the fracture is very illusory. The fineness of the grain and the silkiness of the gloss is very captivating to the eye, but it can be produced by hammering cold. The consumer of steel may be enraptured by the superb fracture of a bar of steel; but, after all, this is only a dodge, depending upon the inclination of the axis of the revolving hammer to the plane of the anvil. The practical consumer of steel must descend from the heights of art and science and take refuge in the commonplace of the rule of thumb, and buy the steel which his workmen tell him is full of "nature" and "body."

Hints Regarding Working Steel.

Salt water is no more likely to crack steel than fresh or soft, if the steel has been properly, *uniformly*, heated. Brine will produce a greater degree of hardness at the proper heat, other things being equal.

Steel requires the same conditions for annealing, whether in bulk, ponderous or otherwise. The *sine qua non* is, heat uniformly to proper heat and as *soon* as homogeneously saturated (not super-saturated) permit to cool as *slowly* and uniformly as practicable.

My experience says: Harden in every case where practicable under a stream of cold water, taking care that the contact is perfect and directed to the *locale* requiring the greatest degree of hardening. It is almost always prudent to move the article constantly, if only slightly.

Wherever water is in impinging motion it is, of course, more rapidly changing its heated for a colder co-efficient, or successive heat extractor, we will call it, and the more extractors receiving heat the quicker the locality is refrigerated and fixed, consequently the hardest.

Very few, if any, drop hammer dies, if properly hardened, require a subsequent tempering.

I have known good gray, or, in some cases, white cast-iron, capable of doing twenty times the amount of work of any kind of steel tried.

My way is to heat all *ordinary* brands of " tool cast-steel " very slowly (and if practical) in a COOL fire, to commence with, gradually letting (by draught rather than blast) both fire and steel increase in temperature together, to as low red as is necessary.—*By* W. DICK.

The Warping of Steel During the Hardening Process.

In heating steel to harden it, especial care is necessary, particularly when the tool is one finished to size, if its form is slight or irregular, or if it is a very long one, because unless the conditions both of heating and cooling be such that the temperature is raised and lowered uniformly throughout the mass, a change of form known as *warping* will ensue. If one part gets hotter than another it expands more, and the form of the steel undergoes the change necessary to accommodate this local expansion, and this alteration of shape becomes permanent. In work finished and fitted this is of very great consideration, and, in the case of tools, it often assumes sufficient importance to entirely destroy their value. If, then, an article has a thin side, it requires to be so manipulated in the fire that such side shall not become heated in advance of the rest of the body

of the metal, or it will become locally distorted or
warped. If, however, the article is of equal sectional
area all over, it is necessary to so turn it in the fire as
to heat it uniformly all over; and in either case care
should be taken not to heat the steel too quickly, unless, indeed, it is desirable to leave the middle somewhat softer than the outside, so as to have the outside
fully hardened and the inside somewhat soft, which
will leave the steel stronger than if hardened equally
all through. Sometimes the outside of an article is
heated more than the inside, so as to modify the tendency to crack from the contraction during the
quenching; for to whatever degree the article expands
during the heating, it must contract during the cooling.
Hence, if the article is heated in a fluid, it may often
be necessary to hold the article, for a time, with the
thick part only in the heating material; but in this case
it should not be held quite still, but raised and lowered
gradually and continuously, to insure even heating.

Pieces, such as long taps, are very apt to warp both
in the fire and in the water. In heating, they should
rest upon an even bed of coked coal, and be revolved
almost continuously while moved endways in the fire;
or when the length is excessive, they may be rested in
a heated tube so that they may not bend of their own
weight. So, likewise, spirals may be heated upon cylindrical pieces of iron or tubes to prevent their own
weight from bending or disarranging the coils.

If a piece is to be hardened all over, it must be occasionally turned end for end, and the end of the holding tongs should be heated to redness or they will abstract the heat from the steel they envelop. Very small pieces may be held by a piece of iron wire or heated in a short piece of tube, the latter being an excellent plan for obtaining a uniformity of heat, but in any event the heating must be uniform to avoid warping in the fire, and, in some cases, cracking also. This latter occurs when the heating takes place very quickly and the thin parts are not sufficiently heated to give way to accommodate the expansion of the thick ones. The splitting or cracking of steel during the cooling process in hardening is termed *water* cracking, and is to be avoided only by conforming the conditions of cooling to the size and shape of the article.

Experiments have demonstrated that the greater part of the hardness of steel depends upon the quickness with which its temperature is reduced from about 500° to a few degrees below 500°, and metal heated to 500° must be surrounded by a temperature which renders the existence of water under atmospheric pressure impossible; hence, so long as this temperature exists the steel cannot be in contact with the water, or, in other words, the heat from the steel vaporizes the immediately surrounding water. As the heated steel enters the water the underneath side is constantly meeting water at its normal temperature, while the upper side is surrounded by water that the steel has passed by, and, to a certain extent, raised the temperature of.

Hence, the vapor on the underneath side is the thinnest, because it is attacked with colder water and with greater force, because of the motion of the steel in dipping. Suppose, now, we were to plunge a piece of heated steel into water, and then slowly move it laterally, the side of it which meets the water would become the hardest, and would be apt to become concave in its length.

From these considerations we may perceive how important a matter the dipping is, especially when it is remembered that the expansion which accompanies the heating is a slow process compared to the contraction which accompanies the cooling (although their amounts are, of course, precisely equal), and that while unequal expansion usually only warps the article, unequal contraction will in a great many, or, indeed, in most cases, cause it to crack or split.—*By* JOSHUA ROSE, M. E.

Tempering Steel.

I have read with considerable interest the different processes for tempering steel, and the different treatments that have appeared from time to time in mechanical journals. It always seemed to me the object to be sought for is to cool the steel as soon as possible after it has been heated to the well known cherry red, and, in doing so, the different solutions offered for a cooling bath are as numerous as the recipes for a toothache. Mercury, no doubt, makes the best bath, and salt water, for many purposes, is equally as good. But one object I have observed in quenching steel, is the time required for reducing the heat. For some moments the heated steel shows its cherry color through the cooling bath. Mercury, being the best conductor of heat, takes away the heat the fastest and hardens it the hardest. If there were any way in which the cold water could be brought in contact with the metal, its heat would the sooner be removed. Warm water hardens almost as well as cold, except for light work. This may be owing to the jacket formed about the heated steel, which protects the steel from losing its heat. This is more particularly noticed in hardening the face of a hammer so that it will not settle in the center, or cave off around its edge. In plunging it into the bath, the center of the face is, to a certain extent, protected by the heat from the outer edge, and remains the softest. The drawing process or tempering being governed by the color of the oxidization that appears on the polished surface, there is no way to distinguish the hard places from the soft that were produced in hardening ; and without further comment, will state that the process of hardening by cooling with water that is brought in close contact with the heated surface by pressure, promises well, and should find its way more effectually into general use. The writer remembers very well when at work in a shop close by a reservoir, where a stream of water rushing through an orifice, under a head of twelve feet or more, was always ready for quenching steel for the purpose of hardening. Hammers were heated as near the right temperature as was thought best and held under the stream where the water would strike square upon the face of the hammer, removing the heat with great rapidity, the heated liquid passing off out of the way and the cooler taking its place, and, owing to the great press-ure, the film of vapor that might otherwise be formed between the heating and cooling surfaces. is broken up. Smooth metallic surfaces, when heated to a low red heat, are protected from coming in con-tact with a liquid by the intervening film of steam which gives an imperfect in hardening, and is known as the spheroidal state of liquids, as observed when cooling sheets of iron by pouring water upon them, the liquid will run about in large drops without break-ing up or boiling. Steel is hardened to a remarkable degree by being forced in contact with almost any cold substance. A flat drill that has been heated at the point, and driven into a lump of cold lead, is as hard as if quenched in a bath of cold water, Any way to remove the heat is all that is required for hardening, and the sooner it is removed the better, and in chill-ing with cold water it is necessary that the steel should be moved about to break up the film, and to keep in contact with the cooling liquid. I have felt an inter-est in the matter of tempering steel, and cannot but feel that this state of things in regard to the close communion between heated metals and their cooling solutions should be more fully understood. — *Cotton, Wool and Iron.*

Another Method of Tempering Steel.

It is desirable to obtain any degree of hardness by a single process if possible.   In some cases, by heating a known quantity of steel to a definite temperature and quenching it in liquid maintained at about an even temperature, the color is becoming dispensed with, the conditions of heating and cooling being varied to give any degree of hardness.   Another and a very desirable method of hardening and tempering, is to heat in a flue of some kind, maintained at the required temperature over the fire, and after quenching, instead of applying the color test, provide a tempering bath composed of some substance heated to a temperature of from 430° to 630°.   By placing the articles (after hardening them) in the tempering bath and heating it to a temperature equal to the color of the temper required, we have but to cease heating the tempering bath when a thermometer marks the required temperature.   A uniform degree of temper will be given to all the articles, and the operation will occupy much less time than would tempering by the color test, because a liquid is much more easily kept at an equal temperature throughout its mass than are the heated sand or hot pieces of metal resorted to in tempering by the color test. Another method of tempering is to heat the steel to a definite temperature and cool or quench it in a liquid having sufficient greasiness or other quality which acts to retard its retraction of the heat from the steel and thus give a temper at one operation. As an example of this kind of tempering, it is said that milk and water mixed in proportions determined by experiment upon the steel for which it was employed, has been found to give an excellent spring temper. Such tempering carefully conducted may be of the very best quality. A great deal, however, in this case depends on the judgment of the operator, because very little variation in heating the steel or in the proportions of milk to water produces a wide variation in the degree of temper. If, on trial, the temper is too soft, the steel may be made hotter or more water added to the milk. If the steel was heated as hot as practicable without increasing the danger of burning it, more water must be added, while if the steel was made red-hot without being hot enough to cause the formation of clearly perceptible scale, the steel may be heated more. It is desirable in all cases, but especially with a high quality of steel, not to heat it above a blood-red heat, although sheer and spring steels may be and often must be made hotter in order to cause them to harden when quenched in water.

Hardening and tempering steel, as applied to cutting tools, are much more simple than when the same operations are required to give steel elasticity as well as durability of form or to give durability to pieces of slight and irregular form of sufficient hardness to withstand abrasion.   One reason of this is that for tools a special and uniform quality of steel is readily obtainable, which is known as tool steel.   Special sizes and grades are made to suit the manufacture of any of the ordinary forms of tools.

As a rule, the steel that shows a fracture of fine, dull grain, the face of the fracture being comparatively level, is of better quality than that showing a coarse or granulated surface, brightness denoting hardness, and fibrousness, toughness.

Very few steels are as yet sufficiently uniform to render it practicable to employ an unchangeable method of tempering, and to this fact is largely due the use of particular brands of steel.

In tempering steel, regard must be had to the quality most essential in the special tool to be tempered.   A turning tool is required to be very hard and is often taken out of the water hot enough to temper itself down to a degree so slight that no color is perceptible, while a spring is required to be very elastic and may be tempered down to a blue.

A scientific explanation of the process of tempering steel has yet to be given without mystifying one by talking unintelligibly about molecular rearrangement and crystalline transportations.

Working Steel.

In making steel tires blacksmiths generally heat them too much. A deep cherry-red is hot enough. Of course you can't make much headway in hammering, but you should heat oftener. It is better to spend time in heating often than to burn the steel, spoil the job and get nothing for it. When steel has been hammered cold and gets black it should never be heated hot enough to raise a scale, because this would open the pores and render it worthless for anything requiring tempering. Heat just to a low cherry-red and draw your temper accordingly. Some smith may say: "It wouldn't be hard enough." Don't be afraid of that; it will be hard enough for anything.—*By* BENNINGER & SON.

Working and Tempering Steel.

To work steel never heat above a light cherry-red for hammering, then hammer light and quick until near black, as this improves the steel and will make tools that will do more than double the work than if not so treated. The hardness of steel is governed entirely by the heat when it is dipped in water; for instance, a piece of steel dipped at a bright cherry color and drawn to a straw, will be very much harder than a piece heated to a dark cherry-red and then dipped and drawn to a straw. Try it.

The forging, hardening and tempering of steel is an

art that but few understand, as its knowledge is only gained by experience, and but few ever give its secrets to others; yet in a few words I will try to give the principal elements to workers of steel, which if followed will save you many losses, and give you a reputation for working steel that will ensure you good and serviceable tools, as well as increase your gains.

Please remember that the heat at which steel is worked and hardened are two of the vital elements to produce good and serviceable tools. If heated above a light cherry-red, some of the vitality of the steel is destroyed, and it would in heating too many times return to iron. If heated too hot when hardening it would fly to pieces, destroying your labor and steel as well as giving you a poor reputation.

Remember also to hammer your work lightly at a low heat, as this improves chisels, drills, lathe tools, and edge tools most wonderfully; also take as few heats as possible, as overheating and too frequent heating reduces the steel to iron by destroying the carbon.

To harden taps, rimmers, chisels and drills, always dip them slowly to the depth desired in as near a vertical line as you can by the eye and hand, then move in a circular position until cold, but never any deeper in the water than first dipped, as this prevents them from cracking, which they would be likely to do if held perfectly still and the water formed a line around them. Do not change the water in which you temper, but as it wastes fill up the tank. If you are

obliged to use fresh water always heat a piece of iron
to put into it and bring it to such a warmth as is perceptible to the hand, as steel is liable to crack when
dipped into cold water, When you have heated your
article to be tempered take it from the fire and examine to see if any flaws are observable in the steel, as
this will prevent your having poor pieces of steel laid
to your carelessness in hardening.

In cutting up steel a thin, sharp chisel should be
used, as a blunt one is liable to splinter or crack the
bar, which will not be seen until it is tempered and
then the labor is lost with the steel.

Colors of different articles for use.—Taps should be
hardened and then brightened by rubbing emery and
oil on the clearance, and then draw on a hot plate or
in a heated ring to a dark straw color.

Dies should be a bright straw color and drawn on a
hot plate or in sand.

Drills for iron should be a dark straw on the cutting
part and the rest a blue.

Chisels for iron should be violet color ; for cutting
stone a purple is required.

Milling cutters should be of a yellowish white.
Gear teeth cutters the same color. The usual way to
dip these is to have a rod with three prongs to pass
through the hole after it is heated to dip with, lower
slowly until all the cutter is under the water about two
inches, then move in a circular position until thoroughly cold, remembering that a great many things

break by taking from the water before they are cold, especially large pieces of steel, as the center retains the heat, and when taken from the water it expands the outside and causes it to crack.

In tempering pieces having a thick and thin edge, always dip the thickest part first. Study the pieces you have to harden and it will help you very much. Large centers in work for tempering should be avoided, as they are liable to cause the end to split open.—*Iron Trade Review.*

Tempering Steel.

Two of the most important processes in blacksmithing, are the hardening and the tempering of steel. Great judgment particularly, as well as experience, is required to temper dies and tools. With good judgment, a person will soon learn to temper; but without good judgment, tempering can never be successfully learned. A man may learn to do one special kind of work, but put him in a large hardware manufacturing establishment, where all kinds of dies and tools are used, with hardly any two requiring the same temper, and without judgment, the difficulties connected with such a position can never be overcome.

To harden and temper a piece of steel, it should always be properly annealed; otherwise it is almost certain to spring or warp. It is a very general idea that you can draw all the temper out of steel, without heating it red hot all over; but such is not the case. Heating the face of a die and covering it up in ashes does not thoroughly anneal it by any means. Possibly in that way you can get it in such a condition that it can be worked; but it will not be very soft, and will not harden and temper as well as if it had been heated all over.

The best way that I ever found to anneal steel (when you do not have a kiln for that purpose) is to heat it all over in a slow charcoal fire; the slower it is heated the better. Do not heat very hot, but all over and all through. Then take it out and cover it up in fine charcoal, and let it remain till cold.

In heating a die for the purpose of hardening, it is not necessary to heat it all over, unless you want to harden it all over. The only way, in my judgment, that dies can be tempered as they should be, is for the one that tempers them to see, from time to time, how they work, as they are being used; and in that way he can tell if they require more or less temper and the particular places where they should be hard or soft.

It is useless for anyone to undertake to tell how to temper everything that is used in a manufacturing establishment; such knowledge can only be acquired by experience, combined with good judgment and mechanical ingenuity. I will try, however, to explain my way of hardening and tempering.

Trip-hammer dies may seem to be very easy to handle, but a blacksmith without experience would meet with many difficulties. Take, for instance, a die seven or eight inches long, one and a half inches thick and four and a half inches wide with several impressions cut in it, leaving several small points which are liable to fly off as soon as they are hardened or when you are drawing the temper.   Now, my way to prevent the corners from coming off, and keep the dies straight is this: I heat my die very carefully in a clean charcoal fire, being careful not to get it any hotter than is necessary to have it harden.   When the proper heat has been obtained, grasp it with the tongs near one end in such a way that it can be put in the water perpendicularly, and while in the water I turn it to a horizontal position and take it about half-way out, letting it remain until it is cool enough on the face to take out entirely for an instant without permitting the temper to run down.   Then I withdraw it and return it to the water several times very quickly until it is cool enough to take out and scour off.   The temper can then be drawn to suit, without any danger of the corners flying off.

The object in putting it in the water perpendicularly is to keep it straight; and, as it cools off all alike, when you bring the back out of the water the heat rushes up toward the back, and expands it, taking all the strain off the face of the die and preventing it from breaking.

By plunging it into the water and withdrawing it very quickly, the face of the die has time to get cool gradually, and the corners are thus prevented from flying off.

This process will work well on any dies or tools hardened in this way. I have tried it hundreds of times with the best of success.—*By* G. B. J.

Tempering Small Articles.

When tempering cold chisels, or any other steel articles, heat to a very dull red and rub with a piece of hard soap, then finish heating and harden in clear, cool water. The potash of the soap prevents the oxygen of the atmosphere from uniting with the steel and forming rust or black oxide of iron. The article will need no polishing to enable the colors to be seen. This will be appreciated when tempering taps, dies or various complex forms not easy to polish. Never "upset" a cold chisel. It is sure death to steel. Many of us have lived on a farm and know something about a bundle of nice, straight, clean straw. If you work it intelligently you can tie it up into stout bands for binding other bundles. You can take hold of the ends of the straw and draw out a handful without harm to the straw. After you have drawn out half that bundle a foot or so, try to drive it back; every blow breaks the straw, cripples and doubles it up, and it will hardly bear its own weight, to say nothing of making a band for other bundles. Just so with steel. If you have a broken chisel to sharpen, draw out and cut off, never upset.   It will cripple the fibers just as the straw is crippled when driven endwise.

Make chisels short for hard, rough work.   They transmit the power or force of a blow much better. Long chisels are apt to "broom up" on the hammer end, as the long steel through which the blow passes has more chance to absorb the force of the blow.

The harder the metal to be worked, the quicker the blow should be transmitted.   Cast-iron works much better with a short steel chisel and light hammer, than if the blow was struck upon a very long chisel with a heavy wooden mallet.—*Age of Steel.*

Tempering Steel.

I have never used any mercury in tempering but have no doubt it answers the purpose.   I was one of the first blacksmiths in this country who worked cast-steel.   The boss under whom I learned the trade made it a part of his business to teach country blacksmiths how to put cast-steel in axes and how to weld and temper it.   He welded with borax melted into a kind of hard glassy substance.—*By* C. W.

Tempering Steel with Low Heat.

Some curious statements on tempering steel are made in a paper published in *Dingler's Polytechnic Journal*, vol. 225, by Herr A. Jarolimek, "On the Influence of the Annealing Temperature upon the Strength and the Constitution of Steel." Hitherto it has been generally considered that to obtain a specified degree of softness it is necessary to heat the hard steel to a particular annealing color—that is to say, to a definite temperature—and then allow it to rapidly cool. Thus, for example, that steel might anneal—be tempered—yellow, it has to be heated to 540 deg. and the supposition was formed and acted upon that it must be allowed only a momentarily subjection to this temperature. Herr Jarolimek says the requisite temper, which is obtained by momentarily raising the temperature to a particular degree, can also be acquired by subjecting the steel for a longer time to a much lower temperature. For example, the temper which the annealing color—yellow—indicates, can be obtained by exposing the hard steel for ten hours to 260 degrees of heat; in other words, by placing it in water rather above the boiling point.

To Temper Steel Very Hard.

As hardness of steel depends on the quickness with which it is cooled, there are better materials than water, which gives an unequal temper; besides the steam bubbles developed interrupting contact; water is also a bad conductor of heat, and if the bubbling and heat did not put it in motion, it would be unfit for hardening. Water with plenty of ice in it gives a hard temper; small tools may be stuck into a piece of ice, as jewelers insert them in a piece of sealing wax. Oil is also used by them as being better than water, as it does not evaporate so easily. The Damascus steel blades are tempered in a small current of cold air passing through a narrow slit; this gives a much more uniform and equal temperature than water. But the most effective liquid is the only liquid metal—mercury. This being a good conductor of heat, in fact the very best liquid conductor, and the only cold one, appears to be the best one for hardening steel-cutting tools. The best steel, when forged into shape and hardened in mercury, will cut almost anything. We have seen articles made from ordinary steel, which have been hardened and tempered to a deep straw color, turned with comparative ease with cutting tools from good tool steel hardened in mercury. Beware of inhaling the vapor while hardening.

Hardening Steel.

Often when great care has been taken in heating a straight piece of steel, and it is put into water or other hardening compound, it comes out crooked; in this case the trouble is entirely in the forging. I will give my reasons for this statement.

Long pieces of steel, such as reamers for boring boxes for axles, are generally forged under a trip hammer. We will suppose the piece of steel to be forged is evenly heated through. The blacksmith takes the bar in one hand, and in the other his hammer, and the helper holds his sledge ready for business. The smith turns the bar back and forth, never turning it entirely over. Now, the hammer and the sledge will draw out the fiber or grain of the steel faster than the anvil. The steel is unevenly forged, and very likely will not be straight, but will be made straight across the anvil. Heat this piece of steel as evenly as possible, and put it into water or other compound, and it will very likely be crooked when hardened.

If a piece of steel is heated evenly, and hammered equally as many blows on all sides, and if, when crooked, while forging, it is straightened by hammering, and care has been used in heating, it will generally come out straight, providing the same care has been observed before it comes to the blacksmith.—*By* C.

Case-Hardening Steel or Iron.

I think the best and simplest method of case-hardening iron is to use prussiate of potash. It is a yellow substance that comes in the shape of flaky, shining flat lumps. Pulverize it till it is as fine as flour ; heat the article to be hardened to a deep red, and put on the potash just where you want it to be hard. Then put it back in the fire, heat to a deep red and plunge into cold water.—*By* J. P. B.

How Damascus Sword Blades Were Tempered.

Perhaps the best method which has ever been discovered for tempering steel, resulting in hardness,
toughness and elasticity combined, is that followed in
hardening the blades of the famous Damascus swords.
The furnace in which the blades were heated was constructed with a horizontal slit by which a current of
cold air from the outside entered. This slit was always
placed on the north side of the furnace and was provided on the outside with a flat funnel-shaped attachment by which the wind was concentrated and conducted into the slit. The operation of tempering the
blades was only performed on those days of winter
when a cold strong north wind prevailed. The sword
blade when bright red-hot was lifted out of the fire and
kept in front of the slit and by this means was gradually cooled in the draft of air. It acquired the proper
degree of temper at the single operation.

To Harden Steel.

A very fine preparation for making steel very hard
is composed of wheat flour, salt and water, using say
two teaspoonsful of water, one-half a teaspoonful of
flour, and one of salt; heat the steel to be hardened
enough to coat it with the paste—by immersing it in
the composition—after which heat it to a cherry-red

and plunge it in cold, soft water. If properly done, the steel will come out with a beautiful white surface. It is said that Stubb's files are hardened in this manner.

Tempering Steel Springs.

The hardening and tempering of springs whose coils are of thick cross-section is performed at one operation as follows: The springs are heated in the furnace or oven described, and are first immersed for a certain period in a tank containing fish oil (obtained from the fish "*Moss Bunker*," and termed "*straights*"), and are then removed and cooled in a tank of water. The period of immersion in the oil is governed solely by the operator's judgment, depending upon the thickness of the cross-section of the spring coil, or, in other words, the diameter of the round steel of which the spring is made. The following, however, are examples :

Number of coils in spring.................................... 5¾
Length of the spring... 6 inches.
Outside diameter of coils................................. 4¾ "
Diameter of steel... 1 inch.

The spring was immersed in the oil and slowly swung back and forth for twenty-eight seconds, having been given thirty-five swings during that time. Upon removal from the oil the spring took fire, was redipped for one second, and then put in the cold water tank to cool off.

Of the same springs the following also are examples :

Example.	Time of immersion in oil	Number of swings in oil.
Second	36 seconds.	46
Third	27 "	36
Fourth	38 "	40

SIZE OF SPRING.

Number of coils in the springs	6
Length of the springs	9 inches.
Inside diameter of coils	$3\frac{1}{4}$
Size of steel	$1 \times 1\frac{1}{2}$ square.

Example.	Time of immersion in oil.	Number of swings in oil.
First	9 seconds.	12
Second	8 "	12
Third	8 "	12
Fourth	9 "	12
Fifth	9 "	12
Sixth	9 "	12

To keep the tempering oil cool and at an even temperature, the tank of fish-oil was in a second or outer tank containing water, a circulation of the latter being maintained by a pump. The swinging of the coils causes a circulation of the oil, while at the same time it hastens the cooling of the spring. The water-tank was kept cool by a constant stream and overflow.

If a spring, upon being taken from the oil, took fire, it was again immersed as in the first example.

In this, as in all other similar processes, resin and pitch are sometimes added to the oil to increase its hardening capacity if necessary.

The test to which these springs were subjected was to compress them until the coils touched each other, measuring the height of the spring after each test, and continuing the operation until at two consecutive tests the spring came back to its height before the two respective compressions. The amount of set under these conditions is found to vary from three-eighths of an inch, in comparatively weak, to seven-eighths of an inch for large, stiff ones.

The springs were subjected to a severe test in a machine designed for that purpose, being compressed and released until there was no set under the severest test.

In the following description of the plans adopted by a very prominent carriage-spring maker will also be found a process termed a water-chill temper, which tempers at one process. The steel used by this firm is "Greave's spring steel." The spring plates are heated to bend them to the *former*, which is a plate serving as a gauge whereby to bend the plate to its proper curve.

This bending operation is performed quickly enough to leave the steel sufficiently hot for the hardening; hence the plates after bending are dipped edgeways and level into a tank of linseed oil which sets in a tank of circulating water, the latter serving to keep the oil at about a temperature of 70 degrees when in constant use. About three inches from the bottom of the oil tank is a screw to prevent the plates from falling to the bottom among the refuse sediment.

To draw the temper the hardened springs are placed in the furnace, which has the air-blast turned off, and when the scale begins to rise, showing that the adhering oil is about to take fire, they are turned end for end in the furnace so as to heat them equally all over. When the oil blazes and is freely blazed off, the springs are removed and allowed to cool in the open air, but if the heat of a plate, when dipped in the oil to harden, is rather low, it is cooled, after blazing, in water. The cooling after blazing thus being employed to equalize any slight difference in the heat of the spring when hardened.

The furnace is about ten inches wide and about four inches longer than the longest spring. The grate bars are arranged *across* the furnace with a distance of three-eighths of an inch between them.

The coal used is egg anthracite. It is first placed at the back of the furnace, and raked forward as it becomes ignited and burns clearly.

For shorter springs the coal is kept banked at the back of the furnace, so that the full length of the furnace is not operative, which, of course, saves fuel. By feeding the fire at the back end of the furnace, the gases formed before the coal burns quickly pass up the chimney without passing over the plates, which heat over a clear fire.

For commoner brands of steel, what is termed a water-chill temper is given. This process is not as good as oil-tempering, but serves excellently for the quality of steel on which it is employed. The process is as follows: The springs are heated and bent to shape on the *former* plate as before said ; while at a clear red heat, and still held firmly to the *former* plate, water is poured from a dipper passed along the plate. The dipper is filled four or five times, according to the heat of the plate, which is cooled down to a low or very deep red. The cooling process on a plate 1½ x ¼ inches occupies about six seconds on an average, but longer if the steel was not at a clear red, and less if of a brighter red when the cooling began, this being left to the judgment of the operator.

Some brands of steel of the *Swede steel* class, will not temper by the water-chill process, while yet other brands will not harden in oil, in which case water is used to dip the plates in for hardening, the tempering being blazing in oil as described. In all cases, how-ever, steel that will not harden in oil will not temper by the water-chill process.—*By* JOSHUA ROSE, A.M.

Tempering Small Tools.

I have had a great many years' experience in the matter of tempering small tools, such as chisels, punches, drills, etc., and I think that I may be able, accordingly, to give some simple directions which will be of use to the trade. Steel for tools of this kind should never be heated beyond a bright cherry-red. The last hammering should be invariably on the flat sides, and at a very low heat; the tool meanwhile being held fairly on the anvil, and blows struck squarely with the hammer. This process is technically known as hammer-hardening, and serves to close the grain of the steel. After this, heat the article slowly and evenly until it shows a cherry-red about one and one-half inches from the point. Immerse the tool edge first into pure cold water, the surface of which is perfectly calm, a short distance, and hold it steadily at that point until the red above the water has become quite dull. Brighten the tool slightly by rubbing on a stone or by any other convenient means, and watch the changes of color which occur. First, blue will appear next to the body of the chisel, then probably brown, after which will come dark straw-color, then light straw-color, and at the edge a quite bright straw-color. Heat from the body of the tool will gradually change the location of these colors. The bright edge will assume a light straw-color; then will follow straw-color, orange, brown, and finally blue.

A word with reference to colors in the matter of tempering. A tool to cut hard cast-iron should be straw-color, or sometimes light straw-color; for soft cast-iron it should be dark straw-color; for wrought-iron, purple; or, if the iron is quite soft, blue may be found hard enough. A chisel treated as last described will wear well and not break easily. Drills may be tempered in the same way as described above. In my own practice, I leave them a shade harder than is required in a chisel. On the other hand punches may be slightly softer for the same work.—*By* SMALL TOOLS.

To Temper Small Pieces of Steel.

Many blacksmiths are bothered to temper small pieces of steel on account of their springing. My way is to temper them in linseed oil, and they give me no trouble. I make a great many very thin knives.

Take a tin can large enough to insert the steel that you want to temper, say a tall two-quart fruit can, fill it with oil. Do not work your steel too hot, for that will spoil any steel. Temper just the same as you would if you were using water, and I think the result will be satisfactory.—*By* VOLNEY HESS.

Hardening Thin Articles.

In hardening any article of steel that is thin or light and heats quickly, it is advisable to remove on a grindstone or emery wheel the scale formed in forging before heating. The scale being of unequal density, if it is not removed it is generally impossible to heat evenly; besides, the degree of heat can be better observed if it is removed.

Sword Blades.

Sword blades are made and tempered so that they will chip a piece out of a stone without showing a nick upon their edges, says a gentleman who has been through the great sword manufactory at Soligen, Germany. The steel, he says, is cut from bars into strips about two and one-half inches wide, and of the required length, by a heavy cutting machine. These are carried into the adjoining forge room, where each piece is heated white, hammered by steam so that about twenty blows fall upon every part of its surface, and then thrown into a barrel of water. Afterward these pieces are again heated in a great coke fire, and each goes through a set of rolls, which reduce it to something like the desired shape of the weapon. The rough margins are trimmed off the piece of steel in another machine, and there is left a piece of dirty, dark-blue metal shaped like a sword, and ready for grinding. This is done on great stones, revolved and watered by machinery, the workmen having to be the most expert that can be obtained, as the whole fate of the sword is in their hands. It is afterward burnished on small wheels managed by boys from twelve to sixteen years old, and when it has been prepared to receive the fittings of the handles, is ready for testing, which has to be done with great care. Any fault in the work is charged to the workman responsible for it, and he has to make it good. It is said that any blade which will not chip a piece out of a stone without showing a nick on itself is rejected.

To Temper Steel on One Edge.

Red-hot lead is an excellent thing in which to heat a long plate of steel that requires softening or tempering on one edge. The steel need only to be heated at the part required, and there is little danger of the metal warping or springing. By giving sufficient time, thick portions may be heated equally with thin parts. The ends of wire springs that are to be bent or riveted may be softened for that purpose by this process, after the springs have been hardened or tempered.

Heating to a Cherry-Red—Points in Tempering.

What is a cherry-red heat? To answer this question I will describe how I do my work. My shop is well lighted by windows and I heat to a cherry-red in the shade on days when the light is good, but on cloudy days I don't heat quite so high. I do not think that in hardening cast-steel it should be heated above a cherry-red in the shade. After hardening, temper thus: for razors, straw color: penknives, slightly bluish; screw taps and eyes, yellow; chipping chisels, brownish yellow; springs, dark purple; saws, dark blue.—*By* JOHN M. WRIGHT.

Brine for Tempering.

Brine for tempering is usually known as hardening liquid, or hardening compound. The tempering is done after the hardening, and is usually termed draw-ing the temper. If good crucible steel is used there is nothing better than rain or soft water to harden with, that is, for tools which are not so thin as to bend, spring, or break when hardening. When thin articles, such as knife or saw blades, are to be hardened, cold raw linseed oil is the best material or compound ex-tant. The bath may be filled entirely with oil, or have a surface of oil say six inches, and six inches or more of oil underneath the water. Clear oil is best, because, when water is present the lower stratum of oil is likely to saponify or become soapy, and loses its cooling qualities.

When the steel is not uniformly hard or lacks the necessary amount of carbon for hardening properly, then re-agents called hardening compounds are used to produce the necessary hardness. Of these compounds there are many, some of value, and more of question-able character. I give a few good preparations. Avoid using hard water at all times.

Chloride of sodium (salt), 4 ounces; nitrite of soda (saltpetre), ½ ounce; alum pulverized, 1 dram; soft or rain water, 1 gallon; when thoroughly dissolved heat to cherry-red and cool off. This process hardens and tempers, or draws no temper.

Another preparation is: Saltpetre, 2 ounces; sal-ammonia, 2 ounces; pulverized alum, 2 ounces; salt, 1½ pounds; soft water, 3 gallons. It is not neces-sary to draw with this mixture.

Another compound is: Corrosive sublimate, 1 ounce; salt, 8 ounces; soft water, 6 quarts. Corrosive sublimate is a subtle poison, so be careful with it.

While the above are of more or less value, the following will ever stand by you. It is in more general use than all the others put together:

Ferrocyanide of potassium, sometimes called prussiate of potash, 8 ounces, pulverized; 6 pounds of salt; 8 ounces of borax, pulverized; soft water, 10 gallons. The potash is poison, but when dissolved it becomes so well distributed in the water that its power as a poison becomes dissipated. For this mixture, as well as all others, use a wooden vessel, or a vitrified earthen vessel. The former is preferable. If prussiate of potash is not at hand, substitute 1½ pounds of crude potash, or two gallons full-strength soap-makers' lye, made by leaching hardwood ashes. In using this compound you will find that the salt and other ingredients are drawn to the surface edges of the vessel and form an incrustation on the outer upper section of the vessel, which you must remove and replace in the water. If in constant use replace the evaporated water with an equal amount *pro rata* of the ingredients. When much scale is deposited in the bottom of the vessel, remove the water to a clean receptacle, and clean the deposit from the vessel; replace the water drawn off and add sufficient water to replace the loss, and add ingredients *pro rata*. This preparation is in use by all file makers, and in it are hardened the smallest files extant. With care (keeping covered when not in use), a bath of this preparation may be kept with proper additions for years. I know of one bath of this kind which (by the necessary additions) has been in constant use thirty years. It is a tank holding about eighty gallons. Its owner would not dispose of it for $1,000. He makes the best files produced in America. For tools of any kind which are not liable to spring in hardening I do not know of a better ordinary process.—*By* Iron Doctor.

A Bath for Hardening Steel.

I have a hardening bath that is good and cheap. It is made as follows : Potassium cyanide, 2 ounces ; ammonia carbon, 1 ounce ; soda bicarbon, 1 ounce ; aqua pura (water), 1 bbl.; sodium chloride (salt), 15 lbs.

I use a coal oil barrel. The plow lay should be of an even cherry-red all over. Hold the lay with tongs at the heel, put it into the water point first, but not too fast or it will spring, and keep the lay under water until it is cold.—*By* E. W. S.

The Lead Bath for Tempering.

Among the many secrets of tempering is the employment of the lead bath, which is simply a quantity of molten lead, contained in a suitable receptacle and kept hot over a fire. The uses of this bath are many.

For instance, if it be desired to heat an article that is thick in one portion and thin in another, every mechanic knows how difficult it is to heat the thick portion without overheating the thin part. If the lead bath be made and kept at a red heat, no matter how thick the article may be, provided sufficient time be given, both the thick and thin parts will be evenly and equally heated, and at the same time get no hotter than the bath in which they are immersed.

For heating thin cutting blades, springs, surgical instruments, softening the tangs of tools, etc., this bath is unequaled.

If a portion of an article be required to be left soft, as the end of a spring that is to be bent or riveted, the entire spring may be tempered, and the end to be soft may be safely drawn in the lead bath to the lowest point that steel can be annealed without disturbing in the least the temper of the spring not plunged in the bath. Springs, or articles made of spring brass, may be treated in the same manner. A great advantage in the use of the lead bath is that there is no risk of breakage by the shrinkage of the metal at the water line, as is often the case when tempered by the method of heating and chilling in cold water.

As lead slowly oxidizes at a red heat, two methods may be used to prevent it. One is to cover the surface of the lead with a layer of fine charcoal or even common wood ashes. Another, and a better plan, is to float on the top of the lead a thin iron plate, fitting the vessel in which the lead is contained, but having a hole in the center or in one side, as most convenient, and large enough to readily admit of receiving the articles to be tempered or softened.—*By* W. H.

Hardening Small Tools.

It is said that the engravers and watchmakers of Germany harden their tools in sealing wax. The tool is heated to whiteness and plunged into the wax, withdrawn after an instant and plunged in again, the process being repeated until the steel is too cold to enter the wax. The steel is said to become, after this process, almost as hard as the diamond, and when touched with a little oil or turpentine the tools are excellent for engraving, and also for piercing the hardest metals.

Hardening in Oil vs. Hardening in Water.

I have made and tempered cutters for straight and irregular molders, sash tools, etc. If tempered in oil they will hold their edges better, cut smoother and longer than if tempered in water. In hardening, the oil cleaves to the steel, which is in consequence longer cooling. The water seems to separate, leaving air spaces between the steel and the water. Water cools quicker and hardens harder than oil and consequently steel hardened in oil must be left at a higher color than when hardened in water.   A good deal depends on the heating of the steel to get a good temper.   While water injures the quality of the steel, oil improves it. —*By* D. D.

Tempering Plow Points.

If the steel is good, nothing will temper a plow point better than good clear water, with perhaps a little salt in it.   Harden at as low a heat as the steel will bear, and do not draw the temper for blunt tools for cutting stone.   Heat your plow points in the same manner.   The great trouble with plow points is in the poor quality of the steel.   You may make the plow points better by case-hardening, which every blacksmith knows how to do, and harden at a low heat without drawing the temper.—*Scientific American.*

Tempering Blacksmiths' Tools.

Some blacksmiths will, perhaps, be glad to know that by sifting prussiate of potash on red-hot iron and cooling it immediately, a temper is obtained hard enough to make a great many of the anvil tools used by smiths.—*By* I. C.

Softening Chilled Castings.

For softening chilled castings my plan is as follows: Heat the metal you wish to drill in the fire to a little above a cherry-red. Then remove it from the fire and immediately place a lump of brimstone (sulphur) on the part to be drilled. You can keep the metal on the fire so as to retain heat and continue to throw sulphur on it until it will be as easy to drill as pot metal is. —*By* F. B.

To Harden Cast-Iron.

Heat the iron to a cherry-red, then sprinkle on it cyanide of potassium (a deadly poison), and heat it to a little above red, then dip. The end of a rod that had been treated in this way could not be cut with a file. Upon breaking off a piece about half an inch long, it was found that the hardening had penetrated to the interior, upon which the file made no more impression than upon the surface. The cyanide may be used to case-harden wrought-iron.—*Scientific American.*

Brass Wire—How Should it be Tempered for Springs?

Brass wire cannot be tempered, if, by tempering, is meant the method of tempering steel springs. The only method to make a brass spring is by compressing the brass by means of rolls, or by hammering. The latter method will be the one that will probably be used. If the springs are to be flat, hammer them out to shape in thickness from soft wire, or sheet brass, somewhat thicker than the finished spring is to be. If the brass shows a tendency to crack in hammering it must be annealed, which can be done by heating to a light red and plunging into water. In hammering use a light hammer, and don't spare the blows.—*By* H.

To Harden Steel Cultivator Shovels.

Shovel blades will harden in good soft water, with a little sal ammoniac in it, say one pound to ten gallons of water, if they are not put in too hot. Steel will harden best at a given heat, and practice alone will teach what that heat is. Clean the blades well, or, better still, polish them ; then cover them with a paste made of salt and shorts, or flour and heat them very slowly.—*By* E. J. C.

CHAPTER V.

FORGING IRON.

Hand Forgings.

Notwithstanding the working of iron is one of the oldest mechanical occupations, the opinion prevails that the blacksmith need not of necessity be a man of much skill beyond what is necessary to heat and pound iron into shape. Yet this is but a small part of the duty required of him. If he is to work metal intelligently he must know the nature of the different kinds, its adaptability for specific uses. One grade of iron is well suited to one class of work and unfit for another. Then, too, welding is something more than the causing of two pieces of iron to adhere. Unless fusion is perfect the work is not well done, and perfect fusion can be obtained only by the proper heat and fit condition of the surfaces. Tempering steel is an important part of the business, and one which few thoroughly understand, or even care to.

In all other departments of carriage-making, patterns can be used with a certainty as guides, but the blacksmith has a large part of his work to do without patterns of any kind other than as general outlines for forms. Beyond this the eye must guide him, and as his work must be performed while the iron is hot, he must act promptly, and unless he is accurate his work must be done over again.

In ironing a carriage the woodwork is placed before him in pieces, and to perform his work well he must decide upon a general line of action before beginning his work. It will not do for him to make one piece and then take up another without previous study. If irons are to be fitted to the wood they must be shaped on the anvil, not on the wood, where, between burning and hammering, the general shape is obtained, but at the expense of the timber. Notwithstanding all that has been written and said against fitting iron to timber by burning, a large percentage of ironworkers in the country never think of any other way. We go into shops and see the blacksmith heat his tire red-hot, place it around the rim of the wheel, and amid fire and smoke "set up" to the rim, while two or three boys are busy with pails of water cooling off the iron. Those who have profited by experience and study find that if the tire is welded to the right length, and bent true, very little heat is required to expand the tire large enough to allow its being placed outside of the felloes, while water poured against the tread of the tire will cool it. In fact, not a few set light tires without using any water, and those who heat the tire but little find that the work is far better than when heated to a point that will burn the wood.

Too many blacksmiths are satisfied if the work is

done so as to pass, regardless as to details and accuracy. These men are a disgrace to their vocation, and they too often regulate wages to be paid, and as the number increases more rapidly than that of the good workman, they will interfere the more seriously with wages in the future.

The young man who thinks of learning the black-smith trade should first learn whether he is physically fitted for the peculiar labor.   If satisfied on that point, he should immediately begin a course of study with special reference to the working of metals.   He should also study free-hand drawing.   Every hour spent at the drawing-board is an hour shaping irons, as he is training the hand to perform the work and the eye to see that it is true.   And at no time should he drop the pencil.   He should keep in mind the fact that the most skillful are the most successful.   We do not mean skillful in one line only, but in all.   The man who can direct, as well as execute, is the one who will make the greatest advancement, and to direct it is necessary to know why a thing should be done as well as how.

The poetry of the blacksmith shop has been a theme for writers for centuries, but there is little poetry in it to the blacksmith who stands at the forge day after day pounding and shaping unless he has studied, and finds new themes in every heat, spark, or scale.   If he can create beautiful forms in his mind, and with his hands shape the metal to those forms, then he can see poetry in his work.   If he is but a machine that performs his work automatically, the dull prose of his occupation makes him dissatisfied and unmanly.—*Coach, Harness and Saddlery.*

Making a T-shaped Iron.

If the blacksmith who wants to learn how to make a T-shaped iron, will take good iron two-thirds as long

Making a T-shaped Iron.   Fig. 128—Showing the Iron ready for Turning.

as his head block, twice as wide and one-eighth of an

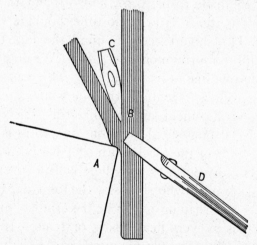

Fig. 129—Showing the Turning Process.

inch thicker than he wants the plate when finished (or

perhaps one and one-sixteenth inches on a light plate),
fuller in one edge one-third from the end, draw off the
short end, next split the long end down to within one
and one-quarter inches of the fuller scarf (if he has an
inch perch), then rest the fuller scarf on the round edge
of the anvil, follow the chisel down with the small fuller and punch, and turn off to a right angle with a

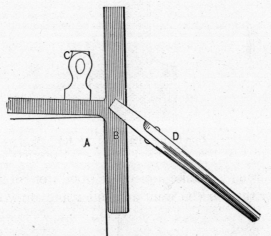

Fig. 130—Showing how the Iron is turned to a Right Angle.

hand hammer, his iron will be so nearly finished that
he will understand what else should be done without
any more directions from me.

The accompanying illustrations will help him to understand my instructions.   Fig. 128 represents the iron
ready for turning; Fig. 129 shows the turning process,
A denoting the anvil, *B* the iron, *C* the fuller, and *D*

the tongs. In Fig. 130, *A* denotes the anvil, *B* the iron, *C* the hammer, and *D* the tongs.—*By* E. K. W.

Another Method of Making a T-shaped Iron.

I will describe my way of making a T-shaped iron without having a weld at the hole that the kingbolt

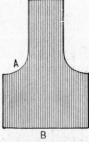

Making a T-shaped Iron by the Method of "J. L." Fig. 131—Showing how the End of the Iron is Fullered and Drawn Out.

goes through. Take a piece of good iron of suitable size for the job you want and fuller and draw out the

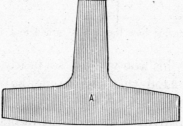

Fig. 132—Showing the T Completed.

end as at Fig. 131. Next place *B* on the anvil and insert the fuller on the two inside corners so as to draw out the ends for the head block, then weld to each end to make it the desired length. Do not cut the inside corners square, but leave them rounding, as Fig. 132, and also a trifle thicker at the center, as this makes it stronger and at the same time gives more support to the kingbolt. I almost always weld at *A*, Fig. 132, by upsetting well, so as to have plenty of stock, and being careful to get a clean heat. I do not remember ever having one break that was made in this way.—*By* J. L.

Forging Stay Ends and Offsets.

To make stay ends I take a piece of good iron 1½ x 1 inch and fuller and forge as shown in the dotted

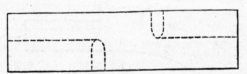

Fig. 133—Showing the Stay End with Dotted Lines for Forging and Fullering.

lines of Fig. 133. It will then be shaped as in Fig. 134. I then fuller and forge as in the dotted lines of Fig. 134, and finish with the file. To make a stay offset take a piece of iron 1½ x ¾ inch, forge as in dotted lines of Fig. 135, punch a hole and split open. Next open as in Fig. 136, and forge as seen in the dotted lines, then straighten up and finish with a file,

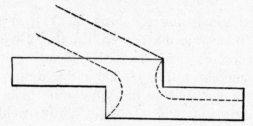

Fig. 134—Showing the Piece as Forged and Fullered.

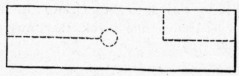

Fig. 135—Showing the Stay Offset with Dotted Lines for Forging.

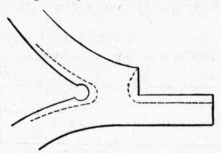

Fig. 136—Stay Offset Opened to Forge as in Dotted Lines.

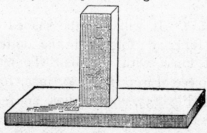

Fig. 137—Showing another Method of Making Stay Ends.

Figs. 137, 138 and 139 illustrate another way of mak-

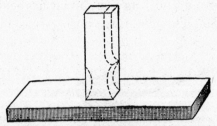

Fig. 138—Showing the Fullering and Forging as by Dotted Lines.

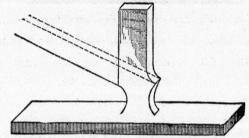

Fig. 139—Showing the Shape after Fullering and Forging.

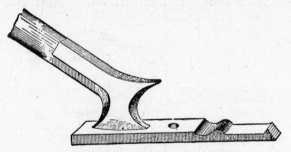

Fig. 140—Showing Finished Stay End.

ing stay ends. Forge a piece of iron, square and small enough to go in the square hole of the anvil; then

forge on the flat head, giving a shape as in Fig. 137.
Next fuller out and forge as shown in the dotted lines
of Fig. 138. This will give a shape as in Fig. 139;

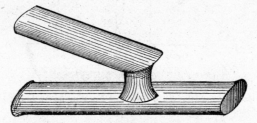

Fig. 141—Showing Finished Offset.

then bend according to the dotted lines in that figure,
and finish with a file. Figs. 140 and 141 show the
finished end and offset.—*By* J. C. H.

Making an Eye-Bolt.

The accompanying illustrations represent my

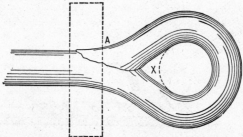

Making an Eye-Bolt.   Fig. 142 — Showing the Old Way of Doing
the Job.

method of making an eye-bolt so that it will be

round in the eye, and likewise very strong at the weld.

Fig. 142 represents the old way of making an eye-bolt and the way it is made now by most blacksmiths.

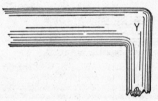

Fig. 143—Showing how the Iron is Turned in E. K. Wehry's Method of Making an Eye-Bolt.

The bolt is simply turned about, the end weld being at A. It will be noticed that the place X is not filled out with iron, and that the hole in the bolt cannot be round unless more iron is used.

By my method the iron is turned down as at Y in

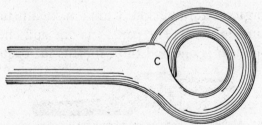

Fig. 144—Showing how the Weld is Made.

Fig. 143. It is made somewhat flat at Y and then turned around as in Fig. 144. A good weld is made at C, and it is worked down to the size of the iron. The eye-bolt is as shown in Fig. 145. The weld will not give and the hole is a round one.   With a little practice, this eye-bolt can be made as easily as the old

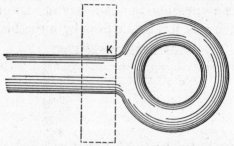

Fig. 145—Showing the Eye Bolt Completed.

style, and can be worked down so that it will fit in a hole up to the eye as shown in Fig. 145 at *K*.   Compare this fit with that shown in Fig. 140.—*By* E. K.

Forging a Turn-Buckle.

In forging a turn-buckle, I first make a mandrel, as shown in Fig. 146.   The part *A* is one and one-fourth inch round, *B* is one and three-fourths inch square.   I

"Tinker's" Method of Forging a Turn-buckle.   Fig. 146 — Showing the Mandrel.

next take some 1¼ x 1½ inch iron, make collars and weld them on the mandrel, and scarf on each side of the collars, with a round pene fuller for the cheek pieces, as shown in Fig. 147.   I then take for the sides some $\frac{7}{8}$ x $1\frac{1}{8}$ iron and cut long enough for both sides, bend in the middle and scarf the ends, and am now ready for welding up. I put one of the collars between the two prongs and take a light heat to stick

Fig. 147—Showing the Finished Buckle and Collar.

them together. I then go back to the fire and get a good soft heat, weld down on the mandrel, finish off with the swage, then cut the end and repeat the process. If the turn-buckle is to be finished up extra nice, you can use the same swage for the sides.—*By* " TINKER."

Forging a Turn-buckle.

My method of forging a turn-buckle, say for a one and one-fourth inch rod, is: First, I take a piece of

Forging a Turn-buckle. Fig. 148—End View of Ferrule Bent for Welding.

one and one-fourth inch square iron and bend it into a ferrule such as is shown in Fig. 148 and then weld into it a prong as in Fig. 149. Then I cut out a place,

as at *A* in Fig. 150, and weld in the other prong.
Next I put in a mandrel and shape it up to the taper,
as in Fig. 151. This makes half the turn-buckle and

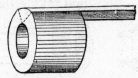

Fig. 149—Showing Prong Welded to Ferrule.

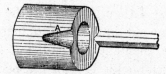

Fig. 150—Piece cut out at *A* for Second Prong.

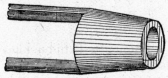

Fig. 151—Showing Second Prong Welded and Taper Forged.

Fig. 152—Showing the Two Pieces Welded at *B B*, and Job Complete.

by repeating the operation I get two of these pieces,
which I weld together at *B B*, and get the finished
turn-buckle as in Fig. 152. In welding the prongs
together to join the two halves, I take one-half and

let my helper put in the mandrel with one hand and tap lightly with a small hammer with the other, and after the welding is done I use the mandrel to handle the forging with while swaging it to finish.—*By* Southern Blacksmith.

Making a Cant-Hook.

I make a great many cant-hooks. For the clasp I use 1 ½ x 1 ½ inch Norway iron. About half an inch from the end I cut it half off, bend over and weld,

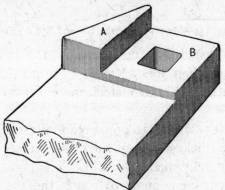

Making a Cant-Hook. Fig. 153—Showing how the Jam and Clasp are Made.

forging rather thin inside of the shoulder. I then take a set hammer and make the shoulder for the hook to strike against.

I leave the jaw about three-eighths inch thick, punch the hole, and trim to suit. The other end is made in the same way. For the hook I use ¾ x ½ x ⅞ x ½ inch steel, cut thirteen inches long. One end should be stove (not bent) and put in the heating tool to get the bill. After taking it out I draw it to a point, punch the hole and bend nearly to a circle. In bending I lay the bill and eye on a straightedge or board as shown in Fig. 154.

I use three bands, the first and second being one

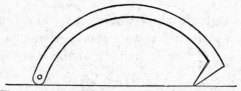

Fig. 154—Showing how the Bill and Eye are Bent.

and one-half inch No. 14 band iron; the third band is two and one-half inch No. 8. For the pick I use seven-eighths inch square steel, and cut it off ten inches long.

In Fig. 153 of the accompanying illustrations *A* indicates the thickest part of the clasp, and *B* is the jaw. This is generally made too thin. The point must not come down far enough to touch the toe ring, but should stand up six inches. In bending the bill there is no sharp corner made which may break the hip when you are pulling it out of a log.—*By* H. R.

How Forks are Forged.

The following is a description of the manner of forging a four-tined manure fork, as practiced in one of the largest establishments in the neighborhood of New York City. The process of splitting and bending as here described may be extended so as to include forks of a larger number of tines.

How Forks are Forged.   Fig. 155—The Blank.

The blank for a four-tined manure fork is simply a rectangular piece of mild steel, as indicated in Fig. 155.

Fig. 156—First Operation, Preparing the Handle Stem.

It is five and three-quarter inches long, one and three-quarter inches wide, and one-half inch thick. The

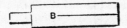

Fig. 157—Splitting the Piece Preparatory to Opening it, as Shown in the next Illustration.

first operation is to draw out the end, leaving a projection, *A*, as shown in Fig. 156, from which the stem

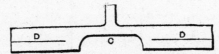

Fig. 158—The Piece Opened Out, Forged Down and Split Again.

for the handle is subsequently drawn. The piece is then split to the line *B*, Fig. 157, and is opened out as in Fig. 158. The thickness is reduced to *C*. All this is done at one heat, and the splitting and opening out is accomplished by a machine termed a splitter. The next operation is to split the piece along the lines *DD* in the engraving.   The parts are then opened out

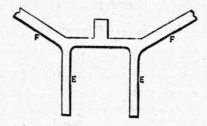

Fig. 159—The Four Tines Roughly Formed.

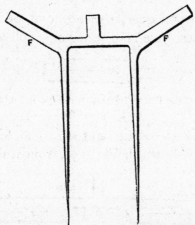

Fig. 160—The Middle Tines Drawn Out.

as in Fig. 159, *EE*, forming, when forged out as in Fig. 160, the middle tines.   After the tines *EE* are drawn out, the ends *FF* are drawn and bent around as shown in Fig. 161. The last operation is to draw out the handle *A* to the required shape. After these several steps have been taken, the tines are formed to proper shape and finally are tempered.

It will be obvious to the practical reader that the

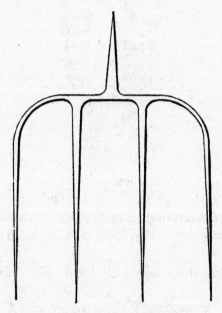

Fig. 161—The Finished Fork.

grain of the steel in this process of forming the fork is kept lengthwise of the handle as well as of the tines. The whole of the forging operations described are performed under the trip hammer, but the forming or setting to shape of the tines is done in a special machine.

Five Methods of Making one Forging.

The sketches given herewith are of a piece of forging of a somewhat intricate character. The different

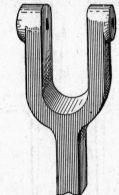

Fig. 162—The Finished Forging.

methods of accomplishing the same result form an interesting study. Fig. 162 shows the finished article.

To make this, says one blacksmith, of ordinary

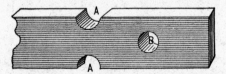

Fig. 163.

refined iron, I fuller it as at *A A*, and punch the hole at *B*, Fig. 163. Then I split it open, as shown by the dotted line in Fig. 164, and open it out as in Fig. 165.

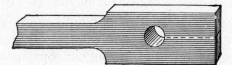

Fig. 164.

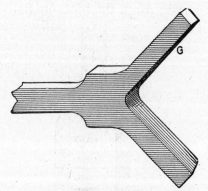

Fig. 165.

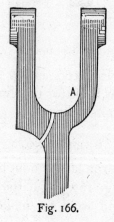

Fig. 166.

Then I bend each arm, as *C D* in Fig. 165, to shape and forge it to size, punching the holes toward the last.   I know of no better way of forging it out of solid iron unless I could get the job roughed out to any better shape by sending it to a shop having a trip hammer to rough the blocks out.   Or it might be a good plan to use lighter iron, forge the piece in halves and weld

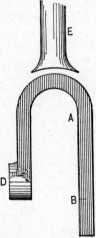

Fig. 167.

them as shown in Fig. 166, as my principal difficulty is in setting the jaw back for the curve *A* in Fig. 166. —*By* YOUNG BLACKSMITH.

METHOD NO. 2.

Take a piece of iron large enough, and bend it to U shape, as at *A*, Fig. 167.   Cut the end as at mark *B*, and bend over and weld to make eyes, *D*.   Then jump-weld the rod *E*.   It will make the smoothest job to jump it, if the iron is thick enough.—*By* H. B.

METHOD NO. 3.

Thinking it a duty, as well as a pleasure, to help my brother blacksmiths, I give you my way of doing the job.

I should take iron of sufficient size to forge the piece *A*, Fig. 168, fullering it in the center, as at *a*, with a large fuller to sufficient depth to make a good

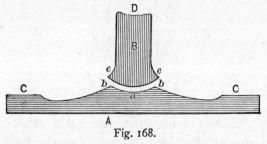

Fig. 168.

weld.   Then, with a small one, fuller it out on each side, as at *bb*, and draw it out long enough to bend to the required shape, leaving a lump, *CC*, on each end to form the eyes.   Then forge the stem *B*, making the scarf at *ee*; overlap the fullering at *a*, and more curved than the fullering at *a*, so that when the jump-weld is made, the stem *B* will first meet the piece *A* at the bottom of the fullering at *a*, and the rest of the surface will come together with the first jumping blows.   This is quite important in obtaining a good, sound weld, as it forces out the air and any loose cin-

ders, etc., that may not have been cleaned off the surfaces. After welding at the center by striking on the
end, *D*, of the stem, weld with a fuller applied at *ee*,
and then bend to the required shape.

There is another and similar way, as follows : Form

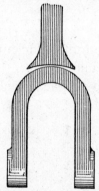

Fig. 169—Method No. 3.

the two pieces as in Fig. 169, leaving it thick enough
to weld and finish. In this case, also, the fullering on
the stem must be more flat than the seat on which it
welds, so that it will be sure to weld in the center first,
and weld on the horn of the anvil.—*By* G. B. J.

METHOD NO. 4.

First take a piece of iron thick enough to give
plenty of iron when fullered at *A* in Fig. 170, and
fuller it hollow there. Then bend it to shape ; take a
piece for the stem and jump it, taking care that it well
laps the fullering at *A*, and let it be more curved than
at *A,* so that it will weld in the center first. To weld,

place the hook on the anvil horn, clean it with a
brush ; bring the stem down on the anvil with a light

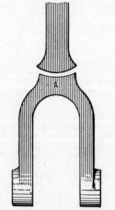

Fig. 170—Method No. 4.

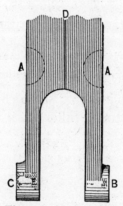

Fig. 171—Method No. 5.

blow to clean off the dirt, etc.; brush it quickly, strike
a few quick blows with a light sledge on the end of
the stem and then fuller round the stem.   Get a good

heat and don't lose a second's time and you'll have a good, sound, neat job.

Some blacksmiths make the weld round at *A* instead of hollow, but I don't see why.—*By* LEATHER APRON.

METHOD NO. 5.

I would like to have blacksmiths try my method, as per Fig. 171. Forge two separate pieces, as *B, C*, in the figure, and weld them at *D*. Fuller *AA* to dotted lines, and draw out the stem.—*By* C. A. S.

Making Offsets.

Take a piece of good iron of the proper size and fuller in half way at *A*, in Fig. 172, then swage down

Making Offsets. Fig. 172—Showing how the Iron is Fullered and Split.

the end *B*, then split with a sharp chisel at *C*, down to *D*. Next with a small fuller work in at *D* and finish

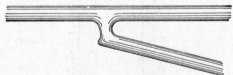

Fig. 173—Showing the Offset Completed.

with a large fuller, then turn off the ends *E* and *F*, and swage down to proper size as shown in Fig. 173. —*By* J. D.

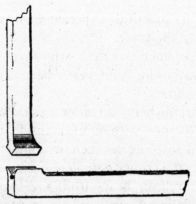

Making a Square Corner. Fig. 174—Ready for the Weld.

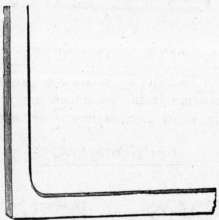

Fig. 175—Completed Job.

To Make a Square Corner.

It requires years of hard study and practice to attain any high rank in our profession, but if brother black- smiths would each make known a little of what they

have learned by practical experience, it would be a
great benefit to the trade.

I have never met any man who had nothing to
learn in blacksmithing, and yet I have known some
very good workmen.

The illustrations herewith show a good way of making a square corner, with a fillet inside if required.
The upset and scarf are as seen in Fig. 174, and Fig.
175 represents the corner complete.

This works well in heavy iron, say two inches by
four inches. It is a V weld in the corner. Be careful to have good clean heats.—*By* R. C. S.

Making a Square Corner.

I send you herewith my method of getting a square
corner up sharp. In the accompanying illustration I
show in Fig. 176 a piece of iron to be bent to a right

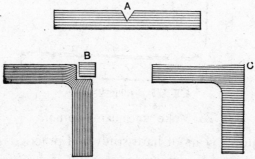

Figs. 176, 177, and 178—"Southern Blacksmith's" Method of Making a
Square Corner.

angle and have a square corner. First I cut it half way through where the bend is to be, as at *A*, then I bend it as shown in Fig. 177, and then weld in a piece *B*, which brings the corner up sharp and square as shown in Fig. 178.—*By* SOUTHERN BLACKSMITH.

The Breaking of Step-Legs.

Builders of heavy wagons with the step-leg at the back end of the wagon experience much trouble from their breaking. They try to overcome this by making them of thicker and wider iron every year, but

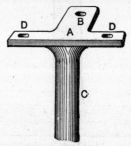

Fig. 179—Showing " Iron Doctor's " Method of Preventing the Breaking of Step-Legs.

they invariably break in the outer hole, and frequently break off the bolts.

In making iron of such a character, at all times avoid, if possible, having holes where the direct strain comes. Fig. 179 shows the proper way to do such work. *A* is the upper part of the leg and fastened on the underside of the tail-bar. *B* is a projection, which

is secured to the central sills. *C* is the shank of the
leg. *D, D, D* are the bolt holes. An iron step
made and secured in this manner with one or two
central braces will last until the wagon is worn out,
and will then answer for another wagon. —*By* IRON
DOCTOR.

Making a Thill Iron.

My way of making a thill iron is to take a straight
bar of iron of the proper width and bend it square

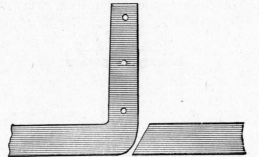

Fig. 180—Making a Thill Iron by the Method of John Zeck.

around, forming the stem of the T, as shown by Fig.
180. I then take another piece of iron of the same
size as the first, cut the end to be welded a little slant-
ing and weld it on at the bend of the first piece with
the long corner out, as shown in the illustration. This
leaves the iron straight on the outside, and when made
in this way thill irons never break, as they often do
when made in the ordinary way.—*By* JOHN ZECK.

Making a T-shaped Iron.

To make a T-shaped iron, I always take the best of iron, Norway or Swedish, for material.

In making a T-shaped, or in other words head-block

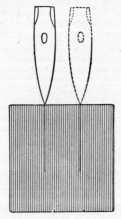

Making a T-shaped Iron.   Fig. 181—Showing how the Piece is Cut.

plates for a one-seated rig, I take a piece of Norway iron 3 x 3 x ¾ inches thick, heat the whole piece at

Fig. 182—Showing how the Corners are Cut.

once, put it on the anvil, and cut with a hot chisel as in Fig. 181, so that the prong will be 1 x ¾ inch.   I

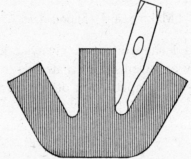

Fig. 183—Showing how the Fuller is Used.

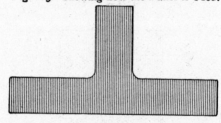

Fig. 184—Showing the Piece after being Fullered.

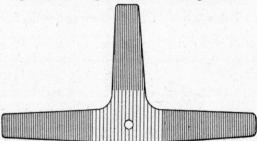

Fig. 185—The Finished T.

next cut away a little of the corner, as shown by dotted lines in Fig. 182. This prevents a seam, and doubtless a bad job. With two heats I bend with the fuller as in Fig. 183, and then draw out according to the shape of the head block, which must govern the thickness and width of the iron. Fig. 184 represents the piece after the fullering.

For larger T's a larger piece of iron is needed. Be sure you have enough iron, as it will be far better to cut off than to weld on. Leave the corner rounded, as it adds strength. Fig. 185 shows the T finished. After one or two trials you can make one in from three to five heats.—*By* L. A. B.

Making a Step-Leg.

Take iron of the size that will fit in the square hole of the anvil, and split it as at *A* in Fig. 186, then bend

Making a Step-Leg. Fig. 186—Showing how the Iron is Split.

it over nearly at right angles with the standing part, take a welding heat and beat down as in Fig. 187, *BB* being the upper part and *C* the leg. Then prepare the pieces *F*, Fig. 188, heat both to the welding point, insert the part *E* in the hole and weld *F* to *D*.

If the square hole in the anvil is not countersunk, make tools as in Figs. 189 and 190. *H*, Fig. 189, is a

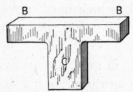

Fig. 187—The Iron as Bent and Beaten Down.

Fig. 188—Showing how the Pieces *F* and *D* are Welded Together.

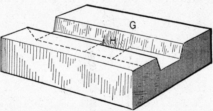

Fig. 189—Showing a Tool used when the Square Hole in the Anvil is not Countersunk.

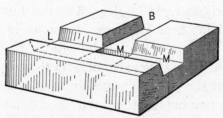

Fig. 190—Another Illustration of the Tools used in Making a Step-Leg.

hole, *L* and *B*, Fig. 190 are recesses, and *M* is a hole. The recesses may be rounded or flat on the bottom,

Fig. 191—Showing one Method of Shaping the Recess in the Tool.

and round at sides as in Fig. 191, or flat on the bottom and beveled on the sides as in Fig. 192.   Beveling or

Fig. 192—Another Way of Shaping the Recess.

rounding are necessary to ensure the ready removal of the iron from the tool.   The holes ought to be slightly countersunk to prevent galling.—*By* Iron Doctor.

Forging a Head-Block Plate for a Double Perch.

My method of forging a head-block plate for a double perch may be of interest to the trade.   It is as follows :

Take good Norway iron 2½ x ⅜ inches, and forge as shown in Fig. 193, on the back of the anvil; then cut out as indicated by the dotted lines, Fig. 193, then split the ends and turn down for perch ends, finish in the corners with files, draw out the ends of the plate, and you have a forging for a double saddle clip as shown in Fig. 194.

To make a Brewster saddle clip take iron the same

size as for the double saddle clip, and use the fuller as
indicated in Fig. 195, then cut out according to the

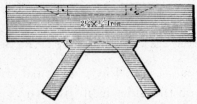

Forging a Head-Block Plate for a Double Perch. Fig. 193—Showing
how the Iron is Forged and Cut Out.

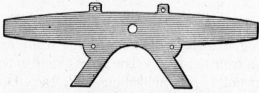

Fig. 194—Showing how the Forging is done for a Double Saddle Clip.

Fig. 195—Showing how the Fuller is used in making a Brewster Saddle
Clip.

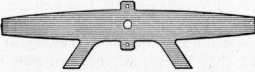

Fig. 196—Showing the Forging Completed.

dotted lines, split the ends as in Fig. 193, and finish.
Then you have a forging as shown in Fig. 196.

I don't claim that this method is cheaper or better

than buying the machine-made articles, but if you want one immediately and cannot get it without waiting two or three days, the next best thing to do is to make it as I have described.—*By* P. R.

Forging a Dash Foot.

My way of forging a dash foot is as follows : I take a piece of Norway iron 1½ x ½ inch and five or six

Forging a Dash Foot by " J. C. H." Fig. 197—Showing how the Iron is Fullered, Punched and Split.

inches long, fuller it at *A* as shown in Fig. 197, then forge out as indicated by the dotted line, punch a small hole at *B*, and then split out as shown by the dotted line. The piece is then ready to be opened

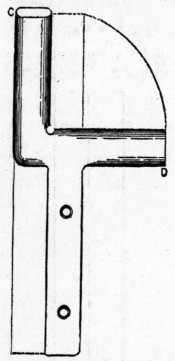

Fig. 198— The Piece Opened Out.

out as in Fig. 198. The corners and ends are then squared by swaging and the rough places are finished with a file. The result is a dash foot as neat and substantial as any one could desire. The welding on is done at *C* and *D.—By* J. C. H.

How to Make a Slot Circle.

I will tell beginners how I make fifth wheels at the factory, I mean those with a slot in them—that is, how I make the slot part.

First make two pieces like that shown in Fig. 199,

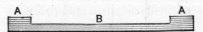

Making a Slot Circle by the Method of " Iron Doctor." Fig. 199—Showing the Shape of the Piece.

the parts *A A* being the same thickness as *B*, but twice as wide. The distance between *A A* is made to suit the turning part of the job. Next weld the two pieces together at *A A* and form the slot *C*, as shown in Fig. 200, *D D* representing the *B* in Fig. 199, and

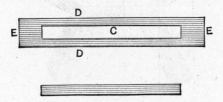

Fig. 200—Showing the Two Pieces Welded Together, and the Piece Used in the Slot.

E the ends welded together. Then weld the slot of the clip and get the right lengths. Then fit a piece of iron of the shape shown in Fig. 201 into the slot so as to fill it up, then heat the whole to a red heat and bend around a former. Then the inside piece will

contract.   The filling is removed when the circle is
complete.—*By* IRON DOCTOR.

Forging a Clip Fifth Wheel.

My way of forging a clip fifth wheel is as follows:
Take a piece of Norway iron and fuller in a recess, as

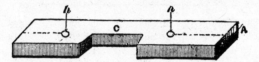

Forging a Clip Fifth Wheel by the Method of "J. C. H."   Fig. 202—
Showing the Piece Fullered and Punched.

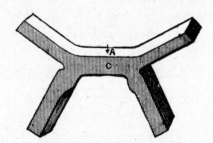

Fig. 203—Showing the Piece Opened Out.

in Fig. 202, then punch in the two holes *h,* and split
to the dotted lines, opening the piece out as in Fig.
203.   Next forge the whole to shape, draw out the
shanks, cut the threads at their ends and then bend to
shape, as in Fig. 204, the face *A* in Fig. 204 being the
same face as *A* in Fig. 203.   Weld at *B* (Fig. 204)

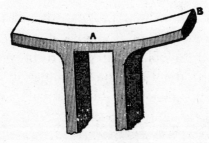

Fig. 204—Showing the Piece Bent to Shape.

the remainder to form the circle, or if the iron is long enough, and it is prepared, it can be made out of one piece.—*By* J. C. H.

Method of Making Fronts for Fifth Wheels.

With reference to the subject of fifth wheel making on a small scale, permit me to offer a wrinkle for the consideration of the craft.

The "bow" or "front" of many wheels used to be

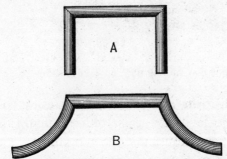

Making Fronts for Fifth Wheels. Fig. 205—Showing the Old Method of Making the Mitre,

of a pattern represented by B in Fig. 205. It was made of ¼ or 5-16 iron. The usual.way to form the mitres (which to look well require to be definite) was to upset the iron into a square angle at each mitre point, as at A, then open out and curve the ends to

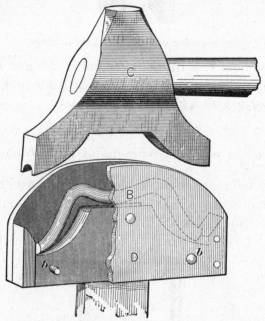

Fig. 206—Showing the Top Tool and Swage Used.

the desired form, and finish the mitres by considerable filing. To facilitate this tedious plan (and it was tedious when thousands were required), I made the tools shown in Figs. 206, 207 and 208. A number of lengths—say 100 lbs.—of the rod, were cut about ⅝ inch for 5-16 inch and ½ inch for ¼ inch longer than the distance (measured with a piece of cord of the same diameter as the iron) between points *B* and *B*,

Fig. 207—End View of the Top Tool.

Fig. 206, and these lengths were bent cold into the approximate shape or form shown by the dotted line *B*, Fig. 206. The swage and top tool being ready, a

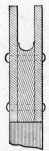

Fig. 208—End V'ew of the Swage.

number of cold shaped blanks were put in the furnace or forge, and the helper taking out one at a time when white hot along the crown or middle, dropped it into the swage, when by two or three smart quick blows with the sledge upon the top tool *C*, Fig. 206, the bow or stay would be complete and ready for welding into the split ends of the circle top. The job I have described is completed without the use of a file. Done by the old plan, filing had been quite an item of expense and it is hardly necessary to say that I never went back to the old method.—*By* W. D.

Making a Fifth-Wheel Hook or a Pole Stop.

To do any work properly and quickly we require the right kind of tools. In making a fifth-wheel hook on a pole stop we need a heading tool, as shown in

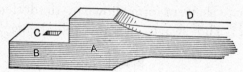

Making a Fifth-Wheel Hook or a Pole Stop. Fig. 209—The Tool Used.

Fig. 209. *A* is the thick heading portion. *B* is the thin heading post. *C* is the square hole. *D* is a section of the hard portion. Take good iron of the proper size, draw down and form the end *D*, shown in Fig. 210, to fit the square hole *C* in the tool. Heat the iron, insert in the tool, and split with the splitting chisel, as at *E*. Next, with a small fuller open up the split, as at *K*, Fig. 211, sufficiently to insert a larger fuller without continuing the split further down. The part *F* is inserted in the tool, and *H* is thrown off. Next take a larger fuller and force down *H*, as at *N* in Fig. 212, *L* fitting in the tool while *M* is still upright. Twist *N* to the shape desired, then repeat and insert the part *O*, Fig. 213, in the tool, hold the

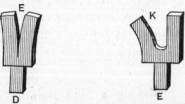

Figs. 210 and 211—Showing how the Piece is Split and Fullered.

sledge on *S*, turn down *P* and dress up the whole with the set-hammer. *R* is the space or recess covering the fifth wheel when the device is used as a fifth-wheel hook, and resting on the cross-plate when it is used as

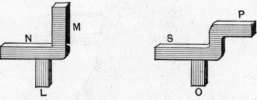

Fig. 2 2—Showing the Next Stage   Fig. 213—Showing the Job Com-
in the Fullering Process.   pleted.

a pole stop. Remove the piece from the tool and round up the end *O* to the proper size for the thread and nut. The square portion is for a fifth-wheel hook, and should be left just as long as the iron is thick through which it passes, less enough to give a set or tension with the nut. The thread should be cut clear up to the square portion. The nut ought to be over the standard thickness to admit of having an extra thread, with a view to getting a better grip.

For a pole stop make the shank the same as you would a bolt. The beginner may require four or five heats to make one. A little practice will reduce the labor to three heats. We have seen experts do them in two heats.—*By* Iron Doctor.

Making a Shift Rail.

The accompanying sketches represent a new and inexpensive method of making a shift rail for buggy seats, as the following explanation will show : Take a

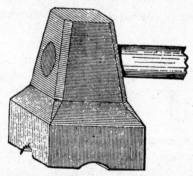

Making a Shift Rail.   Fig. 214—Upper Part of the Swage.

piece of 5/8 by 7-16 inch oval Norway iron, upset it at *A*, in Fig. 216, then take an oval-pointed cold chisel and make a hole in the place where it was upset large

enough to admit a piece of ⅜-inch round iron, with a
collar swaged on one end of it as shown in Fig. 216.

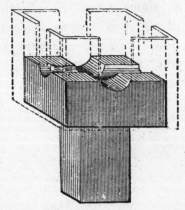

Fig. 215—Lower Part of the Swage used in Shaping the Rail.

Take a good welding heat at the point where the two
irons intersect, and then place in the swage shown in
Fig. 215.   Place the swage shown in Fig. 214 on

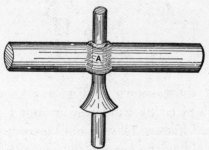

Fig. 216—The Shift Rail Commenced.

top and strike a few blows with a sledge hammer.
The result will be a forging of the kind shown in Fig.

217, ready for welding on the goose neck and arm rests, as shown by the dotted lines. In strength this construction is about equal to a forging made out of solid iron, while it is exactly the same in looks. The swages shown in Figs. 214 and 215 are made the same as other swages employed by blacksmiths,

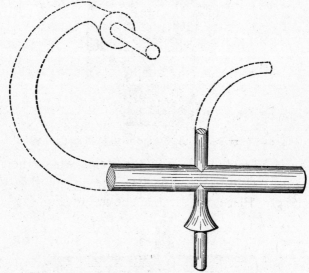

Fig. 217—The Finished Forging Ready for Welding.

except that those shown in Fig. 215 should be provided with a piece of band-iron arranged as indicated by the dotted lines. This should be shrunk around it. It projects above the face of the swage a distance of three-quarters of an inch or more, and serves the purpose of holding the top swage in correct position while taking the weld.—*By* C. T. S.

Making Shifting Rail Prop Irons by Hand.

The following description of some tools for making shifting rail prop irons by hand, with sketches showing

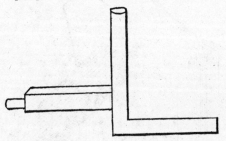

Fig. 218—Showing the Finished Prop Iron.

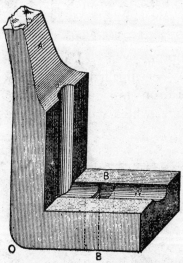

Making Shifting Rail Prop Irons. Fig. 219—Showing the Tool used to give the Iron a Complete Finish.

how to make an iron in the tools and how to prepare
it for the tools, describes my method of making

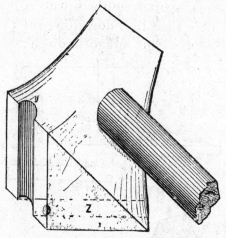

Fig. 220—Showing the Top Swage.

shifting rail prop irons. Fig. 218 shows the prop
iron as it is when finished. To make this take the
proper size of iron and split it out as in the dotted
lines of Fig. 222, which will give two irons as in Fig.

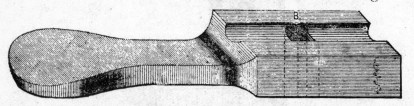

Fig. 221—Showing the Tool to which the Square _A_ is Fitted.

223. With the same heat used in splitting out the
two pieces draw the square _A_, shown in Fig. 223, so

it will fit the square *B* of the tool shown in Fig. 221 ;
now split Fig. 223 as at *X*, and with the same heat
place the square part *A* in the square part of the tool,
Fig. 221, at *B*; then turn down the part *O*, then, with
an ordinary top swage, swage it down ; now take the

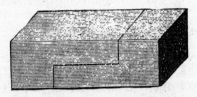

Fig. 222—Showing the Lines on which the Iron is Split

iron out of the tool and reheat it, edge it up and place
it in the tool Fig. 219, and use the top swage, Fig.
220.   The tool, Fig. 227, gives the iron a complete
finish and makes all irons alike at the corners, which
is a big gain where irons are to be duplicated.   The
tool, Fig. 219, is used on the anvil the same as any

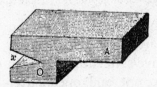

Fig. 223—Showing the Iron Split.

ordinary heading tool.   Hold the corner on the anvil
while swaging the corners; while swaging over the
square part set the square part of the prop iron in the
square hole of the anvil, and so on.   In a short time
any ordinary smith will be able to handle the tools

properly and make a good iron. I do not think it necessary to give any further description of the tools, as I think the sketches will speak for themselves.—*By* H. R. H.

Getting out a Solid King-Bolt Socket.

My way of making a solid king-bolt socket is as follows :

I first make a block as shown in Fig. 226. It is about four and one-half inches long, and if the plate is to be one and one-quarter inches wide, make the block, *A*, two and one-half inches wide and one and

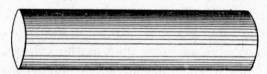

Getting Out a Solid King-Bolt Socket by the Method of "Iron Docto ."
Fig. 224—Showing the Iron before Splitting.

three-quarter inches thick ; make the swage part, *B*, one and one-quarter inches half round ; make the hole nearly one and five-sixteenths inches in diameter at the top and taper to one and one-quarter inches on the bottom, which permits of the easy removal of the iron. Then take round iron one and one-quarter inches in diameter and five inches or more long, as shown in Fig. 224, split, as shown in Fig. 225, three inches down, and open up ; split with a dull chisel or round fuller, swage the joint of round portion just a trifle so as to allow it to enter the block easily, reheat to a moderate heat and then insert the tool in the block. If the square hole in the anvil is not large enough, or a swage-block is not at hand, hold the piece over the

Fig. 225—The Iron after Splitting.

open forging vise and bend the ends down moderately until nearly a right angle is formed. Next cut off the end so that it will be less in length than the block is thick by a matter of three-eighths of an inch, raise a welding heat, insert the point in the block and flatten

Fig. 225—The Block.

or set down into the swage—first with hammer and sledge, striking quick blows so as to weld up any loose-ness, then use the flat hammer to finish—as a result we get Fig. 227—in which A is the plate and B the stem or portion to be converted into a socket. Then

weld in iron of the proper size, draw and swage to a
finish and fit while the iron is cooling off.

I will say just here that it is very improper to fit iron
to wood by burning it on as some stupid blacksmiths

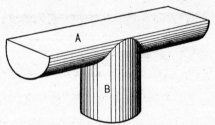

Fig. 227—The Plate and Stem.

do. Hit the iron while it is black hot, and should it
still burn, rub chalk over the portion which comes in
contact with the iron.

The socket is finished inside with two drills, one for
the insertion of the smaller portion of the socket, the

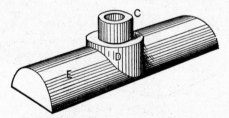

Fig. 228—The Plate and Socket.

other to make a passage for the king-bolt, which in this
case may be five-eighths of an inch. In Fig. 227, A denotes the plates; B the full-sized part of the socket and
the same diameter as the socket; C, of Fig. 228, is the

small portion of the socket which fits in the socket and
is formed by swaging.   Fig. 229 represents a good tool
for turning off the upper portion of the socket ; *A* is
the portion which fits in the drill-chuck ; *B* the waist,

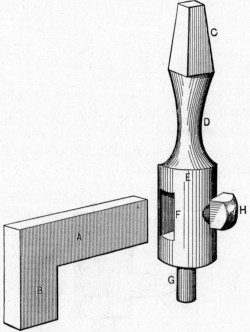

Fig. 229--Showing a Tool for Turning Off the Upper Portion of the
Socket.

about three-quarters of an inch diameter ; two inches
long ; *C*, the body of the tool, one and one-quarter
inches diameter, two inches long ; hole *F* may be one
inch by one and one-half inches for the insertion of the
portion marked *A*, about three and one-half inches

long, one inch by one and one-half inches. *B* is the cutting part. In Fig. 229 is shown a set-screw to hold the cutter fast. The point *E* fits the hole in the socket and acts as a guide. With a little practice the tools shown in Fig. 228 will answer as well as a lathe. —*By* IRON DOCTOR.

Heading Bolts.

I send a sketch in Fig. 230 showing a heading block for an anvil, the mouth of the hole being worn rounded, as shown at *b b*, which would let the iron fill in, as at *c c* in Fig. 231. Now a very litt'e wear there will let the iron fill in enough to make

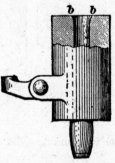

Fig. 230—Showing the Heading Block for the Anvil.

quite a difference in the length of blank required to make a bolt-head to any given dimension. But the extra iron is not of so much consequence as the swell in the bolt neck, which is a great nuisance, especially where both are to be threaded clear up to the head. In the anvil block used in our shop we have steel dies set in the block, as in Fig. 232 at *d*. By

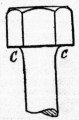

Fig. 231—Showing the Iron filled in at *C C*.

this means different sizes or dies may be fitted to one block. The dies may be turned upside down, by making the dies *d* longer than the recess is deep, so as

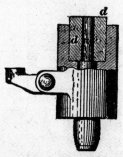

Fig. 232—Showing the Steel Die Set in the Anvil Block.

to stand above the top of the block. We are enabled to heat the dies and close up the holes when they have become too much worn.—*By* J. R.

Heading Bolt Blanks.

In heading hexagon bolts I allow three times the diameter of the iron, providing the heading tool is the proper size. Suppose, for example, a ¾-inch bolt is

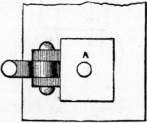

A Substitute for a Bolt-header, as designed by "J. R." Fig. 233—Top View.

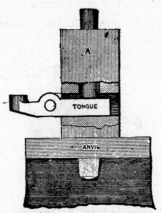

Fig. 234—End View.

to have a stem three inches long. Then in cutting the iron rod into blanks I make the blanks five and one-fourth inches long, which allows two and one-fourth inches of blank length to form the head, the bore of the heading tool being ¾ and 1-64th. The header, or the dies, as the case may be, should by rights be of steel, as cast-iron wears very quick; and after five hundred bolts have been made in a cast-iron die there will be so muchwear that the heads will not come up to size with the above allowance.

A good shop tool for short bolts, which I like better than a bolt-header, consists of a block *A*, Fig. 233, with

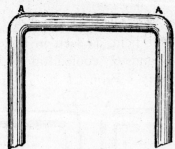

Bending a Cast-Steel Crank.   Fig. 235—Showing the method of Bending at *A A.*

stem to fit in the square hole in the anvil, and having a slot through it to receive the usual tongue. Fig. 233 is a top view of the tool, and Fig. 234 is an end view.—*By* J. R.

Bending a Cast-Steel Crank Shaft for a Ten Horse-Power Engine.

The illustrations herewith will show how I made a crank, the shaft for which was two and one-half inches in diameter.   I made the bends at *A* and *A* first, and shaped as shown in Fig. 235.   I then heated at *B*,

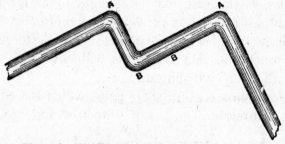

Fig. 236—Showing the Crank Bent at *A*, *A* and *B*.

cooled off *A*, and bent as seen in Fig. 236.   I then heated at *A*, *B* and *B*, cooled off *A*, and bent as shown in Fig. 237.   From *A* to *A* in Fig. 235 I

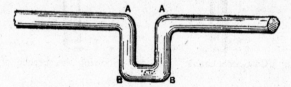

Fig. 237—Showing the Job as Completed.

allowed fourteen inches to make a five-inch stroke.   I straightened so as to turn to two and three-eighths inches, and there was not a cockle or a scale on it.—*By* SOUTHERN BLACKSMITH.

Making a Clevis.

A man can learn his trade with a good mechanic, and then go in another shop and see the same piece of work done in another way, much simpler and easier than his. To illustrate this point, I will explain what I once saw a good workman do. The job I refer to was the making of a clevis. He wished to make a five or six-inch one as follows: Large in the center, tapering forward to the bolt holes, the holes to be flat

Making a Clevis by the Method of "T. G. W." Fig. 238—Showing the Ordinary Way.

on the inside and round on the outside. That required the iron to be half round to form the collar for the bolts. To do this he cut the iron to the length required, drew out the ends, bent it over the horn of the anvil, then over a mandrel, took a heat, welded down, and then hammered it over the horn again. By this time it required another heat, as it needed more drawing, and this way of doing the job took twice the time really necessary for it. He then finished the other

Fig. 239—Showing the Piece as Drawn Out and Flattened.

end in the same way, bent it, and this completed the work, the collar being then as shown in Fig. 238 of the accompanying illustrations.

Now, he could have saved both time, coal and labor by having taken a piece of iron the required size, drawn out the ends, then laid it in a swage and taken

his set ; then flattened it back two and one-half inches,
or one and one-half inches, from the ends, flattening
say three inches in the swage.   This would have made

Fig. 240—Showing the Clevis After Beveling and Welding.

it as shown in Fig. 239 ; and after beveling and welding the collar the holes would have been as shown in
Fig. 240.—*By* T. G. W.

Crank Shafts for Portable Engines.

Herewith I send you sketches of my plan for making crank shafts for small portable engines.

Fig. 241 shows the pieces composing the crank, and

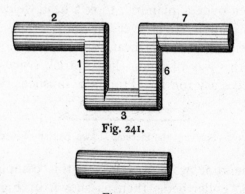

Fig. 241.

Fig. 242.

the other figures the details, having on them the same
figures of reference.

First make two pieces, as shown at 1 and 6 in Fig.

241, and weld Fig. 242 to piece 1; then weld Fig. 243 to piece 1; next weld around the ends of 1 in Fig.

Fig. 243.

244 two straps, these straps being shown at 4 and 5. I weld up the other half in like manner. I sometimes

Fig. 244.

make cranks in this way that weigh up to 150 lbs.— *By* SOUTHERN BLACKSMITH.

Forging a Locomotive Valve Yoke.

PLAN I.

My method of making a valve yoke and stem for locomotive engines requiring but one weld (these parts are usually made with three welds; the saving accordingly will at once be perceived) is as follows: I take a car axle, or any iron of the required size, heat and weld it properly, set it down with a fuller to form the corners, allow for draw between each corner, and then draw to the required size as shown in Fig. 245. I leave plenty of stock in the corners so it can be trimmed with a chisel as necessary. I next bend as shown in Fig. 246. To make the stem I use two-inch square iron, which I twist and weld up the entire length to change the grain of the iron, so that it will not cut the packing or stem. I leave the end for welding on to the yoke as shown in Fig. 246. I take separate

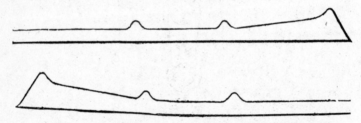

Locomotive Valve Yoke. Fig. 245—The Piece Before Bending.

soft heats on each, being sure to have them clean, and then weld.

Although I use no clamps, I have never had any trouble from the valve yokes springing. I allow that side to come a little long, as it is easier to stave work of this kind than it is to draw it. My reason for considering a V weld the best is that we have more surface to weld in a V weld than we could get in a jump weld; besides, we get into the *body* of the work that is to be done. Any blacksmith who will subject the two welds to a fair test will soon be convinced that a jump

weld will show flaws and break under less pressure
than a V weld. Why do most smiths V steel in bars,

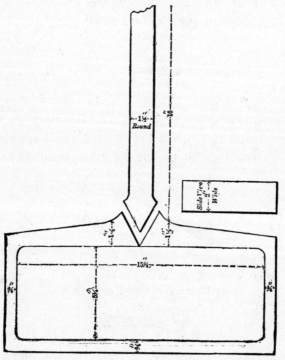

Locomotive Valve Yoke. Fig. 246—Formed, Ready for the Final Weld.

sledges and other similar work if lap or jump welds are
best?

The usual way of making articles of this kind is to
have a weld in each forward corner or in each side,
having a jumped weld for the stem. By the plan that I
pursue a V weld is used, which is the best that can be

made. The oil and steam will soon destroy a jumped weld, as they are frequently unsound. The sketch is reduced from full size. The figures, however, denote the dimensions of the finished work.—*By* R. O. S.

Forging a Locomotive Valve Yoke.

PLAN 2.

I think that the plan I show in the sketch herewith is a good way to forge a locomotive valve yoke, and it has the advantage of having only one weld. The yoke

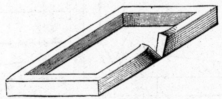

Forging a Locomotive Valve Yoke, "Urknown's" Method. Fig. 247— Yoke Bent and Scarfed Ready for Weld.

Forging a Locomotive Valve Yoke. Fig. 248—Rod Scarfed for Weld.

Forging a Locomotive Valve Yoke. Fig. 249—Rod in Position for Welding.

is forged around as in Fig. 247, and scarfed up for the rod weld, which is formed as in Fig. 248, the weld being made as in Fig. 249.—UNKNOWN.

Forging a Locomotive Valve Yoke.

PLAN 3.

The following plan of making a locomotive valve yoke is followed in my shop: We cut an axle to the

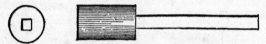

Making a Valve Yoke by the Method of " Novis Homo." Fig. 250— Side and End Views of the Stem after Drawing.

length desired and draw the stem first, leaving it square as shown in Fig. 250. We then draw the other end,

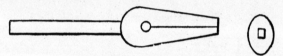

Fig. 251—Side and End Views of the other End after Drawing, Punching and Cutting.

and punch and cut under the hammer until we get the shape shown in Fig. 251. We next split, straighten

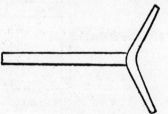

Fig. 252—Showing the Piece Opened.

and open out as seen in Fig. 252. The ends are then drawn out on a table such as is shown in Fig. 253.

The stem is then twisted by placing the opened ends under the hammer, and applying to the square end the lever shown in Fig. 254.   A piece of iron like that

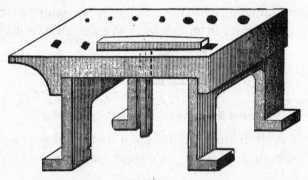

Fig. 253—Showing the Piece Straightened in the Table.

Fig. 254—Showing the Lever Used to Twist the Rod End.

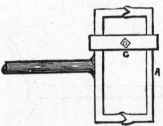

Fig. 255—Showing the Piece *C* Drawn for Welding.

shown at *A* in Fig. 255 is then forged down, the two valves of the yoke are put together, and we weld as shown in Fig. 255, bolting the two pieces together by the clamp *C*. Or we forge the second piece longer on its ends and weld as in Fig. 256.

We have also a face plate designed especially for

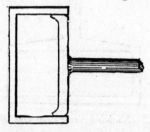

Fig. 256—Showing Another Method of Welding.

making valve yokes. It is like the one shown in Fig. 253, excepting that it has but one hole. In speaking of hammers I mean steam hammers.—*By* Novis Homo.

Forging a Locomotive Valve Yoke.

PLAN 4.

Locomotive blacksmithing is one of the most important branches of the trade, and requires all the skill

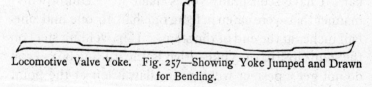

Locomotive Valve Yoke.   Fig. 257—Showing Yoke Jumped and Drawn
for Bending.

and experience that the smith can command. I do not know that I can show a better way than the preceding, but I will attempt to describe my way, which

I think a good one. In the first place, after having got the required size iron, I jump the stem and

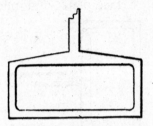

Fig. 258—Showing Yoke Bent and Welded.

draw both ends (all as shown in Fig. 257). The next operation is simply to bend into shape and weld as shown in Fig. 258.—*By* VULCAN.

Forging a Locomotive Valve Yoke.

PLAN 5.

Many yokes lack durability because the oil and tallow used in oiling the valves contain some substance which eats into the fiber of iron if it can get at the end of the bar. I have seen many yokes made in " Unknown's" manner that were eaten in from one-half to one and one-half inches at the end of the stem. If in welding steel on the stem close to the yoke—that is, the stuffing box—you do not get a perfect weld, or if a flaw is left at the point of the steel or the scarfs of the iron, the corrosive substance to which I have alluded will soon eat a hole in the stem, and perhaps all through it.—*By* R. T. K.

Forging a Locomotive Valve Yoke.

PLAN 6.

While I am, as a rule, in favor of the V weld, I do not like its application to the valve yoke, as I believe

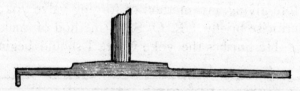

Making a Locomotive Valve Yoke by the Method of "R. D."   Fig. 259
—Showing the Piece Ready for Bending.

it is liable to spring from being so weak in the ends and the opposite side.   I prefer a yoke made on " Unknown's " plan, because that obviates the danger of

Fig. 260—The Yoke Bent.

"springing" while the stem is being welded.   My own method is first to bring to the shape represented in Fig. 259 of the accompanying engravings.   The yoke I make has the two ends and side of the same size.   I then bend as shown in Fig. 260. By this plan I save the time needed to make a corner.—*By* R. D.

Forging a Locomotive Valve Yoke.

PLAN 7.

Before giving my method of forging valve yokes I shall criticise briefly "R. O. S.'s" method of making them. He finishes the yoke where I should begin it.

Forging a Valve Yoke by the Method of "R. O. S." Fig. 261—Shape of Iron at Start.

He says: " I first get out my iron in the shape shown in Fig. 261 (see the accompanying illustrations). I then bend as in Fig. 262." It will be seen that "R. O.

Fig. 262—The Piece Bent to the Yoke Form

S.," in his method, has four corners to form of the right shape and length before welding on the shank *A;* consequently, if he is unlucky—and this may happen to the best of workmen—his labor is all lost, and the iron goes to the scrap pile. No one can weld A to B without stretching the yoke, and when this occurs the

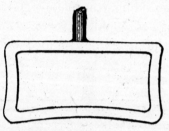

Fig. 263—Showing the Result of the First Error in the Method of " R. O. S."

yoke assumes the shape shown in Fig. 263, thereby making it necessary to go all over the work again.

Fig. 264—Showing the Stem Twisted.

Still, if a former the size of the inside C is at hand (and it ought to be), the yoke can soon be got into shape again.

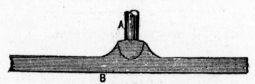

Fig. 265—The Iron Drawn into Shape.

Then " R. O. S." twists the stem A to change the grain of the iron, so that the packing on the stem will

not be cut out.   In twisting and welding up for the
stem as he suggests, you twist with the iron whatever
is in it, and in so doing you make a spiral of the stem
as shown in Fig. 264, and if there is any hard substance left in the iron it is scraped out through the

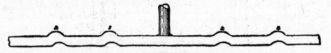

Fig. 266—The Second Stage in the Job.

packing by the motion of the rod, somewhat in the
manner in which a rat-tail file would operate in drawing it back and forth in a hole.   If you do not twist
your rod, although it has sand in it, you get your cut
in one or two places, according to the purity of the
iron.   Twisting does not remove impurities, neither

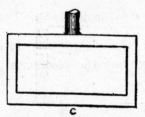

Fig. 267—The Yoke Completed.

does welding, so the time consumed in such work is
lost, for bar iron as clear as steel can be got for what
this twisting and welding would cost.

Perhaps some of the plans of my own, which I shall
now give, may not seem feasible to all of the craft,

but I have found every one of them satisfactory. I have six plans. The first is as follows: I take a piece of good iron, draw it out into shape as shown in

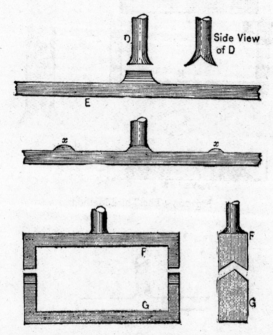

Forging a Valve Yoke, by "J. T. B."   Fig. 268—The Second Method.

Fig. 265, then form as shown in Fig. 266, and weld at C, by splitting as in Fig. 267.

Fig. 268 shows my second way of forging a valve yoke. I jump D to E, by splitting D, then forge, leaving projections at X to bring up the corners, shape

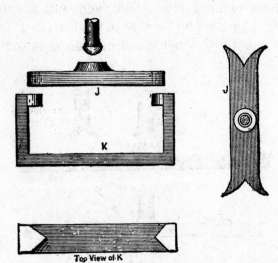

Top View of K

Fig. 269—The Third Method.

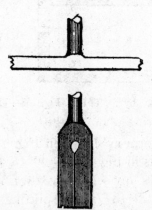

Fig. 270—The Fourth Method.

the bend around, as at *P G*, split *F*, forge a piece *G* and weld *P* and *G* together.

In my third method, shown in Fig. 269, I round the end of the stem, and open the ends of the part *J*,

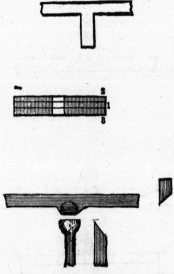

Fig. 271—The Fifth Method.

then forge a separate piece *K*, and weld *J* and *K* together.

In my fourth method, illustrated in Fig. 270, I take a piece of Norway iron, of sufficient size, draw out the shank or stem, then punch a hole, as in Fig. 270, and open out the two ends, thus getting the stem out of the solid.

In the fifth method, as shown in Fig. 271, I take

iron of suitable size, say 1½ x ¾ inches, make the
L-shaped piece shown in the engraving, put all together, and weld them up, and complete the forging in
any of the ways already mentioned.

My sixth method, as illustrated in Fig. 272, is to

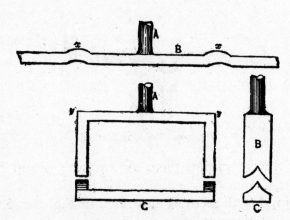

Fig. 272—The Sixth Method.

get out a piece B (Fig. 272) and use the dovetail weld
shown to weld in stem A, the stem being drawn in
sideways ; the corners at x are where the corners y

will come.   I split the ends of *B*, and weld in a piece *C*.

Now all these plans are good and practicable. They show six good methods of putting a shank on a flat bar of iron, and all in keeping with the general custom among skilled workmen.—*By* J. T. B.

Defect in Engine Valve.

The defect in many valves is owing to the fact that the cylinder exhaust port is not made wide enough for

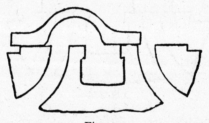

Fig. 273.

the stroke of the valve.   If the valve is worked by a rock-shaft, and there is any room to lower the pin in the rocker arm that carries the eccentric hook, the stroke of the valve can be shortened and a better pro-portion between the steam and exhaust ports obtained thereby.   Shortening the stroke of the valve will pre-vent the edge of the exhaust cavity in the valve from working up close to the edge of the cylinder exhaust port, Fig. 273, and will prevent the exhaust steam from being cramped. Fig. 273 also shows part of the exhaust lap chipped from the valve, which I shall speak of presently. If the valve stroke is shortened it must have the stroke so that it will open about three-quarters of the steam port. It may be well to state that by lowering the eccentric hook pin it will be necessary to lengthen the eccentric rod, or it will throw the valve too much to the front of the cylinder, and make the port openings unequal.

As the valve has an excess of exhaust lap it would

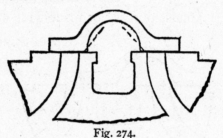

Fig. 274.

be well to take a straightedge and scriber and mark off one-third of the exhaust lap, as shown by the dotted lines in Fig. 274.

Then take a sharp cold chisel and chip off the marked edge, inclining inward to the valve at an angle of 45°, as shown in Fig. 274. By this method there will be a free and easy exhaust, and great compression prevented, even though the engine runs at a very high speed. If the valve stroke cannot be shortened, then chip out nearly one-half of the exhaust lap.—*By* SLIDE VALVE.

CHAPTER VI.

MAKING CHAIN SWIVELS.

Making a Log-Chain Swivel.

DIFFERENT METHODS.—PLAN I.

My way of making a log-chain swivel is as follows: I take a piece of a bar, say three-quarters of an inch square, and flatten it a little and then draw out to three-

Making a Log-Chain Swivel. Fig. 275—Showing how the Piece is Flattened and Drawn Out.

eighths of an inch round, as shown by Fig. 275. I then cut it off long enough to draw out the other end the same way, leaving the center the full size,

Fig. 276—Showing how the Center is Formed.

as shown by Fig. 276. I then punch a hole through it, and I have a mandrel shaped as by Fig. 277. I next take a welding heat, and putting the mandrel through the hole, turn up the two ends as shown in Fig.

278. After getting the ends turned up I finish it up on the mandrel with a light hammer, leaving it as shown by Fig. 279. I then take a piece of ⅜-inch round iron and swage it to half-round at both ends just long,

Fig. 277—Showing the Mandrel.

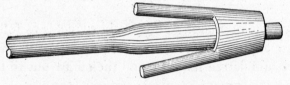

Fig. 278—Showing how the Ends are Turned.

Fig. 279—Showing how the Piece is Finished.

Fig. 280—Showing how the Collar is Welded On.

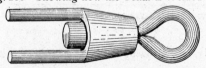

Fig. 281—Showing how the Two Pieces are Joined.

enough to go through the swivel, and with half an inch to weld a collar on. I then turn it around and weld a collar round it just the size of the mandrel, as

shown by Fig. 280, then heat it, drive it through the
hole and open with a punch as shown by Fig. 281.   I
next weld the two ends together as you would a link

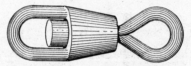

Fig. 282—Showing the Swivel Finished.

(Fig. 282), and you will have a good swivel, as I never
make them any other way, and have found them
always satisfactory.—*By* JOHN ATKINS.

Making a Log-Chain Swivel.

PLAN 2.

To make what I call a ⅜-inch swivel, that is one
for ⅜-inch log chain, I use a piece of good Swedish
iron 1¼ inch by ¾ inch, and 4 inches long.   Then I

Making a Log-Chain Swivel by the Method of "J. H. H." Fig. 283—
Showing how the Fuller Marks are Made.

make fuller marks, as shown in Fig. 283, placing the
marks just far enough apart to allow the middle part
to be square.   I next punch a ⅝-inch hole in the center, and draw the ends as shown in Figs. 284 and 285.
I then bend up the ends, as in Fig. 286. I next take a

good heat and use mandrel shown in Fig. 290. This is made of one-inch steel (machine or Bessemer). It is drawn to five-eighths inch, and the shoulder must be

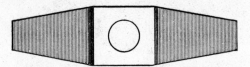

Fig. 284—Showing how the Ends are Drawn.

nice and square if your swivel is to work easily and true. After the piece has been brought to the shape shown

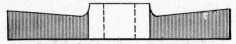

Fig. 285—Another Illustration of the Method of Drawing the Ends.

in Fig. 287, I make the tug by taking a piece of ½ x ¾ inch square Norway iron and forging it half round

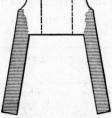

Fig. 286—Showing how the Ends are Bent Up.

for about five and one-half inches, leaving a square piece (about five-eighths of an inch) at both ends to make the head. I then bend it around, take a good soft heat, weld it up and punch the head, which must

be 1 inch x 3⁄8 inch and round.   I then forge the tug
down so as to make it go in the top, as shown in Fig.

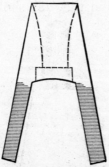

Fig. 287—Showing how the Ends are Flared Out.

Fig. 288—Front View of the Swivel, Showing how the Tug is Opened
Up.

287.   After it has been put in, I take a very thin
punch and open the tug up, as shown in Fig. 288, and

weld the top together.   This makes a very good swivel, and it can't freeze up in cold weather.

The dotted lines in Fig. 287 show how the end must

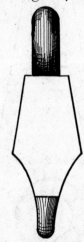

Fig. 289—Side View.

Fig. 290—The Mandrel.

Fig. 291—The Tug Before Bending.

be flared out to give the tug a chance to open.   This is what they call a bar swivel.   The mandrel must be just the right size for the head, and be driven hard enough to let the head of the tug draw out of sight. After the processes described have been carried through, warm the swivel up all over, then take it to the vise to finish it. Fig. 288 is a front view of the

Fig. 292—The Tug Ready for the Swivel.

swivel. Fig. 289 is a side view. Fig. 290 shows the mandrel. Fig. 291 represents the tug before bending, and in Fig. 292 the tug is shown ready for the swivel. —*By* J. H. H.

Making a Log-Chain Swivel.

PLAN 3.

To make a log-chain swivel cheaply and quickly,

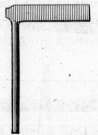

Making a Log-Chain Swivel. Fig. 293—Showing the Iron Flattened and Turned.

take a piece of round iron one size larger than the wire in the chain, flatten about six inches quite thin

and turn at a right angle and a square corner as in Fig.
293. Then chamfer the out corner with a flat punch

Fig. 294—Showing how the Hole is Made for the Swivel,

to get a lap, then commence at the end of the flat part
and roll it up to the round, leaving a hole of about
half an inch for the swivel for a three-eighths inch

Fig. 295—Showing how the Bow is Made.

chain, as shown in Fig. 294. Then cut off the round
about five inches from the corner, scarf the end short,
thin and wide, and turn it on to the other side. Next

Fig. 296—Showing how the Other Piece is Bent and Cut Off.

take hold of the bow thus made, take a good weld
and weld it on the horn as in Fig. 295. Hold your
hand higher than the horn and you will get a tapering

hole. Then take a piece of the same round iron, bend over about three inches, flat them together a little, and turn and weld a ring for a head, finish it up over the corner of the anvil and cut it off so that both ends are

Fig. 297—Showing how the Two Pieces are Joined.

of the same length, as in Fig. 296. Heat the swivel, drive it through, open the ends as in Fig. 297, and turn and weld as you would a link. Then heat the whole and work loose, and the job is completed. Use a light hammer when welding.—*By* HOME.

Making a Swivel for a Log Chain.

PLAN 4.

To make a swivel for log chains, I first forge the

Making a Swivel for a Log Chain by the Method of " C. E. B." Fig. 298—Showing the Piece as Forged and Before Bending.

piece shown in Fig. 298, making the hole by punching. The stem, shown in Fig. 299, should be made large enough to fit the hole in Fig. 298 neatly. *A* is a washer used when fitting the stem in the hole. The

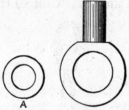

Fig. 299—Showing the Stem and Washer.

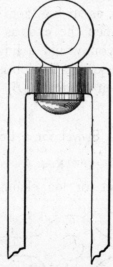

Fig. 300—Showing the Result after Riveting.

washer should be thick, narrow, flat and smooth, so as to secure an easy revolving of the part. The piece shown in Fig. 298 is then bent as indicated by the arrows, and the iron is kept cool excepting where the bends are made. The ends are left open. The next step is to heat the end of the stem, Fig. 299, to a cherry red, and rivet it to the piece shown in Fig. 298.

Fig. 301—Showing the Job Completed.

In doing this use a vise and punch. The punch I use for the purpose is countersunk for a small space on the bottom. The result of this riveting is represented in Fig. 300, and by bending the points together and welding the job is completed as indicated in Fig. 301. —*By* C. E. B.

Making a Swivel for a Log Chain.

PLAN 5.

In making a swivel to a log chain, I take a piece of good iron and forge it as at *A B*, Fig. 302, which are edge and top irons, *B* being a hole. I next forge a piece, *C*, shown in Fig. 303, and put it through the

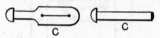

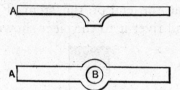

Making a Swivel for a Log Chain, as done by " H. K." Fig. 302—
Showing the Edge and Top Irons.

Fig. 303—Showing the Piece used for the Eye.

Fig. 304—Showing the Finished Job.

hole in *A*, and open out the split to form the eye, and then weld up the ends of *A*, and the job is complete, as illustrated in Fig. 304.—*By* H. K.

Making a Swivel for a Log Chain.

PLAN 6.

My way of making a swivel for a log chain is to:
1st. Make an eye punch of one and one-eighth inch round iron, as shown in Fig. 305. 2d. Take a piece of

good iron 1 ½ x ½ inch, four inches long.   3d. Fuller
and draw ends as shown in Fig. 306.   4th. Bend the

Making a Swivel for a Log Chain.   Fig. 305—The Eye Punch.

Fig. 306—Showing how the Ends of the Piece are Fullered and Drawn.

Fig. 307—Showing how the Ends are Bent.

Fig. 308—Showing how the Eye Punch is Used.

Fig. 309—Showing how the Eye is Made.

Fig. 310—The Finished Swivel.

ends, as illustrated in Fig. 307.   5th. Put in eye punch
and work down, as in Fig. 308.   6th. Make the eye as

shown in Fig. 309. 7th. Square the top end of the
eye and make the washer three-eighths of an inch thick,

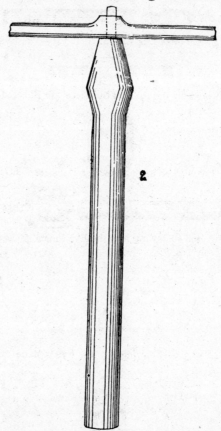

Making a Swivel by the Method of "J. E. N." Fig. 311—Showing the
Shape of the Ends and the Tool used in Bending.

with a square hole. Heat the end of the eye and
washer, put the eye in the vise, put on the swivel, then

put on the washer and rivet. Then weld the swivel. When finished (see Fig. 310) it will not be more than four inches long.—*By* A. S., Jr.

Making a Swivel for a Log Chain.

PLAN 7.

I think the best way is to make the link of square iron, drawing off the ends, as shown at 1 in Fig. 311, and leaving a heavy center in which the eye is to be punched. When the bending is to be done use the

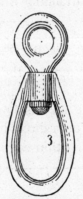

Fig. 312—The Swivel Completed.

tool marked 2, Fig. 311. Then finish on a swage, rivet the swivel eye in hob, weld the ends of the swivel link, and while hot turn the eye around a few times. Then cool off, and the result will be a swivel as shown in Fig. 312.—*By* J. E. N.

CHAPTER VII.

PLOW WORK.

Points in Plow Work.

NO. I.

My method of putting plowshares on stubble plows is as follows : I commence by preparing the landside, as in Fig. 313, and attaching it on the plow in the

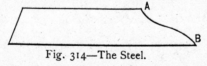

Points in Plow Work.　Fig. 313—Showing the Landside.

proper place. I next cut out the steel, as in Fig. 314, then heat the part from A to B, and drive it over so that when the back of the steel is against the moldboard the line A B will be on a direct line with the landside. I next plate it out to a thin edge from heel to point,

Fig. 314—The Steel.

and then heat it evenly all over so that it will bend easily to the blows of the hammer. In preparing this part of the lay to fit the landside and moldboard, the smith should be very careful to leave no hammer marks on the front side, and he should also be careful to get a good fit, as that is much easier at this stage than when the part is welded on the landside. When this piece of steel is fitted as I have described, attach it to the plow by fastening it at the heel to the brace, and in front by fastening it to the landside with a clamp made after the pattern shown in Fig. 315. This clamp should be made so that after being put on at the point it will be driven tight when about two-thirds of the way upon the lay, thus holding the steel fast to the landside so that it will weld easily.

The next thing to be done is to unfasten the lay from the plow. Prepare a good fire and weld quickly, being careful not to let the piece slip or disturb it any more than is necessary. When it is welded to the top, and before finishing the point, lay a piece of steel from the edge of the point back about two or three inches; this will make the part last much longer. Next finish up the edge and point and edge of the lay, and if it has been held in place you will have a perfect fit.

When it is desired to put on a point, in preparing the point I forge one end of the steel flat and draw it to a thin edge, the other I draw to a point, as in Fig. 316, and then double it so the pointed edge will go on the bottom of the landside. I next weld both sides down solid, draw out to required thickness, cut off the edge of the point at the same angle as the lay, finish up and the point is complete.

Sometimes a lay is brought to the shop that is worn very thin, and some are worn through at the top, near

the moldboard.   In this case I forge the point the same
as I would in the one just described, but leaving the
flat side long enough to reach the top of the lay.   I

Fig. 315—The Clamp.

then bore a hole near the top through both the piece
of steel and the lay and fasten them with a rivet.   I
next heat the piece of steel where it is to be doubled
over, letting the pointed piece go on the bottom of the

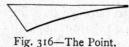

Fig. 316—The Point.

landside, weld up as high as is convenient, and finish
as before.

For the purpose of cooling a lay easily and with more
rapidity, I use a wooden block about eighteen inches

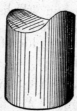

Fig. 317—The Block used in Cooling the Lay.

in diameter and two feet long.   I square one end, place
it upon the floor, and saw the other end to the shape
of a half circle, as shown in Fig. 317.   This cavity is
lined with iron so the wood will not burn.   When the

lay is heated I put it upon the opening and place a piece
of round iron about three feet long and two inches in
diameter upon the part that is to be shaped, one end
of the piece being held in my hand; the helper then
strikes upon the round piece with a heavy hammer
and the lay will bend evenly without leaving marks.—
By T. M. S.

Points in Plow Work.

NO. 2.

I always weld my points on the top instead of the
bottom.   My reason for this is, that the share always
wears thin above the point, and by drawing your point
tapering, leaving the back thick, and drawing the edge
that extends on the face of the share thin and wide,
you make the weak places strong.   All smiths know
that the throat, especially where it is welded next to
the bar, wears thin, and unless you place your point
on the top side, it is soon worn through, and the
share must be thrown aside.   In drawing the shin
piece, the piece that is welded from the point of the
share to the point of the mold should be drawn to a
feather edge where it extends on to the wing and left
heavy on the back, so that when it is welded on it will
scour off and become smooth.   I have seen many
shares that would not scour simply from the fact that
the edge had been left thick, and in welding the smith
made the wing sink in, and left a place for the dirt to
stick.—By W. F. S.

Some More Points about Plows.

That bolts are among the most important things when it comes to repairing plows, I shall endeavor to show in the following remarks.

In all the plows made in factories, that is the steel plows, with very few exceptions, the round countersink key head is used, or else a square neck round countersink head, which is very little better than the key head. It seems to me that plow factories lose considerable profit on this item of bolts.

My plan consists in simply punching a square hole, tapering to fit a square plug head bolt. I hear some one ask how would I punch a tapering hole. I will tell you how I do it. The size of bolt I use for a bar is seven-sixteenths and half inch. Make a square punch a trifle larger than the bolt, so it will go in without driving and will not spoil the threads, then make the die, say for a seven-sixteenths inch bolt, three-eighths of an inch, set it so the punch will pass through the center, now try it and see if it does not make a taper hole fitting a plug-head plow bolt. Make any other size punch and die in about the same proportions to get the taper. You can punch every hole in the mould the same way. Sometimes the corners of the hole will not be cleanly cut out, and in that case take a square pointed punch tapered and tempered, set it in the hole and hit it once or twice.

I think I have shown where two expensive operations with the vise and drill can be saved, and in doing this it is necessary to have only one variety of bolts to use.   Then when it comes to repairing the same there is no turning of bolts in the hole.   If it is so rusted that the nut won't turn it is better to twist it off and put in a new bolt, at a cost of five or ten cents, than to spend a half hour trying to get the old one out, and then have to charge for the time and bolt beside.—*By* DOT.

Making a Plow Lay.

I will describe my method of making a plow lay :

If a new stub on landside is to be made forge it out first.   Sometimes the old one can be used by welding a piece on the point and letting it run upon the top of the old stub.   After the stub is bolted on, lay the slab

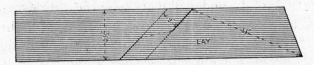

Making a Plow Lay.   Fig. 318—Showing how to Mark the Steel.

of steel on the plow and mark the bevel, then lay the block of a two-inch square on the steel, and mark as shown in Fig. 318 of the accompanying illustrations. Next heat and turn the point and draw and cool the lay so that when the plow rests on the floor the edge will touch over the entire length of the lay.   Next cut out a small piece of steel to lay on the bottom of the point, and punch a hole through the point of the lay, the landside and the small piece of steel, and rivet them all together. Then take off together the entire landside and lay, weld the point first, then take off the

Fig. 319—Showing Clamp for Holding while Heating the Point.

Fig. 320—Showing Point Used
for Bottom of Lay.

long landside and weld the upper end of the stub to the lay, and weld the middle last. Never try to weld from the point up, for the steel will curl or spring up from the stub and prevent your getting a good weld. While heating the point hold it by means of the clamp shown in Fig. 319. Fig. 320 represents the point used for the bottom of the lay. I use borax for a flux.—*Bj* B. N. S.

Laying a Plow.

To describe how I lay a plow, I will begin by calling attention to Fig. 321, which shows how a plow generally looks when brought to the smith to be laid and pointed. There is usually a hole worn in the plow back of the point in the throat, as in 1 in Fig. 321. I forge out a piece of steel of the shape shown in Fig. 322, making it very thick on the side from *A* to *B* and then from *A* to *C ;* I then clamp it to the plow with tongs, as in *D*, Fig. 321, and as shown by the dotted lines. I next heat at E, weld rapidly, take off the tongs, bend the part F under, then put on plenty of borax and weld clear up. The plow is now solid and

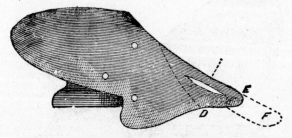

Laying a Plow by the Method of " J. O. H." Fig. 321—Showing the Plow Before Laying and Pointing.

Fig. 322—Showing the Piece to be Clamped to the Plow.

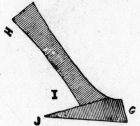

Fig. 323 –Showing the Shape of the Lay Steel.

ready for the lay. I forge out a piece of lay steel of the shape shown in Fig. 323. It is simply doubled up at the point G; I forge then from H to I and J, and

upset at H very heavy, to bring out the worn-off corner of the plow; I then lay it on the bottom of the

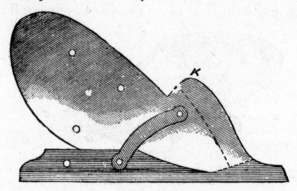

Fig. 324—Showing how the Steel is Laid on the Plow.

plow as shown by the dotted lines in Fig. 324, clamp
it on with tongs at K, put a heat on the point, weld
rapidly, then take off the tongs and weld up solid as

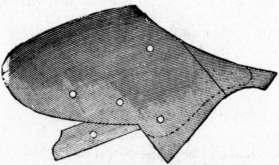

Fig. 325—Showing the Job Completed.

far back as the lay goes. The heat should be put at
the back part of the lay, along the dotted line in Fig.

324, to make a good weld back there. If the job is properly done the share will be lengthened one and a half to one and three-quarters inches. Fig. 325 shows how the plow looks after laying, and the dotted line indicates its appearance before the laying. Most of the laying I do is on Diamond plows. In laying a new share, great care is required to keep it in shape.— *By* J. O. H.

Polishing Plow Lays and Cultivator Shovels.

Perhaps some of your readers would like to know a good way to polish plow lays and cultivator shovels. After pointing shovels and new or old lays I always grind them bright on a solid emery wheel about twelve inches in diameter, with a two-inch face. I then put them on the felt wheel and finish them off so that they look as if they had just come from the factory. The chief point to keep in mind in using emery wheels for a smooth surface like a plow lay is to have a wheel that is soft and elastic. You can never get a fine finish from a hard, solid stone.—*By* "SHOVELS."

Laying a Plow.

PLAN I.

In laying a common plowshare I make my lay of German plow steel about five-sixteenths of an inch thick on one edge, and as thin as I can hammer it on the other. I then sharpen the plowshare as sharp as the thin edge of the lay ; then I strike all the point in separate heats.   If I have no striker, I weld about three inches at a heat, being careful to get the back edge thoroughly welded down and level with the surface of the balance of the share.   If the outer edge of the share is not thoroughly welded, this can be easily done by taking a heat on it while drawing the edge out sharp.   If I have a striker, I weld about four inches at a heat, having the striker strike directly over where the edge of the share meets the lay, thus welding the edge of the share to the lay, while I weld the back edge of the lay to the share with the hand hammer at the same time.

The greatest trouble with most smiths in laying plows is that they leave their lay too thick at the back edge where it laps over the share, so the share gets too hot and burns before the lay gets hot enough to weld. I use common finely pulverized borax for a welding compound.   A good way to test your heat is, when the lay is about to come to a welding heat, just lightly remove the burning coal from the top of the lay and lightly tap its edge along as it welds, keeping up a blast at the same time.   This way of doing not only shows when the lay is in a condition to weld, but the welding is actually commenced in the fire, the share and lay thus beginning to unite as soon as it begins to come to a weld, and therefore is less liable to burn than if it were not settled by the light blows of the poker.   I always leave the out edge of my lay as thick as possible until all is thoroughly welded. Then the plow is ready for the point ; for points I use $1\frac{1}{2} \times \frac{1}{2}$ inch German steel.

I get my point out with the back end as wide as the base it is for, and as thick as the base will permit. I let my point extend back from two to five inches, or sufficient to give the base the necessary strength at the point. I strike the point at separate heats, and when the point is thoroughly welded I work it out well in the throat with the pene of my hammer or fuller, then begin at the point to draw the shoe out, drawing it with a gradual slope from the back edge of the lay to the required edge, keeping the edge on a perfect level with the bar, and being careful to leave the heel of the share and the corners of the point on a straight line, sighting from the heel of the share to the point. —*By* J. McM.

Laying a Plow.

PLAN 2.

To new lay steel plowshares, I select a piece of spring steel and heat one end to a high borax heat, then strike it with my hammer, and if it flies to pieces I put it aside. I don't use high steel. In preparing my steel I partially weld a strip of hoop iron on the edge, leaving it so that where it is scarfed or chamfered the iron will be full with the edge of the steel. I then chamfer the share and weld as usual. It is surer to weld when iron is between the parts.—*By* J. U. C.

Laying a Plow.

PLAN 3.

Repairing plows forms a major part of the black-smith's business in the Pacific States from the first of October until the following May. I will therefore give my plan of "laying a plow," and I hope by this

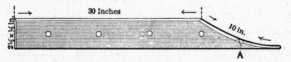

Laying a Plow by "Hand Hammer's" Method. Fig. 326—Showing the Iron Bar drawn from Shin to Point.

means to draw the craft into a discussion of the sub-ject, to our mutual benefit.

I will take a sixteen-inch plow for example.   First cut a bar of iron 2½ x ½ inch and about thirty inches long ; cut on a bevel at one end to save hammering ; take a heat on the beveled end ; draw as in Fig. 326,

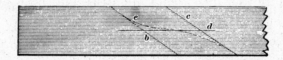

Fig. 327—Showing the Method of Cutting the Steel.

from shin to point about ten inches long, and punch a one-quarter inch hole, as at A.

Second : Clamp the landside thus prepared upon the plow standard in the proper position (the plow

being inverted), and with a slate pencil mark for the
holes, which, when drilled, countersunk and squared to
fit the bolts, can be bolted into place upon the plow.

Third : Take a slab of steel 6 x ¼ inches, lay it on
the plow, parallel with and against the lower edge of
the moldboard, and with a pencil draw a line across
the steel against the landside. This gives the length
and angle at which to cut the steel, as at *b*, Fig. 327.
Then lay the blade of a square two inches wide upon
the steel, parallel with the line *b*, and draw a second
line on the opposite edge of the square, which gives
us the line *c*, parallel with and two inches distant from

Fig. 328—Showing the Pattern.

line *b*. Now find the center of the cross section and
draw the line *d*, then trace with a pencil as indicated
by the dotted line *e*, and upon this line heat and cut
off, which gives you the pattern Fig. 328. Next heat
at *f*, Fig. 328, as hot as the steel will bear, and grasping the pattern with both hands at *g, g, g, g,* strike the
point *h* upon the anvil a few sharp blows, which will
give you the "shape," Fig. 329, after which draw to an
edge, then heat as hot as the "law allows" the entire
length and bend over a mandrel (lying down), the
helper holding a sledge on the back of the pattern
while you hammer along the edge until the curve is

right to fit upon the landside and brace, and along the moldboard where it is designed to go. When cool place the pattern in position and mark for the holes 1, 2, 3, 4, as shown in Fig. 329. After these

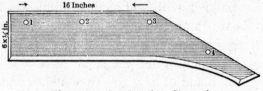

Fig. 329— Showing the " Shape."

holes are drilled, countersunk, and fitted to the bolts, place the parts in position as in Fig. 330, and fasten with a bolt at *I*, and a rivet at *J*. Now you are ready for the last, though by no means least important or difficult operation, *i. e.*, welding, for if you fail in this all is lost.

Finally : Place the work in a roomy, clean fire with

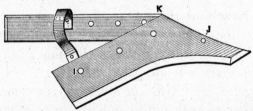

Fig. 330—Showing the Parts Placed in Position and Fastened.

the landside flat down, and heat red at the shin ; then take it to the anvil and hammer it down close ; return it to the fire, apply plenty of borax, and heat to a good welding heat, giving plenty of time to "soak ;" then place it upon the anvil and have your helper catch hold of it at the top of the shin at K, Fig. 330, with the "pick-ups" and squeeze firmly to the landside while you weld with the hammer from the tongs down to the rivet. Next take a heat at the top of the shin where the tongs prevented welding and weld it down, after which weld from rivet to point. The slender point from h to l, Fig. 328, must be turned under; then weld up, which gives strength and shape to the point. Now straighten up the edge, and temper the bolt on the plow.—*By* HAND HAMMER.

Laying, Hardening and Tempering Plows.

I will try to give my practical experience in laying, hardening and tempering the Casaday sulky plowshare; a plow generally used in Texas for breaking old land, and sod as well. When the shares are new they cut from twelve to fourteen inches, and are five and one-half inches wide, measuring from twenty to twenty-five inches from heel to point on the edge. When they are brought to the shop for laying, they resemble Fig. 331 of the accompanying illustrations, measuring from three and one-half to four inches in width. The first thing I do is to lay a piece of iron on the point, which, when shaped looks like Fig. 332. This makes the point of sufficient length and strength to receive the lay, which I make of German or hammered steel, one and one-quarter inches wide by three-eighths of an inch thick, and shaped as in Fig. 333. The heel of the lay is upset to make it heavier and wider in order to supply the deficiency of metal at the heel of the share. I then draw the upper or inside edge of the lay to about one-eighth of an inch, as I do also the edge of the share, and next drill two small holes in the share ; one at the heel, the

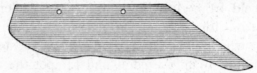

Fig. 331—Showing the Appearance of the Share when Brought to the Shop for Laying.

other about midway between the heel and the point of the share. I then place the lay in position on the under side of the share, mark and drill the lay, and rivet it on. This will hold it in position. I then put it in the fire and heat until I can bring the lay and the share close

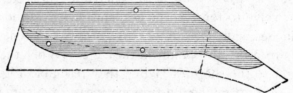

Fig. 332—Showing how the Iron is Laid On.

together, and then turn the lay back from *A*, the top of the share, as shown at *A*, Fig. 333, the object being to thicken the steel, which in many cases is worn quite thin, and requires this extra metal to draw and shape the point. The dotted lines show how the broad or fan-tail points of the lay fit the share when turned back.

I next weld from point to heel, and if when welded the back of the share will not fit the moldboard, I heat the whole share, and while it is hot set it up edgewise

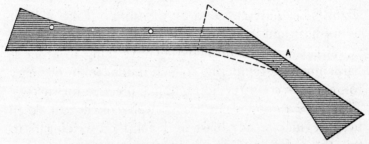

Fig. 333—Showing how the Lay is Shaped.

on the anvil, and strike it on the edge, which will bring it straight. I then begin to shape it at the point, and draw the edge, using the pene of the hammer, or, if the face is used, I allow the edge to project over the round

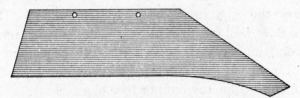

Fig. 334—Showing the Share Completed.

edge of the anvil, to prevent stretching on the edge, which would cause it to curve on the back. When finished and properly shaped it will look like Fig. 334, and be from one-half to three-quarters of an inch wider than the original share. Before drawing it to an edge, I carefully examine it to see if there are any skips or failures, and if such are found, heat, raise the edge, and insert a thin piece of hoop iron, allowing it to project slightly beyond the edge of the skip. Take a light borax heat and it will stick.

With the share finished the next thing in order is hardening and tempering, which if done in the ordinary forge of the country shop requires practice for success. First have a good clean fire of well coked coal, keep up a regular, steady blast as if taking a welding heat, put the point in first, allow it to get nearly red, as it is the thickest, move it through the fire gradually to the heel, and continue to pass it back and forward through the fire until you have an even heat from point to heel about an inch back from the edge. When you have the proper heat, have at hand a trough two and one-half feet long, and holding the share firmly in tongs immerse the edge in the water for an instant. Raise the edge or heel out first, allowing the point to remain a second longer because it has more heat than the edge, but taking care to have heat enough remain in the share to draw the temper to a blue. Have a brick with which to rub the edge, that you may be able to see when you have the proper temper. If there should not be heat enough in the share to do this, hold it over the fire again. Be careful to draw the temper as evenly as possible, for if it has hard and soft places it will wear into scallops.—*By* D. W. C. H.

Laying Plows.

I have been laying plows more or less for sixteen years, and in describing my method I will first deal with the slip share. I first make a lip as shown in Fig. 335. This lip is made of iron one-half an inch thick, and of proper width, forged down to the shape shown, with a bevel for right or left as desired. The joint *A* must be fitted snugly to the plow, so that when bolted on it will be level with the bar on the bottom, and will neither work up nor down at the point. In drilling the hole in the lip, care must be taken to have

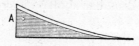

Laying Plows by the Method of "R. W. H."   Fig. 335—The Lip.

the bolt draw the joint together. When finished, bolt on the plow, and swing the plow up by the end of the beam, letting the handles rest on the shop floor. Cut the steel as in Fig. 336, using five-inch steel for twelve-inch plows, five and one-half inch for fourteen-inch, and six-inch for sixteen-inch plows. Heat the steel at *B B* hot as the law allows, and bring the point around to the proper angle, and to the shape of Fig. 337. From *C* to *C* the length should be nine inches for a twelve-inch plow, ten inches for fourteen-inch, and twelve inches for a sixteen-inch plow. The edges of the shares should be drawn with the face to the anvil, making the

bevel underneath. Cut and fit to the lip and moldboard as snugly as possible. It is a good plan to have
the point of the share longer than necessary, so it can
be turned under the back when beginning to weld on.
When your lay is in the exact place, mark the bolt

Fig. 336—Showing how the Steel is Cut.

holes and drill and countersink, then bolt the share to
the plow with a crossbar bolt. Take the landside,
crossbar, and share all off together, just as you would
a solid bar, and with a nice, large, clear fire weld up
the two first heats, then unbolt the share and lip, and

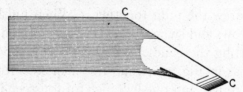

Fig. 337—Showing the Shape Given to the Point.

take off and finish welding to the top; now bolt on the
landside and refit the share, if you have got it out of
shape in making the last welds.

Now I have described how I lay slip-lays. Solid
bars or landsides I treat in the same way, for all the
difference between the two is that there is no lip to

make separately in the solid landsides. In laying the steel on the plow to mark the holes, I let it project over the bar one-eighth of an inch, which gives metal enough to dress a sharp corner in finishing.—*By* R. W. H.

Making a Plowshare.

In making a plowshare, I first get out my steel like Fig. 338. Then I turn the point, as in Fig. 339. I

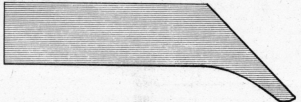

Making a Plowshare. Fig. 338—Showing how the Steel is Shaped at First.

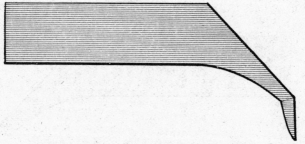

Fig. 339—Showing how the Point is Turned.

do this so that when it is bent back the point will have the same angle as the edge of the share and will not be square or like a chisel, as it will if left straight and

bent back square in the old way. I next bend the
point down and bring it back square with the shin. I
next forge out the bar, and when about finished I take

Fig. 340—Showing how the Flange is Drawn.

a light heat, and clamping it in the vise, draw a flange
on the lip on the inside of the bar as in Fig. 340. I

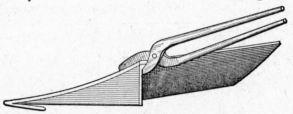

Fig. 341—Showing how the Bar is Clamped to the Share.

now slip the point of the bar under the point of the
share which is bent back, and with a pair of tongs I

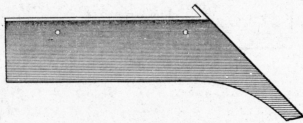

Fig. 342 – Showing the Share Completed.

clamp the bar fast to the share by catching over the
share and under the lip on the bar, as in Fig. 341, and
in this way avoid trouble while welding. I begin at

the point, and when near the top I turn the share over and with the pene of my hammer weld down the lip first, and then with the face of the hammer I strike on top of the share and never have failed to make a good weld in this way.—*By* L. H. O.

How to Sharpen a Slip-Shear Plow Lay.

Take iron ½ x ¾ inch square, thirty inches long, bend it in the center and bring the sides parallel with each other three-eighths of an inch apart, and weld the

Sharpening a Slip-Shear Plow Lay. Fig. 343—The Piece which Prevents the Lay from Springing.

ends. This piece, shown in Fig. 343, is to keep the lay from springing up in the center. I then bolt this piece

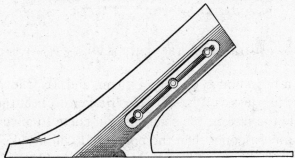

Fig. 344—Showing how the Piece is Bolted.

to the bottom of the lay with the three bolts taken out, or with new ones, as shown in Fig. 344, and then

sharpen the edge of the lay from point to heel. If
there are no rocks where it is used I draw well back
and very thin, and leave as few hammer marks as possible on top.   I always set the edge from point to heel
perfectly level with the landside on a level board or
stone, not by just sighting with my eye.   A level plow
lay is bound to run well, and it will tickle the farmer
all over when it runs well.—*By* G. W. P.

Welding Plow Points.

When making new points or welding old ones that
have ripped, I turn the point bottom upwards, pour in
a handful of wrought iron shavings along the seam,

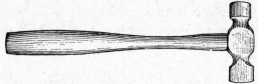

Fig. 345—Hammer Used by "J. W." in Welding Plow Points.

then a little borax on top of them, and lay the point
in the fire just as it is.   If care is taken to heat the bar
a little the fastest, the shavings will come to a welding
heat much sooner than the point, and will be like wax
when the share and bar get to a welding heat. • Then
with a light flat pened hammer, Fig. 345, I settle the
share on the bar, turn it over and with the flat pene
smooth down the melted shavings, making a strong

and neat job. When the point is ready for tempering I lay it down and allow it to cool, then I heat the edge evenly from end to end and set it in the slack tub edge down, taking care that the edge touches the water evenly from end to end. By this means I make a point solid and unsprung.—*By* J. W.

How to Put New Steel Points on Old Plows.

I have thought that someone would like to know how to make plow points last on rocky or clay land in

How to Put New Steel Points on Old Plows. Fig. 346—Showing how the First Piece of Steel is Prepared.

Maine. The farmers use cast-iron plows mostly, and a new point don't last long.

To help the poor farmer and myself just a bit, I new-steel old points by the following method : I use old

Fig. 347—Showing how First Piece of Steel is Bent.

carriage springs or old pieces of sled shoe steel, if I have them. First, take a piece of steel ¼ x 1¾ x 9 inches long for medium size plow, draw down one end thin, about one-eighth of an inch, and punch a five-

sixteenths inch hole one inch from thin end, punch second hole four inches from first hole.   Cut out the other
end with a gouge-shaped chisel, as shown at *A*, in Fig.
346.   Measure three inches from gouge cut end, and

Fig. 348—Showing Second Piece of Steel.

bend back, as shown at *B* Fig. 347.   Cut off four and
one-half inches of same size steel, draw down one end
thin, say to one-eighth of an inch, and punch one-fourth

Fig. 349—Showing how the Two Pieces of Steel are Bolted Together
Ready to Draw Out.

inch hole in thick end as at *C*, Fig. 348. Punch one-
fourth inch hole in long piece, through the fold, rivet
the two pieces together as in Fig. 349.   Take welding

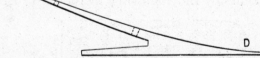

Fig. 350—Showing the Two Pieces of Steel seen in Fig. 349 Drawn to a
Point.

heat on the parts that are riveted together and draw as
in Fig. 350. Take the new point while hot and fit it to
old one, work the first hole on old point drill, countersink and rivet on your new point; drill the second hole

from top through cast iron and steel, countersink, be
sure to cut the rivet plenty long enough to rivet,
put it into the hole, and batter up the end just so the
rivet won't fall out, then heat the point and rivet while
the point is hot; fit new point to old one nicely while
hot. If the old point did not carve the ground enough
drop the end of the new point so as to be on a line
with the bottom of plow as shown at *E*, Fig. 351.

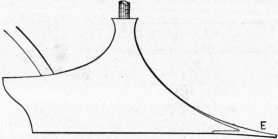

Fig. 351—Showing the Steel Point on the Plow.

Let the job cool before hardening the point. When
done the new point should be from two and one-half to
four inches long from the end of old point; for rocky
ground they should not be as long as for clay. I charge
from forty-five to seventy-five cents per point, according to size of plow, and the farmers say that a point
fixed this way will do better work and outwear two
new cast-iron points, which cost from sixty cents to
one dollar each, thereby making quite a saving.—*By*
Geo. H. Lambert.

Pointing Plows.

I first cut the point out of crucible steel one-fourth of an inch thick, as in Fig. 352. I draw the point to a thin edge as far back as the dotted line extends on

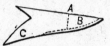

Pointing Plows, as done by "R. W. H."   Fig. 352—Showing the Point.

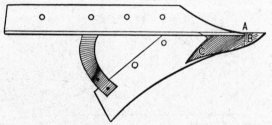

Fig. 353—Showing the Point Applied to the Plow Underneath.

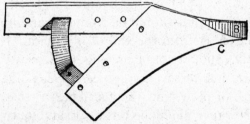

Fig. 354—Showing the Part *B* on Top of the Point.

that edge, then double the point back at *A* for right or left hand, as desired. I also thin out the point *C*. I forge down close, and after thinning the old point out, drive on as in Fig. 354, where the part B is shown on top of the point. In Fig. 353 the point is shown applied to the plow underneath. I next, with a large clean fire, weld on, commencing at the point, welding

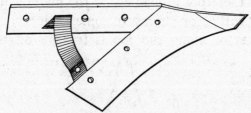

Fig. 355—Showing the Point Completed.

up the bar as far as the point extends, then having part C close to the share, weld up solid, draw out to make a full throat, and finish. Fig. 355 shows the point completed. This makes a very durable point, and always looks well if properly put on.—*By* R. W. H.

Tempering Plow Lays and Cultivator Shovels.

I have a recipe for tempering plow lays and cultivators which I think splendid. It is as follows: 1 lb. saltpetre, 1 lb. muriate ammonia, and 1 lb. prussiate of potash. Mix well, heat the steel to cherry red, and apply the powder lightly. When the oil is dry, cool in water. This leaves the steel very hard and also tough. The mixture is also good to case-harden iron and to make a heading tool.—*By* A. G. B.

Sharpening Listers.

The prairies of the West are plowed, harrowed, and planted in corn with a single machine called a lister, and it is therefore probable that the method of sharpening it will be of interest to some readers.

My way of doing the job is to take off the lister

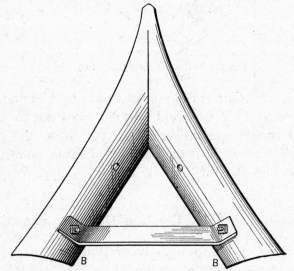

Sharpening Listers.   Fig. 356.—Bottom View of the Lister Shore.

shore, Fig. 356, and after making the brace shown in Fig. 357, bolt this brace on the bottom side, so that the bolts in the back end of the lay will pull it a little. Just here I will add, that as no two lister lays are alike, it is necessary to have a brace for each one, and it is advisable to mark each brace made, so that it can be used whenever the lay it fits comes back to the shop again. The next thing to do in the sharpening operation is to heat at the point and draw thin for three or four inches on one side.   Then change to the other side and draw on that two or three inches more than you did on the first side taken in hand.   Continue changing from one side to the other and testing it on

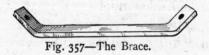

Fig. 357—The Brace.

a level surface.   It can be kept level and the point can be kept down, as the latter can be turned up easily by hammering on the bottom side.

Be sure to keep your lay level as you go on, and also keep it smooth on the top side.   In some localities it must be polished to make it scour.   Always let the lay get cold before you take the brace off, and then it can be put in place again without any trouble.—*By* G. W. Predmore.

Notes on Harrows.

In a harrow I lately made I inserted lengths of one-half inch gas-pipe between the wooden bars, as sleeves on the rods or bolts, as shown in Fig. 358, so that all could be drawn up tight.   It is quite a success.   A

good plan is to mortise in a light strap of iron, say
1 x ¼ inch, directly under the top strap, and bolt or
rivet through, as at *A* in Fig. 359, all nuts on top, to

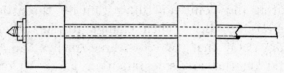

Notes on Harrows.   Fig. 358—Showing a Method of Utilizing Gas-pipe
in Making a Harrow.

keep the ground side smooth.   Fig. 360 is a top view
of the parts shown in Fig. 359.

The narrow hinge shown in Fig. 359 is common,
and can't be beaten.   It allows each section to have a
slight independent motion, can be unhooked at once

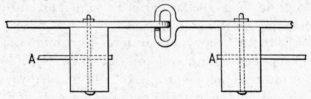

Fig. 359—Showing How the Light Strap is Mortised in and How the
Riveting and Bolting is Done.

by raising one part, and is easily folded over for cleaning.

I don't think it necessary to mortise the teeth holes
out square, as is often done, round ones do well
enough.   A good size of tooth for general work is
½ x ⅝ inch (steel).   This holds well in a five-eighths
inch round hole.   A round hole takes some driving,
but I put a one-fourth inch bolt, or rivet ("wagon-

box " head) and burr, back of each tooth.   It may interest some to learn that in certain parts of Europe an
iron tooth is inserted from below, having a shoulder
to fit against the bottom of the bar and a thread and

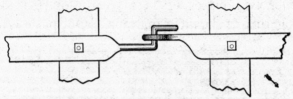

Fig. 360—Top View of the Parts Shown in Fig. 359.

nut on top to hold it.   It is pointed with steel, and
when worn goes to the smith, like a plow, to be laid.

I used a harrow of two-inch iron gas-pipe for many
years, and the teeth (one-half inch square steel) held

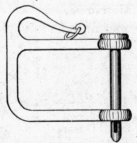

Fig. 361—Showing the Method of Attaching the Doubletree.

perfectly in round holes.   The objection to it was that
the cross-pieces being so low gathered up clods, etc.

The best method of attaching the doubletrees is, I
think, by a clevis combined with a safety-hook, as
shown in Fig. 361.—*By* WILL TOD.

Making a Bolt-Holder and a Plowshare.

A handy bolt-holder which I have occasion to use is made of two pieces of ⅜ x ¾ iron or steel, shape, put together as shown in Fig. 362. One piece is made

Making a Bolt-Holder and Plowshare. Fig. 362—Showing Bolt-Holder Complete.

with a flange to hinge into a slot, which is seen at *A* Fig. 362. The notches are made different sizes so as to hold bolts of different sizes.

With this tool one can hold any plow bolt that has

Fig. 363—Showing Piece of Iron as Used by "J. W. J." in Fitting Plowshare.

a countersunk head, and would be spoiled by the vise. The slot and rivet act as a hinge to take in large or small bolts.

I have a great many shares to make for plows, and every smith knows how hard they are to fit. Instead of staving them, I take a piece of iron, as shown in

Fig. 363, and weld on to the share, Fig. 364. After this is welded on it is an easy matter to fit it with a

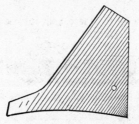

Fig. 364—Fitting Plowshare.

sharp chisel. I use five-sixteenths inch steel.—*By* J. W. J.

Making a Grubbing Hoe.

PLAN I.

The following is my plan of making a grubbing hoe or mattock. Take a piece of iron 2 x ½ inch, and about twelve inches long, cut it as at *A*, Fig. 365, bend

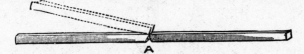

Making a Grubbing Hoe by the Method of Eph. Shaw. Fig. 365—Showing the Iron Cut for Bending Open.

open together and weld up solid to an inch and one-half of one end, then split open and put the steel in as at Fig. 366, then weld the other end for one and one-

Fig. 366—Showing the Piece Split to Insert the Steel.

Fig. 367—Showing how the Iron is Forged.

Fig. 368—Showing how the Forging is done at *G*, on the Other Piece.

Fig. 369—Showing how the Two Pieces are Welded.

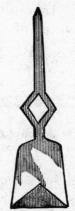

Fig. 370—Showing the Finished Mattock.

half inches together ; this will leave about two inches
not welded as at *B* ; then take a heat not quite hot
enough to weld at *B*, and forge as at *C*, Fig. 367, and
D, leaving the eye, *C*, Fig. 367, closed. Then take a
piece as before like Fig. 365, only ten inches long, and
weld solid together throughout, and forge as Fig.

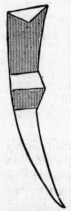

Fig. 371—Another View of the Finished Mattock.

368, *E*. Then take a good welding heat on both pieces
and weld as at *F*, Fig. 369, with steel in as *G*, then
forge and finish up as at Figs. 370 and 371. This
makes a good strong mattock, and is the only way I
know of to make one, unless it is to weld two pieces
together and form the eye, and then twist for the hoe
end.—*By* EPH. SHAW.

Making a Grubbing Hoe.

PLAN 2.

To make a grubbing hoe, take iron 3 x ½ inch, cut as shown in Fig. 372, draw out the ends, bend at *A*

Making a Grubbing Hoe by "Southern Blacksmith's" Method.
Fig. 372—The Iron Cut and Drawn.

Fig. 373 —The Iron Bent to Shape.

to a right angle, bring *B B* together, as shown in Fig. 373, and then weld. This is an easy job, and the result is a good hoe.—*By* SOUTHERN BLACKSMITH.

Forging a Garden Rake.

The question is often asked, Can forks be made successfully of cast-steel ? I can always forge better with

cast-steel than with any other metal.   I have made a
garden rake of cast-steel and it was a good, substantial job.   It is done as follows : Take a piece of steel
one-fourth or five-sixteenths of an inch thick, lay off
the center as in Fig. 374, then punch a hole about as
far from the center as is necessary to give stock enough
to turn at a right angle for the stem to go in the
handle.   Then cut out with a sharp chisel as marked
in the dotted lines *A*.   Then lay off the teeth *B B*,

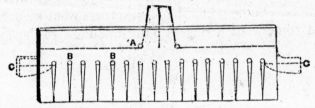

Forging a Garden Rake.   Fig. 374—" Constant Reader's " Plan.

Punch or drill holes and cut out.   The end pieces *C C*
can be turned out straight and drawn out well.   After
the holes and the pieces are cut out, to separate the teeth
turn each tooth (one at a time) at right angles, and
draw out to the desired size.   Then straighten it back
to its place, and so proceed until all the teeth are drawn.
By using a tool with holes in it to suit the tooth you
can give it a good finish on the anvil.—*By* CONSTANT
READER.

Making a Double Shovel Plow.

I will describe my method of making a double
shovel plow : I first make the irons.   The shovels

should be five inches wide, twelve inches long, and cut to a diamond or a shovel shape, as the customer desires. After drawing, bend a true arc from point to top, on a circle of twenty-two inches in diameter.   The plow will

Making a Double Shovel Plow.   Fig. 375—Cross Sectional View of a Ridge-Faced Plow.

then, as it wears away, retain the same position it had when new. I make the faces of plows to suit customers.   Some prefer them flat, others want them oval, and some want a ridge up the middle.   In the latter

Fig. 376—The Clevis.

style a cross section of the plow would look as in Fig. 375.

The next thing to be done is to make four brace rods, two one-half inch, and two ½ x 15 inches. There

Fig. 377—Showing the Standard.

should be ten inches between the center of the eye and the nail hole. I cut threads on the ends of the one-half inch rods, and punch nail hole in end of three-eighths inch rods. I then take three bolts, two one-half inch, one ⅜ x 3 inches long ; one of the one-half inch bolts should be eight inches, and the other seven and one-half inches long. The clevis comes next. I take two pieces of one-half inch round iron, ten inches

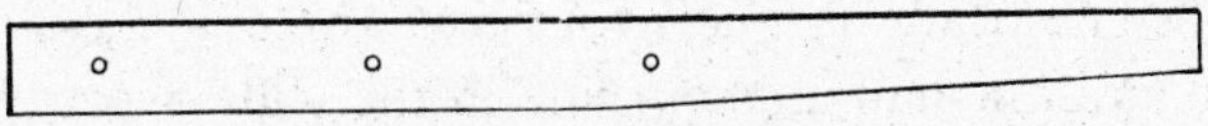

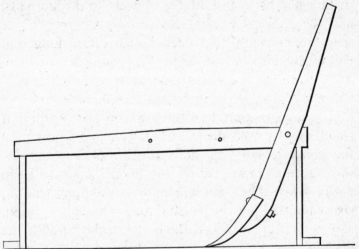

Fig. 378—The Beam.

long, flatten one end of each piece, punch three-eighths inch hole, lay the flat ends together, weld the round ends and bend to shape, when the clevis will look as in

Fig. 379—Showing the Method of Adjusting the Position of the Standard.

Fig. 376. I bore a hole in the end of the beam to admit the point of the clevis. This keeps it firmly in place. The irons are then finished. In beginning on the wood-work, I take two uprights or standards, one three and one-half feet long, and three and one-fourth inches in the widest part, and two inches thick ; the other is of the same dimensions, except that it is somewhat shorter at the top end. I make these as in Fig. 377. The beam is made four feet, three inches long, three and one-half inches wide in the widest part, and two and one-half inches at the point. I bore three holes in the wide part, two holes being one-half inch, and one three-eighths inch, and each being twelve inches from center to center, as shown in Fig. 378. After making the handles I fit the shovels to the uprights, and then take two strips of plank 1 x 2 inches, one strip fifteen inches, the other sixteen inches long, and nail blocks on one end, as in Fig. 379, and nail them down to the floor so that the ends of beam will rest in them, as shown in the illustration, resting the front end on the short piece. I lay the beam on, take an upright, stand it up by the side, as in Fig. 379, and adjust until the shovel stands on floor to suit me. I let the shovels stand rather flat on the floor. They will run better when sharp, but will not wear as long without sharpening. I put the pencil through the hole in beam, and mark the place where the hole is to be bored in the upright pieces. I bore brace holes and take a seven and one-half inch bolt, and put it through the long upright from left to right.

The block put on should be 3 x 3 inches, and two and one-half inches long. Some use iron, but wood is as good and makes the plow lighter. I put the bolts

through the beam and put on a three-eighths inch brace
and a nut.   I put an eight-inch bolt through the short
upright block and beam from right to left, and put a
one-half inch brace through the hole in the upright, as
shown in Fig. 379.   I put the eye of the one-half inch

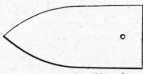

Fig. 380—The Shovel.

brace on the bolt and also use a three-eighths inch
brace.   I use a one-half inch brace in the front upright,
and also one bolt.   I screw the nuts up, bend three-
eighths inch brace down under the beam and against
uprights, rivet the end to the upright, and the plows
will then stay well apart.

In placing the handle on the beam I ascertain the

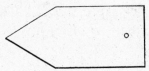

Fig. 381—The Diamond-Shaped Shovel.

height wanted on the upright, bore an inch hole through
the same, and fit the rung in so that it projects three
inches to the left of the upright.   The right handle is
put on so as to come on the outside of the front upright.   I notch the upright to fit the handle and bolt
them together with a five-sixteenths inch bolt.   Then

the clevis is put on and the plow is ready for painting.
Fig. 380 represents the ordinary shovel, and Fig. 381

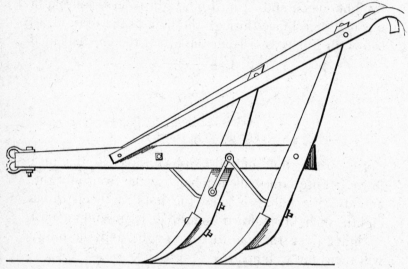

Fig. 382 —The Finished Plow.

shows the diamond-shaped shovel.   The finished plow
is shown in Fig. 382.—*By* C. JAKE.

Pointing Cultivator Shovels.

PLAN I.

We that labor for farmers must know how to do
work on farm implements and machines, and so there
may be many who would like to know a good way for
pointing cultivator shovels.   My plan is as follows:

I take a piece of spring steel about six inches long

and one and one-half inches wide, and draw it out from
the center toward each end to the shape shown in Fig.
383. I then draw out the straight side *A* to a thin
edge and cut through the dotted line nearly to the point.

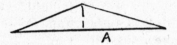

A

Pointing Cultivator Shovels by the Method of " A. M. B." Fig. 383—
Showing the Shape to which the Steel is Drawn.

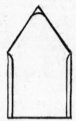

Fig. 384—Showing the Old Cultivator Shovel.

Fig. 385—Showing the Steel After it has been Cut into and Doub'ed
Around.

I next double around as in Fig. 385 and take a light
heat to hold it solid. I then take the old cultivator
shovel, as illustrated in Fig. 384, straighten it out
flat, lay the point on the back side, take a couple of
good welding heats, and finish up to shape as in Fig.
385, making virtually a new shovel.—*By* A. M. B.

Pointing Cultivator Shovels.

PLAN 2.

I will describe my way of pointing cultivator shov-els, and I think it is the best and most economical I ever tried. Take a piece of one-quarter inch plow steel two and one-half inches wide, cut it as shown in Fig. 386, and forge it into the shape shown in Fig. 387.

Pointing Cultivator Shovels.   Fig. 386—Show'ng how the Steel is Cut.

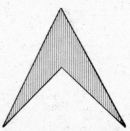

Fig. 387—Showing the Point after the Forging.

Then you will have a point with just the right amount of steel in the right place and with none wasted. I al-ways mark the whole bar with a dot punch before I commence cutting the points.—*By* W. L. S.

Pointing Cultivator Shovels.

PLAN 3.

I cut out my points in one piece as shown in Fig. 388, using good crucible steel. Then I take the shovel to be pointed and draw its point, then half way up each edge I also draw the points shown in Fig, 388,

Pointing Cultivator Shovels. Fig. 388—Showing the Point.

where they lap on to the shovel edge, and cut them to fit under the point of the shovel to be pointed, as shown in Fig. 389. In getting the point in place clamp it with a pair of tongs on the right side of the

Fig. 389—The Point Adjusted Ready for Welding.

shovel, put in the fire on the left side, with the face of the shovel up ; have an open, clear fire ready, put on borax, and let the heat come up slowly, so as not to burn the point underneath. A fan blower is better for this purpose, as you can regulate it to any degree of blast. After welding each point, take a light heat and tap the thin edge of the shovel down snug upon the point and lay it flat in the fire, face up; then take a wide heat (with plenty of borax) over the entire point and weld down solid with quick blows and with a hammer a little rounded on the face. Draw the edges out thin and hold the piece on the

Fig. 390—The Finished Shovel.

anvil so as to bevel from the bottom, leaving the top of the shovel level, as in Fig. 390. After finishing, heat to a cherry red all over, and plunge it in water edgeways and perpendicular, holding it still in one place till cool, then grind the scale off of the face and polish it on an emery belt. Shovels pointed in this way are almost as good as new, and will scour and give perfect satisfaction.—*By* R. W. H.

END OF VOLUME III.

INDEX.

VOLUME IV.

CONTENTS.

PREFACE.

In the present volume we have continued the very interesting topic of jobs of work, and have devoted considerable space to the subjects of cutting, bending, welding and setting of tires, setting axles, resetting old springs, making bob sleds, the tempering of tools; bolts, nuts, the working and welding of steel, etc. The last chapter is wholly given up to the compilation of a set of tables giving the sizes and weights of iron and steel.

CHAPTER I.

MISCELLANEOUS CARRIAGE IRONS.

The blacksmith is often called upon to repair carriages and wagons, or to iron some particular part of each on short notice, and unless experienced in carriage work much valuable time is lost in devising means of performing the work in a satisfactory manner. As a help to such the directions in this chapter for making a variety of irons will be found valuable.

As hammer signals are of interest we preface this chapter with a complete code.

Hammer Signals.

When the blacksmith gives the anvil quick, light blows it is a signal to the helper to use the sledge or to strike quicker.

The force of the blows given by the blacksmith's

hammer indicates the force of blow it is required to give the sledge.

The blacksmith's helper is supposed to strike the work in the middle of the width of the anvil, and when this requires to be varied the blacksmith indicates where the sledge blows are to fall by touching the required spot with his hand hammer.

If the sledge is required to have a lateral motion while descending, the blacksmith indicates the same to the helper by delivering hand-hammer blows in which the hand hammer moves in the direction required for the sledge to move.

If the blacksmith delivers a heavy blow upon the work and an intermediate light blow on the anvil, it denotes that heavy sledge blows are required.

If there are two or more helpers the blacksmith strikes a blow between each helper's sledge-hammer blow, the object being to merely denote where the sledge blows are to fall.

When the blacksmith desires the sledge blows to cease he lets the hand-hammer head fall upon the anvil and continue its rebound upon the same until it ceases.

Thus the movements of the hand hammer constitute signals to the helper, and what appear desultory blows to the common observer constitute the method of communication between the blacksmith and his helper.

Making a Thill Coupling.

My way of making a thill coupling is as follows:

I take a piece of Norway iron, say, for a buggy, three-eighths of an inch by two and one-half inches, then cut off a square block and cut it in the way shown in Fig. 1 of the accompanying illustrations, and in which *A A* denote where the blot goes through. *B*

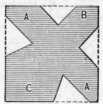

Making a Thill Coupling. Fig. 1—Showing How the Piece of Iron is Cut.

is drawn down and rounded for the lower part of the front side, as shown in Fig. 2. *C* is drawn out to make

Fig. 2—Showing the Coupling Completed.

the cuff which goes over the axle and down on the inside. I find this plan better than depending on welding the lugs *A A* to the other part.—*By* J. A. R.

Making a Thill Cuff.

To make a thill cuff or shackle, take a piece of iron three inches wide and three inches long by five-six-

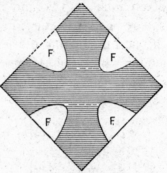

"E. W.'s" Method of Making a Thill Cuff.   Fig. 3—Showing How the Iron is Fullered.

Fig. 4—Showing How the Piece is Bent and Chilled.

Fig. 5—Showing the Thill Cuff Completed.

teenths of an inch thick, and fuller it as shown in Fig. 3.   I then bend up two corners to which the shaft end is to be fastened, and drill holes through for bolts, as in Fig. 4. One of the other ends is drawn out for the clip, with an end shaped for a nut. The other end is also threaded for a nut. The thill cuff is then finished, as shown in Fig. 5. It should be made of the best iron, either Norway or Sligo.—*By* E. W.

Making Spring and Axle Clips and Plates.

As most blacksmiths will be interested in learning a good method of making spring axle clips and plates,

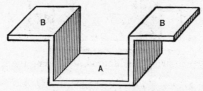

Making Spring and Axle Clips and Plates, as Described by "Iron Doctor." Fig. 6—Showing the Clip.

I will, with the aid of the accompanying engravings, endeavor to show how the job is performed in my

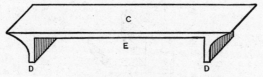

Fig. 7—Showing the Finished Clip Plate.

shop. Fig. 6 represents the clip. *A* indicates where the axle sets, and *B B* are parts of the clip plate. Fig. 7

shows the finished clip plate.   The part *C* sets on the
spring.   *E* is the space between the cars, *D D,* in

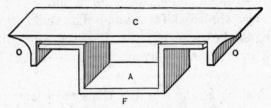

Fig. 8—Showing the Parts Put Together.

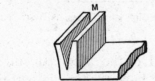

Fig. 9—Showing the Method of Bending the Ends.

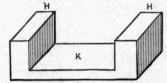

Fig. 10—Showing the Manner of Splitting.

Fig. 11—Showing How the Fullering is Done.

which the clip shown in Fig. 6 fits.   Fig. 8 represents the whole thing put together.   *A* is the spring

plate, F is the axle clip, C C are the spaces between the clip yokes. In making, first bend the ends at HH in Fig. 9, in which K indicates the plate, then split down as at M in Fig. 10, next fuller in with a small fuller as at M in Fig. 11, and then using a larger fuller bring to the shape shown in Fig. 12.

If the best iron is used the bending can be done

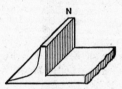

Fig. 12—Showing the Fullering Process Completed.

with one heat, and another will be sufficient for the working out. If ordinary iron is employed more heats will be required.—*By* IRON DOCTOR.

How to Prevent Working of King Bolt, and How to Make a King-bolt Stay.

All carriagemakers have had more or less bother with the head of the king bolt becoming loose in the head block, rattling, turning around and finally making a hole in the block. After some study and experimenting I have overcome the trouble. I have also managed to get up a first-rate king-bolt stay, which will wear a long time without rattling, and does not wear a hole in the king bolt or wear the thread off.

In Fig. 13 I show how I take care of the king bolt.

A is the oblong or elongated head which is let in the head block, *C* is the king bolt or a section of the same. *B B* are holes in the head which I countersink

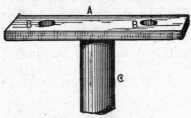

How to Prevent Working of King Bolt. Fig. 13—Showing How the King Bolt is Made.

from the upper side, and put in two five-sixteenths inch bolts which go all the way through the head block and head-block plate and fasten with nuts on the under side.   Since making my king bolts this way I have had no more trouble.

By Fig. 14 I show how I make the king-bolt stay. *B* is the head, with the hole *E* for the passage of the

Fig. 14—Showing How the King-bolt Stay is Made.

king bolt.   *F* is the stay, which may be made flat, oval or round.   I always make mine oval.   By *G* I show a recess in the under side of the nut—done by counterboring—for the insertion of the king-bolt nut, which is so made as to fill the recess which I show by Fig. 15. *K* is the square part of the nut on which the wrench is placed. I sometimes make them six-cornered. *H* is a raised round section on the nut which fits in the recess in the stay head at *G*. The

Fig. 15—Showing the King-bolt Nut.

wear by this means comes on the nut and not on the king bolt. I make an ordinary nut and form the round part with a file. In conclusion, I think I have wrought out something good which all may use.—*By* IRON DOCTOR.

Fastening a King-bolt Stay.

It took me a good many years to learn that if I bolted iron to iron where there was much vibration the bolts would soon break. For years I bolted my king-bolt stays to the reach or reaches with, as I thought, bolts strong enough to hold. Well, they would hold a little while and then the nuts would get loose and drop off, sometimes the reach would split and refuse to hold a bolt. After putting up with the nonsense about long enough, I put on my thinking cap and turned out a pretty reliable stay, which I have

been using ever since.   It is a simple but effective stay.
A, Fig. 16, is the back end, which extends under
the reach enough to take one or two bolts.   *B B* are

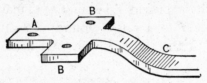

Fig. 16—Fastening a King-bolt Stay as Made by " Iron Doctor."

ears on each side of the plate and form a good solid
clip bar.   *C* is a section of the stay neck.   I make a

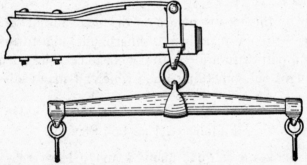

Fig. 17—Showing the Spring Doubletree Described by J. O. Hess.

wide clip (two inches wide), and secure the perch and
stay with the same, and have no further trouble.—*By*
Iron Doctor.

A Good Spring Doubletree.

I send you a spring doubletree (Fig. 17) which I
think is much simpler than any other I have ever seen.
Any blacksmith can make it.   The spring is ten

inches long by one and three-fourths inches wide, and made with two leaves. The spring stands off from the end of the doubletree two and one-half inches. Two bolts are sufficient to make secure.

This will do for ordinary farm work; for heavy work it should be made stronger.

One of these springs will pay for itself in less than a year in easing the wear and strain to horse, harness and wagon.—*By* J. O. Hess.

Making a Pole Cap or Tongue Iron.

To make a pole cap or tongue iron, take two pieces of band iron, fifteen inches long and one and one-fourth by three-sixteenths of an inch, and a piece of

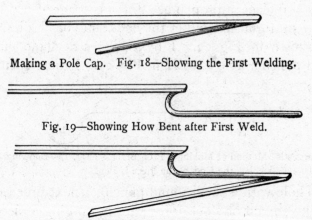

Making a Pole Cap. Fig. 18—Showing the First Welding.

Fig. 19—Showing How Bent after First Weld.

Fig. 20—Ready for Second Bend.

rod iron eleven inches long by five-eighths of an inch in diameter, and weld the rod to one of the flat pieces, as shown in Fig. 18 of the accompanying illustrations. Then shape them as shown in Fig. 19, weld on the

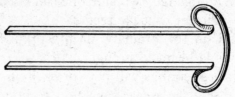

Fig. 21—Showing Pole Cap Completed.

other piece of band iron as in Fig. 20, and bend to shape as shown in Fig. 21. Then the bolt holes are drilled, and the job is completed.—*By* J. M. W.

Making a Prop Brace for a Carriage.

To replace a prop brace for a carriage I use oval iron of right size, upset the ends, and bend one end as shown in Fig. 22. I next take a key-hole punch and punch a hole as at *A* in Fig. 22. I then open up

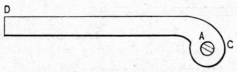

"Earnest's" Method of Making a Prop Brace.   Fig. 22—Showing How the End of the Piece is Bent.

the hole with a small round punch. I next proceed to make an end or stock for a joint by forging a piece of iron so as to make it seven-sixteenths of an inch by eleven-sixteenths of an inch, and then bend the end as at *C*, Fig. 22. I then make a square-lipped drill with a centerpiece one-fourth of an inch round, as shown in Fig. 23, the lip being as broad as I want the joint to be. I next drill a hole three-fourths of an inch in di-

Fig. 23—The Drill.

ameter through the end, as shown in Fig. 24, and with the square-lipped drill make a hole half way through

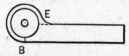

Fig. 24—Showing the Position of the Hole when Drilled.

the end, as shown by the dotted lines in Fig. 24. I next file off the edges, all that the square-lipped drill

Fig. 25—Showing the Piece Ready for Welding.

had left. I file three-fourths of the way down, and file around, beginning at *E* and ending at *B*, Fig. 24, leaving the piece as shown in Fig. 25. I then weld the piece Fig. 25 to the part shown in Fig. 22, *F* being welded to *D*. I next make another piece just

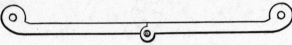

Fig. 26—Showing the Brace Completed.

like the first I have described, put the two together with a large head-rivet, and this makes the job complete, as shown in Fig. 26.—*By* EARNEST.

Making a Pole Socket.

I will describe my way of making a pole socket:

Take a piece of Norway iron at least three inches wide and three-eighths of an inch thick, cut it to the length of four inches, and mark it off with a pencil as

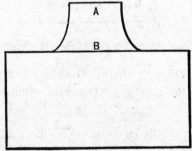

Making a Pole Socket.　Fig. 27—Showing How the Iron is Marked.

shown in Fig. 27. Then mark the pencil lines with a cold chisel, heat the piece and cut it out. Next bend the part *A* down at *B* over the anvil and work the corner up square. Do not use the vise in bending, for it is a mistake to bend any sharp corner in a vise.

Fig. 28—Showing the Piece After the Rounding and Welding Operations.

Then draw out the part *B*, leaving it one-half inch or two inches wide and three-sixths of an inch thick. Next bend it round to a diameter of one and one-half

Fig. 29—Showing How the Piece is Split, Bent and Formed.

inches, then weld, finishing and rounding it upon a mandrel, and it will then be of the shape shown in Fig. 28. Next punch a very small hole at *C*, split it upward as shown by the dotted line, and bend and form each half as in Fig. 29. My boss had another way of making a socket. He took a piece 1¾ x 5-16, and

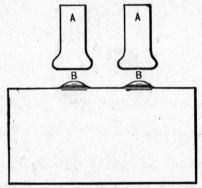

Fig. 30—Showing How the Ears are Welded in Another Way of Making a Pole Socket.

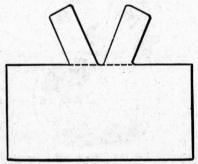

Fig. 31—Showing the Ears as Welded On.

welded on the two ears shown in Fig. 30, *A A* being the ears and *B B* the scarf ends to weld on. When the welding was done as shown in Fig. 31, he did the bending and other work in the same way that I do.— *By* T. J. B.

Making a Staple and Ring for a Neck Yoke.

Many years ago, when I worked as a journeyman in a carriage and wagon shop, I often thought when ironing neck yokes, that I could devise a middle ring for a neck yoke that would be much easier on the horses'

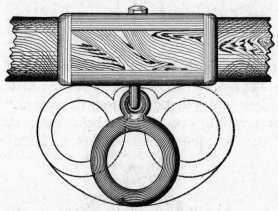

Making a Staple and Ring for a Neck Yoke by the Method of "M. D. D."
Fig. 32—The Finished Ring.

necks than anything I had ever seen. So when I went into business for myself, I put on the first neck yoke I ironed a staple and ring like the one shown by Fig. 32.

All the other rings I know anything about are rigid, or nearly so; not one of them will work like this. It is over ten years since I ironed that neck yoke, and it is

still in use and has never been repaired.   For a spring
wagon this ring will outwear half a dozen leather ones.
I have two ways of making it, but think that Figs. 33
and 34 illustrate the best way.

I get a piece of good Norway iron, of a size to

Fig. 33—The Piece Punched and Split.

correspond with that of the ring wanted, put in the
fulling hammer and work the eye round ; then punch
a small hole and split it down from the hole to the end,
as shown in Fig. 33.   I then bend back the arms
nearly but not quite horizontally, work them round,

Fig. 34—Showing the Piece Ready for Rounding and Welding.

punch and work out the eye, as in Fig. 34.   It is then
ready for turning round and welding, after which I
get a piece of round iron, which also ought to be good,
form the eye bolt or staple, then open it a little and

slip it into the eye, take a weld and draw it down tapering. I then make two plates for the neck yoke,
making the holes for the eye bolt to fit snug; if for a
farm wagon the plates must be longer, and fastened
with two rivets; but for a spring wagon all that is
needed is two wood screws for each plate. After

Fig. 35—Showing Another Method of Making the Ring.

boring the hole I burn it with the eye bolt, being
careful not to get the hole too large, for the eye bolt
ought always to fit tight at first. For a spring wagon
I put on a six-sided nut, for a farm wagon a ferule,
and rivet the end of the eye bolt red hot. To make
the ring as shown in Fig. 35, such good iron is not
needed. In that case I put in the fulling hammer
at $A A$, draw down the arms to B, turn them round

Fig. 36—The Ring in Position.

and weld them, then work out the eye; but if I have
good iron would much rather make them the other
way. Fig. 36 shows the ring in position. There is no
patent on this ring; at all events, I have taken none
out; and I believe I am the original inventor.—*By*
M. D. D.

Making Wagon Irons.

I will give you my way of making iron toe calks that will wear almost forever and outlast two steel ones. Simply heat the calk nearly to a welding heat, dust it with cast-iron and cool in cold water. If done right the surface will be of a light gray color. A great deal of iron about very heavy wagons, whiffletree irons most especially, if treated this way would last much longer, and the cost would be small if it were done at the time of ironing.—*By* H. A. S.

Making Shifting Rail Prop Irons.

I will explain my method of making a shifting rail prop iron. I take a bar of Norway iron one and one-eighth by one-half inch, and draw out or cut it out half the breadth two inches long, as at *A* in Fig. 37; then cut into the dotted line *B*, and bend the end down to

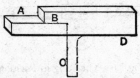

Making Shifting Rail Prop Irons by the Method of "H. N. S." Fig. 37—
Showing How the Bar is Drawn Out and Bent.

the dotted lines *C*. This leaves *B* and *D* at different heights, so I put the end *C* in the square hole of the anvil and drive *B* down even with *D*, as in Fig. 38. Then I draw out the end in the dotted lines *E*, and split at *F* and bend up *F* as at *G*, and swage to the size of iron needed for the rail. I make the upturned

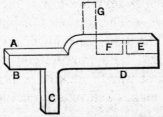

Fig. 38—Showing Further Operations in Drawing and Bending.

end one-half inch round and make the collar and prop piece. Then I have a swage one-half an inch wide to

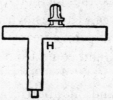

Fig. 39—Showing How the Swage Fits Between the Collar and Prop Piece.

fit between the collar and prop piece, as at *H* in Figs. 39 and 40. I like the collar to be close to the prop

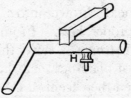

Fig. 40—Showing the Collar and Prop Piece in Position.

piece, as this makes a stronger rail—one that cannot bend. Most of the railings I see have a space or length two inches where I only make one-half inch or five-eighths. The next thing in order is to raise the prop part, which gives the top a nicer appearance when lying down. The top rests or blocks are usually too low, and the bows are lower in the rear than where they part. I do not pretend that this is the quickest or easiest way of making a prop iron, but in my opinion it makes a firm and neat-looking railing. —*By* H. N. S.

Bending a Phaeton Rocker Plate.

The following is the method of making phaeton rocker plates in large factories where they make from one to five thousand pairs a year. These plates are all bent with one heat, and come from the form after they are bent, ready for use. In Fig. 41 I show a straight piece of steel one and one-fourth by five-sixteenths of an inch, drawn at both ends, and ready to be bent.

First, they cut off any desired number of pairs of plates with power shears to the exact length required. Then the ends are drawn out under power hammers. The plates are next thrown into a large furnace and heated to the proper heat. From twenty to thirty pieces are heated at once. After they are hot they are placed on the cast plate between the formers as shown in Fig. 41. Then the eccentric C, Figs. 41 and 42, is pulled around so as to press the small plate X against the rocker plate and the part H of the form. The lever B is now pulled into its place and a pin is placed in the hole *J*, which will keep the lever in position, The lever *D* is next pulled in its place, and pins are put in the holes *K K*; then the lever *E* is pulled around in its place. Then, with a hammer, the rocker plate is levelled and straightened while it is in the

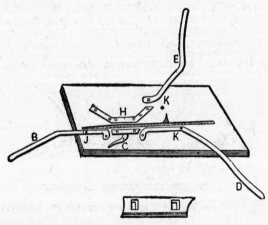

Bending a Phaeton Rocker Plate, as Described by "H. R. H." Fig. 41— Showing the Steel before Bending, and also the Part Marked ✕ in Fig. 42.

former; next the two pins *J* and *K* are taken out, the lever is pulled back, and the rocker plate is taken from the former finished.

In Fig. 42 I show a sketch of the former as it is when the rocker plate is bent between the levers. It does not take much work to make a former of this kind. Have a cast-iron plate the proper length and width, and one and one-half or two inches thick, and plane it level on one side. The levers and other pieces of the form should be made of steel the same thickness as the rocker-plate, and from two to two and one-half inches wide. The levers E, B and D are bolted to the plate with five-eighths inch steel bolts. The part ×, where the eccentric presses the plate, has two slotted holes five-eighths of an inch wide and one inch long, as is shown in Fig. 42. The part H is bolted solid to the plate. The levers B, E and D should have jaw-nuts on the bolts so as to have the levers work easy. The

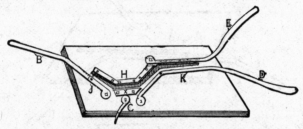

Fig. 42—Showing the Plate Bent Between the Levers.

eccentric C is fastened the same as the other levers, and with a five-eighths inch steel bolt. On the lever B will be seen a mark which is the gauge for the proper length of the front end of the rocker plate. Besides its use in forming, this plate can also be employed as an ordinary straightening plate.—*By* H. R. H.

Shifting Bar for a Cutter.

The shifting bar for a cutter illustrated herewith I have used for some time, and it has been pronounced by competent judges one of the most complete devices for the purpose that has ever come before their notice.

Fig. 43 shows the device arranged for side draft, and
Fig. 44 for center draft. *A A* represent the runners
of the cutter. *B B* show some double acting springs

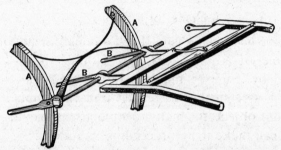

Shifting Bar for a Cutter.   Fig. 43—Arranged for Side Draft.

which hold the shaft in place. The draw-bar is made
of nine-sixteenths inch round iron, with a center stay
running back to the beams. The cross-bar is provided

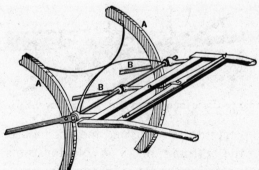

Fig. 44—Arranged for Center Draft.

with three eyes. When the shafts are brought to the
center the third eye catches the end of the draw-bar
and holds the shafts firmly to the runners. The draw-

bar is rounded down to one and one-half inches, and
the thread is cut back of that for screwing into the
draw-iron.—*By* L. P.

A Crane for a Dump Cart.

I have been using what I call a crane for holding up
the pole of a dump cart, and I think the device as
shown by Fig. 45 may be of use to some; it will
prevent sore necks on horses, and this should be a
sufficient object for many people to utilize it.   Any
smith can make it by proceeding as follows :

Take a piece of flat iron the width of the tongue,
make an eye in one end and put a hook on it; now

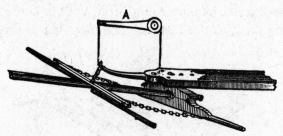

Fig. 45—Crane for a Dump Cart, as Made by "A. H. S."

bolt the pieces on the tongue, one on the top and the
other on the bottom ; make a hole for transom bolt
and another for the crane ; in punching the hole for
the transom bolt make it oblong.   Put your crane in
between the two plates and put a pin in ; bolt a piece
of chain to the cross-bar, raise the pole up and hook
the chain to the crane.   With this device you can

turn the cart around just as easily as if it was not there, and it can be removed in a moment. *A* indicates a side plan of the hooked piece.—*By* A. H. S.

To Iron Front Seat of a Moving Van.

The primary points to be kept in view when ironing the front seat of a moving van, a lookout for general ease, convenience, comfort and security for the driver and his associates on the seat ; I also plan to give strength throughout, and see that the fastening of the work to the body frame is such as to hold it firm and prevent it from working loose.

In Fig. 46, *A* is the outside line of body in front, *B* the base line. *C C*, where the handle is secured to the body frame. *D* is the hand piece of the handle. Make *D* of one-half inch round iron and cover with harness leather, which will insure a safer grip than iron alone. Make *C C* one inch wide and one-half inch thick at the first hole, and taper in thickness to three-eighths of an inch, four inches long, and fasten with three-eighths inch bolts. *E*, *F* and *G* represent the step, *E* where it is secured to the body, *F* the shank, and *G* the tread. Make *E* six inches long, one and one-half inches wide, seven-eighths of an inch thick at lowest hole, and taper to top to one-half inch thick. Fasten with seven-sixteenths inch bolt top, one-half inch bolt bottom. Make the shank *F* seven-eighths of an inch in diameter at the body, and taper to three-quarters of an inch at the tread, and between the body and tread six inches long. Make the tread, *G*, an oval six inches by five and three-sixteenths of an inch thick; round over the top edges to prevent cutting.

In Fig. 47, *K* is the base line of body, *M* the seat

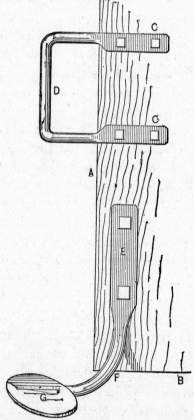

To Iron Front Seat of a Moving Van.   Fig. 46—Showing How the Handle and Step Should be Secured.

rail, L where it is secured to the body, and N the foot which secures it to the seat board. The dotted line R is the space occupied by the seat bottom. P is where

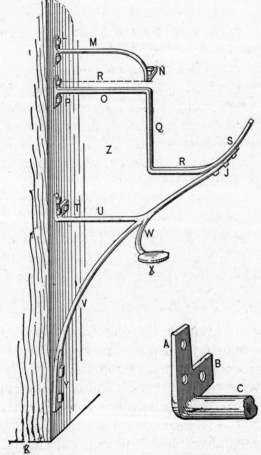

Fig. 47—Showing How the Seat Should be Ironed.

Fig. 48—Showing How T of Fig. 47 Should be Made.

the seat iron secures to the body, O the horizontal foot of the seat iron, Q the vertical part, R the horizontal part of the foot board, and S the bracket or toe piece. U is a safety stay from the stay V to the body, where it is secured to the body. V is the main stay, Y where it secures to the body, W the central step shank, and X the tread. Z is the space in which to set the blanket box, with a gate at each end.

Make M of nine-sixteenths inch round iron, and fasten to body and seat with three-eighths inch bolts; O, Q, R and S of 2 x ¾ inch half oval iron. V and U of 1½ x ⅞ inch oval iron. Step shank W and tread X same as F and G. Fasten at P, T and Y with one-half inch bolts. Make O, Q, R and S in one piece; also, U, V, W and X in one piece, and bolt all together with three seven-sixteenths inch bolts at J. Make T the same as Fig. 48, A and B to bolt on the body to prevent racking. P and Y may be made the same when additional security is desired.—*By* IRON DOCTOR.

Wagon Brake.

For a brake suitable for a light wagon to carry from four hundred to six hundred pounds I should recommend three-eighths-inch round iron. For a wagon that is to carry from seven hundred to one thousand two hundred pounds, one-inch round iron. For a wagon that is intended to carry from two hundred to one thousand five hundred pounds, one and one-eighth inch round iron, and for one that is to carry from one thousand five hundred to two thousand four hundred pounds, one and one-fourth inch round iron. The special feature that recommends the brake made by

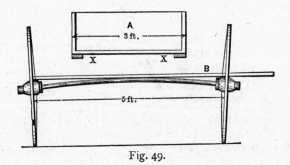

Fig. 49.

me is its simplicity. It is also the easiest for the smith to make of any with which I am acquainted.

In order to explain the brake intelligently, let it be supposed that a brake is to be made in order to fit a given wagon. The first thing I would do would be to get the width of the body, which may be assumed to be three feet from out to out, as indicated by *A* in

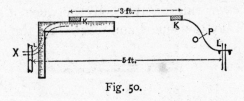

Fig. 50.

Fig. 49, a section of the body of the wagon. Next I get the width between the sills of the wagon, then I get the distance from center to center of the wheels,

or, what is the same, from in to out of the wheels at
the place where the brake blocks are to come. This
is also indicated in Fig. 49. I then take a piece of

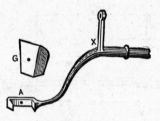

Fig. 51.

board of proper length and width, and mark upon it,
first, the width of the body. Then I would mark the
distance between the sills of the body as shown by K
K in Fig. 50. Now, as the width of body is three

Fig. 52.

feet, and the width from center to center of the brake
blocks is five feet, there will be left the space of one
foot on each side of the body between it and the
wheel. Take the square and place it on the board as

Fig. 53.

indicated at $K X$ in Fig. 50, and measure one foot out
on each side of the body. At X will be the center of
the block. With a piece of chalk make a double

sweep, as shown from K to L, in Fig. 50. This sweep should be the same in its two halves; that is, the curve from K to the cross line marked O should be the same as from L to the same cross line. Next get the length

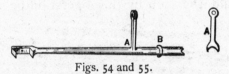

Figs. 54 and 55.

of the iron from this board, and shape the brake over the draft thus constructed. Cut the iron so that each piece will make one-half of the brake, and make the last weld in the center.

In making the brake a choice must be made as to the fastening to be employed for the block. For the

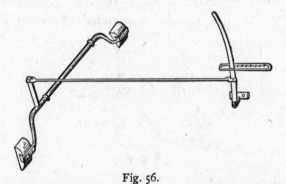

Fig. 56.

sake of illustration we will choose that indicated by A, in Fig. 51. To make this fastening proceed as follows: Heat the iron and split it, as shown at F in Fig. 52. Then forge out the end marked X, as shown at A in Fig. 53. Next place the iron back in the fire, and getting a good welding heat, use a fuller and thus turn back a part for the lip, and swage the iron a trifle thinner back of the lip, as shown at X in Fig. 53. Should the iron by this operation be made too

Fig. 57.

light at the flat part of the lip, indicated by O in Fig. 53, heat it again and upset it until the proper shape is obtained. This iron might be forged out of a solid piece, or of a large piece of iron, and then welded out to the round iron. This, however, I think useless, as the plan I have described is fully as good a way of making it, and has the advantage of being accom-

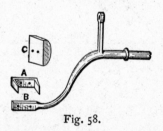

Fig. 58.

plished in one-third the time required for the other. After the iron has been finished as is shown in Fig. 53, turn the other lip as indicated by X, in Fig. 54. This part is then finished. Weld on the lever for the rod as shown by A in Fig. 54. Fig. 55 illustrates how this lever is prepared, ready for welding. Then weld on the collar as shown at *B* in Fig. 54. This collar, *B*, must be welded on so that when the iron is bent, as shown in Fig. 51, it will come even with the inside of the sill of the body, as indicated by *X X*, in Fig. 49. The object of these collars is to keep the brake in its place. In shaping the lips *A* of Fig. 51, they should be made wider on the top than on the bottom, so that they will receive a block, as indicated by *G*. This block is made dovetail, so that it will not

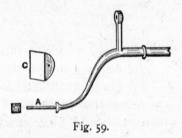

Fig. 59.

give trouble by slipping through the iron when the brake is applied to the wheel. The opposite side of the brake is made in the same manner, save that it does not need the lever *X* shown in Fig. 51. The rod operating the lever is placed only on one side of the body. It is generally placed on the right-hand side.

In Fig. 56 the brake is shown as it would appear when applied to the body. The body itself is omitted because it would conceal the irons, which it is desirable to show. In Fig. 57 two forms of hanging irons are shown for hanging the brake to the body. The iron

A is generally used on very light work, while the iron *B* is desirable for heavy work, such as platform, mail or express wagons. If the iron *B* is used, it must be put on the brake before the collars are welded in place.

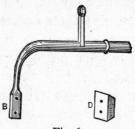

Fig. 60.

In Fig. 58 another method of fastening the block in place is shown. The iron is flattened out wide and two holes are punched in it, as indicated at *B*. Then an iron is made of the shape shown at *A*. The block *C* is fitted to the iron *A*, and block and iron are to-

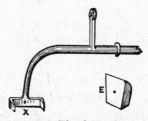

Fig. 61.

gether bolted to *B*. In Fig. 59, at *A*, a collar is shown that is swaged round. A thread is cut on the end of the iron, and the block, made of the shape shown at *C*, is slipped over it and held in place by the nut. This kind of fastening for brake blocks is in general use on heavy work. Still another form for fastening the brake blocks is shown in Fig. 60. *B* is flattened as indicated in the sketch, and the block *D* is bolted on to it by means of two bolts. Fig. 61 shows the use of the block of the general shape shown

Fig. 62.

at *E*, which is very nearly like that shown in Fig. 51. In making this iron, weld on a piece in the same manner as employed in welding a T or shaft iron. Then turn up the ends for the block. In Fig. 62 is shown a detail of the iron used where the lever is fastened.

In making a brake ratchet I proceed as follows: Take a piece of steel one by one-fourth inch, or one and one-

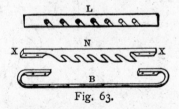

Fig. 63.

fourth by one-fourth inch, according to the size of the wagon. Drill as many holes in it as there are teeth required. Then cut them out, as is shown at *L* in Fig. 62. Finish as indicated by *N* in Fig. 63. After the teeth are in proper shape, twist the flat part at each end, as indicated by $X X$, Fig. 63, so that it can be bolted with the wide side against the body. B shows the shape of the guard for the lever. This is bolted on to the ratchet with the same bolts that hold the ratchet to the body.—*By* H. R. H.

An Improved Wagon Brake.

Having, as I believe, an improvement on that antiquated instrument, the wagon brake, I give it for the benefit of the trade.

The improvement consists in using a cam in such a manner as to hold the wheel tighter than the ordinary

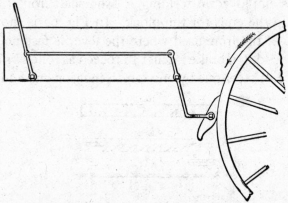

Fig. 64—Improved Wagon Brake Made by "E. L. H."

brake will, while the exertion of force on the part of the driver is much less than in using the common style of brake. The device is shown by Fig. 64.

The friction of the wheel turns the cam, this springs

the brake into the ratchet plate, and it tightens in re-volving until the shoe proper rubs on the tire. The shoe is made double so that when the wheel revolves backward it can be locked by the same process. The lower shoe should be made heavier than the upper one, otherwise it would not fall into the proper position on loosening the brake.—*By* E. L. H.

How to Make a Two-Bar Brake.

My method of making a two-bar brake :

Fig. 65 shows the brake as applied to the wagon body. *A* is the lever which goes across the body, and by the moving of the rod *H* the blocks *B B* are applied to the wheels.

Fig. 66 shows some of the iron work required to make the brake. *F F*, Fig. 66, are two iron plates

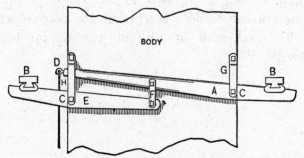

How to Make a Two-Bar Brake. Fig. 65—Brake as Applied to the Wagon Body.

one and one-half by one-half inch and six inches long One goes above and the other below at *F*, Fig. 65.

D, Fig. 66, is an eye bolt which goes in *D*, Fig. 65, and to which the rod *H*, Fig. 65, is attached. Any kind of a ratchet may be used. *G* and *H*, Fig. 66, are iron straps used at *C C*, Fig. 65.

This brake is a very common one in the West, and

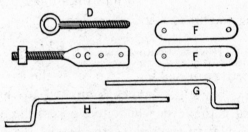

Fig. 66—Iron Work for Brake.

for a box brake is quite as cheap and as good as any in use.

There are single bar, two-bar and three-bar brakes, and we also have single bar brakes for hounds, which can be used with or without the wagon box.—*By* G. W. P.

CHAPTER II.

TIRES, CUTTING, BENDING, WELDING AND SETTING.

Tiring Wheels.

The old-time blacksmith, who heated his tire to a bright red heat, after having given one-fourth to three-eighths of an inch draw to his tire, then deluged the rim with water to prevent its being burned up, would be skeptical as to the usefulness of a tire that is heated to, without reaching, the slightest shade of red, then cooled with a sponge, and water applied to the tire without wetting the wood; but if he looks back to the wood shop he will find that he was altogether in fault. With rims driven on that do not set snug up to the shoulders, there must be something done that will correct that fault, and the tire must do the work, but there never was any need of heating the tire as hot as they were accustomed to. Wheels that are well made have all the dish in them that is required, and any draw in the tire that is more than enough to set the metal snug up to the wood and tighten the ends of the felloes is useless. It is not a part of the blacksmith's work to put the dish in the wheels, but it is the duty of the blacksmith to set his tire in a manner that will adapt it to the locality where it is to be used.

Wheel manufacturers season their timber thoroughly; unless they do so they cannot guarantee its durability. If the wheel is to be used where the natural condition of the atmosphere is dry, the tire can be set so as to hug the rim very tight; but if the wheel is to be used where the conditions of climate are different, the set of the tire must be regulated accordingly. Very many wheels are tired for shipment abroad; if the blacksmith sets the fire on these as close as he would were they to be used in New York, he will learn to his sorrow that he has made a blunder. The wood will expand while in the hold of the vessel, and the spokes will, if light, spring, or, if heavy, the felloe will bulge. The tire is simply a binder to the wheel, and when it is so set that it holds the wood firmly into the position designed it is in condition to perform its work thoroughly.—*Coach, Harness and Saddlery.*

Tire-Making.

The first thing necessary in making a tire is to see that it is straight, especially edgewise. The face of the tire should be straight before going into the bender. There are more tires and wheels ruined by the tire being bent for the wheel with crooks in the tire edgewise than in any other way in tire-making. Some seem to think the crookedness can be taken out more

conveniently after the tire is bent, but this is a mistake. It is almost impossible to take it out after it is bent, because hammering will cause the tire to become flared, like that of a barrel hoop at the parts hammered on. And how would it look to put it on the wheel with either the bends or flare in the tire? Of course, in this case the tire is ruined, and so is the wheel. It is, of course, forced into the same shape as the tire. This kind of tire-making is more apt to be done by smiths who have no machine for tire-bending. Such tire-making is disgraceful, but it is common. The best way I have discovered to straighten the face and edge is to procure a good sized log, about eight feet long, and give it, either by sawing or hewing, a nice face. Then, after the tire-iron is drawn by hand as straight as possible, I take it to this log, and by the use of the sledge-hammer pound out the crooks. After all this I often find the part that was bent considerably twisted, and this is a thing I dread to see. Small a thing as it seems to be to remedy, it is not easy. The twist can be taken out by the use of a blacksmith's large vise and a large wrench made for the purpose. If the twisted parts are made a little hot, the job is easier done. Some smiths seem to think that all this is too much trouble and takes too much valuable time, so make the tire just as the iron may fall into their hand, hoping the dishonest job may never be discovered.—
By F. F. B.

A Simple Way of Measuring Tires.

I would suggest, as an easy way to measure tires, the following plan :

Let *A*, in Fig. 67, represent a section of the tire; now start at *B* and run over the tire with the measuring wheel and it comes out at *C*, as the tire is, say, half an inch larger than the wheel. Now, take a pair of dividers and open them to the extent of ten or twelve inches, or, better still, take a piece of stiff

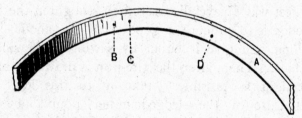

A Simple Way of Measuring Tires.   Fig. 67—Section of the Tire.

quarter-inch wire and bend it to the shape shown in Fig. 68. Then the points are not so liable to be moved by an accidental fall on the floor. Place one point at *C*, then take a center punch and make a mark where the other point touches at *D*, and also at *B*. Now heat and shrink or weld between *B* and *D*, and then, by placing the dividers in *B* or *D*, you can instantly tell whether you are right or not. If the tire is a little too short it can be drawn without reheating, whereas if you had to run it with the measuring wheel it would be so cold that reheating would be necessary. I think that by adopting this plan a smith can save an hour or more on a set of tires, and time is money.— *By* A. M. T.

Tiring Wheels.

After seeing that the tire iron is clear of twists and kinks, I lay it on the floor of the shop, then take up my wheel and set the face of it on the tire at one end of it. I next draw a pencil mark on the side of the rim exactly at the starting point at the end of the tire,

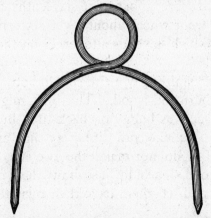

Fig. 68—The Wire Measurer Bent to Shape.

and roll on the tire until the mark of the rim comes again to the tire. I then draw a mark across the tire, one and seven-eighths of an inch beyond the mark on the rim.

I make this allowance provided the iron is five-eighths of an inch thick. This thickness is most commonly used on two-horse wagons. If the tire is greater or less in thickness, I would allow more or less, according to the thickness of the iron.

The height of the wheel need not be considered in allowing for the shrinkage, as a short bar shrinks just as much as a longer one. Some will think one and seven-eighths of an inch is more than is necessary to allow for shrinkage, but if they will observe this rule, they will find it almost correct. To allow more makes waste, and to cut it shorter ruins the wheel. For a hind wheel I give about nine-sixteenths of an inch draw, for a front wheel about seven-sixteenths. This is a matter which depends altogether on the condition of the wheel.

Some blacksmiths say a tire should not be made hot enough to burn the wood. This idea might do with small tires such as buggy or hack tires, but not with large tires. I make my tire very hot and cool it quickly. If I do not make the tire hot enough to burn the wood, I would just draw them on and set them aside, and let them have their own time to cool off.—*By* F. B.

A Cheap Tire Bender.

A cheap tire bender, which may be found very useful in many country shops, is shown by Fig. 69. *A* in the drawing indicates a section of a two and one-half inch plank. The part *B* is a segment of a three-foot

six-inch circle. It is secured to a post with spikes, and
the iron strap _E E_, two by two and one-half inches, is
fastened to the block _A_ and to the post in such a way

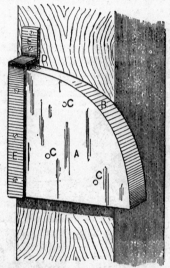

Fig. 69—A Cheap Tire Bender, as Made by " R. C. "

as to leave at _D_ a space of one inch between the strap
and the block. By bending the tire slightly at one
end and inserting this end under the strap at _D_, the
process of bending can be continued and finished easily
and rapidly.—_By_ R. C.

Welding " Low-Sized " Tires.

Smiths sometimes experience a good deal of trouble
in welding "low-sized" tires, from the fact that they

are unable to take a full heat on more than half of the point to be welded. The following is my plan for obviating this difficulty. In Fig. 70, *A* represents the back upper wall of the forge. *B* is the hood or bon-

Welding "Low-Sized Tires," as Done by "Iron Doctor." Fig. 70— Showing the Forge.

net projecting over the tuyeres ; *D* indicates the position of the tuyeres, and *C* is the upper section of the hearth. Fig. 71 represents the plate or anchor on which the brick composing the bonnet rests. To make it I took a piece of old tire two inches wide and about three-eighths of an inch thick, and first bent it on the edge so as to be rounding at the point *H*, and described a part of a circle eighteen inches in diameter, leaving the space *G* just fourteen inches in the clear, and from the corners *E E* to *H* just thirty-eight inches. I then turned down the lugs or corners *F F* eight inches, so as to catch on four bricks, and punched a

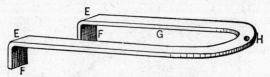

Fig. 71—The Anchor Plate

hole at *H* for the insertion of the bolt *P*, Fig. 72, which I made of five-eighths inch round iron. I split one end and formed the anchor, and next put on a thread and nut as at *M*, Fig. 72. *S* indicates the base plate. The anchor or king bolt is secured to *S* at *M*. The dotted line from *T* to *R* indicates the back wall, and the other dotted line represents the front wall of the chimney, the distance through being fourteen inches. *T* and *R* are the anchors of the bolt and plates, and when the whole is in position a complete truss is made. I removed a few bricks, placed my truss in position and secured it by replacing the bricks, and with a few whole bricks and bats, with the necessary mortar, built or completed the hood, removing the corners before placing them so as to give a smooth finish. I covered the outside with a coat of fine mortar, and smoothed it down with a coat of whitewash. Between the top of the hearth and the bottom of the hood the space should not be more than

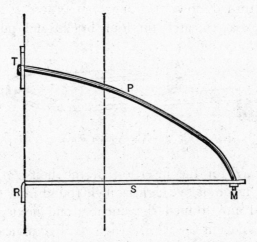

Fig. 72—Showing the Arrangement of the Truss.

twelve or fourteen inches. The bolt T is encased in the brickwork. For tire welding and horseshoeing no better forge hood can be made, and the cost is but trifling. I presume one made of sheet-iron would answer quite well and cost but little.—*By* IRON DOCTOR.

Device for Holding Tire While Welding.

When welding tire I have bothered me to keep
their ends together, as I employ no helper. The little
device which I have represented by Fig. 73 is the
result of my study of how to accomplish the desired
result most easily. For my own use I made the tool
about twelve inches long, and used half-inch square
Norway iron. I cut the bar off twenty inches in length,
upset the ends, and then split them open about one and
one-half inches. By this means the two jaws were
provided. I made the splits about three-eighths or

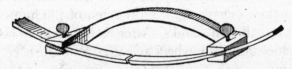

Fig. 73—" D. P.'s " Device for Holding Together Tire Ends While
Welding.

half an inch wide, so as to adapt them to receiving
ordinary light tire. I drilled a hole in the center of
the top of each jaw, cut a thread and put in a thumb
screw. I made the bends three inches from the ends,
and gave the jaws the requisite twist to suit the tool
to the circle of the wheel. In use I put the tool first
to the tire on the side toward the chimney, which
keeps it out of the way of the hammer when the tire is
put upon the anvil. The arch in the body of the

device keeps it out of the way of the fire in heating. It is very satisfactory. I can put on my welding compound and feel perfectly sure of producing the weld just as wanted. I have seen many smiths bothered in welding tire, and think that my device will not be without interest to your readers.—*By* D. P.

Tire-Heating Furnaces.

In setting tires in large shops we proceed as follows. We bring forty sets of wheels in the smith shop, where we have four smiths welding tires. Each of these smiths is supplied with a piece of chalk of a color different from that used by his fellow workers, and each man makes a chalk mark on the end of the hub of the wheel he takes in hand. After he has welded his tire his helper takes the wheel and tire to the furnace. By the time helper No. 1 gets his first tire at the furnace, in come helpers Nos. 2, 3 and 4; so you see there are four tires at the furnace at about the same time. Then we have a man at the furnace whose place it is to heat these tires and keep the furnace going and put the tires on. This gives the furnace a start with four tires. The furnace man puts them in the furnace and places his wheels outside the same, and this he keeps up all day. By the time he has seven or eight tires in the furnace, his first tire is warm enough. He takes it out and pulls it on the wheel; as soon as he has done this, he places it aside, sets another wheel on the tire plate and puts on another tire. By this time there will be four or five more tires ready to be heated, and as he takes a tire from the furnace he places another in. After these tires have been put on by the man at the furnace and are beginning to cool off in the air (for we never heat them so they will burn the felloes), another man takes the wheel and with a wooden mallet raps the tire lightly all around so as to have it down on the rim solid. He also faces the tire with the rim, and when he gets through he stands the wheels in sets. Then the inspector comes and examines every wheel, looking after the weld, dish, joints, etc.; also at the chalk mark of each wheel.

Now if we would allow each man to heat his own tire and put it on the wheels it would require twice as many smiths to weld as it does now, and we would have to pay eight smiths and eight helpers, instead of four smiths and six helpers, as at present, and in place of running five fires we would have to run eight, and these eight would cost (if they heated the tire the *ola way*) three times as much more for coal, and twice as much more for shop room, with no more work turned out. In large shops the heating device pays; in small shops the old way of heating on the forge is cheaper; but let me tell you that you cannot heat a tire as it should be heated (uniformly) on the forge, but you can do this on a furnace.

Where you have from ten to twenty sets of tires to set per day it will pay to put in a furnace.—*By* H. R. H.

A Tire-Heating Furnace.

There are various styles of tire heaters used in different sections of the country. Some of these are for indoor work only, and others are for outdoor uses. The first step toward building an outdoor furnace, such as is shown by Fig. 74, would be to excavate a circle eight feet in diameter, and about two feet deep, and build or fill in with a stone and cement wall to within six inches of the surface.

On top of the stone foundation lay a bed of sand cement and fine mortar well mixed, and sweep it off so

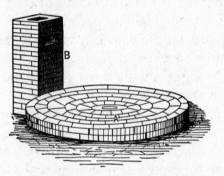

A Tire-Heating Furnace as Made by "Iron Doctor."   Fig. 74—Showing the Chimney and Tire Bed.

that it is horizontal, excepting a small incline to the center. On this bed lay the bricks in fine mortar, two courses. If the "row-lock fire-brick" shown in Fig. 75 of the accompanying illustration can be obtained, they are preferable to any other material. With "row-lock" brick begin at the outside and lay on one course, anchoring and tying them in at proper intervals, and when this has been done place around the whole two spring bands of one and one-half by one and one-fourth inches, secured with a half-inch bolt, or use a single band four by one-half and two securing bolts. This should be done while the mortar is green, so that it can be set up firmly all through. The top must be first cleared off and then covered with a thin slush of fine mortar, which will fill in all cavities. The chimney is built as shown at *B* in Fig. 74, the part *A* being the tire bed. The chimney should be at the base of a

Fig. 75—The Row-lock Fire-brick.

twelve-inch wall, and batten up to four inches, with an eight-inch or twelve-inch flue. At two feet above the tire bed there should be an eight-inch opening in the chimney, which will be alluded to again presently. The next thing to be done is to make the oven. In doing this, sheet-iron of ordinary grade, number twelve or number fourteen, thirty inches wide, is used. With it is formed a circle two inches or four inches less in diameter than the hearth. Fig. 76 illustrates the construction of this and other parts. *D* is a smoke hole

to suit the hole in the smoke-stack. The top is furnished with a strong ring or eye bolt, and a hinged lid

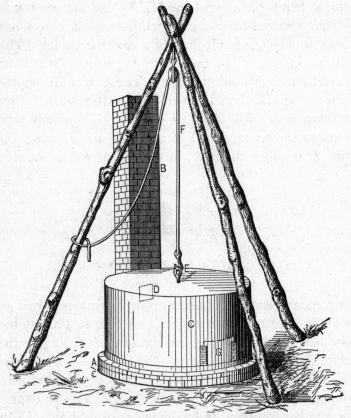

Fig. 76—Showing the Furnace Completed.

taking up about one-third of the diameter. I rivet all
together with one-fourth inch rivets, and put in two

good braces on the under side to strengthen the cover
and to prevent its buckling or bulging, and at the bottom of *A*, Fig. 75 on the outside, it is necessary to
rivet all the way around a plate of one by one-fourth.
On the opposite side I place a vertical sliding door,
with spring attachment to hold it in any position that
will insure a draught.

The next thing to be attended to is the method of
lifting this oven off and on for the removal of the tires.
This is shown in Fig. 76.   I make the tripod of three
saplings, securing them at the top by passing a bolt
through them, and from the bolt suspend the pulley
block, through which passes the wire rope or chain fall
FF hooked into the eye in the top *E*.   *C* is the oven
and *G* the door.   This completes the whole.   Place
the tires in position on the hearth, first raising the
oven ; then place the fuel, lower the oven, open the
door, and start the fire.   As the tire becomes warm
enough for setting, raise the oven and remove a tire
and lower the oven.   The whole operation does not
require more than half a minute.   While one tire is
being set, the others are being heated, and no heat is
lost.

This device is economical in operation, and besides
lessens the cost of insurance.   If the draught is too
strong, a common damper may be put in the smoke-
stack.   The apparatus would work well with wood or
charcoal, and by putting in grate bars, anthracite coal
could be utilized at small expense.   The heater, if

often used, ought to be re-coated with fine mortar slush three or four times a year. To prevent rusting the iron work should be covered with coal tar several times a year.—*By* IRON DOCTOR.

A Tire-Heating Furnace.

I build a tire-heating furnace as follows : Fig. 77 shows the number of courses of brick used, fire brick for the inside court. A brick, I believe, is generally 9 x 4½ x 2½ inches; perhaps a little allowance should be made from these figures for mortar. The walls are two bricks of nine inches thick. The furnace being built to the square should have some old tire iron laid across it to hold up the bricks to cover the top inside,

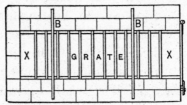

A Tire-Heating Furnace.　Fig. 77—The Base.

leaving an opening of about five or six inches at each end (see *C* and *D*, Fig. 78). The object of this is to cause the flame to spread instead of going straight up the chimney. The grate or bars may be for wood or coal. I use for fuel the chips, old felloes, etc., that would otherwise be in my way. I throw a lot of fuel in the furnace, place the fires on the bars *BB*, put fire to the fuel, and attend to other work while the tires heat. Sometimes we turn the tires, as they heat the fastest at the bottom, but this is not always needed unless they are extra heavy.

The capacity of this furnace is for common two-

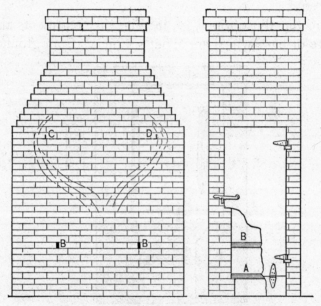

Fig. 78—Side and Front Views of the Furnace.

horse wagons, for two sets of tire, or eight tires, but we can keep setting tires all day by adding fuel and tires, as it does not take much fuel after the first heat.

It operates very well, it enables you to get at the tire easily when it is hot, it occupies but little room, will not endanger property by the fire used, and enables you to set tires at any time without being inconvenienced by wind or mud.

Allow me to say, also, that I do not put tires on wheels unless they are hot enough to expand and drop on without injuring the wheels, as I have seen wheels badly injured by trying to put tires on when they were too cold.

In the illustrations, *A*, in Fig. 78, represents the grate or bars, which are about six inches from ground,

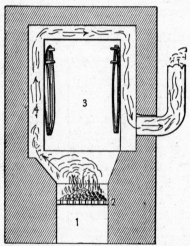

Improved Tire-Heating Furnace.   Fig. 79—Sectional View.

and *BB*, in Fig. 77, represent two heavy bars of iron to hold up tires twelve inches above the fire bars or grate. The door is sheet iron one-eighth of an inch thick and extends over the brickwork about one inch, with six inches cut off the bottom, and is secured with hinges to regulate the draft or inlet of air. The grate should not be within one foot of the door or the other end. If the fire is too close to the door it will warp it so that it will not fit the brickwork good. I use an ordinary latch to keep the door closed and ordinary hinges are bolted to the brickwork and door.

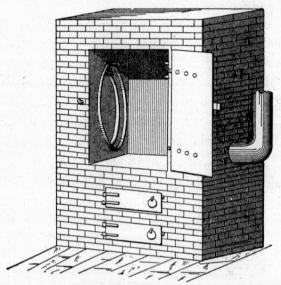

Fig. 80—Front View.

The inside course of brick should be built rather wide up to the grate, to rest the latter on it.

Fig. 77 represents the base. Fig. 78 includes side and front views. The stem of the chimney need not be thicker than one brick.—*By* T. GRIFFITH.

Improved Tire-Heating Furnace.

We present herewith two engravings representing an improved tire-heating furnace used by a large carriage company. Fig. 79 is a sectional view, in which

the various parts are indicated by figures, as follows:
One is the ash-pit, two the grate, three the tire-heating
box, the size of which is fifty by fifty by thirty-six
inches, and four is the flue.

Fig. 80 is a front view of the furnace. It will be
observed that the pins from which the tires are suspended are arranged so that the front tires can hang
inside of the rear ones. This furnace is capable of
heating ninety sets of tires a day.

Making a Tire Cooler.

PLAN I.

I make a tire-cooling frame as follows: *A*, in Fig.
81, is six feet long, and is made two by four or else
three by three. It is nailed to the water box, the lat-

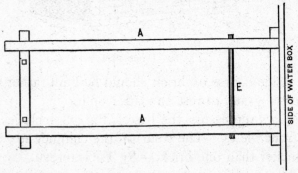

Making a Tire Cooler by the Method of "J. A. R." Fig. 81—Showing
the Frame.

ter being sunk so that the top is two inches above
ground. *A* is sloped to the ground at the back end.

An iron spindle goes through the hub of the wheel and into the holes shown in *B*, Fig. 82, thus holding the wheel up in place while it is being cooled. *B* is of four by four timber. It works on the same shaft with *C*, Figs. 83 and 84, and the trigger *D*, Figs. 82

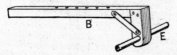

Fig. 82—Showing the Device for Holding the Wheel.

and 83, holds them together at the back end. The wagon wheel is placed on *C*. The spindle is passed through the hub and into the most suitable hole in *B*. The hot tire is then put on the wheel, and both *C* and *D* are raised together until they stand perpendicularly. The lower side (or edge) of the wheel goes in the

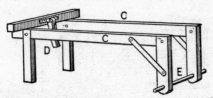

Fig. 83—Showing the Arrangement for Supporting the Wheel.

water in the box. When the tire is cool enough to stick to the wheel, the trigger is raised and *C* falls back to its place, while *B* still stands up like a post. When the tire is cold and trued up, the iron pin is drawn out, the wheel is rolled to one side, *B* is turned back in its place and latched by the trigger *D*, and then another wheel is placed on the frame as before.   Fig. 85 shows the complete apparatus.

The top beam of *B* is about six inches lower than

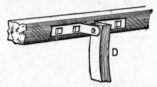

Fig. 84—The Trigger.

the top beam of *C*, in order to give room for the end of the hub and allow the rim to lie back on *C C*. The latter are four feet long and eighteen inches high. The shaft on which they work is eighteen inches from the water-box.

There are, I believe, only two of these frames yet made.   I made both of them, and have been using no

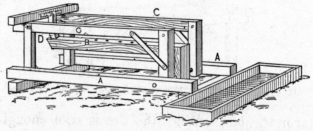

Fig. 85—Showing the Tire Cooler Completed.

other for cooling tires for six years.   One man can cool tires better with this frame than any two men can in the old way.—*By* J. A. R.

PLAN 2.

By using this tire cooler the smith will not be obliged to swallow smoke any more, and he will be in no danger of getting his eyes sore; he will never have a burnt felloe, and he can do his work in one-fourth the time usually required. It can be made at

Fig. 86—Showing How the Iron is Bent.

an expense of about twelve dollars, in the following way :

Make a box of one and one-eighth inch pine lumber, wide enough for the largest sizes of wheels, say five feet, and make it about ten inches longer than it is wide, and sixteen inches high. Put three pieces of

scantling on the bottom crosswise, and extending out
two or three inches.

Take a set of wagon box straps and fasten them on
the outside as you would on a wagon box. Get two

Fig. 87—Showing the Crank.

pieces of one and one-fourth inch round iron, and bend
them in the shape shown in Fig. 86. Weld two
collars on each piece to hold the trestle in its place,
and square one end of each to receive the crank shown

Fig. 88—The Connecting Rod.

in Fig. 87. This crank is made of tire iron. Make
the connecting rod shown in Fig. 88 and the lever,
Fig. 89. Cut a slot in the lever so that a bolt can
be used to fasten it to the connecting rod. Then drill

Fig. 89—The Lever.

a hole in the elbow to fasten it to the box. Fig.
90 represents a piece that is used to go over the lever
in the elbow to make it more solid. Fig. 91 is a

Fig. 90—The Piece that is Fitted on the Elbow of the Lever.

Fig. 91—The Hook.

Fig. 92—The Piece Used in Fastening to the Box the Irons Shown in Fig. 86.

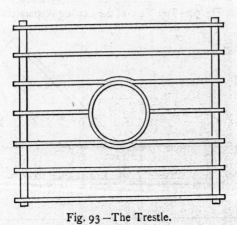

Fig. 93—The Trestle.

hook used on the end of the box to hold the lever
down while the tires are being put on. Fig. 92
represents one of four pieces used to fasten to the box

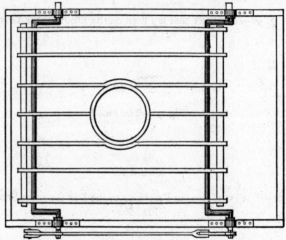

Fig. 94—Top View of the Cooling Apparatus.

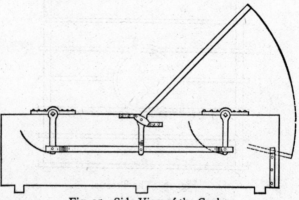

Fig. 95—Side View of the Cooler.

the two pieces shown in Fig. 86. Make your trestle of iron or wood, and twelve inches shorter than the box. By lowering the trestles you will move them to the right side a distance corresponding to the bend in the piece shown in Fig. 86. This bend is eight inches. Raising the lever will draw the wheels into the water. Fig. 93 represents the trestle. Fig. 94 is a top view of the cooler, and Fig. 95 is a side view. —*By* C. M. S.

Tire Shrinking.

In the South we have, as a general thing, very hot, dry Summers, and these, with sand and rocks, destroy wheels quickly. Now, I claim that there is no surer way to ruin wheels than to shrink the tires. Let's see: You have your tire set when very dry if you want them to remain tight. So soon as you get in rain your wheels are dished out of shape. Now you have paid the smith to ruin your wheels. As a remedy for this, I recommend that you have your rims painted, and have it done in time. It is cheaper than shrinking, and preserves the wheel, while the other course destroys it.—*By* NICHOLSON.

Getting the Precise Measurement of a Tire.

To get the precise measurement of your tire, have it cold or at a normal temperature throughout when you measure it with your traveler.—*By* TIRE SETTER.

Shrinkage of Wheel Tires.

I wish to say a few words on tire setting. First, the edge of the tire wheel should be as thin as possible, as it makes a great difference in measuring. A man will not carry his hand so true as not to cross the face of the tire wheel as he runs around the wheel or tire; therefore the thinner the better.

Secondly, do not screw down any wheel that does not have loose spokes, not even those that dish the wrong way, as they can be made to dish the right way by simply planing off the tread on the back and not the front felloe, as that will leave it so the tire will bear hardest on the front, which will dish the wheels the right way. Sometimes it is necessary to cut out a piece of the felloe if it is very bad. To screw down a wheel to stop it from dishing is an injury to it, as it starts all the joints, and it will be looser after the screw is removed than it would be if it were set less tight and left to dish as it naturally would.

Thirdly, as there is a great difference in the shrinkage of tires, they should be measured cold. The draft depends wholly upon the ability of the wheel to stand it. Tires never need any fitting up with sledge and light hammer except at the welds, and that, if care be taken, need not be done. They should be left to cool of their own accord, and no water should be used, as that swells the wood; it does not require much heat to expand a tire. From two to three minutes is enough for light tires to heat in the forge, as they will not then burn the wood, and the wheel can be set up one side out of the way and another one put on the form. A man can do more work by this method than by the other, and it will be better for the wheel, as all the pounding occupies time and injures the wheel. I have never worked on heavy work; therefore I will say nothing about it.—*By* O. F. F.

Measuring for Tire.

For the benefit of blacksmiths who, perhaps, are setting tires in the old-fashioned way (*i. e.*, by guess,) I will give full details of my method.

In taking the measure of a wheel and tire, it is necessary to get the exact measurement of both; therefore, the smaller the mark on your tire wheel the better. A common slate pencil makes the best.

Use a wooden platform to set all light-wheel tires.

Take a half-inch round rod, about two feet long, turn one end and weld it, leaving a loop or eye about three inches long by an inch and a half wide; cut a thread on the other end of the rod about six inches; make a hand wrench for this, with the handle about six inches long.

Fasten a piece of wood or iron (strong enough not to spring) through the center of the platform, and low enough not to strike the end of any wheel hub when the wheel lays on the form.

If the spokes are loose, or work in the hub or rim, it is because the rim is too large, and there should be a piece taken out of it (the amount to be taken out depending on how much the spokes have worked), varying from the thickness of a saw-blade to three-fourths of an inch.

A light wheel should have the rim left open in one joint (the others all to be tight), about one-sixteenth of an inch ; start a small wedge in this joint to crowd all the other joints together. Take your tire wheel and place the notch on the end of the rim at the right side of the joint; measure around toward the right until you come to the joint where you started from ; make a mark on the tire wheel, at the end of the rim, leaving out the width of the joint which is left open.

Place the notch of your wheel on a mark on the inside of the tire (standing inside the line), measuring around to the right, until the tire wheel has taken the same number of revolutions that it did on the wheel, cutting the tire off as much short of the mark on the tire wheel as you wish to give it draft.

Light tires should measure the same as the wheel while hot from the weld ; heavy tires should have from one-eighth inch solid draft for medium to one-half inch for cart wheels : solid draft, *i. e.*, after the joints of the wheel are drawn together solid.

On old wheels, the ends of the spokes often rest on the tire, the shoulder having worked into the rim, thus letting the spokes rest wholly on the tire ; these should be cut off a little below the outside of the rim.

For light wheels, put the wheel on the platform face down ; pass the rod through the hub, bore a hole in a piece of board to put over the end of the hub, running the rod through the hole ; put on the wrench, and draw it down to where you wish the wheel to be after the tire is set ; heat the tire on the forge, heating it all the way around ; when you put it on the wheel, cool it enough so it will not burn the rim ; fit it with a light hammer, holding a sledge on the inside of the rim, and strike lightly on the tire over each spoke as it is cooling.

If a wheel should be turned in toward the carriage, after cutting some out of the rim, put it on the platform, face side up ; place a few pieces of board under the rim, draw it back through, and give the tire three-sixteenths solid draft for a light wheel ; more draft for a heavy one.—*By* YANKEE BLACKSMITH.

Tire Shrinker.

NO. I.

A tool by which any tire can be upset, that is usually taken off from wheels without cutting, is shown by Fig. 96. It is made of two by five-eighths inch tire iron, cut one foot long. The ears are made of the same material. The keys should be constructed of good spring steel. To upset a tire, first heat it and bend a small portion inwards, then put the tire in the

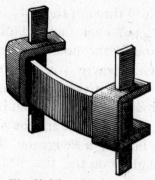

Fig. 96—Tire Shrinker, Contributed by " R. E."

clamp and drive home the keys and flatten down the bent part with the hammer.—*By* R. E.

Tire Shrinker.

NO. 2.

A tire shrinker, which I have invented and which almost any blacksmith can with care build for his own use, is represented by Fig. 97. *A* and *B* are sliding bars, made of five-eighths by one and one-half inch iron. They are so arranged that when the handle of the tool is depressed they slide in opposite directions. *D* and *C* are cross bars, with lips turned up for holding the edge of the tire. They are faced with steel upon the inside, and are notched and hardened the same as the dogs *K*, which work in front of them. *D* is welded solid to *B*, and *C* is welded to A. Both *D* and *C* are provided with a number of holes, threaded for the reception of the set screws which hold the dogs in place, and so distributed as to permit of moving the dogs backward or forward as the width of the tire may require. The two slides *A* and *B* are held in place by suitable straps which pass over them, and which are

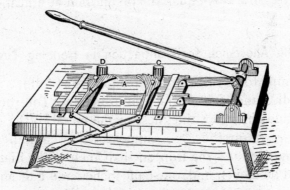

Fig. 97—Tire Shrinker in Use by "R. H. W."

bolted to the bench. The face of the bench is protected by a thin plate of metal placed under the sliding bars. The bars are moved by connecting rods fastened to studs welded to opposite sides of the shaft to which the handle is attached. These studs are about two inches in length. On moving the handle one of the connecting rods pushes and the other pulls. They are connected with the eyes on *A* and *B* by half-inch bolts. Snug fits are necessary. The shaft should be made as short as the dimension of other parts of the tool will permit. It should be square in section at the part where the handle is joined to it. It is bolted to the bench by the end pieces shown in the cut, provided for the purpose. The dogs K K are operated by a short lever handle so arranged that tires may be easily managed by a single hand. A shrinker properly constructed to the design here described will shrink the heaviest tire three-quarters of an inch at a heat.—*By* R. H. W.

The Allowance for Contraction in Bending Tires.

Templeton's rule for contraction is as follows: The just allowance for contraction in bending (on the flat) is to add the exact thickness of the metal to the diameter—*e. g.*, in the case supposed the circumference is three feet and the iron one-half inch. The diameter would be eleven and one-half inches, add half an inch for thickness of tire, giving one foot diameter, or three feet one and five-eighths inches in circumference.

In bending on the edge, ring instead of hoop shape, add the breadth instead of the thickness of the metal to the diameter. Of course there is no allowance here for welding.—*By* WILL TOD.

Setting Tire—The Dishing of Wheels.

My rule for setting tire is to first see that the rim on new wheels or old is wedged down tight on the spoke, then I clip the spokes one-sixteenth of an inch below the tread of the felloe. I saw the felloe joint open from one-eighth to one-quarter of an inch, according to the size of the wheel. I then drive a wedge in the open joint so as to be sure to close all of the other joints tightly, then I measure the wheel and always get the right length. I next place my wheel on the wheel bench. When the wheel is placed over the rod I place a block on the end of the hub, put the tail tap on and screw it down. If it is a light patent wheel I screw all the dish out of it, that is, make it so that the spokes are on a straight line. I make the tire the same size as the wheel when it is to have a red-heat as for light wheels. For new heavy wheels, such as those used on job or road wagons, I allow an eighth of an inch for draw when the tire is red-hot. If a set of wheels is badly dished they can be screwed down to the back side of the wheel. Keep the screw there until the tire is cold, and when the wheel is released it will dish again, but not so much as it did before. If the spokes are sprung leave the wheel on the bench as long as you can.

I heat all my tires, except those for wagons, in the forge. I seldom heat tires hot enough to burn or even scorch the felloes. In my opinion there is no necessity for burning rims. I clip the ends of the spokes because in old wheels they are too long and will not allow the tire to rest evenly on the rim.

When the spokes are too long the wheel will be

dished, because the tire presses on the ends of the spokes instead of on the rim, and the wheel will be rim-bound besides. It is better for the spokes to be an eighth of an inch short than to have them go through the rim. When the spokes are a little short the tire will press the rim down on the shoulders of the spokes.—*By* W. O. R.

About Tires.

The question as to what is the best kind of tire to use is an interesting one. My idea is that the kinds of tire should vary with the localities and conditions in which they are used. If the vehicle is to be used in a city and on street railway tracks, a round-edge steel tire is best. It will throw lots of mud, but it will preserve the felloes.

On sandy roads a bevel-edge iron tire would be preferable, because the wear is all in the center and is caused by the sand coursing down the tire when in motion. On earth roads the square-edge iron tire is the best. If over paved streets or macadam roads, the square-edge steel tire (crucible mild) is by far the best. Its wearing capacity cannot be questioned, and another thing in its favor is that it will not throw mud and dirt over vehicle and occupants. In fact, my experience has taught me that for general purposes the flat-bottom, square-edge tire overtops all others for wear and general utility.—*By* J. ORR.

Setting Tires.

There is no need of riveting. Bend your tire (upset if you like—I don't) so that the ends come properly together, set it in the fire, heat, chamfer both ends with one heat, and set it back for the welding heat. If it is inclined to slip, take a pair of tongs and give it a pinch. It will stay, you bet. If it is a light tire I split the ends and lock them as we lock spring leaves for welding, except that I split once instead of twice.—*By* R. H. C.

Putting on a New Tire.

I put on a new tire in a way different from some other smiths. My plan is as follows: I first see that my tire is perfectly straight and then lay it on a level floor and run the wheel over it, commencing at a certain point and stopping at the same point. I then allow three times the thickness of the tire to take up in the bend, and allow one-quarter of an inch for waste. I cut the tire off, put one end in the fire, heat, and upset well, chamfer and punch, then turn the other end and give it the same treatment. I am careful to upset well. I then put it through the bender, rivet and weld. This is, I think, the easiest way of doing the job, and it can all be done by one man if the tire is not too heavy.—*By* Jersey Blacksmith.

Tiring Wheels.

There is much time wasted, at least in country shops, in the method in vogue of welding tires, viz.: scarfing before bending and pinning.

A much quicker and easier way is to cut the bar the right length, bend the end cold, to allow it to enter the bender, and bend; then track your wheel, if you have not already done so, and then your tire. If you have made a good calculation when you cut your bar you may not have to cut again, but if there is any more stock than you wish for your weld, before scarfing trim off with the fuller if the tire is heavy, or with the hand hammer if light. Then lap according to your own judgment and take a good slow heat and weld.

In measuring the wheel, if there is much open joint insert a wedge sufficient to press all the joints together but one, and start your truck from one end of the rim and run to the other. Thus you get the exact size of the rim : and when you truck your tire, mark the size of the rim on it, and add the amount of stock you wish for the weld, less the draft you want to give, and if there is any over cut it off.

By this method of measuring, as you will readily see, there is only one calculation to make, viz.: the amount of stake required for the weld.

Some object to this way of welding because it leaves a "slack" place each side of the weld, but if you are careful about lapping and heat slowly in a good fire you will not have any trouble.

I do not think it is any benefit to pin even a light steel tire. If it is bent true and scarfed short it will not slip unless roughly handled. If tires are too large or stiff to bend cold, I heat scarf and bend one end before putting in the bender.

In resetting old tires measure both the wheel and tire before heating, then you can see how much it wants to upset and can do it in one heat if it is not very loose. I use the Green River upsetter and can recommend it; it will upset from three-sixteenths to 4 x ⅞ or 3 x 1.

If you have any joint sawed out of the rim, upset the tire on the same side that you saw and the bolts will come very near the same holes.—*By* A Cape Ann Boy.

Setting Tires in a Small Shop.

I have a small shop, only 20 x 30 feet, and not much room to spare in it. So it is likely that my way of setting tires with the space I have at command is worth describing. I have a box twelve inches square inside, ten inches deep, and with a top that is two inches below the level of the floor. The lid is made of inch boards, doubled and riveted together, with a ring in the middle, so that when I want to set a tire I can take up this top, put the hub in the box and let the rim rest on the floor, and thus secure a solid place to set the tire. When the job is finished I replace the lid and have a level floor again, and heat all my tires on the forge and cool in the tub.—*By* A. T. P.

Resetting Light Tires.

For the benefit of the craft I will give my way of resetting light tires (I mean those that are bolted on). In the Summer time tires are apt to become loose, and the wheel will not wear well when this is the case.

I take out the bolts, mark the tire and felloe, and drive the felloe from under the tire till it falls off. I then get some press paper, such as is used in woolen mills, cut it in strips the width of the felloe, and tack it on with small tacks till the wheel and tire measure the same in circumference, or till the wheel is a trifle the largest. I then heat the tire to a black heat, drop it on and let it cool off. If it burns I sprinkle it with a little water. I put the bolts in the old holes. I never make new ones. This job can be done very nicely, and the result is much better than if the tire was cut and welded or upset. The paper I use is hard and about one-thirty-second of an inch thick.—*By* G. W. B.

A Handy Tire Upsetter.

I have a little tire upsetter that I find handy. It is made as follows: Take a piece of iron three-eighths or one-half inch thick and ten inches long and weld on the ears *E* shown in Fig. 98. In these ears drill holes and cut them one into the other to form slots or keyways. Then take a piece of spring steel and draw

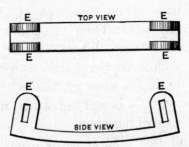

A Handy Tire Upsetter, as Made by "A. L. D." Fig. 98—Showing Top and Side Views of the Device.

it out and make a taper key of each slot. Then put a kink in the tire, lay the upsetter and keys on the anvil

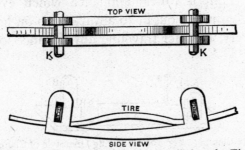

Fig. 99—Showing the Upsetter Applied to the Tire.

all ready, beat the tire where the kink is, and quickly key it on the upsetter as shown in Fig. 99, and by hammering down the kink the tire is upset.—*By A. L. D.*

A Good Way to Upset Light Tires.

An excellent plan for upsetting light tires well and cheaply is as follows : First make a short curve in the tire by placing it on the horn of the anvil and striking on each side. Then place the tire smooth side up over an old rasp, and let the helper grasp the tire and rasp it close to the curve, using a heavy pair of tongs. You do the same on the other side of the curve. Then while it is still hot strike it lightly and quickly with a small hammer.

I have found this plan to work especially well on light buggy tires.—*By* G. W. P.

Tire Clamps.

A tire clamp is a little appliance which every job-bing wagon-maker ought to always keep on hand, and which every wagoner traveling any distance ought to

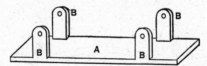

Tire Clamps.   Fig. 100—Showing One Style of Clamp.

carry with him. It is an appliance for securing a broken tire when time or place will not per-mit rewelding or resetting it. The manner of mak-ing the clamp is shown by Fig. 100, which is a flat piece of iron about one and one-quarter by twelve inches. Each of the ears, *B, B, B, B,* has in it a hole for the insertion of a bolt or clinch pin. *A* rests on

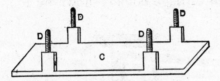

Fig. 101— Another Style of Clamp.

the tire and the ears extending over the felloe or rim. Fig. 101 shows another style of clamp, *C* denotes the

Fig. 102—The Clip Yoke.

plate and *D, D, D, D,* are clips with threaded ends. Fig. 102 is the clip yoke. Fig. 103 is a simple band *E,* which fits the tire. *F, F* are provided with ears,

Fig. 103—Another Form of Clamp.

for bolts or clinch nails. These styles of clamps are easily made, and in making them ordinary iron may be used.—*By* IRON DOCTOR.

A Tool for Holding Tire and Carriage Bolts.

A tool which I have used about ten years for holding tire and carriage bolts is shown by Fig. 104. I put

Fig. 104—A Tool Made by "C. H." for Holding Tire and Carriage Bolts.

steel in the point of the screw, and finish it up like a center-punch. The screw is five inches long, with a handle three inches long.—*By* C. H.

Device for Holding Tire Bolts.

I inclose you a sketch of a tool we made some time since in our shop, which we are using with very satisfactory results. It is for holding tire bolts in old wagon wheels to prevent them turning round when it is necessary to screw up the nut. It is needed in every shop. Such a tool is made as follows: A piece of steel one and one-half inches by three-eighths

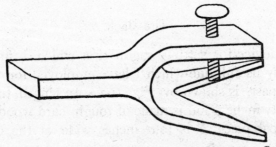

" Apprentice's " Device for Holding Tire-Bolts.   Fig. 105—General
View of the Tool.

of an inch, is split at one end into three parts, each about four inches in length. A hole is tapped in one of

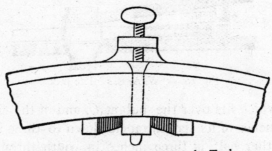

Fig. 106—Manner of Applying the Tool.

them for a set screw, and the forks are then bent into the shape shown by Fig. 105. The manner of using the tool is shown in Fig. 106. It is placed upon the

wheel with the point of the set screw against the
head of the bolt.   When the screw is drawn up tight
it never fails to hold the bolt from turning.—*By* AP-
PRENTICE.

Tire Jack.

A device for setting wagon tires which I find extremely useful, one which I have employed for fifteen
years past, is shown by Fig. 107.   In length the tool
is thirty inches, and is made of tough, hard wood. The
principal piece *B* is four inches wide at the curved

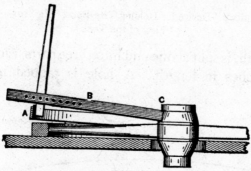

Fig. 107—" W. A. E.'s " Tire Jack.

part, which fits over the hub at *C*, and in the first fifteen inches of its length tapers down to three inches.
The other half is three inches in width throughout.
The slot is one inch in width.   In thickness this piece
is one and one-half inches.   It is provided with five-
sixteenths inch pin holes at different points, adapting
it to use upon different sized wheels.   The lever is

twenty-four inches long, and is of convenient size for grasping in the hand. The face of the part which comes against the tire is provided with an iron plate, thus protecting the wood from burning. The wheel is laid flat upon the floor, with one part of the hub in a hole provided to receive it. The tire is placed in position. Then to draw it into place this device is braced against the hub at *C*, and the iron-shod end of the lever is brought against the tire, as shown at *A*, when, with a very small exertion, the work is completed.—*By* W. A. E.

A Tool for Holding Tire Bolts.

A tool for holding tire bolts I make as follows:
Take a piece of round iron about fifteen inches long, make a hook at one end, and about three and one-half

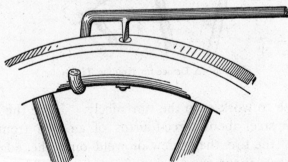

Fig. 108—" J. A. H.'s " Tool for Holding Tire Bolts.

inches from the hook weld on the iron a chisel-pointed piece of steel which is intended to rest on the bolt-head.   By pressing on the other end of the iron you form a clasp which works much easier and quicker than a screw.   Fig. 108 represents the tool and the method of using it.—*By* J. A. H.

A Device for Holding Tire Bolts.

To hold tire bolts while removing the nuts, a better way than putting the wheel in a vise is to take a piece of three-quarter inch sleigh shoe steel, about fifteen inches long, and weld on one end of it, at right angles, a piece of seven-sixteenths inch round iron, long

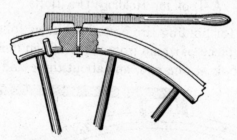

Fig. 109—A Device for Holding Tire Bolts.

enough to work onto the rim nicely.   Have the edge of the steel about three-fourths of an inch from the face of the tire, then screw or weld onto the edge of the steel, about two inches from the hook, a piece with a burred end, Fig. 113.   This tool is a lever which can be used with either hand and will hold a bolt till the nut starts.—*By* E. M. C.

Enlarging a Tire on a Wheel.

To enlarge a tire on a wheel which is too tight, drive the felloe out so that a little more than half of the face of the tire shows for a few inches in length of the tire. Take a small fuller and a hand hammer, set the tire on the anvil, draw one edge of the tire, drive it through to the other side and draw the other edge, but do not draw too much or your tire will be loose.—*By* C. W. BRIGDEN.

A Tool for Setting Tire.

A tool for drawing tire on wheels, in setting tire, is shown by Fig. 109. A glance at the sketch will show its construction. From the rivet to *C* or *A* the distance is three inches. The jaw is hooked to suit, as shown in the illustration. When using the tool slip

Fig. 110—A Tool for Setting Tire.

the lip under the felloe, with the shoulder against the rim, fetch the hook over the tire, bear down and squeeze the handles together at the same time. The handles are two feet long and five-eighths of an inch round. Make the shoulder in the jaw so that it will come inside the hook when the jaws are closed.—*By* JAKE.

Putting a Piece in a Tire.

A smith is often compelled to weld a piece in a tire, and to weld three or four inches in a tire is no easy job if done by one man alone.   I do it as follows:

I cut a piece of iron of the same size as the tire and about twelve inches long.   I open the tire about ten

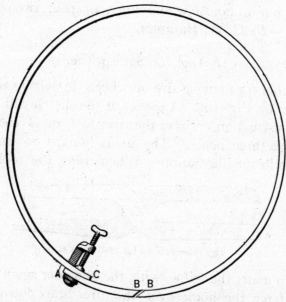

Fig. 111—Putting a Piece in a Tire, as Done by E. K. Wehry.

inches and lay the short piece on the tire or under, as at *A*, Fig. 111.   I fasten the two ends together at *A* with an iron clamp, weld the piece to the tire at *B B*, then lay the tire down, take a traveling wheel begin-

ning at *C* and when I come around cut off what I
need. Or I start the traveling wheel at the end of the
short piece *A* and cut out of the tire as much as
necessary. By this latter plan I avoid getting the two
welds too close together.—*By* E. K. WEHRY.

A Tool for Drawing on Heavy Tires.

A very simple tool for drawing on heavy tires, and one
which experience will tell any man how heavy to make,
is shown by Fig. 112. The part marked *b* is the hook,
which is split so as to straddle the main lever. To use

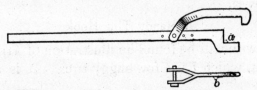

Fig. 112—Tool Made by " S. E. H." for Drawing on Heavy Tires.

the tool throw the hook over the tire, place the shoulder *a* against the felloe and bear down. I use this tool
for setting all kinds of tires from one and one-half to
four inches wide, and like it better than any other I
have ever seen.—*By* S. E. H.

Welding Heavy Tires—A Hook for Pulling on Tires.

I will describe my way of welding heavy tires. I
do not scarf the ends at all. I cut off to the length desired and bend it as round as possible, put one end on

top of the other, take a good clean heat and drive it right down with the hammer. This leaves the tire as heavy at the weld as at any other part and it will never break.

Fig. 113 represents a hook I use to pull on tires.

Fig. 113—A Hook Made by "A. B." for Pulling on Tires.

It answers for all widths. The hook is loose. The way of making it is shown plainly enough in the cut. —*By* A. B.

A Handy Tire Hook.

Herewith will be found an illustration of a tire hook, Fig. 114, which I use for buggy tires. It is made of

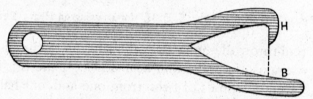

Fig. 114—"E. W. J.'s" Handy Tire Hook.

an old spring two inches wide and one foot long. For tires larger than those used on buggies the hook is made larger in proportion. The brace *B* is one and one-half inches from the dotted line at the point. The point *H* is three-fourths of an inch long. The hole in the handle is used to hang the tool up.—*By* E. W. J.

Putting Tires on Cart Wheels.

I think some of the craft would like to know a good method of putting tires on cart wheels. Say four inches wide, half an inch thick, and sometimes five inches by five-eighths, which is a very hard tire to weld if you don't know how to go to work in the right way. I begin by placing the tire on the floor and then roll my wheel, starting at one of the joints and stopping when I come to the joint again. I then cut it off, first making an allowance of two or three inches. I next see that it is straight edgewise, bend one end down over the horn of the anvil with the sledge, put it in rolls and bend it as near a true circle as possible. If the circle is too small I strike on the outside until the ends are very near even, then I truck my wheel; and then my tire, cut off to the mark, is heated, scarfed and pinned to prevent slipping. I see that the fire is clear, and then set the tire on it, taking care to have a good bed of coke under the tire. I next put two or three shovelfuls of wet coal on both sides of the fire, lay a soft wood board over the tire, each end resting on the coal at the side of the fire, and shovel on wet coal all over it except near to me, or in front. I then blow up slowly. Through the space left in front the operator may watch the tire and put on sand. Be sure to blow slowly, and look at the tire often to see that the edges are not burning. If they are, put on more sand. When it is up to a good soft heat, shovel off the coal and weld quickly. Put plenty of coal on top of the board, for it is not wasted. It can be put back in the

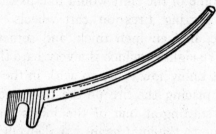

Putting Tires on Cart Wheels. Fig. 115—Showing the Shape of Irons Used by " C. F. N." in Taking the Tires Out of the Fire.

box when the welding is done. Never use a hardwood board. The next thing to be done is to build a fire outdoors; heat and put on the tire, striking a blow over each spoke to bring the joints up. For taking

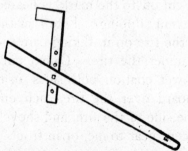

Fig. 116—Showing the Hook Designed by " C. F. N." for Pulling on the Tires.

the tire out of the fire I use two irons made as shown in Fig. 115. These enable me to stand where I will not get burnt. Then I have a hook, as represented in Fig. 116, that I use for pulling on the tire. I catch the hook over the tire, and with the end of the lever on the tirestone pull outward.—*By* C. F. N.

Keeping Tires on Wheels.

As an amateur blacksmith I ironed a wagon some years ago for my own use, and before putting on the tires I filled the felloes with linseed oil, and the tires have worn out and were never loose. I also ironed a buggy for my own use, seven years ago, and the tires are as tight as when put on. My method of filling the felloes is as follows : I use a long cast-iron heater made for the purpose. The oil is brought to a boiling heat, and the wheel is placed on a stick so as to hang in the oil. An hour is sufficient for a common-sized felloe, of which the timber should be dry, as green wood will not take oil. Care should be taken that the oil does not get hotter than the boiling heat, else the wood might be set on fire and burnt. Timber filled with oil is not susceptible to water, and is much more durable. —*By* A. S. T.

Light vs. Heavy Tires.

There is no part of a wheel, and especially a light wheel, that contributes to its lasting qualities so much as the tire does, and yet the kind of tire that the majority of people would prefer, instead of tending to make a wheel durable, has just the contrary effect, for most people overlook the true principle of tiring wheels. They say : " I want a good heavy tire, it will wear longer." True, a heavy tire will wear longer than a light one, if the wheel keeps together long enough to enable it to wear out. But does the heavy tire make the wheel wear longer ? In tiring light wheels with heavy tire the blacksmith will usually give draw, and if too much is given the wheel will dish, and the tire being heavy and strong, will not allow the dish to come out. As it is put in use on the roads, the tire being too heavy and solid to give will cause more dish in the wheel, will get loose, and after being reset will draw still more dish in the wheel. Then where is the strength of the wheel ? A well-dished wheel is bound to go. As soon as the spokes are bent out of their plumb, there is no strength in them, and with a heavy tire striking every obstruction with such a solid blow, what chance is there for the wheel to wear as long as the tire ?

My experience with light tire has been very satis- factory. My plan is to use as light a tire as possible. All the work a tire is expected to do is to hold the wheel in place, and, of course, also to stand the hard knocks instead of the felloe. I put the tire on just the size of the rim, and draw the heat in the tire only at the time of running it, and it does not draw the spokes out of the line in which they were driven. Every- thing just goes together snug, and the wheel is not drawn out of its original shape by undue compression. In striking an obstruction the wheel simply springs, and does not jar. And I contend that the tire will not require resetting more than one-third as often. There is a buggy in Philadelphia that was made in 1878. It has a three-inch hub, scant inch spokes, light felloes, three-quarter inch tread, and one-eighth inch steel tire. The tire has been reset but once since that time, and the spokes are as straight as when they were first driven in the hub. I also know of a buggy with a two and three-quarter inch hub, seven-eighth inch spokes, light three-quarter rims, and tired with light scroll, which has been in use eight years, and the tires have been reset only once. The owner said a short time ago that the wheels were just as good as ever. These are only a few of the instances in favor of light tire that have come under my personal observation. We put three-fourths by seven-sixteenths steel tire on a wheel made with three and a half-inch hub, one inch to one and one-sixteenth inch spoke, one-inch depth felloe, and average sizes to suit. A set of wheels that we have repaired several times has very heavy rims, and seven-eighths by one-quarter tire and one-inch spoke. Whenever the heavy rim and tire strike an obstruction, some of the spokes are broken down at the hub, which requires the tire to be taken off and new spokes put in every time. The rim and tire are so solid and stiff that every jar is bound to make something give, and the spokes being the weaker and having no chance to spring must break, and break they do, and always will unless there is a chance to spring instead of striking so solid. Try the light tire and judge for yourselves, fellow-craftsmen.—*By* C. S. B.

Proportioning Tires and Felloes.

Presuming that the wheel maker has properly proportioned the wheel, the blacksmith in the selection of tire must be governed by the felloe. If the felloe has a three-quarter inch tread, it should have a depth of one and three-sixteenths inches. For such a felloe the tire should not exceed one-eighth of an inch in thickness of steel, and nothing else should be used.

There are two reasons why the tire should be light; first, because a heavy tire loads down the rim of the wheel and operates to draw the spokes by the increased power of the leverage, maintaining the motion of the top of the wheel when the bottom comes in contact with an obstruction. Secondly, a light tire, backed by a felloe sufficiently heavy to support it, will not become set from concussion, and flattened between the spokes. A heavy tire will require a little harder blow to bend it than a light one, but unless the wood is sufficiently firm to support the tire, the latter will set and force the wood back, thus flattening the rim of the wheel between the spokes. There is far more danger from loading down light wheels with heavy tires than there is from using tires that are too light.—*By* EXPERIENCE.

CHAPTER III.

SETTING AXLES. AXLE GAUGES. THIMBLE SKEINS.

The Principles Underlying the Setting of Axles.

As a practical carriage smith I have given much attention to the axle question.   I well remember, when a boy of but nine years of age, of hearing a long argument in my father's shop on setting axles.   I became very much interested in the question at that time. The arguments then presented were as follows: One smith claimed that axles should be set so that the wheels would have five inches swing and a gather equal to one-half of the width of the tire; that the front axle should be the longer, so as to give the front wheels the same amount of swing as the back wheels had on the top.   The second smith claimed that the wheels should have a swing equal to twice the width of the tire, and that the front axle should be the shorter, so as to have the wheels range.   Both of the smiths were good mechanics. I served my apprenticeship with one of them.   As he was my instructor, it was natural for me to set axles as he did.   Before I had completed my apprenticeship, however, I had learned that by setting with an arbitrary allowance for swing was only guesswork. One day, during the dinner hour, I heard a smith talking about "plumb spoke." In an instant I perceived that he had the foundation of setting axles. He, however, believed in making the front axle shorter, so that the wheels would range.

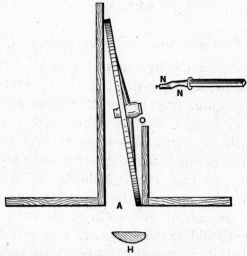

Fig. 117—Example of a Wheel Set so as to be Thrown under the Plumb Line, with an Indication of the Resulting Wear upon the Axle and the Tire.

For some two or three years after the occurrence of this circumstance I set axles as he had recommended, but by practice and observation I learned to do better as I grew older. From close observation I know that a large proportion of the mechanics engaged in wagon and carriage making do not know what is meant by "plumb spoke." In evidence of this, I may narrate an incident which occurred recently. I was visiting one of the largest shops in the West. I noticed a man setting axles. He had finished some forty or fifty, and had as many more yet to do. I asked him how he set axles. He replied, "By the gauge." Then I asked him how the gauge was set, and he confessed that he did not know. I asked him other questions, but he could tell me nothing about an axle, save that he set his axles "by the gauge," and supposed that all axles were set in the same way. This man, I afterwards learned, had worked in carriage factories for five years, yet he really knew nothing of what he was doing.

Before a blacksmith can properly set an axle he must have a rule to be governed by, and the principle upon which the rule is based should be fully understood. The foundation principle underlying axle setting is the "plumb spoke." What I mean by "plumb spoke" is fully illustrated in Fig. 118. After the axles are set, place the wheels upon the axles, standing them upon a level floor as at A. If the square is on a line with the spoke as shown by B, what is called a plumb spoke is obtained. If it is desired to know how much swing the wheel has, a larger square is to be used, as shown by C on the opposite side of the wheel. The space F shows the amount of swing. Fig. 117 shows a wheel thrown under the plumb line, as indicated by the space between the top of the small square

and the spoke marked *O*.   *A* in this illustration shows
the amount of swing.   Fig. 119 shows a wheel which
is thrown out of the plumb line as indicated by the
space *B*.

My custom in setting axles is to set the wheels under
sufficiently to make them run plumb spoke when loaded

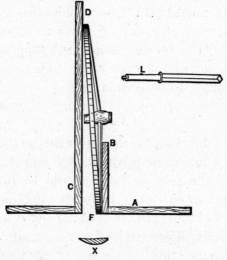

Fig. 118—A Wheel Set to a Plumb Spoke, Showing the Swing, and also
Indicating the Resulting Wear upon Axle and Tire.

and in use.   For a one-inch axle, five foot track, I set
the wheels from three-eighths to one-half inch under
plumb.   If the axle arm has one-eighth inch taper, I
gather the axle a quarter of an inch to the front, one-
eighth inch to each wheel.   A tapered spindle should
always be gathered to the front.   If it is not so gathered

the wheels will have a tendency to crowd against the axle nuts, producing friction.   Gathering tapered axle arms does them no harm; it is the abuse of gathering that spoils many jobs.   In welding axles always have both front and rear axle of one length.   Dish the front wheels just as much as the back wheels are dished at a

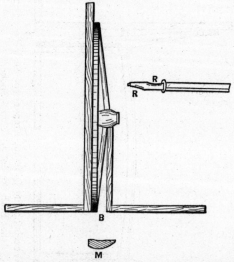

Fig. 119—Example of a Wheel Thrown Out of a Plumb Line, and Showing the Consequent Wear upon the Axle and the Tire.

corresponding height.   This will give the back wheels more swing across the top than the front wheels, but the back wheels will have the same amount of swing at the same height as the front wheels.   If the axles are set under alike the wheels will track.

In setting axles I never pay any attention to the

swing. Plumb spoke is the rule I work on. As already mentioned, I set axles somewhat under plumb

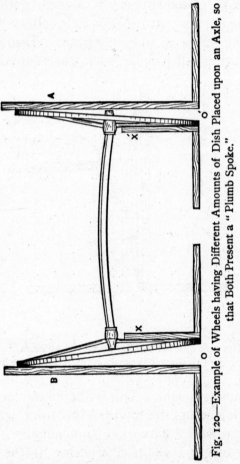

Fig. 120—Example of Wheels having Different Amounts of Dish Placed upon an Axle, so that Both Present a "Plumb Spoke."

spoke, varying from three-eighths of an inch to five-eighths of an inch, the amount depending upon the

size of the axle and the width of the track.   As to the
gather of axles there are various opinions.   From close
observation during many years of practical experience
I believe that gathering axles to the front is necessary
where tapered axle arms are used.   The amount of
gather depends upon the taper of the arm.   The object of setting axles under plumb is to get an even bearing upon both box and spindle.   This is done in order
to reduce friction.   In like manner axles are gathered
so as to obtain an even or horizontal bearing, also to reduce friction. If a wheel is set as much under plumb as

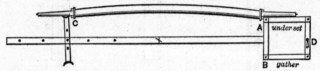

Fig. 121—Gauge for Setting Axles, Described by "H. R. H."

shown in Fig. 118 the axle will wear as shown by $N N$,
while the tire will wear as shown at H.   If the wheel
is set as in Fig. 119 the reverse will occur.   The axle
will wear as shown by $R R$, and the tire as shown
by M.   If the axles are set so that the wheels will run
plumb spoke, as shown in Fig. 118, the axle arms will
wear evenly as at L, and the tire will wear as shown at
X.   From this it will be seen that axles must be set
under plumb, and that they must be gathered enough
to give even bearings on both box and axle.   Not until this has been done will friction have been reduced to
the smallest possible amount.

Fig. 120 shows two wheels of different dish, in position upon an axle. The wheel marked A has a half-inch dish, while the wheel B has a dish of one inch. Both wheels are set upon " plumb spoke " as shown by the squares XX. At O and O is shown the amount of swing which the wheels have at the top.

Fig. 121 shows the construction of an axle gauge which is made of steel. The long part X is made of one and a quarter by five and six-tenths. The parts A, B and D are made of seven-eighths by three-six-

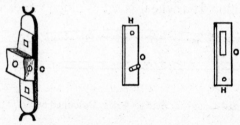

Fig. 122—Details of Construction of Axle Gauge Shown in Fig. 121.

teenths. The gauge shown may be used for any kind of an axle, whether tapered or not. The part C is made as shown by C in Fig. 122, and is fastened to the bar with a set screw. In changing the gauge from a wide to a narrow track, the set screw of C is loosened, which permits the part to be moved along the bar as required. At the opposite end of the gauge a frame is arranged fitting close to the arm of the axle as shown. The side A is for the underset and B is for the gather. At O and O in Fig. 122 the construction of this part is shown. At D, Fig. 121, a slot in one of the pieces

is provided through which a bolt is passed from the
other. By this means the gauge is readily adjusted to
suit axles of different tapers. As a part of the adjusta-
bility of the gauge it should be remembered that each
of the four corners of the frame is held by a set screw,
provided with a jam nut. A gauge of the kind here
described can be made by any smith in two hours' time,
and the cost may be estimated as not exceeding one
dollar and a half.—*By* H. R. H.

Setting Axles.

PLAN I.

I have always understood the term plumb spoke as
meaning a plumb line passing through the center or
middle of the under spoke, in the direction of its
length when the wheels are placed upon the axle, and
standing upon a horizontal plane. I believe the center
line is the foundation principle underlying axle setting.
I believe so because it affords a positive point from
which to work. Now, if I place the square on a line
with the spoke, as directed by those who plumb their
spoke by its back, the lines drawn at right angles from
the spokes, Fig. 123, will clearly show the variableness
of the rule.

To be governed by the center line, of which I have
spoken, gives results that are certainly more reliable.
If, in practice, it is desired to set the spokes of wheels
under or out from a plumb line, we can do so ; but at

the same time we have the advantage of a positive
point from which to calculate our departure from a
plumb spoke.

I will say, in favor of the former rule, that when
spokes are used whose back and front sides are parallel,
or nearly so, there could be no serious objection to it ;
but when the various tapers found on spokes are con-

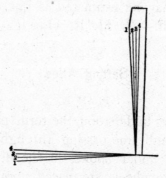

Fig. 123.

sidered, and the great variety of wheels made and in
use, I think a line through the center of the spoke the
most practicable line from which to work.—*By* F.
W. S.

Setting Axles.

PLAN 2.

I am a blacksmith, and I speak with particular reference to iron axles. It is evident, however, that what
is applicable to them may be used also upon wood
axles. The gauge I shall describe may be applied to
any kind of an axle.

It is evident to anyone who has given the matter the slightest thought, that if axles should be made parallel—that is without taper—and the wheels straight—that is without any dish—no set would be required. It follows, therefore, that the main point to be kept in mind in considering this question is that a line drawn horizontally through the center of the axle from shoulder to shoulder (not through the spindles) should always stand at right angles to a line drawn perpendicularly through the center of the lower spoke in the wheels when set up. To bring about this relationship

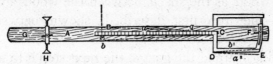

Fig. 124—Gauge for Setting Axles Described by "Hand Hammer."

of parts, the taper and length of spindle, and the height and dish of wheels must each and all be taken into consideration. By the use of the gauge illustrated by Fig. 124, and by observance of the rules I shall present, the above result may be obtained with the utmost precision and in a very brief space of time. Referring now to the sketch, A is a piece of white wood about seven feet long, four inches wide and one-half inch thick. B is an iron about four and one-half feet long, one inch wide and one-eighth of an inch thick. It is offset at C about five inches, and is fastened at that point by a screw, upon which it turns freely. From D to E

the iron is straight and smooth on the edge.   From E to F it is fitted with a circular slot, depending upon C for a center.   Through this slot a bolt provided with a thumb nut F is passed, and is so arranged that while the iron may be moved freely in either direction, it can be readily fastened in place, by means of the thumb nut, at any point. G is also made of iron, and is constructed with a slot through which the wood A passes. A thumb screw, indicated in the sketch, serves to fasten it upon the wood at any desired point.   The ends of G are made to come the same distance from the edges of the wood as the space between the wood and that part of the iron first described, shown between D and E.

Having learned the gauge, the next step is to adjust, so as to adopt it to set some required axle.   First slide G upon the wood A until H rests upon one spindle at the shoulder, while D rests upon the other spindle at the collar.   Suppose, for example, that the spindle is nine inches long from shoulder to nut, and that it has three-sixteenths of an inch taper.   The taper must be ascertained by the callipers.   Find nine inches on the bar B, measuring from C.   For facilitating this operation, I have the bar graduated along its upper edge, as shown in the sketch.   At nine inches, ascertained as above, move the bar upward three thirty-seconds of an inch, or, in other words, just one-half of the taper.   The effect of this movement upon the iron is to move the edge D C correspondingly, since it revolves upon C, resulting as shown by the dotted lines $a\,a^1$. Suppose, further, that the wheels in question are four feet two inches in diameter, and have one inch dish. At a point on the graduated bar B, twenty-five inches or one-half the diameter of the wheel from C, slide the bar B from its present position down one inch, or the full amount of the dish; as indicated by the dotted lines $b\,b^1$, and fasten in this position by means of the thumb nut F. When the gauge has been adjusted in this manner the axle is to be heated and bent at the shoulder, until the straight edge from D to E will bear evenly along the under surface of the spindle, while the iron G rests at H, upon the opposite spindle at the collar. After one end has been set in this manner, turn and repeat the operation for the other. By this means a plumb spoke will always be produced.

Upon the opposite edge of the gauge, Fig. 124, I have a device for adjusting the axle to the gather, which I vary from one thirty-second to one-eighth of an inch, according to circumstances—the more taper and dish, the more gather is required.—*By* HAND HAMMER.

Setting Axles.

PLAN 3.

I wish to say a few words about setting iron and steel axles. In the first place the tires on the wheels should be perfectly true, so that there will be no swinging back and forth while hanging on the spindles. If the axles are to be arched, make the arch as desired and they are then ready to be set or to receive the under and front gather. In doing this I first bend them with the hammer as near to the shape as possible, then put the wheels on spindles, and next use the straightedge to see if the spindles are bent properly. I first drop the measuring stick on the floor to see how far apart the wheels are at the bottom. I then raise the stick up

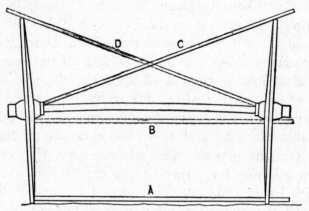

Fig. 125—Setting Iron or Steel Axles by the Method of J. W. Keith.

to the butts of the spokes. Between the rims and the butts of the spokes the distance must be the same when they go in the hubs as shown in Fig. 125. This insures a plumb spoke. On the front end the gather should be half the width of one tire (when it is not over one and one-half inches wide). The narrower the tire the smaller the spindle should be.

To ascertain if the spindles are bent alike measure

with the measuring stick from the back of one hub to the top of the tire wheel opposite, as shown at *C* in the illustration, and then reverse the stick as at *D*. This enables you to tell if both wheels stand alike or not, and also shows just where to bend the one that is not right. Measure in the same way at the front, and this will enable you to make all wheels stand alike.— *By* J. W. KEITH.

Setting Axles.

PLAN 4.

I think my axle setter, Fig. 126, is a great improvement over the old straightedge, as it is easily and

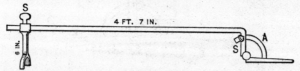

Fig. 126—Setting Buggy Axles by the Method of C. H. Heath.

quickly adjustable for any angle required. It is made of one-half inch square iron. For the joint, use a common carriage top stub joint; make the slide *A* three-eighths of an inch by one-eighth of an inch. No other explanations are necessary.—*By* C. H. HEATH.

Setting Axles.

PLAN 5.

In setting axles I use two tools: *A*, in Fig. 127, is a straight stick of hard wood, about five and one-half feet in length and one and one-fourth inches square. *B* is a piece of iron, ten or twelve inches long and five-eighths of an inch square, drawn down to one-half inch and perfectly round, making a good collar with a nut at the end. About two inches from the end of the wood a hole is bored, and the iron bolted in just tight enough so it will swivel to take up the angle when the gather is made on the axle. At *C* is a slot in which works the half circle. In the slot is a

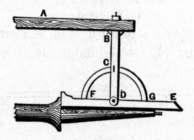

Setting Axles. Fig. 127—Showing a Tool Used for the Purpose by " M. D. D."

steel thumb-screw with a sharp point. Before the slot is made the iron should be upset at that point, so as to make it stronger. There is another slot at the lower end, at *D*, in which is inserted the straightedge *E*, both being fastened with a rivet. If the half circle is properly made and welded at the straightedge at *F* and *G* rightly, all it needs after is a little filing and it is ready for use. *H*, in Fig. 128 is another piece of iron the same length as *B*, with a square loop at the top made to fit the wood snugly, and in which is inserted a thumb-screw, so as to hold it at any length required. At the lower end of the iron is a crotch, which is made to prevent the tool from slipping off the axle when in use. I think this explanation is sufficient for any good workman.

Many years ago, when I worked East, I used a tool to set axles very different from the one just described, and I happen to know that tool is in use in some places now. Nearly thirty years ago, when I first came West,

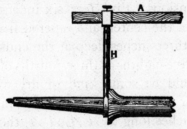

Fig. 128—Another Tool Used in Axle Setting by " M. D. D."

I found the tool I have just described in use; so whatever may be its merits, I feel assured there is no patent on it. I know the tool to be good and handy, and, if taken care of, will last a lifetime or more.—*By* M. D. D.

A Straightedge for Setting Axles.

For setting axles I use the straightedge board with screws as shown in Fig. 129. I set the axles level on the bottom, with no gather, and find that they will run better so than when set in any other way.—*By* W. H. H.

Fig. 129—A Straightedge Board, Made by "W. H. H.," for Setting Axles.

A Gauge for Setting Axles.

There is no guesswork about my method, for it will always set an axle correctly.

Make a batten as shown in Fig. 130, and of the following dimensions: Five feet six inches long, fifteen inches deep in the center, and tapered from the center each way to three inches deep at the ends. The thickness must be five-eighths or three-fourths of an inch. The material should be some kind of dry wood that will not spring or warp. Then set four common wooden screws two inches long at *A A, A A,* the distance between to be the width of the arms on the axle. Have the end marked *S* for the side gather, and that marked *B* for the bottom gather or set, and, after fitting to the axle-bed, set the wooden screws on a line in

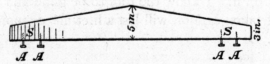

Fig. 130—A Batten for Setting Axles, by "A. D. G."

the edge of the batten, leaving the point screws one-eighth off a straight line or whatever gather preferred.

It does not matter what shape the axle is between the shoulders, this gauge will make the arms exactly the same by inverting from arm to arm. Never strike the arm with the face of your hammer, but use a piece of hard end wood, set it on the arm and strike the wood. The smooth surface of the arm may be spoiled by the lightest stroke.—*By* A. D. G.

Setting an Axle Tree.

First get the length of arm on a straightedge and mark as shown at *B* in Fig. 131 of the accompanying sketches. Next get one-half of the height of the wheels with the tire on, and get the dish of the wheel marked as shown at *C*. From the dish mark draw a line across the arm mark to the point indicated by *A*. Next get the taper of the arm, which, by way of illustration, we may call one-eighth of an inch. Take one-half of the taper, that is, one-sixteenth of an inch, and mark back from the line mark at *B*. Then place the rest on the straightedge with the joint corner at *D*, and mark to the point of the straightedge at *A*, which will give the dip of the axle arm for a plumb spoke.

Fig. 132 represents the gauge, the use of which is described above. It is so simple in its parts that very little description is necessary. The bar is one and three-quarters by one and one-half inches in size. The standard with thumb-nut shown at the right is six and three-quarter inches in height and is fastened to the bar by

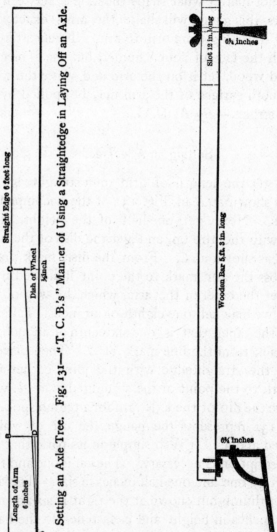

Setting an Axle Tree. Fig. 131—"T. C. B.'s" Manner of Using a Straightedge in Laying Off an Axle.

Fig. 132—"T. C. B.'s" Adjustable Gauge for Setting Axles.

a slot twelve inches in length. The adjustable gauge at the opposite end is made six and three-quarter inches in its shorter arm, to correspond with the length of the standard, while the long arm is made thirteen inches, or of a convenient space for gauging ; the bevel is as above described.

For this end of the gauge I have used an old carriage iron, adding only the thumb screws and other parts necessary to adapt it to its present purpose.—*By* T. C. B.

A Gauge for Setting Iron Axles.

I have a gauge for setting iron axles which I find

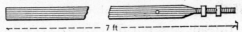

A Gauge for Setting Iron Axles. Fig. 133—The Long Bar with Taps on End.

very handy. Take a piece of bar iron, Fig. 133, one and one-quarter by three-eighths or one-half inch, and

Fig. 134—The Gauge which Slides   Fig. 135—The Inner End Piece for
on Fig. 133.   Fig. 138.

about seven feet long. Next make a piece like Fig. 134, with a slot to fit on the long iron, so that it can

be slipped along it easily. In one side put a thumb
screw, so that it can be held firmly at any point. Now
take the long piece, and forge one end back about
seven or eight inches, as seen in Fig. 134. Forge three

Fig. 136—The Outer End Piece for   Fig. 137—The Top Piece for
Fig. 138.   Fig. 138.

inches of the end down to about half an inch round,
then cut threads and put on two caps, as seen in Fig.
134. Then make Figs. 135, 136 and 137, which go to
make up Fig. 138. The piece shown in Fig. 135 has

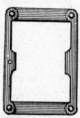

Fig. 138—The Frame that Goes on End of Fig. 133.

a slot, and is intended to slide on the long rod, Fig.
133, also holes in each end for rivets. Fig. 136 is made
similar to Fig. 135, excepting that the slot in the center is longer. There are two pieces like Fig. 137, and

when they are all riveted tightly together we have Fig. 138. Then take Fig. 138, put it on the end of Fig. 133, and with Fig. 134 on the other we have the gauge complete as seen in Fig. 139. The length of the axle is

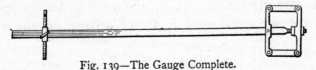

Fig. 139—The Gauge Complete.

regulated by Fig. 134, which slides along the bar, and Fig. 135 works by tightening or loosening the end tap, and thus gives the spindle the set you want.—*By* A. G. B.

A Simple Axle Gauge.

Take a piece of clean body ash, six feet long, four inches wide and half an inch thick, and dress the sides and edges to a straight line and parallel, as in Fig. 140 in the accompanying illustrations. This finishes the

A Simple Axle Gauge, as Made by "Iron Doctor." Fig. 140—**The Gauge Bar.**

gauge bar. Next begin the iron work by taking band iron, one and a quarter inches wide, one-eighth of an inch thick, and making two pieces as in Fig. 141. The part *A* should be from corner to end five inches long, the slot *B* three inches long, five-eighths of an inch wide. The part *D* should be two and a quarter inches long from the corner to the end; the security hole a half inch from the end. The plane *C* should be made twelve inches long from corner to corner. Then make the iron shown in Fig. 142, *A A*, the outer portion forming the recess *B;* the swell is for the insertion of set screw rests, *C C*, for setting on the axle

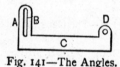

Fig. 141—The Angles.

spindle. To make this iron, take two pieces three-quarters of an inch by one-eighth of an inch, as shown in Fig. 143—*A A*, the ends; *B B*, the halves of the recess —and then weld on the swell *C*, drill it and fit a set screw. Then open the unwelded ends so that they measure each one and three-quarter inches from the bar to the center of the curve, as at *C C* in Fig. 142.

Fig. 142—The Standard.

Next make the parts shown in Fig. 144, by welding a five-sixteenths of an inch bolt, one and a half inches long, into a plate of band iron two inches square by one-eighth of an inch thick, welding in a tool. On the opposite side jump (weld) another bolt of the same dimensions, as at *A*, which is the plate, *B B* being the bolts. In the plate drill four holes and counter-

sink them for three-quarter by nine-inch screws, and
then fit on each bolt a thumb nut C. When this
piece of furniture is complete let it into the gauge
bar at the end marked X in Fig. 145, distant from
the end of the bar to the center of the bolt two and a
half inches, and in the center of the width of the bar,
one bolt passing through the wood. Next cut two
hard leather washers one and a half inches in diameter,

Fig. 143—Showing the Two Pieces Used in Making the Iron.

with five-sixteenths of an inch hole, and two iron
washers one inch diameter with five-sixteenths of an
inch hole. The parts shown in Fig. 142 are placed on
the end of the bar marked Y, Fig. 145, and secured
to it with the set screws. Next place one of the axles
as at F, B, E, on the bolt and apply a straightedge so
that when the end marked F is distant on the outer

Fig. 144—Showing the Iron Parts for the Other End of the Gauge Bar.

edge one and three-quarter inches from the gauge bar,
and the other end of the straightedge rests on A, you
can bring down that end to strike on the straightedge,
as shown in the dotted line L, which gives the exact

position to insert the securing bolt. Both sides are finished in the same manner, the dotted line *K* serving as did the dotted line *L*.

The gauge is then complete, and by means of the set screw *H* you are prepared to move the standard, shown in Fig. 142, along to any position on the wood gauge bar, and so allow of it accommodating itself to suit any length of axle.

The tool is operated in the following manner: With a pair of calipers take the taper of the spindle, then be sure that the plane *B*, Fig. 145, is on a line with the

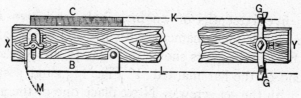

Fig. 145—The Axle Gauge Completed.

standard *A*, as much as the spindle tapers from the shoulder to the point next the thread. Move the plane *B* from the bar *A* at its end, as shown by the dotted line *M*. Next get the dish of the wheel by placing a straightedge across the face of the wheel and measuring from the inner side of the straightedge to the face of the spoke at its intersection with the hub. If the spokes are dodged or staggered, take your measurement from the inner side of the straightedge to half the distance of the dodge of the spokes. Then move out the plane *B*, Fig. 145, just as much more as your wheel dishes. Then place your standard or measure at the shoulder on the upper side and apply the plane *B* to the other spindle. When it—the spindle—conforms to plane *B* the spindle is in a position to give you a plumb spoke. For ascertaining that your axle sets alike on both sides—that is back and front—move out the plane *C* as much as your spindle tapers. If the axle spindles are straight they will agree with the gauge on both sides.

If the spindle has no taper the calipering process is not necessary. To set your axle narrower than a plumb spoke, drop the plane a trifle more. To create gather, set the plane *C* out a trifle and apply to the rear part only.—*By* IRON DOCTOR.

How to Set Buckboard Axles.

Buckboards are used a great deal in the State of Vermont. If the axles are set correctly they are easy running, having the additional advantages of being light and cheap.

We will commence with the forward axle. On account of the buckboard settling or sagging when laid, if the axles are fastened at right angles with the slats or boards the forward axle will turn back and the hind axle forward; so if the forward axle is set the same as for a wagon, the axle being rolled back will have too much gather. In my opinion the forward axle ought to be set with no gather at all, and if it be necessary to turn the arms down, they ought at the same time to be turned back somewhat. From this statement of the case it is evident that a man should use his own judgment in a point of this kind. The rear axle, for reasons given above, will roll forward, which, if the axle is set as for a wagon, will serve as backward gather, which any blacksmith knows is not right. To remedy this the hind axle ought to have considerable gather. This must be calculated with reference to the sag of the buckboard. It should have enough, so that when it is loaded the wheels will have no more tendency to run off than to run on.—*By* A Boy Blacksmith.

To Lay Out Thimble Skein Axles so as to Secure Proper Dish to the Wheels.

If you want to stand the wheels on a plumb spoke, the proper plan is to use a skein that has a plumb spoke taper. All others are imperfect, and in my opinion are not fit for use. All the skeins with which I am acquainted, excepting one brand, are tapered too much. They require the outer end to be raised up in order to arrive at a plumb spoke. Now if the outer end of the arm be raised higher than the shoulder, the tendency will be to work the wheels off, which requires an unnecessary amount of gather to counteract. This causes the wheels to bind, and results in heavy draft. I

will now present my way of making thimble skein
axles.   I first take a thin piece of stuff, say five-sixteenths of an inch thick, and shape it to fit skein as
shown in Fig. 146.   I then draw the perpendicular

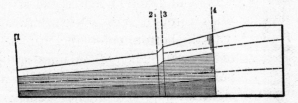

Fig. 146—Pattern for Laying Off Axles to Receive Thimble Skein.

lines 1, 2, 3 and 4 shown in the sketch.   I then lay
out an eight-square or octagon for each of these lines,
as shown in Fig. 147.   This is done by making a square

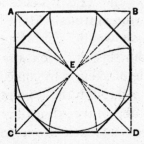

Fig. 147—Diagram of Cross Sections through Axle.

with sides of the length of the cross section.   Draw
the diagonal lines.   Set the compasses to one-half the
length of one of these diagonal lines, and from the
corners of the square as centers strike arcs, cutting the

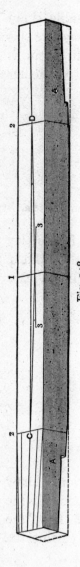

Fig. 148.

sides of the square as shown. Connect the points thus obtained, which will complete the figure. Mark points on pattern corresponding to lines 1 and 2 of Fig. 146. Cut a small notch at end at 1, and prick through at 2. Next draw a line with the bottom points the entire length of pattern. Then draw lines at upper points from 1 to 2, after which make eight square points on lines 3 and 4. At top make small hole through and draw line from 3 to 4. Then draw a line through center of 1 and 2 the whole length of pattern, as shown dotted in Fig. 146. With the pattern thus prepared, take the axle, which should be straight on the bottom. Mark across the center as shown by 1 in Fig. 148. Measure from this line each way to where the inside of skein is to come. Draw the lines 2, 2 through these points. Through the centers of these lines draw *C, D* as shown. Measure back from where skein is to come the space of twenty inches from each of the lines indicated by 2. Make marks one-eighth of an inch back from center line as shown by 3 and 3. Place a straightedge on the center of 2 and the point 3, which is twenty-eight inches away, and draw line from 3 to end of stick. This will give the gather. Now place pattern upon axle so as to have the center line on pattern on gather line of axle. Mark against pattern for lines to taper to ; mark by notches at end and through holes on line 2, by which to get lines for reducing the corners. Then mark both sides with pattern as shown in Fig. 148 at *A* and *A*. Next work off the top, and then lay out the top by pattern in the same general manner, after which take pattern and mark sides of axle ; work off the corners; then the axle will be ready to round up. That there will really be very little to do may be seen by inspecting the lower part of Fig. 147. If it is desired to have the timber to last well inside of the skein, point it with red lead and varnish it before cutting on the skein. This treatment of the wood will prevent the rust from injuring the wood.—*By* * * *

To Set Axle Boxes.

The best plan I have ever found in fastening a pipe box that has turned in the hub and worn away so that it cannot be wedged, is to clean out all the grease and rotten or splintered wood, wrap the small end of the box with oilcloth or leather, and drive it tight in the hub. Then center the large end just as you want it, and take good clean sulphur, perfectly clear of sand and dross, melt it and pour around the box. I have found this to hold a box when wedges would not. The sulphur must be pure and clean.—*By* J. F. McCoy

How to Lay Off an Axle.

Suppose we have an axle to make for a wheel with a thimble like that shown in Fig. 149 of the accompanying illustrations, three inches in diameter at shoulder, and one and one-half inches at the point. First get the length of the axle between the shoulders, and the amount that should be taken off the point of the spindle. To do this set the wheels up as shown in Fig. 151, on the floor or some suitable place, and just as you want them to set on the axle when finished. Be sure to set them on the floor the right distance apart, which is five feet from "out to out" in this lo-

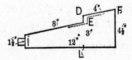

How to Lay Off an Axle.   Fig. 149—Showing the Thimble.

cality, though it varies in different places; and confine them in this position. Then take a straightedge, straight on the bottom, but beveled on top, as shown in Fig. 150, so it will easily enter the box. Put it in the hubs as shown in Fig. 151. See that it rests on the point on each box at *P*. It will not touch the back part of the box at *A*. The distance from the bottom of the box to the straightedge at *A* is the amount to be taken off the point of the axle at *B*, Fig. 153. The distance between the boxes on the

straightedge is the distance between the shoulders of
the thimbles when on the axle. Mark the distance on
the axle at *C, C*, Fig. 153. Then get the thickness of
the thimble at the shoulder between *D* and *E*, Fig.
149. Do this by measuring from *F* to *D*, outside,
and from *F* to *E*, inside. The difference in these
measurements is the thickness of the shoulder between
D and *E*. Say it is one-half inch, mark this inside *C*,
Fig. 153 at *G*, and mark across the tops and down the
back side of the axle at *G*, as here is the place to cut
down the shoulder. From *G* mark the distance from
E to *F*, in Fig. 149, to *H* in Fig. 153. Here is where
the thimble will come on the wood. Then get the distance from *E* to *F*, Fig. 149, inside, and having this,
then measure from *H*, Fig. 153, toward the point and
saw off one-half inch shorter to prevent the wood binding at the point. Then draw a line parallel with the
bottom of the axle, and three eighths or one-half inch
from the bottom, as at *J, J*, Fig. 153. This is the
line to measure from. From the intersection of *J, J,*
and *G* measure the diameter of the thimble inside on
G, which in this case would be three inches. From
J, J, at the point, measure the distance of the straightedge from the box at *A*, Fig. 151, represented at *B*,
B, Fig. 153. Draw a line from *F* through the intersection of *J, J* and *G* to the bottom of the axle, which
is to be cut off to this line. From one and one-half
inches from *B*, this being the inside diameter of thimble at point, draw the line *K* to the line *G*, three

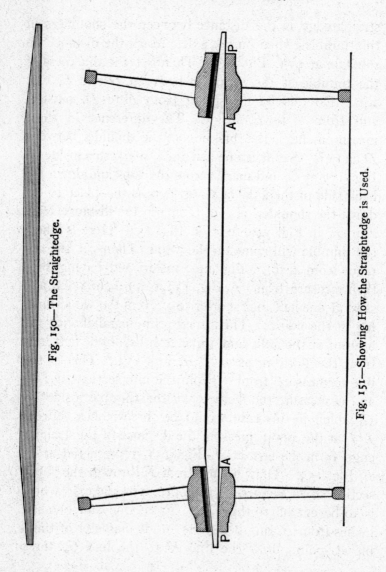

Fig. 150—The Straightedge.

Fig. 151—Showing How the Straightedge is Used.

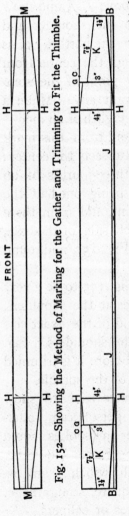

Fig. 152—Showing the Method of Marking for the Gather and Trimming to Fit the Thimble.

Fig. 153—Showing the Method of Measuring for Cutting Down the Shoulder and Fitting to the Thimble.

Fig. 154—Showing the End of the Axle Before it is Finished.

Fig. 155—A Gauge Used in Rounding the Spindle at the Shoulders.

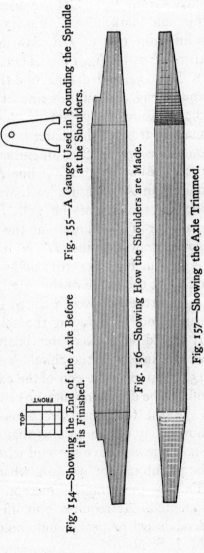

Fig. 156—Showing How the Shoulders are Made.

Fig. 157—Showing the Axle Trimmed.

inches from *J, J.* Get the distance from *L* to E, Fig.
149, and mark it on *G*, Fig. 153, above *J, J,* and draw
a line from this to *H.* Saw down the shoulder and
trim off, as in Fig. 156. Then turn the bottom up, as
in Fig. 152, and draw a line through the center from
end to end. From this line at the point of the spindle measure the gather, if you want any. Make a
mark in front of the center line one-eighth of an inch—
one-sixteenth is better for gather—and from this mark
draw the line to where the line *H* intersects the center ;
and from *M* measure each way three-fourths of an
inch at the end of the axle, this being one-half the
diameter of the thimble at the point, and from these
points draw the lines *H, H* at each side of the axle,
as seen in Fig. 152, trim off as in Fig. 157, and round
off to fit the inside of the thimble.

I find the gauge represented in Fig. 155 to be a very
handy tool in rounding the spindles at the shoulders.
It should be made of thin board and of the exact size
of the inside of the thimbles at the shoulders. Fig.
154 represents the end of the axle before it is trimmed
off. The dot represents the center of the spindle.

In the foregoing directions I have tried to show
how to lay off an axle so that any person can understand me. I have not said whether the spokes should
be plumb or not, nor just what the gather should be.
This is the simplest method with which I am acquainted. It requires only the square, straightedge,
scratch awl or pencil, and compasses or calipers.—*By*
M. J. S. N.

Setting Wood Axles.

I have worked in a good many shops, but have never yet met anyone who employed the rule I use. I will describe my method, for the benefit of all brother mechanics who are interested. I draft my axles according to dish and height of wheels. I measure from the hub or collar on spindle, half of the diameter of the wheel. I then draw a line about one-eighth of an inch more than half of skein at collar, inside from bottom edge; I draw it more than half, in order that the taper on bottom edge of axle may run back to the rim on the skein. I gather wood axles from one-sixteenth to one-eighth of an inch, and set the hounds so as not to roll the axle in coupling or in its natural standing position. Referring to the diagram

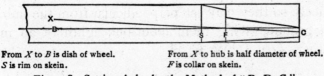

From *X* to *B* is dish of wheel.   From *X* to hub is half diameter of wheel.
S is rim on skein.   *F* is collar on skein.

Fig. 158—Setting Axles by the Method of "R. D. C."

for explanation in connection with Fig. 158, it will, I think, make the rule as above given fully understood. Measure half diameter of wheel from *F* to *B*. Set compasses on line *C B* to get size of axle to fit skein. After obtaining inside size of skein set compasses to half diameter, and taper the axle to fit.—R. D. C.

Making and Setting Thimbles on Thimble Skein Axles.

My rule for making and setting the thimbles on the thimble skein axle is, to make the bottom of the axle straight. Strike a line from one end to the other; get the size needed to make the spindle to fill the skein at the point; move the center up and forward one-eighth of an inch, retaining the original center at the shoulder; then proceed to lay off the spindle and dress off on bottom and back, tapering from the shoulder of the thimble to the point; then dress off the front and top until it fits perfectly, and put it on with white lead.

This rule is for straight wheels or those slightly dished; if much dished leave the spindle straight on the bottom and take one-eighth of an inch more off at the back. Of course the method must be varied to suit the wheels, so they may set perpendicular from the hub to the ground, giving them about one-eighth of an inch gather.—*By* D. W. C. H.

Thimble Skein Stay.

The closer two smooth surfaces come together the more they will cling to each other, forming a perfect joint ; and so it is in fitting axle arms to thimbles. If you have no machine skein fitter, you will have a tedious job before you to make a perfect fit, but fit it you must as near perfect as possible. Bore a hole of the proper size to retain a firm hold on the thread of the bolt. Then give the arm a coat of red lead and linseed oil, which will stick tighter to the arm and thimble than any other cement I know of. This will fill the slight inequalities that still remain after the fitting, and will also prevent water from getting in and forming oxide of iron, which is injurious to hickory axles. If you have no press to put them on with, drive them on as firmly as you can, screw in your skein bolt, and your skein will stay.

Some blacksmiths make a bolt with a hole punched in the end to take the bolt that comes down through the bolster, with thread on the other end, and nut on to screw up the skein with. It is a bad way, to my mind, as it not only causes extra labor to let in the bolt in the arm, but weakens the axle where it should be the strongest.

Putting skeins on hot is not practicable. The skein expands and allows it to go on further than it should, and when the skein shrinks to its original size it is very liable to burst.—A LONG FELLOE.

Setting Skeins.

I first make my timber of the desired size, being careful to get it perfectly straight. I next find the center on the bottom and at each end, then take the straightedge and lay a straight line on the bottom and both ends. I next lay off each end to the size of the skein. I begin to lay off on the bottom and take an eighth of an inch more off the back than off the front. This will give a gather quite sufficient and will suit wheels with three-eighths or one-half inch dish. Some may think that I raise the point of the skein too much, but I raise it in order to get the wheels in three or four inches at the bottom.—*By* H. D.

The Gather and Dip of Thimble Skeins.

First straighten the axle on the bottom perfectly straight. At the back end of skein put a center prick mark, and taper axle from there to the end one-fourth of an inch and allow one-sixteenth of an inch for forward gather. I center with a fine seaweed line, which is better, in my judgment, than a straightedge. I learned to set skeins from the inventor of the first ones made.—BROTHER WOOD BUTCHER.

The Gather and Dip of Thimble Skeins.

My method for setting iron axles is to have the wheels four inches wider at the top than the bottom of track. To get at the gather use a straightedge, and give just as little as you can by measure, from the end of the axle to the straightedge.—IRON ROSTER.

Giving an Axle Gather.

Well, my idea of this matter is, that when I set an axle I set it so that the spoke from the hub to the

ground will be plumb.   If you will examine an axle
which has no gather, you will see that it will wear on
the back side next to the collar and on the front side
next to the nut.   We give it gather for the same
reason that we give it tread, to make the bearings even
on the axle.   If it had no gather one wheel would be
trying to get out one side of the road, and the other
the other side of the road.   This is my idea, and I give
it for what it is worth.—*By* A. W. MILES.

Finding the Length of Axles.

No. 1.   Measure from the back end of the hub to the
face of the spoke, then double the length and subtract
it from the width of the track.   If dodging spokes,
measure half the dodge.   This gives the length between the shoulders.

No. 2.   Take the distance of the track from center
to center, and establish the length of the axle so that
the hubs are the same distance apart less the length of
one hub.

No. 3.   To get the length of wooden axles between
the shoulders, first measure from the face of the spoke
to the large end of the hub (or where the shoulder
comes) on each wheel; add these two distances together, and to this sum add the width of one spoke at
the rim of the wheel.   Take this amount from the desired track (from centers) and the remainder will be
the length between shoulders in the center of arm on

the front side.   If the wheel is very dishing it will be a trifle longer on top and a trifle shorter on bottom.

No. 4.   My method of getting the length of a wooden axle is to measure the width of track on the floor, and stand the wheels on the track, plumb up to the spokes, then measure from one hub to the other, which will give the exact length of the body of the axle, and when the wheels stand in this position I pass a straight-edge through both hubs, and that gives the set under for the axle.   I allow one-sixteenth of an inch for gather.—*By* J. D. S.

The Gather of Axles.

Spindles are tapered in order that the vehicle can go over uneven surfaces with the least possible binding or friction.   The gather partially answers the same purpose, for without gather the motion of the wheel would carry it toward the outer end, causing binding or friction on the nut or linch pin.   The gather serves as a support to the wheel, giving it the proper position under the load, so that it may be carried with the least possible strain.   Too much gather is as bad as not enough. With regard to the proper mode of obtaining gather in iron axles opinions differ somewhat.   Wheel measurement is generally resorted to.   Some wheelwrights use a certain measurement for the axle for a wooden axle, no matter what the kind or height of wheel may be or how much taper the spindle has.   Others use an axle set for setting iron axles, but in my opinion none of these axle

sets is desirable unless the mechanic using it knows
how to change it to suit the height of the wheel and
the taper of the spindle.   Surely if an axle be set for
a wheel measuring four feet six inches, with a very
small point, it would not be right for a wheel measuring
three feet.   Change the taper of a spindle and you
change the gather.   The accompanying illustration represents a method I use for attaining the gather, etc.
In Fig. 159, *A* denotes the axle ; *B* is a line drawn
far enough up from the bottom to come to the center

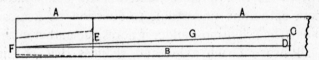

Fig. 159—" A. O. S.'s " Method of Ascertaining the Proper Gather.

of the point of the spindle ; *C* denotes the height of
the wheel ; *D* is the point where you obtain your
gather.   You ascertain the difference, or how much
wider your wheels are at the top than at the bottom,
when the under spoke is standing plumb, then you get
the height of your wheel from the point of the spindle,
measure half the difference in width of the bottom
and the top of the wheels, draw the line *G* to the
point of the spindle, then, using the line *G* as the center of the spindle, size your spindle at the butt and point
and you have the proper gather.   Give your spindle
half as much gather forward as it has up and down and
you will have a good running wagon.—*By* A. O. S.

Should Axles be Gathered?

Who was the first to "gather" an axle arm, or what led to the "gather" are questions not easily answered, but of all fallacies in connection with carriage building, none obtained a stronger foothold than this one of "gather." Old-time wagon makers said it was to keep the wheel up to the back shoulder, and by so doing protect the linch pins, but their experience failed to sustain their theory. Yet the idea was handed down from master to apprentice, and until a comparatively recent date none undertook to question its necessity. To-day the scientific builder ignores the gather entirely on all heavy coach axles, and reduces that on light axles to a minimum, recognizing that the only earthly use of the gather is the necessity of overcoming the throwing out of the forward edge of the wheel by the springing of the axle, one-sixteenth, or at the outside one-eighth, of an inch difference between the front and back of the felloe being all that is required. The true principle is to have the rims describe by their tread on the ground absolutely parallel lines at perfect right angles with the axle bed, and no wider than the true width of the tire. And just in proportion as the wheels deviate backward or forward from these lines, so is the draft increased.

Advocates of gather say that if the arms of axles were perfectly straight gather would not be needed, and it is because of the taper that the gather is necessary.   They are not bold enough, however, to ask that the gather be made equivalent to the taper, and thus throw the front end of the arm on a line parallel with the front of the bed.   If they do this they will set their wheels so much in that they would scarcely re-volve at all on roads where they cut in to the depth of four to six inches.

Take an axle arm ten inches long, having a taper of one and one-quarter inches, or five-eighths of an inch each side, and set the arm forward to bring the front straight, the front of the wheels, if three feet ten inches high, would be six inches nearer together than the backs; a situation that none would venture to ad-vocate because of the greatly increased draft.   And yet every fractional part of an inch that would lead to that situation adds its percentage of the increased draft.

The revolution of the wheel is from an absolute center, even if the bearings be on a cone.   So that the taper itself has nothing whatever to do with the run-ning on or off of the wheel.   A plumb spoke and a straight tread are the two essentials for an easy running vehicle.   And it is time that the trade got rid of the " talking " chucking of the arm and the cramping "gather."—*By* PROGRESS.

The Gather of Axles.

I am now in the shadows of fifty years.   I have stood at the anvil for considerable over half of that time, and I want to say a word in regard to the gather of axles. As far back as the time the *Coachmaker's Magazine* was published in Boston (in the fifties), I remember an article on the gather of axles that settled that question beyond controversy. I will state its points briefly :

The question was asked by the editors : "How much gather is necessary for the easy running of carriages?" It was answered by a number of the trade, and a division of opinion was made evident, and to settle the matter an inclined plane was constructed up which a buggy was pulled by a rope running on a pulley; upon the other end of the rope was a bucket into which were put weights enough to pull the buggy up, with five-sixteenths inch gather. The amount of weight in the bucket necessary for this was noted ; then the axles were taken out and the gather changed, leaving one-eighth gather, and it was found that the same buggy could be run up the same incline with less weights in the bucket, which proved that a buggy with one-eighth inch gather would run easier than it would with five-sixteenths inch. I do not give my buggy axles over one-eighth inch gather. I set them about three-eighths inch under what I want them to track, if I want them to track four feet eight inches outside. That will give me a plumb spoke. I make them three-eighths of an inch narrower, because when I hang up the body and one or two persons get in, the axle will settle a little in the center, which will throw the wheels out correspondingly on the bottom, and so when on the road I have my track right and my spoke plumb.

Setting iron axles is a difficult job, whether the axle be light or heavy. A few years ago there was built in Central New York a heavy wagon to run on a plank road. Its first trip with a load disclosed the fact that something was wrong with the axles. They would heat and the team was obliged to labor very hard to draw the load. The wagon was returned to the shop and carefully looked over. The axles were measured and pronounced all right, but on the next trial the same results followed. The axles were taken out and another set put in with the same result. The wagon was finally taken to another shop and was looked over, the axles were measured, and the owner was told that if he would leave his wagon it would be made to run and without heating, and that the same axles would be used. Now note the result. The last man found about three-quarters of an inch gather. He took the axles out and reduced the gather as much as he could without leaving the wheels as wide in front as at the back. The axles after that ran all right and never heated. If a wheel runs on the front of the shoulder enough to cause friction it is just as bad, if not worse than if it ran on the nut by running out on the bottom.—*By* H. M. S.

Making a Wagon Axle Run Easily.

The younger members of the trade may be interested in knowing how to make a wagon that will run easily.

The secret of doing this is to get the set and gather so that the wheel will stand in such a position that it will not bind on the axle arm.

Set your axles so that the faces of the spoke will stand plumb, that is, so that the width close under the hub and the track on the floor will be the same, if the wheel stands under, the axle and will wear most on the under side-end, next to the collar and on the top side the end next to the nut. Or if the wheel stands out on the bottom the axle will wear *vice versa*. In either case it makes the wheel bind on the arm and, consequently, run hard. It also wears the tire thinner on the over edge.

A very small amount of gather is sufficient for ordinary axles. If the axle arm is as large at the outer end as at the collar it will not need any collar at all, but as our axle arms are made tapering it is necessary to give them a little gather, so that they will not tend to crowd the axle nut too hard. From one to three-fourths of an inch, according to the weight of the job, will generally be sufficient; a heavy axle having, of course, the most gather.

It is also very important to get the gearing together square and true.

The way many men judge whether a lumber wagon runs easily or not is by the chucking noise. You can easily make one rattle loudly by cutting away the hub so that the box will project one-eighth of an inch beyond the hub. This allows the box to strike the collar and so make an unnecessary amount of noise.—*By* BILL.

That Groove on the Top of an Axle Arm.

Fifty years ago quite the larger part of the axles made were not turned. The blacksmith bought the drafts in the rough, and fitted to each were two short boxes about one and one-half or two inches long. There were two boxes in each hub and a hole was punched for a linch pin. This was what was used mainly fifty or sixty years ago. But after a time there was an improvement on the box. One going through the hub was used, and these were called "pipe boxes," and I can well remember when orders were received for axles like this: "Send me ten sets one and one-eighth by six and one-half axles with pipe boxes," otherwise they would receive axle drafts. These axles with pipe boxes had a nut on the end. The nut had to be square with the square of the axle, and a hole drilled through the nut and axle. It seems but a short time since we could not sell an axle without this hole through the nut. But to the groove: When axles with leather washers began to be used, either half patent or a common axle with pipe boxes, these boxes were made to fit. They were ground on the axle to bear the entire length, so that the fit was perfect. With the box washered up with leather on each end, and the nut screwed up so that there was no play endwise, the box must be kept free from dirt to run easy. But dirt would certainly get in the box, and if there was no place for the dirt to stop it would in time become hard and stick the wheel. The groove was made to stop all dirt in the box and leave the box free to turn easily on the arm. Originally the groove was not intended for oil, but to catch the dirt.

There are those now who make axles with boxes ground to fit, and the groove is of great value. But when axles are made with boxes fitted very loosely, the groove is of no earthly use.—*By* C.

Broken Axles.

By far the greater number of broken axles in the larger towns take place just inside the hub of the wheel,

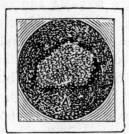
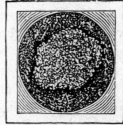

Fig. 160—End View of Broken Axle.   Fig. 161—End of Broken Axle, Dark Portion Showing Old Crack.

where the square and round part of the axle meet, or at the shoulder.

Of the many broken axles which we have examined within the past two years, we have failed to find one which could be considered a new break. In almost every case at least one-half of the substance of the axle had been cracked through, leaving only the central portion to sustain the load.

Fig. 160 represents a very common appearance of an axle after it is broken. The lighter portion in the centre shows the new crack; outside of that will be a black and greasy surface, *A*, showing that the break had been under way for a long time and had penetrated to such

Fig. 162—Front Axle of Fire Engine. Dark Portions Show Old Cracks, Light Band the Final Break.

a depth that the sound metal in the center was at last unable to stand the strain.

Fig. 161 shows a different arrangement, where the axle has probably had a greater load, and the broken part bears a greater ratio to the old crack *A* than in the previous case.

Not long since, in running to a fire, a steam-engine was disabled and thrown on to the curb-stone by the breakage of the front axle. We examined the break and found the fractured part in the condition shown in Fig. 162. The body of the axle had been cracked from the two sides. These old cracks had worked toward the center until only a narrow strip in a diagonal direction was left, as shown in the engraving.

A large majority of people seem to think that with a heavy cart a broken axle is inevitable. Axles do break, and every teamster at some time finds himself laid up with a wheel in the ditch. We believe, however, that broken axles are not a necessity ; and we have never seen an axle broken which, on examination, did not show faulty construction as the direct cause of the breakage.

A great deal of nonsense is current in regard to "crystallization" of iron when it is strained or has to bear constantly repeated shocks. The statement is often made, even in scientific papers, that iron subjected to even light blows will crystallize after a time and become weak and "rotten."

The amount of strain which iron can safely sustain is measured by what might be called the spring of the iron. When, after a piece of metal is stretched and the tension taken off, we find that the iron goes back to its original size, no harm has been done. If the strain has caused the iron to become lengthened on one side so that it does not return to its original condition, it has been harmed and breaking has already begun. In all engineering structures great care is taken to proportion the metal to the load in such a way that the iron will never be strained to the point where it will take a "set." In other words, when the strain is taken off the iron is expected to return without damage to its original form. "The limit of elasticity" is the limit of load which the iron will bear without being permanently stretched. As long as we keep well inside this

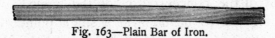

Fig. 163—Plain Bar of Iron.

point there seems to be no limit to the life of the iron. In fact, in ordinary practice, this limit is never reached.

Bearing this fact in mind, it is easy to explain how it is that axles improperly shaped break under light loads so easily and so frequently. If we take a bar of iron like that shown in Fig. 163 and bend it, the fibers all stretch along one side; and if we do not bend it so as to cause it to "take set" it returns to its original form without injury. If we now weld four pieces of iron upon this bar, in the form shown in Fig. 164, we shall find that when we undertake to bend it to the same extent as before, all the stretching of the fibers is concentrated at the one point A; consequently, an amount of bending which did not harm the plain bar

Fig. 164—Plain Bar with Four Bars Welded Upon It, Leaving Gaps at Center.

will in this case break the fibers on one side or the other, at the bottom of the openings between the bars which were added.

In this we have precisely the same effect as is

obtained by nicking a bar of iron to break it on the anvil.   In that case the bending of the bar is all done at a single point and the fibers break at the surface on account of the concentration of the strain.   All the stretching has to be done at a single point.   It is a well-known fact in carpentry that a large stick of timber, scored with a knife on the side that is in tension, will lose a large proportion of its strength.   A sapling, two or more inches in diameter, if bent sharply can be cut off easily and quickly by a pocket knife, if the cut is made on the rounding side. A piece of timber, nicked as shown in Fig. 165, is in such a condition that the

Fig. 165—Weakened by Nicking.

greater portion of the stretching when the timber is bent has to be done at the very point of the nick, consequently a few fibers have to take all the strain and yield quickly, and as others follow the breaking is rapid.

We have seen that the single bar of iron is stronger when of equal section throughout than one of much greater thickness deeply nicked on opposite side.   We have also seen that it is necessary to distribute the bending over a considerable surface, in order that the fibers of the iron may not be overstretched at any one point.   Examinations show that car axles broken before their time have almost invariably been finished

with a " diamond-nosed " tool, which left a sharp corner
at the point where the journal joined the axle and
where the metal was subjected to severe strain.
Consequently, any bending which took place was concentrated in the metal at the corner, and a crack at
once began. The means for avoiding this are to be
found in so shaping the metal that the strains are not
concentrated at a single point, but distributed along
the whole length of the metal as much as possible.

The broken axles that we have mentioned, as well
as all that we have examined, have been, without

Fig. 166—Axle with a Sharp Corner at the Point where Arm and Collar
Meet.

exception, of the form shown in Fig. 166. By inspection it will be seen that the shoulder joins the arm
with a sharp corner, and this corner invariably acts
precisely like a nick in a bar of iron that is to be broken
upon the anvil. Every blow or strain that bends the
axle does all the work of bending at this point.
Consequently a crack commences and usually runs all
around the axle, as the blows come from all directions.
Every successive blow tends to increase the depth of
the crack, until at last the solid metal is so reduced in
quantity that a heavier shock than usual takes the axle
off.

If, instead of finishing with a sharp corner, we put
in what machinists call a "fillet," or an easy curve, as
shown in Fig. 167, the strength of the axle will be

Fig. 167—Well-Rounded Curve Between Arm and Shoulder.

greatly increased and there will be much less tendency
to break at the shoulder.

Fig. 168 is a section of an axle which shows how
greatly this rounding, or fillet, at the shoulder increases
the strength.   The illustration is of a very large car-
wheel axle, some four inches in diameter by eight

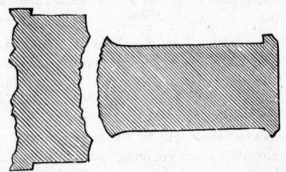

Fig. 168—Axle of Stone Car.   Break Rounding Out into Solid Metal.

inches long, which was broken under a stone car on
one of the Canadian railroads.   The axle was so heavily
loaded that it was bent even when the car was standing

still, and of course at every revolution the bending took place on all sides. Instead of breaking off square across, and in the shortest line, the fillet increased the strength of the metal at the shoulder by distributing the strain. The axle finally began to crack inward from about the middle of the fillet and broke in the peculiar manner shown, the break rounding into the solid metal.

The journal, as the part upon which the bearing rests is called, had a convex surface projected some little distance into the body of the axle. This break, although it began probably when the car was first loaded, took a long time for its completion, and on the outer edges of the crack the surfaces were hammered down smooth all around by their constant opening and shutting as the axle bent. This axle would probably have broken at once had there been a sharp corner at the shoulder where the strain could have commenced a crack at right angles to the journal. As it was, a breakage was only completed under the most severe usage, and after a long time. The axles fitted up with a rounded corner, which we have shown, may be expected to last until they are worn out, when they are properly proportioned to the work they have to do. The blacksmith, in his work, should constantly bear in mind that any piece of metal subject to strains should be free from "re-entrant angles," *i. e.*, his work, where it is subjected to strains, should not have nicks which may be considered as the beginning of cracks.

Round corners, with curves of as great a radius as convenient, are preferable.

Repairing Large Iron Axles.

I will tell you how I repair large iron axles when the spindles are broken at or near the shoulder. I first clean off the grease and then screw the nut on solid in place, gripping it endways with a good pair of tongs.

I then let the helper take the tongs and spindle to the opposite side of the forge. I lay the axle on the forge with the broken end in a clean fire, and let the helper fit on his piece and push a little to hold it in place. I then turn on the blast and put some borax on the point. As soon as it comes to a light welding heat the helper gives a few taps on the end of the tongs with a pretty heavy hammer. As soon as I think it has stuck a little, I take off the tongs, apply plenty of sand and bring it to a good heat. It is then taken to the anvil and the helper strikes a few good blows on the end of the spindle with the nut on, at the same time I use the hand hammer on the point and then swage down to the size and shape required, and smooth off. I have welded a great many this way and never failed to get a good job. If any of the smiths have a better way I would like to hear from them.—*By* F. B. C.

CHAPTER IV.

SPRINGS.

Resetting Old Springs.

After our butcher, or baker, or grocer, as the case may be, has used his wagon a few years it becomes too old-fashioned to suit him, so he will order a new one, and in many cases will give his old one in part payment at a very low price. Sometimes it can be sold as it is and will bring a fair profit. But a better plan is to repair and touch it up and then sell it. It will then bring perhaps as much profit as a new one. It may, perhaps, need new wheels and spindles, sometimes, perhaps, a new body, the gearing or braces generally being good. But what of the springs? They may be settled very badly, and perhaps some leaves are broken. These may be welded, but I prefer to put in new ones, and then I know they will give satisfaction. Now, to explain how I set the spring. I first take it apart and mark the leaves with the center punch, so as to get each one back to the same place with the least trouble in fitting. I then take the temper out of the first or main leaf and fit it with the hammer on the concave spring block to the shape of Fig. 169. It should have a sweep of three inches; that is, a line drawn from eye to eye should be three inches from the line to the arch in the spring for one of thirty-six inches in length.

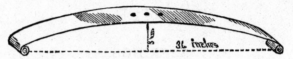

Fig. 169—Showing the Main Leaf Hammered to Shape.

Then I temper it and next put the leaf in the spring bench (Fig. 170), stick pins through the eye at X, and spring the leaf half an inch with the screw A. I heat the second leaf to a cherry red, lay it on the first leaf, clamp at the center B with a screw clamp, and fit it down by pinching with the tongs, one in each hand, and with a helper to do the same on the opposite side. I fit it close all over, then take out the first leaf and put in the second one. I do not give quite so much

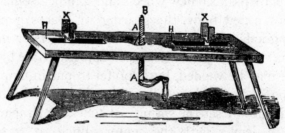

Fig. 170—The Spring Bench.

spring to this, for being shorter it does not require so much. I fit the third leaf to it and so go on, giving each a less spring than the preceding one. When the leaves are bolted together the spring will have a sweep of four or four and a half inches.   To temper it, beat it to a cherry red, dip it in oil, and pass it back through the fire to let the oil blaze off ; then put on more oil and blaze it off again.   This will make a tolerably high spring temper.   To make it milder, blaze off the oil for the third time ; take single leaf at a time.   The pieces $X\,X$ are fastened with tail nuts below and move back and forth in the slots $H\,H$ to suit the length of the spring being set.—*By* J. O. H.

Welding and Tempering Springs.

I have a method of welding and tempering all kinds of steel springs, especially buggy springs.   At least I can say that I have mended hundreds of them and have never yet failed in such jobs, nor have I had one come back to me on account of imperfection.   I will give the best description I can of how the job should be done or how I do it.

In the first place I take the two broken ends and put them in the fire, and heat the ends hot enough to get all the paint off the steel, for steel cannot be welded if there is paint on the parts.   Then I heat and up-set about three-fourths of an inch back, then hammer out the ends in chisel-pointed shape and then split them, as in Fig. 171 of the accompanying cuts. I next take one end and hammer the center down and the the sides up.   Then I take the other end and hammer the center up and sides down as in Fig. 172.   I next

turn them together, as in Fig. 173, getting the laps together as close as possible.   I next heat to a cherry
red, put in some borax, let it dissolve a little, then put
on some iron filing (I never use steel filing).   The next

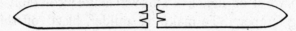

Welding and Tempering Springs by the Method of "A. W. B."
Fig. 171—Showing the Ends as Split.

step is to put the pieces in the fire, and take a very
slow heat.   I put on a little borax now and then, but
do not hurry in heating, and watch my heat very closely.
I bring them to a little more than cherry red, and when

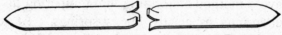

Fig. 172—Showing How the Ends are Bent.

they are soft enough to weld lay them on the anvil
quickly and strike the blows as quickly as possible.
Sometimes I have to take a slight second heat.

When I wish to temper, I heat the steel so hot that
it will almost throw a piece of pine stick into a blaze

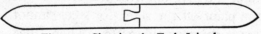

Fig. 173—Showing the Ends Joined.

when rubbed on it, and then dip it into lukewarm soft
water.—By A. W. B.

Mending Springs.

I have lately discovered why springs always break
at the point where smiths weld them.   The smith, in

mending a broken spring, Fig. 174, usually draws each
end out, leaves them square, then welds them together,
and tells his customer that the spring will never break

Mending Springs.   Fig. 174—Showing the Break.

where the welding was done.   In Fig. 175 the leaf is
shown as welded, and *A*, the square end of the leaf, is
about an inch from the place where the spring was
broken.   In a few days the customer comes back with
the spring broken again, and this time as shown in Fig.

Fig. 175—Showing a Faulty Method of Mending.

176.   The smith says it was not broken where he welded it, but it broke where one end was welded across
the leaf.   The smith welds the spring again, but in a
little while it breaks as before, and then the owner de-
cides to try the skill of some other smith, but the re-

Fig. 176—Showing the Spring Broken Again After Being Welded as in
Fig. 175.

sult is the same, and he is finally convinced that it
would have been better for him if he had bought a
new spring instead of trying to get the old one mended.

But the trouble was due entirely to the method of welding.   The smith should have drawn the ends as

Fig. 177—Showing the Proper Method of Mending.

shown in Fig. 177 and made at each end a hole, *B B*, for a rivet.   He should put the pieces together tightly and weld with a good clear fire.   When the job is

Fig. 178—The Job Completed.

done it will look as shown in Fig. 178, and the spring will *not* come back to the shop in a few days.—*By* E. K. W.

Fitting Springs.

My method of fitting springs is to hold the plate next to the one to be fitted, in the vise or let the help-er hold it on the anvil, and then heat the plate to be fitted red-hot half way, put on the other plate, hold firmly with the tongs, and pinch the two plates to-gether with two pair of tongs.   I proceed in the same way with the other end, and then put the set in and temper.—*By* E. A. S.

Construction of Springs.

To those blacksmiths who are in the habit of making their own springs the sketches, Figs. 179 and 180, will show how to improve upon the old way. The improvement consists of making the tit at the end of the leaf, and solid at that. This keeps the leaves in place

Fig. 179—The Old Way.

Fig. 180—The New Way.

better than the old plan, and besides the springs are not nearly so likely to break as when made in the old way.—*By* D. F. H.

A Spring for Farm Wagons.

I will try to describe a good, easy spring for use in the country on light and heavy farm wagons. Take four old side springs, or any other that are long enough, or have new ones made to order. Turn ends for hangers, out of three-fourths or five-eighths rod iron. These go astride the bolster outside the stake. Some blacksmiths put them inside, but they do not make as good a spring when put on this way. The hangers should be spread at the bearings, so as not to hang plumb, as will be seen in Fig. 181. If there are no holes in the springs I use four bolts, two on each side, putting them through the plank with heads on top.   On

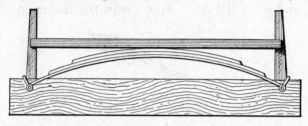

A Spring for Farm Wagons.   Fig. 181—Showing Spring in Position.

the under side of the spring the bolts are fastened through common axle clip yokes.

Fig. 182 is the hanger, with the nuts, *A A*, to keep

Fig. 182—Showing Hanger and Nuts for Holding Spring in Place.

the spring from working off. Fig. 183 is the plank with slots in end, in which the wagon stakes work freely and to which the spring is bolted.

Fig. 183—Showing Plank with Slots for Wagon Stakes.

Sometimes smiths are troubled to make small wooden wedges.   I have a simple method which I give for their benefit.

Split the wood to the size and length of which you want the wedges. Make a block like Fig. 184, and screw in the vise. Lay the blocks that are to be made

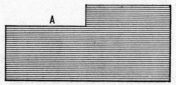

Fig. 184—Showing Block for Making Wooden Wedges.

into wedges on Fig. 184 at *A*. You will have no trouble then to make the wedge with draw shave.— *By* E. B. P.

A Wheelbarrow with Springs.

I presume many of the craft have never ironed a wheelbarrow with springs, and perhaps have never

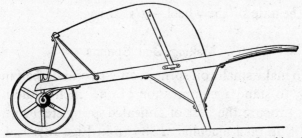

Fig. 185—A Wheelbarrow with Springs, as Made by " Lunkhead."

seen one. The accompanying illustration, Fig. 185, needs no explanation, except to state the size of the springs, which is 1¼ by ¼ inch spring steel. They can be applied to any ordinary wheelbarrow. The springs prevent the constant jar and the danger of the falling out and breaking of articles carried on the wheelbarrow. It also prevents the jar to the arms.— *By* LUNKHEAD.

Springs for a Wheelbarrow.

Everything nearly, even to our planet, has springs, why not wheelbarrows? How a spring is arranged is shown by Fig. 186. *B* is the front end of the shaft, *C*

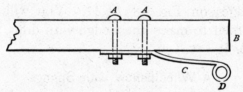

Fig. 186—A Wheelbarrow Spring as Made by "Dot."

is the spring fastened by the bolts *A, A, D* is a hole for the axle of the wheel.—*By* DOT.

Making Coil Springs.

To make small coil springs, only two and a half inches long, to stand a compression of one inch without setting, procure the best of annealed spring steel wire and coil it up on a machine as shown in Fig. 187. *A* is a piece of one and a quarter inch plank and two pieces of iron. *C, C* are holes bored through them to receive the rod *B*, which is the size of the inside of the desired coil. At *D* there is a hole to receive a removable pin, and at *E* is a hole through which the end of the wire

is inserted.   The wire is held so as to coil on the rod
B while the rod is turned by an assistant.   The coil is
wound solid, and when wound the full length of the
rod to *C* is easily taken off the rod by cutting the wire
with a file at each end and removing the pin at *D*.
The coil can then be pulled off the end of the rod.
One end of the coil may then be put into a vise, and
while the other end is grasped by pinchers the coil can
be stretched out until it is opened as much or more
than it is desired to be when finished.   I then cut the
strings the proper length, measuring by the number of

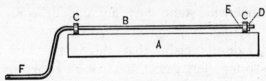

Making Coil Springs.   Fig. 187—Showing How the Wire is Coiled.

coils, regardless of the length it may be, as I have
found that when finished a certain number of coils
gave the length required, regardless of the length that
the stretching might leave them.   I then hold the
springs in tongs over an ordinary blacksmith's fire until
they are at an even cherry red and then drop them into
linseed oil.   I next put them into an iron dish with
enough linseed oil to cover them and hold them over
the fire till the oil is boiling, and the springs when
lifted out are all on fire; I then take the springs out
quickly and drop them into cool oil.   I next put them
on a machine, shown in Fig. 188, in which *A* repre-

sents a lever hinged at B.   The spring C is put on the pin *D*, and by pressing on the lever *A* till the spring is pressed entirely together, the springs that have been tempered properly will open out just alike, while those that are too soft will stay together, and those made too hard will break.   The good springs will be uniform in

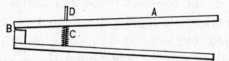

Fig. 188—Showing the Machine for Testing the Temper of Springs.

length and will stand any amount of compression without setting.

Now, I do not claim that this is the best way to make a spring, but I do know that by this process I am enabled to make a first-class spring at a very small cost for appliances.—*By* H. A. F.

Working Car Spring Steel into Tools and Implements.

It has become common of late to work old car springs into agricultural tools, but experienced blacksmiths find it difficult to handle these springs, because the steel of which they are made is so hard.   But it can be easily welded with borax or a mixture of salt and clean welding sand.   Great care must be taken to avoid getting the heat too high when salt and sand are used.   Raise the heat to a shade above cherry red as regular as you possibly can, dust over with a thin coat of sand and salt, return to the fire and raise the heat until it seems to be a low welding heat. Then take the work to the anvil and give it a few quick, light blows. Repeat this operation two or three times to insure a good weld before you draw it much, raising the heat a little each time. Then you can draw to the proper shape without difficulty.

In hardening tongue plows, etc., made of car spring steel you must be very careful or it will crack when you put it in the water. Have lukewarm water with a good amount of dusted charcoal and salt in it. Hammer the steel equally on all sides, and for all the higher qualities of car steel heat to a low red. When you put it in the water keep it in constant motion until it is cold, and then temper to a grayish blue.—*By* J. M. WRIGHT.

Tempering Locomotive Springs.

To temper locomotive springs use the following materials: Eight ounces gum arabic, four ounces oxalic acid, two pounds fine salt, two and one-half pounds brown sugar and fifteen gallons whale oil. Heat the leaves of the spring red hot, but not so as to burn or overheat.

Plunge into the mixture and let lay until cool. In using the above mixture it will have to be employed in an iron tank. The best method for testing a spring is to put it under a locomotive and let it be used practically. If it is not tempered properly it will soon show evidence of it.—*By* SPARK.

Tempering and Testing Small Springs.

My plan is to heat the springs to an even heat; then cool in water. Now coat it with beef tallow and return to the fire and heat until the tallow blazes and burns off. Then lay the spring back on the forge to cool. To test the spring, take a piece of the same steel as the spring, bevel it to a V-shape, and by closing the ends in a vise you can give it any desired test.—*By* B. T. W.

Making and Tempering Springs.

My method of making and tempering small springs is to first select for the job the best of cast-steel, then in forging I am careful to hammer all sides alike and not to heat above a cherry red. I have three ways of tempering. One plan of mine is to heat to a dark cherry red and harden in water that is a little warm; to draw the temper well in a crucible or some other suitable vessel heat enough to cover the spring, and immerse it in this heat until both are of the same heat. Then lay the spring on the forge to cool. Another plan is to harden as in the second method, but in drawing the temper pass it backward and forward through the fire until *in the dark* it is just a little red, then lay it on the forge, covered with dirt, and let it cool.—*By* J. E. F.

Tempering Springs.

My way of tempering springs for use above or below water is as follows: I first forge from good cast-steel, hammering edgewise as little as possible, and then heat evenly in a charcoal fire; I do not blow the bellows but simply lay the spring in the fire and let it come to a cherry red. I next dip it in pure lard oil, then take it out and hold it over the fire while the oil blazes all over the spring. I then lay it in the dust on the forge and let it remain there until it is cold. Then the job is done. Springs should never be filed crosswise, but should be always filed lengthwise for a finish. —*By* D. L. B.

Tempering Coiled Wire Springs.

A good way to temper small coiled wire springs, as practiced in factories where many have to be done, is to heat an iron pot filled with lead so that the lead is a full red, or sufficiently hot to heat an immersed spring to the requisite temperature for hardening, which can be done by quickly immersing the hot spring in water or lard oil. Then, for drawing to a spring temper, heat a small vessel of linseed oil to its boiling point. Dip the springs in the boiling oil for a few seconds— time according to thickness—and then into cold oil.

Tempering a Welded Wagon Spring.

I heat the welded end of the spring from the end to the center hole (it is not easy to heat the whole length in a blacksmith's fire, nor is it necessary to temper in the center, as there is no spring at that point) to a " cherry red " by passing it back and forth through the fire. Immerse end first in a tub of clear water and hold still until cold. Then draw the temper by passing over the fire back and forth until a pine stick rubbed over the surface of the spring will burn and show sparks of fire. Now, while hot, clamp the welded leaf to the one that fits upon it (it having been fitted before hardening), and if it prove to have sprung you can hammer it upon a block or the anvil until re-fitted; lay it down to cool in the air. A spring treated in this way (with very rare exceptions) will hold as well as it did before breaking, and often better.—*By* HAND HAMMER.

Tempering Buggy Springs.

To temper buggy springs, try the following plan : Prepare a wooden box four feet long, eight inches wide, one foot deep; fill it one-third full of water, and over this pour raw linseed oil. While the springs are hot immerse them in the oil, and hold them there about one minute; then let them go to the bottom.— *By* A. L. D.

Tempering Steel for a Torsion Spring.

A piece of steel three-eighths of an inch or larger, for a torsion spring, could be oil-tempered in an ordinary smith's fire. I think a good plan would be to build an ordinary fire and put an iron plate over it, supported by bricks, which form an oven above it. Then the steel can be heated on the top of the plate.—*By* J. S.

Forging and Tempering Small Springs.

If I use sheet steel I am careful to have the length of the spring cut lengthwise from the sheet, for then the grain of the metal does not run across the spring. If I forge springs I make them from small flat bars of good spring steel, and am very careful not to heat the steel too much. In tempering, heat to a light red and harden in oil. I save all refuse oil and grease, and keep it in an iron dish for this purpose. When the springs are hardened, put them in a pan, an old sheet-iron frying pan with a handle is as good as anything; put some oil in with them, hold the pan over the forge fire, shaking it in the meantime until the oil takes fire and burns with a blaze. If the springs are heavy repeat this operation once more. Shaking the pan so as to keep the springs in motion will insure an even temper.

To test the springs, take an iron casting, drill holes in it and insert wire pins so as to hold the springs firmly in position as they would be when in the pistol, then fix a lever to operate on the end of the springs the same as the hammer would, then bend them two or three times. By bending them rather more than they would be bent in use and letting them back suddenly, you can pretty well determine their quality. If it be desired to ascertain the number of pounds required to bend the spring, attach a common spring balance between the lever and the spring.—*By* WESTERN GUNSMITH.

How to Temper a Small Spring.

My plan is to heat the spring to a light red, dip it in water, not too cold, then make a small fire with some fine shavings and hold the spring over the flames until it becomes black all over, then hold it in the fire until the black coating disappears. The spring must then be swung in the air until it is almost cold.—*By* H. K.

Tempering Small Springs.

The following is my way of tempering small springs: When the spring to be tempered is finished to proper shape, heat it to a cherry red, cool it in water (rain water is the best), then hold it over a gentle fire until it is warm. Then apply tallow and burn it off over the fire. Repeat this process of burning off the tallow two or more times, then cool in water, and the spring is ready for use.—*By* W. G. B.

Tempering Revolver Springs.

PLAN I.

I take a taper file, or any file that is of good steel, and test the spring by breaking off a little of the point with my hammer, and if it looks well I forge it to the shape it should be when in the revolver. When finished I heat it to a light cherry and cool in water. I make it as hard as possible, and then pass it to and fro in the fire, turning it often to heat it evenly, until I can just see its shape in the dark.   It is then laid aside to cool.   If I temper springs in the daytime, I get a box or barrel to put them in, so that I can see when they are of the right color, without exposing them to the light.   The night is, however, the best time for such work, because then the degree of heat is more obvious. I have tempered a great many springs in this way, and always with success.—*By* C. N. Y.

Tempering Revolver Springs.

PLAN 2.

I will give my method.   Forge the springs in required shape, then heat to cherry red, then immerse in linseed oil (I do all spring tempering in oil).   To draw the temper to required degree, hold the spring carefully over the fire so that it will heat evenly, till the oil burns away, then withdraw it from the fire, put more oil on with a brush or stick, hold to the fire again.   Burn the oil off in this way three times and again immerse in oil. The spring will then be ready for use.   Great care must be taken not to overheat the steel when it is worked, and proper material must be used.   I generally use a three-cornered file.—*By* A. G.

Making Trap Springs.

If a blacksmith wishes to make the best trap spring that can be made, let him go to his scrap heap, get a piece of wornout Bessemer steel tire, and forge the spring from it at a low heat, shaping it after the New-house pattern. To temper it, heat to a cherry red and cool off, then wipe it dry, cover it with oil and hold it over the blaze of the fire, moving it backward and forward to get the heat even. When the oil seems to have entered into the steel, put more on and hold over the fire again until it is burned off. Then cover the spring in the forge dust and let it cool.—*By* W. U. A.

How to Make a Trap Spring.

In forging a spring, care should be taken not to overheat the steel, or hammer at too low a heat. It should be forged at a cherry heat as near as possible, and hammered alike on both sides. It should never be hammered edgewise when near its required thickness. A gradual, even bend of the spring is very essential, so that the strain will not come too much in one place. One end of the spring can be punched to receive the jaws, while the other must be split, drawn and welded. When the forging is done, then comes the tempering, of which there are various ways. Some temper in oil ; others rub the spring over with tallow, burning it off two or three times.

Springs tempered in this way may do very well when used upon dry land, but are liable to break the first time the trap is set in mud or water. My way of tempering I consider preferable, but it renders the spring more durable. I heat it as evenly as possible in a charcoal fire, turning it frequently in the coals. When

I obtain an even cherry red heat I plunge it edgewise into strong brine, not too cold. I draw the temper in the blaze of the fire, turning it over and over all the while, until a faint red is discernible when held near the bottom of a nail keg, with the top partly covered. The proper degree of heat can be better ascertained by rubbing a rough stick across the edges of the spring. When the sparks appear freely, I cover it up in the dust of the forge and leave it to cool. When cold I put the ends into the vise and gradually shut up the spring. If I find there is not an even bend, but too much strain in any one place, I grind the thick part before closing the ends. Springs made in this way I have found to be reliable in any circumstances. I make my springs of old flat files.—*By* W. H. BALL.

Making and Tempering a Cast-Steel Trap Spring.

My plan is to work the steel at a low heat. Forge your spring so it will be right when flattened. Do not edge it up after you commence to flatten it ; harden the spring at as low a heat as it will harden ; ignite some pitch or other resinous substance, hold the spring in the blaze till it is coated with lampblack, and then proceed to draw the temper and continue till the lampblack peels off.—*By* S. N.

Tempering Trap Springs.

My plan is to heat the spin just to the point when you can see that they are red in the dark. The heat must be even ; then plunge them into warm water and let them remain until cool.—*By* C. B.

Tempering Springs and Knives.

To temper trap springs to stand under water. In forging out the spring, as I get it near to its proper thickness I am very careful not to heat it too high and to water-hammer as for mill picks. When about to temper, heat only to a cherry red, and hold it in such a way that it will be plumb as you put it in the water, which prevents it from springing. Take it from the water to the fire and pass it through the blaze until a little hot, then rub a candle over it upon both sides, passing it backward and forward in the blaze. Turn it over often to keep the heat even over the whole surface, until the tallow passes off as though it went into the steel ; then take it out and rub the candle over it again (on both sides each time), passing it as before. through the flame, until it starts into a blaze with a snap, being careful that the heat is properly regulated. —*By* J. L. C.

Tempering Gun Springs.

So many methods for tempering small springs have been described that it seems useless to mention any more. Still I will venture to give one. To temper a mainspring for a gun, after forging, filing, etc., harden it in soft water, then make it bright, then heat a piece of iron one by three-eighths of an inch to a good red; lay spring on it edgewise, and as the iron turns black, the blue should be passing over the spring. Then set the iron and spring aside together to cool. A little practice will enable anyone to perform the job with the assurance of a good temper. Always use cast-steel.— *By* H. S.

Tempering Mainsprings for Guns.

My method for tempering mainsprings for guns is as follows: Heat the spring to a good red and plunge it in the water, then take a fat pine splinter and smoke the spring well all over, next heat it until the smoke burns off, then dip the spring in the water. I have followed this method for ten years and have found it satisfactory.—*By* A. F. M.

CHAPTER V.

BOB SLEDS.

Making Bob Sleds.

The ironing of bob sleds is something the novice has to be careful about. He must proceed slowly, and feel his way carefully to the finish. To have the runners parallel with the surface of the roadway, he must find the center of gravity for each bob; all are not alike. Different lengths require different positions of the bolster through which the sag-bolt passes in securing the body to the bobs. The draft of the front bobs being by the shafts or the tongue (pole) permits the setting of the front bolster farther ahead on the front bob than is set the bolster on the back bob, as the back bob is drawn by the bolster only. If either bolster is half an inch farther ahead than its proper position, the bobs will "nose" or "plow," that is, work down on the front. An error the reverse of this, that is, putting the bolster back of the proper position, will cause "jumping," lifting in front and falling to the earth again. To ascertain the proper position when first ironing bobs place a horse in the shafts, put a little tallow on the runners and draw them over the floor. One or two experiments will place you nearly right,

Then take your measurements and reserve them for
future use. From this one experiment you can base
future calculations. As your runners increase in length,
correspondingly place the draft ahead or forward ; as
the runner decreases in length, correspondingly move
the draft back on the bob.

The drawing to one side is due to two causes, one
of which we explain now. The second cause will be
explained when we reach the coupling of the body to
the bobs and the securing of the bobs with the stays
and irons.

The first cause is the misplacement of the shafts.   I

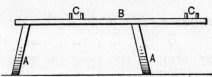

Making Bob Sleds.   Fig. 189—Showing the Position of the Shaft Bar.

now allude to sleighs for country roads, where the
horse can only travel in the beaten track, which necessitates the setting of the shafts to one side. In cities
where the snow is usually level, because of great
traffic, the horse can travel immediately in front of the
sleigh. In Fig. 189, *A, A* represent noses of the front
bobs, *B* the shaft bar, *C, C* the jacks. The jacks must
be placed in such a position that when the horse is
attached and doing his work, the front bob will run
directly forward.

It will be noticed that the long end of the bar is to

the right side, which is to facilitate turning out to the
right side of the road when meeting teams.   Were the
long end, or projecting end, on the left side, a greater

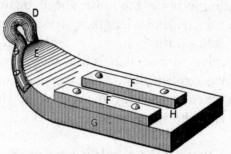

Fig. 190—Top View of the Brake.

detour would have to be made, so that the bars might
not interfere.   Besides, in places where the snow is
always quite deep, if the long end were not on the
right side it would be next to impossible to turn out.
If the jacks be placed too far to the right, it will cause
the nose of the front bob to crowd to the left ; if too

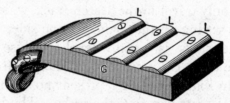

Fig. 191—Bottom View of the Brake.

far to the left, the nose of the front bob will crowd to
the right.

To get at the right position, measure your sleigh

track. Then stand two horses before your sleigh in the position they would occupy, and mark the position of the hind feet, remove the horses and place the shaft in such a position that if a plumb line be dropped from the center of the shaft bar it will touch at the center of the track, between the feet of the right-hand horse. When you once have the measurement, record it. It will last as long as you build sleighs.

I now refer the reader to Fig. 192, in which M, M

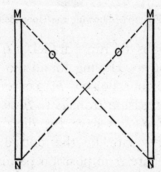

Fig. 192—Showing the Front and Back of the Bob.

represent the front of the bob, N, N the back of the bob. In putting together, have them square and prove them so, as shown by the dotted diagonal lines O, O. Fig. 194 represents the bob bottom up, and as you put on the stays, P is the bar, R, R are the posts. Prove them square by the dotted diagonal lines S, S. If you are right up to this point, and the shafts are properly placed, there will be no danger of your bobs "sliding"—moving from one side to the other—pro-

vided they are properly coupled to the body, an operation I illustrate in Figs. 195 and 196. I will begin
with Fig. 196. The body must be perfectly or strictly
square at all corners, or you will find much trouble in

Fig. 193—Showing the Hoop Bolt.

getting your bobs to run parallel. *E* represents the
front of the body. Having found the proper position
to place your front bolster *F*, secure the same temporarily ; then measure from *E* to *F*, as per the dotted
parallel lines *d, d,* and have the distances equal, and
prove you are square by the dotted diagonal lines.
When right, secure *F* in position permanently. Then
place the back bolster *G* in position temporarily, and

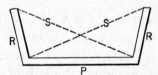

Fig. 194—Bottom View of the Bob.

have it equi-distant at each end from *F*, as per dotted
lines *b, b,* and prove correctness by dotted diagonal lines
g, g, and when correct secure permanently. This finishes the fastening of the bolster to the body.

The next part of the programme is shown by Fig. 195. Place the body on the bolster, the bob standing on the floor. Have the bar and bolster parallel with each other, the bolster having been squared on the bob by the same process as the bars were squared on the body. Then measure from each bob on its outer side to the outer ends of the body and get the distances equal. T is the body ; Y, Y are the body corners at the sides; U, U are runners. Prove as per the dotted diag-

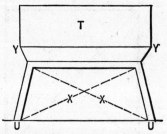

Fig. 195—Showing How the Bobs are Coupled to the Body.

onal lines X, X. If all these precautions are taken your bobs will run as straight as an arrow.

About brakes. There are a number of appliances. The best is the wide skid or shoe shown in Fig. 190, in which D represents an iron eye of the proper size, with straps on each side of the part of the shoe at the curve E, or it may be so made as to go over top and bottom. G is the body of the shoe—six inches wide, one and one-half inches thick, twelve inches or more long. The pieces F, F are eight inches long, two inches high. They are bolted fast to the shoe. The inner piece is bolted to the inner edge, and there is space enough between the two to allow the runner to enter readily.   The projection is on the outside, so as to catch on the unbroken or rough snow.   On the bottom, secure at equal intervals pieces of half round or half oval iron transversely, as indicated by Fig. 191.

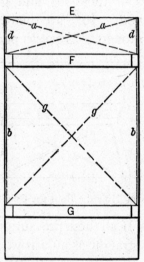

Fig. 196—Showing Another Stage in the Coupling Process.

Attach a chain at the eye D, and secure the chain to the body so as to allow of the brake adjusting itself to the front of the runner, which will throw a pressure on the heel of the shoe of the back bob and thus produce friction.   The great width of the braking shoe, and the fact of its projecting over the rough and unbroken snow, together with the transverse bottom bars, will be sufficient to bring any ordinarily loaded sleigh to a standstill on any ordinary hill. When hills are unusually steep two transverse pieces eight inches apart are better than three. I have found one quite sufficient. Fig. 193 is a hoop bolt on which the shoe brake is hung when not in use. The front ends of the back bob should have a chain running up to the body so as to lift the nose up when dropping into holes, but slack enough to give the bob sufficient play to suit the unevenness of the road.

In securing the back bob it should be remembered that it acts much like a ship rudder. If the nose is too much to the right it will crowd the front bob to the left, and if too much to the left, vice versa.—*By* IRON DOCTOR.

Hanging Bob Sleds.

In my opinion the bunk on a forward traverse should not be over two inches back of the center of the run, but the hind sled should be hung further back. If your sled is four feet on the run, I think it should be hung six inches back of the center. Some say eight inches. You will find that when sleds are hung in this way the shoes will wear very near even on the whole surface. If you get on a stone or hard ground, your sled will not stick as it would if hung in the center. And if you get into deep snow the hind sled will follow the front one very much easier than it would if it were hung nearer the center.

The reason the front and rear sleds should not be hung alike is that, as the team is hitched to the front sled, the front of the forward sled does not bear as hard on the road as the front of the hind sled would if they were hung alike. I think anyone can see that to have a sled run easy the shoes should wear even. If one does not understand the principle of hanging sleds, just take a hand sled and slide down hill three times: the first time sit over the front beam (if you don't sit on the snow before you get to the bottom of the hill you will be lucky), the next time sit over the middle beam, and the last time sit nearly back on the hind beam. You will find that the last time down you will ride much the easiest, and your sled will go the farthest. You can see after this trial how a hind traverse would work hung forward of the center.—*By* W. L. P.

The Tread of a Bob Sled.

I have been in the sled-making business for ten years, and have a reputation second to none for build-

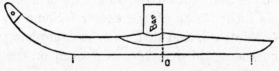

The Tread of a Bob Sled.　Fig. 197—The Front Bob.

ing well-hung and easy running sleds. My rule for placing the bars is as follows:

I find the center of tread by applying the straightedge to the runner, then place the front bar forward of the center, as shown in Fig. 197, and place the hind bar on the center, as in Fig. 198. I generally use the

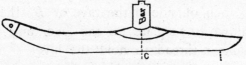

Fig. 198—The Rear Bob.

Bartlett patent. It makes the strongest and easiest running sled in the world.—*By* G. W. R.

A Brake for a Bob Sled.

In making a sleigh brake, I get the width from outside to outside of the raves of the rear bob, next take a piece of one and one-fourth inch round iron, six inches

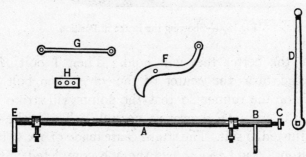

A Brake for a Bob Sled, as Made by "E. H. A." Fig. 199—Showing the Parts in Detail.

longer than the sled, and then jump on a piece of 1½ x ⅝ inch, six inches long, as at *E*, Fig. 199,

with a hole half an inch from the end.   Next I weld a
collar on, *A*, to keep the brake in place when on the
sled ; then make a two-eyed bolt to fasten the brake to
the rave.   This I slip on *A*, and jump on a piece of
1 ½ x ⅝ inch, outside of the rave at *B*; then I draw
the bar down to a square for the lever, and put on a
nut having a thread to hold the lever *D* in place.
Next, I make the brake hands *F* of a piece of common
steel, 2 x ½ inch.   The wider the digging points are

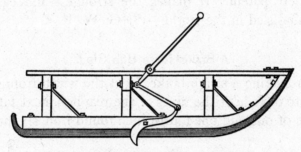

Fig. 200—Showing the Brake in Position.

made, the better they will hold.   Then I bolt *A* to
the sled over the center of the rave, then bolt the
hands on the runner so that the points will strike the
center of the rave as near as possible.   The brake can
be adjusted to suit.   The straps *G* are made of 1 x ¼ inch
tire iron.   Fig. 200 shows the job completed.   This
brake is operated with a rope as the driver sits on top
of his load.   When he pulls, the hands dig, and when
he lets go, the load carries the hands up out of the
way.   This brake will never fail.—*By* E. H. A.

An Improved Sled Brake.

I make a self-acting break for a sled that is very simple and effective, as follows: A, Fig. 201, is a movable nose of the same size as the runner, to which it is bolted at G. It may extend above the runner, as shown, if desirable. D is the brake, swinging on the pin at E. C is a rod connecting the brake with the

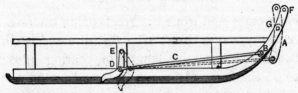

Fig. 201—An Improved Sled Brake, as Made by " E."

lower end of the movable nose. When the load presses upon the team, the movable nose, turning on the pin G, acts upon the break, as indicated by dotted lines. Any simple device may be used for confining this nose to the runner at B when the brake is not in use.—By E.

Fitting Sleigh Shoes.

The quickest and best way that I know of fitting sleigh shoes is to heat them evenly as far back from the end as they are to be bent. Have a strip of tin the width of the runner and long enough to cover the whole bend of the runner as far as the iron is heated. Place this strip on the runner, and fasten it, if necessary, with a small brad. Have at hand a pair of tongs large enough to take in the runner and the end of the shoe. Let a helper hold these together with the tongs while you bend down the shoe, hammer slightly, if necessary, and you have a perfect fit without burning the runner. If you have no help, the end of the shoe can be held to the runner with a clamp.—ANONYMOUS.

Centering Bob Sleds.

I have made and ironed a great many traverse runners, and my way is this: After the hind end is clipped for backing I take the length of bearing, plus four inches on the forward end, and place the center of the bunk on the center of this measurement, placing both bunks alike. The plan gives general satisfaction.—By S. F. G.

Plating Sleigh Shoes.

I am an ironworker, and would like to say for the benefit of blacksmiths and others that one of the best

Fig. 202—Plating Sleigh Shoes.

ways to plate sleigh shoes is to use one-eighth Norway iron, one-half inch wider or more than the steel to be plated; lay the steel in the center of the iron, heat and form round the steel, Fig. 202, S representing steel and I iron. Form as you weld. Shoes plated by this method can be made lighter and stronger, and in case they spring when hardening can be bent in any direction without cracking.—*By* D. F.

Hanging Traverse Runners.

My plan of hanging traverse runners is to hang them from two to six inches back of the center, measuring from the shoe where it strikes the floor. If the rear bob draws from the top it may be hung a little farther back than the front one. The longer the knees are, the farther back they should be hung to run well. By looking at the shoes of some that are almost worn out, anyone can generally judge where to hang them. I think that twenty-four pairs out of twenty-five are hung too far forward for the good of the team obliged to draw them. If the shoe is all worn out on the nose, and as thick as when new at the heel, it shows that there is something rotten in the state of Denmark.—*By* G. W. B.

CHAPTER VI.

TEMPERING TOOLS.

Making and Tempering Dies or Taps.

Knowing that many blacksmiths are troubled with dull and battered dies that are unfit for business, I venture to give my method of putting them in order.

If the dies are too badly worn or defective, take a piece of good cast-steel, forge it down nearly to the size of the dies and cut it off a trifle longer. Get a piece of one and one-half or two-inch gas pipe, eight or ten inches long, plug up one end, heat the pieces of steel to cherry red, pack them in the pipe with fine charcoal, plug the other end, heat the whole to a good red and hold the heat fifteen or twenty minutes, then bury the whole well up in the fire over night. They will be soft enough to work quite well next morning. Then dress them up with the file to the proper size and length; cut the end slots with the hack saw and fit them nicely in the plate; remove them and file notches in the faces large enough so the tap can be started steadily; return to the plate and cut good full threads with a sharp tap of the desired size.

Then cut out the throats with the hack saw and file,

and temper as follows : Heat the dies to a cherry red and drop them into a vessel of raw linseed oil. When cool take them out, polish, and draw on a hot iron to a medium dark straw color.

I find that, as a rule, it is best to buy taps, yet sometimes one is wanted for a special job, and it is inconvenient to buy it. Taps may be made on the same general principles, that is, by making the steel the proper size and shape, cutting the threads and then working out the grooves with the hack saw, chisel and file. Care must be taken in drawing the temper on taps to heat very slow, otherwise the edges of the threads may draw too soon and be too soft, which, of course, means a bad job.—*By* F. W. S.

Tempering Drills.

PLAN I.

For tempering drills, take a half ounce of sulphate of zinc, three-fourths of an ounce of saltpeter, one-eighth of an ounce of prussiate of potash ; pulverized together, used as a mixture into which to dip the drill when heated to a dark cherry red, will prove satisfactory for your purpose. The article should be dipped into the mixture so as to cover all the parts which it is desirable to harden, the same as though melted borax was used. After dipping the drill, return it to the fire, increasing the heat to what is commonly called bright cherry red. Then dip into clear, soft water, into which about half a pint to the gallon of common salt has been dissolved. I have never had experience in dressing drills for quartzite, but good steel hardened in this way will cut glass very readily.—*By* B. H. B.

Tempering Drills.

PLAN 2.

I will try to describe, for the benefit of many, the way in which I temper small drills. I learned it from experience, and think there is no better plan. I dress the drill to the desired shape, then heat to a cherry red and insert it gently in a cup of warm water, which should be placed on the forge for convenience. I then take it out, and when the temper runs down to a dark straw color, dip it into a can of common lard or grease, such as we use in cutting threads, and cool it off above the cutting edge. This rule is good for chisels, punches and all kinds of small tools. I have tempered drills in this way that would drill through one and one-half inch wrought iron. I think they are less liable to heat than those tempered in water alone.—*By* J. W. J.

Tempering Drills.

PLAN 3.

My way of tempering drills for chilled plow metal is worth telling.

When the drill is hot I rub in cyanide of potassium, the drill being hot enough to melt it. I then heat it so that it will be a dark cherry red when held in the light, and cool it off in warm, soft water, made with very strong brine. I don't draw the temper. The drill will look white, but the drug makes it hard and tough. I use the drill dry, and never turn it backward, for if I did the edge would fly.

I have tempered mill picks in the same way, and with good results. I generally make my drills of old files, but good, plain cast-steel is better.—*By* J. W. J.

Tempering Drills.

PLAN 4.

To temper a drill so that it will drill a hardened saw blade, heat the drill in a charcoal fire to a cherry red, and quench it in spring water, to which is added a handful of salt, then make the drill bright, and draw to a light straw color.—*By* W. R.

Tempering Drills to Drill Saw Plates.

After learning the grade of the steel and what heat it will stand, procure the best drill steel and forge out to shape. Leave it as heavy above the drill point as it can be, and still be clean in the hole after it is drilled. Have your drill tapered or beveled, so that when the heel of the bit is cutting, the point will be through the plate. File up sharp with a very fine file. The cutting edge should be sharp and smooth. If a coarse file is used, it will leave a rough edge that will cut in soft iron well enough and in steel would crumble. Procure a block of lead, heat the drill to a cherry red and drive it into the lead, say half an inch, and then leave it to cool. If the steel is good it will never be too soft, and may sometimes be too hard. If too hard, don't try to draw the temper, as it will then be too soft on the cutting edge. Temper over, and don't heat quite so hot, and you will soon learn what heat the steel will require. I have one that has drilled a great many holes and is sharp yet. Never use this drill on iron, as it will fly like glass, and there is as much to keep in mind in using a drill for this work as in tempering it. Always use a hard wood block under the plate to be drilled, and it should be one on which the saw will rest only when it is under the point of the drill. Never force the drill, and use plenty of oil. When the heel of the drill is about through, turn it and feed very cautiously, or you will break your drill or crack your plate if it is thin, and that crack will not be seen until the saw has been run some time.

I have had saws brought to me that had been drilled and had had a piece of brass or copper riveted in the drill hole. They cracked again farther down. Never plug a hole that has been drilled in a saw plate. I have never seen a saw crack below the drill hole if drilled properly. When a saw is cracked it is cracked further than the naked eye can see, so you must get the course of the crack and drill in that course, say one-half of an inch further down. Then your saw will never crack again unless it goes to pieces.—*By* W. G. R.

Tempering Drills for Saw Plates.

Concerning the tempering of drills for drilling saw plates, my advice is to harden the drill and bring it to a straw color. Use turpentine instead of oil, be careful not to give the drill too sharp a point, and you will have a tool that will drill any ordinary saw plate. Even glass may be drilled with it by using a bow-drill.—*By* D. W. C. H.

Tempering Taps.

Heat the tap in a clear fire to a dark cherry red. Use the blast sparingly, and do not heat too quick, but give the tap time to "soak," so that it will be thoroughly and evenly heated all through. Now dip it endwise and all over in water till cool. To draw to the proper temperature (a dark straw or purple color), hold the head of the tap in a hot tongs, passing it backward and forward and round about over a clear fire, keeping it covered at the same time with oil, which you can apply by having a small piece of rag tied on the end of a little stick, which you can from time to time dip in the oil as you rub it on the tap. The oil will regulate the temper evenly, and keep the "teeth" of the tap from heating sooner than the body of it. The above is what we might call the straightforward way of doing the job; but in order that someone who is not regularly accustomed to doing such work may not fail, I will give a few hints or suggestions that may not be amiss.

As a precaution against cracking in hardening, it would be well to rub the tap while hot, and just before tempering dip it in a paste made of flour and prussiate of potash, or yeast, to protect the tap from a too sudden cooling. It would be well to have the chill taken off the water before dipping, or, in other words, to not have the water real cold. Remember not to let the tap get too hot; don't let it get too hot and then cool again before dipping; heat slowly and harden at the *lowest heat it will harden at.* Keep this in mind, and you need not have any fears that you will spoil the job. Now, after having it hardened, you will proceed to draw the temper. Rub the sides or grooves of the tap with a piece of sandpaper, so that you can see the temper more plainly as it comes. Hold the head of it in a hot tongs and keep the oil applied as I have said above, until you bring to the desired temper. All manner of taps, either large or small, can be hardened and tempered in the way described.—*By* I. A. C.

Tempering Taps and Other Small Tools.

Take an old piece of steam pipe, or other iron cylinder, about fifteen or eighteen inches long and large enough to admit of the tongs holding the tap being passed into it. Plug up one end of this pipe solid with some non-combustible substance such as a bit of clay and bung it in the fire with the open end toward you and slightly higher than the closed end. Take care that no bits of coal get down into the pipe.

Now grasp the tap by the square end made for the reception of the wrench (in no case must it be held by the threaded end in the tongs), and as you see that the pipe is red hot insert the tap and by turning the tongs keep the tap slowly revolving in the pipe and when it looks as though it were red hot pull it out and thrust it into a nail-keg or some other handy dark corner and see if it is heated all over evenly. This is important. By a little attention you will soon get in the way of noticing the cooler portions by their slightly darker color. Repeat these operations until you are sure you have an even but not a high heat (say a dull red). Then plunge the tap point downward into a bucket of clean soft water and hold it still until it is as cool as the water. With a few times trying we believe you will find this an easy way to harden a tap or other small tools in a common fire without risk of burning or injuring the steel. Now polish the shank and flutes of the tap, and by again inserting it into the hot pipe you can easily let down the temper to any degree of hardness required. In the latter case do not have the pipe too hot, as it will make a better tap to let the temper down slowly and evenly.—*Industrial World.*

Recutting and Tempering Old Dies.

Heat the die in a clean fire to avoid a cherry red heat, not hot enough to scale, for that would open the "grain" of it, and therefore cause it to crack in hardening, or render it more liable to break while using.

Cover the die while hot with a little sawdust first, and then cover all with ashes to keep out the air, and let lay until cold. Or another way you can anneal. Put the die or dies in a piece of iron pipe one and a half or two inches in diameter and eight or ten inches long; have one end of the pipe closed up. Now put the pipe in the fire, and while heating put in some little pieces of old leather, or hoof parings, or charcoal, either one will do if you haven't got the others, or you may put equal parts of all in if you have them. Heat all to a cherry red heat. Plug the pipe up with a piece of iron, and let it lay covered up in some convenient place with ashes until cold. After having them cut the next thing in order will be to temper them. Now, with this operation you must be careful or you will have your whole job spoiled. Heat them in a clean fire to a red heat; just hot enough that they will harden, and *no more*. As a precaution against cracking you may cover them with prussiate of potash or with a paste made of soap and oil. If you have neither paste nor potash you may throw a little salt in the water you harden in, and if you have not heated them too hot there will be no danger of their cracking. After being hardened rub them on sand or on a grindstone to brighten the sides so that you may see the temper better.

To draw the temper you can heat a piece of iron, hold it in the vise, place the dies on it, and turn them from one side to the other with a little rod until they are brought to a dark straw color.

Try this plan now, and see if you won't succeed "on a small scale."—*By* I. A. C.

Recutting and Tempering Dies.

PLAN I.

The best plan of recutting and tempering old dies for cutting threads, when the taps are perfect and the dies are hand-plates, is to cut them by filling the sides between the dies with lead. If they are machine dies, three or four to the set, a tap with a spiral flute is the best. These flutes can be made in the lathe or with a file. A tap of this kind is best for cutting either hand or machine-made dies. To temper them, heat them slowly in a clear fire to a cherry red, or at the slowest heat at which they will harden, cool them in clear water with the chill off, then brighten and draw to a temper at a straw color over a piece of hot iron.—*By* R. T. K.

Recutting and Tempering Dies.

PLAN 2.

For recutting and tempering old dies, my advice is to heat the dies a light cherry red, then cover them in air-slacked lime or dry loam till cold. To anneal, place your dies in the plate, put your large tap in the vise, run the dies on the largest part of the tap till the thread in them is sharp, file out the vents, harden at a low heat, rub them with tallow and draw temper till the tallow burns off, and then cool.—*By* S. N.

To Temper Cold Chisels, Taps, Etc.

When tempering cold chisels or any other steel articles, heat to a very dull red and rub with a piece of hard soap; then finish heating, and harden in clear, cool water. The potash of the soap prevents the oxygen of the atmosphere from uniting with the steel and forming rust or black oxide of iron. The article will need no polishing to enable the colors to be seen. This will be appreciated when tempering taps, dies or very complex forms not easy to polish. Never "upset" a cold chisel. It is sure death to the steel.

Tempering Butchers' Knives.

PLAN 1.

My way for tempering a butcher's knife is as follows: I heat it slowly to a cherry red, being careful that the heat is distributed evenly over it. I then dip it in oil with the back downward, and then draw to a dark straw color.—*By* J. B. H.

Tempering Butchers' Knives.

PLAN 2.

A good method of tempering butcher knives is to securely fasten the knife to be tempered between two pieces of iron about three-fourths of an inch thick, and a little longer and wider than the knife. Then heat irons and all together until it becomes a bright cherry red ; then dip the whole in water. By this method you can harden thin pieces of steel without warping.— *By* H. G. S.

Tempering and Straightening Knife Blades.

I have seen in books several good articles on tempering edge tools, but I have not observed any directions for straightening knife blades, etc., after they have been immersed in water and without changing the color.

After the immersion in water an edged tool is apt to spring. It should first be brightened with sandpaper or by being rubbed on a brick. Then the convex side must be laid on a bar of hot iron, and while one end is held by the tongs the other should be pressed on with something that will straighten it. The blade need not remain on the iron long enough to change color. The temper can be drawn on the hot iron until the right point is attained.—*By* W. J. R.

To Temper Knife Blades.

PLAN I.

To harden thin blades without warping them out of shape, be very careful about heating. Heat in the blaze, evenly all over, and then plunge perpendicularly into a tank of raw linseed oil. Be particular to plunge into the oil perpendicularly, and draw the temper on a hot iron. Another way is to heat and harden the blades between two straight pieces of iron.—*By* D. D.

To Temper Knife Blades.

PLAN 2.

To get the temper of knife blades uniform requires skill on the part of the workman. The nearer all parts of the blade are heated and cooled alike the more uniform will be the temper. They are generally cooled in oil, to harden them. This method does not give as good results as when water is used, but reduces the liability of cracking and warping. The temper is drawn in various ways, on sand, and in revolving ovens, and in hot animal oil. In the first method the degree of temper is regulated by the color; in the second, by color and degrees of heat, and in the last, by degrees of heat, which is found by a pyrometer or thermometer, and sometimes by some substance which will melt at any known degree of heat. There has, as yet, no way been found to harden knife blades and get a good cutting edge, without warping them out of shape.—*By* W. B. & Co.

Tempering Mill Picks.

PLAN I.

Perhaps some reader has mill picks to temper, and has no good recipe for tempering them. When sharp and ready to temper, get a pail of rain water and a bar of common, cheap yellow soap. Heat the pick to a cherry red, and cool it by sticking it in the soap. Cool it until the soap gives it a white coating. Do this three times in succession. Then heat it the fourth time to the same color and plunge it in the rain water. Don't draw the temper.

I don't know what property the soap contains that is of benefit to steel in this way; but if anyone will give this a careful trial, he will use no other means for tempering mill picks.—*By* J. A. RODMAN.

Tempering Mill Picks.

PLAN 2.

Being both a miller and a blacksmith, I have had considerable experience in tempering mill-pick work, and believe that I have at last found out the best way of doing it. In the first place, you employ a good quality of steel; secondly, the steel must be very carefully worked, using charcoal only, as stove coal would destroy the carbon in the steel, and thereby render it brittle. Never heat the steel above a red heat, and after the picks are made, water-hammer the ends well, and let them cool off. Have in readiness an iron vessel containing mercury (three inches deep), and place this vessel in a bath of ice water, to keep the mercury as near the temperature of the water as possible. Now heat three-fourths of an inch of the points just to a color, and set them straight down into the mercury. Let them cool there, and do no drawing.—*By* W. P.

Tempering Mill Picks.

PLAN 3.

Take three gallons of water, and of ammonia, white vitriol, sal ammoniac, spirits of nitre and alum three ounces each, six ounces of salt and two handfuls of horse-hoof parings. When this mixture is not in use keep it in a jar and tightly corked. Heat the pick to a dark cherry red and cool it in the liquid just described. Draw no temper.—*By* H. M.

Tempering Mill Picks.

PLAN 4.

For tempering mill picks, I take six quarts of salt water, one ounce of pulverized corrosive sublimate, three handfuls of salt, one ounce of sal-ammoniac. Mix, and when dissolved it is ready for use. Heat the picks to only a cherry red, plunge in the fluid just described, but do not draw to any temper. In working them be very careful not to heat them; work with as low a heat as possible. In drawing, there ought to be a good deal of light water-hammering. In heating picks I find charcoal much better than blacksmiths' coal, because the former does not heat so quickly, and so there is less danger of overheating.—*By* G. V.

Tempering Mill Picks.

PLAN 5.

My recipe for tempering mill picks is one I obtained from an English miller, who had used it for thirty years, and would try no other. It is as follows: Salt, half a teacup; saltpeter, half an ounce; pulverized alum, one teaspoonful; soft water, one gallon. Do not heat above a cherry red, nor draw to temper.—*By* I. L. C.

Tempering Mill Picks.

PLAN 6.

To dress a mill pick, it is necessary to have a smooth anvil and a hammer with its face slightly rounded and very smooth. Great care must be taken in heating, for too high a heat will spoil the whole job. What hammering the edges will require should be done at first before the steel is thinned any, because blows delivered on the edge of hard steel crush the steel more or less, according to the number and weight of the blows. The body of the steel is partially separated and very much weakened, although it will not show any flaw when fractured.—*By* H. BUCK.

Tempering Mill Picks.

PLAN 7.

I use pure rain water in tempering mill picks, and get better results than I can with any composition I have ever tried. I draw down thin and even, leaving no light or heavy places in them, and in the last heat I wet-hammer with a light hammer. I hammer as much on one side as on the other. I heat very slowly to a dark cherry, and immerse in water that is about the temperature of the air. I am very careful as to how I immerse the picks. If it is done too quickly, circular cracks will form around the edge, and if too slowly, cracks will appear straight in and back of the edge. I heat them only as far up as I wish to temper, and then cool them off all over. I then rub them bright and hold them over the fire until they are warm—not warm enough to change the color, but sufficiently to make them tough.—*By* W. J. R.

One of the Secrets of Hardening.

"The best mill pick man he ever knew always withdrew the steel from the water before its temperature was reduced to that of the water, leaving enough heat remaining in the steel to dry off the water in about two seconds." This I believe to be one of the secrets of expert hardening, and I have somewhere read that steel treated thus will bend, providing that the bending be done while the steel is still warm, but that the bending cannot be proceeded with after the steel has once got cold after hardening it. It has been stated that the file-makers utilize this fact by drawing the files from the water when at about eighty to a hundred degrees, and pouring cold water upon the outside of the curve of warped files, so as to contract the same, and therefore help to straighten the files.—*By* T. H.

How to Temper an Axe.

Having had fifteen years' experience in axe work, I will, for the benefit of the inexperienced, give my way of tempering.

Some seem to suppose that with an edge tool everything depends upon the temper. This is a great mistake. While tempering is a very essential part, it is no more so than is the forging. Unless the steel is properly worked and refined with the hammer, there is no temper in the world that will give a nice, smooth cutting-edge. With a thick axe almost any temper will stand. If too hard it is too thick to break, if too soft it is not likely to bend. But when an axe is made thin, as it should be to cut easy, no haphazard way of tempering is going to answer the purpose.

The right temper is in a thin axe a very essential point, and can be obtained only with the greatest care. In making over an axe, after the finishing touches have been given to the steel, I grind out the hammer marks before tempering, as this can be done much easier before than after, and the temper can more readily be seen. Having a good charcoal fire I put in the axe with the bit towards me, watching closely the extreme edge to make sure that the steel does not get too hot. If it is overheated the fine grain of the steel is injured, and cannot be restored. I am careful to keep dead coals against the edge until the axe is of a bright red to within about half an inch of the edge. I then take a firm grip upon the head with the tongs and put the bit into the coals, moving it round, and turning it over (without any blast) until a perfectly even heat is obtained. When at a bright cherry heat I plunge it at once into a tub of brine to within half an inch of the eye, and move it slowly about until the steel is cold.

If properly hardened when taken from the brine, the steel will be a grayish white. After wiping, I brighten up the bit by rubbing it with a piece of grindstone, also by scouring it in sand. I then proceed to draw the temper, the most important part of all. Some set the axe upon the head in the fire and let the temper run down as they would with a drill or cold chisel. But this is a bad way, and those who follow it are fifty years behind the times. Axes tempered in this way will grow soft after grinding a few times, as everyone must see. Besides, this method of drawing the temper is attended with many difficulties. My way is to level down the fire, seeing that there is no blaze; I then set a brick up edgewise each side of the fire, and lay across a one-fourth inch wire upon which to rest the bit; I place another brick in front for the head to rest on, and lay the axe down flat over the fire. The axe should be from four to six inches above the coals, according to the amount of heat.

The temper should be drawn slowly, in not less time than five minutes, and ten or fifteen minutes would be better.   As to the color that marks the point to which the temper should be drawn, I know nothing reliable, for in making over old axes we find different grades of steel.   I sometimes leave the temper at a dark straw color, at others at a deep blue.   Were I to be governed solely by the color, I would prefer a mixture of copper color and blue.   But the smith who in making over axes relies exclusively upon the color in drawing the temper must expect to meet with many a failure. The only sure and reliable way is to use a nicking tool.

I use the pene of a small hammer for that purpose. When the temper is at a dark straw color, I take the axe from the fire and tap it lightly upon the edge.   If the pieces fly I pronounce it too hard, and put it back and draw it lower, then try it again, and continue to do so at short intervals, until the sharp ring of the steel dies away, and pieces no longer fly off, but turn over, and readily fly when tapped the other way.   When this point is reached, I plunge it in water or lay it aside to cool.

Before cooling, it would be a good idea for a new beginner to put the axe in the vise and try the edge with a rasp.   He will soon learn in this way when the right temper is attained.   If the steel yields to the rasp the temper is too low.   The axe should be kept the same side up in drawing the temper.   I prefer brine to water for tempering, To one-half barrel of water I add some four quarts of salt. The "chill' should be taken off in Winter, or the tool is liable to crack in cooling.

Now, one word about grinding, as there is not one man in ten that knows how an axe should be ground, to stand. In the finishing process the stone should run towards the grinder, and the axe be kept in constant motion, lest it be ground too thin upon the edge for Winter use.—*By* W. H. BALL.

Tempering a Chopping Axe.

For the benefit of those blacksmiths who are with-out aey good method for tempering a large chopping axe, I would say: Get ten or twelve quarts of soft rain water. Put the same in a clean pail or tub. To this add one pint of common salt, letting the salt dis-solve before the mixture is used. Heat a piece of iron and plunge it in the water. This is done simply to take the chill from the water. Now heat the axe over a slow fire to a dark red-hot. Place about three inches of the axe in the water, and, while holding it in this position, keep moving about, that is, do not hold it constantly in one place. After it has cooled to the depth mentioned, take it out and rub the cooled part on a brick or stone, so as to enable you to see the tem-per draw toward the point. When it is down to a dark blue at the keen edge, plunge it deep into the water, and after it has cooled off it is ready for use. One great trouble with smiths when tempering edged tools is that they take the heat on the end or edge to be tempered too short, and, at the same time, they get the tool hotter at the points than it is back of them. The main thing to be remembered in tempering is to heat the steel to a uniform and even degree throughout, and to get as long a temper on the piece to be tempered as it is possible to get. A large tool with only one-fourth to three-fourths of an inch of temper will break, nine chances out of ten.

To illustrate what I mean by a short temper, I will relate a few instances of tempering that came to my notice a short time since. A certain smith had sharpened and tempered a screw-driver and cold chisel from four to six times, and still both would break. After he had experimented to the extent of his patience, failing to get either tool to stand satisfactorily, he came to me and complained that the steel was not good. I asked him if he had not overheated it. He thought not. So, after satisfying myself, I sharpened both for him at his own fire. In tempering the screw-driver, I cooled the point up to about one inch, and let it run down to what I thought was the proper temper, which was a dark blue. His helper has since used the tool on about one gross of screws, and it is as good yet as when first sharpened. I also gave the cold chisel about one inch temper, and it has not broken since the trouble the owner had with it. The difficulty in this case was that both tools had been cooled only about one-fourth of an inch back of the point, which gave the short temper. The result was as described. I explained these points to the owner of the tools, who admitted their correctness after being convinced by seeing my experiments.—*By* H. R. H.

Tempering Axes.

PLAN 1.

To temper axes heat the poll in a charcoal fire to a little more than a cherry red, then change ends and heat the bit in the blaze to a cherry red all over. Be sure to heat it all over. When hot enough cool the bit only, in a salt water bath. Plunge it in the water at once; if you don't, there may be a fire crack that will spoil it. If done right the steel will look like silver. Scour with a brick and put the poll in the fire endways. Use no blast and let the temper run to a blue. Then you will have an axe that will cut.—*By* H. A. S.

Tempering Axes.

PLAN 2.

My way of tempering axes is as follows: I split the iron poll to receive the steel, heat the axe bit up to the eye to a peculiar red heat, plunge into salt brine and fresh water until it is cold, and then draw to brown yellow over a charcoal fire.—*By* C. K. H.

Tempering Axes.

PLAN 3.

To have a good axe steel must be worked at a low heat and hammered all over even before heating to harden. If there is no grindstone hammer, and file to an edge. Brine is the best fluid to harden in, but fresh water will do. In hardening, the axe should be given a little swing, letting one corner strike the water first. Then brighten the steel and let the temper run down to a shade below a dark blue.—*By* J. W. C.

Tempering Axes.

PLAN 4.

My way of tempering a chopping axe, that I have tried for the past four years and which has always proven successful, is as follows: Take six pounds of tallow and two pounds of beeswax, and one ounce of finely pulverized sal ammoniac. Melt the tallow and beeswax together, and then put in the sal ammoniac. Pour the mixture into a sheet-iron box, which, for convenience, should be two feet long, four inches wide and four inches deep. A box of these dimensions will hold enough of the mixture for tempering any sized axe, hoe or other tool. When the axe is ready for tempering, heat to a white red; then put it into the mixture deep enough to cover the steel all over. Let it remain from one to two minutes, then put in the water the same way. Then draw to a blue color and return to the mixture as before. Then hold it over the fire until it becomes dry, and then put it back in the water to cool. Never heat the steel more than to a light red when forged out.—*By* T. G.

Tempering Axes.

PLAN 5.

To temper axes I heat the edge to a bright red, then, when it is all ready to temper, I use the following composition : Three gallons of soft water; two ounces of prussiate of potash ; quarter pound of saltpeter and one pound of whale oil.

This should be kept in a small barrel and stirred well just before using. I then heat the axe to a cherry color, and very even, and then draw to a purple, and I have an axe as good as a new one.

But another point must be kept in mind, and it is this : All axes are not of the same steel. By hammering you can tell whether the steel is hard or not. If it is soft do not let the temper come down so low as when it is hard.—*By* B. T. C.

Tempering Axes.

PLAN 6.

I have had over fifty years' experience in work of this kind. I am now seventy-two years of age. I will venture to explain my way of tempering a chopping axe for the benefit of tool makers and blacksmiths. It is my custom to make axes very thin. I would heat the axe over a fire in the blaze until it is heated through even and to a moderate cherry red. I would then dip it into a solution of salt and water nearly to the eye. As soon as it is hardened, and as quickly as possible, I would put it over the blaze again, until there is no danger of cracking. I would then rub it off clean, and let the temper run down. In the first place, it will look as if the tempering is done. The workman should not be deceived by that. If he waits a little he will see a brass or copper color coming down again. Let this come down to the edge, and then to a light pigeon blue. When this stage is reached, cool the eye of the axe, so that it will not run any lower. Finally, hang the axe up until it has cooled off sufficiently for handling.—*By* A. H.

Tempering Axes.

PLAN 7.

My method is to temper in beef tallow. After drawing out I heat the axe to a medium bright cherry red, have a kettle of tallow ready and dip it in the same as if in water ; I let it remain till the blaze has nearly left the tallow, then take the axe out, brush off the grease, lay the axe on the fire and draw the temper to a deep blue. I have some rifle powder ready, and often sprinkling a little on the edge, let the temper run down till the powder flashes, and then cool in water.   If the steel is hard I let the powder flash the second time.   I draw out from ten to twenty-five axes every year, and hardly ever miss if the steel is good.   I have followed this plan successfully for over fifteen years.—*By* J. L. R.

Tempering the Face of Hand Hammers.

To those who wish the best method of tempering hand hammers, I would say that it is impossible to get the center of a hammer face too hard.   Of course we cannot harden the center without hardening the outside, and if we permit the hammer to remain in this condition the edges will chip off.   To avoid this we must temper the outer portions, giving it either a straw color, copper color or blue, according to the work which we propose to do with the hammer.   To draw an even temper, make a collar of bar iron, the thicker the better for the purpose, just large enough to slip over the hammer.   After it is finished, polish the sides of the hammer so that when it is slipped in to the collar the temper will be drawn quickly. Of course the face of the hammer must also be smoothed off, so that the colors can be distinguished easily.   Now heat the collar to a white heat and slip it quickly over the hammer.   When the proper color is seen on the outer edges, slip off the collar and cool your hammer at once in whatever liquid you have on hand for that purpose. Care must be taken that the center of the hammer is

not also heated so as to destroy the original hardness.
If a hammer is tempered all over, so that the edges will
not chip, it will be too soft in the center and the face
will sink in at that point after use.—*By* M. EHRGOTT.

Tempering a Hand Hammer.

My method of tempering hand hammers is this : Put
one quart of water in a small can that will hold the
hammer also.   Heat the hammer all over, evenly, to a
bright red. If you wish to temper both face and pene,
put a punch in the eye and let the face down in the
water as far as you wish the temper to extend.   Hold
the hammer so about half a minute, then turn it over
and treat the pene in the same way. Change back and
forth from face to pene until the center is black, then
slip the hammer off the punch into the can, and let it
stay until cold.   I make all my own hammers, and
they never crack or break in the eye.—*By* J. N. B.

Tempering a Hammer.

My way is to first heat the hammer to a cherry red,
and then dip it in clear water. In drawing the temper,
I use a fine, sharp file for testing it, judging in this
way when it is drawn enough.—*By* J. B. H.

Tempering Blacksmiths' Hammers.

Tempering a hammer is a job which a great many
men cannot do as it should be done.   I was that way

myself until one Winter, when, while traveling in Iowa, I learned from the foreman of a shop there the following method of tempering: After the hammer has been dressed in good shape and everything ready to temper, get an old coffee pot, or some vessel with a small spout attached; heat your hammer to an ordinary heat, and holding it over the slack tub, pour water from the coffee-pot spout into the center of the face until cold. This hardens the center to a greater depth than it can be hardened by plunging the whole face of the hammer into the tub in the ordinary way. The temper can afterwards be drawn on the edges.—*By* S. E. H.

CHAPTER VII.

PROPORTIONS OF BOLTS AND NUTS, FORMS OF HEADS, ETC.

Bolts and Nuts.

Bolts are usually designated for measurement by their diameters at the top of the thread, and by their lengths measured from the inner side of the head to the end of the thread, so that if a nut be used, the length of the bolt, less the thickness of the nut and washer (if the latter be used), is the thickness of work the bolt will hold. If the thread be within the work and no nut, therefore, be necessary, the same rule as to length holds good, because the depth of the thread in the work is equivalent to the nut; hence the thickness of work that a bolt will hold is equal to the length of the bolt from the inside of the bolt head to the inner radial face of the nut when the latter is screwed upon the bolt, so that the end of the bolt has emerged to the distance that the end is rounded or chamfered off. It is assumed in this case that the end of the bolt passes or screws into the work to a depth equal to the depth of a nut which should equal the diameter of the bolt.

A black bolt is one left as forged. A finished bolt has its body, and usually its head also, machine finished, but a finished bolt sometimes has a black head.

A square-headed bolt usually has a square nut, but if

the nut is in a situation difficult of access for the wrench, or where the head of the bolt is entirely out of sight, as beneath a secluded flange, the nut is often made hexagon. A machine-finished bolt usually has a ma-

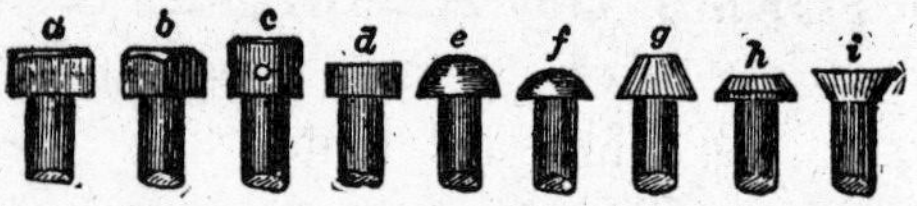

Fig. 203—Various Forms of Heads.

chine-finished and hexagon nut. Square nuts are usually left black.

The heads of bolts are designated by their shapes, irrespective of whether they are left black or finished.

Fig. 203 represents the various forms : *a*, square head ; *b*, hexagon head ; *c*, capstan head ; *d*, cheese head ; *e*, snap head ; *f*, oval head, or button head ; *g*, conical head ; *h*, pan head ; *i*, countersink head.

Bolts are designated as in Fig. 204, in which *k* is a

Fig. 204—Designations of Bolts.

machine bolt, *l* is a collar bolt, *m* is a cotter bolt, *n* is a carriage bolt, and *o* is a tire bolt.

In Fig. 207, *s* is a patch bolt, *t*, *u*, *v* are plow bolts, and *w* is an elevator bolt.

A tap bolt is one which screws into the work instead of requiring a nut. The distance its thread enters the work should be at least equal to the diameter of the thread, and in cast-iron about one and a quarter to one and a third times the diameter, on account of the difference in strength of the thread on the wrought-iron bolt and the cast-iron thread in the hole. Tap bolts have usually hexagon heads, and are left either finished or black, as circumstances may require.

A stud or standing bolt is formed as in Fig. 205.

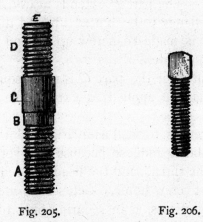

Fig. 205.   Fig. 206.

The threaded part A is to screw a tight fit into the work, the stud remaining firmly fixed. The plain part B is intended to enter the work, the bore of the thread in the hole having the thread cut out to receive it. By this means the shoulder between B and C will abut against the face of the work, and the stud ends E will all protrude an equal distance through the nuts, providing, of course, that the thickness of the flange bolted up, and also of the nuts, are all equal. Another method of accomplishing this result is to cut a groove where B joins C, a groove close up to the shoulder, and extending to the bottom of the thread, so that the thread may terminate in the groove. By this means the shoulder will screw fairly home against the face of the work, while the plain part B is dispensed with, and clearing out the thread at the entrance of the hole becomes unnecessary. The part B extends nearly through the hole in the flange to be bolted up, and the fit of the thread at D is made to screw up a good working fit under hard pressure.

In some practice the part C is made square, so that a wrench may be applied to extract the stud when necessary.

A set screw is formed as in Fig. 206, the diameter of the head being reduced because the working strain falls upon the thread, and the head is used to merely screw the set screw home. Set screws are employed to enveloped pieces, as in securing hubs to shafts the enveloping piece is threaded to receive the screw whose end, as the set screw is screwed home, is forced against the piece or shaft enveloped. This end pressure is apt to cause the end of the screw to spread, rendering it difficult to unslack or screw back the screw. To avoid this the following methods are resorted to :

Sometimes the end is rounded, so that the pressure falls on the middle or center of the screw only, but as this reduces the area of contact, increases the liability

to spread, and allows the screw to become loose, a
cup recess of about half the diameter of the screw is
provided.   A better plan is to chamfer off the end of
the thread for a distance of about two threads, or the
thread may be turned off the end of the screw for the

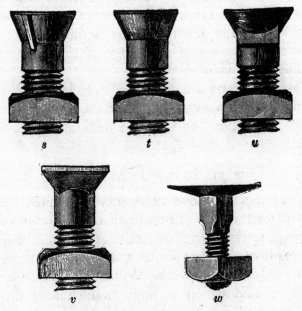

Fig. 207.   Designations of Bolts.

same distance.   A still better plan is to cup the end of
the set screw, as shown in Fig. 204, so that the screw
end will compress a ring in the shaft.   Set screws
should be of steel, with the points, at least, hardened,
which enables them to grip the shaft more firmly, and

obviates the spreading. But if made of wrought iron, they or their ends should be case-hardened.

The term cap screw is applied to the screws made especially for the caps of journal boxes or bearings. They have square or hexagon heads, and are usually machine-finished all over. The part beneath the head is left cylindrical for a distance varying according to order, but usually nearly equal to the diameter of the screw, the thickness of the flange of the cap usually equaling that diameter.

Machine screws are designated for diameter by the Birmingham wire gauge, and have their thread pitches coarser than those on standard bolts and nuts.—*By* J. R.

Bolts and Nuts and Their Threads.

Up to the year 1868 there was no United States standard for the sizes of bolt heads or nuts, or standard pitches of screw threads for bolts. As a result, threads were made of different forms and pitches by different makers. In 1868, however, William Sellers & Co., of Philadelphia, designed an angle and pitch of thread, and a standard size of bolt head and nuts, which was recommended for adoption as the United States standard by the Franklin Institute, and subsequently, with a slight modification in the sizes of bolt heads and nuts, adopted by the United States Navy Department as a standard, which is now known as the United States standard. At the present time the matter stands thus:

There are three forms of thread in use in the United States. The first is shown in Fig. 208. It is known

Fig. 208.

as the V thread, or sharp V thread, its sides being at an angle of sixty degrees. This thread is in more com-

Fig. 209.

mon use than any other, being the standard for gas and steam pipes, and is in very general use.

The second is that referred to above as the United

Fig. 210.

States standard thread, its form being as in Fig. 209. The sides are at an angle of sixty degrees. The depth of the thread is divided off into eight equal divisions.

The top and bottom division is taken off, so as to leave
a flat place at both top and bottom.   The application

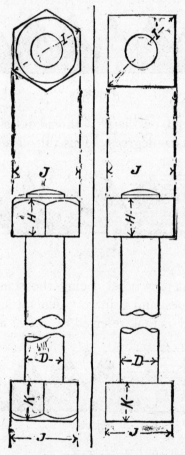

Fig. 211.

of this thread is continually increasing, prominent tool-
makers keeping tools and dies in stock for cutting it,

United States Standard Dimensions of Bolts and Nuts.

BOLT			BOLT HEAD AND NUT				
Diameter — Nominal, D	Diameter — Effective *	Standard number of threads per inch	Long diameter, I, or diameter across corners — Hexagon	Long diameter, I, or diameter across corners — Square	Short diameter of hexagon and square, or width across, J	Depth of nut, H	Depth of bolt head, K
$\frac{1}{4}$	.185	20	$\frac{9}{16}$	$\frac{23}{32}$	$\frac{1}{2}$	$\frac{1}{4}$	$\frac{1}{4}$
$\frac{5}{16}$	.240	18	$\frac{11}{16}$	$\frac{27}{32}$	$\frac{19}{32}$	$\frac{5}{16}$	$\frac{19}{64}$
$\frac{3}{8}$	.294	16	$\frac{13}{16}$	$\frac{31}{32}$	$\frac{11}{16}$	$\frac{3}{8}$	$\frac{11}{32}$
$\frac{7}{16}$	.345	14	$\frac{29}{32}$	$1\frac{3}{32}$	$\frac{25}{32}$	$\frac{7}{16}$	$\frac{25}{64}$
$\frac{1}{2}$	.400	13	1	$1\frac{1}{4}$	$\frac{7}{8}$	$\frac{1}{2}$	$\frac{7}{16}$
$\frac{9}{16}$	.454	12	$1\frac{1}{8}$	$1\frac{3}{8}$	$\frac{31}{32}$	$\frac{9}{16}$	$\frac{31}{64}$
$\frac{5}{8}$	.507	11	$1\frac{7}{32}$	$1\frac{1}{2}$	$1\frac{1}{16}$	$\frac{5}{8}$	$\frac{17}{32}$
$\frac{3}{4}$	.620	10	$1\frac{7}{16}$	$1\frac{3}{4}$	$1\frac{1}{4}$	$\frac{3}{4}$	$\frac{5}{8}$
$\frac{7}{8}$	.731	9	$1\frac{21}{32}$	$2\frac{1}{16}$	$1\frac{7}{16}$	$\frac{7}{8}$	$\frac{23}{32}$
1	.837	8	$1\frac{7}{8}$	$2\frac{5}{16}$	$1\frac{5}{8}$	1	$\frac{13}{16}$
$1\frac{1}{8}$	.940	7	$2\frac{3}{32}$	$2\frac{9}{16}$	$1\frac{13}{16}$	$1\frac{1}{8}$	$\frac{29}{32}$
$1\frac{1}{4}$	1.065	7	$2\frac{5}{16}$	$2\frac{27}{32}$	2	$1\frac{1}{4}$	1
$1\frac{3}{8}$	1.160	6	$2\frac{17}{32}$	$3\frac{3}{32}$	$2\frac{3}{16}$	$1\frac{3}{8}$	$1\frac{3}{32}$
$1\frac{1}{2}$	1.284	6	$2\frac{3}{4}$	$3\frac{11}{32}$	$2\frac{3}{8}$	$1\frac{1}{2}$	$1\frac{3}{16}$
$1\frac{5}{8}$	1.389	$5\frac{1}{2}$	$2\frac{31}{32}$	$3\frac{5}{8}$	$2\frac{9}{16}$	$1\frac{5}{8}$	$1\frac{9}{32}$
$1\frac{3}{4}$	1.491	5	$3\frac{3}{16}$	$3\frac{7}{8}$	$2\frac{3}{4}$	$1\frac{3}{4}$	$1\frac{3}{8}$
$1\frac{7}{8}$	1.616	5	$3\frac{13}{32}$	$4\frac{5}{32}$	$2\frac{15}{16}$	$1\frac{7}{8}$	$1\frac{15}{32}$
2	1.712	$4\frac{1}{2}$	$3\frac{5}{8}$	$4\frac{13}{32}$	$3\frac{1}{8}$	2	$1\frac{9}{16}$
$2\frac{1}{4}$	1.962	$4\frac{1}{2}$	$4\frac{1}{16}$	$4\frac{15}{16}$	$3\frac{1}{2}$	$2\frac{1}{4}$	$1\frac{3}{4}$
$2\frac{1}{2}$	2.176	4	$4\frac{15}{32}$	$5\frac{15}{32}$	$3\frac{7}{8}$	$2\frac{1}{2}$	$1\frac{15}{16}$
$2\frac{3}{4}$	2.426	4	$4\frac{29}{32}$	6	$4\frac{1}{4}$	$2\frac{3}{4}$	$2\frac{1}{8}$
3	2.629	$3\frac{1}{2}$	$5\frac{11}{32}$	$6\frac{17}{32}$	$4\frac{5}{8}$	3	$2\frac{5}{16}$
$3\frac{1}{4}$	2.879	$3\frac{1}{2}$	$5\frac{25}{32}$	$7\frac{1}{16}$	5	$3\frac{1}{4}$	$2\frac{1}{2}$
$3\frac{1}{2}$	3.100	$3\frac{1}{2}$	$6\frac{7}{32}$	$7\frac{19}{32}$	$5\frac{3}{8}$	$3\frac{1}{2}$	$2\frac{11}{16}$
$3\frac{3}{4}$	3.317	3	$6\frac{5}{8}$	$8\frac{1}{4}$	$5\frac{3}{4}$	$3\frac{3}{4}$	$2\frac{7}{8}$
..	3.567	3	$7\frac{1}{16}$	$8\frac{21}{32}$	$6\frac{1}{8}$	4	$3\frac{1}{16}$
$4\frac{1}{4}$	3.798	$2\frac{7}{8}$	$7\frac{1}{2}$	$9\frac{3}{16}$	$6\frac{1}{2}$	$4\frac{1}{4}$	$3\frac{1}{4}$
$4\frac{1}{2}$	4.028	$2\frac{3}{4}$	$7\frac{15}{16}$	$9\frac{23}{32}$	$6\frac{7}{8}$	$4\frac{1}{2}$	$3\frac{7}{16}$
$4\frac{3}{4}$	4.256	$2\frac{5}{8}$	$8\frac{3}{8}$	$10\frac{1}{4}$	$7\frac{1}{4}$	$4\frac{3}{4}$	$3\frac{5}{8}$
5	4.480	$2\frac{1}{2}$	$8\frac{13}{16}$	$10\frac{25}{32}$	$7\frac{5}{8}$	5	$3\frac{13}{16}$
$5\frac{1}{4}$	4.730	$2\frac{1}{2}$	$9\frac{1}{4}$	$11\frac{5}{16}$	8	$5\frac{1}{4}$	4
$5\frac{1}{2}$	4.953	$2\frac{3}{8}$	$9\frac{11}{16}$	$11\frac{27}{32}$	$8\frac{3}{8}$	$5\frac{1}{2}$	$4\frac{3}{16}$
$5\frac{3}{4}$	5.203	$2\frac{3}{8}$	$10\frac{3}{32}$	$12\frac{3}{8}$	$8\frac{3}{4}$	$5\frac{3}{4}$	$4\frac{3}{8}$
6	5.423	$2\frac{1}{4}$	$10\frac{17}{32}$	$12\frac{29}{32}$	$9\frac{1}{8}$	6	$4\frac{9}{16}$

* Diameter at the root of the thread.

recommending its use and doing all in their power to further its universal adoption.

The third form, Fig. 210, is the English, or Whitworth thread, which is adopted by some of the prominent bolt makers, by some influential private firms, as R. Hoe & Co., of New York, and by some railroads. The sides of the thread are at an angle of fifty-five degrees, the depth of the thread is divided off into six equal parts, and with a radius of one of these parts a circle is described, cutting off one of the parts at the top and at the bottom, and giving to the top and bottom a rounded form.

The foregoing table, in conjunction with Fig. 211, explains the United States standard sizes for bolts and nuts and the pitches of the threads.

Turning Up Bolts.

I want to give you a couple of hints that will be found quite acceptable in country shops where bolts are turned up. The first is to use a dog, fastened to the face plate as in Fig. 212 of the accompanying engravings. This saves screwing and unscrewing a loose dog every time. The second is to bend all cutting-off and facing tools as in Fig. 213, so that they will well clear the dog.

These points may not be new to some, but I think they will be found as useful to others as they were to me.—*By* F. J. L.

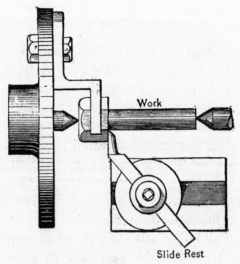

Turning Up Bolts by the Method of "F. J. L." Fig. 212—Showing the Dog Fastened to the Face Plate.

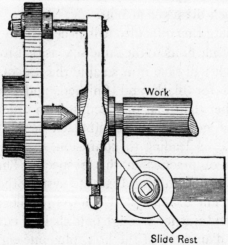

Fig. 213—Showing the Method of Bending and Facing the Cut-Off Tools.

Sizes of Bolt Heads.

In determining the sizes of bolt heads we have the following to consider : So far as convenience in the use of the bolts is concerned, it is desirable to have the diameter across the flats of the heads the same for those left black as forged, as for those machine-finished, so that one solid wrench will fit all the heads, whether black or finished, of a given diameter of bolt.   But in this case bolts that are to have their heads machine-finished must be forged larger, to allow for the metal cut away in finishing the same.

Hence, if all bolt heads for a given diameter of bolt were forged to the size necessary to allow for this finishing, those not finished will be larger than those finished, and two sizes of solid wrenches will be necessary for each diameter of bolt.

To obviate this difficulty it is necessary to forge the heads of black bolts to the same size as that for finished bolts, which will save iron, enable the use of one size of wrench for black and finished, and involve no trouble other than that of specifying in ordering bolts whether the heads are to be left black or finished. It is unfortunate, as leading to confusion, that there is no uniformity of practice in this respect. Thus in the " Sellers" or " Franklin" Institute system the rule is as follows : " The distance between the parallel sides of a bolt head and nut for a rough bolt shall be equal to one and a half diameters of the bolt, plus one-eighth of an inch. The thickness of the head for a rough bolt shall be equal to one-half the distance between its parallel sides. The thickness of the nut shall be equal to the diameter of the bolt. The thickness of the head for a finished bolt shall be equal to the thickness of the nut. The distance between the parallel sides of a bolt head and nut, and the thickness of the nut, shall be one-sixteenth of an inch less for finished work than for rough."

The United States Navy Department, which adopted this Sellers system so far as the pitches, angles, shape of bolt thread and diameter of finished bolt heads is concerned, varied from it by adopting the system of making the standard for black or rough bolt heads of the same size as those for finished heads, and this is undoubtedly the most convenient for use.—*By* R. J.

An Apparatus for Making Rings.

A simple and convenient apparatus for making small rings in lots can be made of two and one-half inch gas pipe, as shown at *A* in Fig. 214, with a slot at *F*, a collar at *G*. A hole is made in the bench at *B*, Fig. 215, to admit the end of the pipe. A post *E*, with a slot large enough to admit the pipe, is placed just outside the collar *G*, and a brace *C* is nailed on the post and bench to hold the pipe against the bench, A pin *D* is put through the post above the pipe to prevent it being lifted out while in operation.

To use the apparatus proceed as follows : Heat one
end of the bar and loosen it down about one inch,
forming a hook, place the hook in the slot *F*, let one

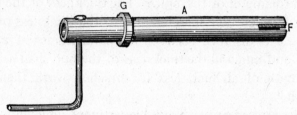

An Apparatus for Making Rings.   Fig. 214—Showing the Pipe Used.

man turn the crank while another leans on the bar near
the pipe.   The bar is wound into a coil, which can be
taken off the pipe by withdrawing the pin *D* and lift-

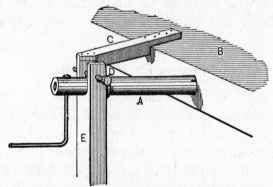

Fig. 215—Showing the Apparatus Ready for Use.

ing out the pipe.   Place the coil diagonally across the
point of your shears, and every clip will give you a
ring.   The rings can be made larger or smaller by cut-

ting them with the gap more or less open.   They will
be cut scarfed ready for welding, and a few light blows
will bring the nicks together.   One heat alone is
enough to weld and finish up.

To Make Rings Without a Weld.

Steel rings without a weld have become a staple article of manufacture.

One method of making these rings may be described by taking as an illustration a ring twelve inches
in diameter, two and one-half inches wide across the
face and one and one-eighth inches thick.   This will
answer all purposes for description, for although, if it

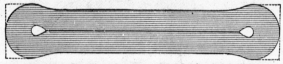

Fig. 216—Showing the First Steps in the Making of Solid Steel Rings.

were to be a milling cutter, the thickness would, of
course, be much greater in proportion to the width of
face, yet the operations in forging would be the same.

In making this ring from the solid stock we propose
to take a piece of suitable size and length, punch a hole
in cach end, split the piece from hole to hole, open out
the split, and hammer up the sides and ends, until the
stock in the ring is of the right size and shape, and the
diameter is that which is required.   A representation
of this bar, after the ends are punched, is given in Fig.
216.

The piece is then "upset" on each end enough to make it half an inch thicker, for two and one-half inches back ; the holes are punched, either with a five-eighths inch pear-shaped, or a rough punch, one and three-eighths inch from the ends, and the corners are then cut.

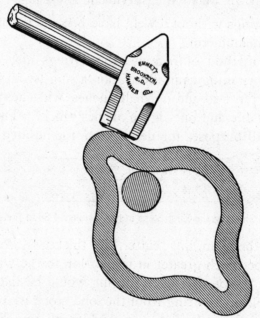

Fig. 217—Showing the Method of Knocking Short Crooks Out of a Ring.

The next thing to be done is to split it, which is done by marking it through the center with a straight line when it is cold enough to use a cold chisel, and then heating it and cutting half way through on each side. The more nicely this is done, the less trouble it

will be to work the sides.   A good, but not a regular
heat is then taken all over, to open it.   If the ends are
much longer than the sides are thick they give unnecessary trouble in opening.   In this case they should
not exceed one and one-eighth inches.   All that is
wanted of the length is to get stock to fill up the lank-
ness caused by changing the punched circle of five-

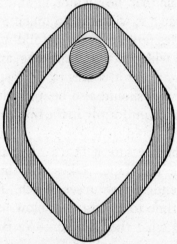

Fig. 218—Showing How the Ring is Bent to Avoid Short Crooks.

eighths of an inch to the full circle of the ring.   When
it is opened out to the shape shown in Fig. 217 by
driving larger pins into it successively over holes in the
swage block, it can be got on the horn of the anvil,
and a ten-pound sledge brought to bear to knock out
the short crooks, which are liable to get in if the piece
does not have just the right kind of a heat on it, when

it is opened out. If it is properly heated, which will be when it is the hottest at each extreme end, it can be made to open out as shown in Fig. 218. There will be much less trouble in finishing a piece which is thus opened.

There will be a tendency to upset and get smaller if the ring is hammered on the outside with too light a sledge, while neither heavy nor light blows, if struck with a heavy sledge, will tend so much to produce this effect. It is desirable to have a solid mandrel of the proper size on which to round the ring, and this is especially necessary when it comes to the last and finishing heat. A furnace should also be provided for heating which will heat it uniformly in the finishing up process; for if one side is cold, it is not easy to stretch the other side against the pressure it bears. In hammering on a solid mandrel, the taper takes up the stretch and hinders the tendency to upset, which, if not counteracted, causes time to be lost and blows spent without accomplishing what they should.—*By* B. F. SPALDING.

How I Made a Cast-Steel Cylinder Ring.

The ring when finished was of the following dimensions: diameter, seven inches; width, one and three-eighths inch; thickness, one-fourth of an inch. The only steel I had was a piece of one and three-fourths inch square. I first split about five inches, then opened it with mandrels until I could get it on the horn of the anvil. I next drew the end until I got it round, and then drew it to the proper size. It was nearly two inches wide when finished, and that gave plenty of room to chuck in the lathe. I next turned it to its proper

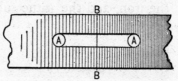

Fig. 219—Making a Cast-Steel Cylinder Ring by the Method of "Dot."

size, and had yet to cut the slot and to cut the steel in two as shown at the dotted lines Fig. 219. I first drilled two one-fourth inch holes as at *A*, and then with a hack saw I cut from one hole to the other, first filing down one side. To get the saw blade in after finishing the slot I cut across as shown at the dotted lines *B*. I sprung it to place carefully without tempering and found it had enough spring to come back to its original position.—*By* Dot.

A Device for Making Rings.

The accompanying illustration, Fig. 220, represents a

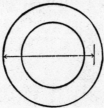

Fig. 220—"A. L. D.'s" Device for Making Rings to Measure.

device of mine for making a ring the exact size of any

I already have.   I measure from one center of the iron to the opposite outside as shown in the cut, and multiply this measurement by three.   This will give the length to cut the iron, and the same rule is good for all sizes.—*By* A. L. D.

CHAPTER VIII.

WORKING STEEL. WELDING. CASE HARDENING.

Steel Work.

In making the cutters which are used in cutting out from leather the various regular and irregular pieces which are used in making boots and shoes, suspender ends, and many other things, the stock used is sometimes like that in a scythe, in having a part of it composed of iron, but while the steel of a scythe is preferably laid with iron on each side, it is better for that

Steel Work. Fig. 221—Sectional View of Cutter Stock for Dies.

used for these cutters to extend up on one side, as shown in section in Fig. 221 of the accompanying engravings.

This stock is bent and formed in such a manner that the edge, which is on the inner side, is exactly of the shape which is to be cut out. The customer gives the cutter-maker a pattern of just the size and shape wanted, and expects that the piece which the cutter cuts out will be exactly like it,

Let us suppose, for the purpose of illustration, that the pattern is the sole of a slipper, Fig. 222.

As the sole is cut out in one piece, the length of stock required for the cutter is found by measuring around the outline of the pattern with a flexible rule and allowing, over this, four times the thickness of the thick part of the stock.   The ends are scarfed, and it is then lightly heated and bent around, as most convenient, in a rough and ready fashion to some form, so as to bring the weld at the heel.   The scarfs are fitted, and when a good borax heat has been taken, it is

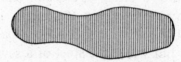

Fig. 222—Showing the Shape of the Inside of a Cutting Die.

brought out on the horn, and the first blow given to it is to weld the edge.   It is right here that the success of the whole operation is involved.   If the edge is not perfectly welded, the tool is absolutely worthless, for the edge is the part to which all the rest of the tool is auxiliary.   At first thought it would seem that the stock was too thin on the edge to get a good weld there, but this is not found to be the case, and there is little attempt made to thicken it up before welding. As it is thin it must weld, if it welds at all, just where the weld is needed; while if it were thicker, and there was considerable stock left on it to be ground, or filed off, it might occur that the very part taken off would be all that was welded, and when it was removed there would then remain an unwelded edge. The expedient of using iron filings in welding is not usual with skilled workmen. After the edge is thoroughly secure, the cutter is skillfully formed into shape; care being taken to keep the opening, on the edge side, considerably smaller than on the back, so that when the pieces are cut out, they will drop through easily. There is

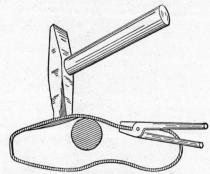

Fig. 223—Showing How the Edge is Drawn In.

no trouble about "drawing in" the edge to make it smaller than the back. It is done by letting the piece rest on the horn and then hammering the edge side down just beyond where it rests, as in Fig. 223. Another way is to hold the piece so that it rests on the horn a little back of the edge, and then the edge can be lightly hammered down as in Fig. 224. The first way is the best, but not the easiest. The last is apt to concave the piece too much near the edge, a fault that shows itself when the tool is somewhat worn. A very little practice will enable the workman to do the job with facility, either way, after he once tries it and understands the theory. It is necessary to be sure to have the stock long enough to commence with, in order that the back may be large enough to let the piece go easily through after it is cut.

When the cutters are formed, they are fitted with

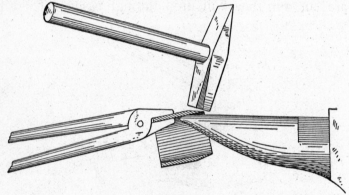

Fig. 224—Showing Another Method of Drawing In the Edge.

iron backs. These are sometimes made to be used by hand with a blow, and sometimes by power with a press. Fig. 225 shows a back for a hand cutter. It will be seen that it is a job which requires good iron. A piece of round iron for the handle is jump-welded on to a piece of flat iron, from which the spider is afterwards forged and cut out. It rests on the top edge of the cutter, and ears come over and down the side and are fastened through with rivets, as shown in the figure.

The cutter is cleaned and finished inside before it is hardened.   The hardening is done in oil, and then the temper is evenly drawn.   The handle may then be riveted on and the edge may be nicely ground and finished afterward.   There is no unnecessary finish put upon the rest of the tool.   It simply receives a coat of paint.

Where is the cutting edge of the cutter?   Is it on

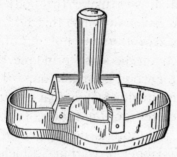

Fig. 225—Showing the Attachment of the Driving Shank to a Cutting Die.

the surface of the tooth, or is it buried some distance below the surface?

It is certainly on the surface of the teeth when you begin to use it, but the stock which will form the edge after the first edge is ground away is then buried beneath the surface, but that will not be the case if you do not grind off the face, but sharpen by grinding off from the tops of the teeth ; then the faces of the teeth which remove the stock you are operating upon will always be hard.

It is a fact that if a goodly quality of wrought iron

is used, a good cutting edge can be got by case hardening.

What is a case-hardened edge, in fact, but blister steel, made by the same process as that by which the carbon is best introduced into all really good blister steel ?

The method of making large cutters which is most generally adopted, is to make the body of the cutter of either iron or steel, and into this body cut gains or recesses for the reception and holding of inserted teeth or cutters, much on the same principle that the large rotary cutters for wood are made on. The advantage of making them in this way is that the frame or foundation of the cutter does not have to be heated and hardened, and therefore is not subjected to the strain or liable to the danger of warping, which inevitably accompanies this operation.

There is, however, another way of making large cutters which I would not advise the timid or unskillful workman to attempt. This does not possess the advantage of requiring no heating to harden the teeth, and yet is considered by some as a very good way of making such tools. This method is to make a steel band of sufficient size to cut the teeth in and also give stock to support them. This toothed ring is sometimes tightly fitted and fastened to an iron center, as shown in Fig. 226, and sometimes an iron center is welded inside to it. It is sometimes asserted that a better method than this is to weld a steel band on the iron center, as it is closed around it, and finally to bring the band together and weld it either with a cross V, a butt, or a scarf weld; but to this method there is this objection, that it is a very risky business to make a cutting tooth, or the root or edge of a tooth, in a weld of any kind, and then undertake to harden it.

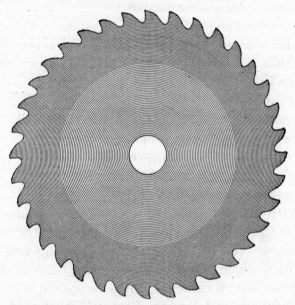

Fig. 226—Showing a Twelve-Inch Solid Steel Ring with Iron Center.

It appears to be much the safest way to make rings, in which teeth are to be cut, of solid steel; for there being then no weld where the teeth are to be, all of that fertile source of danger vanishes at once; and if it is decided to fit and fasten the centers without welding them, there is nothing to be apprehended, except the usual uncertainties of hardening. To make these as few and slight as possible, the steel must be heated to a low degree such as will barely suffice to harden it, in order that the change in the temperature which takes place suddenly when it is quenched may be no more than will answer the purpose, for from this sudden change much of the danger arises. Now it is well known that steel which has a large percentage of carbon will harden at less heat than that which has less, and therefore it is advisable that when it is to be hardened, it should be high in carbon. Make sure that nothing has been omitted that should be done before the piece is hardened. The hole should be bored out ; three small half-round key seats should be cut under the centers of three teeth ; the spaces between the teeth should be left rounding on the bottom, as sharp corners and even file scratches sometimes start cracks ; the sides should be trued up to the proper thickness. Having made sure that nothing has been forgotten which will necessitate taking the temper out after the cutter is hardened, it may be packed in an iron box with charred leather, from which all pieces of metal have been removed—I have known zinc shoe nails, remaining in the leather, to melt and get on the work and prevent it from hardening. The box should then be well covered to prevent the carbon from getting out, and also to keep the air from getting in. The box may then be put into a charcoal fire, or into a furnace, and kept at a red heat for three or four hours. The piece may then be taken out. It should be of a heat that will look red in the shade, but not in the sun, and should be at once immersed in clean soft water, cool, not cold, 55° to 70° F. It should be held there as long as a tremor is felt. Immediately upon the cessation of this, it may be quickly removed to a vessel of oil of sufficient capacity to prevent the heat from rising, and there it should remain until the next morning. It should then be found hard, and unaltered in shape and sound. It may be heated to start the temper and relieve the tension, as the case may require, either as hot as boiling water, or it may be, nearly to a straw color, and while it is thus expanded it should be put in the right place upon the iron center, which if made of the correct size it will shrink tightly upon without being strained.—*By* B. F. SPALDING.

The Art of Welding.

I have some remarks to offer on the subject of welding iron and steel which may not be entirely devoid of interest to your readers. The operation of welding is required in almost every piece of iron work used in the construction of wagons, cars, bridges, dwellings, etc. More than half of the blacksmith's daily labor is expended on the work of welding. Hence the importance of thoroughly understanding this branch of the business, and of performing the operation in a workmanlike manner. Upon the character of the welding depends, in a great measure, the wear and strength of iron work. The art of welding is one attended with some difficulties. It is acquired only by years of careful study and practical experience. It is not so easy to master as the superficial observer might suppose. The successful smith puts into his work an amount of care and judgment that would hardly be expected by those who are not practically familiar with the trade. Many smiths are very careless in welding, and the bad work they produce frequently results not only in loss to their employers, but in damage to reputation. The difficulties in producing solid welds are many, and should be carefully studied by all who desire to succeed at their trade. A perfect weld cannot be made if any foreign matter comes between the two parts to be united. Hence the necessity of care in this direction. It costs no more in the way of fire to heat two pieces of iron or steel, so as to make a perfect weld, than to make a poor one, an argument which should convince everyone of the economy of good work. The losses attending poor work of this kind are to be figured up under several heads. Repairing is necessary. This causes loss of time in returning the work to the shop. The defective weld may have caused an accident. Cases have occurred in which persons have been killed by reason of poor welding. In returning imperfect irons for repair, freight or express charges are involved. After they reach the shop time is required in taking them apart and again in putting together after the poor work has been made good. Still other items might be enumerated, but enough has been presented for illustration. A defective weld is an expensive piece of injustice, and always results in pecuniary loss to the employer, and a loss of reputation to the individual smith. There is no valid excuse for a smith having broken irons with bad welds coming back for repairs in any considerable numbers.

If the weld is worth making at all it is worth making well. I admit that there are exceptions in welding as in everything else, and that a good smith in some cases may make a weld which he thinks is solid, but which is not. There is no excuse, however, for a smith to have broken irons coming back to him continually. Such a condition of affairs is traceable only to carelessness. Much of the defective work is due to over heating or not heating enough. Still other is due to carelessness in knocking the cinders from the irons before placing them together. Another difficulty is working with a green or new fire, or a fire full of cinders and dirt. In order to make a clean and solid weld, the cinders, which naturally accumulate while the irons are being heated, must always be knocked from them before they are placed together. A smith should not use a tool of any kind on his irons after they are welded, until he has again cleaned the scale from them. No good smith will try to weld his irons if his fire is not in proper shape. It always pays in the end to have a clean and well coked fire before undertaking to weld.

In carriage and wagon blacksmithing the smith's ability is often tried to its full extent. He has not simply one brand of iron and steel to work, but a variety of brands. Experience, however, if he pays strict attention to his business, will soon teach him the nature of the various irons and steels with which he works, so that in time there will be no difficulty in accomplishing the desired results, whatever may be the material in hand. One difficulty which new beginners encounter is the tendency to keep pulling the irons in and out of the fire to see if they are hot enough. This alone is sufficient to insure a bad weld. Continuous poking around in the fire causes the irons to accumulate dirt and cinder, while it also tears the fire to pieces. Carelessness in matters of this kind frequently results in no hot coal around the irons, and in some cases with the bare blast striking the irons. A good welding heat is only obtained by the greatest care in little details of this kind. The smith must keep his irons between hot coals continuously while obtaining a weld heat. By so doing he can get a clean and good job ; otherwise, he will fail.—*By* H. R. H.

Getting a Welding Heat.

I would like to tell the readers after having worked at my trade eleven years, and from my experience, I am able to say that success in blacksmithing depends chiefly on close observation, hard work, forethought and the ability to profit by the mistakes of others.

As regards the color of iron at a welding heat, that depends on the quality of the iron and coal employed. In our shop we use Piedmont coal, and when we get a fresh supply we cannot always tell when our iron is at welding heat by looking at the color, and so we often make mistakes. The best way to find out if your iron is hot enough is to take a small (say three-eighths) rod and feel the iron with it. When it is right for welding you can pick it off very easily with the rod.—*By* Novis Homo.

Case Hardening.

PLAN I.

Case hardening consists in the conversion of the surface of wrought iron into steel. The depth to which this conversion takes place ranges from about one sixty-fourth to one thirty-second of an inch. The simplest method of case hardening is to heat the work to a red heat and apply powdered prussiate of potash to the surface. In this process the secret of success lies in crushing the potash to fine powder, rubbing it well upon the work, so that it fuses and runs freely over the work, when the latter must be quenched in cold water.

It is essential that the potash should fuse and run

freely, and to assist this a spoon-shaped piece of iron is often used, the concave side to convey the prussiate of potash and the convex side to rub it upon the work. If by the time the potash fuses the work has reduced to too low a heat to harden, it should be placed again in the fire, the blast being turned off, and worked over and over till a light blood-red heat is secured, and then be quenched in quite cold water.

Work case hardened by this process has a very hard surface indeed, and appears of a frosted white color, resisting the most severe file test.   Since, however, it is an expensive process, and is unsuitable when the article is large and of irregular form, what is termed box hardening is employed.   This consists in packing the articles in a box, inclosing the case-hardening materials.   The box is made air-tight by having its seams well luted with fire clay.   The case-hardening material most commonly used is bone dust, a layer of which is first spread over the bottom of the box.   A layer of the pieces to be hardened is then placed in the box, care being taken to so place them that when the bone dust is consumed the weight of the uppermost pieces will not be likely to bend the pieces below them, or to bend of their own weight ; and it follows that the heaviest pieces should be placed in the bottom of the box.

A better material, however, is composed of leather and hoof, cut into pieces of about an inch in size, adding three layers of salt ; the proportions being about four pounds of salt to twenty pounds of leather and fifteen pounds of hoofs, adding about one gallon of urine after the box is packed. The box lid should be fastened down and well luted with fire clay. It is then placed in a furnace and maintained at a red heat for about twelve hours, when the articles are taken out and quickly immersed in water, care being taken to put them in the water endways to avoid warping them.

Articles to be case hardened in the above manner should have pieces of sheet iron fitted in them in all parts where they are required to fit well and are difficult to bend when cold. Suppose, for instance, it is a quadrant for a link motion ; fit into the slot where the die works a piece of sheet iron (say one-fourth inch thick) at each end of the slot, and two other places at equi-distant places in the slot, leaving on the pieces a projection to prevent them from falling through the slot. In packing the quadrant in the box, place it so that the sheet-iron pieces will have their projections uppermost ; then, in taking the quadrant out of the box, handle it carefully, and the pieces of iron will remain where they were placed and prevent the quadrant from warping in cooling or while in the box (from the pressure of the pieces of work placed above it).

Work that is thoroughly box case-hardened has a frosted white appearance, and the fanciful colors sometimes apparent are proof that the case hardening has not been carried to the maximum degree. These colors are produced by placing charcoal in the box and heating to a lesser degree.

Sheehan's patent process for box case-hardening, which is considered a very good one, is thus described by the inventor.

DIRECTIONS TO MAKE AND USE SHEEHAN'S PATENT PROCESS FOR STEELIFYING IRON.

No. 1 is common salt.
No. 2 is sal soda.
No. 3 is charcoal pulverized.
No. 4 is black oxide of manganese.
No. 5 is common black rosin.
No. 6 is raw limestone (not burned).

Take of No. 1, forty-five pounds, and of No. 2, twelve pounds. Pulverize fine and dissolve in as much water as will dissolve it, and no more—say fourteen gallons of water in a tight barrel—and let it be well dissolved before using it.

Then take three bushels of No. 3, hardwood charcoal broken small and sifted through a No. 4 sieve. Put the charcoal in a wooden or iron box of suitable size made water-tight.

Next take of No. 4, five pounds, and of No. 5, five pounds, the rosin pulverized very fine. Mix thoroughly No. 4 and No. 5 with the charcoal in your box.

Then take of the liquid made by dissolving No. 1 and No. 2 in a barrel as stated, and thoroughly wet the charcoal with the whole of said liquid and mix well.

The charcoal compound is now ready for use.

A suitable box of wrought or cast iron (wrought iron is preferable) should next be provided, large enough for the work intended to be steelified.

Now take No. 6, raw limestone broken small (about the size of peas), and put a layer of the broken limestone, about one and one-half inch thick, in the bottom of the box. A plate of sheet iron one-tenth of an inch in thickness is peforated with one-fourth inch holes one inch apart. Let this plate drop loose on the limestone inside the box. Place a layer of the charcoal compound, two inches thick, on the top of said peforated plate. Then put a layer of the work intended to be steelified on the layer of charcoal compound, and alternate layers of iron and of the compound until the box is full, taking care to finish with a thick layer of compound on the top of the box. Care should also be taken not to let the work in the box come in contact with the sides or ends of the box. Place a suitable cover on the box and lute it with fire-clay or yellow mud. The cover should have a one-fourth inch hole in it to permit the steam to escape while heating.

The box should now be put in an open fire or furnace (furnace preferred), and subjected to a strong heat for five to ten hours, according to the size of the box and the bulk of iron to be steelified. Remove the pieces from the box one by one and clean with a broom, taking care not to waste the residue, after which chill in a sufficient body of clear, cold water and there will be a uniform coat of actual steel on the entire surface of the work to the depth of one-sixteenth or one-eighth of an inch, according to the time it is left in the fire. The longer it is left in the fire the deeper will be the coat of steel.

Then remove the residue that remains in the box, and cool with the liquid of No. 1 and No. 2, made for the purpose with twenty gallons of water, instead of fourteen gallons, as first used with the charcoal compound.

The residue must be cooled off while it is hot, on a piece of sheet iron or an iron box made for the purpose. Turn the residue into the supply box, and it will be ready for use again. The more it is used, the better and stronger it will be for future work.

There is nothing to be renewed for each batch of work but the limestone, and that, after each job, will be good burned lime.

This process does not spring nor scale the work, nor make it brittle, as the old method of case hardening does. That has been proved.—*By* JOSHUA ROSE, M. E.

Case Hardening.

PLAN 2.

One of the prime requirements in case hardening is, that the article shall be well polished. If the iron is not quite sound, or shows ash holes, it is hammered over and polished again. The finer the polish which is imparted to the surface, the better will be the results in case hardening. The articles are next imbedded in coarse charcoal powder in a wrought-iron box, which should be air-tight. Sometimes, instead of a wrought-iron box, a pipe is employed. This is really preferable, because it can be turned, thus allowing the heat to be applied more uniformly. After the articles have thus been prepared, the box or pipe is exposed for some twenty-four hours to a gentle cherry-red heat. Sometimes a flue steam boiler is used for this purpose, or the heat may be obtained in any other place where a fire is maintained uniformly. By exposing the articles to the heat for the period named, a hard surface of about one-eighth of an inch in depth is obtained. If so much time cannot be given to the operation, or if deep hardening is not required, the articles may be imbedded in animal charcoal, or in a mixture of animal charcoal and wood charcoal, and exposed for a much less period of time. Four or five hours will be found sufficient to make a good surface of steel. It is frequently necessary to case harden a single article, which necessitates a very different operation from that which we have just been describing.

The charcoal is finely pulverized and mixed into a paste with a saturated solution of salt. The tool, whatever it may be, is then well covered with this paste and dried. Over the paste is laid a coating of clay moistened with salt water, which is also gently dried. The article thus prepared is now exposed to a gradually increasing heat, until it is brought to a bright red, but not beyond it. This heat will be found sufficient to give a fine surface to small objects. In all cases the article is plunged in cold water, when it has been heated the proper time and up to the proper degree.

While the operation of case hardening as we have described it is very simple, it is not so easy a matter to select the qualities of iron by which the best results will be obtained. If the iron is of coarse fiber, the hardened and polished surface will be unsound; if the iron is impure, it will be brittle after being hardened. The best iron for the purpose is one of very fine and close grain. The test by which its quality may be determined is as follows:

Heat a piece a little beyond the heat by which it is to be hardened and plunge it into cold water. If it retain its fiber and malleability after this test, and is free from ash holes, it is safe to conclude that it is entirely suitable for the purpose of case hardening.

CHAPTER IX.

TABLES OF IRON AND STEEL.

Table of Sizes of Irons of Different Forms Used by Carriage, Wagon and Sleigh Makers.

Twenty-five years ago the sizes of merchantable iron were limited in number, and it was necessary for the blacksmith to forge the greater portion. Ovals and half ovals were almost unknown; at the present time ovals, under the general heading, can be procured from regular stock, suited to most purposes. Half ovals are divided into two classes, the second being known as flat half ovals. Some of the sizes here given are not always procurable in the open market, but large manufacturers have no difficulty in procuring them at the mills when ordering in quantities.

FLAT.

$\frac{3}{8}$x$\frac{5}{8}$	$\frac{7}{8}$x$\frac{5}{8}$	$1\frac{1}{8}$x$\frac{3}{4}$	$1\frac{1}{2}$x$\frac{5}{8}$	$1\frac{3}{8}$x1	$1\frac{1}{2}$x1	2 x$\frac{1}{2}$	4 x$\frac{1}{2}$
$\frac{1}{2}$x$\frac{1}{4}$	1x$\frac{1}{4}$	$1\frac{1}{4}$x$\frac{7}{16}$	$1\frac{1}{4}$x1	$1\frac{1}{2}$x$\frac{1}{4}$	$1\frac{3}{4}$x$\frac{3}{8}$	$2\frac{1}{4}$x$\frac{3}{8}$	$4\frac{1}{4}$x$\frac{1}{2}$
$\frac{3}{4}$x$\frac{7}{16}$	1x$\frac{3}{8}$	$1\frac{1}{4}$x$\frac{5}{16}$	$1\frac{1}{4}$x$1\frac{1}{8}$	$1\frac{1}{2}$x$\frac{3}{8}$	$1\frac{3}{4}$x$\frac{1}{2}$	$2\frac{1}{2}$x$\frac{1}{2}$	$4\frac{1}{2}$x$\frac{5}{8}$
$\frac{3}{4}$x$\frac{1}{2}$	1x$\frac{1}{2}$	$1\frac{1}{4}$x$\frac{1}{2}$	$1\frac{3}{8}$x$\frac{5}{8}$	$1\frac{1}{2}$x$\frac{5}{8}$	$1\frac{3}{4}$x$\frac{3}{4}$	3 x$\frac{1}{2}$	
$\frac{7}{8}$x$\frac{1}{2}$	$1\frac{1}{8}$x$\frac{3}{8}$	$1\frac{1}{4}$x$\frac{3}{8}$	$1\frac{3}{8}$x$\frac{7}{16}$	$1\frac{1}{2}$x$\frac{7}{8}$	2 x$\frac{3}{8}$	$3\frac{1}{2}$x$\frac{1}{2}$	

SQUARE.

$\frac{1}{4}$	$\frac{3}{4}$	$\frac{9}{16}$	$1\frac{1}{4}$	$1\frac{3}{8}$	$1\frac{3}{4}$
$\frac{3}{8}$	$\frac{7}{8}$	1	$1\frac{5}{16}$	$1\frac{5}{8}$	2

ROUND.

$\frac{5}{16}$	$\frac{7}{16}$	$\frac{5}{8}$	$\frac{7}{8}$	$1\frac{1}{8}$	$1\frac{3}{4}$
$\frac{3}{8}$	$\frac{9}{16}$	$\frac{3}{4}$	1	$1\frac{1}{4}$	2

PRACTICAL BLACKSMITHING.

HALF ROUND.

$\frac{9}{16}x\frac{3}{8}$	$\frac{5}{8}x\frac{3}{8}$	$\frac{3}{4}x\frac{3}{8}$	$\frac{7}{8}x\frac{1}{2}$	$1x\frac{3}{8}$	$1\frac{1}{8}x\frac{5}{16}$	$1\frac{1}{4}x\frac{5}{8}$	$1\frac{5}{8}x\frac{7}{8}$	$1\frac{3}{4}x\frac{3}{4}$

OVAL.

$\frac{3}{8}x\frac{1}{4}$	$\frac{5}{8}x\frac{3}{8}$	$\frac{3}{4}x\frac{3}{8}$	$\frac{7}{8}x\frac{7}{16}$	$1\ x\frac{5}{8}$	$1\frac{3}{8}x\frac{7}{8}$
$\frac{5}{8}x\frac{5}{8}$	$\frac{5}{8}x\frac{7}{16}$	$\frac{3}{4}x\frac{7}{16}$	$\frac{7}{8}x\frac{1}{2}$	$1\ x\frac{3}{4}$	$1\frac{1}{2}x\frac{3}{4}$
$\frac{1}{2}x\frac{1}{4}$	$\frac{5}{8}x\frac{1}{2}$	$\frac{3}{4}x\frac{5}{16}$	$\frac{9}{16}x\frac{5}{16}$	$1\frac{1}{8}x1$	
$\frac{5}{8}x\frac{5}{16}$	$\frac{3}{4}x\frac{5}{16}$	$\frac{3}{4}x\frac{3}{8}$	$\frac{9}{16}x\frac{7}{16}$	$1\frac{1}{4}x\frac{5}{8}$	

HALF OVAL.

$\frac{5}{16}x\frac{3}{16}$	$\frac{7}{8}x\frac{3}{8}$	$1\frac{1}{2}x\frac{1}{4}$	$1\frac{1}{4}x\frac{3}{8}$	$1\frac{1}{4}x\frac{5}{8}$
$\frac{3}{8}x\frac{3}{8}$	$1\ x\frac{3}{16}$	$1\frac{1}{2}x\frac{3}{8}$	$1\frac{1}{4}x\frac{5}{8}$	$1\frac{1}{2}x\frac{3}{4}$
$\frac{5}{8}x\frac{1}{4}$	$1\ x\frac{5}{16}$	$1\frac{1}{2}x\frac{7}{16}$	$1\frac{3}{8}x\frac{7}{16}$	$1\frac{3}{4}x\frac{3}{4}$
$\frac{7}{8}x\frac{5}{16}$	$1\frac{3}{8}x\frac{3}{16}$	$1\frac{1}{2}x\frac{1}{4}$	$1\frac{1}{2}x\frac{1}{2}$	

BAND IRON.

$1x\frac{1}{8}$	$1x\frac{3}{16}$	$1\frac{1}{2}x\frac{3}{16}$	$1\frac{1}{4}x\frac{1}{8}$	$1\frac{1}{4}x\frac{3}{16}$	$2x\frac{3}{16}$	$2\frac{1}{8}x\frac{1}{8}$	$2\frac{1}{4}x\frac{3}{16}$	$2\frac{1}{4}x\frac{5}{16}$

SHEET IRON.

No. 10.	No. 12.	No. 14.

Table Exhibiting the Weight in Pounds of Square Bars, Wrought or Rolled, to each One Foot in Length.

Sizes of Cross Section in Inches.	Weight in Pounds.	Sizes of Cross Section in Inches.	Weight in Pounds.	Sizes of Cross Section in Inches.	Weight in Inches.
$\frac{1}{8}$	.053	1	3.380	$1\frac{7}{8}$	11.883
$\frac{1}{4}$	.211	$1\frac{1}{8}$	4.278	2	13.520
$\frac{3}{8}$	.475	$1\frac{1}{4}$	5.280	$2\frac{1}{8}$	15.263
$\frac{1}{2}$	.845	$1\frac{3}{8}$	6.390	$2\frac{1}{4}$	17.112
$\frac{5}{8}$	1.320	$1\frac{1}{2}$	7.640	$2\frac{1}{2}$	21.120
$\frac{3}{4}$	1.901	$1\frac{5}{8}$	8.926	3	30.416
$\frac{7}{8}$	2.588	$1\frac{3}{4}$	10.352		

Table Exhibiting the Weight in Pounds of Round Rolled Iron to each One Foot in Length.

Diameter in Inches.	Weight in Pounds.	Diameter in Inches.	Weight in Pounds.	Diameter in Inches.	Weight in Pounds.	Diameter in Inches.	Weight in Pounds.
$\frac{1}{8}$	.041	$\frac{3}{4}$	1.493	$1\frac{3}{8}$	5.019	2	10.616
$\frac{1}{4}$	.165	$\frac{7}{8}$	2.032	$1\frac{1}{2}$	5.972	$2\frac{1}{8}$	11.988
$\frac{3}{8}$	.373	1	2.654	$1\frac{5}{8}$	7.010	$2\frac{1}{4}$	13.440
$\frac{1}{2}$	.663	$1\frac{1}{8}$	3.360	$1\frac{3}{4}$	8.128	$2\frac{1}{2}$	16.688
$\frac{5}{8}$	1.043	$1\frac{1}{4}$	4.170	$1\frac{7}{8}$	9.333		

The weights in the tables above are for sizes divided by one-eighth. For proportions not specified, of one foot in length, of the form prescribed, multiply the weight in pounds of an equal length of square rolled iron of the same size, if the weight be sought of

Iron, round rolled, by 7855
Steel, square " " . . . 1.0064
" round " " 7904
Cast iron, square rolled, by . . 1.1401
" " round " " . . .7271

If the weight of a flat rolled or wrought bar is required, multiply the sectional area in inches by the length in feet, and that product, if the metal be

Wrought iron, by . . . 3.3795
Cast " " . . . 3.1287
Steel, " . . . 3.4

If the weight of a bar of steel is required, the

length of which is six feet, breadth two and one-fourth inches, thickness three-fourths of an inch (reduce fractions to decimals), and the statement will be

$$2.25 \times .75 \times 6 \times 3.4 = 34.435 \text{ lbs.}$$

Table of Sizes and Weight per Foot in Length of Iron for Tires.

Size.	Weight per Foot in Length.	Size.	Weight per Foot in Length.	Size.	Weight per Foot in Length.
⅝x⅛	.264	1⅜x¼	1.161	2 x¾	5.069
⅝x¼	.528	1⅜x⅜	1.742	2½x⅜	2.851
¾x⅛	.316	1⅜x½	2.323	2¼x½	3.802
¾x¼	.633	1½x⅜	1.901	2¼x⅝	4.752
¾x⅜	.950	1½x½	2.534	2¼x¾	5.703
⅞x⅛	.369	1½x⅝	3.168	2½x½	4.224
⅞x¼	.739	1½x¾	3.802	2½x⅝	5.280
⅞x⅜	1.108	1⅝x⅜	2.059	2½x¾	6.336
1 x⅛	.422	1⅝x½	2.746	2½x⅞	7.393
1 x¼	.845	1⅝x⅝	3.432	2¾x⅝	5.808
1 x⅜	1.267	1⅝x¾	4.119	2¾x¾	6.970
1 x½	1.690	1¾x⅜	2.218	2¾x⅞	8.132
1⅛x¼	.950	1¾x½	2.957	2¾x1	9.294
1⅛x⅜	1.425	1¾x⅝	3.696	3 x⅝	6.337
1⅛x½	1.901	1¾x¾	4.435	3 x¾	7.604
1¼x¼	1.056	2 x⅜	2.534	3 x⅞	8.871
1¼x⅜	1.584	2 x½	3.379	3 x1	10.139
1¼x½	2.112	2 x⅝	4.224		

To make a practical application of this table in its application to wheels, first ascertain the diameter of the wheel on the tread, and multiply that by 3.1416, that being the established ratio of the circumference to the diameter. For convenience, 3 1-7 is used, but where accuracy is desired the whole number and decimal is preferred to the whole number and fraction.

On this basis a wheel four feet in diameter will have a circumference of 12.566. The statement would be

$$4 \times 3.1416 = 12.566.$$

Another point to be considered is the addition of the thickness of the tire when determining the diameter; thus a four-foot wheel with a half-inch tire would have a diameter of four feet one inch. Light tires one-fourth of an inch thick and under should have one inch added to their length when that length is twelve feet, adding or decreasing in that ratio as the length is increased or diminished.

A light wheel four feet in diameter, tire three-fourths by one-eighth inch, would require three pounds and nine hundred and ninety-six one-thousandths; for convenience the weight of the one inch extra is added to the total of the weight of the actual measurement.

Statement: $12.566 \times .316 = 3.970 + .026 = 3.996$ pounds.

A wheel of like size, the tire one by one-half inch, would have a diameter of four feet and one inch and a circumference of fifteen and one hundred and seventy-three one-hundredths feet.

Statement: $4.83 \times 3.1416 = 15.173.$

The weight of the tire would be twenty-five pounds and sixty-four one-hundredths.

Statement: $15.173 \times 1.690 = 25.64.$

WEIGHT OF METALS IN PLATE.

The weight of a square foot one inch thick is, if of

Malleable iron, . . .	40.554 lbs.
Common plate, . . .	37.761 "
Cast iron, ...	37.546 "

Or for any other thickness, greater or less, in the same proportion. Thus a square foot of common plate one-eighth of an inch thick would be 4.720 pounds.

Six square feet of that thickness would weigh 28.32 pounds.

Statement: $37.761 \div 8 = 4.720 \times 6 = 28.32$.

Table of Carriage Bolts, Standard Sizes.

$\frac{1}{8}$, $\frac{3}{16}$ and $\frac{1}{4}$ Diameter.	$\frac{5}{16}$ Diameter.	$\frac{3}{8}$ Diameter.	$\frac{7}{16}$ Diameter.	$\frac{1}{2}$ Diameter.
Length.	Length.	Length.	Length.	Length.
1	1½	2	2	2
1¼	1¾	2¼	2¼	2½
1½	2	2½	2½	3
1¾	2¼	2¾	2¾	3½
2	2½	3	3	4
2¼	2¾	3¼	3½	4½
2½	3	3½	4	5
2¾	3¼	3¾	4½	5½
3	3½	4	5	6
3¼	3¾	4½	5½	6½
3½	4	5	6	7
3¾	4½	5½	6½	7½
4	5	6	7	8
4¼	5½	6½	7½	8½
4½	6	7	8	9
5	6½	7½	8½	9½
5½	7	8	9	10
6	7½	8½	9½	10½
6½	8	9	10	11
7	8½	9½	11	12
7½	9	10	12	14

Table of Tire Bolts, Standard Sizes.

$\frac{1}{8}$ and $\frac{3}{16}$ Diameter.	$\frac{1}{4}$ Diameter.	$\frac{5}{16}$ Diameter.	$\frac{3}{8}$ Diameter.	$\frac{7}{16}$ Diameter.
Length.	Length.	Length.	Length.	Length.
1	$1\frac{1}{4}$	$1\frac{1}{2}$	2	2
$1\frac{1}{4}$	$1\frac{1}{2}$	$1\frac{3}{4}$	$2\frac{1}{4}$	$2\frac{1}{4}$
$1\frac{1}{2}$	$1\frac{3}{4}$	2	$2\frac{1}{2}$	$2\frac{1}{2}$
$1\frac{3}{4}$	2	$2\frac{1}{4}$	$2\frac{3}{4}$	$2\frac{3}{4}$
2	$2\frac{1}{4}$	$2\frac{1}{2}$	3	3
$2\frac{1}{4}$	$2\frac{1}{2}$	$2\frac{3}{4}$	$3\frac{1}{2}$	$3\frac{1}{2}$
$2\frac{1}{2}$	$2\frac{3}{4}$	3	4	4
$2\frac{3}{4}$	3	$3\frac{1}{2}$	$4\frac{1}{2}$	$4\frac{1}{2}$
3	$3\frac{1}{4}$	4	5	5
$3\frac{1}{4}$	$3\frac{1}{2}$	$4\frac{1}{2}$	$5\frac{1}{2}$	$5\frac{1}{2}$
$3\frac{1}{2}$	4	5	6	6

END OF VOLUME IV.

INDEX.

ADVERTISEMENTS.

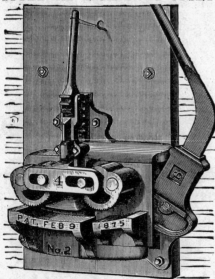

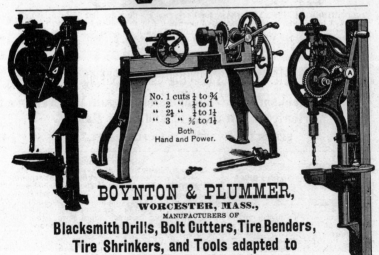

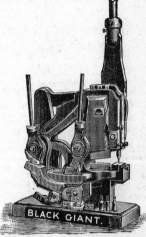

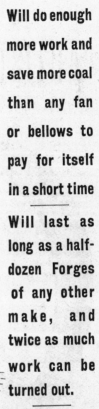

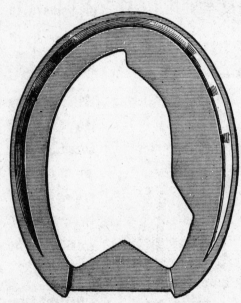

VOLUME I.

Practical Blacksmithing.

Is a new book compiled from practical articles which have appeared from time to time during the last few years in the columns of "THE BLACKSMITH AND WHEELWRIGHT."

Volume I. relates to Ancient Blacksmithing, and gives illustrations with descriptions of some ancient tools; tells how Hammers Should Be Made; gives Plans of Blacksmiths' Shops, and a variety of plans of Forges, and the best way to build Chimneys. Illustrations with descriptions of a great variety of Tongs, Hammers, Punches and Cold Chisels are given.

Two prize articles on Blackmiths' Tools, which have appeared in "THE BLACKSMITH AND WHEELWRIGHT," are printed in full.

There are five chapters in the book, each complete in itself.

Chapter 1 treats of Ancient and Modern Hammers. Chapter 2, Ancient Tools. Chapter 3, Chimneys, Forges, Fires, Shop Plans, Work Benches, etc. Chapter 4, Anvils and Anvil Tools. Chapter 5, Blacksmiths' Tools.

There is no book like it in the language; in fact a work on blacksmithing has never before been published in this or any other country. The book is bound in extra cloth with ink side stamp and gold back, and will be sent, *postpaid*, to any part of the country on receipt of price, One Dollar. Address

M. T. RICHARDSON, Publisher,

84 and 86 Reade Street,   NEW YORK.

VOL. II.

Practical
- - Blacksmithing.

Chapter 1 treats of **iron** and **steel**, their antiquity and great usefulness, the strength of **wrought iron** and **steel**, the **rotting** and **crystallization** of **iron, heating steel, testing iron** and **steel**, with illustrations; treatment and **working of steel; hardening steel**, with illustrations; how to **select good steel; restoring burnt steel; cold hammering iron.**

Chapter 2 treats of **bolt** and **rivet clippers**, giving several ways of making these tools, accompanied by numerous illustrations.

Chapter 3 treats of **chisels** and **chisel shaped tools**, and is elaborately illustrated. Tells how to make all kinds of chisels, including clipping and cold chisels.

Chapter 4 treats of **drills and drilling**, tells how to make several styles of drill presses, each plan being accompanied by one or more illustrations. It also tells how to make and temper stone drills, and gives many hints about drills in general. There is an article on drifts and drifting.

Chapter 5 treats of **fullering** and **swaging**, giving the principles of fullering. This has numerous illustrations.

Chapter 6 treats of **miscellaneous tools,** and gives the principles on which edged tools operate, and hints on the care of tools, tongs for bolt making, home-made fan, how to make a pair of pinchers, handy tool for holding nuts, and handy tool for countersunk bolts, how to make clinching tongs, tongs for holding ship lays, accompanied by illustrations.

Chapter 7 is a continuation of **miscellaneous tools.** It tells about the shapes, with illustrations, of **lathe tools, useful attachment to screw stock dies,** wear of screw threading tools, tool for wagon clips, false vise jaws for holding rods, making spring clips, handy tools for making joints, tool for holding bolts in a vise, tool for making singletree clips, tool for making dash heels, mending augers and other tools, attachment to a monkey wrench, handy tool for finishing seat rails, tool for putting yokes on clips, how to make a candle holder, making a bolt trimmer, making a spikebar, how to make a tony square and easy bolt clipper, tool for pulling on felloes, a handy clincher, a bolt holder, making a cant hook, making screw boxes for cutting out wooden screws, mending a square, crane, an improved swage block, repairing augers, clamp for holding countersunk bolt heads, clamp for framework, tool for holding bolts, hints about callipers, vise attachment, a bolt set, a home-made lathe. The descriptions of the way to make all these different tools are accompanied by illustrations.

The price of this volume, in extra cloth binding, the same as Vol. I., to wit—**One Dollar,** and a copy will be sent to any address on receipt of price. In ordering be particular to specify that you want *Vol. II. of "Practical Blacksmithing."* Address

M. T. RICHARDSON, Publisher, 84 and 86 Reade St., N. Y.

VOLUME III.

Practical Blacksmithing.

It has been our aim in compiling Volume 3 of PRACTICAL BLACKSMITHING *to make it even more interesting and instructive than the two previous volumes. We have given in detail, directions, accompanied by many illustrations, as to how to make the tools most useful to blacksmiths.*

CHAPTER 1—Treats of Blacksmiths' Tools ; the preservation of same ; Bench Tools ; Tongs ; Tools for Farm Work ; Tools for holding Plow Bolts ; Tools for holding Plow Shares, etc.

CHAPTER 2—Gives various illustrations of Wrenches, and descriptions for their use.

CHAPTER 3—Gives illustrations and descriptions for Welding, Brazing, and Soldering.

CHAPTER 4—Describes the various uses of Steel ; Tempering, Hardening, Testing, etc.

CHAPTER 5—Illustrates and describes Hand Forgings.

CHAPTER 6—Illustrates and describes the making of Chain Swivels.

CHAPTER 7—Treats on various points on Plow Work, with illustrations.

The price of this volume, bound uniform with Volumes I. and II. is $1.00, and a copy will be sent to any address on receipt of price. In ordering be particular to specify that you want VOL. III. OF PRACTICAL BLACKSMITHING.

M. T. RICHARDSON, Publisher,

84 and 86 Reade St., New York.

VOLUME IV.

PRACTICAL BLACKSMITHING.

This volume completes the Series of Four Volumes. Like its companion volumes, it is handsomely printed with clear, large type on good paper and contains over 200 illustrations.

CHAPTER I.—Is devoted to **Miscellaneous Carriage Irons, Hammer Signals, etc.**

CHAPTER II.—Tells about **Tires, Cutting, Welding, Bending and Setting.** How to make a Tire Heating Furnace.

CHAPTER III.—Treats of **Setting Axles, Axle Gauges and Thimble Sk⋅ins.**

CHAPTER IV.—Tells about **Springs.** How to make and reset. Different ways of Welding.

CHAPTER V.—Describes **Bob Sleds.**

CHAPTER VI.—Treats on **Tempering Tools,** including **Mill Picks, Drills, Taps, Dies, Knife Blades, Chisels, Axes, Hammers, etc.**

CHAPTER VII.—Gives proportions of **Bolts and Nuts,** forms of **Heads, etc.**

CHAPTER VIII.—Treats of **Working S eel, Welding, and Case Hardening.**

CHAPTER IX.—Gives Tables of **Iron and Steel,** including size of iron, and different forms used by **Carriage, Wagon and Sleigh Makers.**

It is bound in extra cloth, with ink side stamp and gold back, and will be sent postpaid to any part of the country, on receipt of **ONE DOLLAR.** In ordering be particular to state that you want VOLUME IV. of PRACTICAL BLACKSMITHING. Address,

M. T. RICHARDSON, Publisher,

84 AND 86 READE STREET,

NEW YORK.

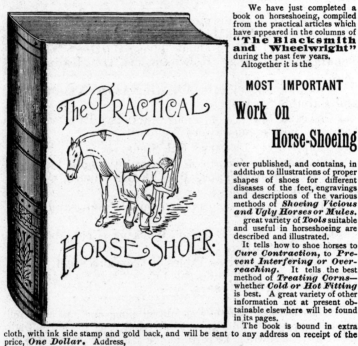